The History of the Borough of Newport

The History of the Borough of Newport

From Swamp to Super-town

by

Haydn Davis

Acknowledgements

Thanks to Solo Syndications Ltd of Kensington for permission to use the Daily Mail graphic of the ancient boat discovered at Magor in 1995.

Also to Chris Barber, copyright holder of the Fred Hando Collection, for the reproduction of St Julians House.

The following are mentioned for their help and guidance in other various shapes and forms:-

Mr Jack Strath (deceased)
Mr Roger Cucksey (Newport Art Gallery)
Mr Haydn Jones (Port Manager, Alexandra Docks)
Mr Gerry Healey (Linen Hall Library Belfast)
Mr Edwin Gimlett
Mr George Homfray
Members of the staff of Newport Reference Library.

Dedication

To the countless Newportonians past and present who never realised that their town had a history.

Foreword

'Little is known of Newport's history. I have asked the Borough Librarian for books on its history and I was told that, except for Sir Joseph Bradney's history of the County, he did not have any.'
   Lord Raglan
   March 1939

'An epic novel could and should have been written about Newport. But this place has never yet received full justice from creative artists and it is time that it did.'
   Jack Jones
   Welsh writer 1959

'Newport has no history society. I wonder if this is because it is ashamed of its history or it has no history.'
   President of the Monmouthshire
   Local History Council
   June 1965

Contents

Preface

History has no beginning and no end. It appears out of the mysterious, swirling mists of antiquity and advances relentlessly towards an ever retreating horizon, pausing only momentarily in every lifetime. Its recording can be a matter of the utmost complexity, requiring careful analysis of all that appears to have substance, and discriminating investigation of all that is hearsay – the drawing of a line between fact and fantasy. But not discarding the unproven entirely for it has not been unknown for eminent historians through the ages to cast doubt on details included in the broader fabric of acknowledged fact.

In legend is found the story of the ancient days before man acquired the ability to keep records or even to recognise the use for them. When the importance of such communication dawned, its earliest manifestations were in cave drawings or in stories passed by word of mouth from generation to generation by raconteurs many of whom were not above replacing more uninteresting but truthful items with more colourful but less reliable material. Such is the stuff of which legend is born!

The time when fact became more easy to identify than fiction brought with it the great opportunity for man to realise that in the past lays the key to much of the future, but the advantage was too rarely taken. Instead, the choice was made to embark on century after century of senseless wars and rebellions in the greedy pursuit of power, estate and even the Crown itself. The result was an incalculable waste of time, national wealth, human life and the wholesale destruction of intrinsic knowledge, relics and artefacts which, had they survived, would have swelled the archives beyond the wildest dreams of the most dedicated historian!

Every castle, house of religion and ancestral home that Owain Glyndwr plundered – and they were vast in number – lost anything up to two centuries of painstakingly kept documentation, and when Oliver Cromwell's Model Army eventually ended the siege of Abergavenny Castle,a fabulous library was mindlessly burned to ashes.

To a great extent Newport has suffered in a similar way although more as a result of gross indifference than violence. More than likely this is responsible for a note of cynicism that has insisted on inserting itself here and there throughout the narrative.

There are histories and histories. On the one hand keen and dedicated scholars immerse themselves wholeheartedly in the past, much travelled in their search for clues in far flung archives and in the ancient debris that lies beneath the very ground that we walk upon. Their books are masterpieces, meticulously cataloguing historic incident and filling the gaps with intelligent conjecture based upon what little is known. These are the real historiographers whose role in life is twofold: primarily to satisfy their own thirst for unravelling bygone mysteries and secondly to present their findings to the rest of us so that we may be aware of the great wealth that we have inherited.

On the other hand there are the amateurs who work within much more confined horizons, to whom the past is not an all-consuming career, whose interests lie only in their natal surroundings and who are only concerned that this locale has not been sufficiently explored or exposed for native edification. There are few places left in this land that have not undergone this treatment.

For instance, every city and almost every town in Wales have their recorded histories standing proudly on their library shelves.

So where is Newport's? Do not bother to search, friend, because your labour will be in vain. In many a Welsh history book it is difficult enough to find any mention of Newport in its index!

Eminent Newportonians *have* written books about the town but these are mainly descriptive of their own lifetimes. These works contain a wealth of contemporary information but span only an eye-blink in time. In fact, most of them were composed in the 19th Century and therefor repeatedly plough the same furrows.

Why does Newport not give greater account of itself? Why indeed!

There are those in the town who are much better equipped than I to tell the story, but for some unknown reason Newport has been an anathema to them all. No one has yet emerged to take up the challenge and no one expresses any interest in encouraging it. It is almost as if the town is generally regarded as of insufficient repute to warrant such a memorial!

Hence this stopgap of an attempt that comes from the 'on the other hand' stable. It is undoubtedly amateurish, devoid of the usual text book detail and only as accurate as the memories of the many long gone contributors who have found time to leave behind an anecdote or two. It is, however, first in its field and a work that I hope will cultivate pride in Newport's past, appreciation of its present and hope for its future.

At this point it is felt necessary to mention a certain feature of the first chapter which deals with those aforementioned ancient times. The leading source of information for this period (5th to 11th centuries) is the Anglo-Saxon Chronicle, believed to have been inspired in the 9th century by Alfred the Great, the first literate king.

It follows that much of the Chronicle's earlier content must have been concocted to a large extent from old Saxon traditional beliefs, from the tattered works of a few long deceased intellectuals which managed to survive the destructive attentions of successive barbarian invaders, to informed guesswork and even stabs in the dark by some of the more imaginative compilers. The completed Chronicle itself suffered the loss of vital passages and the fabrication of others!

The content of the portion relating to the centuries prior to the commencement of writing is therefor generally regarded as suspect and of much less value than those years contemporary to the teams of monastic scriveners. It is also the case that the Chronicle is almost exclusively a *history of England* and as such only fleeting comment may be found of incident outside the Danish and Saxon boundaries. That being so, it would appear that this monumental record is not a very reliable source of events in Wales!

So it is that certain happenings purporting to have taken place in, or in the vicinity of Newport — but without that elusive factual foundation . have been included in this chapter. After all there must be something about these accounts that has caused them to endure for over a thousand years!

In conclusion, an explanation is offered on the subject of the illustrations that have been used to supplement the text. Recent years have seen a proliferation of Newport pictorial publications which have rendered almost unnecessary the use of actual photographs in this book. The town's visual appetite for late 19th and early 20th century images in black and white or sepia is more than amply catered for. Nevertheless, to coat the bare bones of this history, recourse is made to items hitherto hidden away from public gaze in remote corners of the archives. They consist on the whole of old sketches (some refurbished for the sake of clarity) from long forgotten town journals, enlargements of very small scale ancient maps and even the author's own humble attempts to add perspective. Sadly they are all too few in number but, hopefully, fresh on the scene!

Now read on.

Chapter One

On this anvil, out of blood and torture, the destiny
of these islands was forged.'

Anon.

A truly historic town would certainly have commenced its life, back in the mists of time, as an ancient tribal camp, the site chosen for its water supply, safety from attack and all round convenience. Future incumbents would have decided that they could not better the choice of their forefathers and would have built on the ruins of the old, time and time again until, eventually, they produced a city that could truthfully boast of its origins in the pre-dawn.

Newport is not such a town. Its only authentic history spans less than a thousand years - a mere pinprick in time!

Not much more, for that matter, is known with certainty of the surrounding area of Gwent before the arrival of the Romans, who for the 450 years of their presence, carved their epitaph everywhere in stone for posterity to enjoy.

It would be admirable if Newport could claim some affinity with the Yorks and Canterburys of this world but, singularly, this kind of historical longevity seems only to be reserved for those places that were the earliest to succumb to foreign invaders. Certainly there is rumour that one of the most ancient of cities was Caerleon on the Usk, where for many centuries before the Romans made it their great military centre and port, it was said to be a leading seat of tribal government allowing no other township to flourish in its shadow.

How better then than to set Newport's scene with a beginning in folklore?

It is suggested that some 1,500 years before Christ there was a race of people who built a substantial town by the ancient ford across the River Usk. They placed it on the lower slope of a high hill, just out of reach of the lapping waters of each great tide that raced daily across the marshes from the River Severn and up the long (town) pill just south of the ford.

The story goes that these ancient folk were of sufficient intellect to be respected throughout the land for their teaching, their justice and their ability to rule wisely. Eventually they earned such widespread deference that this place became the chief seat of government for much of Britain.

That is the extent of the legend, but from what is known of the earliest occupiers of South Wales it is highly improbable that they would have settled in an area so open to attack or so close to a river noted for enormous tides that frequently inundated the lowlands. Furthermore, Stow Hill being a ridgeway, there was not space for the convenient spread of an encampment on its narrow spine.

The fort that was typical of these tribesmen was the open summit of a hill. The notable one in the Newport area was in the suburb now known as The Gaer, and has been known variously as Maes-y-Gaer, Gaer Fort or Tredegar Fort. To reach it one must travel on, past St Woolos Church at the top of Stow Hill, continuing a short distance along the ancient highway to the west until suddenly it skirts the foot of the green hillside which is crowned by the tumulus of the old camp site. Around the fairly flat top there is room for a sizeable encampment to be laid out, with an impregnable line of ditches and embankments encircling the slopes. A panoramic view in all directions allowed ample warning of danger and there was easy access to thick forests teeming with game and to the crystal clear, salmon-rich waters of the River Ebbw that flowed round the south western base. It was one of many like

1

fortifications situated on practically every individual height in South Wales and from the relics found thereon was obviously of Celtic origin.

The earliest known immigrants from the Continent to this area were the Iberians, a race of small, dark people who apparently originated in Greece and also settled heavily in Northern Spain to found the Basque race. They brought with them crude skills in farming and implements in bronze, a metal that was previously unknown on these shores.

When a further seven centuries had passed, in about 600 BC, the country received the Celts whose many tribes had already spread from the west to settle most of what came to be known as Gaul. Crossing the Channel came two separate branches of the same race - the Goidels or Gaels who settled in the north, and the Brythons who spread across the south. In contrast to the Iberians the Celts were a tall, fair haired race with a much more advanced husbandry, due partly to their knowledge of iron making. The Brythons were the people with whom the Romans first had to deal so they coined the name Britannia for the country where they found them.

Gradually the Brythons absorbed the Iberians in a menial capacity. One branch, however, retained its identity longer than most, despite interbreeding, to become the proud Silures who put down their roots in South Wales in the area that was to stretch one day from West Glamorgan to Gwent. Here they remained, fiercely independent and determined to defend their homeland to the death. Some sort of small settlement may have existed a few miles up from the mouth of the Usk, but it was not to be permanent. Here doubtful reliance is placed on the writings of Geoffrey of Monmouth (1100 to 1154) the mediaeval chronicler whose fertile mind often wove fantasies into semi-legends and presented them in a factual light. He would have it that in 406 BC the Silurian king, Belinus, founded the city that was one day to be known as Caerleon three miles upstream from the Usk ford. Presumably he felt that his capital should benefit from the more convenient access and freedom from flooding. Needless to say, from that time onwards the settlement at the ford – if it ever existed – ceased to exist without trace except for the beaten track that led up from the river crossing.

To say that the ancient Celtic encampment at the Gaer was the beginning of Newport is something of an overstatement because for centuries after its occupiers had disappeared into prehistory nobody lived by the River Usk ford except perhaps one or two hardy individuals who managed to survive by fishing but who could not lay claim to any indigence in the area. The immediate surround of dank marsh and floodplain was a dismal prospect whose immediate effect was to hurry the traveller on his way!

So it remained until the next great invasion.

Came the year 55 BC and probably the most momentous event in the history of the British Isles. Julius Caesar was the first Roman leader to step ashore at the head of his army but this visit and another, a mere twelve months later, were not so much invasions as scouting trips. Wales was not disturbed on either occasion.

However, nearly a century later, in 43 AD, the Emperor Claudius despatched his general Plautius leading 20,000 men to overwhelm the tribes south of the River Thames and open the way to the Valley of the Severn. This time the Romans meant to stay!

This was the testing time for the Silures of Gwent who found themselves about to face the greatest military machine that the world had ever seen. The contest appeared to be totally one-sided. The Silures were much inferior in armament and in fighting strategy but they had the advantage of their familiarity with the rough terrain and their savage determination to defend and hold on to that which was theirs. What was now needed was a leader who could match the discipline and precision of the Legions with unstinting bravery and native cunning.

Fate introduced Prince of Gwent, Caradoc or Caractacus as he was known to the Romans.

Son of another great Silurian warrior, King Cymbeline, Caradoc harried the Romans for years, giving them as good as given in at least thirty pitched battles along the Welsh border. It was beginning to look as if he would never be bettered when he was betrayed by Cartismandua, Queen of the Brigantes, jealous of his success and seeking to ingratiate herself with the Legions. In 50 AD, Caradoc was captured following a mighty battle at Caer Caradoc near Church Stretton and taken in chains to Rome. There he was treated with the respect befitting a valiant, defeated enemy and lived as a freeman for the rest of his life.

In the meantime there was nothing to suggest that the Usk crossing (for that was all it was) benefited in any way from the Roman occupation. Caerleon obviously offered the more attractive proposition as a highly strategic site for a military outpost and following its establishment the legions placed their next coastal fort twelve miles farther west — there are no remains of Roman foundations beneath Newport's Norman castle as there are beneath that of Cardiff!

The Roman Empire embraced Christianity as late as 323 AD but, almost up to the last minute, inhuman attempts were made to stamp out the heathenism of the Druids and the beliefs of the increasing number of Christian converts and replace them with the heathenism of the Roman gods. There had been many waves of savage religious persecution in the Roman Empire but by the early years of the fourth century AD it looked as though it might be ending. It had hardly touched Britain up until then but suddenly the Emperor Diocletian (284 to 305 AD) gave it its last gasp in the northernmost outpost of his empire. The full weight of the scourge did not fall upon Britain as it did on neighbouring Gaul but that is not to say that the few examples which touched nearer home were not carried out with any less ferocity.

Several centres of heavier Roman occupation have their own horrific tales to tell, one or two fairly well authenticated. That which allegedly took place on the outskirts of the then unnamed River Usk village has no stronger support than is suggested by its endurance in local legend but several noted authorities on Romano-British history have dignified the event by agreeing that it *plainly* did happen in the year 303 AD, inexplicably, on the eve of the Roman Empires s own conversion to Christianity!

A large group of Christian Britons were gathered for worship at Caerleon when soldiers fell upon them and took them to prison. When it was found that the prison was too small to hold them, the Roman officer ordered them to be put to death. The massacre was carried out with the utmost cruelty. The terrified Christians were pursued for a distance of nearly one and a half miles towards Newport, all the while being hacked to pieces and drenching the road with their blood.

Among these poor innocents were Julius and Aaron, two devout assistants to the Bishop Amphibulus. They were among the last to fall, at the site of St Julians on the bank of the Usk. The Bishop himself is said to have escaped, making his way to Verulamium to warn Archbishop St Alban of what had happened but he arrived only to be murdered in the company of his superior and a group of religious colleagues. The city outside which this vicious martyrdom was enacted was afterwards renamed St Albans.

In memory of SS Julius and Aaron a chapel was eventually dedicated to each, one on the site later occupied by a barn at St Julians Farm and the other believed to be near the old Roman camp at Penrhos Farm Caerleon. A modern church, dedicated to SS Julius and Aaron was built in 1926 at St Julians Avenue Newport, making use of stones taken from the old St Julians Farm Buildings.

Threatened at home by invading Goths and Vandals, the Romans withdrew completely from Britain in 410 AD, leaving the way clear for the Germanic tribes who had been awaiting this opportunity for centuries, constantly beset as they were by famine and pestilence in their homelands. The Britons, so long being used to the protection afforded by the Romans, were out of practice in their own defence and at first they found great difficulty in containing the new invaders who quickly gained secure foothold on the southern shores. Resistance gradually stiffened, however, and became more united as the bestial hordes looted and burned their way inland, despoiling the churches of the hated Christians and depriving them of their lands.

The conflict went on for over a century until the barbarians became well established in several small kingdoms which were expanding into the larger Wessex, Mercia and Northumbria - but, as yet, no inroad into Wales! There were many skirmishes along the border but the Saxons found to their cost what happened if they tried pursuit into the mountain strongholds. They were now calling the Britons 'Welsh' (strangers or foreigners). The Britons called themselves 'Kymry' (comrades).

In 490 AD or thereabouts a powerful chieftain named Glyws ruled the territory known as Dimetia.

Many think of Siluria as having borders coinciding approximately with modern Gwent but it went much farther than that. Along its Bristol Channel coast it stretched from the River Wye to the Towey and it was there that Dimetia began, taking in all the rest of south western Wales.

Glyws had seven sons, all as bold and fiercely warlike as their father but for one of them a much different future was supposedly in store. It is here that the realm of myth is re-entered, for the popular story can hardly be more than that, and there is a much more reasonable alternative.

Anyway, of this son, Gwynlliw, it was said that piracy was his speciality. For this purpose he kept a fast sailing vessel in a narrow pill situated near the mouth of the River Usk, and would venture out with his cut-throat crew to attack any passing ship that appeared to be a worthy prize. This 'pill of Gwynlliw' eventually received the name Pillgwenlly, giving its name to the whole district surrounding it.

Gwynlliw married Gwladys, daughter of the King of Brechiniog (Brecknock) and they had a son who they named Cadoc. When he reached adulthood Cadoc became a holy man and succeeded in persuading his father to renounce his dissolute way of life and to devote himself to the worship of God. Up to here the story sounds factual but then it wanders into the realms of implausibility.

One night an angel appeared to Glynlliw in a dream and advised him to forsake all his worldly possessions. He was further required to make his way to the summit of a nearby hill where he would find, grazing, a white ox with a black spot between its horns. Where he found this beast he was to live and labour in the service of the Lord!

The prediction in the dream proved correct so Gwynlliw and his wife built a small cottage and church in wattle and daub on top of the hill overlooking the sea. When the pious, old man died he was buried there and it has been the site of churches ever since.

A pleasant little tale, but somewhat predictable when one considers that legends involving white cattle with black markings can also be found in parts of Cornwall, Ireland and Scotland. A breed of this description was known to the pre-Christian Celts. They were probably related to the great, long-horned aurochs some of whose remains were found deep in the excavations for the Alexandra Dock entrance lock. Mystical qualities were attributed to them by their ancient herdsmen. However, this version of the life of Gwynlliw is completely at odds with another which has had much the same airing through the ages.

In it, Gwynlliw was not lured to the top of Stow Hill by any dream; he had always lived there in a permanent camp where he plotted all his villainy. From this excellent vantage point he was able to espy rich cargo ships sailing towards the Usk and to ports higher up the

Severn. He was then able to quickly descend the hill by way of a well beaten track (Belle Vue Lane), race down the marshy Mendalgief to his harbour pill and commit his acts of piracy. This suggests that whilst resident on Stow Hill Gwynlliw was an unreformed character and it leaves the manner of his conversion very much in question.

Even the mound that existed on the summit of the hill until 1848 has been credited to Gwynlliw as the 'twyn' on which the chief's tiny house was built. Otherwise known as Gwynlliw's Tump, this theory has been confuted as future paragraphs will show.

Rightly or wrongly the age of Gwynlliw has been placed in the sixth century AD. One can gain some idea of the extreme smallness of the first Church of the Stowe by comparison with the larger Cathedral Church of Llandaff, already built at that time and only 28 feet long by 15 feet wide by 20 feet high!

The name, St Woolos, carried by the 20th century cathedral church, is the latest in a long list of translatory deviations from the original Gwynlliw. One of the most inexplicable was a documentary reference to the church in 1551 as St Olaves! In the 1630 Survey of Newport it was St Gaules and thereafter there were variations such as St Ollas and St Wollas, until the late 18th century when references began to appear to St Woolos, its present form. For the record, there is no firm evidence as to what it was called in its earliest years and one is left to wonder why the latinised version, St Gunleus, appeared as late as 1881 on the ordnance survey map of Newport.

During its long and chequered history the church suffered despoliation and destruction at least five times up to the end of the eighth century at the hands of Irish pirates, Saxon and Danish raiders. In 1065, Earl Harold (afterwards King Harold of Hastings), making a punitive expedition into Gwent, found that frightened inhabitants had stored their valuables in the church before fleeing to the hills. The soldiers could not be held in check and caused great damage in the course of their looting. A few years later, Prince Caradoc of Caerleon destroyed the long suffering building, and then came remission until 1172 when Prince Iorwerth included its burning in his terrible revenge on King Henry II. It is not hard to imagine why a building leading such a precarious life should have continued to be built in no more permanent materials than timber and thatch. Easy and cheap replacement was so often needed before some sort of order was restored to the area. If the legend of Gwynlliw is to be given any credence at all, it means that, except for the large abbeys and Minsters, the top of Stow Hill is one of the oldest church sites in Britain. This is based on documentation and archaeology suggesting that very few churches were founded before the end of the 9th century and, when they were, they were Saxon built, containing an increasing amount of stone in their construction. There is believed to be a fair amount of Saxon stonework beneath the floor of St Marys Chapel in the Newport Church.

In 1402, Owain Glyndwr sacked St Woolos in his nation-wide orgy of destruction. This was the last occasion of its really severe maltreatment, although it did receive slight external damage during a minor siege by Oliver Cromwell's army in the 17th century. The Commonwealth troops were not known for church vandalism.

The sea used to come much closer to the hill called Stowe and consequently, on the occasions of the highest tides, the church closely resembled a lighthouse perched on a cliff top. Its prominence made it a beacon for Britons, Saxons, Danes and Normans alike as they contended with the notorious waters along the Wentloog levels. In later centuries it is believed that a light was kept burning on the church tower (for much of its early history it was towerless) as an aid to night navigation and to serve as a warning of enemy approach. Even night travellers along the highway found it reassuring to have the pitch darkness lifted, if only for a short distance.

The walls of the church have in their time played host to Kings Canute, Harold, William the Conqueror, his son William Rufus and, on two occasions, Henry II as he made pilgrimage to St Davids and passage to Ireland.

In 1093, King William II (William Rufus) was seriously ill in Gloucester and was tended by the monks of St Peters Church. As a token of his thanks for their successful ministrations he gave them St Woolos Church at Newport together with 15 hides of land. A hide was defined as the amount of land required to sustain a free peasant farmer and his family and could be anything from 60 to 120 acres according to local custom, so the area of this gift could have been anything between 900 and 1800 acres. It remained in the ownership of St Peters for the next six centuries. One of the quainter obligations of this agreement was that the Newport church had to provide the Convent of St Peters with 20 marks per annum for the supply of French wine and wastel (a fine white bread).

It is on record that, 150 years after King William's gift, the Lord of the Manor of Morganwy and Gwynllwg, Earl Gilbert de Clare, repeated the donation 'to God and the Church of St Peter, Gloucester, for the good of my soul and that of my wife Isobel'. Just how he could give what had already been given is not clear.

The 5th and 6th centuries were the most violent of times seeing the emergence of many ultra-bold leaders from the ranks of the Britons and eventually producing the most colourful figure of all. It was once again the fanciful imagination of Geoffrey of Monmouth, that sketched the romantic, dreamlike adventures that were to influence and expand future accounts of this legendary Celtic king at the hands of celebrated classical authors throughout the middle ages.

Unfortunately there is not one scrap of solid evidence by documentary or archaeological discovery to show that such a character ever lived. Nevertheless it generally agreed that some great chief was very active at about the stated time but he belongs to the whole Celtic nation and not to any one of the British branches. This, however, does not prevent regional pride from staking claims. Gwent is able to make as good a case as any.

Prince Arthur was born in the latter part of the 5th century and he was crowned king at Caerleon at 15 years of age. A kind, just and wise ruler, he was revered by the multitude of brave knights who flocked to his banner. The philosophy that he instilled into his subjects was the advancement of all aspects of honour and chivalry in the deepest convictions of the Christian faith.

Following a series of damaging incursions into his domain by the Saxons, the young King Arthur led a massive force across the border. Under his overall command he had the armies of the Kings of North Wales and of South Wales with the two kings acting as his adjutants and in AD 516 he inflicted a crushing defeat on the Saxon English at Mount Badon (Mons Badonicus) which has never been identified but which is believed to have been somewhere near Bath.

In numerous other encounters with his enemies it was rare indeed for Arthur to find himself on the losing side and with this reputation it is not surprising that he is claimed in other parts of Britain as the local hero. Romantically he is associated with Tintagel in Cornwall, Glastonbury in Somerset, with Kent, Windsor and Cumbria. Not that any defence is needed of Arthur's Gwentian heritage, but is it by coincidence that his Welsh queen's name was Gwenhwfar (how like Guinevere) and his most trusted adviser was the Welsh prophet Merlin of Maes Aleg (Bassaleg)?

In modern times the site of King Arthur's Round Table was popularly believed to be at the Roman amphitheatre, Caerleon, and the Ordnance Survey gives its blessing to this by labelling its maps accordingly. It seems that King Arthur set a precedent that was to last a long time. By the end of the 8th century, Offa, King of Mercia, was still finding the subjugation of the Welsh to be a most frustrating project because he built his Dyke from the

Dee to the Wye with the notion that 'if you can't beat them, confine them!'

Another 200 years were to pass before the tussle drew to an end in virtual stalemate, but even in the final days the antagonists met in clashes that were no less fierce.

In 918 AD, for instance, a grim battle was reputedly fought over the site where Clarence Place now stands. It was at the time when the Mercian Saxons were fighting furiously on their northern boundaries to prevent invasion by the Danes from the Danelaw (the occupied northern territories of Britain).

King Owain of Brecon raised an army to help the Danes against his old enemies and to deal with this threat at their rear, the Saxons withdrew a contingent from their front line and sent it into Wales. The expedition was successful, Owain was defeated in his own stronghold and the victorious Saxons commenced their return journey. It so happened, however, that Morgan, Prince of Glamorgan, received intelligence that the war party intended to cross the ford over the River Usk, so he set up his ambush on the river bank.

In those days the surface of the track was 12 feet lower than today. It sloped gradually from approximately where the Cenotaph now stands to the low water mark and at high water the tide encroached well up the track. On the western side the gradient was gradual up to half way along the modern High Street.

As soon as the whole Saxon force had crossed to the east bank Morgan sprang the ambush and a bloody battle ensued. Each side numbered about a thousand men and they fought for several hours while the tide rose behind the Saxons to cut off their retreat. When it was all over, the Saxon survivors were taken prisoner and thereupon provided the greatest of shocks to their captors when it was revealed that their chief was a woman, none other than Athelflaed, Regent of Mercia, daughter of King Alfred the Great and sister of the reigning King Edward the Elder with whom she shared command of the Saxon armies! This was probably not her first foray into Welsh territory since the defence of the western Mercian boundary had been her responsibility for some years.

The consternation and embarrassment of the Welsh must have been great indeed for, despite their ferocity in battle, they still retained a high regard for the teachings of someone like King Arthur and his ideas of chivalry towards the fair sex. These warriors were completely unused to women who went into battle with their men, much less as their general! They could do no other than to free Athelflaed and her followers and allow them to go home.

This is another of those stories on which the Anglo-Saxon Chronicle has no comment and which has arrived in the 20th century by some circuitous route through the ages, but the year is correct and contemporaneous to the characters. Who then put them together in a locality where it was logical to find both warring factions? It would have been surprising indeed if the proud, warlike Athelflaed and her band of survivors had allowed their humiliation to reach the ears of the Chronicle's recorders. In any case, the Lady of Mercia (another of her titles) did not have to keep her secret long because she died a few months later at Tamworth and was buried at Gloucester.

Some of the defeated Saxons, especially the wounded and disabled, chose to stay and were allowed to settle on the western bank of the Usk ford where they built and worked a mill on a site that eventually became the junction of Mill Street and Shaftesbury Street. Milling operations continued here for a thousand years until they had to make way for 20th century development. The mill wheel was probably powered by the Nant-y-stelth or Malpas Brook which started as the Crindau Pill some distance north of the ford and divided into two streams, one of which flowed in a southerly direction from Barrack Hill, parallel with the river almost back to the ford. This stretch was, in the late 18th century adapted as a section of the Monmouthshire Canal.

Histories of the Welsh borderlands for this period mention many such clashes between Welshman and West Saxon but the situation was well on the way to its resolution. Eventually it cooled to a point where two very different, volatile peoples came to coexist in suspicious harmony. There is little in present day Newport to point to any Saxon influence but this can also be said of any number of towns situated in the heart of Saxon occupied England. Unlike the Romans the Germanic tribes were not noted for building to last. In any case, the immigrants to Uskside were in short number and were probably absorbed very quickly into the manners of the tiny Welsh settlement. However, there are signs which are just as significant as anything that could be expected to emerge from the soil and these are reflected in some of the un-Welsh names given to areas of the town and shown on early maps. They are discussed later.

When the first Germanic invasion took place in the 5th century, three separate tribes were involved, namely the Angles who settled in the east, the Jutes who settled in Kent and the Saxons who stayed south, creating the Kingdom of Wessex and later pushing to form Mercia. Christianity came to each at different times but by 655 AD it was universally accepted and the tribes all merged, linked as they were by language and culture. They were now only divided by petty jealousies, boundary disputes and the greed of individual chiefs. They had truly become the English and the British had become the Welsh!

Gwent Welshmen and Mercian Englishmen, both now practising the Christian faith, developed smoother relations. The area on the Usk ford became known as Dinas Newydd (New fort or enclosure) suggesting that some sort of fortification, probably of wood and probably Saxon inspired, was standing on the western bank. After all, it was only 16 miles to the Mercian border (River Wye) so it was inevitable that the area would soon become somewhat anglicised with interchange of population not totally frowned upon. A further measure of the degree of acceptance was the complete rebuilding by the Saxons of the church on the Stowe either on a long vacated or derelict site.

The difference between the Welsh and the Saxons was the reason for the latter making their homes on the River Bank in the first place. They were farmers who chose the fertile land near water; the Welsh were not interested in agriculture and preferred the higher ground where their herds could graze. Records that do exist, such as they are, show that all Saxon villages followed the same plan. An outer circle was used as common pasture while the inner part comprised three large fields and the living accommodation.

Two fields out of the three were used for different crops each year: one for wheat, one for rye or oats and the third was left fallow to recover its strength. Rotation followed.

The fields were divided into strips so that each man had his fair share of the good and the bad. Cereal, peas, beans and fruit were grown. Some cattle were put in the outer pasture, sheep were grazed on the moorland, pigs were raised in the forest and there was plenty of fish and game. Sugar was unknown so bees were kept to provide honey for sweetening and the making of a drink called mead. In the autumn animals were slaughtered, meat salted or smoked to last throughout the winter. Everyone had the right to take wood from the forest for fuel or building.

The foresters and swineherds had to be extra vigilant in the forests which abounded with wolves and continued to do so for centuries to come. Many locations exist today which were then merely clearings in the heavily wooded areas close to the edges of many villages. They still carry in their modern names the suffix 'bela' meaning wolf, a creature that was still being hunted in the area as late as the year 1500. Newport has its own memento of the times in Courtybella - *Cwrt-y-bela* - *Haunt of the wolves*.

The local chief or aeolderman usually owned the water or wind mill, and allowed the villagers to use it for grinding their corn. He also supplied farming equipment and oxen for the ploughs in return for which the people gave two or three days to work for the chief. Money although known was little used - no Saxon hoards in Dinas Newydd. Smiths, millers, carpenters, shepherds and other tradesmen, who were always giving services to others, received their rewards in local produce.

The women in Saxon villages were truly maids of all work. They toiled long and hard, cleaning the ramshackle houses, baking, brewing, salting meat, making butter and feeding the livestock; they also prepared wool from fleeces, spun, weaved and knitted it into clothing. Skins were tanned into leather and furs made into wall or floor coverings.

Peaceful coexistence was the watchword within the village but outside was a different matter. Quarrels between settlements were quite common so it was essential to provide some sort of defence. Every man could be called upon to fight when needed and many of the young men preferred this to working in the fields so they became permanent retainers to the lord. Called 'thegns' (thanes) meaning servants, they were given military training and lived at their lord's expense. The thegns of a lord who, through conquest, became very powerful, were rewarded by grants of land which became their own. They then became freeholders, ceorls or churls - the term did not then carry its modern derogatory implication. Their underlings were the serfs and below them came thralls (slaves), prisoners and criminals.

The living accommodation of these folk was very primitive. The typical house was little short of a hovel made from wooden branches and thatch bound together with mud, and with a beaten earth floor. This explains why so little Saxon building has survived the test of time.

There was one thing above all others for which the Saxons had a deep-rooted love and that was governing by assembly. They regularly held meetings or 'folk mootes' to discuss matters of gravity and concern to the community. Leaders were elected, law breakers were tried and rough justice dispensed. It was a form of local government and a legal system in the very early stages of development.

Here then was the tiny hamlet of Dinas Newydd, the name given by the local Welsh inhabitants and used now because it is not known if there was a Saxon equivalent — unless it was the one described in the following paragraphs.

A strong Saxon element was indicated by the church, mill and fort which they allegedly built. Furthermore, a little higher up the track on which stood the 'milne' (Mill Street) they erected their 'geldenhall' (guildhall or meeting place) where all the folk mootes were held. Old maps of Newport show a meeting house at this spot (near the bottom of Queens Hill) up to the early 19th century. Gild or geld was the name given to a fraternity which paid a levy or tax on geldable land to the lord of the manor. Today, the corruption of that name is 'Goldtops'.

Joining Goldtops to Mill Street is a stretch of road bearing the name 'Pentonville'. It has been suggested that this derives from the joining of two Saxon words : 'pyndan', a dam on a mill stream, and 'vil', a small group of dwellings. There are a mill and a mill-stream close by and it is fairly certain that the street of the milne was the very first piece of urban development in ancient Newport.

After William the Conqueror's invasion, the Saxon and Anglo-Welsh serfs (for that is what their Norman masters made of them) lived on, outside the castle walls, in the tiny cluster of houses which they knew as Pyndanville — ergo present day Pentonville!

The land extending from Pyndanville to Gwynlliw's church on Stow Hill had been owned by the church since the 6th century. It comprised several fields, namely, Dragon Field (site of Newport railway station), Six Acres, Beanswell, Cae Croch and Church Field.

The church had always allowed them to be worked and tilled, bond free, for the benefit of the poor. The Saxons, on their arrival, allowed this to continue as an act of charity or, as they termed it, 'beneweork' (good work). On Coxe's s map of 1802 these fields are marked 'brendekyrg' (church fields) and the similarity between the two Old English words may have some significance.

- 0 -

The many clashes between Saxons and Welsh were born in bitter hatred and had continued in unabated fury as the invaders aimed at complete subjugation, but several centuries of stalemate brought the realisation that compromise was the only answer. The men of Mercia seemed happy, eventually, to be accepted in the border areas as long as they did not pursue their ideas of territorial gain. Besides, towards the end of the 8th century they needed to turn their attentions towards the much more serious threat from a new enemy!

In the year 795 AD the first of the dreaded Northmen appeared on the east coast of Britain and began a reign of such terror, blood-letting and devastation as no country had ever seen. The brooding barbarians from Norway, Sweden and Denmark (known collectively as Vikings or pirates) crossed the North Sea and descended like a pestilence, showing no mercy in an orgy of pillage and slaughter. They hated Christians so the riches of the churches were their obvious targets with the priests being murdered at their altars.

However, it was 877 AD before South Wales received the first visit from the 'black pagans', a name descriptive of their dark coloured boats and clothing.

Gwent suffered badly in this attack, but apparently the Danes under their leader, Hubba, found the country so wild and the people so poor that they changed their minds about staying for the winter. Only a year later Gwent was hit once again by the fleeing remnants of the Danish army routed by King Alfred at the Battle of Ethandun (Edington, Wilts).

In 891 AD, a large force landed near Llantwit Major and advanced on Gwent destroying everything in its path. Waiting for them with a large army was Welsh prince, Morgan Hen, and after a fierce battle fought somewhere between Newport and Caerleon, the Danes were forced to flee back to the bases that they had made in Ireland. It was a typical trait of these people that they never forgave anyone who caused their downfall so just one year later they returned to get their revenge, this time wreaking havoc and putting the whole of South Gwent, including Caerleon, to the torch!

915 AD saw another large party of Vikings enter the River Severn. They were led by the two chiefs, Ohter and Hroald, and on landing they spread at incredible speed into the interior, laying waste and murdering indiscriminately. However, their insatiable greed was their undoing and, having overstretched themselves, they were caught and annihilated by a combined army from Caerleon, Hereford and Gloucester . another pointer to the softening of relations between occupiers on either side of the border! There must also be significance in the fact that during all these years of bloody invasion and counter invasion in Gwent there is never any mention of the establishment of any community nearer the mouth of the River Usk than Caerleon!

The end of the first millennium saw the throne of England in the occupation of a very weak and feckless king. Ethelred the Unready was aptly named and, in 994AD he was guilty of an act that must have caused his great, great, great grandfather, the old Dane-fighter Alfred the Great, to turn in his grave.

The Danes who had made their bases on the coast of France were attacking furiously in support of there kinsmen in the northern English kingdom of Danelaw. Ethelred in his naivety believed that they could be trusted so he offered them a huge bribe (those days equivalent of £15,000) to go away and leave him in peace. King Olaf of Norway kept his promise and took his army home, but King Swegn of Denmark took the money and with his fleet sneaked off round to the Bristol Channel and made one of the last major attacks. Again Gwent suffered cruelly!

So drew to a close the bloodiest period of history that Gwent had ever known. The barbarians from over the sea finally gave up the game and joined their kinsmen who had settled on the north coast of France to make the transformation from Norsemen to Normans in time for their return in the great, conclusive invasion nearly two centuries later.

The Vikings, Danes, Norwegians, Swedes whatever had been far worse than the Saxons, Angles or Jutes in their invasive heyday. They were the most cruel, savage and merciless of any who had ever crossed the Dinas Newydd ford, but so many had done so over a long period that it was inevitable that a further dimension should have been added to the racial mixture of the district.

There was a time-encapsulated reminder of this dark period when excavations were taking place in 1878 to create the timber float at Newport's Alexandra Dock. Under eight feet of soil an ancient boat was uncovered and at the time it was believed to be of Danish origin. An interesting account of the find is given by Newport historian and former Director of Education, David Oates, in his 'Story of Gwent'. He writes: 'The vessel appears to have been about seventy feet long and was constructed for speed rather than for strength as it is only slightly put together'.

Its size would seem to indicate something other than the local coastal trading craft. It was made of oak planks held together with iron nails and carbon dating of the only surviving piece of timber dates it from 950 AD. Given a plus or minus factor of 50 years this vessel was probably afloat when the Bristol Channel was teeming with attacking Norsemen and could easily have been one of the longships that took part in those last desperate attempts at Danish penetration.

It was found half a mile from the River Ebbw and a mile from the River Usk which gives some indication of how the courses of the two rivers have changed in a thousand years.

What might have caused the abandonment of this vessel?

It is interesting to speculate.

Were the crew all killed in the onshore fighting?

Were they drowned by a fast incoming tide as they struggled back across the marshes loaded down with plunder? Is it possible that they got lost and had to be picked up by another ship? Or were its occupants killed or captured somewhere else in the Bristol Channel leaving their craft to drift until the tides left it high and dry on the Wentloog marshes?

The answers can never be known but it is a little awe inspiring to think that there may be still in existence in the local museum a tiny piece of an object that featured in the lives of those barbaric wild men from the north, and which may have been part of the very vehicle that brought them to the River Usk!

As the 10th century drew to a close one could be forgiven for imagining that a reasonable if not wholly satisfactory road system was in being in order to have coped with the many thousands of human feet and horses' hoofs which apparently had found no trouble in travelling the great distances demanded by their endless conflicts.

Prior to the advent of the Romans, most of the lowlands consisted of swamp or thick forest, so it was little wonder that the ancients built their highways to cling to the high chalk ridges. The very word *highway*, although now assigned to describe a main road at any altitude, sounds most appropriate for what existed in those far off days. The main highway through Gwent was such a road.

Known as Akeman Street, it came from the east, over the Wentwood ridge to Christchurch and then, crossing the Usk ford, it continued up the beaten track that would become Mill Street, across the fields to Barrack Hill and onward, Glassllwch to Bassaleg. This route was safe from the enormous tidal surges - over 40 feet - that swept in regularly from the Bristol Channel.

An extract from 'Historic Newport' by James Matthews (1910) describes this phenomenon as it was in the 18th century:-

> **'The marshes within the confines of the Crindau Pill were nothing better than a swamp and formed almost an island near the mill; the marshes from Town Pill to Pillgwenlly were a water-soaked and swampy fen, a veritable quagmire; the Town Pill ran up to the present day Bryngwyn Road, making Stow Hill a peninsula; and the sea came up nearly to Bassaleg Church. The land within the embankments of the Caldicot and Wentloog levels extending from Goldcliff to Cardiff and the land whereon stands almost the whole of Newport is reclaimed.'**

If this is a true picture of the area in the 18th century it is small wonder that Newport's recorded history started as late as it did!

When the Romans constructed their excellent communications network, it included a ferry from Abonae (Sea Mills) near the mouth of the Bristol Avon, to Sudbrook in Gwent where a fine, 20 feet wide, paved road carried on through Venta Silurum (Caerwent), via Penhow, the Wentwood ridge, Christchurch and thence to the barracks of the 6,000 strong, 2nd Augustan Legion at Caerleon.

When building their roads the Romans almost always broke new ground but occasionally they used lengths of old roads repaired and resurfaced. This was the case with Akeman Street up as far as Christchurch, but here the Roman road branched off to their fortress at Caerleon and, after passing through, swung round on the western bank of the River Usk to emerge at Malpas, a name for which there appears to be two possible derivations. Some say that the Romans called the place 'Malus Passus', the bad pass noted for the boggy, low-lying ground at Pillmawr which, even well into the 20th century, could be covered by high tides.

Archdeacon Coxe, circa 1797, thought otherwise. He travelled this road on the back of a donkey and wrote that the Welsh called it 'Malp Aes' meaning a 'plain within hills', a description that the reverend gentleman felt was much more fitting. From this point the route carried on up Penylan (Barrack Hill), along Alltyryn, Ridgeway and Glasslwch to Pye Corner, Bassaleg. This was the Via Julia Maritima.

It should not come as a surprise to learn that these brilliant engineers, centuries ahead of their time, also tackled the formidable problem of the high tides. There is positive proof of their involvement in throwing up a flood barrier along this part of the Severn coastline. A carved stone, found at Goldcliff Priory in 1878, tells of the construction of 31½ paces of sea wall by the century of Statorius Maximus - tantamount to an artist proud enough of his work to sign it! This particular work party probably lived in a temporary camp while the job lasted. There is no evidence of Roman settlements on the moors but in 1959 excavations for the Uskmouth Power Station unearthed a large amount of Roman pottery which proved to have been manufactured in Europe.

Sadly, after the departure of these gifted men, and incredibly for the next fourteen centuries, the making and maintenance of roads found no priority whatsoever so that they fell back into the summer moraines and winter morasses of old.

The 11th century was a relatively quiet period for Gwent even though the whole of Britain was to see momentous change with the coming of the Conqueror!

The throne passed from Ethelred very briefly to his son Edmund Ironside and then to Swegn, king of the victorious Danes, whose own death after only a few months, gave the crown to his son, Cnut (Canute). A short dynasty of Danish kings followed with Canute's sons, Harold Harefoot and Hardicanute but the latter died childless and the Witan, in 1042, deciding to continue the Saxon ascendancy, gave the crown to Edward the Confessor, second son of Ethelred the Unready. This reign ended in January 1066 and Harold Godwin, Earl of Essex, became the last Saxon king of England, setting the scene for the final denouement at Senlac Hill, Hastings, a few months later.

Thus, while the throne of England was changing hands eight times, little effect was felt in Gwent which was seeing plenty of action among its own royals!

Wales had always had more than its fair share of self styled kings and princes. During this particular era it was literally awash with them! There were kings of North Wales and South Wales; there was even a 'chief' king of Wales. There were princes of North and South Glamorgan, Upper and Lower Gwent and of Brecknock. They were all continually in contention with each other over their titles and the extent of their domains. Nowhere was there a country where the native population could be said to be less united! All their troubles were of their own making and this constant bickering was undoubtedly the basis of the disunity that eventually opened the gates of South Wales to the Norman flood!

In 1,000 AD, the chief King of Wales, Meredydd, died and King Aeddan of Gwent felt that the superior title should be his. The King of Gwynedd objected and killed Aeddan in battle. Rhydderch, nephew of Aeddan, stepped into the breach and elected himself King of South Wales as well as of Gwent. Gruffyd, who had succeeded his father Llywelyn as King of Gwynedd, now wanted to be King of all Wales and he took up arms against every other prince for the privilege. They, in turn, banded together and sought the help of Harold, Saxon Earl of Wessex, who was glad of any opportunity to gain influence in Wales. Gruffyd was defeated in 1063.

On his way home, Harold dallied at Portscuit (Portskewett) in Gwent. He was labouring under the entirely false impression that the Welsh were now subservient enough to allow him much more freedom of action in their territory, so he built a lavish hunting lodge for his king, Edward the Confessor. To confound his hopes Prince Caradoc of Caerleon razed the lodge to the ground and slaughtered everyone connected with its construction. It was during Harold's punitive pursuit of the raiders that St Woolos Church happened to be in the line of fire and suffered a looting.

At this time, as far as can be gathered, the Welsh were still only predominant in the foothills of the eastern and western valleys of Gwent and the higher ground in the valley of the Usk. At the ford, Pyndanvil was still just a scattering of hovels and cultivated fields between church and mill.

Ominously, the year was 1065!

13

Chapter Two

The Normans

The result of the Battle of Hastings came as a great shock to the Saxons for they were firmly convinced that they would be the victors; the likelihood is that they would have been were it not for the treachery of Harold's brother, Tostig. It was he who, landing in the north at the head of a Danish invasion force, caused Harold to force march his troops from their vantage points on the south coast to Stamford Bridge in Yorkshire where they fought a brilliant and victorious battle. But luck deserted the Saxons when, at the very moment of victory, the prevailing winds changed direction in favour of the waiting Norman invasion fleet and they were landing at Pevensey before Harold's main army could get back!

In a journey taking nine days the Saxons had raced 200 miles to the north, fought and defeated the Danes, retraced their steps at full speed over another nine days to London and then covered the last 60 miles to the south coast in a further two days! It was an incredibly brave but totally exhausted Saxon army that faced William, Duke of Normandy, at Senlac Hill on October 14th 1066.

This was only the first of many shocks that the Saxons were to suffer. Very soon after his victory, William took firm and irreversible steps to consolidate the occupation of his new kingdom. He decided to reward all his faithful barons, in particular those who had fought alongside him at Hastings, with grants of land taken from the Saxons. His philosophy was simple: confiscation of property was a punishment for those who had fought against him and also for those who, whilst not having fought against him, had not fought for him! Either way they were considered to be traitors against their lawful king. All Saxons who, in their own society had been freemen, could only remain so by payment of heavy fines or else become serfs or villeins of their Norman masters.

It was William's intention to create a new feudal system. It had to be an improvement on the one he had left behind in France where a baron's followers swore allegiance to their feudal leader and not to the king. This practice led to situations where the king found great difficulty in obtaining support in disputes with his barons. William knew this from personal experience as he had, on several occasions as Duke of Normandy, defied the King of France. So, with this in mind, he gave large estates to his Anglo-Norman barons, but only after exacting from them and their retainers an oath of allegiance to him directly.

It must rank as the biggest give-away in British history. Although the original Norman invasion force had been massive, the aristocracy numbered only about 5,000 and between them they received the whole of England in parcels commensurate with services rendered. The king's share naturally dwarfed all others! No estate was ever situated in one locality. They were made up of huge tracts of land scattered over wide areas so that any baron with mischief in mind could not marshal his forces in a central place. A prime example was that of the very powerful Robert de Mortmain who was granted 793 manors but in 20 different counties!

A few exceptions were made to the general rule and the reason was the, as yet unconquered country of Wales.

In the early years of his reign, King William I was beset by a host of problems at home and abroad. The English still were not completely subjugated and there was trouble from the feudal barons in his Dukedom of Normandy. He was not therefore keen or indeed ready to take on the Welsh so he created three great Marcher Lordships at Chester, Shrewsbury and Hereford with the titles Lords Baron to match. These Lords of the Welsh Marches (borderlands) were given much greater power than any of the other barons, based on the premise that they would be kept too busy to use it against the king. They were given free rein in their methods of containing the fiery Welshmen on behalf of the king, provided that they did it at their own expense and with their own retainers. Understandably, these lordships became almost minor kingdoms in their own right and continued to grow more powerful as new territories were conquered across the border.

Each new slice that was obtained was protected by a newly built castle and 169 were built in Wales in a few years. In Gwent alone 25 sprang up at intervals along the Rivers Wye and Usk. More castles appeared in Gwent than in any other county.

It was during this period that one of the disputes between Welsh princes did untold damage to their own cause.

Prince Caradoc ap Gruffyd of Caerleon – he who had destroyed Harold's hunting lodge at Portskewett – was deprived of the kingship of South Wales by Meredydd. To regain the title he enlisted the aid of Iestyn, Prince of Glamorgan, and then asked the Marcher Earl of Hereford, William Fitz Osborn, to be an ally. The latter jumped at this easy chance to further Norman influence in Wales and the combined force fought a battle on the River Rhymney, defeating and killing Gruffyd. The Normans had therefore advanced unopposed across the full breadth of Gwent, farther than ever before, and at the invitation of one Welsh prince in his domestic quarrel with another!

In accordance with the policy encouraged by the monarchy – that any territory taken in Wales should belong to the taker – it would appear that the baron whose men first occupied South Gwent was Robert Fitz Hamon. Whether he was part of the Earl of Hereford's force against Prince Gruffyd, or whether he took advantage of the diversion to make an independent incursion is not clear. Suffice it to say that in the year 1093 Robert Fitz Hamon became the first Lord of the Norman Manors of Morganwg (Glamorgan), Brecon and Gwynllwg (the area between the Rivers Rhymney and Usk), which included the tiny village by the ford. He kept Morganwy and the southern part of Gwynllwg tightly under his control but from Machen northwards he left in the hands of the Welsh, subject to the payment of heavy dues.

One of his first concerns in his newly acquired domain was to look to its security and almost straight away he set in motion the building of Cardiff Castle, to stand on the foundations of the old, ruined Roman fort, in those days much closer to the shore of Cardiff Bay. This was to become the principal seat of the Lord of the Manors but at the same time something similar, if not so ambitious, was planned for Newport.

The Fitz Hamon fortification was not the one which now stands in ruins on the bank of the River Usk. It was not even close but set on the summit of the Stowe a short distance from the church of Gwynlliw with a clear view of the country for miles around. This, the first Newport Castle was of the type known as motte and bailey and took the form of a high mound of earth surrounded by a ditch from which the earth originally came. On the flattened top would have been a wooden tower enclosed in a stockade. This mound survived the centuries until 1848 when it was swallowed up by the spoil excavated from the new railway tunnel that passed immediately underneath. At that time the mound stood in Fir Tree Field and when the tunnel's soil had been spread about,there was only the slightest tumulus protruding.

A large house named Springfield was later built nearby and its generous garden encompassed the ancient site. Mr Octavius Morgan who lived in The Friars, just opposite to the entrance drive of Springfield (Friars Road), asked the occupier, his old friend, Mr Gething, to mark the spot when he landscaped his garden and this he did with a cairn of large stones. Unfortunately this rear edge of the garden fronted the newly developing Stow

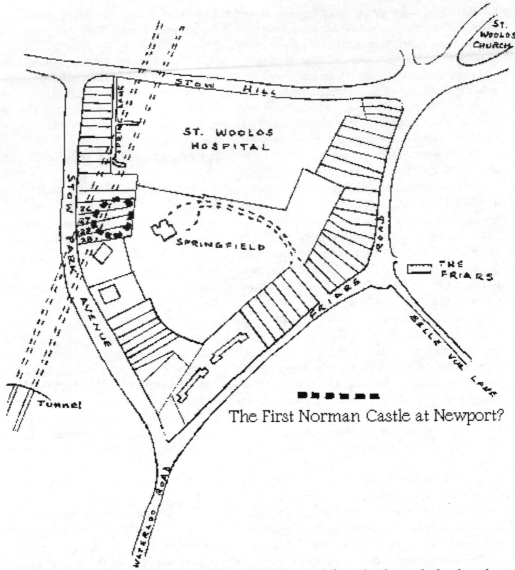

The First Norman Castle at Newport?

Park Avenue and was sold to the builder who obliterated the cairn beneath the three houses numbered 27 to 29 Stow Park Avenue!

For the benefit of the reader who is interested in Springfield House, it once occupied the ground on which the modern block of wards of St Woolos Hospital (Springfield Wing) now stands and its entrance drive was the same one that now leads into the hospital from Friars Road.

The chapter dealing with the legend of Gwynlliw puts forward an alternative idea on the origin of this ancient mound.

The Welsh-Saxon village of Dinas Newydd (Pyndanvil?) was now firmly established as a Norman feudal community, the inhabitants of which had to face life under an entirely different set of rules. The village, as one supposes it existed, has already been described. Under its Saxon aeolderman it had been used to one kind of feudal system ; the Normans introduced another, a much harsher regime although King William had toned it down somewhat from the more brutal, continental version.

16

Previously the ceorls or freemen had owned their own land and had only looked to their own lord for protection whilst giving small services in return. This idea was alien to the Normans and had no part in their feudal methods.

The villagers now found that they were reduced to the level of serf in its most menial sense; they were no longer free; they were bound to the land and could not leave it even when it was sold; they were forced to work two or three days a week on their lord's land for no payment and they could not give their daughters in marriage without their lord's consent. They were completely in their lord's power. He could fine them, flog them or humiliate them in many other ways. Life was made very unpleasant for both Welsh and Saxons, having become slaves to men who despised them and who spoke a language that they could not understand.

William I, hard man though he was, was also a fair man and did not believe in severity for severity's sake. He introduced judicial measures into the new feudalism which were not at all popular with his barons because they were not wholly weighted on their side. There are several instances recorded in the pipe rolls, of manorial barons being fined for vicious beatings of their villeins. The Marcher barons, however, were a law to themselves and had much greater problems to contend with in the violent borderlands that they were expected to control. Their treatment of their villeins was probably only on a cruelty par with the lawlessness that surrounded them.

It may well be that Dinas Newydd and Pyndanvil, its suburb in villeinage, came in for slightly better than average treatment from the Lord of Gwynllwg, Robert, Earl of Gloucester, because there is evidence to suggest that he developed a certain liking for his Anglo-Welsh vassals. This may be due to the fact that he was half Welsh himself on his mother's side.

At this point Newport's story has still hardly begun but it has reached the commencement of a lull that lasted for many years. That is not to say that it was a time totally without incident but what was worth chronicling more often than not involved only the ruling classes. The lot of the common herd stood still drabness unabated; the little township never expanded and the population remained static. The quality of life only improved for those in charge – the barons and the lesser nobility – as they grew richer and more powerful off the backs of their forced-labour serfs who had become second class citizens in their own country!

There was some small consolation and a little hope for the future in the fact that the Normans were slowly becoming more willing to make selected bondsmen into freemen, albeit under the more restricted rules of the manorial system. One of the main conditions for those who qualified was that they should be members of a Saxon 'fyrd', a feudal levy raised to form part of a baron's defence force and ipso facto expected to fight against one's own kin were the situation to arise! Every man from the age of sixteen to sixty was eligible.

Robert Fitz Hamon, Lord of Gloucester, Morganwy and Gwynllwg, had an only daughter, Mabel, who had two apparent claims to fame. First, she caused Peterstone Church to be built and endowed with 60 acres of land which she gave to the Abbey of Bristol; second, she married Robert Fitz Henry, who succeeded to the Fitz Hamon estates inherited by Mabel on her father's death in 1107. Fitz Henry was created Earl of Gloucester in 1122.

Robert was the illegitimate son of King Henry I and therefore half brother to the Princess Matilda whom he supported in her long devastating war against her cousin Stephen in order to regain the Crown which she, as the deceased king's only true offspring, felt was rightfully hers. It is not inconceivable that many Dinas Newydd men, good and true, spent much of their time fighting in one of the Earl of Gloucester's fyrds during those terrible 18 years.

Like Robert, all the other barons took sides and, without a strong king to preside overall, they put the country to the sword in a savage orgy of settling old scores, questing for larger estates and gaining power over each other. Vast regions of prime land were devastated and famine spread across the land. A clearer picture of the situation in 1137 is given in the Anglo-Saxon Chronicle

'Then was corn dear, and flesh and cheese and butter, for there was none in the land; wretched men starved with hunger. Never was there more misery and never heathens acted worse than these. The earth bore no corn; you might as well have tilled the sea, for the land was all ruined by such deeds and it was said openly that Christ and his saints slept.'

Probably little of this privation touched Lower Gwent – at least there is no evidence of Matilda's wars being waged in the Valley of the Usk or of these lands of her cousin being laid waste. Left alone the small community would have been self sufficient even if kept short by the growing demands made of it by its lord in his battles. Nevertheless there may possibly have been some change when the wars ended in stalemate and, in 1138, the Earl of Gloucester's estates were confiscated. For a little while the Manors of Morganwg and Gwynllwg were in the hands of the Crown but were shortly restored when King Stephen, in order to safeguard his tenuous position, was forced to pardon all those who had opposed him, and agreed to Matilda's son becoming his heir.

The early 12th century saw a remarkable period of reconstruction. Between 1100 and 1113 AD the Normans rebuilt many of the old Saxon churches in stone where the material previously had been timber. Their castle-like design and, in many cases, crenellated towers, suggested and often proved that they were intended to be used in a second line of defence. Cases were known of garrisoned churches. St Glynlliws Church did not apparently receive the full treatment: reconstructed it was, but without a tower – probably because Fitz Hamon's castle was only a short distance away.

There was no let-up in the building of castles and in 1126 the Earl of Gloucester decided that a much stronger structure was needed at the Usk ford than any old timber fortification that previously existed. It seems probable that the main reason for this was that marauding bands of Welshmen continued to make regular attacks on Caerleon which was then still the principal town of Gwent. Blocking the path across the ford would have gone some way to allaying that threat. It may also have been in Earl Robert's mind that considering his own violent style of life, such an enterprise would not come amiss if he had a more substantial stronghold to which he could retire when he was in the area on manorial business.

The castle that stands on the river bank today is not the original. No trace of the original remains as it has been overbuilt, rebuilt and redesigned at various times through the ages.

The 12th century version was erected on the west bank of the River Usk just where the water level was hardly more than shin deep at low tide. It was constructed of rubble and stone which could have come from either or both of two quarries, one on Stow Hill just below the church and another where the barracks now stand.

There was a courtyard or green, surrounded by a wall which seems not to have been too intimidating because it was heightened at a later date. On three sides was a wide moat that filled at each high tide through inlets made in the river bank. The River Usk itself made up the fourth boundary. There would obviously have been gates but it is impossible to say how many or if they were in the same places as those of the later castle which will be described in a later chapter. There was definitely no west gate but when eventually one came into being it had no connection with the castle or the defence of the town.

It was the arrival of Newport Castle that caused the misconception that has lingered down the years. The Welsh called the castle 'Castell Newydd' or 'Casnewydd' meaning a new castle, presumably to avoid confusion with Caerleon and its old Roman castle. Of course it could just as easily have been a comparison with the decaying motte and bailey on Stow Hill. The name actually referred only to the building and everything within its walls for there was nothing outside except the serfs' community. This state of affairs seems to have deceived most of the mediaeval historians and travelling diarists who reported with conviction that the 'toune' was surrounded by stone walls. This belief was even fooling some into the 20th century!

In 1907 for instance, during excavations for the building of the new Savoy Hotel on the corner of Station Approach, stonework of great antiquity was uncovered and was presumed - rightly so - to have been part of the castle. Immediately, the architect of the project, Mr Gardiner, produced a plan reflecting his idea of the building in the 12th century. It depicted a great wall wide enough on which to patrol, with several watchtowers, enclosing the area from Stow Hill in the west to the Town Pill in the south. Huge fortified gates bestrode all roads in and out, and their positions approximated to Thomas Street (North Gate), the bridge (East Gate), the Town Pill (South Gate) and Stow Hill (West Gate).

Beside the facts that the West Gate was not built until the 14th century and was certainly not part of any wall, and the North Gate did not exist until the restoration to Owain Glyndwr's damage in the 15th century, it is inconceivable that such enormous bastions should not have left substantial remains about the town. Far older walls have survived over much of the British Isles, but even the great excavators of the 18th century – the canal builders found no trace when they carved their way through this part of the town.

But no more talk of ruins for the time being!

It was said that inside the castle lived no more than fifty souls made up of Norman gentry, their ladies, servants and tradesmen involved in the day to day running of the building. This was the New Castle and it is extremely doubtful if there was ever any intention of the name embracing a wider area than that enclosed within its walls.

The Normans themselves called the area Novus Burgus which meant a new fortified town and this must have been an appellation for a larger district than just the castle. Giraldus Cambrensis, Chaplain to King Henry II and Archdeacon of St Davids, certainly thought so for, in his writing of a visit to Newport in 1171, he referred to St Woolos Church by another of its many names – Ecclesia Novo Burgo.

Within a few years of the completion of the castle, one solitary house was erected just along the track near the end of the south wall. This was the home of the Murenger, the official delegated to collect murage, a toll or tax required to pay for the upkeep of the castle walls (Mur : French : wall).

The original murenger's house ceased its function in 1324 but the building remained until its demolition in 1816. At that time the public house now named 'Murenger House' in High Street stood alongside having been built nearly 300 years later in 1541, probably as the residence of the first High Sheriff (Sir Charles Herbert) after Henry VIII created the County of Monmouthshire in 1535. But even this building was completely demolished and rebuilt in the early 19th century.

The Reverend E Nicholson, in his 'Cambrian Traveller's Guide (1840)' wrote:-

'An old building called the Murengers House was left standing till the year 1816. The edifice which was ornamented in front with shield and arms carved in stone over an antiquated doorway, has been taken down. It was a building of one storey only with a handsome freestone front and portico.'

19

The Murenger House 1903

This makes three things clear: the present inn called 'The Murenger House' was never the home of the murenger; it is not the building erected in 1541 being of much lesser antiquity and furthermore it does not even occupy the same site as the 12th century original, although quite close!

Its proximity to the castle can be gauged by the fact that a portion of the old wall was exposed during the building of the first High Street Post Office in 1844. Archbishop Coxe's sketch plan of the castle shows that the end wall, running south to north, was approximately 240 feet from the river and, if the width of the moat is included, this would have put it almost on the line of the future Thomas Street. From this it is fair to assume that the pattern of Newport's few early streets conformed to the shape of the greater area of the castle.

The road from the bridge paralleled the south wall of the castle and continued over Stow Hill to Bassaleg but immediately at the end of the south wall it was joined at right angles by another track which passed along the moat at the back wall, into Mill Street, through Pyndanvil and up Milne Hill (Queens Hill) to the north. Thus it would appear that to round the corner of the castle wall was almost akin to turning into Thomas Street. The murenger's house stood just the other side of this junction – in 1324 almost certainly the only dwelling on the road!

The list of Newport's historic buildings is woefully short but at least those that are recorded have reasonably well documented and plausible reasons for their existence except, that is, for one!

There was another set of buildings in the form of a small castle, standing a couple of miles outside the feudal township, on the eastern bank of the River Ebbw, one mile or thereabouts from its confluence with the mouth of the Usk. It was very close to Tredegar House although separated by the river and obviously of much greater antiquity. Nothing is known of its original purpose but there is a theory that it was the work of a henchman of Baron Robert Fitz Hamon at about the time that the latter built the first Newport Castle on top of Stow Hill, the two fortifications being used in conjunction with one another.

It receives no mention anywhere until discovery by John Lelande and Thomas Churchyard in the 16th century. The former called it Castle Behan and the latter called it Greenfield (Maesglas). Lelande gave the following description:-

'A goodlye seate, a tour, a princelye pyle, built as a watch or saftie for the soyle, by river stands from Neuporte not three myle . . .'

It does not seem to have been a castle of importance judging from its size, or situated as it was in an area containing little worth defending. Lelande may have had the right idea in calling it a watchtower for it was ideally placed to give early warning of any craft clandestinely entering the River Ebbw out of sight of the town.

When Archbishop Coxe saw the remains in 1800 he referred to them as Castell Glas (Greencastle) and said:-

'Little remains now but a small square tower with a stone spiral staircase and some adjacent apartments now used for housing cattle. Several doorways in the gothic style are visible. The tenant in his time remembered vessels ascending the river to unload at a stone wall about five feet high along the river'.

21

All that remains of Castell Glas Maesglas

He also stated his belief that this had been a place of great strength and security during the civil wars (probably those of Edward II in the early 14th century). By the early 20th century the ruins were part of Maesglas Farm, close by the farmhouse and completely ignored as having any historical value! It is on record, however that before the Second World War this site was scheduled as an ancient monument. So much for preservation in a town that needed it more than most!

Wherever a new castle appeared, the traders and merchants were soon to follow and Novus Burgus was no exception.

Trading, even in its most basic form, was never a strong point of the Welsh or the Saxons. They were content just to tend their herds and till their fields, sustaining themselves and their families by virtue of the callused hand and sweat on the brow. It was the Danes who had been the traders and wherever they settled had grown up the great centres of commerce, as were the towns of Leicester, Lincoln, Nottingham and Derby, situated in the old Danelaw kingdom of the north.

Towns usually developed from villages after a market was added and then took their direction from whatever industry took root. The market attracted pedlars and itinerant salesmen with packs on their backs containing ornaments, woven cloths and other luxuries. An annual fair brought greater benefits from farther afield and merchants from Flanders, Venice and Genoa began to appear with their fine silks, velvets and precious stones.

As the needs of the people increased, fairs and pedlars were not enough. Markets had to be held in the most suitable places, two or three times a week. The choice venues were those to which goods could easily be brought from the surrounding country. Entrances to valleys, crossroads, the mouths of rivers, bridges and shallow fording places were ideal.

The situation of Novus Burgus in the 12th century was made to measure for such development. The new castle with inhabitants who demanded more of the good things of life, persuaded pedlars to stop where previously there had been nothing to gain. As there

22

was no other place to display their wares they set up their trays and small tables on the side of the track past the castle walls. The High Street of the future was in the course of being conceived!

With an avaricious eye to the profit and in accordance with the custom in all similar communities, the Lord of Gwynllwg took steps to control this influx by the institution of a weekly market, subject to the payment of stallage tolls. Members of the Abbey of Gloucester were exempted and also burgesses of the town. It was only a matter of time before an annual fair was organised to commence on August 15th (the Feast of the Assumption) and to last for fifteen days.

The presence of the market caused many changes. As visitors grew more numerous, officials had to be appointed to oversee the correct conduct of business and to make rules for fair dealing. Additional tradesmen such as carpenters and blacksmiths were needed for market repairs and so the first service industry became present where no form of industry had thitherto existed. Many merchants found it more convenient to live near a permanent market and often attached their stalls to their houses, thus creating the first shops.

Protection by the lord of the manor increased in importance as prosperity grew and consequently the trading area clung more tightly to the castle. In these circumstances it was a natural sequel when the Normans decided that the ford, which was the main route to the market and which was impassable due to the tide for much of the day, should be bridged.

Fifty seven years or thereabouts after the building of the castle, the first bridge was erected over the River Usk in the tiny, Anglo-Welsh, Norman-dominated township of Novus Burgus. There were those who would still occasionally use the ford but for all practical purposes it ceased to exist after having served the ancient Britons for thousands of years, the Romans for some 400 years, raiding parties of Danes and Saxons for 220 years and finally the Normans. The latter had already demonstrated what prolific builders they were, but so too had the Romans who, in their small regard for the area, had deemed it unworthy of a bridge. It had taken 600 years to create the enhancement that made the difference!

Constructional timber was cut in the forest between Caerleon and Usk. To withstand the pressure of the enormous tides and fierce currents, the trees that supplied the legs of the bridge must have been massive, although from a little distance the overall effect would have been spindly and rickety.

The carriageway was of edge to edge planks and very narrow, but just wide enough for two carts to pass. It must have been a harrowing experience for anyone with a heavily laden, horse-drawn vehicle to be right in the middle of a 500 feet span, with the timberwork creaking and groaning in protest against the huge forces exerted below, with nothing but a flimsy rail preventing a plunge into the racing torrent. One has only to stand in a similar position, behind the safety of the heavy concrete parapet of the 20th century bridge at high tide, to get a graphic idea of the 12th century traveller's ordeal!

Despite the obvious signs of instability however, there is only one recorded instance of any of the old wooden bridges collapsing of their own accord or being carried away by tidal forces. There were several occasions when they were deliberately brought down, but on the whole their construction seems to have been sound. As it happens, the Norman bridges at Newport through the ages received little if any mention of being renewed or repaired but it is hard to credit that such structures would be long lasting.

The King of England was now Henry II, great grandson of William the Conqueror, and first of the Plantagenets. During his reign he featured in two incidents where Newport supplied the background.

William, 2nd Earl of Gloucester, had become Lord of the Manors of Morganwy and

Gwynhlwg following the death of his father, Robert, in 1147. The King had asked him to supply a company of his Welsh archers, who were noted as the best in the whole of Britain, to help in a campaign against the troublesome Rhys, Prince of South Wales. Henry's passage with his army through Newport was watched with great interest and a large crowd of local people gathered to witness the accuracy of an ancient prophesy.

Gerald Cambrensis tells that Merlin, the great King Arthur's friend and adviser, had predicted that one day a mighty freckled-faced prince, intent on invasion, would succeed in crossing a ford of the Nant Pencarn (River Ebbw) and by so doing bring about the complete subjugation of Wales. Since Henry was both mighty and freckled-faced, and as the ford was in a dangerous condition, everyone was eager to see if the prophesy would be fulfilled. Needless to say, Henry did make a successful crossing but since Merlin's day the main road had been realigned to a new, safer ford just a mile or so north of the old ford, and it is highly questionable if the King would have risked the loss of his cavalry and foot-soldiers in the swamps and dangerous eddies of the older crossing.

This campaign against the Welsh was fruitless and, as Henry made no further efforts against them, it may be said that Merlin miscalculated. But he was not always wrong for he did forecast in relation to Gwent that one day rivers would be made to flow over mountains and that ships would sail over them. This sounds like a very accurate description of the canals which came to join Newport to the upper valleys and Brecon at the end of the 18th century.

By 1173, Prince Iorwerth ap Owen was causing untold problems for the Normans in Gwent, but King Henry felt that nothing would be gained by another offensive; instead he decided to rely on diplomacy.

He invited Iorwerth and his sons to a peace conference on the Welsh border. They accepted and were granted safe passage. Owen, eldest son of Iorwerth, was on his way and about to cross the bridge at Newport when some of the castle's garrison attacked and killed him. Whether this was a premeditated act at the orders of William, Earl of Gloucester, or accidental, the result was predictable and immediate. Iorwerth and his youngest son broke off relations with King Henry, returned in haste to the fastnesses of Wales and, gathering a huge army descended on Gwent with fire and sword laying waste from the Severn to Hereford and from the Rhymney to the Wye. How Newport was effected is not recorded suffice to say that it stood right in the way of this bloody, revengeful tide!

It is interesting to note that despite all the reports of damage caused by the constant Welsh attacks over the years, Caerleon seemed to have fared pretty well, although it changed hands regularly as counter-attack followed counter-attack. This presumption is based upon another eye-witness report:-

'Many remains of its former magnificence are still visible; splendid palaces which once emulated with their golden roofs, the grandeur of Rome, for it was originally built by the Roman princes, and adorned with stately edifices; a gigantic tower, numerous baths, ruins of temples and a theatre, the walls of which are partly standing. Here we see, both within and without the walls subterraneous buildings, aqueducts and vaulted caverns; and what appeared to me most remarkable, stoves so excellently contrived, as to diffuse their heat through secret and imperceptible pores.'

Gerald gave this account following a visit made in 1188 but, like several other of his writings, doubt can be cast upon it. Apparently, 50 years earlier, Henry of Huntingdon also visited Caerleon and reported that he saw no trace of the city walls!

Nearly 700 years were to pass before another opinion from an impeccable source gave the impression that little had changed. Seated at his desk in the Hanbury Arms on September 16th 1856, Alfred Lord Tennyson wrote: 'This is a most quiet half ruined village of about 1500 inhabitants with a little museum of Roman tombstones and other things.'

The reason for Gerald's presence was the Third Crusade.

A year earlier, in 1187, news had been received that the Saracens, under their leader Saladin, had overrun the Holy Land and taken Jerusalem. In order to recapture it a new crusade was proclaimed and King Henry II sent Baldwin, the Archbishop of Canterbury, into Wales to preach the crusade. Gerald Cambrensis was invited to accompany him, probably because being Welsh himself (born in Manorbiere), it was thought that he would soften reception to a Norman Archbishop. A number of other noted archbishops were in the party which travelled down from Hereford, preaching at Abergavenny, Usk, Caerleon and finally arriving at Newport. Some historians dispute this, saying that Newport was not on the itinerary, but there is no doubt that Gerald was in Caerleon on this occasion and it is hardly likely that an important manorial township nearby would have been ignored. Anyway, after a nights rest, the eminent clerics gathered to preach their sermon before the Norman gentry, the native dignitaries and the lined-up soldiers from the castle.

Where this assembly took place is not known for certain. The obvious place was the most important local church and this would certainly have been St Woolos, except for the fact that it was still suffering from Prince Iorwerth's disastrous attack in 1172 to avenge his son's death. The church still stood roofless and largely unrepaired. Although it was somewhat undignified for such a high ranking cleric to address his congregation in the open air, there was no alternative.

At places popular for religious meetings it was customary to erect a stone, wayside cross, and such a cross stood halfway up Stow Hill where Havelock Street now joins it. Near the site today stands Cross House (the Baneswell Social Club). A portion of the head of the cross is in Newport Museum, having been found in the bed of the River Usk in 1925 during the building of the new roadbridge. Buried 21 feet deep in the mud and 130 feet from the town bank, it is believed that the cross was broken off and thrown from the bridge by Parliamentary forces carrying out the provisions of a 1643 decree. The base was removed to St Woolos in the 1930s, leaving the original site totally unmarked. The Museum's dating places it some 250 years after the Crusade so this may not be the original cross.

There is disagreement over Newport's response to the sermon. Gerald had said: 'the men of Gwent were accustomed to war, famous for valour and more expert in archery than any others in Wales.'

Some sources say that the recruiting campaign was a huge success but the general consensus is that for all their courage not many of the townsfolk nor of their country kin folk, showed willingness to forsake their homes in order to follow the Archbishop to his subsequent death in the Holy Land.

By now, the ownership of the manors and Newport Castle had become complicated by the death in 1183 of William, Earl of Gloucester. His only son, Robert, had predeceased him so the estates went, undivided, to Isobel, the eldest of three daughters. Unfortunately she happened to be married to John, 3rd son of King Henry II, and the future, infamous King of England. He was then known as John Lackland because of his lack of title and estate (the term used was 'portionless'). His good fortune in succeeding to his wife's considerable estates did not automatically bring with it the Earldom of Gloucester but he took it anyway and was allowed to keep it.

It was therefore under this title that John acted as regent to his brother, King Richard I (Lionheart), during his absence abroad for nine of his ten years on the throne. John was Lord of the Manor of Gwynllwg for the whole of the time that he was grossly mismanaging the realm, and committing the terrible deeds that have branded him the worst monarch that this country has ever had! However, in 1199 King Richard died, John became king and almost immediately divorced Isobel – but not her estates which he kept in his hands until his death in 1216. The effect of his ownership on the manors and their population can only be guessed at by comparison with his contemptible attitude to the country as a whole; record of incident in Newport for this period is sparse and remained so for the next 40 years.

To avoid any further confusion caused by the several name changes of the town it is proposed to refer to it only as Newport from hereon. It is impossible to say when this name first arrived or indeed when the maritime trading status was sufficiently raised to merit the title of port. It could have been around the year 1348 when Ralph, 1st Earl of Stafford, instituted the Westgate Tolbothe for the collection of levies on all goods entering the town and on cargoes from ships. Nothing appears in writing however until 14th century documentation of the redistribution of the Morganwy and Gwynllwg Manors.

After King John's death, the manors were handed back to his ex-wife, Isobel, but she died childless in 1217 so her estate passed to her sister, Amice, widow of Richard de Clare, Earl of Hertford. Their son, Gilbert, succeeded as the Earl of Gloucester and Hertford until his death in 1230 and this marriage of estates made the De Clare family one of the biggest landowners in the realm.

For nine years the widowed Countess Isabella was in control and then she too passed on. From 1239 a few years of stewardship by other relatives followed until Isabella's son, Richard de Clare received full title and held it from 1243 to 1262, a period in the later years of which Newport formed the backcloth to events which might have changed the course of British history.

At this time the district of the Marches around Newport was in a dreadful state. In 1247 Mathew Paris, the celebrated chronicler, wrote:

The Welsh employed themselves in pillage, slaughter and incendiarism and only laughed and ridiculed the efforts made by the English for their suppression. The frontiers are reduced to a desert and inhabitants fall by the sword; castles and houses were consumed by fire, and woods were felled by axe and by spade; flocks and herds fell victim to the butchers or died of starvation.

Peter de Montfort, father of the Duke of Leicester, was in command of Abergavenny Castle and he wrote to the King to the effect that all around his seat was devastation. In 1258, conditions were made more miserable by a great storm that destroyed most of the crops throughout the county.

The new King of England after John was his son, the third Henry, and as he was only nine years old the country was in the regency of two Earls Marshal of England and, it must be said, was ruled wisely and well.

It was when Henry III took over the full management of his kingdom in 1227 that he began to show what a weak, foolhardy and totally extravagant king he was to become. His court overflowed with toadies drawn from relatives and foreigners. He filled every vacant post of authority with his French wife's uncles and cousins. He gave away royal estates as presents.

Rome became an obsession with him and he fell completely under papal influence, so much so that he drained the Treasury and the Church's coffers in order to send gifts. He paid 135,000 marks (£50,000) to the Pope to obtain the Kingdom of Sardinia for his youngest son Edmund, a position that was never taken up. He waged an expensive and totally pointless war against France. In the midst of a severe famine he took corn that had been purchased by his barons in Germany to alleviate suffering, and sold it elsewhere for his own profit! The tales of his shameful behaviour were unremitting and eventually his demands of his barons drove them to extreme action.

From among them, as leader, emerged Simon de Montfort, Earl of Leicester, and his close ally, Richard de Clare, Earl of Gloucester. A demand was made that a committee should be formed to draw up terms for reforming the State and obtaining the king's confirmation of Magna Carta signed by his father. From 1259 to 1264 negotiations took place with the king, but in vain. Henry broke promise after promise until armed conflict became the only answer. The Barons War began.

- O -

In 1264, Earl Simon's army faced the Royalists at Lewes and after fierce fighting all day through the streets of the town, claimed victory with King Henry and his son Prince Edward as prisoners.

The old Earl of Gloucester had died in 1262 so it was his son, Gilbert de Clare, known as the Red Baron, who fought at Lewes alongside De Montfort, although their relations were becoming strained. A final split in the alliance came a few months later.

The young Earl Gilbert had for some time been growing disenchanted with De Montfort who seemed to be overreaching himself in taking authority into his own hands. He had for instance taken over the wardenship of all the Marcher castles and installed in them his own supporters. There was also a personal reason for the rift and this was connected with the Earl of Leicester's designs on De Clare lands in South Wales, which had originally belonged to his wife's family. Many barons suspected, rightly or wrongly, that the Crown itself was at stake ! The Earl of Gloucester finally broke away and renewed his support for the king and his son Edward, both of whom De Montfort was taking with him wherever he went.

It was at Hereford Castle that Gloucester and his friend Roger Mortimer found them and secretly effected the escape of Prince Edward to Ludlow where he raised forces loyal to the King and commenced to harass Earl Simon, driving him southwards into Gwent. De Montfort was repelled in an attack on Monmouth Castle but he managed to take Usk, although not for long as this was a De Clare fortress in the heart of De Clare lands. Driven out, he headed for Newport and easily captured the castle which for some reason was only lightly garrisoned at the time.

By now De Montfort's army had been augmented by that of LLywelyn ap Gruffyd, the last, great, native Prince of Wales – a strange alliance but one which the Welsh prince obviously felt would benefit him in his lifelong fight for independence from the Crown of England. Preparations for escape were now made. There was only one way and that was across the Severn.

Prince Edward's spies informed him that rescue ships were crossing from Bristol to the Usk.

In readiness for embarkation Earl Simon marched his army down the east bank of the River Usk to Goldcliff, but he arrived only to witness the sinking of his seven ships in the river mouth by Prince Edward's fleet, newly arrived from Gloucester. It could be said that Uskmouth had experienced its one and only naval battle! The beleaguered Barons' Army was now forced to retreat back up the River Usk, fighting a desperate rearguard action against Prince Edward's soldiers who had landed to continue in hot pursuit.

Those today who know these low-lying moors, interlaced with drainage ditches locally referred as reens, may find it difficult indeed to visualise the scenes enacted on that day in 1265, across what was then a vast, unenclosed, waterlogged plain. Many hundreds of men with horses and supply wagons overflowed from the narrow, pot-holed, country tracks and turned the already marshy terrain into a gigantic sea of mud. The return journey would probably have been even more hasty with the curses of the heavily weighed-down knights hardly heard above the squealing of terrified horses, kicking and plunging frantically as they struggled to free themselves from the morass.

The parishes of Goldcliff, Nash and Liswerry would have presented a scene of men scattering like a nest of disturbed ants and, close behind, another huge force trying to make up ground through the great man-made bog already churned up twice by its quarry! One can only wonder at the effect that all this mayhem, taking place outside its walls, would have had on the inmates of Goldcliff Priory. Their situation must have placed them in the thick of things!

The Priory had by then been established by the Benedictines for 150 years and even if quite small was very active. It stood on top of the 'gold' cliff, the only cliff as such to be found along that stretch of the River Severn, and so called by Gerald Cambrensis because of the effect of sunlight on its reddish grit and embedded mica chippings, covered in modern times by massive sea defence masonry. The Priory's later history is extremely vague; it became unused after Henry VIII's disestablishment of religious houses. In 1710, however, Hill Farm was built on the exact site and it is said that in the farmhouse cellar there was an original monastery wall inset with a window.

Although only a small cliff as cliffs go, the height of the gold cliff above sea level made it the ideal vantage point from which Simon de Montfort was to watch for his ships and then to see them being sunk in the Usk rivermouth.

Once the bulk of his fleeing army was back across the River Usk and into the little township of Newport, the wooden bridge was fired and by the time of Prince Edward's arrival, was totally destroyed. It is anyone's guess as to the feelings of the burgesses of the town, but undoubtedly they were none too pleased at losing the main access from the east, not to mention the untold damage done by hordes of fighting men living off the land, driving away the livestock for food and trampling down the planted fields!

The final act in this drama was played out many miles away in England having received most of its impetus from the events that took place in and around Newport. Simon de Montfort, Earl of Leicester, now finding escape across the Severn denied to him, fought his starving army through the mountainous regions of North Gwent to Hereford from where he hoped to reach his son's army at Kenilworth, not knowing that this son had already been killed and his army dispersed.

At Evesham, Prince Edward caught up with him, surrounded the remains of the baronial army and in a series of tactical moves cut it to pieces. De Montfort was offered a honourable surrender but, refusing, he and another of his sons fought on to the death.

So ended the life of a man thought of by many as the greatest Englishman (he was French-born) in history due to his concern for his country and for what he achieved during the few short years when he held higher authority than the King. His Barons' Parliament was seen as the very first attempt at a truly representative, legislative body such as the House of Commons was eventually to become. Even his death which ended the Barons War, did not wipe out the seeds of democracy that were sown in his lifetime.

Newport saw him and felt his presence, and if he had by chance passed through the town as victor rather than vanquished, a change of events could have been unleashed that would have resulted in a mutation of history that would have had far-reaching, escalating effects to this very day!

But, returning to the havoc that the war must have wreaked on Newport, no record has survived of the rebuilding of the bridge on this occasion but it must have been the top priority for a town that had become so dependent on it. In actual fact it was to be another 59 years (1324) before revocation of its tolls (pontage) brought written acknowledgement that a replacement had been made.

Given a little time to recover after its gruelling experience in the Barons' War, Newport found one redeeming feature. King Henry III, once more safely ensconced on his throne, showed his gratitude for the help given to him by the Earl of Gloucester and the burgesses of Newport whatever form that had taken by paying for the erection of the first short, stumpy tower on St Woolos Church. On the face of it this appears to have been a magnanimous gesture until one remembers Henry's previous record of financial dealings, and then the suspicion arises that somehow the squirearchy of the town might have been inveigled into treating itself in the king's name!

Chapter Three

The Middle Ages

The last decade of the 13th century held further troubled times for Newport. The year 1295 saw the death of the lord of the manor, Gilbert of Gloucester, but in the years immediately preceding, he was involved in military actions in and around the town with Morgan ap Meredydd, son of Meredydd ap Gruffyd, Lord of Machen.

It will be remembered that when the first Norman overlord, Fitz Hamon, invaded Gwent in 1093, he left the area from Machen northwards in the hands of the Welsh with a certain amount of autonomy. This had led to a shaky but peaceful stability for the next 200 years until Gilbert de Clare decided to dispossess the Welsh chieftain and bring the Machen estates back under the strict control of the Gloucester earldom with all the rigours that that involved. Naturally, Meredydd objected strongly and sent his son at the head of an armed force down the western valley to attack Newport.

What sort of action ensued can only be gauged by clues in an inquisition of the deceased earl's estate in 1296. This was the usual stock-taking of assets taken 'post mortem', and it showed that fighting had been carried into the town.

The evidence was that of 256 burgages, 66 were noted as destroyed by warfare - a burgage being anything for which the lord received a rent, not necessarily being built upon or lived in. There was damage to the mill and the low income from beer suggested that a corn crop had been obliterated.

The next earl, also a Gilbert, was only four years old when his father died in 1295 so he could not immediately enter into his inheritance. His mother Countess Joan of Acre, daughter of King Edward I, would normally have held the estate during Gilbert's minority but she had antagonised her father, making him withhold them from her. Her offence was that she had remarried within a year of her husband's death to one of his squires, much against her father's wishes. However, just before his own death in 1307 he relented and gave back the earldom to his grandson, the sixteen year old Gilbert de Clare.

The new king, Edward II, was Gilbert's uncle and only seven years older; they spent much of their childhood in each other's company. They became close friends and as Gilbert grew into a dashing military leader, it was not surprising that he and his Gwent archers were always at the king's right hand. So it was that at the early age of twenty-three, Gilbert met his death at the Battle of Bannockburn in 1314, due to a moment of indiscretion occasioned by a difference of opinion with the king over the tactics to be employed. The young earl advised that battle should not be joined with the fresh, well dug-in, Scottish army until the English troops had rested from their long march. Edward did not agree and accused his old friend of cowardice, stinging the hot-headed Gilbert into leading a brave but extremely foolhardy cavalry charge from which he did not return.

The Welsh manors were leaderless once again and as there was no male heir they remained so for the next three years while the Crown contemplated the inheritance.

Earl Gilbert had three sisters and in 1317 the decision was made that the estates should be theirs, but not in partnership. For the first time, the Morganwg(Glamorgan) manors were severed from those of Gwenllwg (Gwent) and this action gave Newport real township status as the principal town of the manor - a position that only Cardiff had enjoyed when the manors were combined. The documentation required for the division showed for the first time the town's modern name: 'Dominium de Newporte in Wallia', (Lordship of Newport in Wales).

Eleanor was married to Hugh Despenser and their share was Glamorgan; Margaret was married to Hugh de Audley and they were given Lower Gwent together with Newport and its castle. Elizabeth, the youngest daughter and her husband Roger Damory, received the Lordship of Usk. This might sound a fair arrangement but one could not reckon without the nature of Despenser the Younger, so called to distinguish him from his father, Hugh Despenser the Elder, Earl of Westminster.

The term 'robber baron' is a product of the 20th century and has been used in several different connotations, usually in a jocular vein as evinced in pantomime or in the popular, romanticised idea of the mediaeval hero's traditional enemy. But they did exist and from what one can gather, Despenser was the epitome!

He too had been a childhood friend of King Edward and of course his wife was the king's niece. Somehow, taking advantage of these personal relations, he managed to dominate the king almost completely, bending him to his will and obtaining all sorts of special favours. The king accepted his advice above that of all others and this made the earl the most hated among his peers. Despenser was mean, grasping, avaricious and intent only on increasing his already massive land holdings. He was entirely without scruples and often resorted to trickery and legal chicanery to snap up estates which for any reason, had become vacant. Eventually, by the most underhand methods and questionable means of persuasion, he had acquired estates yielding him four to five thousand pounds a year, making him the richest and most powerful of barons.

He was most upset by the division of the De Clare lands in South Wales for he had imagined that through his wife, the eldest daughter Eleanor, he would have obtained the whole inheritance for himself. However he was not chagrined for long. This was Despenser after all, and in 1320 he persuaded the king to force his brother-in-law, Hugh de Audley to cede Lower Gwent (and Newport) to him. Not content with this however, Despenser coveted every other manor in sight and this proved to be his undoing when the rest of the barony realised that due to his extraordinary influence with King Edward, he stood every chance of fulfilling his ambitions. They took the law into their own hands!

Hugh de Audley, Roger Damory, Henry Bohun, Earl of Hereford, Roger Mortimer and other leading Marcher lords joined forces with the family of Prince Llewelyn Bren of Machen who had been treacherously executed by Despenser. The huge force flying the king's banner consisted of 800 men-at-arms, 500 hobelers (light horse) and 10,000 foot. They attacked Newport on 4th May 1321, taking the castle after a four day siege during which everything in the neighbourhood belonging to Despenser was destroyed! Damage to the castle cost £600 to repair which in 14th century terms was quite considerable. The attackers ruined the manor's corn crop and it took more than 300 oak trees from the Caerleon forest to carry out local repairs in the district. This might suggest another wrecking of the bridge!

Moving on into Glamorgan the baronial army destroyed Despenser castles at Cardiff, Caerphilly, Llantrisant and elsewhere, laying waste to his lands and chattels wherever they found them. This great show of feeling was accompanied by a petition to King Edward for the banishment of the Despensers, both father and son. In the face of such determination the king could not find the courage to refuse.

Hugh de Audley once more assumed the mantle of Lord of the Manor of Newport and Lower Gwent but the crafty King Edward insisted that as it was banishment by the Crown that caused the estate to become vacant, then that estate was rightfully forfeit to the Crown. To which De Audley replied that as far as he was concerned the estate had never been legally vacated by him in the first place and in defiance of the king he stood his ground!

In the following year, 1322, the king, weak and fickle as ever, reinstated the Despensers and raised an army strong enough to face the barons when they came to seek retribution. The two armies met at Boroughbridge in North Yorkshire and victory went to the king. The senior baron, the Earl of Lancaster, was executed almost immediately outside his own castle of Pontefract; Roger Damory, Lord of Usk was sentenced to a like fate but being married to another of the king's nieces, he was reprieved. Mortimer was imprisoned while his case was considered. Hugh Despenser, back at his old games and with the king's help, found rich pickings among the forfeited estates of the 'treasonable' barons!

Edward's queen, Isabella, and the twelve year old Prince of Wales, were in France in 1325, sent by the king to pay homage to Isabella's brother, the French king, Charles IV. For some time the queen had been conducting an affair with Earl Mortimer who now escaped from prison to join her in France where they pooled their hatred of King Edward and the Despensers, and began to plot their downfall. In September 1326, Isabella publicly renounced her marriage vows and together with Mortimer and a band of 700 co-conspirators, crossed the Channel to England, where they found great support from those discontented with the king's rule. Realising that the weight of opinion against him made resistance pointless, King Edward and the Despensers fled westwards. Hugh Despenser the Elder was ordered to defend Bristol but the garrison mutinied and handed him over to his pursuers. Showing no respect for his 90 years of age they executed him where he stood in his full armour! Meanwhile, the king and Despenser the Younger crossed the River Wye and tried to escape from Chepstow by sailing first to Lundy and then to France but several days of adverse winds forced them to come ashore and continue their flight into Despenser's Glamorgan stronghold. On November 16th 1326 they were captured at Neath Abbey, en route to Caerphilly Castle, by the Young Earl of Lancaster who was still seething at the execution of his father at Pontefract, and brought back to Monmouth Castle. Eight days later, in Hereford, Hugh Despenser was tried, found guilty and hung, drawn and quartered on a fifty foot high gibbet, one of the highest ever built for an execution. The King was taken to Kenilworth Castle where he was made to relinquish the Great Seal of England, symbolic of giving up the Crown. Subsequently he was moved to Berkeley Castle, ostensibly for an indefinite period of imprisonment whilst the complexity of his position was considered. Roger Mortimer and Queen Isabella now ruled the country as regents for Prince Edward who was still only fourteen years old. Mortimer always felt that his position would be in jeopardy while the ex-king was alive so he had issued orders of which Isabella was possibly unaware, that Edward's stay in Berkeley Castle should be made as rough, cold, hungry and insanitary as possible in the hope that his end would be hastened. However, Edward's stamina proved stronger than was expected so Mortimer impatiently sent assassins to finish the task, with instructions to leave no mark that would suggest foul play.

During the night of September 23rd 1327, Edward was finally despatched by a red hot iron thrust into his bowels. His fearful screams of agony awakened the villagers well beyond the walls of the castle! The following day his body, outwardly unmarked, was placed on public display to show that he had died a natural death.

Hugh de Audley received back his Lordship of Newport together with the Earldom of Gloucester which was especially recreated for him and which curiously was never passed on. Thus the sequence of inheritance returned to traditional lines and life by the River Usk returned to normal or as near normal as those tempestuous times would allow. De Audley became a very important official in the king's service and served in several foreign countries on diplomatic and military missions. His manors were called upon often to support the king.

In 1332 the Earl took a Welsh contingent to fight in Ireland and a year later, Newport was ordered to supply a hundred men for service in the Scottish wars. At home in 1338, Newport Castle received orders to prepare for a Welsh assault but this seems to have been a false alarm. In 1346 the Lordship volunteered a hundred men for the French campaign; in 1362 the Irish campaign called for thirty archers and in 1370 the town was warned to be armed against a French invasion!

- 0 -

Growth of the town has already been touched on insofar as it depended on its visitors and the trade that they introduced. There are no population statistics for those days or indeed for any period before 1791 except for the unsubstantiated figure of 460 in the year 1711 as mentioned by James Matthews in 'Historic Newport' .However, a little hypothesis does no harm, and if it is based on the very few established facts loosely related to residency, and a study of what is known of the rest of Britain, it may be possible to arrive at a not unreasonable offering.

It has been estimated that the population of England, Scotland and Wales was in 1086 (the Domesday Survey) only half what it was under the Romans. Depopulation appears to have been at its most severe in the 6th, 7th and 8th centuries as people suffered from famine, disease and the worst excesses of the satanic, Dark Age invaders. Under these circumstances it is logical to assume that the lower stretches of the River Usk did not feature in this exodus for the very good reason that there was nothing there to depopulate!

Between the Domesday Survey and the late 13th century the total population of Britain increased from 1½ millions to about 5 millions but Newport did not share in this renaissance for the likely reason that with its flood-prone river banks, ugly mudflats and unhealthy marsh lands it was ill favoured with assets that would promote a growing population. This adds more weight to the theory that the first stirrings of a town came almost by accident in the late Saxon era and hardly more than a century before the first Norman soldier crossed the ford.

There is no way of telling if Newport's population of 750 in 1791 had been constant for any length of time, or if this figure was the result of a sudden 18th century surge. After all, the national population had risen from about 5 millions to nearly 8 millions in the previous 60 years chiefly due to a famine free period, a much improved birth survival rate and a plummeting death rate. Newport however could not claim to be a contributor to these statistics – the acquisition of only 750 heads in 600 years can hardly be described as 'healthy' growth, especially in view of the fact that the population of the rest of Wales shot up by 50% during the 16th century alone!

In 1293 there were 247 burgages in the town but a large proportion of them were not residential. These would have been the strips of rented agricultural land, barns, cattle pens, quarries, fishponds and even areas along the castle moat rented to thatchers for their supply of reeds and osiers. It follows that the number of burgages on which people actually lived was considerably less than the total.

In 1750 there were only 178 houses so, by the use of some extrapolation between the two dates and including a little influence from national population trends, it might not be too unreasonable to settle on a figure of between 30 and 40 houses in the 14th century. Families were inclined to be large both from the point of view of ignorance of birth control and the need of members as a potential source of extra income to the family and further protection against decimation by disease and starvation. So, with a conservative estimate of say five persons in each household surviving early demise (and allowing for an equal number who did not) the population of the riverside village could well have been reckoned at something between 150 and 200. If this was anywhere near accurate it means that the town's population increased, incredibly, by less than 100 per century over 600 years!

No great store should be put by such heterogeneous calculations. As far as Newport is

33

concerned, only the flimsiest evidence is provided by an indeterminate starting point in time, among a scattering of crude shacks around a small castle, and the complete absence of birth, death and migration records over seven centuries. In these circumstances even the most inspired speculation can only be the most arbitrary. Even if such records ever existed, in whatever form, they are long gone from any archives that may have been housed in castle, cathedral or tollbooth vaults. Owain Glyndwr, numerous marauding Welsh princes and generations of the borough's inept, self-seeking mediaeval corporations have much to answer for!

Compared to Newport the average medium sized town in England (Bristol for example) in the middle ages had 2,000 to 3,000 inhabitants but it must be remembered that any population quotations up until the first national census in 1801 must be the product of educated guesswork.

Most histories written about the early development of the coastal areas of Wales make little or no mention of Newport. Cardiff and Swansea achieve regular references as small but prospering ports, but by far the greatest credits go to Tenby, Pembroke, Carmarthen and Milford Haven. Obviously Newport had little to offer in the Tudor world of big business and marine commerce.

The places that consistently did well were those where there was easy access to the main trading commodities of the day: wool, woven goods and leather; no wonder then that the more westerly of the Welsh ports were so favoured, situated as they were so conveniently for the thriving Welsh cloth industry. Newport's day *would* come but that day was still nearly two centuries away. Meanwhile, no incentive, no change and no growth!

Squalid, insanitary living conditions, undoctored illness and disease, ignorance and a phenomenal birth mortality rate all contributed to Newport's stand-stills, go-slows and sometime regressions, but from which ever way it is looked at it is only too apparent that the town's demographic record was widely divergent from that of the nation as a whole.

Since the days of Baron Robert Fitz Hamon, their first Norman master, Newport's inhabitants seemed to have found some favour with his successors and received from them more concern than many of their ilk in other parts of the kingdom. The earliest of granted privileges remain vague but later barons all seemed eager to confirm and improve much of what had gone before.

The device used to confer such liberties was known as a charter and was usually given only to the king to grant. Since, however, Newport was situated in the Welsh March, its charters did not require royal sanction because of the autonomous authority originally given to the Marcher barons by William the Conqueror.

In 1324, the notorious Hugh Despenser uncharacteristically secured for his Newport burgesses exemption from all tolls, murage, pontage, picage, pavage, quayage, terrage, lastage, stallage, tronage and other dues levied on traders or their merchandise in any lands ruled by King Edward II. This even extended to Aquitaine in France and each burgess was issued with a strip of parchment showing name, calling, residence and qualification – a passport to freedom from taxation! This was the event which disposed of the need for the murenger and the house that went with the job.

It was a truly handsome package in an age of lord and lackey and one that was regularly confirmed by successive lords of the manor in 1342, 1359, 1394, 1423, 1465 and 1497. For such primitive times the lives of all those resident in Newport were reasonably regulated. Admittedly they had to go to bed when the curfew bell tolled; their only indoor entertainment were the miracle plays performed in church on holy days, and in the open air there was little else but dancing round a maypole to the music of pipe and tabour.

34

Cross bowman on the ramparts
of Newport Castle

Merchant seaman of Old Newport

A citizen of Old Newport

Lady of Old Newport

35

All in all however they knew only too well that they possessed privileges that had to be guarded jealously against insinuation by newcomers, unless they had special qualities to offer the town.

The burgesses were even permitted to produce carly by-laws subject to the baron's approval. One of the first was to become a permanent part of the town's constitution until repealed in 1711 by a much more enlightened borough council. It empowered the burgesses to escort undesirable characters to the manor boundary and eject them into the county from which they came. Undesirables in this context was meant to describe those who were old or infirm and who might become a drain on the local poor rate to which they had contributed nothing. It was also meant to work against persistent trouble-makers but in this respect it was open to abuse and the good burgesses were not above fitting any innocent who displeased them with this description! As the years rolled by, this ordinance was operated with increased vigour especially when it was found that its manipulation could be financially rewarding to unscrupulous authority. No doubt the part it played in the restriction of residency to only a chosen few, was relevant to the population debate!

- 0 -

The year 1338 saw the commencement of the Hundred Years War against France over Edward's III's claim to the French throne through his French mother Isabella, and his attempt to regain territories in France that the Plantagenets had always regarded as theirs. The war did not really last continually for a hundred years but consisted of a series of campaigns stretching through the reigns of five English monarchs.

On June 25th 1346, the king ordered payments to be made to Ralph, Earl of Stafford, the then incumbent of the Newport and Gwynllwg Manors. Ralph had earlier volunteered 100 fighting men from his Welsh manors as follows:-

2	knights bannerets (having with them some of their own retainers)	4 shillings a day.
16	knights	2 - do
31	esquires	1 - do -
50	bowmen on horseback	6 pence a day

Total 99 with the Earl himself making the hundred.

The payment in modern terms was extremely handsome. An earl's fee would have been eight shillings a day but in this case Ralph received nothing because he was a volunteer and presumably paid his own expenses.

The Newport contingent attended divine service, left the castle by the drawbridge into High Street (or whatever it was then called), crossed the river bridge and, via Christchurch and Gloucester, headed for Southampton where a huge fleet of sail awaited them. Two months later, on August 26th 1346 at the village of Crecy in France, 100,000 Frenchmen and their allies faced 25,000 travel-weary Englishmen, Welshmen and Irishmen. Ralph, Earl of Stafford, led his Newport battalion in the forefront of the first division of the sixteen year old Black Prince.

The heavily armoured French knights and their well-rested foot-soldiers attacked in waves all through the day but each charge faltered and broke under the devastating firepower of the Welsh archers. The arrows darkened the sky like flocks of birds and stocks of them grew so low that they had to be torn from the bodies of the slain and used again! The range of the great bows was measured in hundreds of yards and the force of their delivery could pin a man to his horse through his armour!

When the battle ended a most astonishing sight was revealed. The French king, retreating, left over 20,000 dead and wounded in the field amongst whom were numbered two allied kings, five princes and five dukes! British losses, as near as can be ascertained, were not much more than a hundred including but two knights!

When the news was received of this incredible victory in the face of such enormous odds, the whole of Britain set about rejoicing. Newport town and the surrounding area of Gwent went wild in the knowledge that its sons had played such a vital part in the French defeat and had suffered few casualties. One can only imagine their reception when weeks later they appeared, worn out but happy, over the brow of Christchurch Hill to commence the descent to the bridge. Bonfires were lit on every hilltop including Twyn Barlym, and night became day around Newport Castle as hundreds of blazing torches illuminated its walls!

On April 2nd 1347, in recognition of the valiant part that he and his Welshmen had played, Ralph, Earl of Stafford, was honoured with the additional title of Earl of Hereford. Two years later he was one of twenty-six peers who founded the Order of the Garter and his arms, a shield charged with a chevron on each facade, were partly adopted in Newport's coat-of-arms. Little did the country suspect in its moment of greatest jubilation that within a further two years it would be stricken by the most loathsome abomination that ever contaminated the earth!

The great plague entered the country in 1348. Only named the Black Death from the 19th century, it came probably by way of Weymouth, its journey having been only slightly delayed by the Channel, from Europe where it was raging. This bubonic plague originated deep in Asia and spread like lightning across all frontiers. Within a very short time the disease had the whole of southern England in its grip.

The first large city to be smitten was Bristol where eventually there were not enough living to bury the dead and the grass grew waist high in the streets! Countless corpses lay and rotted where they fell in ditches and hedgerows! In Europe, an estimated twenty million people died in two years and Britain lost between a third and a half of its population! The speed of proliferation of the virulent scourge was frightening, taking as it did no more than two to three days from the first symptoms to death!

Neither did it respect class or creed; the nobility was decimated and even royalty was touched when the king's daughter was taken. The clergy seemed to be especially prone, due probably to living in close confinement and to their willingness to tend the afflicted. Two archbishops of Canterbury succumbed. Priories and monasteries all over the land were left empty with their farms wasted and their animals allowed to wander and starve! Whole communities vanished from the face of the earth and there were no beneficiaries to inherit the possessions of the dead. Not content with all this, the awful pestilence carried a sting in its tail — it showed a preference for youth and wiped out a larger proportion of the flower of the land than its elders!

The best evidence of the Black Death's visitations in Gwent come from surviving manorial accounts for the year 1349. Those which are available show that Abergavenny suffered most with the Manors of Monmouth, Usk and Caldicot only a short step behind. Rent receipts were shown as less than a third of a normal year. Further analysis reveals why, and gives an interesting insight into the life of the times. For instance, no rents were paid in respect of clay pits as presumably there were no potters left to dig and mould the clay; fishponds were valued as nil because nobody had stocked them; many freemen's burgages were unworked because their occupiers had flown from the plague spots!

Unfortunately, proof such as this is not preserved for Newport but it could not have escaped lightly, surrounded as it was by areas known to be badly ravaged. Some slight protection may have been achieved by the indefinite closing down of the town's fairs and markets, and the strictest implementation of the by-law to exclude outsiders. Ultimately however, no amount of restriction on movement could halt the progress of the flea of the black rat!

Few exceptions are likely to have been made but it is easy to imagine that the simple, frightened burgesses would have been easy prey for the many travelling quacks, herbalists and mountebanks who put in an appearance: 'disguised in oriental garb, who brought with them terrible stories of the spread of the plague, at the same time unfolding their little carpets on the ground, offering for sale their oyles, souvereigne waters, herbs, drugs and simples which they declared to be never failing remedies" (James Matthews - 'Historic Newport').

It may be of relevance here to observe that with all the extensive excavation which took place in the town in the 19th century and continuing in the 20th, there is no record of the discovery of anything resembling a plague pit. Could it be that during the period of the great plague the town gave up its dead to the huge receding tides that regularly cleansed its shores?

The plague returned again on at least three occasions in the next twenty years. In 1348/9 there is a record of its being in the vicinity of Newport when it killed Ifor Hael, Lord of Bassaleg and Wern-y-Cleppa. and Nest his wife, at Bishton. Ifor had extensive estates (built up from those which his ancestor had been allowed to retain for services to the early Normans) but he had no children, so everything passed to a nephew from whom all the Morgans of Tredegar were descended. In 1361 the plague wiped out the Bishop of Llandaff, his staff and several other well known dignitaries, at the Bishop's House in Bishton – a place to steer well clear of it would appear!

The 1369 visitation has no mention.

- O -

Hugh de Audley died in 1347 and his estates fell quite legally into the hands of a man for whom he had no liking.

In earlier days, when leading military expeditions in the service of the king, the man who was almost always at De Audley's shoulder was Ralph, 1st Earl of Stafford. In due course he became a close family friend and so made the acquaintance of Margaret, Hugh de Audley's seventeen year old daughter and only child. She was, in modern parlance, an excellent catch, being the sole heiress to a third of the immense De Clare estates, plus the not inconsiderable lands held by De Audley in his own right. Stafford like many other ambitious noblemen, was well aware of Margaret's potential but in the absence of evidence to the contrary, it would not be fair to say that this was the only consideration in his mind when he abducted her and made her his second wife. He did after all know her well enough to have developed an intimate relationship. Predictably, her father was outraged at the elopement and sought the aid of the king who ordered a commission of 'oyer and terminer'(to hear and to judge) Little came from this except the information that Ralph had used over 20 men to steal his bride. No action was taken, the marriage was allowed to stand and De Audley came to terms with it, no doubt mollified by the news that the Earldom of Gloucester was to be revived in his favour (1337).

The Westgate Tolbothe (after anonymous drawings)

Thus, through Margaret Stafford, Ralph became the next overlord of Newport and Gwynllwg not the happiest of inheritances because it was accompanied by the Black Death!

Immediately however, he had one special duty to perform.

Apparently the first inroads were being made into the realisation of Newport's potential as a centre for promising shipping industry and as a gateway for the entry of cargoes and wool, skins, leather, wines and lead. Customs duties had to be levied on such commodities and these were not local taxes but belonged to the king, thus making them fair game for avoidance. No one was above playing this game, from the most upright, ship-owning merchants and their unprincipled sea captains down to the receivers and consumers in large country houses or lowly taverns!

In 1348, as some measure towards tightening up the collection system, Ralph, Earl of Stafford, had a customs house built near the bottom of Stow Hill with a gated archway across the main road. This was the western entrance to the town and came to be known ever afterwards as the Westgate - without being related in any way to the castle or defence of the town. This customs house was originally a small, single storied building of red grit and sandstone with the Stafford coat-of-arms over the frontal arch. It received the title 'Westgate Tolbothe'. At that time there was nothing standing between Stow Hill and the river bank, and over this open ground the customs house had admirable views of the several quays stretching for a short distance down-river from the bridge and the Town Pill. In later years a first floor was added over the archway to make a residence for the earl's bailiff. This building carried out its duties for the next 173 years and then, for a further 278 years until 1799 it was the town jail.

As Newport was now regarded as busy enough to warrant a customs house it is difficult to understand why in later centuries writers maintained that in those days there was very little traffic on the River Usk. Scott in his very meagre 'History of Newport 1840' says:-

'Although Elizabethan historians have said that Newport was a port from which vessels 'sayled to Bristowe, this is deemed apochryphal by many who suppose that no shipping visited Newport before 1780.'

and

'About the year 1700, tradition says that only a coracle of the poor fisherman, or occasionally a trading smack, was seen upon the bosom of the Uske.'

The fallacy of such statements was fully exposed by the ancient customs books of the ports of 'Bristowe' and 'Caerdiffe', and a return of shipping compiled in the reign of Elizabeth I. These records give the impression that the River Usk was alive with craft of all shapes and sizes throughout the 16th and 17th centuries.

Newport-owned ships were listed as

100	tons	Green Dragon and White Eagle
40	tons	Lyon and Griffon
34	tons	Black Lyon
30	tons	Samuel, Speedwell and Stephen
26	tons	Marie Rose
24	tons	Trinity

In addition, not exceeding 20 tons were: Angell, Barthewe, Cock, George, Hare, Jones, Swallow and Xpian.

Caerleon-owned vessels were : Dolphin, Jesus, Joseph, Margaret, Marye and Marye Catheryne. There were besides, numerous others navigating the Usk from English, Irish and Continental ports.

Trading vessels of 100 tons were big by 15th century standards and only Bristol (8) and Newport (2) could boast such craft. However, busy as it was, Newport was not then regarded as a fully-fledged port; neither was Caerleon although it had become a most important centre through which much of the agricultural produce of Wales and midwestern England was distributed to Bristol.

The Westgate Arch rediscovered during the building of the third Westgate Hotel
(sketched from a photograph taken on 31 July 1884)

By decree of King Henry IV, afterwards confirmed by Henry V, Bristowe and Caerdiffe were designated 'great portes' and all other havens as their sub-ports or 'creekes'. Thus, Newport was a creek of Cardiff which received credit for all the foreign trade entering the River Usk. The situation remained so until a Commission dated 12th June 1822, recognising the vastly increased status of the town, 'set out' the town as a port in its own right and released it from the shackles of the smaller and less busy Cardiff.

If further proof is needed of the abundance of shipping using the River Usk in mediaeval times, it is only necessary to look at the shipbuilding industry that flourished along its banks, especially with so much suitable timber available in nearby Wentwood and the Forest of Dean. Registration of Newport's own ships did not come until the 19th century but it is certain that most of those sailing regularly out of town from the earliest days were built on Uskside. There is ample evidence here that Newport 's maritime heritage did not start as late as the writings of some of those 'passing through' historians would have one believe!

Having given a brief account of the origin of the first customs house or Westgate Toll Booth as it was quaintly called, attention should be drawn to an element of mystery that has never been satisfactorily explained but which casts suspicious light on the way in which 'honest' business may have been transacted by those who should have known better! It makes for interesting speculation anyway!

The original building having become a prison, was adjoined by an inn in 1709. In 1799,

41

both structures were demolished and replaced by the second Westgate Inn. This in turn was pulled down in 1884 and the present Westgate Hotel built. During the reconstruction, the 500 year old arch was exposed and a spiral stone staircase leading to the remains of a tunnel that went under Stow Hill. Photographs were taken on 31st July 1884 before these relics were obliterated for all time, but the contractors, not being of a very inquisitive nature, filled in the tunnel and nothing more is known of it. One can question its purpose nevertheless, and there is a possible but wholly hypothetical answer.

A manor house called Westgate House once stood facing the Toll Booth on the approximate spot where the tunnel might have surfaced. When it was built and for whom is not known. It certainly stood there in 1533, the home of George Morgan, bailiff of the castle, and could have been built up to 100 years before that. The question is: was the tunnel a link between the manor house and the toll booth where much money was handled, or was it built in a later age for some shady purpose involving the prison or the inn and the occupier of the manor house? Whatever the reason, the very presence of the clandestine route suggests corruption in high places!

For a further 25 years Newport remained in the hands of the 1st Earl of Stafford but inevitably in 1372, his son Hugh inherited as 2nd Earl and his term in office was notable for two gracious acts at his instigation.

First in 1377, he granted land between Stow Hill and the River Usk shoreline to the Hermits of St Augustine of whom Hugh's father, Ralph, had been a patron and had, in 1344, established a priory in Stafford. This order also called themselves the Austin Friars. By this time there were 130 houses of the Austin Friars in England; Wales had two and they were both in Gwent - the Priory at Llanthony near Abergavenny, and the Friary at Newport. Together with the land were given 32 burgages and the free Chapel of St Nicholas. The first prior was Brother Thomas Leche, nationality unknown, but believed to have been brought from the priory at Stafford. From that time on, the burgesses of Newport became used to the sight of black-gowned and hooded friars in the few streets of the town.

The Austin Friars were also the reason why the town did not see fit to provide any sort of refuge for the poor, as the monastery was made a haven for the sick, blind and destitute. The friars even built an isolation hospital for contagious diseases, well out of town in the wild wastes of Liswerry and carrying a name that lingers on today in the Spitty (Hospital) Fields.

Hugh Stafford's most memorable act came on the 14th April 1385 when he, with the full authority vested in a Marcher Earl, granted the town of Newport its first, formal charter.

On this momentous day in the town's history, Hugh Stafford was present in his castle and called before him all the more important burgesses of the town to witness the placing of his seal on the charter, which in addition to confirming the exemption from tolls and taxes already enjoyed under the Despenser administration, gave many more liberties never before granted in the old feudal society. Assembled before the Earl were clergy, reeves, their deputies and representatives of every trade and craft. Local gentry from outside the town witnessed the event.

The main provisions of the charter were:-

The burgesses were to elect their own reeve who was to preside over the hundred court as well as the piepowder courts. They were also permitted to form a guild representative of all trades, to rule on weights and measures, the town's ordinances, the making of regulations for the selling of bread and ale, and the holding of a 15 day fair commencing on 9th August each year. To the fair would be attached a piepowder court.

The constable of the castle was authorised to act as the town coroner and to attend sessions of the borough courts in order to ensure that all fines due to the lord were properly directed. Borough boundaries were designated and burgesses were to be permitted to let any land that they owned to anyone they wished.

The Earl listened sympathetically to additional pleas from the burgesses and made further concessions regarding freedom from custody in the castle, trial by jury of fellow burgesses in their own courts and avoidance of appearances in the Earl's court, something that had been bleeding the tenants of more money than they could afford. It seemed that the Earl was desperately anxious to boost the loyalty of his followers, and no doubt his feelings were strongly influenced by the experiences of the nobility in the recent Peasant's Revolt (1381).

Although Hugh Stafford's charter was only the conception of their emancipation, the burgesses found themselves for the first time firmly in control of their own commercial, economic and legislative affairs. Almost immediately, Newport's first ever market was held in the castle bailey.

At this time in Mill Street, which was the main thoroughfare of the village, there were several small shops carrying on the trades of baker, cordwainer, cooper, barber, fletcher, scrivener etc. There were also three small alehouses showing on their signboards the names White Lion, White Swan and King's Arms. The shops all had to close on market and fair days so that as many people as possible could attend and swell the lord's funds.

Before concluding the subject of the charter, it is necessary to explain one expression used in it.

The term 'piepowder' was an anglicised version of the French 'pied poudreux' meaning literally 'dusty foot', being descriptive of the travel-stained boots of the visiting pedlars and merchants. The courts which carried this name were intended to deal with such itinerants when they were involved in the petty offences of drunkenness, brawling, dishonest trading or vagrancy, and they were all punishable by fines payable to the lord's exchequer.

The manor - and so far Newport was still only the small corner of one such where the largest group of people could be found - has up to now received all too few mentions. Now, in order to remove any misunderstandings of the life that manorial organisation generated, it is necessary to go into greater detail.

The fact of the matter is that the manor was the be-all and end-all of everyday life in mediaeval times. Everything revolved around it; everyone depended on it. It was the big business of those days and it was analogous to the big business of today.

The Earl was the chairman of the company and his largest castle was his company headquarters from which he made frequent visits to oversee his often far-flung branches. His children (if he was so blessed), when into maturity, were the board of directors; the elected steward or reeve was the company accountant and manager whose duty it was (assisted by his bailiff) to protect all manorial privileges, to keep the chief accounts of household and farm, to superintend the domestics and all departmental heads and above all to keep the manor in profit! His accounts were kept on skins or parchment and at the end of each year they were tacked together in one household roll. It is from remnants of a few of these that a record of the period is obtained.

The Earl's business was conducted through divisions separately responsible for agriculture, forestry, game, fisheries and building, and those who worked in these divisions were known by a variety of titles. Following the bailiff there came a head harvest man who was elected by the tenants, ate at the lord's table and kept a horse in the lord's stable. After him, in some sort of seniority, came farriers, huntsmen, approvers, foresters, masons,

43

paviours, haywards (fences and gates), shepherds, ploughmen, swineherds, carters, threshers and farm labourers.

If the business was sound and healthy it would be profitable and would provide a living for each and every member of the firm and a firm investment for his lordship. It behove the management therefore to run a happy ship by taking good care of the crew.

The manor of the year 1400 bore little resemblance to that of 1100. After the Norman invasion the manor had been ruled, iron-fistedly, by a baron who looked upon on his Welsh and Saxon vassals as foreign barbarians suitable only for slave labour. Three hundred years later the occupiers were in receipt of rights, albeit still under the overall control of their lord, but sufficient to give them some choice in guiding their own destinies.

It has already been established that it was false to assume that the lord of the manor resided almost permanently in his headquarters in Newport Castle. As in most manors the earl was an absentee landlord, living in his most imposing castle on his most important estate, usually somewhere in England. This was especially true of Newport which was only a rather insignificant part of the massive De Clare holdings extending throughout South Wales, Southern England and the Midlands and even including a more modest claim in Ireland.

The lord of the South Wales manors would put in an appearance in this part of the Marches mainly when there was some event of great importances to attend, a vital decision to be made or to recruit men for his military ventures. On these occasions he stayed in Newport Castle, never his residence but more a symbol of his authority. During his absences he left all administrative duties to his elected officials and relied heavily on the bailiff or steward of the castle to maintain the efficiency (and thereby the profitability) of the whole organisation. The results were recorded in the documents (rolls) to be set forth whenever the lord wished to peruse them and particularly to produce an annual balance sheet to demonstrate one year's progress against another.

Obviously the system was open to abuse and clever manipulation. It was quite easy, for instance, for the accountant to 'forget' to enter the occasional sale of a load of timber, or to 'lose' an animal from the pound, and he could have a field day with favours from visitors to the town, especially if they wished to keep out of the lord's courts! Several times over the years the condition of the accounts showed by their deficiencies that all had not gone smoothly. Thus there are records of warfare, plague, famine, drought, and when none of these were the cause, just plain bad management!

One example of the state of the Newport manor comes from 1386 when Hugh Stafford caused the first thorough assessment to be made of his estates. Newport was shown to be worth something like £21 in rents from burgages, the town mill and fisheries. With between 200 and 300 burgages in the town an idea can be gained of the individual rents charged - some were as low as a farthing - and the business was apparently booming!

A similar appraisal in 1400/1401 by Edmund, 5th Earl of Stafford, gave a value of over £57 with takings from burgages, small leases of land, fisheries, beer tax, fines from courts and other. This account was rendered by Roger Thomas, Reeve of the town, and gave the general impression of a busy, prosperous place and a worthy asset to its lord. How fortune can change almost overnight! A year later, after Owain Glyndwr's disastrous attack, the value of the town was assessed as nil and all further seigniorial evidence from that date onwards implies that Newport never fully recovered from this incident until well into the 16th century. However, not all the blame could be laid at Glyndwr's door!

When the Black Death finished its ravages, the four million population of Britain had been halved; the work-force was reduced proportionately, labour was in very short supply and burgages, being widely vacated, gave much reduced rents or service in lieu. The lord of the manor found that he no longer called the tune as he had when labour was plentiful and cheap. The workers now realised only too well their own inflated worth and consequently the price they demanded for their services went steadily higher. They were now asking for a fixed wage instead of payment in kind or commutation of rent. The lord found that he *had* to pay or he could lose a harvest, and if it came to it, half a harvest was better than none at all!

Under circumstances such as these the manors were never to be the same again, and even began to break up as more and more tenants' strips were combined into larger areas and leased to wealthier burgesses rather than let them remain vacant and unprofitable year after year. The middle class farmer was on the way! (Farm: Latin - firma:fixed payment).

Certain it is that Newport never again made profit, although with the right kind of guidance it might have done. At least one person thought this way because, a century after Glyndwr, when the manor had once again become a Crown holding and was stifling in managerial indecisiveness, one David ap Morgan Kemeys, was so confident of his powers in estate management that he offered King Henry VIII nearly £7 a year for the opportunity. This was £1 more than the estimated worth of the borough at the time.

It is easy to generalise but even allowing for the regular, depressing end of year results shown in successive manorial rolls, Newport, whilst not being the most energetic of market towns, was certainly not in the league's relegation zone!

- O -

Only a year after his grand gesture Hugh, the 2nd Earl of Stafford, died and a period of instability was introduced into the family's control of its affairs. The next four earls were under age when they came into their inheritances and even when they reached their majorities, most died as very young men. This meant that for 37 years the manors were constantly in the care of less than dedicated regents, just at the beginning of a most turbulent time in the town's history. Its problems were never at a lower ebb and nothing less than a man of iron was needed.

The 3rd Earl of Stafford was Hugh's eldest son, Thomas, who was a minor until 1390 and lived only a further two years. William, his brother, became the 4th Earl for only three years and never came of age. His twin, Edmund, was also a minor until 1399 and it was during his short spell in office that the real tragedy for Newport occurred!

Owain Glyndwr was the descendant of Llywelyn and other Welsh princes. His name meant 'Owen of the Glen of Water', probably derived from his home estates in the beautiful but rugged Valley of the Dee. He could well have called himself Prince of Wales but had no inclination to do so until it was forced upon him. Many regard him with mixed emotions in the light of the barbaric turn that his uprising took, but in actual fact he had a fairly genteel upbringing, loved books, studied law at Oxford and joined the court of King Richard II as one of the royal squires. He even had a knighthood conferred upon him.

When the king was deposed in 1399, Owain retired to his Welsh estates to live as he hoped the peaceful existence of a country gentlemen, but it was not to be!

His English neighbour, Reynold Lord Grey, no friend of Owain, made a series of plundering attacks across his borders, driving out his tenants. A complaint to the new king, Henry IV, was useless because Lord Grey was a royal favourite. Shortly afterwards, the king sent a letter to Glyndwr asking for his military help in the Scottish wars but Grey intercepted the message, telling the king that Glyndwr was ignoring it and should be arrested for treason. It was Lord Grey's attempt to carry out this very act that turned a border dispute into a major conflagration that was to engulf the whole of Wales.

The Welsh were already smarting quietly under the harsh rule of the English who had imposed upon them a set of regulations that were draconian in the extreme:-

No Englishman was allowed to be convicted on the word of a Welshman.
No Welshmen was allowed to marry an English woman.
No Welsh child was allowed to be apprenticed to any trade anywhere.
The assembly of bards or minstrels was illegal.
The old custom of 'Cymmortha' ie. the meeting together to assist each other in the harvest, was declared illegal.

In addition, exceptionally high taxation was ruining the home economy so, when they heard of the Glyndwr rebellion, Welshmen everywhere flocked to his support, giving him a substantial army with which he ranged far and wide in the Principality, hitting the English estates with unbelievable ferocity.

His modus operandi in every case was to burn and destroy anything owned by or of use to, the English, and to leave nothing on the land to sustain a pursuing army. In the course of operating this strategy a lot of innocent families suffered badly, both from the violence and the local famine that was sure to follow. Devastation was usually complete even to churches, priories etc and public opinion has been unanimous throughout the succeeding years that the burning of structures held sacred was indefensible!

Early in the year 1402, a bright comet appeared in the sky and this was interpreted by the bards as favourable to Glyndwr's cause. It certainly did not favour Newport!

In the summer of that year, the Glyndwr hordes entered Gwent from the north and scorched the earth down the valley of the Usk. After laying waste to Crickhowell and Abergavenny they arrived at Newport and meeting little opposition from the undermanned garrison, they destroyed the castle, the mill and the bridge, badly damaged St Woolos Church and the Austin Friary, drove off all the livestock and burned acres of standing crops. Those burgesses who took refuge in the forest returned eventually to find the town a blackened ruin! It was a savage attack and the most terrible ever inflicted on the town. It is somewhat incomprehensible therefore to find that the majority of historians have treated the incident as insignificant and hardly give it passing mention in tracing the course of the Glyndwr uprising in Wales.

It is of interest to note that possibly the last sighting of Owain Glyndwr in South Wales was in Gwent not far from Newport in about 1408. He tried to free his son who was held in Usk Castle, but was defeated by King Henry IV in a battle on Pwll Melyn Hill with the loss variously reported at from 800 to 1,500 men. He was last seen being helped away into the mists by his family, leaving another son dead on the field.

From then on his activities began to decline and eventually he retired permanently into his North Wales mountain stronghold. In 1415 he was offered a free pardon by King Henry V, who had always held a grudging respect for the old Welsh prince, but, independent to the last, Owain refused and died a year later.

Many felt that he gave nothing to Wales, only an ideal of freedom accompanied by incalculable misery and material damage. The vast majority of poor Welshmen must have welcomed the arrival of Owain Glyndwr on their doorsteps as their parents had welcomed the Black Death — both had much the same effect!

There were, however, men around Newport who sympathised with the Glyndwr cause. A fifth column must have existed in the town because it was known to be the point of delivery for much of the money collected in England to support the rebellion. In 1403, for their treason, Ieuan ap Jenkin Kemys, William Flemyng, Gruffyd ap Llewelyn and Llewelyn ap Morgan, all influential inhabitants of the area, suffered forfeiture of their lands. The last named, Morgan, lived approximately where Tredegar House stands today and his lands were the early beginnings of the Tredegar Estate. Somehow this family — always the opportunists — had recovered their estate by the end of the 15th century.

On 21st July 1403, King Henry IV faced Owain Glyndwr and his English and French allies at Shrewsbury. The battle was won by the king but, by a strange and coincidental quirk of fate, Newport's lord, Edmund 5th Earl of Stafford, was killed fighting for the king. In the short space of twelve months the Glyndwr jinx had claimed his town and his life!

In that same year, the Royal Army was billeted in Newport, whether before or after the Battle of Shrewsbury is not known, but apparently King Henry found conditions so desperate in the town that he sent messengers to the Sheriff of Bristol ordering ships to be loaded with flour, ale, wine and salted fish and sent across the Severn with extreme urgency.

The scene that met the eyes of the townsfolk of Newport on returning to their homes was awesome indeed! It must have reduced them to the depths of despair. All the houses were ruined, with only the occasional stone wall or chimney surviving; the fields of once-golden corn were black and still smouldering; there was no life, no everyday farmyard sounds and no birdsong. Amidst all this desolation the castle stood like a burned out beacon, roofless and gutted, with ugly smoke-stains streaking up the grey stone from empty eye sockets of windows. As bad as anything else was the absence of the town's main lifeline, for the river bridge too had gone.

Those burgesses who chose to go first to St Woolos Church to give thanks for their deliverance, found that that also had been desecrated. Did they but know it, but every church on the moors in the Caldicot and Wentloog Levels had been savagely destroyed.

The immediate priority was shelter from the elements, as summer was ending and colder days approaching. It is impossible to say what the winter weather of 1402 was like, but there is evidence to suggest that during most of the time that Owain Glyndwr was rampant, it was cold, windy and very wet in many parts of Wales. In fact, it was common talk among the English soldiers that Glyndwr possessed magical powers and could even summon up storms to fight for him! There were indeed many thunderstorms with heavy rain and flooded rivers, and once, the king's tent blew away in a howling gale! In these circumstances the English rarely had any success against their enemy in his own territory.

But to return to the rebirth of Newport — for such is the only way to describe it — when simple temporary shelters had been erected, the clearing up process began. Debris had to be shifted, tools and farming equipment salvaged and many items repaired. It was a prolonged and arduous business and one can only view with the deepest admiration the resilience with which the townsfolk approached their task. In any similar disaster situation occurring in modern times, help would be pouring in within hours, but nothing then existed in the way of emergency services and all government resources were concentrated on pursuing the perpetrators of the outrage.

Finding sufficient food during that first year must have been an almost insurmountable problem but somehow it was resolved. It may be that the supplies requisitioned from Bristol by the king, helped in some measure.

A degree of normality would not have been too long in coming, but the rebuilding of the town's principle structures was to drag on for many years.

In 1403 the one big obstacle to clear planning for the immediate future was the death in battle of Newport's lord, Edmund. His son, Humphrey, was hardly twelve months old so the manor was in for yet another long period of guardianship before there was once more a firm hand on the tiller. What was more, this chaperonage was shared by two women, Humphrey's widowed mother, the Countess Anne, and Queen Joan, the second wife of Henry IV, who between them must have used numerous anonymous advisers and their even more numerous conflicting ideas.

47

For a start, the lordship was valueless and the castle uninhabitable. Three years later the situation was little changed. The damaged Westgate Tollbooth had been patched up and was being used as the seat of local government, as it would be for the next twenty years until the castle was sufficiently repaired. There was still very little income from burgages or court proceedings, and the outgoings in 1406 were very heavy – the cost of temporary repairs to the castle and payments to Sir Gilbert Denys and his garrison of 120 men, came to over £200!

The rebuilding of Newport's bridge was not hurried. Its next mention was in 1418 when the Bishop of Hereford, stating that the crossing was in very poor condition, appealed for contributions to a building fund. In exchange he offered indulgences of 40 days. An indulgence offered by the Church was a special favour giving total or partial remission of temporal punishment for crimes, after confession had secured exemption from religious penalties.

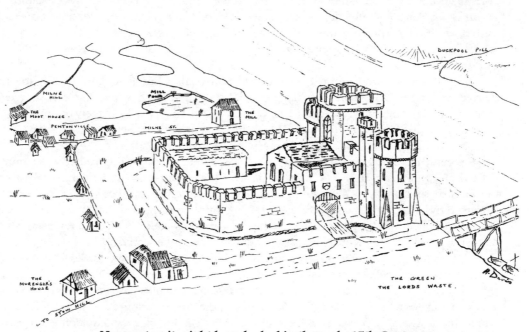

Newport as it might have looked in the early 15th Century

A new bridge was definitely built by 1435 but apparently it was one of a series of inferior structures thrown up with no thought given to durability. In 1488 the Bishop's appeal was repeated, and at the same time it is recorded that a lease was granted for a burgess to run a ferry while work was progressing.

Graphic: Philip Argent

A Bristol Channel 'cray' commonly seen on the river Usk at Newport in medieval times. This is an artists impression from the Daily Mail of one uncovered in the foreshore mud of the River Severn at Magor, Gwent in August 1995.

The castle was under reconstruction and refurbishment for nearly fifty years. The early works until 1422, when Earl Humphrey came of age, were of the most basic nature – roof repairs, weather proofing etc but once the Earl took charge, more urgent order and planning emerged.

A regular team was employed comprising 24 carpenters at 6d per day, boys to help at 2d per day and 22 masons at 4d per day – ludicrous by present day standards but quite generous at the time. Altogether over £500 was spent on the castle, ranging from sums like £1-13s-3d and £4-4s-11d for minor repairs, to £150 for adding a withdrawing chamber for the lord, to the central Chapel Tower.

In 1435, the South Tower was rebuilt and the aforementioned chamber in 1448. For these purposes, small single-masted boats called 'crays' were used to bring sawn stone blocks from the Bristol quarries of St Vincent Rocks and Dundry, and stone and slate from Penarth and Bridgend. Ordinary walling stone and rubble came from the Stowe quarry, and oak timber from the Henllys Forest.

Amongst other things, the north wall of the castle was demolished and rebuilt three feet higher than before. It was finished off with battlements, the crests of which were made of ragstone from the quarry of St Mary Redcliffe, Bristol. The total cost was £20-9s-3d! A new opening was made in this wall and, in his 'Excursion through South Wales and Monmouthshire', E. Donovan said:-

A great gateway in prevailing Gothic style appears on the north side opening to the moat, the communication between which and the bank directly opposite was formerly maintained by a drawbridge. The excavation it bestrided is still very wide and deep.'

There were three towers dominating the bank of the River Usk, the largest of the three was solid and square and flanked by smaller turrets standing at each corner of the battlements. In its base at high tide level, was a Gothic arched water gate with a portcullis that raised into a slot in the chapel above. This gate gave access to a chamber 46 feet long into which boats could sail for loading and unloading.

The two smaller towers were octagonal and supported on alternate faces by massive, triangular buttresses. Built into the walls at the rear of each tower were stone, spiral staircases ascending to various levels and the roofs. Attached to the wall joining the North Tower to the Chapel Tower was the great hall and withdrawing chamber from which a door opened into the chapel; from this point a narrow passage within the other curtain wall led into the South Tower.

Running at right angles from the South Tower and attached to the south wall was a building containing various other rooms and offices used mainly in administration of the manor. Set into the middle of this building was the arch of the South Gate with its drawbridge. Directly over the gate was the 'hundred' room where the hundred courts were held; it was also used as the exchequer office, and in 1522 a document refers to 'the chequer chamber above the Bridge Gate'. In the archway beneath was the porter's lodge and a prison for criminals. Also in this rear projection, close up to the tower, was a massive, circular oven of solid stone, three feet high by eighteen feet in diameter. It is known that all mediaeval castles had a huge capacity for bread baking and, in siege conditions, the oven was as essential as the well!

The only other buildings within the castle walls were the stables and soldiers' quarters which extended from the North Gate the full length of the north wall. Elsewhere in the castle bailey was a well and the entrance to a stairway leading underground to the vaults and the water gate.

It was now a fairly imposing edifice, refurbished and enlarged but still small when compared with other castles in the Marches. When all the works were finally completely in 1457, the interior of the castle was probably quite dignified in appearance with handsome, well appointed apartments. The ceilings, especially in the chapel, were finely vaulted and the arched windows on either side of the fireplace in the great hall, contained decorative glass. The large chapel windows, typically ecclesiastical, were extraordinarily grand. For much of the 18th and 19th centuries they were boarded or bricked up as many old sketches show, but now, opened up again, one can imagine their former glory.

The wide moat along the south wall would have had the effect of creating a much larger gap between the South Tower and the bridge than exists today, but this could be accounted for by the early bridges being less than half as wide as the modern crossing.

It would appear that in addition to the gates already mentioned, which were actually openings in the castle walls, there was a third gate across the end of the bridge known appropriately as the 'Bridge Gate'. Over the years there has been confusion among some writers who have wrongly described the South Gate by this appellation whilst others have referred to it as the more sensible 'East Gate' (of the town, not of the castle!)

Archbishop Coxe, on his journey through Newport in the early 19th century, says:-

'The pivots belonging to the hinges of the East Gate, near the bridge, are clearly discernible in the walls.'

Lelande, three centuries earlier said:-

'there is a great stone gate by the bridge at the este end of the toun'.'

Buck's very realistic view of the castle, sketched in 1732, clearly shows the huge stone archway in which the gate was set.

Of course, no castle was ever complete without its secret passageway and Newport Castle was no exception, having one which was so secret that it has remained undiscovered to this day!

Simple, mediaeval folk loved tales of mystery and magic and often invented their own Underground escape routes with their suggestion of intrigue, adventure and heroic figures outwitting villainous authority, were a favourite imagination associated with supposedly impregnable fortresses. Newport Castle's tunnel must have been an engineering wonder, extending as it reportedly did, under the bed of the River Usk to emerge distantly, somewhere in the parish of Christchurch – St Julians House was frequently mentioned. It featured mainly in a legend of the Cromwellian attack on the town when the Roundheads were gathering on the eastern bank of the river. A dark stranger, so it goes, approached the soldiers and offered to show them this 'back door' to the castle; the fact that it took a direct frontal assault to force final surrender speaks for itself!

Apparently, however, this was not the only tunnel of which the castle could boast; it *was* the most famous, although there has never been proof of its existence. Others turned up centuries later and for these there were reputedly genuine eyewitnesses.

Between 1890 and 1899 Newport Castle comprised part of Lloyd & Yorath's brewery. This was the last in line of several commercial usages which started with Mr Allfrey's brewery in 1820 and then went through other similar occupations besides that of tan house and nail works.

In the grounds was the old well from which the breweries extracted their water and in

1891 its level dropped alarmingly. Mr Harry Jones, a brewery foreman descended the well and below its normal level he discovered the entrance to a stone-walled tunnel that appeared to head in the direction of Shaftesbury Street. Apparently, Mr Jones and another man, holding candles, walked the tunnel against the flow of the stream to its source at the well in Thomas Street. Quite how this could have been achieved with the canal (also below ground level) in between, was not explained. In 1931, another man, an employee of the Borough Engineer's Department, this time draining an overfull well, rediscovered the tunnel. He said that it forked, with one branch going on towards Thomas Street and the other going left towards the Old Green Hotel which then stood on the corner of High Street and Dock Street.

The reason for the existence of these tunnels was never established and in any case they afterwards disappeared without trace. In 1951, eighty five year old Mr Henry Jones was brought back to the castle grounds but could not pin-point the well that he had been down sixty years before! Furthermore, the extensive and fairly deep excavations made in the 1970s right across this area to create the new, Old Green Crossing, failed to expose any old, underground workings!

Opposite to the South Gate, on the other side of the beaten track that would one day become High Street, was the Castle Green which extended as far as the Town Pill. Here, for the first three quarters of the 20th century, was the Old Green Crossing, a block of shops and Screw Packet Lane leading to Bangor and Baltic Wharfs. All this disappeared in the 1970s when redevelopment created a new dual carriageway with pedestrian subways and overhead walkways.

Although he must have been heavily preoccupied with his building problems and the financial worries which were now a constant feature of the Newport lordship, Earl Humphrey still found time to study the welfare of his townspeople. There were rather fewer of them than in his grandfather's day judging by the annual accounts which still showed 61 decayed burgages in the borough.

The Earl was only five years out of his minority when his thoughts turned to the granting of a further charter. On 3rd April 1427, the 6th Earl of Stafford's Charter was presented and the first paragraph, translated from the Latin, is reproduced in part here:-

'For the Burgesses of Newport in Wales (Newporte in Wallia). Humphrey, Earl of Stafford, Lord of Tonbridge and Gwynllwg to all faithful ones of Christ who shall inspect the present Charter. Greetings. Know that we have inspected the Charter of Lord Hugh, late Earl of Stafford, our grandfather in these words . . .'

The Charter went on to define and confirm all the liberties granted in the earlier 1385 Charter, and redesignated the town boundaries. This was achieved by the use of place names that have long since been abandoned and which bear no relation to any in the town today. It is fortunate however that they survived to be used on an old map of the liberties of Newport, circa 1800, and so it is quite possible to trace that original town boundary and follow it by reference to the districts which now occupy the same positions as the ancient charter names.

Commencing at the most northerly point:

The Rock Bryngelond	Bottom of Barrack Hill, Malpas Road to northern end of Queens Hill
	to
Coumycheshul	Gold Tops
	to
Corteyscroft Lower Baneswell	
	to
Brendekyrch	Upper Baneswell, around St Woolos (Clifton Road) leaving the church outside the borough.
	to
Kyngeshul (Kensal lands)	Vicarage Lane and Clytha Square
	to
Mullond	George Street, junction with Commercial Road due north
	to
Crokesland	Emlyn Street due east
	to
Parkpull	Ebenezer Terrace
	to
Groundesende	Canal Parade and the river bank and thence due north up the centre of the River Usk to the mouth of Crindau Pill and south-westerly back along the brook to the Rock, Malpas Rd.

For students of mediaeval nomenclature, a list of some of the burgesses witnessing both charters is produced as follows:

<u>1385 Charter</u>

Lord Nicholas de Stafford, Lord Nicholas Shireborn, John Frenyngham, John de Wexcombe, John Sewell, John Kemeys, John de Bauham, Llewelyn ap Morgan, Thomas ap Ivor, Roger ap Adam and William Flemyng.

<u>1427 Charter</u>

John Gresly, Robert Strilley, William Thomas, John Merbury, Hugh Erdeswyk, Robert

Greindour, John Russell, William Burley, Thomas Arblaster, John Bedulf and John Harpur.

Others whose names crop up from time to time in the affairs of the borough during this period, were: William Berne, Hugh Berne, Morgan ap Rosser, William Kemys, Roger Kemys, Griffith Taylor, Thomas Davy, Richard Adam, Miles Scull, Thomas Vaughan, Ralph Dory, John Clerk, Jenkin Vethyk and Richard Batten.

These named burgesses and many others who remain anonymous knew only too well that they were now the beneficiaries of great privileges. The very significant clause in the Charter was:-

> **'We grant also to our burgesses . . . that no one may hold open stall of any merchandise, nor tavern nor butchery nor do the trade of a master craftsman or victualler in our town unless he be sojourning with our burgesses and received within their guild.'**

Concurrent with these conditions other statutes being passed forbade non resident merchants from trading in cloth, groceries or mercery within any borough, so altogether the burgesses found that they were now in the very strong position of being able to develop their crafts with very little competition.

The 1427 Charter was presumed lost for over 400 years, but it came to light in a most unusual way.

At a London auction sale in the late 19th century, a gentleman from Stafford purchased an ancient document (in remarkable condition) which carried the names Newport and Wenllwg. Seeing also the name, Earl of Stafford, this gentleman believed that the document referred to Newport and Wenlock in Shropshire. It was put on exhibition at the Archaeological Institute in Shrewsbury where Mr Octavius Morgan saw it and proved it to be Newport's 1427 Charter of Inspeximus and Confirmation of the earlier Charter of 1385. Mr Morgan presented the newly discovered charter to Newport Corporation in 1885.

In 1444, Humphrey was created Duke of Buckingham by Henry VI. The Wars of the Roses began in 1455 and immediately, at the Battle of St Albans, the Duke lost his only son and heir, fighting for the House of Lancaster. As if this were not tragic enough, the old Duke himself was killed in 1460, fighting for the same cause at the Battle of Northampton.

Once again the lordship of Newport passed to a minor, Humphrey's grandson. Henry, who had no say in matters until 1473 by which time the town had passed through a further 13 years indifferent financial performance under the absentee management of Richard Neville Earl of Warwick, and Sir William Herbert, the future Earl of Pembroke.

However, Henry did not let the grass grow under his feet when he gained control, even if the rest of his ill-omened life was of little political appeal. Without ado he emulated both his grandfather and great grandfather in granting Newport its third charter. Dated 16th September 1476, the Charter of Henry, 2nd Duke of Buckingham and 7th Earl of Stafford, restated and confirmed all the liberties granted in the previous charters and went on to give further assurances to burgesses who might be charged with offences outside the town.

In essence, such miscreants could only be tried in the town's own courts by a jury of their fellow burgesses, and this was of special advantage to the more daring of the townsfolk who ventured regularly into the forbidden Royal Chase of Wentwood to procure the odd item for the pot!

Penalties in an outside court would have been dire for any person found 'in the manner of Stable-stand (with bow bent ready to fire), of Dog-draw (tracking a wounded deer with a hound on a leash), of Backbearend (carrying away game on one's back) and Bloodyhand (the self explanatory origin of red-handed).'

The reeve was given sole authority to make arrests or to execute any of the lord's writs within the town. Permission was given to build a gaol.

Reeves of the town had always elevated themselves with the more prestigious title of mayor, although this had never found favour with past lords of the manor. Now however, the Duke sanctioned use of the title, but it was well into the following century before it became the official title of the head of the borough.

Although it fulfilled that purpose, this charter made no mention of being a confirmation of the other charters.

It was witnessed by:-
Nicholas Latimer Richard Darell
William Gatesby Thomas Biggings
William Fisher
Thomas Cheym
John Gunter and others.

In 1482 the Duke awarded a further six free burgages to the Austin Friars, making a total of 60 in all given by his family over the previous century. The whole area was one day to receive notoriety under the name of Friars Fields. These were some of the Duke's more reputable acts, but events were to follow that gave serious doubt to his judgement and for which he eventually paid with his life.

Because he was a Lancastrian, and despite being married to Catherine Woodville, sister-in-law of King Edward IV, the Duke of Buckingham was deliberately excluded from all public activities, and this caused him to put his unused talents to work for Richard, Duke of Gloucester, in his ruthless pursuit of the Crown. These were the most treacherous of times and Richard's infamies were legion. He was prepared to stop at nothing to reach his goal and in the process committed unspeakable crimes to eliminate his rivals. In 1478 he had already contrived the murder of his elder brother, the Duke of Clarence.

King Edward IV died in 1483 and his son, Prince Edward, was too young to rule so Richard of Gloucester, his uncle, was made Protector of the Realm. In this capacity he had the young King Edward V and his younger brother taken to the Tower of London, ostensibly for their protection. Meanwhile the Duke of Buckingham took it upon himself to spread doubts about their legitimacy. Shortly afterwards, the boys disappeared mysteriously and their uncle was crowned King Richard III. Although never proved, the suspicion was strong that Buckingham was deeply involved in their cruel murder. He was after all, Constable of the Tower at the time.

Whatever the truth of the matter, it was not long before Henry realised that in the light of the enormous weight of public opinion against the King's cold-blooded actions, he was now the wrong man to support. He therefore changed sides and joined in a plot to topple Richard from the throne and replace him with Henry Tudor, Earl of Richmond. In 1484, leading an army made up mainly of Welshmen from his own manors, Buckingham crossed over into Herefordshire and came to the River Severn which he found to be in the fullest of floods. The situation was for a long time afterwards spoken of as 'Buckingham's Great Water' and it proved to be his final undoing when his men, miserable and hungry, started deserting in droves. The Duke himself was separated from his allies and captured. King Richard had his old friend beheaded as a traitor at Worcester on 2nd November 1483.

The Duke's widow, Catherine, married Sir Jasper Tudor, half-brother to King Henry VI. This explains his interest in Newport where he was responsible for rebuilding St Woolos Church and adding the final storey to its tower.

An act of attainder was placed on the vast Buckingham estates, making them forfeit to the Crown and so they remained for two years until 1485 when Richard III was defeated and killed at the Battle of Bosworth Field. The new king, Henry VII, at once lifted the attainder and restored the estates to Edward, 3rd Duke of Buckingham and 8th Earl of Stafford. The country now had a Welsh king and Newport, for the first time, had a Welsh lord – Edward had been born in Brecon Castle.

The little township by the Usk was not to know it then but it was about to embark on its final term as a feudal lordship, once again with a child at its head. The Duke did not come of age until 1498 but in the next 23 years he reached the supreme heights of his noble calling.

The year 1509 saw the accession of King Henry VIII and Buckingham was made Lord High Constable of the Realm and a privy counsellor – it was in these capacities that he carried the Crown at the coronation. As a direct descendant of Edward III he was regarded as the most powerful man in the country after the king himself. This was not altogether to his advantage as he had on one occasion in the reign of King Henry VII, been spoken of as a possible successor and in his knowledge of this, Henry VIII was ever wary of him. It was not surprising therefore that when the envious Cardinal Wolsey threw his great influence behind a campaign to discredit Buckingham, the trumped-up charges of treason were treated as proven and the Duke pronounced guilty. He was sentenced to death and beheaded in the Tower in May 1521.

Again the estates, including the Newport lordship, were confiscated and this time annexed to the Duchy of Lancaster.

Thus came the end of an era, the last of 428 years and a dynasty of 19 feudal lords, two of whom had been kings, near half had earned reputations for great valour, near half for acts of ignominy and almost a third had come to violent ends. Newport was never again to pledge fealty to a single, omnipotent lord!

Chapter Four

The Reformation and the Elizabethans

Newport in the 15th and 16th centuries was a very small town of diverse fortunes according to whichever historical references one chooses to consult.

It will be remembered that opinions differed over the importance of the town as a port and the amount of maritime trade it conducted. The same scepticism applied to the amount of lawlessness in the borough. Some antiquaries felt that whilst the Welsh March was a hotbed of serious crime, Newport seemed to suffer far less in this way, its burgesses leading fairly well ordered lives. This conclusion was based on court records scattered throughout the latter part of the 15th century and further engendered by a singular aspect of the judicial system which had the effect of largely diminishing the lists of court cases. Other sources certainly do not support the contention that life in the town was all sweetness and light; there is a catalogue of accounts of violence and dishonesty throughout this period – so much so that it was brought to the attention of the highest in the land!

In 1476, King Edward IV issued orders that the citizens of Newport had to give assurances as to their future law abiding conduct on pain of considerable sums to be forfeited if they defaulted. Apparently the previous monarch, King Henry VI had taken action of a similar kind against the town!

One has only to examine the contemporary impressions of the duties of the chief law officers ie. the mayors, to obtain the merest idea of the problems:-

'The most pressing problem for the reeve in the turbulent Tudor Age was the effective suppression of crime and lawlessness.'

'Mayors often had to enlist the aid of outside county magistrates in the never-ending struggle to maintain order in the borough.'

'One of the mayors jobs was to arrest pirates!'

The 1500s were notable for the fact that during most of the period 30 extremely violent crimes involving riot, murder and rape were referred to the highest courts whilst countless others were dealt with at a lesser level. Some of the incidents contributing to the seamier side of Newport 's reputation will be recalled but first it is necessary to consider the manner in which the age dispensed its justice.

Before the town received its charters, the chief law officer in the feudal community was the Earl or his bailiff; one or the other presided over a Manor Court or Court Baron as it was often known. They were usually held at three-weekly intervals and were intended to deal with cases of debt, breach of contract, trespass, assault and petty theft. The lord or his deputy was the final arbiter and notice was taken of a jury made up of the more senior burgesses. The fines that these courts generated were treated as part of the lord's manorial income and as other financial sources depreciated, they became the most important and, indeed, the largest part of that income. No wonder then that justice often seemed to take second place to profit!

The town charters modified the system.

An ancient term inherited from the Saxons for a subdivision of land was the 'hundred' based on the area of land needed to sustain a hundred families or a hundred hides of land .

one to each family. By reason of its growth in status due to its charters, Newport was redesignated a hundred in its own right. It was not unnatural therefore for the manor court to be retitled the hundred court and later, in the 16th century, the town court.

Besides the trials of wrongdoers and the settlement of disputes, these court sittings were also used for the witnessing of legal documents such as leases or sales between burgesses, and other financial transactions of interest to the whole town. The periods between courts varied from town to town but it is known that in Newport they were convened every fifteen days without fail throughout the whole of the next two centuries.

Presiding over each meeting would be the mayor and present also would be the lord's bailiff, the constable of the castle and a jury of burgesses, all playing to a packed house of other burgesses who were there for both the latest news and the entertainment!

Whilst admirably serving the purpose of the times, these courts often allowed an element of duplicity to enter their workings. This arose from the fact that some burgesses and, indeed, some mayors were not above putting justice temporarily aside in order to settle old scores on behalf of themselves, relatives, friends or employees. Those who felt strongly enough that they had received an unfair hearing or judgement, had the right of appeal to a higher court in Westminster, often the Court of the Star Chamber no less, and the grounds of such appeals that are still on record are couched in terms hinting broadly at prejudice and hypocrisy. It seems however that this did not always work; many petitions fell by the wayside under the pressure of backstairs cunning on the part of mayors and bailiffs!

In addition to the hundred court there was a higher echelon of judicial administration in every town and Newport was no exception. As one of the measures to curb the powers of the barons and eliminate feudalism, King Henry II, in the 12th century, had instituted a legal system whereby the country was divided into at least six portions called circuits, each visited as regularly as possible by pairs of itinerant judges from the King's Court to hold Great Sessions and to ensure that justice was administered fairly and quite independently of the local ruler. Ideally such visits would have taken place at least once a year but as far as Newport is concerned, there are only three surviving rolls for the Great Sessions held in the town. These are for the years 1432, 1476 and 1503 but although lacking the written evidence, it is known that Sessions were held on at least ten occasions between 1441 and 1535.

Today the presiding justices would have been called circuit judges and were even then known as 'justices in eyre' (circuit). A strange custom grew up about these Sessions. Anyone would have expected them to have thrown up enough cases over the years to have supplied long lists of burgesses and the fines exacted from them. However, due to the curious system adopted, this was not the case. Apparently it was usual at the opening of the Sessions for the inhabitants to petition for the potential fines to be redeemed for a lump sum payment. If the sum was acceptable the Sessions were dissolved without a case being heard, unless something as serious as murder or rape was listed.

Redemption fees usually exceeded 1,000 marks, a considerable amount even if shared by all the burgesses and tenants. Being able to buy one's way legally out of trouble may not have served the cause of justice but it certainly swelled the lord's coffers with the minimum of labour!

Newport' s mayor or reeve — the titles were used concurrently and often as a matter of personal taste — was a man of many parts. This he had to be in order to cope successfully with the seemingly inexhaustible requirements of his profession. Comparison with his modern equivalent is to liken chalk with cheese, the latter being merely a municipal figure-head with sedentary duties, and the former a jack-of-all-trades, business man, accountant, magistrate, diplomat, buffer between lord and burgesses and a forceful riot-breaker in the streets! In 15th and 16th Newport it was essential for the mayor to be a most dominant personality.

His career always started in another kind of court known as a court of selection which convened every year on the first court day after the Feast of St Michael. Very often, at the termination of a hundred court, the courtroom filled once again with burgesses to witness and take part in a ballot to choose three names from which the steward of the castle would select the mayor for the next twelve months. But even here, in the sanctity and dignified atmosphere of the courtroom, with his term only just about to start, the new mayor could experience a foretaste of his year to come!

For instance, in 1581, local squires objecting to the choice of mayor, sent armed retainers into the selection meeting to force the issue. Ten years later, the election was severely disrupted by a violent group who wanted their favourite mayor to serve a second term!

Since the drawing up of the reeve's original and fairly onerous duties in the early charters, a number of statutes had added to them considerably, in particular those dealing with the collection of revenue.

The first charter commanded that on fair and market days, all visiting merchants had to set up their stalls in the few streets of the town and nowhere else. This was to facilitate the task of the mayor and his several bailiffs in collecting the lord's toll from which the burgesses of the town were exempted ie pontage, pavage, stallage, quayage, lastage, terrage, tronage and many others. Then there were the 'chenses' payments by non-burgesses (called chensers) to obtain permission to trade in the town at any time. 'Tolnetum Pyxidis' was another lucrative tax payable by merchants who only came for the markets and fairs.

Picture the scene on a market day:-

The narrow main street and the few beginnings of its offshoots, packed with humanity almost unable to make progress in the crush; the goods set up on stalls which were probably only handcarts or boxes; pedlars with trays hanging from their necks; illegal beggars, pickpockets and cutpurses furtively threading their ways where the crowd was thickest and the pickings richest.

The castle green was used mainly for horse trading, and would be milling with country folk, combing and grooming their animals to show them at their best to prospective buyers. Here too, the saddlers and harness makers made their pitches. Elsewhere in this throng were the other animals brought in from the country for sale : pigs, cattle, sheep and poultry. Human cries and animal noises; dogs barking and sudden shouts with the crowd parting to make room for a fight caused by drunkenness or dishonest dealing, closing in to get a better view and then parting again to admit the mayor's peacemakers; the overpowering stench of unwashed bodies, decayed vegetable matter, butchers' offal and tripes, animal excrement all made ten times worse in very hot or very wet weather!

Public conveniences in any shape or form were unknown, so the personal needs of the crowds during a long day must have sorely aggravated the problems. When all was over and all but a few had vacated the scene, the state of the streets must have been one of malodorous filth! The four or five men who were employed to clean up after such occasions certainly earned their wages - a sum of five shillings per year was assigned to be shared amongst them!

It was through such a jostling mob that the mayor and his bailiffs had the burdensome task of forcing their way in order to collect the usual tolls and taxes applied to the 'foreigners', and the even more unenviable duty of arresting those who resisted or evaded payment, those who were trading dishonestly, those who drank to excess, gambled. fought, and everyone who broke any of the town's many ordinances. In pursuit of these duties it was not unusual for the mayor himself to be attacked!

All these miscreants had to be hauled away, some resisting violently, to the prison in the castle to await their appearance in the next piepowder court where the mayor also presided as magistrate, as arresting officer and as a witness against many of those whom he had arrested. As if this were not enough, there were numerous other duties such as checking the quality of bread, ensuring that pauper boys received apprenticeships, ordering a poor rate, apprehending horse thieves and one that must have occupied a large proportion of the mayor's time the fixing of the price of ale and assessing the ale tax.

There was no central brewery as such, but there were many brewers, some making ale only for the use of their own families and others brewing for sale. Ale was an essential part of the diet and what is more it ensured that the drinker was imbibing water that had been boiled. This made good sense when so much disease was waterborne and one imagines with horror the unmentionable substances that may have gone down the town's wells on market days!

Ale was a brew that in Tudor times did not contain hops for flavouring, therefore was of an indifferent and vapid taste that nevertheless was easily acquired by old and young alike. Hops, although known, were not yet grown and were very expensive to import from the Continent. The cost of barley too was rising rapidly and between the years 1500 and 1547, several monarchs, particularly Henry VIII, courted popularity with the masses by preventing these costs from being passed on through the price of ale. Statutes were enacted to control prices, and the final obligation for maintaining the rules fell on the overburdened shoulders of the mayor. This was not the end of the matter however, for he also had to levy and collect the lord's tax on the brewing of ale. A sizeable income was derived from this.

The tax was known as 'assise cervisie' and was assessed in two amounts. Burgesses who brewed paid the lesser assize of 1½d for each brewing and non-burgesses paid the great assize of 1/1½d per brew. There were often a hundred or more brewings in a year, and there were side effects even to this innocuous undertaking that added to the general shabbiness of the town.

Brewers (and bakers) naturally used a great deal of corn, barley and other cereals in the manufacture of their products, and in the 14th century the raw materials were often processed and refined on the premises. It was not an unusual sight in Newport therefore to see large quantities of grain heaped in the roads outside brew houses and bakeries where it had landed after being thrown out of an upper storey opening to be winnowed of its chaff by the breeze.

One other of the mayor's major commitments, although by no means the last, was to manage a fund for the repair and upkeep of the bridge. Monies for this purpose were received from donations, bequests and chantries. The latter require explanation.

Devout burgesses who could afford it, left sums of money to pay for the singing of masses in their memory by chantry priests. Sometimes the bequest was large enough to subsidise a chapel, almost invariably screened and containing an effigy of the founder on a stone chest. There were three known chantries in St Woolos, in the names of Morgan ap Rosser for whom a fee of £6-17s-4d per annum was received, and Jenkin Clerke and Morgan David Gwilym Meyrick paying £5-9s-10d for both. According to Thomas Wakeman in his 1839 account of Newport's ancient houses of religion, this latter chantry was the equivalent of £90 in 1839 terms, so, viewed another 150 years on, it would represent purchasing power in excess of £2,000!

Considering this seemingly endless list of bounden functions, who then one may ask would want the job of mayor from choice? It was certainly not from a craving for financial reward which was, incredibly, an irregular fee of 2d per day only when the mayor performed duty and a shilling a year for his manorial accountancy!

The attraction is more likely to have come from the hidden perquisites which successive mayors had discovered over the years and kept carefully hidden from the lord of the manor. There is no doubt that the mayor was in a very strong position to line his own and his relatives' pockets and to cover his tracks, as long as he kept the township in profit to the lord's satisfaction! This is known to have been not a difficult task when for the whole of the 16th century the manorial income hovered around £15 per year.

Because of the reduced population the mayor was ideally situated to snap up vacant parcels of land at advantageous prices and to add them to his family's estates. As a knock-on effect, the increasing farmland acreages in his ownership brought great prestige in a community that was in Tudor times rapidly moving from feudal to agrarian policies. The wealth of the manors was being redistributed by clever men who were willing to work hard and take certain risks. A new social class was gradually emerging.

Throughout the 16th century, private estates began to build up, many in the hands of families whose names featured regularly amongst those who held or had held office in the borough administration. The Morgans, the Herberts and the Kemys were leading examples!

~ 0 ~

Having drawn attention back to churches through mention of chantries, it now seems wholly appropriate to discuss those that administered to Newport's mediaeval, religious needs.

St Woolos is well enough known. It was standing a little taller at the beginning of the 16th century having had an extra storey added to its tower in 1480. Today a cathedral church, it still stands relatively unscathed and readily available for anyone to visit for worship or for architectural or historical inspection. There were however other religious houses of which no vestiges remain and about which the various authorities are at odds in their opinions of their usage and position in the town.

One thing all are agreed on: St Laurence was the town church, St Woolos being outside the borough, and was situated in Mill Street. It was first referred to by name in 1535 but in a deed dated 1449 certain burgages were described as being 'in the parish of St Laurence '. Where in Mill Street the church stood is not absolutely clear but in 1850 Wakeman reported:-

'In the gable end of a building now forming a flour mill in Mill Street, opposite the Pontypool Railway Station, are the traces of a large gothic window, which from its size and form was apparently of the 14th century.'

In 1534 it was said that its possessions were worth £2-15s-4d including a brewhouse and tanhouse. With the mayor and corporation as its patron it was obviously looked upon as the borough church. In 1671 its remains, together with the churchyard, were sold to William Morgan.

The chapel of St Thomas almost certainly ceased to exist before the Reformation. Its situation is more obscure but there are some clues. A certain property deed in the time of Henry VI described its subject as 'being near the East Gate, between the Brigge Tower and the Chapel of St Thomas'. The Brigge Tower was obviously the castle tower nearest to the bridge, placing the chapel on or near the river bank. Lelande in 1540, wrote :'there was a house of religion by the key beneath the bridge', but for some unknown and annoying reason he found no necessity to identify it further.

Little else can be said of this chapel except that it may have been the Austin Friars Chapel of St Nicholas, rededicated when the Benedictines took over to their patron, St Thomas.

Apparently the Austin Friars were poor managers and were letting the Friary run down, so it was put in the care of the more efficient Benedictine Order. It may well be that ancient Thomas Street received its name from the chapel. The vagueness surrounding its situation is compounded by Coxe's map of Newport, circa 1802, whereon the name 'St Thomas Chapel' appears halfway up Queens Hill, followed by a question mark! On his journey through the town, did the Reverend Coxe find other remains of an ecclesiastic nature at this spot?

The free Chapel of St Nicholas was more clearly defined in view of its status as part of the Austin Friars.

It will be remembered that in 1377 the 2nd Earl of Stafford had endowed a monastery for the Hermits of St Augustine on the River Usk bank below the Town Pill. He had done this because he was a patron of the Order which had existed in the town since 1339 and which was finding difficulty in surviving. Their old chapel was rebuilt and they received 32 burgages to which succeeding earls added a further 28. These 60 plots of land became the open meadows later known as the Friars Fields. There were probably between eight and eleven friars in residence. This much is fairly positive but now the facts become much less reliable.

Just below St Woolos Church, at the top of what is now Belle Vue Lane, was another ancient friary. How or when it came into being is not known. Archbishop Coxe would have it that this was a second Newport monastery for the White Friars of the Carmelite Order; Wakeman on the other hand maintains that it was for the Dominican Order of Friars Preachers which was obligated to convert the Jews. This latter opinion was the subject of research in the early 1930s when the English Dominican Order stated that there was no record of a Dominican priory ever existing at Newport (South Wales Argus 12th January 1932).

All that eventually remained of these premises was a manor house known ever after as The Friars which was conveyed in 1547 as a private dwelling. There is no record of when it ceased to be used for religious purposes or the nature of the order that vacated it. The whole question of The Friars is shrouded in mystery but one thing is certain — there is not a shred of evidence to connect it with the Austin Friars!

At the start of the 19th century the house was occupied by Doctor Anthony Hawkins followed by Thomas Protheroe, Newport's town clerk. From 1839 to 1888 Octavius Morgan lived there. He was brother to Lord Tredegar and a renowned antiquary; during his occupation he rebuilt and extended the house in the Elizabethan style. It is now part of the administration complex of the Royal Gwent Hospital and when its grounds were being excavated to provide foundations for a new nurses hostel, archaeologists found the site of the old Stowe Quarry from which came the stone that built the original Friars and much of ancient Newport.

But back to the other friary that stood on the river bank below the bridge : all researchers have reached the same conclusion about one aspect of the Austin Friars history in Newport. Some time before the 1377 endowment, the Hermits planted an avenue of trees stretching from somewhere near the bottom of Belle Vue Lane to the friary on the river bank. It was once suggested that this avenue connected directly with The Friars on Stow Hill but no proof exists of this. Eventually the trees grew into a beautiful grove through which the friars could stroll in their contemplations. Its route roughly followed that taken much

The Austin Friars - sketched circa 1840 by Mr J Lee. Site cleared 1860 onwards.

later by Poplar Row (suggestively named, afterwards becoming Ebenezer Terrace) and Club Row (Lower Kingsway), to enter the Friars Fields at the southern end.

In 1534 King Henry VIII introduced his Act of Supremacy with its subsequent dissolution of the monasteries. The king's constant quarrels and final break with the Papacy, coupled with his desperate shortage of money, caused him to declare himself supreme head of the Established Church and then to proceed to convert much religious wealth to his own use. The smaller monasteries were the first target and orders were given to close them down, confiscate their lands and strip them of anything of value, even to the lead on their roofs!

Two of the king's commissioner's, Doctors John Vaughan and Adam Becanshaw, held a three day inquisition in Newport to assess the town's religious houses. Their findings went into a compilation known as the 'Valor Ecclesiasticus', a great national register of all houses of religion and the revenues attached to them. St Woolos Church, appearing under the name of St Gunleus, showed an annual income of £8!

In 1538, another of the king's visitors, Doctor Richard Ingworth, Bishop of Dover, made a remarkable trip, receiving the surrender of religious houses in Denbigh, Bangor, Llanfaes, Ludlow, Brecon, Carmarthen, Haverfordwest and Cardiff, arriving finally at Newport. From start to finish this journey took only three weeks and on September 8th he accepted the keys of the Austin Friars from the prior, Richard Batte, to close the buildings after an existence of nearly 200 years.

King Henry, determined to wring every last penny from his new source of revenue, ordered the cutting down of the majestic grove of trees, to be sawn up for sale on the spot where the avenue ended within the Friars Fields and just south of the chapel. By this action the king was instrumental in creating a timberyard and sawpits that remained on the same site until well into the 20th century!

Nothing escaped the Royal net although some of the results were disappointing in the extreme. The Friary bell for instance was sold to a Morrice Vaughan for 35 shillings but the total furnishings of all the cells raised only a quarter as much!

When Archbishop Coxe was passing through in 1802, he gave the following description of what he found in the Friars Fields:-

'... remains of several detached buildings containing comfortable apartments and a spacious hall with Gothic windows neatly finished in free stone; the body of the church is dilapidated but the northern transept is a small and elegant specimen of Gothic architecture. It is now occupied by a small cyder mill and the press is placed in a small recess which was once a chapel separated from the transept by a bold and lofty arch. The gardens are enclosed within the original walls.'

Some of the ruins of the Austin Friars were still standing in 1850, and about ten years earlier a Mr J Lee had sketched them. His drawing shows a very run down Tudor manor house with outbuildings. In 1860 Newport Corporation purchased the site for £7237-18s-10d, razed the buildings and commenced redevelopment of the area. What a great pity that the preservation of ancient monuments had no place in the schemes of the 19th century's town fathers. Here was one of the few remaining testimonials in stone to an important phase in Newport's history, seemingly presenting no problem to repair at a worthwhile cost for future generations to enjoy!

James Matthews, chief librarian and noted town historian, had firm views on the subject:-

'Here a sigh of soft requiem, or funeral dirge, may be expressed in silent grief, both for the departed preachers and the great loss Newport sustained in not possessing one particle of this edifice to memorialise the past'.
(Williams Monthly October 1907)

Newport suffers more than most from a lack of 'concrete' evidence of its past. Imagine therefore what might have been if the Victorians had been more enlightened. When the massive redevelopment of the town centre took place in the 1970s and 1980s it would have taken only a slight adjustment to the architects' plans to have sited a genuine, Tudor manor house alongside the Central Bus Station!

On the death by execution of Edward, 3rd Duke of Buckingham, in 1521, the Welsh estates including Newport were forfeit to the Crown. This meant that the town's overlord was to be King Henry VIII and his first action was to order an assessment to be made of his new assets. This was normal procedure in such circumstances but in view of his severe financial problems the king would have been uncommonly interested.

It was also in the same year that the Westgate Tollbooth ceased its function and commenced a new life as the town prison, to be known for the next 270 years as the 'Clock House'.

Newport figured in the survey as having:-

'A proper castle with three towers adjoining just to the water of the haven, the middlest tower having a vault or entry to receive into the said castle a good vessel. In the said castle is a fair hall, proper lodgings after the water side and many houses or offices. How be it, in manner all is decayed in covering and floors, especially of the timber work. There is good plenty of free stone and rough stone lying within the castle for

repairing same, if so it shall be required. Over the castle gate is the chequer chamber and under the same is the porter's lodge and prison for punishment of offenders and transgressors which houses, of necessity, must be maintained and well upholden. The said toune of Newport is a burgh and a proper toune and hath a goodly haven coming into it but well occupied with small crays (one-masted trading vessels) whereunto a very great ship may resort and have good harbour'.

So was the town described by the king's commissioner in 1521 but, as impressive as it sounds, it must be read in conjunction with the remarks of John Leland when he passed through a few years later. He said 'the fairest of the toune is all one street. The toune is in ruine!'

Leland was the first authentic antiquary. He travelled the length and breadth of the country for nine years from 1534 to 1543 describing many ancient buildings which were still flourishing; but he reported so many that 'tendith to ruine' that he may possibly have been confused when he described Newport in this way.

On the other hand, Thomas Churchyard gave a slightly different picture some 50 years later. In his 'Worthiness of Wales' he wrote of the town:-

'A toune nere this, that buylte is all a length,
Called Neawporte now there is full fayre to viewe;
A river runnes, full nere the castle wall;
which seate doth stand for profit more than strength.
A righte royal bridge there is of timber newe;
Nere church there is a mount behold you shoulde. Where sea and
lande to sighte so plaine appears,
That men there see a part of five fayre shires.
As upward hye, aloft to mountain top.
This market toune is buylte in healthful sort
So downward Loe is many a merchant's shoppe,
And many sayle to Bristowe from that porte.
Of aunciente tyme a citie hath it bin;
And in those daies a castle hard to win.
Which yet shews fayre, and is repayred a parte,
As things decayed must needs be helped by arte'.

A great debt is owed to Mr Churchyard for passing on his impressions of the period, but it is feared that there were times when he not only wrote of what he saw but also of what he heard and when most of his informants were simple, superstitious folk, he must have accepted as gospel some of the local hearsay. For instance:-

' . . . of aunciente tyme a citie hath it bin, and in those daies a castle hard to win.'

This conclusion displays a poor knowledge of local history for it is certain that when the castle was newly built in the 12th century, there was virtually nothing outside its walls except St Woolos Church and a small collection of serfs' hovels. A confusion with Caerleon is here indicated.

Even 'a right royal bridge of timber newe' is questionable in 1587, for this is the year that the bridge is reported to have collapsed through disrepair 'to the utter decaye of the toune' - and it remained in this state for the next ten years for reasons that will be explained in a forthcoming chapter.

In 1536, King Henry VIII introduced his Act to effect the union of England and Wales, bringing monumental changes to the British legal and local government systems. Nowhere was its effects more dramatic than in the Welsh Marches. By this act, England and Wales were divided into shires or counties. The Lordships of Newport, and Gwynllwg were combined with the other Gwent manors to form Monmouth Shire and a new sheriff was elected to govern it on behalf of the Crown. The Welsh counties were grouped into four areas and made to form a legal circuit for a new assize system. The Shire of Monmouth was excluded from Wales and added to the English assize.

In each circuit area the travelling Royal Justices held two Great Sessions each year, each of six days duration, to deal with cases of treason, petty treason, murder, felony, riot, rout, extortion and embracery (putting pressure on a jury). The half-yearly courts were supplemented by four Quarter Sessions dealing with slightly less serious crimes.

As significant as all these things were, the most revolutionary aspect as far as Newport was concerned was the complete sweeping away of four and a half centuries of rule by powerful Marcher Lords in the Welsh Marches. They had in any case been a source of embarrassment to successive monarchs for many years and Henry VIII finally succeeded where all others had not found the courage to try. The granting of charters now became a Royal prerogative only.

In 1547 King Edward VI, succeeding his father to both the throne and the Lordships of Newport and Gwynllwg, gave the latter together with Glamorgan to William Herbert who was elevated to the peerage in 1551 as Baron Herbert of Cardiff and Earl of Pembroke.

It was to the Earl — post mortem in 1567 — that is owed another glimpse of the old town from an enquiry into his estates and this time some streets and place names were distinguished.

Starting at 'Crookes Gate' (The Westgate Clock House Gaol) and working up High Street on the right hand side, there was 'Cornes Lane' (Corn Street), 'Skinner Lane' (Skinner Street), 'St Laurence Lane' and the Castle Green. From the same point at the bottom of 'Church Street' (Stow Hill) on the left hand side of High Street, was 'Payneswell' (Baneswell), 'Histingiste Ditch' (The Town Pill?), a burgage called 'Longheye', Crookes Cross (possibly the site of an old gallows) and then the Castle and Bridge Gate. Somewhere near Cornes Lane was the 'Spittehouse' or hospital of the Austin Friary.

This was the actual walking order in which the survey listed these features and whilst Skinner Street and Corn Street remain to this day, St Laurence Lane had to make way for the building of the canal basin near the Town Pill in 1795.

- 0 -

The town remained practically unchanged for the whole of the 16th century. Its short single main street was frequently filled with jostling crowds. mostly on business, often in pursuit of pleasure, visiting their 'town cousins' or just passing through. This was the normal, everyday side of the town's life and one would hardly credit that there was a black side that from time to time filled the same streets with violence of a particularly vicious nature.

On many of these occasions the opposing factions were made up of the same two powerful, local families. There was no love lost between the Morgans and the Herberts, and this presented considerable problems in a town where it seemed that almost every other person carried one or the other of these names. It was the strangest of vendettas – no one being sure of how the hostility first started - but carried on with apparent relish by the younger element over several generations. The elders did little to discourage this animosity although some of them found themselves at times in positions of authority which required that they should intervene. Often they shared the same judicial bench and various committees with each other, and even intermarriage was not entirely frowned upon.

These were the descendants of the shrewd Newport burgesses who had surreptitiously milked the lordship of a proportion of its wealth ever since the first town charter had provided increased opportunities to do so.

The young men of most branches of the families were privileged, often heavy drinkers, womanisers, swaggerers and fanatics about the superiority of their own families above all others. Consequently, as they seemed to have everything and to have done everything, taunting each other to the point of fighting appeared to be an excellent way of burning up their excess energy. To this end they were supported by large bands of armed retainers that were illegal but which nevertheless the landed gentry seemed able to keep with little fear of prosecution.

In November 1532, John Sissyllt (Cecil), a servant of Walter Herbert, murdered Roger David Tewe in Newport. The deputy steward of the castle, George ap Morgan, declared the murderer's goods forfeit to the Crown. There is no record as to what was done to the murderer himself. Walter Herbert protested strongly in defence of his servant and with a band of his supporters was making the situation very ugly when George Morgan's brother, Sir William Morgan of Llanmartin and Pencoed Castle, arrived in the town and confronted the protagonists. In his capacity as a Commissioner of the Council of the Marches, he placed an injunction for good behaviour of both parties under a penalty of 500 marks. This quietened the situation temporarily but it went on smouldering for nearly three months until it finally burst into flames on the morning of 23rd February 1533.

Being a Sunday, George Morgan was coming down Stow Hill on his way from divine service at St Woolos Church when he saw his dog mating with another which belonged to Walter Herbert outside the former's house near the bottom of the hill. Some believe that the Herberts had deliberately set up the occasion but whether by accident or design, George Morgan set about separating the hounds in no uncertain manner and as he did Walter Herbert drew a knife and stabbed him through his arm and side. He then fled the town to avoid apprehension.

Sir Walter Morgan issued another injunction which was again ignored – it was almost as though he made a hobby of issuing unenforceable injunctions!

Walter Herbert was the steward of the Lordship of Magor, an area that he allowed to become the refuge of numerous unsavoury, even murderous criminals. Several days after the incident involving the dog he returned with at least 50 thieves and outlaws from Magor. He had also spread the word among all country branches of his family and they came with their own ruffianly retainers to assemble at St Julians, the home of Walter's brother, William. The whole party numbered something like two hundred.

Hearing of their approach sometime in advance, the Morgans destroyed all the deck planking of the bridge to make it impassable but, nothing daunted, the Herberts turned and at great speed made their way through Caerleon and Malpas village back to Newport where they poured into Mill Street and High Street.

The Morgans were waiting in force, armed to the teeth with bows, billhooks and pikes. A major riot ensued and soon hundreds of men were fighting furiously in the narrow streets. The home of George Morgan, Westgate House on Stow Hill, was surrounded and the Herberts shot over 300 arrows into it killing one and injuring several of the servants.

Someone even took a pot-shot at Sir William Morgan as he tried once more to declare one of his interminable injunctions!

The fighting went on for hours until the real object was lost and then the bloodthirsty adversaries turned their fury on the innocent townsfolk, committing wholesale robbery, murder and rape. At the height of this mayhem it was beyond the control of William Llewellin, the mayor and his small band of bailiffs; there was no mention of the calling out of any castle garrison. These honest folk just had to stand aside and watch helplessly as the Gatehouse was broken open in a search for arms, and the prior of the Austin Friars badly beaten. To intervene would have meant serious injury or even death!

The women of Newport were apparently made of sterner stuff or else they relied heavily on their femininity to protect them. As it happened the thuggery that surrounded them was indiscriminate but nevertheless they marched in a column through the thick of the battle carrying a banner on which were depicted the Crucifix and an image of St Gwynlliw. The intention was that all who set eyes on the banner would be impressed enough to 'Give reverence to the Almighty God and eschew all rancour and malice . . . '

By all accounts this was not the first occasion on which the women had made such a display, and neither would it be the last!

The fact that the made-up banner could be produced at such short notice was further evidence that there was good reason for it to be kept at the ready and a reflection on the volatility of life in the Newport of the Middle Ages!

Gradually the tumult died down and the Herberts cleared the town, taking with them all the wounded but leaving behind those who had fallen and were lying hidden. The dead of both sides were left where they had fallen until they could be counted and identified by the town officials. Two unfortunate serving girls who happened to venture out as the retreating Herberts were galloping past, were swept up across the pommels of the saddles and carried off in the direction of Glamorgan 'and there subjected to the grossest usage and no more heard of!'

There was only one place where such a serious complaint could end and that was in the highest court in the land, the Court of the Star Chamber. The sworn deposition of George ap Morgan pleaded self defence and accused the following:-

The brothers Charles, Thomas and Richard Herbert
of Troy, Monmouth,
John Herbert of Abergavenny,
John Herbert, Bastard,
Miles Mathew,
Thomas Bawdrip of Glamorgan,
and a thousand others!

This was obviously at least a fivefold exaggeration and it will never be known why most of those named were identified by their place of residence whilst for poor John Herbert the second, his parental status served that purpose! Maybe it was a comment on the way in which the Morgans regarded him in particular!

Those who had committed murder were named as:-

Morgan Thomas, Thomas Herbert, Philip Herbert, Richard Philip, David Forten, John Mors and John William *alias* Pell.

Walter Herbert's reply was a complete rejection of the Morgan complaint, starting with an apology for the affair with the dogs and maintaining that he came to Newport with only six men to effect a reconciliation! Amazingly there is no record of how the Star Chamber dealt with this case.

Make no mistake about it — this was real, frightening warfare on the streets, offering danger and death to peace loving citizens and innocent travellers alike. Although not directed against the State and not involving such great numbers it was infinitely worse in terms of mindless brutality and damage to the town than the much more publicised and grossly overrated Chartist Riot three centuries later. By comparison the latter only qualifies as a minor disturbance!

- O -

The ancestral homes of these feuding families are deserving of attention if only because both of them survived into the 20th century. One however lost the battle against an unfeeling and extremely myopic planning authority; the other is still in use.

Crindau House, on the western side of the River Usk was not in those days inside the borough but stood on the right hand side of the road leading to the village of Malpas, a stretch known as Crindau Pitch. This was the lower slope of a steep climb which loosely

Crindau House 1860
Lithograph by Elizabeth Harcourt Mitchell

followed the line of the present Brynglas Road (at that time the main track out of Newport to the north). The area must have taken its name from the house because the Welsh equivalent of Crindau: 'Crindy', meant a round or compact house.

It was a pleasant, Tudor manor house standing in a large acreage with the River Usk forming one boundary at the bottom of an almost sheer, 80 feet, wooded slope. The original residence built for Edward ap Howell ap Jenkin in Queen Elizabeth's reign, passed to his son, Thomas ap Edward and his wife, Margaret Morgan of Pencoed Castle Llanmartin. Their son, John Edwards, left the house to his only daughter, Katherine, who married Miles Herbert, a future notorious mayor of Newport. His eldest son, William, had an only daughter, Katherine, who married Humphrey Morgan of Llantarnam. So, the Herberts' occupation of Crindau House gave way to that of the Morgans who eventually sold the estate to Mr Gregory, owner of an early Newport brewery. He put the run-down building into good repair but not in character for he replaced stone slab roofing tiles with slate and removed

69

several of the original, attractive lattice windows.

The 300 year old manor house and eleven acres of land was purchased in 1889 by Thomas Ponsford and from then on was gradually absorbed into the mass building of working class terraces as Malpas expanded to become a suburb of Newport.

Today, Crindau House may be found, converted partly into a private dwelling-house and partly into a working mans club, tucked away in Chelston Place, a short cul-de-sac just off Redland Street. On a gatepost is proudly displayed its blue plaque of antiquity which states:-

Borough of Newport Crindau House 1580 on moulded porch entry initials H M with date probably refer to Humphrey Morgan of Llantarnam who married Katherine Herbert, heiress of Crindau Newport Civic Society.

St Julians House on the other hand was a Herbert House right from the start, having been built in the reign of Henry VIII by Sir George, a younger son of Sir William, 1st Earl of Pembroke. Another Sir William died in 1592 and left his estate to his only daughter, Mary, subject to the strangest of conditions:-

'My will is that whensoever Marye my daughter doth marrye that then she shall take to husband a gentleman of my Sirname Herbert and if it shall happen that she doe marrye or take to husband any other person than shallbe a gentleman of my Sirname Herbert, then I give and bequeathe all my lands, tenements and hereditaments whatsoever in the County of Monmouthe to William Herbert the eldest sonne of my Uncle, Miles Herbert, and then if there be no heires, to William the 2nd sonne of my Uncle Miles Herbert, and if there also be no heires, to Thomas, 3rd sonne of my Uncle Miles Herbert and if again there be no heires, to Edward the younger son of my Uncle Miles Herbert.'

So Mary had to marry a man named Herbert in order to inherit her father's estates. Old Miles Herbert must have been rubbing his hands in anticipation at the very strong possibility that everything would come to his sons, the Crindau Herberts. For six years they waited and then to their utter chagrin in 1598, Mary married Edward Herbert of Montgomery who was only fifteen years old but who was destined to become a talented and intellectual member of the nobility.

This young man was described as:-

'The historical, the philosophical, the right whimsical peer: a man at once and together the negotiator, the scholar, the statesman, soldier, genius and absurdity of his time and nation.'

He was a very handsome man and especially favoured by Queen Elizabeth I. His impressive talents were further recognised by King James I who elected him Ambassador to France and kept him abroad for many years on diplomatic missions. This however may have been a ploy for the king's own benefit for Herbert was also a suspiciously close friend and favourite of James' Queen, Anne of Denmark.

St Julian's House 1955, taken from the Fred Hando collection.

For his services, he was created Lord Herbert of Castle Island (Ireland) in 1624, and Baron Cherbury in 1629. His latter years were spent alternately at his castle in Montgomery, at St Julians in Newport and at his house in Queens Street, London, where he died in August 1648 having directed that his body be buried at 12 O'clock at night in the Church of St Giles in the Fields 'without pomp or other ceremony than is usual'.

St Julians House stood in solitary splendour about two miles out of Newport close to the east bank of the River Usk, between two short, narrow pills which sheltered the Herbert's boats. It was on the site of the old chapel built where the martyrs Julius and Aaron were reputedly murdered by the Romans.

Stretching away towards Christchurch was the deer park and St Julians Wood. There was a private track to Newport passing by Duckpool Farmhouse on its way to join the main highway to Newport Bridge. From there it was but a short step to the Murenger House which had become the Herbert's town house. In the early 19th century this track became the new Caerleon Road.

St Julians House and estates survived a threat of extinction by Oliver Cromwell and remained in the Herbert family's ownership until the grandson of Edward, Henry Herbert, died childless leaving everything to a nephew, Francis Herbert. His son, Henry Arthur, was created Lord Cherbury in 1743 and Lord Powys in 1748. He was the last in line of the St Julians Herberts, and after his death the estate was sold into other hands.

A few centuries later another St Julians House was built and to avoid confusion was called Higher St Julians, but some historians confused the two. The newer house, an imposing mansion, stood in its own grounds with a long driveway (still existing) to an entrance near the bottom of St Julians Avenue. It was the home of Joseph Firbank, the railway contractor who founded the Firbank Estate much of which became the St Julians Housing Estate. The house was never destined to be a serious competitor to the old St Julians Manor House down by the river, for it was demolished in 1933 to provide the site of houses in Heather Road and Elaine Crescent.

St Julians house lived on for another 40 to 50 years becoming ever more dilapidated, finding use only as a coalyard and storage premises, especially when the nearby M4 Motorway was being widened. There was always a chance while it remained standing that a miracle might happen to give the venerable old house a new lease of life and present Newport with another historic building to add to the sorry few that have been preserved more by luck than any serious thought for the heritage of the town.

St Julians, as seen by Archbishop Coxe in 1800

In 1951, St Julians was scheduled as a Grade III listed building under the terms of the Town and Country Planning Act 1947. In the 1980s it was sacrificed on the altar of private enterprise and its demolition guilefully contrived. On the old foundations a block of elegant flats was erected with the address of 'Marine Court', off Haisbro Avenue, still quite an idyllic spot, and the residents are fortunate indeed to enjoy the same relatively unspoilt views that, 400 years earlier belonged exclusively to the Herbert family!

A local greybeard who lived nearby and who was witness to the 'wanton' destruction, reports an interesting fact that only came to light when the roof was removed. Apparently the guttering did not direct the rainwater away from the house, but had ducts that were pointed inwards to a vast, lead-lined reservoir in the roof-space.

If the point of this was the augmentation of an inadequate well-water supply it may be that many of the unexplained ailments that beset the Herberts were due to generations of flying or creeping creatures which had finished stiff-legged and belly upwards in this penthouse pool! On the other hand, the symptoms could merely have been those of lead poisoning! The overwhelming pity of it is that this appalling vandalism of a heritage was ever allowed to occur and furthermore, that so far nobody seems to care!

~ 0 ~

Entry into the latter half of the 16th century was heralded by a period of raging inflation initially encouraged by the monetary policies of King Henry VIII, his debasement of the coinage and the sudden fluctuation of silver prices around the world. The price of food rose by 290%, wages by only 60%, and things did not begin to settle down until well into the long reign of Elizabeth I. Even then, in one decade the cost of living shot up by another 33% but although this makes conditions sound serious, in real terms it was not so bad.

For instance, an artisan could earn four shillings a week and a shilling would still buy 7 bushels of wheat, 3 pounds of rice and 2 bottles of cider. Alternatively, the same shilling would buy 3,000 bricks or a tooth extraction from a travelling dentist! In other respects this era contained events that were not only the most colourful, the most epic, the most scientific and the most artistic but also some of the most shameful in British history!

Between 1577 and 1588, Francis Drake circumnavigated the globe, redrew the map of the world and destroyed the Spanish Armada.

Galileo and William Shakespeare were both born in 1564, the former's revolutionary theories being finally proven and accepted in the world of astronomy, and the latter by the age of 36 having written 23 of his most famous plays. The same period produced Christopher Marlowe, Edmund Spenser and Sir Francis Bacon, three more of the most illustrious names in English literature.

On the debit side, Sir John Hawkins started the evil and barbaric trade in negro slaves!

This stirring sequence of events included many more, mainly concerned with the discovery of new lands and the spread of England's world trade – all happening during a period of 50 years when two queens, Mary I and Elizabeth I reigned.

Through these momentous times Newport dozed fitfully with spurts of awareness only when parochial occasions caused temporary hiccups.

The year 1581 was notable for the first confirmation of the town's Lords Marchers' charters by a reigning monarch. It took place when Queen Elizabeth was travelling in Wales. On 10th September, at Margam Abbey, she placed the Royal Seal on the document which restated all the privileges that the burgesses of Newport had been enjoying.

It is interesting to note some of the exempted tolls mentioned in this document because they appear to be additional to those previously listed whenever the charters have been discussed. They comprised a ware-carrying toll, a breaking-up-of-the-ground-for-fixing-stalls toll, a wool-weighing toll, a mastage toll and a lord's land-tillage toll! Taken together with all the others, one could be forgiven for imagining that the old lords might have considered a breathing-of -manorial-air toll but reluctantly cast it aside due to difficulty of collection!

Curiously, in one of Newport Corporation's 19th century minute books, there appears an explanatory list of these tolls long after most of them became extinct. They are reproduced here exactly as written:-

    Stallage **Is to be quit of certain customs exacted for the street taken or assigned in fairs or markets.**

    Chimage **Is a toll that is paid for a man's passage through a forest to the disquiet of the wild animals.**

    Pontage **Signifies sometimes the contribution that is gathered for the repairing of a bridge sometimes the toll that is paid by the passengers crossing.**

    Panage **Is that money that the agistors (feeders of cattle) of forests do**

gather for the feeding of hogs within the forest, and is taken for all manner of mast trees within the forest on which the hogs do feed.

Piccage **Is the payment of money, or the money paid for the breaking of ground to set up booths and standings in fairs.**

Murage **Is a toll -tribute levied for repairing and building of public walls.**

Lastage **That is to be quit of a certain custom exacted in fairs and markets for carrying things where a man will.**

Passage **Is when a town prescribed to have a toll for such a number of beasts, or for every beast that goeth thro' their town or over a bridge or ferry maintained at their cost.**

As previously stated there were dozens of these tolls and it is too much to expect that this narrative should identify every last one of them - it is hardly credible that the town accountant could keep track!

In the absence of any solid evidence to the contrary, it must be assumed that life in Newport continued during these years pretty much as usual with the markets keeping the piepowder courts busy and the fortnightly town courts having full schedules of minor felonies, thefts, assaults, poaching etc.

There is little information on the incidence of lawlessness in the town at this time because court records at all levels are woefully lacking. Nevertheless, given the town's reputation for violent street affrays over a long period, the Quarter and Great Sessions must also have had their quota of serious cases to deal with. Areas outside but adjacent to the borough boundaries were teeming with ruffianly ne'er-do-wells and the young bloods had already shown how utterly disrespectful they could be to the poor, working-class girl found alone and unchaperoned. Kidnappings and rapes were probably not that infrequent!

There were also strange goings-on in the borough administration where the pillars of society were shown to be less than upright and the position of mayor suddenly became unusually popular, despite the stressful nature of the job! Most mayors served for only the standard term of twelve months and were probably very relieved when it was over. Occasionally some spent two terms in charge of the town for no good reason that has become apparent – although no doubt they finished up much better off than when they started. One person however, was mayor for a record four terms and was not above using strong-arm methods to secure these appointments!

The few surviving records of submissions to the Court of the Star Chamber of cases in Newport are all in respect of serious affray.

In 1576 the complainants were the Burgesses of Newport, and the defendants, Morgan Griffiths, Morgan Edwards and others. The charge was 'the use of force to intimidate electors and causing the town to be in uproar during the election of the Mayor and bailiffs'.

In 1581 Miles Herbert was just terminating his first year of office and the Selection Court was in session to choose the next mayor when a band of armed men burst in and wrecked the chamber causing many of the honest burgesses to flee. The real reason for this action was never revealed but the outcome was the re-election of Miles Herbert for 1582! This time the complaint was made by Sir William Herbert of St Julians against Rowland Morgan,

Henry Jones and others, the charge reading : 'disturbing the council whilst around the council table electing a mayor'.

Eight years afterwards, in 1590, Miles Herbert managed to get himself elected yet again and when a year later the Court of Selection was in session and had actually chosen Morgan Griffiths as the new mayor, another unruly gang of ruffians appeared chanting 'Miles Herbert, Miles Herbert' over and over again, terrorising the burgesses into re-electing him for his fourth term! It would appear that for a decade at least, Newport was in no position to deny the wishes of the unscrupulous tyrant of Crindau!

There is only one more surviving record of Newport's involvement with the Star Chamber and the year is believed to be 1609. That is not to say that there had not been others in the intervening quarter of a century because the neighbourhood's disruptive element was known to be thriving at that time and regarded its wild incursions as seasonal sport!

Walter Griffin of Llanfrechfa, gentleman and deputy sheriff, made complaint against Giles Morgan and other male members of the Morgan family. The charge was that of cutting open Griffin's nose and lip (said afterwards to be only part repaired), armed resistance, falsification of a jury's evidence and the attempted abduction of the daughter of Rowland Williams of Llangybi!

Miles Herbert's mysterious affection for the job of Mayor of Newport could have had several explanations and the clue to one of the most likely may lie in the continuing story of the River Usk bridge.

The last time that the bridge was said to have been extensively repaired was in 1488, although one suspects that whenever the word 'repaired' was used in reference to this crossing it would have been more accurately described as 'patched up!' Whatever maintenance it may have received since that year, it was not sufficient to prevent the fifteen arch bridge collapsing in 1587 'to the utter decaye of the toune!'

The mayor's fund for the upkeep of the bridge was still regularly receiving income from gifts, legacies and chantry properties. The amounts varied between extremes – as little as two shillings from the least wealthy philanthropist to the very generous £100 given by Sir William Morgan to be used to purchase a grove of standing timber in the nearby forests in readiness for the rebuilding, if and when it should become necessary.

As this possibility became fact in 1587, all the local squires and country gentry subscribed magnificently to the fund but when the bulk of the money was required, it was found that the mayor, Miles Herbert, had appropriated it to his own use! It was in an effort to elect a new mayor who could demand the release of this money that the uproar in the Selection Court took place and Miles Herbert's cronies forced his re-selection.

Newport Bridge never did get rebuilt out of local resources. The town remained bridgeless for over ten years and eventually, in 1597, it was found necessary to petition Parliament for an Act to enable the bridge to be built. The Act made the new bridge the responsibility of the county at large and its maintenance that of the county magistrates.
The town was obviously no longer capable of shouldering the burden of the frequent heavy expense involved in the upkeep of something upon which the economy of the whole region depended.

The archives are bare of any information as to the treatment of Miles Herbert after his near bankrupting the town!

The Old Market House, built 1585 and demolished 1793.

Only two years before the bridge disaster Newport had been congratulating itself on the acquisition of a fine new market house or guildhall, which became the new centre of local government. Its opening in 1585 was most fortuitous for a couple of years later the town was devoid of building funds!

Executive and courtroom accommodation hitherto supplied by the castle, was now made superfluous, giving further impetus to the decline of that ancient edifice.

It appears that the Market House was built astride of the main road, which was diverted round both sides to merge again at the back. This was quite adequate for 1585 because High Street, as narrow as it was, was not yet hemmed in by houses on either side so there was ample room for market stalls and for travellers to pass. This road was not known as High Street at the time in question; for many years it was called Bridge Street and fifty years later, during the Cromwellian Commonwealth, it was known as Monmouth Street.

The Market House was of a design commonly found in Tudor market towns and in many can still be seen remarkably preserved. Stone built, two storied, the upper floor comprised the meeting hall and courtroom and was larger than the lower, thus forming an all round overhang supported by four archways on either side and two across each end. This cloistered area was in great demand as the best, covered market stallage. The chamber above had two large fireplaces and a large window over each of the twelve arches below. The ponderous, pantiled roof and the town clock, set in the massive gabled end added the final touches of mellow stateliness one would expect of a town's civic building.

The Market House served the town for the next 208 years, standing in the middle of High Street at the corner of Thomas Street, approximately where the Kings Hotel and the old Post Office face each other today, and only becoming redundant in 1793 when its island site was causing great congestion in a very busy main street.

The Lord of the Manor of Newport from 1547 to 1570 was William Herbert, 1st Earl of Pembroke. He derived a healthy income from rents, tolls and court fines but it was a subdued lordship in comparison with its former Marcher glory. Like the old days however, the Earl still sought to increase his power and wealth and was ever on the alert for ways to do so. Opportunities were supplied unwittingly by Henry VIII's Act of Supremacy which had undertaken to transfer all religious wealth to the Crown. Not all of this could be accounted for by the King's Commissioners. The buildings presented no problem but the land holdings were a different matter because in many cases the religious authorities, resistant to the confiscations, withheld or destroyed records of their lands. This happened on a grand scale all over the country and as a measure to redress the situation, the king set up a system to investigate the 'concealments' as they were called. A vast network of paid informers was employed.

The evasions were privately encouraged by wealthy landowners who could see the advantage of having unclaimed acreages, ripe for the taking, on their doorsteps. William Herbert was such an opportunist and from 1551 onwards, by means of clever manipulation of conveyancing and the use of loyal accomplices, he added large areas of concealments to his estates.

The Pembroke Estates also profited by honest means. In 1582, for loyal services to Queen Elizabeth, Henry the 2nd Earl, was given the manors of Liswerry and Libenhet (Libeneth), once part of the De Clare's great Lordship of Usk. Documents of the period concerned with these areas are interesting for demesnes that have been preserved in name almost intact to the present day:-

Alweaye, Bishpoole, Ladye Hill, Ringley (Ringland), Hendrey (Hendre), Couldrey (Coldra), Pulpan (Pwllpan Farm Llanwern), Summerton and Traston.

Chapter Five

A Royal Charter and the Common Wealth

The dawn of the 17th century saw dynasties change from Tudor to Stuart and the first in the new line of monarchs was to prove highly instrumental in the reshaping of Newport's future.

Queen Elizabeth died in 1603 after a reign of 45 memorable years. She was unmarried and childless, as had been her deceased half-brother (Edward VI) and half-sister (Mary I), so the heir to the throne had to come from farther afield. Thus it was that the Crown of England went to King James VI of Scotland, son of Mary, Queen of Scots the second cousin whom Elizabeth had committed to the headsman' s axe for her designs on the English throne. Ascending as King James I, the Scottish king added further cement to the union of the two countries.

The few years surrounding this event were momentous for Great Britain. Elizabeth's 1600 Charter of the East India Company had heralded the future domination of India; the foiling of the Gunpowder Plot in 1605 saved Parliament and the Crown ; Virginia, colonised in 1607, opened up the North American continent to the possibility of becoming the most promising - not to mention the most extensive - overseas possession! In Newport the year 1606 would be remembered for a much different reason!

At about 9 am on the morning of January 20th there came in the Bristol Channel and the River Severn the highest tide for many a year. Driven by storm-force winds it quickly breached what passed for coastal defence works at several points and covered the whole of the moors from Caldicot to Cardiff in a surging spate, three feet deep. What effect this inundation had in the town is not recorded but bearing in mind what has already been said of the normal high tides in the Usk, it does not take much imagination to picture the consternation of the townsfolk as, within sight of the Westgate, large waves rolled across the Pillgwenlly marshes. It has been written that at its height the flood lapped at the edge of Bassaleg Churchyard and this being so it must have washed through the ground floor of Tredegar House!

Elsewhere, outside the town, some 2,000 people were believed drowned and an eye-witness gave this account of the calamity:-

'Upon Tuesday being the 20th January 1606, there happened such an overflowing of waters, such a violent swelling of the seas, and such forcible breaches made in the firme land in the counties following – that is to say in the counties of Gloucester, Somerset Monmouth, Glamorgan, Carmarthen and divers and sundry other places of South Wales, the like never in the memory of man hath ever been seen or heard of. For about nine of the clock in the morning, the same being most fairly and brightly spread, many of the inhabitants prepared themselves to their affairs. Then they might see afar of huge and mighty hills of water tumbling over one another as if the greatest mountains in the world had overwhelmed the low villages and marshy grounds. Sometimes it dazzled many of the spectators that they imagined it had been some fog or mist coming with great swiftness towards them, and with such a smoke as if mountains were all on fire, and to the view of some it seemed as if millions of thousands of arrows had been shot forth all at one time. So violent and

swift were the outrageous waves that in less than five hours space most part of those countries (especially the places that lay low) were all overflown and many hundreds of people, men, women and children were quite devoured; nay, more, the farmers and husbandmen and shepherds might behold thir goodly flocks swimming upon the waters~dead.

It will be noted that the above account dates the disaster as January 20th 1606, as do the plaques in the various moorland churches. The actual date was in the year 1607 due to the custom at the time of dating the beginning of each year from March 25th.

James I was probably the most informed and educated monarch that the royal lines had yet produced. He had been a child prodigy and it was said that at the age of ten he could read the Bible in Latin, translate it into French and back into English. It is then, one of the idiosyncrasies of the age that such wisdom could be accompanied by such blind unenlightenment, for the king believed implicitly in witches and witchcraft; he even wrote a book to reinforce that belief! No wonder that during his reign this ugly superstition reached its zenith and hundreds of innocents were pursued and murdered.

Newport it seems did not suffer in this way; at least there has never been any reference to a local pond with a ducking stool, much less a public burning, and none of the notorious witchfinders were known to have passed this way. On the contrary, the reign of King James I, and especially its 20th year, was probably the most auspicious in the town's history. In 1623 Newport was granted its first, outright Royal Charter!

It opened with the following paragraphs:-

James by the Grace of God, King of England, Scotland, France and Ireland, Defender of the Faith, to all whom the present letters shall come. Greeting:

Whereas our borough of Newport in our county of Monmouth is an ancient and populous borough and the Mayor, bailiffs and inhabitants thereof have had, used and enjoyed various liberties, franchises, immunities and honours both by the charter of Henry, Duke of Buckingham as also by reason of divers prescriptions, usages and customs had and used in the borough in times past, And whereas the said Mayor, bailiffs and inhabitants of the aforesaid borough by their humble petition have shown us that, notwithstanding through the lack of certain liberties necessary and proper for the government of the said town, it happens that not only are they oppressed by the poverty but also the rule and government of the same town is daily ruinously burdensome. And therefore they have humbly supplicated to us insofar that we should graciously extend to them in the premises of our royal favour and munificence and that we, for their greater convenience and utility and for the good rule and government of the borough aforesaid, shall deign to grant the confirmation of all the ancient liberties and privileges with the amendment of the defects aforesaid and the addition of certain other liberties and privileges as it may seem to us more expedient . . .'

This last paragraph guaranteed all the provisions of the previous charters regarding the freedoms granted to the Newport burgesses.

No official of the Crown could take proceedings against any burgess who was exercising these rights. Burgesses retained their rights to hold and dispose of their property without let or hindrance. Trading privileges were safeguarded, and non-burgesses were not allowed to trade within the borough except at markets and fairs. An additional fair was conceded so that there were now two each year at the Feast of the Assumption (15th August) and at the Feast of St Leonard (6th November) but each fair was curtailed to two days duration. All existing tolls continued to be levied by the borough which also retained control of the Courts of the Piepowder.

Then followed the drastic new provisions that had the effect of converting Newport from a small township with restricted self government, threadbare administration and precarious financial status, into a substantial borough. The town was entrusted to the care of a corporate body of townsmen to hold property on behalf of the burgesses, and to maintain law and government through a mayor and twelve elected aldermen. The Charter nominated John Priddy as the first incorporated mayor and actually named the twelve aldermen. The mayor was to serve for twelve months until his successor was sworn in on the Monday next before Michaelmas, when the names of two aldermen were to be presented to the Lord's steward for final selection of the new mayor.

Aldermen were to serve for life while of good behaviour, and new aldermen were to be appointed by the mayor and the existing body of aldermen. Any burgess refusing this honour would be liable to a fine.

Only aldermen could remove the mayor and only the mayor could choose or dismiss officers of the Corporation.

The mayor, the steward and two senior aldermen were to be appointed justices of the peace to keep the King's peace, enquire into felonies and, for the first time, hold General Sessions within the borough. This created a self regulating magistracy and a self perpetuating Corporation.

It was the duty of the mayor and aldermen when summoned to the Guildhall, to make reasonable laws and ordinances for the government of the borough, to fix fines for offenders and to order imprisonment or distraint.

To give further guidance in legal matters to the council, a new official called the Recorder was appointed to hold office for life. He was the equivalent of the modern town clerk and the first one Edmund Morgan, was named in the Charter. After his death the power of selection was vested in the mayor and aldermen.

The number of town bailiffs was increased to two.

These provisions then, were the essence of Newport's new ruling structure and the salient points were to form the backbone of the town's administrative development for the next 212 years, until the Municipal Corporations Act of 1835 swept away all vestiges of charter-granted powers and imposed a uniform system on all boroughs.

There appears to have been some confusion over the respective custodies of Newport's two surviving charters.

The story has already been told of Octavius Morgan's providential discovery, in Shrewsbury, of the 1427 Charter of Humphrey, 6th Earl of Stafford. Of this there is no doubt and a series of articles in the South Wales Argus gave full details of the circumstances. However, accounts appeared in other reputable histories which implied that the 1623 Charter of James I experienced an identical disappearance and salvation, even to the exact date and the identity of the discoverer! In this misinformed report it was said that the missing charter was found in the archives of the Tredegar Estate Office on its removal to new premises in 1861. Its presence there for over 200 years was put down to the fact that originally it would have been normal for the town mayor to keep custody of such an important document, and many members of the Morgan family had held this post over the years.

There was still one restriction that the town council found frustrating and that was the retention by the Lord of the Manor (then Philip, 4th Earl of Pembroke), of the right to receive all the tolls, fines, chenses and profits from fairs; within a short while a solution was found to this problem.

In 1627, the mayor and aldermen negotiated successfully with the Earl for the fee farm of the borough. This meant that the Manor of Newport was leased to the Corporation for 21 years for a fine (premium) of £45 and an annual rent of £4. This enabled all tolls 'including killage and pitchage' (another two!) to be used for the benefit of the inhabitants. The fee farm was to be renewed regularly at the end of each term.

The new-look Newport Borough Corporation lost no time in tackling the duties demanded of it by the Royal Charter. From the date of their very first meeting after incorporation, Mayor Priddy and his aldermen began producing ordinances covering all aspects of the town's everyday life, intended to protect the health, peace and prosperity of its burgesses.

The town was still not growing; as a matter of fact, its population was the lowest it had been for two centuries. By all accounts Jacobean Newport was not a very attractive place in which to live, except to its own born-and-bred sons who knew nothing else but the small cluster of insalubrious dwellings which they lived in until they fell down in decay and which were then rebuilt in exactly the same form on exactly the same sites. Nevertheless, these citizens must have been passionately proud of their dirty streets and seedy surroundings, and seized every opportunity to discourage outsiders unless they could pay heavily for the privilege of settling or trading in the borough.

It was in such an atmosphere that the town council, from its market house/guild hall, promulgated a phenomenal number of rules and by-laws which by present standards may give cause for amusement but which, in their day, were meant as a serious reflection of the times. In the years following 1623, the town's rule book grew fat and unwieldy, overburdened by ordinances that overlapped their subjects, had been made redundant by changes of circumstance, had proved impracticable or were otherwise in need of amendment. These councils seemed loath to repeal anything that their genius had created!

In 1711 however, the town council sat in a series of extraordinary sessions to carve some order from the chaos, and eventually produced a comprehensive restatement of the town's ordinances, revised and updated, pruned and streamlined; even so, the result was still 52 by-laws for the tiny community! It only requires a brief description of half of them to paint another vivid picture of conditions that prevailed and incident that could have been instrumental in causing the necessity for such regulations.

In general, the by-laws formed groups under headings relating to specific aspects of community activity:-

The Markets

Provision was made for the supply and accuracy of brass measures and scales.
Trading was restricted to market places only.

Bulls had to be baited before the flesh was exposed.

(This was an extremely cruel practice carried out under the totally false belief that it would somehow improve the quality and flavour of the meat. The fact was that it also gave macabre entertainment to a watching public which was unconcerned with the moral issues

81

involved. In 1847, during the building of the first High Street Post Office, excavations uncovered a large, flat stone in which was embedded a rusty iron ring – the original town bull ring to which the tortured animals were tethered).

All bad meat had to be burned.

Butchers had to bring for inspection the hide, lights, head, heart and liver of any animal sold.

Fishmongers' wares had to be inspected by 'seizors'.

Many of the regulations drawn up in respect of foodstuffs were motivated by fear of the spread of plague which in 1666 had returned with a vengeance to London and other cities. It was essential to keep a very careful watch for unwholesome meat and rotten fish!

Conduct on Sundays

All inhabitants were compelled to attend the established church except 'those so unhappy to dissent, who must attend some properly licensed place'. Such places were the Market House, the Mill Street Chapel and the house of Barbara Williams.

The penalty for not attending St Woolos was one shilling and that for dissenters not attending their places of worship was ten shillings!

To set a good example, the mayor, aldermen, bailiffs and constables with maces and halberds to attend them, should walk to divine service at St Woolos in gowns and cloaks.

There were to be no vain recreations. No games such as futballe, bowles, trippet*, shoulebord (shovelboard), wrestling, cards or dice.

*Trippet was a game sometimes called 'tip cat' and still popular in the 20th century. A short, thick stick was sharpened at each end and laid on the ground. One of the tapered ends was struck with a longer stick causing the 'cat' to spring into the air in front of the player who, with a second swipe, would try to hit it as far as possible.

There should be no dancing or music, (raids were carried out on assemblies where pipes and drums accompanied singing and dancing).

No travelling, drinking or trading during divine service.

Council Procedures

Every alderman and burgess, when called by the mayor, should attend in gowns or cloaks or decent apparel without aprons.

Burgesses were expected to serve as constables or bailiffs with a £2 fine for refusal.

There was a £10 fine for declining to be an alderman and a £200 fine for declining to be mayor.

Promiscuity

No one should allow other people's servants into their homes after 8 pm.

No one should give more than three nights lodging to unmarried women 'begotten with child'.

To keep out prostitutes it was ordained that no spinster was allowed to live in the town unless she owned lands, had money or good employment.

Hygiene

Surprisingly few of the many laws were directed towards the cleanliness of the town and they hardly touched on matters of public health. A town sewer was unheard of but there were makeshift open gullies into which anything could be tipped to make its own laborious way into the Town Pill and consequently the river.

There were four by-laws dealing with dunghills in the streets and eminent citizens were regularly accused of letting them pile up in front of their houses and stables.

Pigs and horses were not allowed to wander in the streets.

The washing of clothes was forbidden near the town's wells.

General

One of the more surprising ordinances appeared under this heading and its presence is one more pointer to there being a serious problem with lawlessness. It was an offence for any burgess *not* to keep defensive weapons in his house! Anyone could then be called upon at any time to help the mayor keep the peace. Penalty for non-compliance – 10 shillings!

Inhabitants were expected to cut their hedges and keep the causeways in front of their houses clean and repaired up to the centre of the roadway.

They should pay taxes for the repair of the church roof, the Market House clock and the free school.

They should not:-

Commit street nuisances,
Play unlawful games,
Curse in public,
Get drunk and cause affrays,
Bake bread unlawfully,
Take part in scandalmongering.

Apparently, to be guilty of this last offence it was only necessary to spread the word that a man was a rogue or that a woman possessed the evil eye!

In order to qualify as a bona fide burgess of Newport, one had to have been born in the borough, to have married the daughter or the widow of a burgess, to have served a seven year apprenticeship to a burgess or to be sponsored by burgesses and pay a £2 admission fee.

Many laws regulated the conduct of houses where ale was brewed or sold, and yet drunkenness was rife. These houses, which had to be licensed, were identified by an ale-rodd, a tall pole erected outside the front door. If wine was also available a bush or some such greenery would be tied to the top of the pole. This was almost certainly the origin of such well known public house names as The Bush, The Ivy Bush and The Hollybush.

If an ale licence was withdrawn it was the constable's job to cut down the pole, and in so doing he stood a very good chance of being sorely attacked by disgruntled customers - sometimes even by the alehouse keeper himself or herself (for it was a popular job for a woman).

Licences were revoked for many reasons : harbouring vagrants, selling over-priced ale and allowing disorder to name but a few.

Some by-laws reflected the times, and they were changed to suit them accordingly. For instance, it was a crime known as malignancy to pray aloud for the monarchy during the period of the Commonwealth and after the Restoration it was punishable to speak admiringly of the days of Cromwell.

Opportunity was also taken in the council chamber to reiterate the 1536 ordinance against 'foreign' millers. The steward of the manor had ruled that burgesses were to use only the lord's mill to grind their corn. This suggests that the only mill in Newport was still that which had stood at the castle end of Mill Street since before the Norman invasion. The strict implementation of this rule created a favourable monopoly for the lord of the manor and deprived the townsfolk of the benefit of competitive prices. A similar action was taken on behalf of the town's tannery and before long other bodies were receiving protection for their monopolies. Two notable cases were those of the Company of Starchmakers in the forbidding of starch manufacture by non-members, and the Company of Soapmakers in the unauthorised production of soap. No doubt these were regulations that had the effect of making the fortunes of some members of the corporation or their families!

Most of the infringements to this bureaucratic proliferation were punished by fines or revocation of licences but there were occasions when the infliction of pain and public humiliation was ordered irrespective of sex. A whipping post was present near the Market House and later outside St Woolos Church.

Vagrancy was a common whipping offence and was carried out by the constables. They then had the duty of escorting the vagabond to the county boundary from whence he had come and there handed over to the constables of that county who would mete out similar treatment. If the poor unfortunate had happened to have crossed several such boundaries on his way to Newport, he would likely receive as many scourgings before arriving back at his starting point!

Although appearing to be drowning in a sea of red tape, there was some small compensation for the burgesses of Newport who had to watch their step (literally in those polluted streets) every moment of the day. They were allowed to graze their animals, free of charge, on the community-owned, 33 acres of the town marshes (the present site of Shaftesbury Park and its surrounding streets), and on the Town Mead, a small, circular meadow split by the mill stream, outside the North Gate of the castle at the end of Mill Street.

- 0 -

William, 3rd Earl of Pembroke died in 1630 and his widow, the Countess Mary, commissioned James Palmer to make an assessment of her Welsh manors. A photostat copy of the original is available at Newport Reference Library, and in James Palmer's own handwriting it covers 29 Monmouthshire manors including Newport. This survey, a century after the one made for King Henry VIII, makes very interesting reading and throws a lot more light on the mid 17th century town.

The folios take the form of a listing of burgages, their holders' names and the rents paid. Many of the rentals must have been for houses in which burgesses lived but unfortunately they cannot be identified because in those days the numbering and naming of residential burgages was most unusual if not non-existent. There are approximately 165 entries within the borough boundaries, some for one or more burgages and some for half burgages but poor quality of the script does not allow the exact number to be ascertained. The rents indicate an average of one shilling per annum per burgage, and six to seven pence for a half burgage. The lowest rent is one penny to the Prior of Goldcliff, and the highest is eight shillings for a multiple of eight burgages.

Significantly, the holders of the largest numbers were the most eminent citizens Thomas

Morgan, Sir William Morgan, Aldermen Roger Williams, Maurice Nicholas and John Priddy (ex mayor). Other aldermen named are Thomas Harris, Morgan Meyrick and John Johnnes. Several non-residents feature, such as Thomas Morgan of Mathern, William Thomas of Caerleon, Alexander James and John Fownes, both of Bristol and probably connected with the shipping trade on the River Usk wharves.

Surprisingly, three women appear in this almost exclusively male catalogue: Ann Lewis, Katherine Watkin and Ann Nicholas who must have been a lady of substance for she held ten and a half burgages – more than any of the men! There may have been some significance here in that the terms of office of two mayors named Nicholas came just before and just after the survey!

Three further items are worthy of mention. The castle was rented to Baron Edward Herbert of Cherbury for five shillings a year, the burgesses collectively were in possession of the marshes and : 'Edward Close, labourer, hath erected a cottage on ye Lord's waste in a place called Corne Streete and amerced two pence'.

One thing was very noticeable in this survey of 1630. Not a single member of the Herbert family now appeared to live in the town and perusal of the last wills and testaments of leading members of the local families reveal no reference to bequests of property in the town. A certain Miles Herbert (the embezzler of the bridge fund?) still lived at Crindau on the road to the village of Malpas. The Kemys family too had apparently vacated the town but were fairly thick in the areas of St Brides, Marshfield, St Mellons and Caerleon. The family seat was at Kemys House, built in 1623 in the parish of Kemys Inferior. The trend was obviously to shake the filth of Newport's streets from one's boots as soon as the town provided the necessary affluence to do so!

The survey was set out in some weird sort of directory order that must have been quite clear to its author and his contemporaries but which makes little sense today:

'**On ye east of ye highway from Crookes Gate to ye Bridge,**
Within Cornes Lane,
Within Skinners Lane in ye little bayly,
Within ye Greate Bayly,
Below St Laurence Streete,
On ye west part of ye High Streete,
Beneath Paynes Gate,
Beneath ye new gate in ye little bayly,
In ye Greate Bayly,
Without Hurstons Ditch (Histingiste Ditch in the survey a century earlier)
Crookes Gate to Payneswell,
From Payneswell to the Marshes north out of ye North Gate,
Within ye highway beginning at Rood Hill on ye south part,
From ye gate about (?) until ye Mill,
Ye Mill ye far side of ye way,
On ye north part of ye way from beginning to out ye way till ye Mill,
From Rood Hill by Bryngelond to ye Mill,
Maders Croft,

---

* Rood Hill has been identified in several old publications as present day Barrack Hill but this is not the case because the former was within the borough and the latter well without. Mr John Wood's 1836 survey map of Newport shows Rood Hill to be a short stretch following the borough boundary and crossing a field in a south-westerly direction, roughly from the junction of Queens Hill and Dos Road to the end of St Marks Crescent, passing en route through the grounds of Queens High School and the old County Hall.

From St Gaules** well by Kingshill*** Greene Lane, Corne Streete, Pill Lane, Skinners Lane, St Laurence Lane

The first houses to be built in High Street were said to have appeared in 1624. Before this, the burgesses lived either within the castle walls or in the area of the old villeins' enclosure (Mill Street and Pentonville), which to many was still symbolic of wearing a badge of servitude which they were desperately anxious to cast off. There is, however, an entry in the 1630 Survey to the effect that :'ye houses of Harry Thomas and Alexander James were built 35 years before, near the Market House in ye Lord's waste'.

The use of bricks as building materials had died out completely when the Romans left Britain but since the beginning of the 16th century they began a revival in the Eastern Counties and the larger cities where stone was difficult to obtain and was in any case very expensive once it had been quarried, dressed and hauled long distances. Wherever suitable clays became available brickworks sprang up, creating employment and supplying a cheap mass-produced building block of manageable size.

Newport's supply of building stone had always been adequate and when necessary had been augmented by ship-borne cargoes from across the River Severn. However, when the advantages of brick became apparent, it was no trouble to rediscover the local sources that the Romans had exploited at St Julians, Malpas and Caerleon. Consequently all further artisan and working class cottages erected in the town tended to be of brick and tile instead of timber which was becoming in short supply in the receding forests.

There were no cellars to these houses until after 1600 when cider started to gain popularity as a beverage. Ale was brewed and drunk within a very short time, but cider needed as much as a year to mature in a cool, dark place. By the 1680s all new houses began to adopt a symmetry of which most earlier versions were lacking; front doors were placed exactly in the centre of facades, windows more evenly distributed and two chimneys became a regular feature. On the debit side, most of the attractive timber-work died out.

Dozens of small manor houses for the landed gentry and lesser squires sprang up on their estates in the countryside around Newport and a fair proportion of them still exist today having taken the form of period farmhouses in states of repair varying from dilapidated to nicely renovated. Many of the 16th and 17th century barns also still exist, some serving their original purpose and others converted into the smaller farmhouses and cottages.

~ O ~

King Charles I ascended the throne in 1625 and in twelve years succeeded in uniting practically the whole nation against himself! He married Henrietta Maria, the Roman Catholic daughter of the King of France and thus became too tolerant of her religion for most people's liking. The Queen had no knowledge of English manners and customs but was allowed to interfere increasingly in matters of state.

Charles believed implicitly in the divine right of kings to govern and for parliaments to obey royal commands without question. This concept put him constantly in contention with his parliaments which, to make matters worse, were puritan almost to a man and therefore rabidly anti-Catholic. He continually sought ways to make money for his various schemes

----

** Another name for St Woolos
*** Also known as Kensal Land and being the track which became Vicarage Hill down to Cardiff Road. A large house called Kingshill stands there today.

Newport Castle in the 17th Century

many of which were ill-conceived; he frightened many of the nobles by his attempts to retrieve vast tracts of church lands that they had acquired, legally or otherwise; he created new taxes that were disapproved by Parliament and he vetoed many laws that Parliament tried to pass. His close advisers, the Earl of Strafford and Archbishop Laud were hated to a point that eventually led to their executions!

The affairs of the country became so confused that when Parliament dissolved in 1629 after the same quarrels that had caused the dissolutions of its predecessors, no further parliament was called for the next eleven years and King Charles governed alone!

One of the king's major problems was the deteriorating condition of his navy and the increasing duties required of it by the maritime authorities on both sides of the Bristol Channel which was infested with smugglers and bloodthirsty pirates. No ship trading in these waters was safe, and hardly a day passed without one being captured, taken to pirate headquarters on Lundy Island and held to ransom. Bristol, Swansea and Cardiff complained bitterly . Newport was included in the petitions but only as a 'creeke' of Cardiff. To raise money to improve his fleet, King Charles resorted to a different kind of taxation.

One of his favourites was 'ship money' which he levied several times on all the coastal counties of England and Wales. This was a most unpopular tax and in 1626 £2,000 was fixed for Monmouthshire. A meeting of justices of the peace in Newport that year authorised a letter to be sent to the king saying, tongue in cheek, that despite an intensive search no ship belonging to the county could be found! The king seems to have got round that sort of excuse in 1634 by extending ship money to *all* the inland counties.

Civil war was not far away when the next administration (the Long Parliament) commenced its sessions in 1640. Charles still disobeyed, ignored or vetoed most of its attempts at lawmaking, but on 4th January 1642 he went too far when he burst into Parliament with 400 soldiers to arrest five members who had opposed him most strongly.

This was an unforgivable and disgraceful breach of privilege but it was unsuccessful because the so-called traitors had received advance warning and made good their escape.

Shortly after this incident Charles decided that he had no option but to declare war on Parliament. Leaving London he marched north and, on 22nd August 1642, raised his standard near Nottingham Castle.

Monmouthshire was predominantly Royalist but when the news filtered through, Newport's lord, the 4th Earl of Pembroke, declared himself against the king, pledged £1,000 and 40 horses and placed his castles of Newport, Usk and Abergavenny at the disposal of the Parliamentary Army. All the other castles in the county were Royalist and most of the gentry, including Lord Edward Herbert of Raglan, Sir Trevor Williams of Llangibby and Sir William Morgan of Tredegar House, joined the Royalist Army.

The ordinary working man in Newport, like his counterpart in every other part of the country, knew very little of politics and probably cared even less. He was ill informed on all matters that originated far away at the seat of government in London, for he had no access to the rough news sheets that circulated among the nobility. The snippets that he did receive from travellers and itinerant traders were often weeks old and embroidered out of all proportion by the constant telling. It was not surprising therefore that the simple town dwellers and countryfolk, in their belief that their masters knew best, would almost certainly give their support to the party that was popular with the local ruling classes and would change their loyalties accordingly. This was not uncommon in the Civil War and many a true-blue Cavalier officer at the outset was found commissioned in Cromwell's Model Army at the end. Some changed sides more than once!

The Earl of Pembroke, having committed himself to the Parliamentary cause, was elected Lord Lieutenant for Monmouthshire and ordered to remove the county magazine with its arsenal and ammunition, from Raglan to the safety of Newport Castle where the King's men could not use it or, as Oliver Cromwell himself said : 'beyond the reach of the Marquis of Worcester!' As it turned out, it proved to be an impossible task because although the Earl tried several times to carry out this order, he was thwarted by the concentration of king's supporters in the area. In any case there would not have been much point because it was only a matter of a very short time before Newport became a Royalist town. This came about when a force led by the Marquis of Hertford crossed the Bristol Channel from Minehead and quickly took over all the castles which were not already in Royalist hands.

On November 4th 1642, 7,000 Royalist soldiers left Cardiff and marched to join the king at Oxford, their columns negotiating the steepness of Stow Hill and passing along the narrow main street of Newport to create quite a display for most of the day. Unfortunately the progress of such an army could not be a well kept secret and the advance guard was ambushed and defeated by waiting Roundheads at Hereford. The rest of the force was badly mauled near Tewkesbury and had to retire back into Wales.

It is a fact, although not a very much publicised one, that Welsh casualties were very heavy in the Civil War. Excluding those confrontations and sieges that took place on Welsh soil (and there were not a few in the south), almost the whole body of infantry troops which suffered such appalling losses in a matter of only two hours at Naseby in June 1645 were Welshmen!

Two years of the war having gone by, Newport was still little effected. The whole county remained one of the most loyal to the king and on several occasions received visits from him. Even he, however, felt the chill that was creeping into his welcome.

One of the reasons for this disaffection was the attitude of the Royalist troops who were stationed in and around Newport. Their commander, Colonel Sir Charles Gerard, was overbearing and foolish in the treatment of his hosts and failed to curb his soldiers' from excesses such as looting, drunkenness and rape. Moreover, they were billeted in local households, everywhere free of charge, and those same households were expected to pay heavy additional levies to finance the war! For example, in December 1644, from his headquarters in Newport Castle, Colonel Gerard issued demands for lump sums of £1,000 and £1,650 each month and his troops went about collecting these amounts with great cruelty.

Compare these exorbitant sums with what had gone before.

The County Public Records Office possesses original letters written on 27th January 1644 by Colonel Richard Herbert, Governor of Newport Castle. The recipients of these letters are not stated but the instructions in them are quite specific:-

'It is ordered by the Commissioners that the sum of £60—0s—0d be assigned monthly for the garrison of Newporte. The sum to be allotted by the Burrough of Newporte £27~10s~0d and by the Townshippes of St Wollas, Bettws and Malpas £27~10s~0d, in all £55~0s~0d . . .'

Unfortunately, at this point the writing becomes indecipherable but enough is apparent to understand just how savage were the demands of Colonel Gerard before the year was out.

A similarly worded letter in the same spidery handwriting, demands a sum of £266-13s-4d from the hundreds of Wentloog, Rumney, St Mellons, Peterstone and Marshfield, to be paid to the garrisons of Chepstow, Abergavenny and Monmouth.

On another tack, one letter appears to be an appeal directly to King Charles, beginning: 'This humble petition of the Commissioners, Gentry and Freeholders of the County of Monmouth . . .'

Again the handwriting leaves much to be desired but here and there it can be ascertained that help was required by way of a royal loan to repair 'bridges damaged by plunderings' and to make good some damaged sea walls at Newport.

The growing antagonism towards his command was so noticeable that Colonel Samuel Tuke, Commander of the Northern Horse, writing to Prince Rupert from Abergavenny, said:-

'I have no trust in this county generally ~ the greater part are niggling traitors ~ their tenants rise, disarm and wound our men for coming to quarters assigned to them'.

If further proof was needed of the change of heart in Monmouthshire, it came when a thousand newly enlisted men were gathered in Newport to be harangued by Sir Jacob Astley. He was the replacement for Colonel Gerard forced on the king by public protest. When the order was finally given to commence the march to Hereford to fight against a Scottish army, there was outright refusal and nothing would prevail on the troops to go!

Shortly after this mutinous display outside the walls of Newport Castle, King Charles visited South Wales to see the signs of disquiet for himself.

As has been stated, the Military Governor of Newport at that time was Colonel Richard Herbert of St Julians. His father, Baron Herbert of Cherbury, was getting too old to take an active part in the war. When the king passed through on July 16th 1645, Colonel Herbert turned out the castle garrison of 50 men to line the route from the bridge and help to swell the small crowd of curious onlookers. Before proceeding to Cardiff the king was wined and dined by the 85 year old Sir William Morgan at Tredegar House.

In Cardiff the king held meetings with his Commissioners of Array who were responsible for recruiting militia to the Royalist Army. He was told that there were no problems but it was a half-hearted assurance on the part of the Commissioners for they knew only too well the harm that had been done by the heavy handed actions of Gerard and Prince Rupert.

A week later on July 23rd, the king, making the return journey, narrowly missed capture by Roundhead troopers at Crick House as he waited for news of a ship to carry him over the River Severn. The diaries of his chaplain, Doctor Bailey, relate that the king had hardly passed out of one door as his pursuers entered by another! He therefore returned hurriedly to Newport where he received no royal reception but was glad to accept two nights hospitality at the house of Mrs Priddy, the widow of a former mayor. This house was situated on the corner of Stow Hill and a side lane which was afterwards named Charles Street in the king's honour.

The castle was no longer used on such occasions because it had deteriorated to such an extent that it could no longer offer the comfort worthy of a king. This fastidiousness was not just a royal prerogative for Oliver Cromwell too preferred the accommodation of a house in the town on his several overnight sojourns. The building in question became known as Cromwell House and it stood on Stow Hill until demolished in 1895 for the building of the Tredegar Hall (now Majestic Buildings).

The fall of Newport to the Parliamentary Army was an event of little account. The town actually changed hands several times but was never the subject of a great classic battle for possession as were the towns of Raglan and Chepstow. The castle in the former suffered a ten week siege with a barrage of sixty cannonballs a day being blasted over the walls; the latter was starved into submission and then subjected to a senseless slaughter carried out on Sir Nicholas Kemys and his surrendering garrison!

Newport, on the other hand, had more in the nature of nuisance value, lying in the path of the several advances or retreats of each army, with a small castle that was difficult to defend and which prudence advised to vacate insofar as its strategic importance was concerned. Every time the Royalists took over, the hills, forests and moors around about became saturated with Roundheads, hiding until it was their turn once again to reoccupy the town!

As Governor of Newport, Colonel Herbert's task was not an enviable one. Up until the war started Newport Castle had been fast falling into decay and now, in order to provide another bastion of Royalist defence, its commander did what precious little he could to strengthen its fabric.

When the first Government troopers appeared on the skyline above the town at Christchurch, they were not in a hurry to approach nearer but camped by a windmill on Fairoak (Christchurch Hill) from where they overlooked the bridge and the castle. From this vantage point they considered their plan for the taking of the town. It could not have escaped their notice that signals were being exchanged between the castle and the tower of St Woolos Church, marking the latter as another building of military importance to be captured. The attack when it came was all too brief; the castle was easily overrun and its far from illustrious career ended once and for all!

Meanwhile, a party of Roundheads with one or two pieces of artillery, surrounded St Woolos and demanded its surrender. They found the doors locked and heard shouts of defiance from within so preparation was made for a bombardment to winkle out the tiny garrison. There is no direct evidence that any violent assault took place although outward signs of damage suggest the impact of some cannonballs and the story has oft been repeated that this is how the statue in the niche on the west front lost its head.

The total loss of the head made the figure impossible to identify but there are two main contenders for possession of the torso. First is Jasper Tudor, Lord of the Marches and of the Manor of Newport by dint of his marriage to the widow of the disgraced 2nd Duke of

Buckingham and builder of the top storey of St Woolos Church tower. The second contender is King Henry II who gifted the first tower to the town. The only evidence pointing to either is in the statue's dress, bearing as it does, the mantle of a Knight of the Garter; and the three shields below the battlements in the upper stringcourse on three sides of the tower, having three trumpets on clarions in pale, another the Crown of St George and the other the Royal Tudor Badge, the double rose. None but a royal personage would have borne or put up that badge.

Inside the church, at the time of the attack, there was some breakage to monuments and effigies but this was probably more from heat of the moment boisterousness as the doors were battered in, than a spirit of wantonness.

After the town was secured for the Parliamentary forces early in 1646, Colonel Herbert's loyalties were obviously suspect. He was the subject of two letters written by Oliver Cromwell. The first, to Major Thomas Saunders the local commander in Brecon, was an order to seek out and capture Sir Trevor Williams of Llangibby who had apparently become something of a renegade to the warring factions, having started out as a supporter of the king, changed over to Cromwell to play a leading part in the siege of Raglan Castle and then reverted once again to the Royalist cause to recapture Chepstow Castle. The letter advised that Colonel Herbert almost certainly knew of Williams' whereabouts and should be approached at St Julians for the information.

The second letter, to Herbert himself, was couched in words that did not imply the greatest of trust. Very bluntly, Cromwell told him : 'If you harbour or give aid to any offenders, your treasonable nest (St Julians) will be burned about you!'

So Newport's far from illustrious war ended. Baron Edward Herbert of Cherbury and his son Richard survived safely but not entirely unscathed. They suffered forms of retribution from both sides. On the one hand, for his lack of positive support, the Royalists had destroyed the elder Herbert's ancestral home, Montgomery Castle; on the other, on 30th June 1648, both father and son were fined £2,574, 'for adhering to the king against Parliament'. They were both fortunate in that no order was made for the sequestration of their lands - the fate of many Cavalier landowners who lost vast estates to Roundhead gentry.

The Civil War had started as much for religious reasons as those of a political nature. The established church was Anglican and lived in constant fear of a resurgence of Roman Catholicism - hence the hatred of Parliament for the power which the Catholic Queen Henrietta wielded over the king.

In 1649, when the war was over and the king executed, the country was virtually a republic for the next eleven years although it was never declared as such. The term used was Commonwealth, changing to Protectorate after 1654. Oliver Cromwell was never the president but the Lord Protector; he was even offered the kingship but he refused as it had never been his ambition and he knew full well that the Army would not stand for it.

The monarchy's parliaments had all been mainly Puritan and much of the trouble leading to Charles' downfall had been inspired by the Puritan versus orthodox Anglican controversy. Puritanism was deeply rooted in the Anglican Church's hysterical abhorrence of Roman Catholics and had been growing for over a century, until now it was a force to be reckoned with. The orthodox variety was a branch, grown apart, with many contrasting beliefs born out of the obsessional anxiety about the aims of the deviant doctrines, and introduced in an effort to eradicate them. To begin with, there was no trust in bishops or their courts. Puritans felt sin should not be punished by religious penalties but in very severe sentences decided in lay courts of law. There was a fanatical pursuit of the purge of sin and, indeed, many new sins were thought up! Puritans loved 'fire and brimstone' sermons, and were noted for their canting piety and their hypocritical repression of any form of enjoyment or entertainment. They were also taught by their religion that second only to their worship came enterprise and hard work. This identified it from the Cavalier form of Anglicanism which was much more tolerant; it might even be said that whichever branch of the religion was practised, it drew the line between the two social classes.

Little has been recorded of the effect that the Puritan regime had on the life of Newport except that which was reflected in the town ordinances of the time (churchgoing, treatment of dissenters, playing of games etc). What cannot be disputed is the fact that the attack on the established Anglican Church in Monmouthshire was pursued with much more vigour than anywhere else, suggesting that those who resisted Puritan principles were much more determined and more thickly distributed in Monmouthshire than any other county. Certainly more church livings were confiscated, more clergy thrown out and more fraud and injustice perpetrated in the name of the new religion than in any other part of the kingdom.

It is fortunate that a certain anonymous gentleman decided to try his hand at writing a novel based upon events occurring around him in Monmouthshire. His work, in a clear, educated hand gives a graphic description of how he saw the Puritans who lived in and around Newport. Again, thanks are due to the County Records Office for preserving the notebooks of this literary Cavalier, who was undoubtedly putting himself at great risk by putting pen to paper in this way!

Here is his account:-

'The Puritans were ignorant as far as learning or science went, reading no book but the Bible and works published by their own body, and their views on religion were most narrow and selfish for they put the most wrongful interpretations on passages of scripture, and would wrest individual and particular texts to apply to their arguments when, if they had taken the whole and entire passage, would have argued directly opposite to them.

In dress their simplicity was the most affected and boastful, and their private carriages the most ostentatious that seemed to say, 'admire me for my sanctity'. their visage was drawn out to the very fullest length and would have turned generous wine to vinegar, so acrimonious was their aspect.

Their conversation was interlaced with phrases and passages, innocent amusements and recreations they condemned, and baptism of their children and disciples bestow no names but those of greatest celebrity in the Bible and generally chose those which were the longest or whose meaning was the most puzzling'.

Thus spoke an eye-witness who has passed on to future generations what is undeniably as true to life a picture of the Newport and Monmouthshire Puritan as can be found anywhere.

If the Commonwealth profited little else for Newport, at least something came from its legislation.

In 1650, the Act of Propagation of the Gospel in Wales appointed Commissioners to look into the Welsh clergy and to eject ministers who were found to be immoral or hostile to the Commonwealth. As it came about, the Bishop of Llandaff lost his living and so did 45 clerics in Monmouthshire whose crimes were said to be those of using the orthodox Book of Common Prayer, drunkenness, ignorance of the Welsh language, non-residency and malignancy (praying for the king).

The Commission was authorised to elect replacements at salaries of £100 a year. In addition, the Act established 60 Free Schools in Wales to teach both sexes English, Latin and Greek. Newport was granted one of these schools.

Chapter Six

The Restoration and the Industrial Revolution.

'The privileges of the Freemen tended greatly to the impoverishment of the Community and there is much cause for thankfulness that we live in these later days of freedom and thought, speech and freedom of trade'.

Conyers Kirby
Borough Engineer of Newport
22nd August 1871.

The Restoration came about primarily as a backlash against religious persecution and the masses of legislation that intruded so drastically into everyone's privacy. By 1660, the people were ready for a change from the repressive and melancholy way of life inflicted on them by their Puritan overseers.

Oliver Cromwell, the iron man of the Protectorate, had died; his son, Richard, after temporarily donning the Protector's cloak, had been forced to flee the country and the Model Army was riven by internal quarrels. Eventually, General Monck, the Governor of Scotland, emerged to put an end to what he called 'the intolerable slavery of sword government', and made arrangements for a new, unfettered parliament to be called.

Its first measure was a vote in favour of the restoration of the monarchy. Prince Charles, in exile on the Continent, was approached with proposals which he accepted in a declaration made from Breda, and on May 29th 1660 he entered London amid great excitement and with 'the ways strewed with flowers, the bells ringing, the streets hung with tapestries and the fountains running with wine!' The Commonwealth was ended and Charles Stuart mounted the throne of England to reign as King Charles II.

The first new governing body was known as The Cavalier Parliament and it lasted, remarkably, from 1661 to 1679. In religious matters it proved to be more severe in its attitude to the rivals of Anglicanism than the Puritans had been to theirs. The chief minister of Charles II was Lord Clarendon who was responsible for four Acts between 1661 and 1665 which were intended to curb mightily the activities of those who did not or would not practise orthodox Anglicanism. Special concentration was placed on the Puritans both as revenge for past humilities and to ensure that they never again became a threat.

By the first of these acts, the Corporation Act, no one could be a member of a town corporation or a member of any parliament unless he took Communion according to the rites of the Church of England, and swore an oath denying the lawfulness of taking up arms against the king. This immediately deprived the Puritans of their hold upon the towns and the House of Commons.

The Act of Uniformity obliged every clergyman and schoolmaster to take a similar oath declaring 'an unfeigned consent and assent' to the whole of the Book of Common Prayer in which 600 anti-Puritan alterations had been made! Over 2,000 clerics refused to obey this command so were dispossessed of their livings and thereby fell foul of the Five Mile Act forbidding them to settle within five miles of their former livings or any corporate town.

The Conventicle Act banned all religious meetings other than those of the Church of England, under pain of imprisonment for the first two offences and transportation for life for the third!

At his nonconformist chapel in Mynyddislwyn, Henry Walter had so impressed the Puritans with his tub-thumping sermons, promising the everlasting fires of hell to all sinners, that they promoted him to be Vicar of St Woolos. At the Restoration he refused to recant and consequently the new legislature withdrew his comfortable living. For some reason the provisions of the Five Mile Act were not enforced and he was allowed to live in Pillmawr House at Malpas. Here he remained until the Toleration Act of 1689 permitted freedom of worship to all denominations except Roman Catholic as long as their meetings were held in specially licensed houses with their front doors unlocked. Then, Henry Walter came out of retirement at the age of 78 and thereafter was a very active member of the Mill Street Chapel.

The aforesaid Corporation Act worked most effectively in its aim to keep local government free from Puritan influence but it also had an unforeseen, adverse effect as evident in Newport as anywhere.

What the Act produced was to become known as the 'closed corporation' and this was the result of placing the town's affairs in the hands of a restrictive, privileged group from the established church. Thus, a mayor with friends or relatives swelling the aldermanic ranks found it no problem to be elected for several years in succession. The financial inducement was not great but the incentives for members of closed corporations to remain in office must have contained more than just a feeling of great responsibility for the welfare of the borough. This had been situation normal in Newport for many years and the Act only served to give permanence and respectability to an otherwise corrupt system. To give some idea of the tiny number of Newport councillors that wielded such power, it is on record that they could all sit comfortably around a remarkably small table in the not too spacious council chamber of the Market House!

In the next half-century this obviously became a national problem to Parliament. In two further acts (1711 and 1729) mayors were debarred from holding office for more than two successive years.

~ 0 ~

By the beginning of the Restoration, the Lordship of the Manors of Newport and Wentloog had descended to Philip Herbert, 7th Earl of Pembroke. When he died in 1683 the manors and the earldom parted company, the title passing to Philip's brother, Thomas as 8th Earl, but the estates going to the 7th Earl's only child, a daughter named Charlotte, wife of Thomas, Viscount Windsor.

Apparently the old Earl had been very improvident in his lifetime and he bequeathed to his daughter such enormous debts that it required the sale of the bulk of the estates to satisfy the creditors. In 1710 therefore, a decree of the High Court of Chancery ordered Viscount Windsor and his wife to make the sale. The purchaser at £9,000, was John Morgan, a London merchant, who also owned an estate at Ruperra. He was a descendant of the Morgans of Tredegar and a founder of the modern Tredegar Estate.

By this time Puritanism had been neutralised and Papism was the new witch-hunt, lasting in lessening degrees for well over another hundred years after the Act of Toleration had relaxed attitudes towards other persuasions. Very severe laws were passed against the Catholics and in 1699 the celebration of a mass by any priest was made punishable by imprisonment for life!

King James himself was an Anglican converted to Catholicism and his second wife, Mary of Modena, was Catholic also. Parliament was prepared to tolerate them, but only so long as their religious beliefs were kept in low profile, and so long as there was every chance that this would be the last reign of a Catholic monarch. That hope was dashed however when a royal male heir, James Edward, was born - obviously to be brought up in the Catholic faith!

Almost immediately, Parliament's reaction was to send an invitation to James' eldest daughter, Mary, and her husband Prince William of Orange - both Protestant and both grandchildren of King Charles I - to accept the English throne, ruling jointly and not in any form of consortship.

In 1688, James was ousted, the reigns of William III and Mary II began and a clause in the 1689 Bill of Rights forbade Catholics thenceforth from ascending the English throne. By this action it has been calculated that over 60 persons have since lost what would have been properly entitled claims to the succession.

The 18th century was ushered in by yet another protracted period of conflict in which Britain became involved. The War of the Spanish Succession lasted from 1702 to 1713, saw the movement of mighty armies across most of the frontiers of Europe and gave rise to the momentous victories of John Churchill, Duke of Marlborough, as efforts were sustained to curb the rapacious territorial ambitions of France. The Treaty of Utrecht did not prove to be the final answer for during the remainder of the century no less than 56 years were spent in seven great wars wherein England and France were the main protagonists.

This was the shadow under which ordinary people lived at that time but it did not unduly influence things in Newport. Gone might be the real history makers of the town the intrepid knights who had led the local men to deeds of great valour on foreign shores; so too had vanished the eminent families with their recurring, colourful and often roguish characters; similarly the last had been seen of the crippling civil wars that had racked the country for centuries and which on several occasions had touched the borough with dramatic effect.

Newport was now entering a time in its affairs when it was becoming increasingly difficult to distinguish a framework on which to build anything other than a vague diary of events of no great moment and of little consequence to the future. Nevertheless, despite the absence of excitement and the scarcity of recorded incident, no history of the town would be complete without even the most trifling occurrences of the time. It is proposed therefore to offer this part of the chapter in the form of a chronological list giving as much or as little as can be gleaned from the contemporary chroniclers.

1704	The town was described as having 192 tenements - all grotesque, gable-ended, penthouse style.
1709	The first Westgate Inn was built adjoining the existing Clockhouse or town jail.
1711	The Hon Viscount Morgan paid for the repair of the town clock on the Market Hall.
1718	Problems in local politics did not appear to have lessened - in fact it might

be said that financial chicanery was on the increase! The statutes restricting the mayor's terms to two terms were being blatantly disregarded by Newport's closed corporations and at least six mayoralties up to 1746 lasted from three to seven years.

The admittance of new burgesses and freemen was a lucrative business with a charge of 20 shillings for the former and 40 shillings for the latter (non-residents who were allowed the freedom to earn their livelihood in the town). There was ample scope here for items to be conveniently lost to public scrutiny! These newcomers were supposed to be sworn in before the mayor and a quorum of aldermen in the council chamber, but on many occasions it was asserted that the only person present was the mayor himself. Worse still, some of these ceremonies were carried out in a private room of the mayor's house with no witnesses and the obvious conclusions to be drawn. The situation remained thus until the end of the century by which time the entry fee for a freeman had risen to a mammoth £18!

This form of municipal avarice had the eventual effect of killing the layer of the golden eggs and applications for entry dropped alarmingly just at the time when the town's fortunes were beginning to burgeon. The whole fee system was ultimately abandoned in 1815 in order to give wider trading facilities to a rapidly expanding population.

1722.   At this time a master pewterer was operating in Newport. Edward Earle was well known nationally and he specialised in the large pewter plates called chargers. Unfortunately he lived at a time when the great potters were entering into the competition with cheap china-ware for the masses.

Looking well ahead and foreseeing the profit to be made from a regular riverboat service, the Morgan family bought a smack of 40 tons and christened it 'The Tredegar Boat'. This was the largest vessel built up to that time in Newport and it was intended for trade with, and the carriage of passengers to Bristol. In this year however, according to Scott's History of Newport, the Tredegar Boat foundered at the mouth of the River Usk and 36 passengers, mostly farmers, were drowned. It was reported that all the bodies recovered were buried in St Woolos churchyard but neither this fact nor the actual number of casualties can be substantiated.

Some time afterwards, Mr Kemys set up in opposition to the Morgans with another smack at moderated or reduced fares. She was named Moderator and gave her name to her home berth, Moderator Wharf (end of Corn Street).

1739.   A 36 year old John Wesley arrived one day in Newport to preach the Gospel. This was his routine for most of his life - often a pulpit in two different towns each day. On this particular occasion he was not very impressed and had this to say:-

'I preached this morning on What must I do to be saved?' to the most insensible ill-behaved people I have ever seen in Wales. They are ignorant of the Gospel as any Creek or Cherokee Indian. One ancient man, during the greater part of the sermon, cursed and swore almost incessantly and, towards the conclusion, took up a great stone which he many times attempted to throw!'

Other contemporaries of Wesley, trying their luck at preaching outside the Westgate Inn, fared even worse, being plastered with thrown filth and refuse, and having their clothing torn before beating hasty retreats. Examples such as these speak volumes of the disregard that was felt for nonconformist dogma.

In 1748, Wesley was again in the town and must have noticed some improvement for he stated that he found the people 'ripe for the Gospel.' Aged 72 and some 27,000 sermons later in 1775, he returned once again to Newport and found a huge, rapt congregation awaiting him. Afterwards he remarked:-

'I reached Newport at about eight o'clock and soon after I preached to a large and serious congregation. I believe it is five and thirty years since I preached here before, to a people who were as wild as bears. How amazingly the scene is changed!'

1743.   'Corporations in England' (published in May) listed Newport as having a mayor, two bailiffs, twelve aldermen or common councilmen, a recorder, a town clerk and two serjeants-at-mace.

1750.   An old map drawn in this year shows 158 tenements and denotes the Kings Head Inn, the Heathcock Inn (built on the green opposite the castle and sometime known as the Bridge Inn) and Pyes Shop on the site occupied in modern times by the Corn Exchange. This excellent bakeshop stood until 1848 and was noted by all the children for its mouth-watering gingerbread.

The map also depicts for the first time a narrow lane between Market Street and Skinner Street in which stood the extremely ugly town house of the Herberts of St Julians. From the Griffin coat-of-arms carved over the door the street received its name.

In the 45 years following 1750 the number of tenements increased by only 43!

The area of the town marshes increased from 33 to 44 acres. By 1789 there were 106 shares worth nine shillings and sixpence each, but by 1806 the value had increased to seventeen shillings each. For many years successive corporations had had selfish designs on this large, very valuable piece of land within the borough boundary. They had almost convinced themselves that they owned it in their own right and not as custodians on behalf of the burgesses as directed in the old charters. There were several underhanded attempts by the mayors to release the marshes for financial reward and even the gentry were not above stealthy acquisition of land properly owned by the burgesses, as a future chapter will show!

1760.   The tidiness of the town was still giving cause for concern and charges were continually being brought against offenders. In July, John Cobb who was landlord of an unspecified inn, was fined one penny for 'nuisance coming down from his boghouse to the Green!'

1777.   The dispensation of justice in the borough appears to have been erratic insofar as the penalties meted out were concerned. In June, being found guilty of nothing more than breaking down someone's hedge, Alice Morgan was ordered 'to be stripped from her waist upward and whipt at 12 o'clock at the whipping post in the borough, with thirty lashes until the blood issues forth.'

Not long after this, two other women were flogged privately in the town jail for scandalmongering. Severe penalties indeed for such trivial offences especially when crimes such as assault or poaching were just as likely to be punished by stern reprimands or the fine of one penny!

1790.   The whole town turned out to see the biggest ship ever to sail upriver to the Town Pill. It was a new acquisition of the Tanner family of the Blaendare Works at Pontypool and was probably involved in the first importation of iron ore from abroad.

1793.   The old Market House had dominated High Street for 208 years but had been giving concern due to its great age and dilapidation causing it to become unsafe. Many petitions for its removal were placed before the Marquis of Abergavenny, the new Lord of the Manor and owner of the building but they all fell on deaf ears. Quarter Sessions injunctions had repeatedly been served on the Marquis but he had ignored them all. Finally a vexed corporation took the law into its own hands and carried out the demolition itself!

Aside from its age and dangerous condition the hall had become an increasing embarrassment in an expanding town wherein its commanding position caused a serious blockage of the main street and brought proceedings almost to a halt on market days. There was now no official council meeting room in the town and no plans to erect one, so for the next fifty years the old carpenter's guildhall above the Carpenters Arms was used for this purpose.

1799.   The first Westgate Inn and the adjoining Clockhouse Jail were demolished. The second Westgate Inn arose on the site but the new jail was rebuilt in Mill Street - still by tradition to be known as the Clockhouse despite having no clock!

- 0 -

A new form of public transport in the shape of the stagecoach was introduced in Britain during the Commonwealth. The first scheduled service began in 1658 running from the George in Aldersgate to such places as Salisbury, Exeter and Plymouth - very slow, very uncomfortable and very expensive!

It was not until 1774 that the first stagecoaches passed through Newport on long distance routes, leaving on Monday and arriving in London on Saturday evening, Two services usually ran through the borough : one, starting at Cardiff, came via St Mellons and Penylan Bassaleg, to Pye Corner, over Stow Hill and down to High Street where the Kings Head was purpose-built as a coaching inn. Immediately opposite was the mail office and the bags were carried across the road to the coach. This site was therefore the obvious place for the future General Post Office.

The second stagecoach from Cardiff did not have a stop in the town and in fact bypassed the town centre by travelling from Pye Corner up High Cross or Glasslwch Lanes, along what is now Ridgeway and Allteryn View, down Barrack Hill and out through Malpas to Hereford and Worcester.

The other service, from Worcester to London, came in from Malpas, over the dangerously steep Crindau Trip (Brynglas Road) with its precipitous drop to one side, up Barrack Hill, through Queens Hill, Mill Street and finally Thomas Street into High Street and the Kings Head. Eventually the Queens Hill stretch was abandoned in favour of the improved and realigned Marshes Road from the Castle North Gate.

Once across Newport Bridge there was only one road eastward and that was by way of Fairoak Hill, through Christchurch village via Catsash, down to Penhow and on to Gloucester and Bristol. Each route was made the more arduous by the steep hills leading out of the borough (Stow Hill, Barrack hill, Crindau and Christchurch) and therefore it was usual to find a stable at the foot of each one so that extra horses could be temporarily harnessed for the long, hard pulls.

Forty years or so later all this had changed. The new Cardiff Road was opened up from the end of Commercial Street in 1812. This not only took Stow Hill out of the coach route but it made it easier for the Morgan family to reach Tredegar House at Ebbw Bridge. Thitherto their only road had been from St Woolos down the difficult and dangerous 'trip' which is now Waterloo Road.

A new low-level Chepstow Road from the meadows which became Clarence Place, through Maindee, opened in 1817.

Before 1825, the only road to Caerleon was via Christchurch and down the steep and narrow 'Black Ash Path' at the side of the church, but after that year, the new Caerleon Road opened - also from Clarence Place - paralleling the River Usk and following the route of the old private track of the St Julians Herberts. At the same time the new Belmont Hill replaced the Black Ash Path as the main road from Christchurch to Caerleon.

99

Public transport and the roads are inseparable subjects and for centuries both were virtually non-existent - at least the condition of what passed for roads was too atrocious to allow little more than very restricted wheeled traffic. These were the days when the pack-horse reigned supreme!

After the Romans abandoned Britain in the 5th century, their magnificent road system was allowed to fall into decay. Their various successors reverted to the ancient tracks and added some of their own but none were engineered or given durable surfaces. It is a sad reflection on the historic development of this country that over 1300 years had to pass before any serious thought was given to the national provision of an easier negotiable highway system! By the 18th century all roads had deteriorated to the point where progress could only be made in the best seasons of the year, and then only upon a good horse that could pick its way deftly around the great stones, cavernous holes and deep mud pools that made treacherous every inch of the way. But even astride the nimblest mount a very early start was necessary by every traveller who wished to avoid being caught up in the struggling pack-horse teams!

For many years it had been the responsibility of parish authorities to maintain their roads from point of entry to point of departure. The local farmers were expected to donate six days free labour a year, and they objected strongly to having to pay in this way for damage that they themselves had not caused. Most of the benefits were going to travellers and foreigners to the parish. Many of the gentry who held this responsibility held the parsimonious and extremely narrow view that their roads did not require levelling because their own carriage wheels fitted neatly and ran smoothly enough in the furrows that they had ploughed over the years!

But if the roads were that bad then, what could they have been like a few hundred years earlier when it was customary for them to carry thousands of men-at-arms from one war to the next? The thought defies imagination but Newport High Street gives an illustration in a curious little story passed down from the 14th century.

It happened that one dark Friday night, a Jewish merchant fell into one of the huge holes that pitted the main road through the town. He was not found until Saturday morning and then resisted all efforts to rescue him, protesting vehemently that it was the Jewish Sabbath and therefore nobody should work on his behalf. Hearing of this , Lord Richard de Clare, who happened to be visiting his manor at the time, vexedly gave orders that the Jew should be left where he was 'but we shall not help him tomorrow either for then it will be the Christian Sabbath and we shall not work for him!'

So it was that on Monday morning, when the good townsfolk of Newport lifted the Jew from the hole, the poor fellow was found to have died of exposure!

The High Street had improved considerably since those days but elsewhere the roads were so utterly wretched and damaging to the economy that it was at last decided to place the responsibility for their maintenance squarely on the shoulders of those who caused most of the wear and tear.

Between 1750 and 1790 there were at least 1600 statutes dealing with roads. In 1755 came the first Monmouthshire Turnpike Act which related only to the town of Monmouth. Three years later, the second Turnpike Act dealt with Newport and district.

The preamble to this act contained a list of roads described as 'in so bad, ruinous and founderous condition and in many cases so narrow that it is very dangerous and difficult for horses, coaches, carts and carriages to pass'. It was further added that the improvement of these roads would be extremely beneficial to the areas served.

Newport's share included lengths of highway from the Rock and Fountain Penhow, through the town by Tredegar House, Castleton and St Mellons to Rumney Bridge; also from

Bedwas Bridge to Bassaleg, through Newport to St Julians and Caerleon; and from Risca through Newport, through Malpas to Llantarnam as far as the road that joined it to Caerleon.

Turnpike Trusts were introduced by this series of acts, and members or trustees were chosen from local justices of the peace and the several members of parliament of adjoining counties.

When the Turnpike Acts were being promoted in 1754, Valentine Morris, MP, of Piercefield Park Chepstpw, being questioned in the House of Commons, was asked:-

'What roads are there in Monmouthshire?'

'None'

'How then do you travel?'

'In ditches!'

This was a definite turning point but while improvements came they came only slowly and gradually - more so in some areas than others. In 1784, thirty years after the Turnpike Acts, Mr Arthur Young, President of The Agricultural Society, travelling from Gloucester, was very critical of English roads but when he entered Monmouthshire he was horrified at what he saw.

'What am I to say of the roads in this country - the turnpikes as they have the assurance to call them and the hardihood to make one pay for? From Chepstow to the halfway house between Newport and Cardiff they continue mere rocky lanes, full of hugeous stones as big as one's horse, and abominable holes. The first six miles from Newport they were so detestible and without either direction-posts or milestones that I could not well persuade myself I was on the turnpike but had mistook the road!'

On 28th May 1790, 'the ruinous state of Newport's roads and highways' was drawn to the attention of the Surveyors of the Highways, John Brewer and John Howells, who were instructed to oversee the repairing of the said highways in the most expeditious manner for the sum of £100! The first road to be 'attacked' was to be Mill Street!

When Scott visited Newport in 1802 he noted a 500 pound stone bulging from the surface of Fairoak Hill where it had been used to plug a correspondingly large hole! It was still a far cry from the surfacing techniques of John McAdam whom, coincidentally, fortune had ordained to be born in the very year that Newport's Turnpike Act was being deliberated.

Two tollgates were installed very quickly in the town, at Queens Hill and Stow Hill; this latter one known as the Stowgate Toll would have stood on the end of a terrace called Llanarth Cottages, now approximately at the St Woolos end of York Place. Three more turnpikes appeared after 1812, in Clarence Place at the junction of the new Caerleon and Chepstow Roads, Marshes Road at the end of Mill Street and at Cardiff Road. None of these buildings have survived but as they all followed a similar pattern it is possible to recreate the image of one by looking at a typical example which stands in the grounds of the Welsh Folk Museum at St Fagans where it has been carefully and cleverly restored after removal from its original home in Aberystwyth.

The single-storied, white-painted, stone and slate building is narrow and lozenge shaped with just one door in the end and windows down each side. It contains one large room which did duty as an office, kitchen, living and sleeping space for the toll-keeper and his family. Outside, the strong, wooden gate is set at right angles to the front door and extends the full width of the road. The cost of the building was said to be £40 to include the gate. Larger turnpikes were constructed in later decades on the newer, busier roads and one of these, with an upper floor, can be seen today, a dwelling-house still in good order, standing near the Newport end of Caerleon Bridge.

On the wall of each turnpike was a big black notice board on which were painted in white, the rates of toll. Not every passer-by was liable; the board showed an appreciable list of exemptions chief among which were:-

Members of the Royal Family,
Soldiers going about their military duties,
Mourners attending a funeral in another parish,
Church-goers,
Carts returning vagabonds to the place from which they came,
Horses going to or returning from the plough,
Carts carrying manure for improving the ground, but not lime (presumably this proviso was to prevent builders from claiming that some of their materials should be exempt).

At intervals along each of the appropriate roads, small stone blocks like mile stones were placed with the words 'Turnpike Roads' carved into them. Their intention seemed to be that of reminding travellers that they should have money ready to pay tolls varying between a halfpenny and six pence according to type of carriage animal or load.

In later years the turnpikes became a great source of irritation, especially in the poorer agricultural areas where the toll-keepers were grossly insolent and the continual demand for tolls at gates only two to three miles apart, ate seriously into meagre incomes. In 1843, in West Wales particularly, many turnpikes were attacked and destroyed by gangs of men dressed as women; these disturbances were named Rebecca Riots after a biblical quotation. Newport, however, was little affected except for one incident at the Stowgate turnpike when its gate was torn down and hurled into a nearby garden. The probability was that so soon after the Chartist Riots, people's thirst for violence was thoroughly quenched!

The turnpikes served their purpose but were bound eventually to give way to advances in the fields of road management and financing. They remained until fairly late in the 19th century but by 1879 all of Newport's tollgates had closed for ever.

- 0 -

Each return to discussion of the topography of Newport -centuries apart - has revealed the same, small, unworthy town, really no more than a village, where apparently time had stood still. It was still sustained by its markets, fairs and cottage industry if ever there was one; the way in which many of the inhabitants earned a living remains a mystery but there must have been ample scope in the providing of services to the small number of members of local society whose affluence demanded the attention of tradesmen, farm labourers and armies of servants. There was, however, nothing that guaranteed real growth. The population had made very little headway (only 750 by 1791) and the evidence was strong of self aggrandisement and corruption by its prominent citizens.

The one short street from the castle to Stow Hill had thrown out a few offshoots in the names of St Laurence Lane, Crosskeys Lane (sometime known as Bakehouse Lane - now Market Street), Griffin Street and Corn Street, all leading to the run-down wharves on the river bank between the bridge and the Moderator. These narrow byways, together with the oldest of them all, Mill Street, comprised the total extent of the town.

Stow Hill commenced its climb on one side of the Westgate Inn and Clockhouse, and on the other side was a short stretch of road known as Westgate Street that petered out in an unmarked track losing itself in the wet wilderness of the Pillgwenlly marshes.

That there was the intention to make something more useful of this track there is no doubt, but the incentives for the reclamation of this dismal floodplain were not yet in the minds of the 18th century planners. As far as Pillgwenlly was concerned there was still only one sure way of reaching its furthest extremity and that was by an arduous trek up Stow Hill, down Belle Vue Lane and along the often impassable Mendalgyffe.

Visitors to the town at that time who recorded their impressions, were obviously uninspired by what they found.

1760

The old town was without a vestige of trade, insignificant of influence and wretchedly dirty and mean in appearance; its streets were narrow, dark and unwholesome and a universal lethargy seemed to pervade the minds of its inhabitants.

Anon. as quoted in E. Hunt's Directory of
Bristol, Newport and Welsh towns

1848

1796

'The situation of the town is happily and conveniently chosen on the banks of a large and navigable river; and where the mineral treasures of the hills may be conveyed by canals for exportation.'

Williams' 'History of Monmouthshire.'

1802

'It is a long, narrow and straggling town, built partly in a flat on the banks of the Usk, and partly in a declivity. The streets are dirty and ill-paved; the houses in general wear a gloomy appearance.'

The Reverend Coxe.

1802

'A canal has been completed to the canal basin for the more ready conveyance of coal and iron from the mountains to the quays. Newport will appear contemptible from the slovenly mode of loading and unloading upon stages which totter under the work; and the vessels are lying on the bank at once steep and filthy; it is to be hoped that the spirit of enterprise will not rest with the completion of the canal, but contribute for the convenience of proper quays and safer berths.'

G W Manby 'Picturesque Guide'

'From Tredegar Park we cross the Ebwy by a long, narrow bridge and presently entered Newport, a dirty ill—built town nearly comprised in one long street winding down a bank of the River Usk.'

Barber's Tour.

Whilst Williams in 1796 held the most flattering opinion those who came shortly after him were not so optimistic. It was left to Mr Manby to visualise a Newport operating under a spirit of enterprise that was soon to fulfil his wishful thinking.

The town was now on the threshold of an era in which it was to be dragged out of the slough of stagnation where it had languished since its foundation at the end of the Dark Ages. There were several factors contributory to this upsurge.

First and foremost was the proximity in the county of rich reserves of minerals without which the industrial revolution, then in its infancy, could not have taken place, although the immediate demand was occasioned by the voracious military appetite in the Napoleonic Wars. Water transport was still the only way to move loads quickly around the country so there was desperate need of a nearby deep-water port. Newport filled this role admirably. Finally came the arrival of the men of vision capable of putting all these natural assets to work, by creating the investment and new-found technology which were to cause the greatest economic explosion ever seen in the world up to that time. It was genesis for the great ironmasters!

Iron-making had been known for well over 2,000 years. The Celts left evidence of their knowledge in their hill forts; the Romans were prolific users, not only in their armour and weapons but also in their tools and road-building equipment. Remains of ancient furnaces and hearths together with beds of clinker, have been revealed beneath what were the remote floors of dense forests and this makes the vital connection between the essential ingredients of iron-making - the presence of ironstone and limestone in the ground, an unlimited supply of timber for the charcoal to fuel the furnaces and a convenient water supply.

The hills and valleys of South Wales possessed vast quantities of all four but until the early 18th century they had not been seriously exploited. Up until then, the production of iron had been more on a domestic basis, for agricultural purposes but with several hundred cannon and thousands of swords and pikes thrown in for good measure whenever one of the inevitable wars erupted. Of course, the second half of that century saw great changes occurring, none more so than the problem of the disappearance of large expanses of woodland in the runaway consumption of timber for charcoal.

Attempts had been made since Elizabethan days to manufacture iron with pit coal instead of charcoal but no suitable process had been perfected. Now however, several astute entrepreneurs, working entirely independently of each other, were successful in producing a good quality metal by the use of coal only. The result was a demand for the fuel as never before seen. The sinking of many new pits and drift mines followed and, in company with the advances made by James Watt with his steam engine and Arkwright in his steam driven mechanisation of manual industrial processes, the iron and coal industries expanded to alter the whole face of the economy of the British Isles.

Between 1765 and 1786, four major ironmasters took leases on all the mineral rights in the Upper Taff, Rhymney, Sirhowy and Ebbw Valleys. The companies formed were Dowlais, Cyfartha, Plymouth and Penydarren (all at Merthyr, then the largest town in Wales). The last of these companies belonged to Francis Homfray of Worcester and his two sons, Jeremiah and Samuel, the latter of whom was destined to play a leading part in Newport's amazing 19th century climb into the leading rank of world seaports. By 1800, seven major ironworks became established in Monmouthshire : at Rhymney, Sirhowy, Tredegar, Beaufort, Ebbw Vale, Nantyglo and Blaenavon. The Tredegar works was acquired in 1789 by Jeremiah Homfray and the Ebbw Vale works was started by his brother, Samuel, in 1794.

The consequent output of many thousands of tons of iron, coupled with the coal from the pits (which had seen a 400% increase over the previous century) gave rise at once to a serious problem that Newport experienced as the major port of dispatch. The one great drawback to the position of these works, 18 to 20 miles from the coast at the tops of rugged

104

valleys, had to be eliminated if the highest efficiency, output and investment potential were to be achieved.

Once again the roads were to blame. The journey down the valleys was a terrifying and never-to-be-forgotten experience: only pack-horse trains, usually driven by women, could get the unimpressive loads of iron and coal down to the wharves on the River Usk, and the trip would take several days! Dates of delivery could not be accurately specified to the local dockside let alone to the ultimate destination. Weather conditions would upset a schedule for weeks or months! Transport from point of manufacture to point of consumption was not only erratic but very costly and certainly provided the most serious obstacle to the advancement of Monmouthshire's industrial ambitions. But in the 1790s these were no longer insurmountable problems, having been encountered and conquered thirty to forty years earlier in the industrial North and Midlands.

That great coal owner, the Duke of Bridgewater, using much of his own capital, had captured the expertise of Dutchmen skilled in drainage and the building of inland waterways, and coupled it with a vast army of 'inland navigators or navvies' to pioneer the digging of a network of canals which had revolutionised the transport systems in South Lancashire and the West Midlands. Even the most wild and challenging regions held no fear for the clever engineers as they fed their artificial rivers through tunnels, across towering aqueducts and by a series of stepped locks, up and down the hills. The time had indeed arrived in Wales for the accuracy of Merlin's 1,200 year old prophesy to be tested!

Throughout 1791, meetings were held in the Kings Head Inn at Newport to discuss the viability and financial implications of a canal system to connect the ironworks and coalfields of North Monmouthshire to the quays of the River Usk. Present at the first meeting were all the interested parties, the major land owners such as Sir Charles Morgan and the Duke of Beaufort, the iron and coal magnates and representatives of Bristol shipping companies. There were also some who were unconnected with the iron and coal trades but who, besides seeking profitable investment, could see only too well the advantages accruing to their own industries from easier access to the South Wales coast and a good Bristol Channel port. Notable among these latter gentlemen was Josiah Wedgewood, the wealthy Midlands pottery magnate who became the major shareholder, but who did not survive to see his investment mature

The engineer who was commissioned to design and plan the project was Thomas Dadford junior, and he presented his ideas together with a detailed costing of £108,476. For this, a canal would be dug from Pontnewynydd near Pontypool as far as the Town Pill Newport, a distance of eleven miles with a branch, also eleven miles long, from Crindau Malpas, to Crumlin.

Incorporated in the work was to be the construction of 41 locks to Pontnewynydd raising the level of the canal 435 feet, and 32 locks to Crumlin raising the level 358 feet. On the latter stretch, at the Cefn Rogerstone, no less than 14 locks were required to raise the canal 168 feet in half a mile! In addition, 57 bridges and several short tunnels were necessary.

This was truly a herculean feat of engineering for those days and must have inspired the greatest awe in the listeners at those early meetings. Nevertheless the sum of £51,000 was quickly pledged and the new Monmouthshire Canal Company was formed. At the beginning there were 1,200 shares valued at £120,000, but within ten years of the canal's opening there were 136 investors holding between them 1806 shares. The leading shareholders were J & T Wedgewood of Etruria Staffs with 213½ shares, Sir Charles Morgan Bart with 85½ shares and the Duke of Beaufort with 78 $\frac{1}{3}$ shares. Arrangements were made to approach Parliament for the necessary legislation and finally, in 1792, the Monmouthshire Canal Act entered the statute books.

The preamble to the Act named 110 proprietors of land which had to be purchased and one of them was Thomas Dadford senior, father of the canal's chief engineer, which might suggest that his original acquisition had been the result of being privy to valuable inside information. After all, this was not the first canal that both father and son had been involved in! Furthermore, if there was a decent profit to be made from land acquisition even before the investment started to bloom, Sir Charles Morgan was certain to have been in for a major share due to the bulk of the acreage required running through Tredegar land. Apparently with the land bought at fivepence per acre and claims for other land 'damaged' by the works, the Tredegar Estate benefited by the princely sum of £1244-4s-9½d - more than enough to replace the £10 a share outlay of Sir Charles' original investment and a clear illustration of the somewhat unfair advantage that the vast wealth of the Morgan family gave to them personally under the veil of shrewd business management. During the 18th and 19th centuries there were to be several examples of how clever, almost bordering on unscrupulous, manipulation of such power added riches to this grand estate!

Work commenced on the canal in 1793 and by 1798 the whole project was completed, not only to the satisfaction of its sponsors but also, it would seem, to the utter relief of all the inhabitants of the villages and hamlets near where it passed. Whilst much of the digging had been given over to local farmers, it had still been necessary to employ hundreds of imported navvies whose drunken carousing had terrorised most of the small communities in the neighbourhood. However, after this nuisance had passed, these same communities settled down to enjoy the new, unlimited supply of washing, bathing and even drinking water that had meandered into their lives.

The first navigable stage of the canal to Newport opened in 1796. It entered the borough by way of a tunnel under Penylan (Barrack) Hill (through which in his impetuous youth your author several times made the perilous voyage on a ramshackle, home-made raft). From here it made use of the old bed of the south-flowing branch of the Malpas Brook, suitably widened and straightened, until it passed under Mill Street and the Castle Green, obliterating for ever St Laurence Lane, bisecting the Kings Head garden and finishing just short of the Town Pill in a new basin excavated at the end of Griffin Street, adjacent to the old Blaenavon and Beaufort Wharves (in modern times renamed Baltic Wharf).

The basin formed a fair extent of enclosed water where the narrow longboats could unload, reload and be warped about for their return journeys. It was the first artificial area of inland water to be constructed in pursuance of the town s trading policies and therefore it may loosely but truly be described as Newport's first dock in the heart of the old town.

The completion of the basin had been more expensive than anticipated so work was suspended while application was made for further powers. The following year brought the passing of the second Monmouthshire Canal Act and work recommenced on carrying the canal over the Town Pill - probably the most formidable challenge in the whole undertaking, but nevertheless, one that could not be avoided if the waterway was to proceed down-river.

To begin with, the Pill itself had to be lined and culverted from High Street to the riverside, with a heavy iron floodgate at the entrance. The canal was carried over on a massive, stone aqueduct laid on the soil of the filled-in pill. All the stone came from the Stow Quarry and it was at first thought that the great weight and pressure of the canal water would cause subsidence and seepage into the artificially packed but softer soil of the pill beneath. As it happened, the driving of hundreds of wooden piles and the most effective 'puddling' in the clay of the canal bed, dispelled all the engineers' fears.

Pile-driving was an expensive and laborious task, not only because of the numbers involved but also because, in the absence of the not yet available steam power, each pile had to be driven by means of a weighty ram hoisted repeatedly by windlass.

The completion of the aqueducted channel was effected in 1804 and was followed by the filling in of the town basin, an act that changed the face of that part of the town and added a large slice of useful, improved land where, prior to the arrival of the canal there had been only rough, riverside terrain and the great 'muddy fissure' as for centuries the Town Pill had been known. Now tidied up and levelled, this area was brought into use for the further development of the borough.

Corn Street was relegated from its status as a main thoroughfare to that of a side street and was replaced by Skinner Street, curving round into the new Canal Parade, Club Row and Poplar Row with their terraces of canal workers' cottages, soon to become the town's main approach to Pillgwenlly. Nowadays, most of this route is buried under Kingsway of which Ebenezer Terrace (Poplar Row) is an extension. Skinner Street is now a secondary shopping street and Canal Parade, a slum clearance project, demolished and over -built in recent years by Docks Way; this perimeter road, void of houses, starts at the river bank side of the Kingsway Leisure Centre and breaks new ground along the old route of the canal, skirting the Old Town Dock to Dock Parade in Pillgwenlly. An old stone garage and store, standing at the beginning of this road has the look of an early, original canal building.

Whilst work was progressing on the Town Pill in 1802, a third Canal Act was applied for and obtained in order to continue the canal onwards to a point nearer the mouth of the River Usk then known as Prothero's Wharf but which today is the site of Penmain Wharf, recently converted into a works car park. After a twelve months delay in order to comply with certain conditions laid down in the 1797 Act, work commenced on the final stage.

From its entry into the borough as far as the town basin the canal was constructed in cutting but all the work authorised by the third act had to be on embankment due to the ground over which it passed being three to four feet below the level of the highest tides. Thus, in its early days the Pillgwenlly section resembled the high level Dutch canals with the new jetties on one side and a sharp drop to the marshes on the other! Its proximity to the river bank and the jetties necessitated another massive piling operation in the notoriously wet and erosive Pillgwenlly soil; the whole length had to be lined with hewn stone! The crossing of Jack's Pill called for identical treatment to that of the Town Pill - more so in fact because it penetrated a lot farther inland (as far as the future Commercial Road), making the culverting process that much greater.

After Jack's Pill, the canal swung away from the river bank to cross the triangle of land formed by the sharp elbow bend of the river. In 1808 it came to its terminus at a point that would one day be the junction of Potter Street and Castle Street, but it was given a small extension in 1818 by the Tredegar Wharf Company to a basin just short of Prothero's Wharf; this, today, would appear to have been somewhere within the curtilage of the Newelco works (previously Uskside Engineering) in Church Street. In order to make this extension, and because of the lowering of the land level by a further five feet, another lock had to be provided. This became known as the Potter Street Lock after the street that was to become one of the first to be built on the giant Pillgwenlly development. Today, Castle Street represents the route of the last couple of hundred yards of the bed of the canal from the Potter Street Lock which straddled Potter Street.

When the final main phase of the canal was completed in 1808 it brought the total cost of the Monmouthshire Canal to £280,000 which, whilst in early 19th century terms sounds like a colossal risk, was in actual fact one of the most profitable enterprises that big business was to see for many a long day. But it was not only the great iron, coal and shipping tycoons or their shareholders who saw the benefit.

Newport Castle and Bridge (the Heathcock Inn to the left) from a drawing by
George Shepherd 1795.

Many thousands of common folk, locals and 'drifters' alike, had gained much needed employment and previously unheard of, relative security for their families and this continued for nearly half a century to give permanent work to the host of bargees and their crews, lock keepers, inspectors, boat repairers and canal maintenance men -even down to a small number of mole catchers with the job of preventing the furry little creatures from undermining the canal banks!

This prosperity was further transferred to those involved indirectly, in the business of catering for the needs of this new labour force, whether through their daily sustenance, their clothing or the tools of their trade. The ale houses were a particular case in point and their increase in numbers along the line of the canal and its towpaths was truly remarkable. The names of some which still exist testify to their origins as places of rest and refreshment for the honest toilers of the waterways. No doubt the ownership deeds of many of the nearby older residences can show evidence of this connection.

Almost as if shamed by these almost daily feats of engineering on the parts of others in their town, Newport Corporation was galvanised into a long overdue, but most progressive act of its own.

~ 0 ~

In 1799, at the height of the canal activity, the old wooden bridge was seen to be so dilapidated that it was declared unsafe and ordered to be dismantled. A noted young bridge architect of the day, David Edwards, was commissioned to design and build a new bridge at a cost of £10,165, a sum quickly raised by the county. Mr Edwards must have earned his reputation by example but to the Reverend Coxe, who crossed the new bridge just before it was finished, his sole attribute apparently was that 'he was the son of the celebrated architect who constructed the bridge at Pont i ty Prid near Caerphilly in Glamorgan!' One other fact known about this talented son however was that his roots were probably not too far removed from Newport because his sister, Mrs Francis, became the landlady of the Red Cow Inn which stood facing the castle on the site later occupied by the Old Green Hotel. This was a well conducted tavern, not to be confused with its namesake of later years in Canal Parade which acquired an extremely notorious and evil reputation.

Construction of the bridge was completed in little over a year. During that time all London-bound traffic was diverted via Malpas and Caerleon. Then, in the year 1800, Newport came into possession of the finest bridge in its history!

A brief mention of the bridge a few years afterwards recalls that in the yard of the Heathcock (later the Bridge) Inn, was planted a notice-board detailing the Lord of the Manor's tolls for bringing animals to the markets. Furthermore some idea of the state of the River Usk could be gleaned from a statement that the waters below the bridge were thronged with moored boats fishing for the salmon that abounded! The best salmon pool was said to be adjacent to the length of bank that became Rodney and later London Wharf, off Clarence Place. Even as long after as 1832 the Monmouthshire Merlin reported the catching of a trout 4 feet 10 inches long between Newport and Caerleon!

The centre span of the new bridge was of 72 feet, those on either side of 62 feet and the two abutting on each shore were of 55 feet. The carriageway was still quite narrow but there were pedestrian footways on each side and strong stone parapets to inspire confidence. Serving the town for the next 125 years, the 475 feet long bridge required only widening in 1866 to contend with the tremendous increase in traffic that half a century would generate. There was however one detail overlooked by the proud, new bridge owners and this was to cause irritation to the townsfolk for the next ninety years!

The passing of the canal under the Castle Green had thrown up many hundreds of tons of spoil. Much of this was used to fill the hollows of what remained of the castle moat and the rest was spread about to give the canal tunnel adequate cover. The net result was a raising of the ground level at the town end of the bridge so that it stood seven feet above that of the approaching carriageway. This severe slope became known to everyone who ever negotiated it as the notorious Newport 'dip!'

Extreme nuisance it may have been to the serious traveller and trader but to some it was the source of great sport and amusement.

All loaded carts or horse-drawn vehicles experienced some difficulty in leaving the bridge over the sudden, steep incline that confronted them at the end of an easy crossing. Market days must have been particularly irksome with traffic jams stretching back past Clarence Cottages almost to the bottom of Christchurch Hill -remember that the separate Caerleon and Chepstow Roads did not come into existence until 1812. There was only one way for vehicles to get across and that was to stop at the centre, whip the horses or give a great heave to raise the momentum, and then to make a swift run at the slope. Sometimes it worked and sometimes wagon or coach faltered. It was then that the local lads who often loitered nearby for just such an occasion, would rush forward, put their shoulders to the wheels and with wild cheers, lift the vehicle almost bodily over the hump!

When the first horse-drawn omnibuses came into service, it was a matter of great annoyance to the passengers that they had to alight and sometimes add their weight to the shove!

With hindsight it would appear that in a period when the town was filled to overflowing with engineers, contractors and experts in the pick-and-shovel game, there would have been no trouble in levelling the dip at an acceptable price, but the fact remains that successive town councils allowed the incongruous situation to persist until 1893!

- 0 -

In a matter of six or seven years the whole of Newport's outlook changed. The turn of the century upheaval took a plodding little community by the scruff of the neck, gave it a good shaking and deposited it among the front runners of the great race that was just beginning. A portent was in the increase of population which in 1801 stood at 1,087, over 300 more than ten years earlier, and which despite sounding inconsiderable, was indeed an explosion by comparison with centuries past!

The 1802 Canal Act had also included proposals for the building of a tram-road to link the Sirhowy Furnaces, through Tredegar Ironworks directly to Newport after first connecting with the canal terminus at Crumlin. This was to be effected by bringing the single track down the valley a matter of ten miles to Tredegar Junction (one day to become Pontllanfraith), and then in a north-westerly direction for about four miles through an opening between the two valleys to Crumlin. The tram-road to Newport would branch off at Pontllanfraith.

Most of the other ironworks, by a series of tram-roads taking routes not inordinately toilsome despite the ruggedness of the terrain, had reasonable access to the canal at Crumlin. Sirhowy however was not in such a fortunate position; hence the need for an easier link with its seaport.

In its first year of operation (1796) the Monmouthshire Canal had carried 2,900 tons of coal, 2,000 tons of iron ore and 1,528 tons of timber, slate and limestone. A single boat carrying a 25 ton load could make the trip from Pontypool to Newport in one day. Something had to be done to give the Sirhowy works a similar advantage.

The initial 14 mile stage of the tram-road cost £30,000 and it was in 1808 that the final rails were laid, allowing the first trams to make the journey between Tredegar and Crumlin. Before long, loads of iron, two tons to a tram, were streaming down the Sirhowy and Tredegar valleys in small horse-drawn teams with as many as a dozen men on each to act as brakes on the steeper inclines. The experiment proved to be so successful that it was quickly decided to continue the railway down to Newport and in 1812, after passing through Tredegar Park, it arrived at Cwrt-y-bella Farm on the north western extremity of the Pillgwenlly Marshes. Here it divided, being originally called Cwrt-y-bella Junction, at the site of the future Great Western Railway's Ebbw Junction.

The main tram-road proceeded straight on into the town along the new Cardiff Road, coincidentally opened the same year, past the equally new Salutation Inn, along the curve of Poplar Row and Club Row to its terminus on the canal at the bottom of Llanarth Street (Blaina Wharf). On its way the line passed over several roads by means of level crossings. The other branch line headed south east from Cwrt-y bella on a route down the Mendalgief that would eventually come to be known as Courtybella Terrace, to terminate at the Pillgwenlly canal basin.

The construction of both branches gave rise to the same problems that the canal builders had had to face in this low-lying area. The eastern and southern sides of Pillgwenlly Marsh were now contained by embankments supporting the canal and the new river jetties . The Mendalgief stretch of tramway provided the western boundary, so it too had to be placed on an embankment seven to eight feet above the surface of the marsh. Pillgwenlly therefore was now virtually enclosed by tidal barriers, and consequently ripe for the reclamation that was to provide a fine, new suburb for the town.

Now, without going into great biographical detail, it is only fitting that some background should be rendered of the men behind these great innovations - they who contributed most to the rise of Monmouthshire as a leading industrial county and Newport as a flourishing seaport of world renown. They were the men of vision, already referred to, noted for their uncanny business flair, inventive powers, far-sightedness and personal drive. Their financial prowess obtained for themselves huge personal fortunes, allowing them to reinvest in and improve their own commercial interests and also to subsidise or encourage other grand schemes which, starting as ripples in the local pond, eventually lapped as large waves on far distant shores.

First there was the celebrated family of the Morgans claiming descent from Cadifor Fawr, Lord of Cil-Sans, who died in 1089. His third son, Bledri, who lived in the 12th century apparently found favour with the Normans who, for services rendered, made him a grant of land in the Bassaleg area. Through Bledri's sons the Morgans divided into the several Monmouthshire branches well known in and around Newport, but last heard of in this narrative in 1710 when John Morgan, merchant of London and Ruperra, acquired large additional estates in Monmouthshire, Glamorgan and Brecon as the price of settling the debts of the 6th Earl of Pembroke. The genealogy of this family from then on is as follows:-

John Morgan of Ruperra
to
John Morgan (nephew)
to
Sir William Morgan (son) 1700-1731
to
William Morgan (son) 1725-1763 - unmarried.
to
Thomas Morgan (uncle) 1727-1771 - unmarried.
to
Charles Morgan (brother) 1736-1787 - without issue.
to
John Morgan (brother) 1742-1792
to
Jane Morgan (sister)

The male line became extinct on the death of John in 1792 but Jane, his sister, had married Sir Charles Gould, a famous legal gentleman and former Judge Advocate General, who applied for and was granted, a royal licence to take the name and coat-of-arms of Morgan and, by the same token, to become the new head of the House of Tredegar.

The large house in which Sir William Morgan had entertained King Charles I in 1645 was probably built about 1500 by Sir John Morgan. In 1664, William Morgan decided to build himself a new house partly on and partly adjacent to the old. The original plans were said to be those of Inigo Jones although this gentleman died twelve years before the rebuilding; all the oak carving was by Grinling Gibbons. Finished by 1674, Tredegar House was the first substantial brick house in Monmouthshire.

By his marriage to Jane, Sir Charles Gould Morgan inherited upwards of 40,000 acres of land in the counties of Monmouthshire, Glamorgan and Brecon, and he immediately set about the exploitation of the industrial potential in his mountains and valleys to add new wealth to his already vast fortune. It was through his interest in granting leases of land for ironworks and coal mines that he became involved in encouraging ideas for the improvements in transport systems. He promoted the building of the Monmouthshire and Brecon Canals, and he was one of the powers behind the Sirhowy to Newport tramroad the last mile of which was to become known as the 'Golden Mile' because it passed through the deer park of Tredegar House and was subject in years to come of considerable sums paid as tolls to the Tredegar Estate.

The unusual fact about these substantial tolls was that they were tax free. In the true Tredegar tradition of appearing benevolent whilst at the same time ensuring that a great deal of his charity remained firmly anchored in the ancestral home, Sir Charles wove a clever scheme into his involvement with the valley railroads.

Under the terms of the Sirhowy Act, the Park Mile was built at the personal expense of the Estate - Sir Charles maintained that it cost him £40,000 which to some would seem incredible for the laying of a single mile of track on land that did not have to be bought! The bargain included freedom of the tolls from parliamentary and parochial taxes. By 1889, the tolls, calculated by reference to tonnage of iron, coal etc had reached £55,000 a year and it was only then that Lord Tredegar, under pressure from the newly-established Monmouthshire County Council, undertook to pay a parsimonious £200 a year! By 1919 the Estate was receiving £19,000 a year!

On January 1st 1923, the Golden Mile passed into the ownership of the Great Western Railway and it was then estimated that during the years of its existence, the tax concession that no other railway shared, had cost ratepayers over £50,000!

Now back to Sir Charles Gould Morgan and, coincidental with his arrival on the scene, there came Francis Homfray, ironmaster, formerly of Wollaston Hall Worcester, who in 1782 had leased an old foundry and forges at Cyfartha, just to the north of Merthyr. With him were his two sons, Jeremiah and Samuel, both expert ironmasters in their own right, and by dint of hard work and a trained labour force brought from the Midlands, they made the venture prosper.

In 1784 they were joined by another brother, Thomas, and they took another lease on one of the richest iron ore deposits and built a new works at Penydarren, a short distance from Cyfartha. Here they produced large quantities of top quality iron and made their family home in a new mansion near the works and aptly called Penydarren House.

Jeremiah Homfray later became estranged from brother Samuel and left the partnership to found the Ebbw Vale Ironworks but he could not settle and after dabbling in several other ventures connected with iron-making (during which time he became High Sheriff of Glamorgan), *Sir* Jeremiah Homfray stretched himself too far. He was declared bankrupt in 1813 and in order to dodge his creditors he fled to Boulogne where he died and was buried in 1833. It was however, Samuel Homfray who emerged as Newport's other leading benefactor.

Fresh from his triumphs in becoming sole proprietor of the Penydarren Works, perfecting further refinements in the iron-making processes and in part promoting the construction of the Glamorgan Canal, he found himself moving in the same exclusive circles as Sir Charles Morgan Bart. of Tredegar House and they soon established a firm friendship. It came as no surprise therefore when a closer relationship was welded by the marriage of Samuel Homfray to Jane, the daughter of Sir Charles. This union not only had the effect of joining two wealthy families, but also of combining the ownership of immense mineral resources with the expertise required to extract and use them.

An early perquisite of the marriage was the granting to Samuel Homfray in 1800 of a lease of about 3,000 acres of land at the top of the Tredegar Valley, on very generous terms. This resulted in the building of the enormously successful Tredegar Ironworks

Before very long, Sir Charles and his son-in-law were working energetically together on many projects of improvement and modernisation, investing large sums of their own capital and raising the rest by forming companies and issuing shares. Their highly successful Monmouthshire Canal and Sirhowy Tramroad have already been described but they were also deeply involved in the Brecon to Abergavenny Canal which had been extended in 1808 so that its 33 mile length connected with the Monmouthshire waterway at Llanvihangel-Pontymoile.

One of the better known stories that illustrates Sam Homfray's pioneering spirit and which loses nothing in its endless repetition, concerns an incident that arose out of his keen interest in experiments with steam power.

The famous Cornishman, Richard Trevithick, was a close friend of Homfray and an employee at the Penydarren Works where he was encouraged to use the full resources of the workshops to build prototypes of his high pressure steam engines as a means to their eventual introduction into industrial processes. There was at one time great rivalry bordering on bitterness between Homfray and Richard Crawshay who now owned the huge Cyfartha Ironworks. The former of these two formidable ironmasters had promoted a pack-horse tramroad from Merthyr to Navigation (later to be called Abercynon) in order to avoid using the latter's canal.

In 1804, Richard Trevithick assured Homfray that his recently tested 'high pressure tram engine' could make the nine mile trip down the tramroad to Navigation, hauling ten tons of iron, more quickly than could be achieved on the canal. A wager of 1,000 guineas was struck between the two ironmasters and on 21st February 1804 the attempt was made. Not only was the ten tons of iron carried on the trams but also seventy enthusiastic Penydarren employees who wanted to experience this novel 'first'.

At a steady five miles per hour, stopping only once for a mishap when the tall, brick smokestack badly damaged an unforeseen, too-low bridge, Trevithick's engine puffed triumphantly into Navigation -technically the first journey by any steam locomotive on a railway anywhere in the world - and Sam Homfray was 1,000 guineas richer! It was just as well that the bet did not cover the return journey because the primitive engine was defeated by the circuitous bends and steeper inclines that were faced going up the valley!

- O -

The new transport systems were operating for only a short space of time before their presence was felt in the rapidly increasing weight of iron, iron ore, coal, limestone and other goods that they carried to the Uskside jetties at Newport.

After the opening of the canal in 1797, each boat with a 25 ton load was making five trips a fortnight from the termini in the valleys to the Newport basin. In that first year, 7,000 tons of coal alone were shipped from the town, whereas ten years later the figure had reached 150,000 tons and had caused the population to double!

The regular coastal trade rocketed and much bigger vessels were frequently to be seen on the River Usk. The original wharfage nearest to the bridge was no longer adequate. The whole length of the western bank needed to be opened up to cope with the anticipated armada. New quays and jetties were built to augment those that the canal had already generated and eventually it was a common sight along the river bank to see an unbroken line of colliers, ore carriers and all manner of other freighters, presenting a forest of masts, spars and rigging as far as the eye could see!

When Archbishop Coxe travelled through Newport in 1800 he noted that despite all this feverish activity, the only road to the southernmost of the new jetties, on the edge of the Pillwenlly meadows, was still only the one following the curve of Corn Street into a continuation called Mountjoy Road, named presumably because the only building anywhere along its length was a dwelling named Mountjoy House, recorded as last being occupied in 1774. This is the first to be heard of this road and appropriately it brings another element of mystery to the history of the town.

Scattered throughout Newport's archives are references to James Blount, Lord Mountjoy and in several of these brief mentions he is described as an Irishman who 'until his death in 1593' owned a house and land in the town. This information is based upon the evidence of a letter that Blount wrote to his old friend, Sir Edward Stradling of St Donats Castle asking for some printed books; this in itself suggests a man of some wealth because such books were only just becoming available in bulk as Caxton's new printing press got to grips with the demand. They were therefore very expensive. The letter extended a warm welcome to Sir Edward and his wife on the occasion of a visit to Mountjoy and 'Joyesland', and the final paragraph included the words 'from Newporte this last day of August 1577'.

The mystery here is that the Lords Mountjoy were not an Irish family but hailed from Derbyshire and Worcestershire, although Charles, the son of James, fought in several campaigns in Ireland. What is more, nowhere in the family history of the Mountjoys can a connection be made to the Newport house and so the story that goes with it must necessarily remain in doubt. James Blount, 6th Lord Mountjoy, actually died at Hook in Dorsetshire in 1581, which suggests that the above mentioned letter is chronologically feasible. Perhaps in such questionable circumstances it is best to salvage a little consolation in the notion that Newport has a small corner that *just might be* named after the ancient castle in Spain from which the Mountjoy title was taken. The name survives in three streets abutting the junction of Cardiff and Commercial Roads.

The old Mountjoy Road of yore became narrowed and almost lost beneath the sudden burgeoning of canal and dock workers cottages, but a section of it became represented by Union Street (off Llanarth Street) and a neat little terrace of villas known as 'Jaynes Buildings' ~ Mr Jayne being a reputable builder in Victorian Newport ~ until all were swallowed up by the modern library, art gallery and entrance to the Kingsway Shopping Centre in John Frost Square.

It was becoming more obvious, rapidly so, that if anything further was to be made of the Pillgwenlly wastes, a much less unencumbered route had to be provided, if only in the first instance to relieve the congestion of the canal towpath as it was chosen as the most direct way to reach the wharves nearer to the river mouth.

Sir Charles Gould Morgan died in 1806 but his mantle was immediately donned by his son, Charles, who at 46 years of age was well inured to his father's ways and full of the same ambitions. He straightway formed the Tredegar Wharf Company with a board of directors comprising himself as chairman, his brother-in-law Samuel Homfray, Rowley Lascelles and Richard Fothergill, all with deep interests in iron and coal; between them they quickly pledged basic capital of £16,000.

Within a year Sir Charles granted the Company 200 acres of the Pillgwenlly marshland on a 99 year lease at a nominal rent, for the purpose of long term development. It was almost as if a town plan were being drawn up of the type for which modern local authorities are noted, but such niceties were then unknown. This was merely the start of a well orchestrated series of events, cleverly co-ordinated and put together in a manner most likely to lead to the efficient and speedy completion of a huge commercial jig-saw puzzle.

No time was lost in laying a rudimentary basis for what was intended to be a fifty foot wide, mile long road from the old town centre, between the Westgate Inn and Skinner Street, to Prothero's Wharf on the far side of the water-logged, half mile square depression that was Pillgwenlly. The first stretch took shape very quickly, covering as it did the least troublesome subsoil from the Westgate to Mountjoy. This area was not so wet or low-lying, and for many years had been found useful as meadows for the grazing of cattle. Even so, a great deal of infilling was required to be tamped well down on a bed of wooden faggots.

By 1808, the road was started and had reached a creditable length before the first building, the Weslyan Chapel, was erected on its frontage. This was eventually pulled down to make way for Newport's first Woolworths (today occupied by Boots fine department store). It is strange now to think that this very central position was then considered to be 'out

114

of town'. The swift erection of a chapel however reflected the urgency that Newport's non-conformist following placed on the obtaining of their own purpose-built places of worship instead of being forced to share specially licensed houses and halls. Within ten years the new road and a side lane (Charles Street) became well endowed with the chapels of several other dissenting persuasions, scattered among a growing number of small houses and workplaces.

Chief among these new places of worship was the splendid Tabernacle Chapel which dominated High Street for over 150 years, from its foundation in 1822, through a reconstruction at the end of the century, a severe fire in 1960, rebuilding in 1961 to final demolition for town centre redevelopment in the 1970s.

As work on the new road proceeded, the citizens of Newport must have viewed it with wonder for never before had they seen a road of such great breadth, straightness and smoothness. In the early days they called it 'The Broadway'. Would that those good townsfolk had continued to have their way, for today the town might have been graced with principal streets named 'Upper and Lower Broadway' instead of the hackneyed 'Commercials' that every town in Britain seems to boast, and which conjure up in the mind's eye pictures of older, shabbier thoroughfares.

By 1812, Commercial Street was finished to the highest standard prevailing in those days but progress on its extension from Mountjoy to Pillgwenlly could not be maintained due to serious problems arising from the necessity to build the biggest embankment yet. The amount of hardcore and spoil required to carry the road across the last half mile of bogs, ponds and quagmires was enormous and certainly far more than was available locally. It could only be accomplished by the mass importation of material by sea, and so from then on ships brought in much of the ballast from all over Britain and the Continent, either as whole or part cargoes.

The task was long and arduous, and even after many more years the highway was never finished in the style of its first half, remaining a pot-holed, debris-covered ridge. After dark, its unlit length was also the haunt of vicious thugs waiting to beat and rob any sailor who foolishly chose this way back to his ship!

The massive operation of ballast-tipping was to continue for nearly half a century in order to fill the great sunken bowl to the level of the canal and tram-roads, and to give it the stability necessary to support the hundreds of houses intended for the Pillgwenlly 'new' town. Modern developers, ignorant of this aspect of their town's history, are often bewildered when they delve deeply into the substrata of the suburb and find strange substances, alien to Welsh shores, that their probing drills uncover.

On the visible evidence of the fine, new road arriving at Mountjoy in 1810, the Turnpike Trustees were persuaded to form another new main road from that point to the bottom of the Waterloo trip near Courtybella where it joined up with the coach road to Castleton, St Mellons and Cardiff. This new Cardiff Road replaced the old route over Stow Hill and through Bassaleg. The turnpikes at Stow Gate and Waterloo Gate were subsequently closed down.

In the midst of all this activity, the year 1811 was notable for very little other than one occurrence which in itself hardly rated a mention except that it was to be the first of a chain that had far-reaching effects almost to the point of disaster for the town. It was in that year that a 27 year old John Frost, who had been brought up in Newport by his grandfather, Tom Frost cordwainer, returned from educative apprenticeships in London and Bristol to open a drapers shop in High Street.

By contrast, 1812 was the most eventful of years! While Napoleon Boneaparte was at the gates of Moscow and about to commence his catastrophic retreat, Cardiff Road was opened and Commercial Street became temporarily known as Cardiff Street. The outlook for this freshly opened up end of the town was so decidedly rosy that it caused a shrewd, speculative builder to obtain a lease of land right on the junction of the three main roads, and there he built the Salutation Hotel to stand as a popular public house and landmark until it disappeared 150 years later under a much enlarged and quite complicated junction (afterwards known for uncertain reasons as Gilligan's Island) created to contend with the 20th century traffic arriving from Kingsway and the newly built George Street river bridge.

The spirit of enterprise was never so widespread in Newport as it was at that time, and it surfaced again through the medium of Mr William Stewart who on 1st October 1816, circulated a pamphlet proposing that a passenger boat, for the first time ever powered by steam, should ply daily between Newport and Bristol. The scheme suggested a vessel of 70 tons burthen, driven by a 20 horsepower engine and costing £2,000.

Two cabins were to be provided, the one aft being the more elegant, furnished with a library of select books, a popular magazine, interesting pamphlets, a daily newspaper, maps of neighbouring counties and a telescope - all for a fare of five shillings. The forward berth would cost two shillings and would obviously be much less comfortable. Only limited quantities of refreshment were to be carried 'to ensure decorum among the passengers!'

The proposed service was advertised as a long awaited alternative to the weekly market boats (under sail) and also to the much more expensive stagecoaches. The latter were given a real drubbing in Mr Stewart's pamphlet in order to prove his point. Besides the considerable cost and slowness of the journey, he said, it could do no good on reaching the Passage (Beachley) to leave the warm interior of the coach in order to embark in an open boat 'exposed to the piercing winds, and washed by the muddy waters of the Severn!'

Wreck of the 'Severn' steamer, Newport Bridge, May 1844

A sample balance sheet was provided to show a likely net annual profit of £1,778 and gentlemen were exhorted by the great advantages to trade to come forward and make a good investment. It is not clear if this idea made Mr Stewart's fortune or indeed if any more came of the venture, bearing in mind that steam engines had not then come into general use for transport on land let alone the sea!

What is certain is that the first steamship to regularly visit Newport, commencing in

1822, was the Bristol-owned 'Cambrian', followed a year later by the 'Lady Rodney', built in Liverpool for a small syndicate of Newport and Pontypool businessmen. The voyage to Bristol took 4½ hours and twelve trips a week were made in summer, six trips a week in winter. The Lady Rodney kept this up for 31 years and gave her name to the wharf from which she sailed. A fellow-traveller did not lead such a charmed life!

Immediately opposite Rodney Wharf, on the town bank, there was a gentle slope where, at the end of what was to become known as Screw Packet Lane, stood a low timber quay almost leaning against the bridge. This was Beaufort Wharf on whose site is now situated a wide, paved area of riverside walk and the 'Wave' monument. But in 1844 it was the scene of a serious ship-wreck!

During these times, a fast steam-packet named the 'Severn' had started a service from Bristol to Newport. Built originally for the Bristol to Chepstow run, her route was changed to compete with the Newport-owned packet-boats and she did, in fact, succeed in reducing the fares by a half! Fitted with four watertight compartments and high pressure engines driving a single, powerful screw, the Severn could carry 60 passengers across the Channel in unparalleled speed and comfort.

On May 4th 1844, she arrived at Beaufort Wharf and, in mooring, her captain neglected to first warp her round to face downstream in readiness for her departure. Consequently, when fully loaded, the attempt was made to turn her against a five knot incoming current. This manoeuvre might have been achieved successfully but a cable snapped, fouling the propeller and causing loss of steerage that allowed the tide to carry the helpless vessel on to the stone buttresses of the bridge. The impact stove in both the ship's bow compartments and she began to settle, held firmly by the fierce tide, broadside on to the bridge, her tall smokestack towering above road level and presenting a fearful picture of disaster to the shocked onlookers!

The report in the following issue of the Monmouthshire Merlin gave its correspondent the opportunity to be most dramatic; the Illustrated London News carried a most imaginative artist's impression of the disaster, and one eyewitness's quote was poetically turned into 'frantic shrieks of wild despair came rolling on the burdened air!'

Fortunately there was plenty of help on hand, both from the crowded riverbank and from the dozens of small craft put into the water by the masters of nearby, moored ships. All passengers were saved and later on the Severn was hauled upright with great difficulty, pumped out, patched up and towed back to Bristol.

For at least three centuries, shipbuilding and repair had been an important industry along the town reach of the River Usk which with its tremendous tidal rise almost to the top of its banks, and a fall that all but exposed its bed, lent itself admirably to the launch of the new and the careening of the old.

The registration of shipping did not become compulsory until 1786 so until then records of vessels, names, burthen and place of construction were, to say the least, unreliable. However, it is widely accepted that most ships' home ports in those days were where they were built, and it has already been established that many of Newport's merchants owned their own ships in the 14th and 15th centuries. None were large; ten to fifteen tons were probably the average but when the Elizabethan world began its expansion, bigger, sturdier, ocean-going traders were called for. Soon Newport's Uskside echoed to the sound of shipwrights sawing oak timbers and driving home copper nails; the air was filled with the acrid odours of charcoal fires and molten tar. Sail-makers thrived, rope-works flourished and ships' chandlers made handsome profits. Orders came from other coastal towns which lacked the appropriate facilities and eventually Monmouthshire gave up its mineral wealth to the nearest suitably equipped town that could provide them.

In the year ended 5th July 1820, 4,211 vessels cleared Newport's wharves. This evidence was used to petition the Treasury Commissioners and persuade them that 'because Newport is now one of the greatest shipping places of coal, iron and tin in the Principality, independence of Cardiff is now urgent'. Thirty years later, the number of ships using the port in twelve months was over 10,000!

This was the golden age for Newport's shipbuilding industry and between 1823 and 1884, over sixty craft of from 40 to 270 tons and numerous smaller, unspecified vessels were built on Uskside. Leading yards were those of Johns, Tudor, Morton, Johnson, and Pride & Williams; later came Perkins, Willmett and Hall.

The peak was reached in 1867, but after 1870 a decline set in which was only temporarily lifted by orders for a few screw-driven schooners placed with Mordey & Carney and the Usk Building Company Ltd.

Tragedy seemed to stalk Newport's shipping and in the worst period, from 1860 to 1870, the wrecks of 84 vessels belonging to the port were reported. They foundered for all sorts of reasons - storms, cargo fires, collisions - but several disappeared without trace and one of these was Newport's finest, the 682 ton 'Crawshay Bailey', which vanished en route from Batavia to San Francisco in 1869.

It goes without saying that with Newport's universal reputation for trading, these disasters occurred in places as far apart as Chile and Shanghai, the Mediterranean and the St Lawrence River. If all the other ports of Great Britain suffered losses anywhere approaching Newport's, it gives cause for one to wonder at the romance of the great sailing ships. Even the good old 'Moderator', built a century before these calamitous years and giving her name to one of the town's best known wharves, went the same way. After so many years of sterling service, Mr Gething's 53 ton coaster foundered in home waters and to this day her timbers lie buried deep in the River Usk mud. Where precisely is not known but at Caerleon there was once a bathing place known to older inhabitants as 'the Moderator!'

The richness of creative incident in 19th century Newport can fairly be described as unsurpassed in all other eras combined. This is probably true also in its comparison with most other towns of Victorian Britain. The seething activity that overtook the west bank of the River Usk knew no bounds and, as its many attractions drew thousands of new inhabitants, the town was soon to outstrip Merthyr as the largest in Wales and for a long time to withhold the title from its nearest rival, Cardiff. An unprecedented demand for accommodation began to stretch the old charter-ordained boundaries.

Today, late in the 20th century, there is hardly a building standing that existed a hundred years ago except for the castle, some houses of religion and a few taverns - the latter only surviving by the sacrifice of time-honoured names for modern and in most cases uncharacteristic, puerile titles. Those that failed to survive, and the characters who briefly occupied them, when flamboyance and vulgarity reigned in perfect partnership, are deserving of a whole volume to themselves!

Chapter Seven

The Nineteenth Century

Public Health, Public Houses and Slums.
The Stowe Fairs, Street Lighting, Gasworks, The Docks and the
Great Dock Road.

With the town's major schemes reaching fruition, the Corporation seemed to become much more aware of its hygiene problems and set itself the task of doing something positive about them.

No consideration had ever before been given to an organised system for the disposal of household refuse, human sewage or the stinking ordures accumulated in a town where the streets were so often filled with farm animals. For some time up to the end of the first decade of the 19th century one man had been employed as a scavenger, the council paying him a pittance and expecting wonders for it. His solitary donkey-drawn dung cart with the offensive scrapings of the streets, toiled daily between the town centre and the Marshes where its contents were spread about the fields. It was a most unsavoury task and one on which one man and his donkey were not likely to make any visible impression. Time then to introduce another character who several times during those years made his appearance in a variety of guises.

Moses Scard applied for the job of town scavenger and the credentials that he presented to the public health committee must have been convincing enough for him to be granted a contract at a fee of £400 per annum. This was an enormous sum, so presumably it included amounts to cover the running costs of several underlings and their donkeys!

In 1839, Moses Scard was heard of again as one of the special constables in the thick of the fighting in the hallway of the Westgate Hotel during the ill-fated Chartist Riot. When the battle was over he emerged to take charge of a party that was collecting the hundreds of weapons dropped in the streets by the fleeing rioters. By the 1860s he leased a farm from the Tredegar Estate at Courtybella and received mention in the Newport Gazette when he appeared in court to confront the stealer of one of his sheep. Thereafter, his family ran a thriving corn merchants business in North Street and must have achieved some prominence to have had a nearby street in Baneswell named after them -an honour usually only accorded to ex-mayors and aldermen!

But to return to the town's early sanitary problems - the record increase in population in such a short space of time caused the position to become so critical that, at last, a plan was devised for a town drain. The outcome was understandably primitive and could by no means be described as a 'system', unless a single, short length of open drain qualified as such! It was dug out in 1809 from the Kings Head to the canal, and in 1813 was extended by means of a covered culvert to Mill Street. This meant that much of the old town sewage was now directed into the canal which, in effect, began to serve as the main sewer!

This was the situation for years afterwards, but there came the day when the inhabitants at the 'new' end of the town found it more convenient to take their refuse, including the contents of their night soil boxes, along past the Salutation Inn and tip it down the sides of the Commercial Road embankments to form foul smelling ditches which needed regular treatment with quicklime. There were still, however, the lazy ones who continued to use their front doors and bedroom windows to drench the roadways that passed their terraces!

Cholera was the inevitable outcome, and Newport was hit by serious outbreaks in 1832 (population 7,062) and in 1849 (population 19,000). The latter visitation came just after the Town Corporation had been given powers under the Public Health Act 1848, to raise finance for sanitary improvements on the security of the local rates.

With this money guaranteed, a scheme was put in hand immediately to provide main drainage for the town. The cost was £12,000 and the works lasted for eleven years until the new sewer was opened in 1859. There were then drains from the top of Stow Hill, Baneswell and the Friars Fields, seven miles of brick and earthenware pipes and five outfalls into the River Usk. Seven years later, in 1866, (population 25,000) came Newport's third and worst cholera outbreak, killing 69 and making hundreds seriously ill. Obviously, in spite of the new drainage system there were still lessons to be learned in the matter of town hygiene. Nevertheless, with all its shortcomings it was the forerunner of modern Newport's sewage disposal system and all subsequent extensions were grafted on to these humble beginnings.

Shortly before the completion of this work, and as a result of an extensive survey which obviously brought to light its inadequacy, a report dated 23rd June 1856 was made to the Borough Council recommending rebuilding and extensions proposed to cost £16,000 plus interest on a loan over 30 years.

The courses of fresh water streams with outlets into Forge Pill (Marshes Road mill stream), the Town Pill, Jacks Pill, and Pill Gwenlly were utilised in the scheme and thereafter became culverted channels for raw sewage. In this way the sluice gate on the face of the stone culvert built in 1802 to support the canal at the Town Pill, became the outfall of a sewer!

Old plans held at the Civic Centre show the stream that fed this pill to have a strangely convoluted course seemingly dictated by a meandering which, starting somewhere above upper Bridge Street, ran under the Cambrian Road Brewery, crossed beneath High Street, along the backs of properties in Griffin Street, under the canal and so through the sluice of the Town Pill into the river. This ancient watercourse, which somewhere along its line probably had connection with the Baneswell Pump, carried (and at the date of writing still carried) untreated sewage from most of the town centre!

- 0 -

Within two years of the opening of the Salutation Inn (1812), another tavern made its appearance - the first beerhouse in Commercial Street. The Parrot, at the corner of Charles Street, was later rebuilt and renamed The Talbot Hotel but in its original form its rooms were often used for town council meetings, sometimes as a police station and later as part of a small music hall that was attached at the rear.

Indeed, Newport's thirst was well taken care of and the building of public houses seems to have been treated as of equal importance as all other projects. In the twenty years following the opening of the two afore- mentioned inns there were added such illustrious names as the Union Inn, the Bush Inn, the Ship and Pilot, the Tradesmans Arms, the Custom House and the William IV. After 1822 and up to 1847, six inns sprang up in Market Street alone; these were the Trout, the Old Ship, the Market Tavern, the Bluchers Arms, the Shipwreck and the Crosskeys. At the other end of the scale, the 'vile and noxious' region of the Friars Fields was giving its custom to the Globe and the Red Cow in Canal Parade where the drinking was often incidental to the transaction of 'other business!'

In 1831, Newport Castle became a brewery and by 1847, with the population standing at 17,000 and the number of residences at 2,230, there were 300 public houses in the borough! If this were not enough, the 1835 street directory lists the names of 74 individuals and describes them as 'beer retailers' - among them John Frost who, besides his High Street drapery, ran a Market Street off-licence.

No wonder then that the 1836 town survey map should show that another large brewery had appeared, the Cambrian, at the back of High Street with an entrance in Baneswell Road (the young Bridge Street). This brewery was owned by Mr Harry Yorath whose name was perpetuated when his firm became well known well into the 20th century as Lloyd & Yorath Ltd. Someone once heard Mr Yorath recount the fact that in his youth he had caught sizeable salmon in a stream that ran along Cambrian Road!

The weather may have had something to do with this great demand for liquid refreshment for, during these years, there are reports of many hot summers. Take 1820 as a case in point - when the intense heat caused dozens of horses to drop dead between the shafts!

Having alluded to Friars Fields as a place of notoriety and evil, one deserves an explanation of how this once hallowed ground earned a reputation that reached even the attention of Punch Magazine and in 1851 caused those respected columns to describe the area as: 'the sombre dens of the proletaries around the market of Newport.' This report and the widespread circulation of the publication must have made Newport the subject of much detrimental tittle-tattle in many a drawing room.

The truth of the matter is that, prior to 1818, this area of ground, desirably situated near the centre of the town, was somehow allowed to fall into the hands of unscrupulous jerry-builders who quickly converted it into the town's first purpose-built slum! Without any form of control or town planning, and without regard for anything but maximum return for the minimum outlay, several terraces of awful, tiny tenements were thrown up, squeezed together so that not one inch of space was wasted. No heed was given to essentials like ventilation, water supply or sanitation, and expense was further reduced by the non-provision of windows and backyards. The whole dark, smelly complex was known as 'The Devil's Half Acre' and it was said that one landlord owned twenty rat-infested, disease-ridden tenements which housed somewhere in the region of 400 persons!

The 1836 map of the town gives the name of these grim alley-ways as 1st and 2nd Rows, and shows that access to them was gained through two narrow openings from Commercial Street (later to become known as Austin Friars and Friars Street), and a rear entrance from Canal Parade.

Without doubt the atmosphere of this brooding warren has never been better captured than in the words of James Matthews in his 'Historic Newport'. The following lengthy paragraph says it all:-

'Hereupon arose that insalubrious, badly—lighted, badly~drained 'plague spot', 'vile rookery' and that 'delightful' neighbourhood of Friars Fields. Here, for a long period, thousands were enticed into that 'man-trap' where they were taken in and 'done for,' the wind having got into their pockets, they were relieved of all their money, banknotes, cheques, watches and valuables, as if by magic. The fraternity that once resided in this humble suburb of Newport were those masculine, ungainly~shaped, unprepossessing, amazonian denizens and smiling nymphs of the pavement, who went about generally with their eyes in 'mourning' which spoke volumes as to the gentleness of their lives, some of them having earned for themselves aliases such as ~ 'the Duchess'; Nancy Bwlch'; 'Mary the Cripple'; 'Ann the Doctor'; 'Annie the Sawyer' who was the 'sawbones' to the doctor aforesaid; 'Julia the Slattern'; 'Amelia the Smut'; and 'Mary the Pickaxe'. The other members of this community were the prison-cropped looking gentlemen - 'crack files' 'bullies, 'leaders of rows and

fights in the Fields, and rogues who plundered henroosts, broke into warehouses and waylaid honest travellers, chief among whom were ~ 'Dick Cochin'; 'Bill the Fighter'; 'Bill the Drummer'; and 'Evan the Milkman', with the broken beak. All the above resided here when they were not temporarily lodging either at the 'hole in the wall' (Carpenters Arms Lane lock-up) or in the 'Clock-us' (Mill Street) or performing healthy exercises at, or were residing in the 'Stone Jug' (Usk Jail).'

One, Hannah Willis, stole a jug of gin from the Tredegar Arms and was sentenced in July 1836 to seven years transportation. Another, Amelia the Smut, received ten years of the same for the theft of a watch in 1838. Ruth Harris, a prostitute aged twenty four, received fourteen years transportation for stealing a watch and £1-14s. As she was being led away she was heard to say to the prosecutor, 'Mind thee, if ever I come back, I'll mark thee', upon which His Lordship recalled her to the dock and as the sentence had not yet been recorded, he amended it to transportation for life! Much subdued, the woman s only further comment was, 'I don't care much for that!'

How many, one wonders, of Newport's present day antipodean cousins owe their existence to a moment of folly in a South Wales slum?

The citizens of modern Newport should consider themselves lucky indeed as they stroll in the sunshine, between the trees and flowerbeds of John Frost Square, and muse to themselves that they are treading the same ground that those disreputable, villainous characters walked in surroundings of such extreme squalor.

The 1830s were noted as years of great malfeasance in the town and, other than the type of transgressions already catalogued, vandalism was rife. For most of 1836, a gang of ruffians was roaming Newport by night causing mindless mayhem and damage. Inoffensive, out of town Clarence Place received a visit when the homes of Doctor Gwillim and Mr Birch were broken into and severely despoiled.

The same gang rampaged around the big houses on Stow Hill, tearing up valuable trees, shrubs and fences in the gardens of Kingshill, Tivoli House and Reverend Isaacson's Vicarage.

Bearing in mind that the borough had not yet formed a police force, press comment was not in the least surprising. The Monmouthshire Merlin had this to say;-

'We have more than once alluded to the want of a police force in this town, which we believe to be the worst protected in England. In saying this we do not wish to reflect upon the man who is now employed and his aide who are very efficient in their way!'

So Newport, with its violent slum population, 300 public houses and an unremitting crime wave, was reliant on two watchmen (one part time) for the safety of the innocents and their property!

But with all this villainy so common as to have become resignedly acceptable, there was another kind which though not uncommon along the muddy shores of the Usk, was more romantically associated with the rugged coasts on the other side of the Bristol Channel. There were many such occasions when vigilant excise officers discovered the illegal landing of goods with the intention of evading the payment of customs duties. Favourite spots were around the mouths of the Rivers Usk, Ebbw and various other little creeks in their vicinity. One of the earliest of these incidents to be recorded took place on 7th September 1649 when 2,000 lbs of Barbados tobacco were landed at Redwick and seized by John Byrd, the Newport Collector of Customs. Consignments varied in size but some were considerable: like the

9,804 lbs of tobacco and 40 gallons of brandy apprehended at Goldcliff on 8th April 1784. This was taken into Newport under armed guard to protect it, it was said, 'from the desperate set of people who inhabited the country around!'

Two months later, at the same place, 130 gallons of rum and brandy came in. So it went on for the next 50 years until, on June 22nd 1833, the Customs searchers made the biggest killing of all!

On that night, the schooner 'Kate' of Bristol was seen to discharge cargo into a house known as 'The Windblown Tavern' at Nash Point. The Customs Comptroller and three of his men raided the premises and captured 264 casks, each containing 4 to 6 gallons of brandy – about 1,100 gallons in all! Such coups sounded easy to achieve but it was highly dangerous to underestimate the ruthlessness of the smugglers. Clashes were often of the most violent nature and customs officers knew they might be fighting for their lives!

Besides these daring night landings on the wild Monmouthshire shores, there were many others where the ships ran openly in to the River Usk wharves, unloaded legal cargoes and then sneaked their contraband into neighbouring timber and boat yards – owned by respectable Newport gentry who, it was widely known, condoned and profited from the arrangements. The local excise men thought that they were highly successful in their dockside searches but the publicans of the town would have it otherwise, knowing full well that there were always cheap casks of brandy, rum or Irish whiskey available for the asking!

~ 0 ~

What one tends to overlook in the Newport of the early 19th century, is that whilst its stature grew in every other respect, it was still contained within the same physical boundaries as laid down 200 years before in the Charter of James I – even the exploding suburb of Pillgwenlly was still outside the borough, in the parish of St Woolos (the old Manor of Wentloog).

Once, in mediaeval times St Woolos had been, if anything, a more forward and spirited township than its cousin down on the bank of the Usk, and was often referred as the township of Stowe. It had had its own mayor and, apart from its beautiful old church, also had many attractions for the burgesses of Newport, not the least of which were the annual Stowe Fairs, grandiose indeed in comparison with anything of like nature held at the bottom of the hill. Stowe was an Old English word for a place of trade or market and from the earliest times these fairs were held under the auspices of the Abbots of Gloucester.

The Stowe Fairs of later years are believed to have originated as the sole survivors of the two fairs granted to Newport in the 1623 Charter. They had given a much needed boost to commercial life in an area where the population was thin and scattered. Everyone had a central point where they could come together, do business and then, at a certain hour, finish off with a bout of relaxation and merry-making. They were also occasions for the local squires to make brief appearances in order to give the impression of taking an interest in their 'inferiors'.

The fairs more than satisfied the trading demands of the sleepy little town that had for so long hibernated alongside the River Usk, but the increasing prosperity of the port, its swelling population, ever busier markets and the final sweeping away of all barriers against foreigners setting up shop in the town, were all contributory factors to their demise.

Once a year, Newport was almost denuded of its inhabitants as the great exodus was made to the neighbouring township, where, among a hundred stalls serving refreshments, would begin a hectic day of buying, selling, bartering, singing, dancing and – it almost goes without saying – drinking! For the duration of the fair the humdrum routine of everyday life was forgotten and the top of Stow Hill was vibrant with laughter and good humour.

Casks of ale abounded, not only in the nearby inns or the booths within the field, but also in the doorways of practically every cottage along the way as householders tried to make a little profit on the day. It was not unexpected therefore, after a late night and early morning of hurly-burly and rumpus, to find the field filled with the recumbent bodies of those who had indulged themselves to excess!

The historian, Scott, attended the 1847 fair and he afterwards wrote:-

'The spirit of fun and frolic of the old Stowe Fair went out with the last generation and is remembered now but in tradition.'

As the wilder element took over, it became the established rule to elect a mock 'Lord Mayor' who presided over the boisterous pleasures of the fair, seated on a roughly made throne. For the duration of the proceedings his word was law and anyone who usurped his authority or failed to pay the visitor's toll, might be tossed into a nearby, stagnant pond or placed in the stocks for revilement by insult or rotten fruit! Those of Jewish persuasion were favourite targets and, as many of the itinerant travellers were of that faith, they suffered heavily of these indignities. On one occasion even Sir Charles Morgan of Tredegar House only just escaped his turn in the stocks by payment of a guinea.

There were, however, moderate men who would have dearly loved to have stopped the Stowe Fairs, but fought shy of action in the face of those who found rude enjoyment under the vicarious reign of the 'Lord Mayor.'

One who exercised the authority to put his foot down without fear of reprisal, was the Vicar of St Woolos, the Reverend John Evans, and he placed restrictions on ruffianly activities on land adjoining the church. His successor, the Reverend Isaacson, went a step further and refused permission for the fair to take place anywhere near the church. As late as 1861, Newport Corporation was still debating remedies for the 'scenes of debauchery and dissipation which take place there!' (Newport Gazette 11th May 1861). Apparently the subject was not treated very seriously and this particular meeting broke up in laughter when the Mayor, James Brown, remarked :'I should be very sorry to interfere with ancient institutions of our country in the slightest degree'. It was not long after this that the Fairs ceased for good due to the usage of the fields being barred to them.

Standing opposite St Woolos Church was the Old Tythe Barn, a large thatched roofed building which for the duration of the fair was used as a theatre where travelling groups of actors performed the popular one-act plays of the day, and comedians entertained 'with drolleries and farces'. The Six Bells Inn became part of this site.

Behind the barn, the Stowe Fair was held on land called Molly Rosser's Farm, an extensive area that sloped down to Cardiff Road.

Most of this land is today occupied by the Royal Gwent Hospital, but the top end was for many years, up until the 2nd World War, used for the grand, annual hospital fetes which may have set ghosts a-dancing on that same turf that once hosted the Stowe Fairs.

One of the colourful characters who would almost certainly have put in an appearance at the fairs, was the town crier. Newport was known to have one although all records refer to the town 'bellman'. Strange to relate, Newport's first crier was a woman; there is no record of her date of appointment but her name was Sarah Gardner and she held the position until 27th September 1762.

Her successors were:-

John Taylor	1762	
John Jones	1804,	also hayward of the marshes
Thomas Morgan	1824	-ditto-
George Williams	1833	-ditto-
William Williams	1857	- ditto -

How long the last named held the post is not known, but he died in 1891 and not only was he positively the last of the town's bellmen but also the last of the town's ancient order of freemen. His bell is preserved in the town museum.

- O -

Another serious drawback to the quality of life in the town was the very poor standard of lighting in the streets. For many years reliance had been placed on a makeshift system of oil lamps suspended from poles, unstable and few and far between, which were the only source of illumination after nightfall. The tiny pools of light that they shed seemed to accentuate the larger areas of blackness and made every night-time excursion one of peril, especially in the vicinity of the Friars Fields. Too often, on dark wintry evenings, the lamp-shields were no match for the gusting winds, and the wicks sputtered easily to extinguishment.

On 24th September 1824, the Gaslight Establishment held its first meeting in the Town Clerk's office under the chairmanship of the Mayor, Mr William Williams. As a result of this and further meetings, a private company was set up with an original capital of £2,500 at £25 a share.

A site for a gasworks was quickly obtained in Mill Street and on 8th July 1825, the first proposition for the lighting of the town was minuted:-

> **'The gentlemen of the Committee who consented to call on the inhabitants of the town to collect subscriptions for the lighting of the public streets and highways with gas, reported that they had succeeded in obtaining £50 or thereabouts. For this sum they stated that they could put up ten lights and keep them lighted with gas from 29th September 1825 to 29th September 1826 from sunset to sunrise'.**

The Newport Improvement Act was an act for lighting, paving, repairing, cleaning and law enforcement and, as a preliminary to the lighting of the town by gas, it proposed strict rules for the laying of gas mains i.e. penalties for trenching the roads and not relaying the surface neatly and smoothly. This ruling came somewhat as an anachronism in a town which had thitherto never enjoyed the luxury of a smooth street!

By 1835, the old town was 'brightly lit' by a gas company wholly under the direction of private enterprise, and various individuals took renewable leases as they tried to improve the service. The early years were marred by one serious incident; during a fierce storm in 1837, the gasometer was blown clean out of its supports. Several men were killed and Newport was flung into darkness for a week!

After tight negotiation with the Corporation, the Company's initial charge for street lighting was £3-5s-0d per lamp, per annum, with the condition that the lamps remained unlit on five moonlight nights in each month from March to October each year.

In 1843, the directors applied to Parliament for an Act of Incorporation and when it received Royal Assent on 31st May , the Newport (Monmouthshire) Gas Company was born under its first chairman, Thomas Prothero.

The supply was not then metered. Consumers entered contracts for fixed numbers of lights on each premises and paid an agreed sum, quarterly in advance, for a certain number of hours each day. If anyone was caught switching on before or after these times they were immediately cut off! A very popular man was the official hired to spy out the offenders!

Another new Act in 1855, authorised expansion into parts of Christchurch, Malpas and St Woolos. By 1866, increasing demands were more than the Mill Street premises could cope with so a second gasworks was built at Crindau. In 1870, a special main was laid in William Street to supply a temporary hospital erected there for victims of the 1869 cholera epidemic.

By 1900, there were 1,056 public lamps lit by gas but they had already begun to be run down in deference to the increasing use of electricity.

- O -

Newport was the setting in November 1829 for another unofficial and largely unpublicised 'first'.

Each year, Sir Charles Morgan held a renowned cattle show at Courtybella Farm, and Samuel Homfray, who at that time lived at Bedwellty House near Tredegar, intended that his family and friends should make their entrance in grand fashion. This was the son of the Samuel Homfray who had helped to form the Tredegar Wharf Company and who died in 1822, and therefore the nephew of the current Sir Charles.

Anyway, Sam Homfray purchased for his Tredegar Ironworks one of the new steam locomotives for the purpose of drawing tramloads of iron down what was then the longest railroad in the world! For this one special occasion the trains were carefully cleaned up and converted for passenger use. Installed precariously on uncomfortable plank seats, the party, dressed in all its finery, left Tredegar at 7 am on this chilly November morning to ensure timely arrival at Newport, but fate decreed otherwise.

The journey proved long and arduous due to numerous breakages and distortions of the rails. A gang of workmen, taken along for emergencies, spent most of their time on the track with hammers and crowbars. Derailments were frequent as the little engine, pushed to its limits to keep on schedule, caused vibrations to which the tracks were wholly unused. By midday the train was only as far down the valley as Blackwood, and it was not until evening was closing in that it entered the last mile through Tredegar Park where it promptly lost its smokestack, broken off at the boiler by a low, overhanging tree branch. This was the end and the journey had to be continued on foot. It was a very tired, cold, bedraggled party which finally entered Tredegar House! The ladies in their billowing silk and satins and large feathered hats, must have presented a particularly depressing spectacle!

As disastrous as this outing may have been however, and although it has not earned a mention in the record books, the fact remains that Sam Homfray's 'passenger train' made its historic run a year before that of the first passenger service in Great Britain, introduced on the Manchester to Liverpool Railway.

It may even be that Mr Homfray had an eye on the record of 35 miles per hour set by George Stephenson's 'Rocket' that same year. Who is to say that but for the extremely rough terrain, the poor quality of the track and the unpruned trees of Tredegar Park, the record might have been given a close run?

Apparently the state of the permanent way became much improved within a few years. Mr Kyrle Fletcher, Newport's well known antique dealer and historian, recalls that by 1834 the Sirhowy Tram Road and Monmouthshire Canal had started to serve the community in ways unthought of when the priorities were merely to get the coal and iron to the docks.

On market days, huge trains drawn by eight-horse teams made the journey from

126

Tredegar, through Risca, bringing hundreds of eager shoppers in search of bargains and the latest fashions from London and Bristol. The journey must have been unimaginably uncomfortable with planks laid across the coal trams for seats and, when trains met, the hard push backwards for one of them to a passing place! At eventide, the terminus at Cardiff Road was choked with queues of tired, heavily-laden buyers and others who had celebrated in another way, all waiting to make the long return journey.

A similar service was supplied to travellers from Abergavenny and Brecon by means of passenger-carrying narrow-boats on the canal. At first the ticket office was at the Old Green terminus, but by 1848 the Town Directory was advertising canal services to the north from Moderator Wharf (the boats of Rowe or Wallace), Tredegar Wharf (Haines', Edwards' or Richards' boats) and Bristol Packet Wharf (Ann Prosser's boats).

These were journeys for the staunchest and most determined only for it took ten hours down to Newport and fourteen back up to Brecon with only one redeeming feature and that was the stretch of canal along the Blorenge slopes, which in summer gave incomparable views across the Usk Valley.

It was only a matter of time before even the vastly improved docking facilities of the port began to show inadequacy.

The ironworks and coal mines had increased production tenfold and the communication systems were busier than ever envisaged. Many more barges were needed on the canals and there were nose-to-tail wagon trains on the tramroads. Although Trevithick's first steam locomotive had made its test run in 1804, it was not until 1830 that a regular service, making a record two trips a week from the heads of the valleys, was seen on Newport's tramroads. All this added to the congestion on the River Usk wharves whose own efficiency was often impaired by the waywardness of the tides.

The solution was obvious. There was desperate need for additional berthing facilities, preferably in still waters; to this end an inland dock, unaffected by tides, was promulgated by a consortium consisting of a Mr Jones, R J Blewitt, Mr Blakemore and Samuel Homfray. The Newport Dock Bill received assent in 1835.

Tuesday, December 1st 1835, found the town in a state of great excitement and fervour; by midday several hundred people were gathered on the site of the new dock. At 12.15 pm, to the accompaniment of St Woolos Church bells, several salvos of gunfire and loud cheers from the massed townsfolk, the mayor, Mr John Owen, took a brand new spade and cut the first sod to commence operations that were to take six years to complete at a cost of £200,000, raised by shares and loans.

There is no record of how much work was done on that first day because, in honour of the occasion, the navvies were allowed to broach several free casks of the Castle Brewery's best ale and the scene was set as if a fair was taking place!

The site chosen was an area east of the Pillgwenlly canal basin, on the wasteland formed in the great bend of the River Usk. It required some degree of filling as it was still very much below the level of the highest tides, but at least this was something of an advantage where the actual dock had to be excavated.

Access to the site was a big problem for the hundreds of workers involved. 'Pill Road' (Commercial Road) was even then, 25 years after its commencement, a dangerous, pot-holed road, littered with piles of rocks, having steep drops down the sides and completely unlit at night. On the other hand, the canal towpath was narrow, often blocked by working horses, and totally unsuitable to take large bodies of men to and from their work, especially during the severe winter conditions of 1835, 1836 and 1837. It so happened however that the workers themselves sorted out this difficulty and in so doing became the unwitting architects of a new road that otherwise might never have come into existence.

127

After negotiating the filthy household slops and refuse thrown into the roadway at Canal Parade, Club Row, Poplar Row and Fothergill Street, the workmen ignored the canal towpath to their left and Commercial Road to their right, and blazed a trail straight up the middle, across the unballasted marshland. Once this route had been established, artificially tamped down by the daily tramping of a thousand boots, the first spoil excavated from the dock was laid to raise the track on to an embankment level with the canal, the tram road and Commercial Road. This then was how the great Dock Road came into being - unplanned, unsolicited and never to have its own official opening ceremony!

In 1817, one solitary building was erected in the depths of the Pillgwenlly marsh, near the canal. It was placed there for the benefit of both canal, dock and river wharf workers so it comes as no surprise to learn that it was a public house. The first of Newport's several well known canal-side taverns, this was the Union Inn and it was not unexpected that the dock builders' 'private' road should make a bee-line for a place whose cheery, lighted windows guided them to their workplace during the darkest hours. The northern end of the new dock was just the other side of the canal. with access over two small angled bridges.

Older generations of modern Newportonians who knew this location as 'Octopus Bridge', may not also be aware that the Riverview Club, standing on the opposite side of Lower Dock Street, was previously the Richmond Hotel which in turn occupied the approximate site of the old Union Inn.

During the construction of the new dock it was necessary to move nearly 140,000 cubic yards of earth which was spread around the surrounding area. It was probable that Prothero's Wharf disappeared beneath this inundation, causing the canal to end at Kings Parade. From start to finish it was a mighty operation of back-breaking labour, every shovelful of soil removed by human endeavour in hundreds of horse-drawn loads.

On several occasions work was suspended because of abnormally high tides that swamped the huge excavation. In 1837 there was a flood and a serious land slip, whilst in the winter of 1840 nearly the whole of Pillgwenlly, except for the canal and tramroad embankments, was under water! Drainage, drying out and repairs added considerably to cost.

Eventually, in 1842, the finishing touches were added by Messrs Rennie, Logan & Co., the last of several contractors, and the project was pronounced ready for the grand opening. The whole complex, including warehouses and wharves, covered 24 acres of which 4½ acres were water.

On Monday, 10th October 1842, the town was agog. The streets were full at an early hour as the crowds gathered to watch the inaugural procession that was starting from Caerleon where the Chairman of the Dock Committee, Samuel Homfray, now lived at Glen Usk House. All those who wished to join in were instructed to fall in at Duckpool Lane, and by the time the procession was passing through the town it was a mile long!

The streets were a riot of colour with flags and garlands at almost every window-sill. It was a scene of celebration such as had never before been seen in Newport. Everyone rejoiced, bands played, cheering was tumultuous and the whole parade one of great pomp and style, made all the more of a spectacle by the grand, bedecked coaches of the dignitaries, the prancing horses and the liveried coachmen. Leading were the Mayor and his Corporation, followed by the mace bearer, Newport Police and contingents from all the various clubs and guilds headed by their banners and flags. Next came the carriages of the Tredegar family, and the Lord Lieutenant of Monmouthshire with his bodyguard in brightly hued uniforms.

At 10 am, with everyone assembled at the Dock and the tide almost at full flood, the watergates slowly opened. The clamour recommenced, the guns roared, the band struck up, the cheering resounded and a line of ships entered what was at that time the most extensive, man-made area of inland dock water in the world, capable of accepting the largest, ocean-going ships.

The first ship in was the 800 ton Newport barque 'Great Britain' owned by Joseph Latch, a recent town mayor, and fated to be lost only six months later (30th March 1843) in a fearful Mid-Atlantic storm.

Those first-user vessels, berthed at their various wharves, were thrown open to the hundreds of curious 'landlubbers' and the dock water gates were closed against the receding tide.

Celebrations continued all that day with boat races on the River Usk and a regatta in the new dock. At 5 pm there was a banquet in the Kings Head Hotel for all the dignitaries, chief among whom were the Mayors of Newport and Cardiff, the High Sheriff, the Lord Lieutenant, Samuel Homfray, Sir Charles Morgan, Colonel Whittingham (Army), Captain Foote (Royal Navy) and representatives of the Church.

Town Dock 1842

At the Town Hall a grand ball was held. Over 180 guests danced the night away to the music of the Cheltenham String Band. Other celebratory functions were held all over the town, at the old Masonic Hall, the Foresters, the Oddfellows and many other clubs. A huge beacon was lit on Twynbarlwm and brilliant firework displays erupted in Park Square (for the children) and at Rodney Wharf (for everyone).

The results of this great engineering construction were more effective and far-reaching than its innovators could ever have hoped for. In the first year of operation, 12,033 tons of iron were shipped, and in the next four years this had increased to over ten times the output of all the ports of Great Britain a century earlier! It was however no time for counting chickens or resting on laurels.

Cardiff's annual output in 1846 was lagging 130,000 tons behind that of Newport, but in the matter of only a few years was able to leap ahead by reason of the greatly increased docking facilities provided by the Marquis of Bute. Newport's progress was maintained at the same rate year after year until its fine new dock was simply unable to cope. It therefore became necessary to expand the wharfage, and in 1858 an extension of nearly 8 acres was dug out to increase the total surface water area to over 12 acres.

These works lasted for over two years, cost £77,000 and when completed the great basin extended from Dock Parade almost to George Street. The opening ceremony took place on 2nd March and was graced by the presence of Brunel's famous ocean liner 'The Great Britain'.

As was usual, a public holiday was declared, celebrity dinners were held all over the town and the night sky exploded in a dazzling display of fireworks!

Old Town Dock 1991

- 0 -

By 1864, Newport's sea trade had again become too great for the dock's capacity and it did not require much forethought to realise that with the vast resources of mineral wealth lying north and west of the town, and the growing frequency of the arrival of much larger ships to collect that wealth, the continued prosperity of the port depended more and more on its not being left behind in the dock accommodation stakes.

The much vaunted, inland haven that had been the pride of Newport only 20 years earlier, was now too small! According to the 1851 Census, the town itself was larger than Cardiff, exceeding its population by over 1,000 and its accommodation by 200 dwellings. If the expansion was to continue, greater wharfage for shipping had to be provided, and for this reason, in 1865 with Parliamentary powers having been obtained, Lord Tredegar formed the Alexandra Dock Company. At the ceremony on 28th May 1868, Lady Tredegar cut the first sod. The celebratory parade contained 15,000 people and, spread along its three quarters of a mile length, were eight bands!

For several years afterwards adverse circumstances threw serious doubts upon the wisdom of the promoters. Soon after the commencement of the project a deep trade depression set in, triggered off to some extent by the end of the Franco-Prussian War. For five successive years there was no increase in shipments, and coal exports actually decreased each year. The erstwhile boom centring around the new dock began to waver, displaying a marked lack of confidence by its backers and an increase in reluctance to invest further. Funds ran out and work was suspended.

It was at this point that Sir George Elliot MP entered the arena. An indomitable powerhouse of a man who lived locally at Belle Vue House, Cardiff Road, he was a co-founder with Lord Tredegar of the Alexandra Dock Company. The shrewdest of business brains and the intuition of the expert financier, coupled with the ability to retain perfect composure in any crisis, caused him to invest further large sums unhesitatingly, and to charm others, including Lord Tredegar, into doing the same. In this way confidence in the Dock programme was revitalised and the brakes came off completely when Sir George made known his further plans for a scheme to open up coal-bearing districts to which Newport had had no previous access. The Pontypridd, Caerphilly and Newport Railway was about to be born!

The period of construction had extended over seven years but, at last, on 10th April 1875, the new dock was opened by the Mayoress, Mrs Benjamin Evans, in the absence of Lady Tredegar who could not leave the side of her dying husband. Pressure on an electric switch caused the sea gates to open and three ships, the 'George Elliot', 'Lord Tredegar' and 'Lady Tredegar' sailed in to make a circuit of the great expanse of water.

A public breakfast was held in the Victoria Hall (afterwards the Lyceum Theatre and now the site of the Cannon Cinema, Queens Square or Bridge Street, to give it its correct address).

Digressing slightly, it is felt worth mentioning a topographical oddity of this district that may have the effect of clearing up some confusion later on. It has been known by a variety of names as the years have rolled by: Baneswell Square (Overseers of the Poor Rate Books), Victoria Square (1836 Survey), Tredegar Square (various street directories) and Queens Square (modern but colloquial).

The annual Mayor's banquet (for which the Mayor had to foot the bill out of his own pocket!) created either a gastronomic paradise of over 40 rich food items or a disgusting display of waste and gluttony - depending from whichever side of the social fence it was viewed. But the Alexandra Dock banquet surpassed all!

On occasions such as this, Victorian gentry liked to be indulged almost to an immoral degree. There was always a large crowd outside the building that played host to the sumptuous affair, enviously watching the elegantly attired gentlemen and their bejewelled wives as they descended from their carriages. Many of these onlookers, possessed of pinched and sickly countenances, little realised that the objects of their admiration were about to sit down to a feast that would have fed the poor and hungry of Newport for a year!

The menu was a work of art;-

Soups
Real turtle (clear), Oyster, Boars head or Julienne.

Main Courses
**Mayonnaise salmon, Spring lamb, Tongues,
Lobster salad, Fowls and Béchamel sauce, Roast fowls, Turkey a la
Royale, Roast duckling, Braised beef, Ham decorated, Forequarter of lamb,
Turkey.**

Desserts

Blancmange, Madeira jelly, Trifle,
Charlotte a la Russe, Raised pie of pigeon,
Raspberry cream, Tipsy cake, Meringue, Lemon jelly, strawberry
cream, Hothouse grapes, biscuits.

From this glittering function the Mayor sent a telegram to HRH The Prince of Wales:-

'The Mayor of Newport has the honour, most respectfully, to inform His Royal Highness, The Prince of Wales, that the Alexandra Dock, named after Her Royal Highness The Princess of Wales, has just been successfully opened in the presence of 40,000 people of all classes, and amid the universal rejoicings of the inhabitants of Wales'.
Within two hours came a reply:-

'The Prince of Wales, Sandringham, to the Mayor of Newport, Victoria Hall, Newport Mon.

'I thank you very much for your telegram and I congratulate most heartily the inhabitants of Wales on the undertaking'.

Thus the famous name of the Dock was established and renowned world-wide; but all was not yet over!

The 28½ acres of water were contained in a space 2,500 feet long by 500 feet wide. The entrance lock was 350 feet long and 65 feet wide, with a depth of water over the outer sills of 35 feet for spring tides and 25 feet for neap tides. The various gates on the lock were worked by hydraulic power supplied by twelve sets of engines. Three electric lighthouses provided illumination.

On the western side of the dock were eight hydraulic hoists with weigh-bridges and high and low level railways. The loaded trucks traversed by their own momentum an incline at each hoist, terminating in what was termed a 'cradle'. Each truck was weighed before entering the cradle ; it was then raised, tipped and the empty truck, instead of descending to the level it originally left, stopped midway, was turned into a siding and ran downhill again by its own weight into another siding. Coal shipment was therefore a continuous process with empty trains forming as fast as full trains arrived. On other quays there were powerful hydraulic cranes for the loading and shipping of the rest of the business of the Dock Company - iron ore, timber and grain.

A graving (dry) dock , 515 feet long, was added in 1878 with an adjoining iron foundry, boiler-making shops and large fitting and repair shops, the best equipped of their kind in Britain. In 1879, a timber float for the storage of timber in bulk, was opened. This was 2,600 feet long and 150 feet wide, and on excavation was found to be the graveyard of a thousand year old, possibly Danish, sailing ship.

Not long afterwards, an unfortunate disaster marred the reputation of the great dock. In 1882, two steamers, the Constantine and the Primus, entered the entrance lock together and promptly became jammed tightly against each other, immovable between the side walls. They remained like this for a fortnight, trapping 65 other vessels inside the dock! All their owners claimed large sums in compensation from the Newport Dock Company.

132

A south basin of 20 acres was added and opened in 1892; soon afterwards the area was increased to 95 acres, and it became necessary to identify the old and new water surfaces, separated by a swing road bridge, as the North and South Alexandra Docks. So far the, the total length was 1,500 feet, width 640 feet and the average depth 30 feet. The entrance lock was now 503½ feet long and 72 feet wide.

The trade expansion and good fortune that all these works allowed the town to enjoy, was truly phenomenal and is expressed in the following table and notes which refer only to the original Old Town Dock

	1843	1874
Number of Vessels entering	148	1,380
Registered Tonnage	36,712	421,772
Tonnage of coal shipped	32,575	490,835
Tonnage of iron shipped	12,033	131,914

Newport Alexandra dock entrance

In 1875, the first year of operation of the Alexandra Dock, coal shipments alone from Newport were 983,474 tons increasing over the next ten years by 235% to 3,290,980 tons, and of this, 2,225,434 tons went through the new dock!

With regard to shipping, 1,043 vessels representing 365,367 tons register, entered the dock in 1876; by 1885 this number had risen to 2,006 ships of 1,248,862 tons register. On this point it is interesting to note that in the former year, there were only 63 steamers of over 750 tons but by 1885 the number had become 700!

In 1906, the General Manager of the Alexandra Dock and Railway Company said 'As compared with the huge liners that now visit Newport, we can afford to smile at the appellation *'leviathans of the deep'* which was given to the then considered monsters which entered the newly constructed dock in 1842'.

The final extension added another 75 acres. The year, ominously, was 1914 and the contractors, Messrs Easton Gibb of Westminster, employed 2,800 men, day and night for two and a half years, When finally completed the dock contained 130 acres of deep water. The new entrance lock was the biggest in the world, measuring 1,000 feet long in two compartments of 600 and 400 feet. Two huge timber jetties curved out across the foreshore on either side of the great, outer entrance gate; one was 750 feet long and the other 450 feet, to facilitate the handling of vessels docking early or late on tide.

Lord Tredegar's steam yacht 'Liberty' brought Prince Arthur of Connaught (the first Royal visitor for centuries) to the Alexandra Dock for its official opening on 14th July 1914.

Chapter Eight

The Chartists

'The whole physical force agitation is harmful and injurious to the movement . . . All this hurry and haste, this bluster and menace of armed opposition can only lead to outbreaks and to the destruction of Chartism!'
William Lovett
National Chartist Leader.

John Frost was a man dedicated to the achievement of ideals which, for his day and age, would have seemed unthinkable. He was a man of the people, concerned only for their welfare and quality of life, but his growing hatred of the privileged classes engendered a fanaticism that often blinkered his judgement. Many of his ideas possessed genuine merit but he all too often made accusations that he could not substantiate, charges which earned him heavy fines in the libel courts and one six month prison sentence. Up until 1835 he campaigned unceasingly by letter, by broadsheet and by public speaking, against Corporation misuse of the burgesses' property and funds.

The ordinary people loved him; he was reckless and headstrong but he was always on their side and said what they liked to hear, even if the facts were often generously embroidered with exaggeration!

When he stood in 1835 as a candidate in the first council elections under the Municipal Corporations Act, his popularity among the masses made it a foregone conclusion that he would obtain a seat and this he did in no uncertain manner - by topping the poll! Then, in the most powerful position he could ever have expected to hold, on equal terms with the most influential men in the town, John Frost, displaying all his old impetuosity, unleashed the full fury of his tongue and his pen on his council colleagues. It did not help when six of them, the ones he mistrusted most, were straight away made aldermen!

Almost everyone else on the council was decried for an obsession in 'what we can be paid for this or what we can be paid for that!' and for being rich men, elected by the power of their money and having no interest in the poor. He denounced the 'so-called gentlemen of Newport who have very little pretension to antiquity of family!'

There was undoubtedly more than a grain of truth in his rantings but Joseph Latch, the first co-operative mayor in 1835, took personal space in the Monmouthshire Merlin to reject these accusations, and to state that many eminent citizens would testify to the fact that he had often offered to serve his term of office for no salary at all!

The 'blue' party argued that it would be better for the borough to have gentlemen in charge who were 'possessed of the rateable property, because they were more likely to watch carefully over the expenditure, and to prevent all unnecessary taxation of the inhabitants.'

John Frost vehemently rejected this line of reasoning, saying that such was not supported by the facts anywhere where rich men ruled, and he quoted the National Debt, the East India Debt, Corporation Debts and Turnpike Debts. 'All is debt!' he thundered and went on to point out that every one of these debts was contracted by rich men; a great part of the money was borrowed and kept by those who borrowed it, foisting the repayments off on those who could ill afford them, 'and we are told that rich men are the more fit to manage our affairs!'

John Frost's birthplace: The Royal Oak Inn, Thomas Street

On another occasion, in quieter vein, he said:-

'I hope we shall see many young men of Newport distinguished for their knowledge, for their eloquence, for their public spirit, for their hatred of repression; that we shall see them taking the lead in public matters and employing their acquirements for the good of the community.'

Two men in particular bore the brunt of his consuming passion. The one was Thomas Prothero, Town Clerk for 29 years, County Treasurer for 26 years, High Sheriff and Justice of the Peace; the other was Thomas Jones Phillips, a fellow councillor.

Prothero was born in 1780, in humble circumstances in Usk. Trained as a lawyer, he was in Newport only a short time when fate and a certain amount of luck contrived to draw him to the attention of Sir Charles Morgan of Tredegar. His work for the noble baronet combined with a natural fawning attitude, caused his rapid rise to become the Agent to the Tredegar Estate, a position of great prestige and authority that Prothero milked to the full. In 1807 he became Town Clerk of Newport and in the exercise of this and his full-time occupation he obtained further approbation as the Agent to the Kemys Estate, Deputy Recorder, Treasurer of the Caerleon Charity, Deputy Sheriff of Monmouthshire, Clerk to Newport Harbour Commissioners, Turnpike Commissioner, Chairman of Newport Gas Company, Magistrate and, in 1846, High Sheriff of the County. As well as being a fully practising solicitor and banker, he was a ship-owner and if some references to him by John Frost were to be believed, an ironmaster and coal owner to boot! It was no wonder then that this exceptionally busy man should amass a great fortune and live in such grand houses as the Friars and Malpas Court!

John Frost was in no doubt that sharp practice, inside information and hard-hearted manipulation of his power over the Tredegar Estate tenants, was the basis of Prothero's good

136

fortune and he took every opportunity to malign him as the archetype of all oppressors of the working classes.

Thomas Phillips was another product of a poor home. His father had been a labourer in the Ebbw Vale Ironworks; it was probably a delusion of grandeur that led the son to lay claim to descent from Sir Davy Gam of Agincourt fame. Because he was a partner in the firm of Thomas Prothero he was tarred with the same brush in the eyes of John Frost. Little did Frost know then, that in a few short years he would face Phillips in the major confrontation of the century!

John Frost had no patience with such men and brewed up within himself enormous frustration at their inflexibility and rooted prejudice.

Strangely enough, he was his colleagues' choice to be Mayor of Newport - only his second year in office - and his conduct in this elevated position left nothing to be desired in dignity and decorum. He was also honoured by being made a justice of the peace but, due to his radical ideas and Chartist associates, he was threatened by the Secretary of State, Lord Russell, with the removal of his name from the register of magistrates. His reply was in such impudent terms that the threat was carried out!

If it was in the minds of those who chose him as mayor that the greater responsibility would have some long term calming effect on his turbulent nature, and produce in him a more passive approach to his civic duties, it did not work! The end of his year of mayoralty saw the uncaging of the same, intransigent beast.

The next phase of John Frost's career has been the subject of intensive analysis, documentation and debate over a century and a half. Any serious student of the man s life, his aims and ambitions, may take a choice from hundreds of sources, many of which have been described as 'wishful claptrap' and in so doing, receive numerous contrasting opinions based upon the interpretative judgements of his biographers to whom he could be hero, villain or a mixture of both. It is probably more appropriate to speak of him as a man of his time, misplaced in time.

The great Reform Act of 1832 promised so much but delivered so little to the poor working classes who were fully expecting some relief from their miserable lot. For many years they had been suffering untold hardships in the squalid hovels, lacking all basic amenities, in which their employers forced them to live.

Surprisingly, wages were not an issue in the 1830s, they were quite generous but were totally absorbed in the factory 'truck shops' where workers were compelled to pay inflated prices or lose their jobs. These shops had been made illegal in 1831 but the South Wales ironmasters and coal owners seemed able to operate theirs with impunity.

As some measure towards improving these conditions, it was widely expected that the working man would get a larger share of the franchise and consequently more representation in Parliament. Instead, the vote was extended only to men owning property with a worth of £10 (a substantial sum in those days). Effectively therefore, only the middle classes became enfranchised. Overwhelming disappointment gave way to bitterness and anger when the poor realised that the means of obtaining reforms through the ballot box was still withheld from them.

A group of better educated, working class radicals formed themselves into the London Workingmen's Association, with the avowed aim of uniting the oppressed working force into a formidable opposition. In 1838, the Association published the People's Charter and thenceforth all members became known as Chartists. The six points of the Charter were:-

The vote to be given to all men over the age of 21.
Voting to be by secret ballot.

There should be 300 constituencies, each of an equal number of electors.

Parliamentary elections should be held every year.

The ownership of property to be abolished as a qualification for membership of Parliament.

Members of Parliament should be paid.

These points were all perfectly reasonable except the fourth, which by any standard of intelligence was completely impracticable. It would be impossible to prepare for a general election every 12 months, and to expect each Member of Parliament to vacate his seat before he had hardly warmed it would have resulted in no government at all!

The London Association sent out missionaries to every part of the country to teach Chartist theory, and the accent was always on peaceful persuasion. Leading Chartists in England, such as William Lovett and John Collins, had never believed that there was a violent answer to the achievement of their aims.

The man whose task it was to convert Monmouthshsire was the 25 year old Henry Vincent, who wandered far and wide in the county addressing huge open air meetings and enthralling his audiences with his startling eloquence. He was not a Welshman but a London born Northerner who the people of Monmouthshire took to their hearts, especially the ladies because of his handsome looks and the fact that he held strong feminist views.

This 'Young Demosthenes', as he was labelled, followed the Association's peace policy assiduously but his firebrand type of oratory, whilst quietly drawing the doubting moderates into the fold, had the opposite effect on the violent faction and only inflamed their demands for stronger action. When he was really in full flight, Vincent often described the ruling classes as 'drivelling idiots and contemptible, insidious knaves!'

It was inevitable that he and John Frost should become good friends, just as it was inevitable that the latter should embrace Chartism as the vehicle that would carry him to the fulfilment of all his dreams.

In Newport, Chartist lodges were established in public houses such as the Parrot and the Bush in Commercial Street, where meetings were held under the fanatical William Edwards known as 'the mad baker,' and the secretaryship of Samuel Etheridge, whose printing shop was thrown wholeheartedly into the production of Chartist propaganda.

In August 1838, the great Charter, reinforced by over a million and a quarter signatures, was presented to a Parliament that promptly rejected it. This led to disturbances in many parts of the country -nothing however that worried the authorities unduly. Following this setback, the extreme partisans in Monmouthshire renewed their activities in conversion and subversion, and despite valiant efforts by the recognised Chartist leaders to play down the feelings of bitterness, the rabble rousers in the valleys began to gain the upper hand.

Due to address a meeting at Pentonville on the evening of 25th April 1839, Henry Vincent issued a printed handbill exhorting the people : 'Keep the peace - I charge you. The slightest indication of tumult would afford our enemies the pretext for letting their bloodhounds upon us!' Wise and prophetic words indeed!

For some time the authorities had been sabre-rattling; Chartist lodges were raided, meetings broken up and speakers prosecuted. According to John Frost, the special constables and the magistrates who made up the raiding parties were consistently drunk on duty and savage in the use of their truncheons. It was only too easy to become an unwitting suspect and innocent people were caused to suffer in this way.

There is in existence a remarkable document signed by 71 employees of the Cordes Dos Works and dated 2nd May 1839. Apparently it was produced to deny allegations that firearms and other weapons were being manufactured in the works. What is remarkable about this document is that although put together at a time when few ordinary working men could write, there are not many signatures represented by a cross and all others display legible handwriting!

With tension increasing and affrays becoming more frequent, authority decided that it was time for stronger action. On May 7th, as Henry Vincent was addressing another meeting in Newport, he and several others were arrested, charged with unlawful assembly in breach of the peace, and committed for trial at Monmouth Assizes.

A few weeks earlier, Capel Hanbury Leigh, the Lord Lieutenant of Monmouthshire, had seen signs and received information from various sources, including Thomas Phillips the Mayor of Newport, that led him to believe that an armed insurrection was a growing possibility. Taking no chances, he requested Parliament to send a company of troops to the town. On 10th May, a detachment of the 29th Regiment arrived by ship from Bristol. It comprised one field officer, two captains, four subalterns, a surgeon, seven sergeants and a hundred and five other ranks. The commanding officer was Major the Honourable C.A.Wrottesly. There was not yet a barracks in Newport so the troops were billeted in the new workhouse which was only 12 months old, near St Woolos Church. A month or so later this contingent was withdrawn and replaced by just over 70 men of the 45th Regiment.

News of Vincent's arrest spread like wildfire from lodge to lodge and from valley to valley. If it was the idea of the authorities that taking the Chartist leader out of circulation would quench the fires, they soon found out that the opposite was the case! Driving the cause further underground only had the effect of stirring up the ferment.

The anti-Chartists of the county, and in particular those of Newport, had set up a fairly comprehensive system of secret agents and informers in the Chartist strongholds. Samuel Homfray was a member of Newport Town Council, owned Tredegar Ironworks and at that time lived in Bedwellty House in the heart of the simmering trouble spots. He employed hundreds of men and his company financed a Tredegar police force so he was in an excellent position to maintain a network of informers, recruited from loyal employees who could mix freely in conspiratorial circles. Thomas Prothero too was receiving regular confidences from his own group of paid agents.

Stories were soon arriving of the secret collection and manufacture of weapons of all kinds. Mysterious packing-cases were delivered to Newport and were immediately spirited away to the north. Evidence was afterwards discovered that they contained guns from English firms. At iron foundries as far apart as Pillgwenlly and Ebbw Vale, pike blades were secretly forged and sold at a shilling each. There were hints of dark caverns on the high slopes of Mynydd Llangynidr, above Beaufort, with strange lights seen bobbing across the mountainside after dark. It is said that one of the caves used as an armoury was named John Frost's Cave - complimentary no doubt for there is no evidence that he ever ventured that deeply into these wild regions.

Henry Vincent and William Edwards were sentenced to twelve and nine months respectively, and two other members of Newport Working Men's Association to six months, to be served in Monmouth Jail. Intelligence leaking back to the authorities suggested that an attempt to liberate them was imminent. As it turned out, no such attempt was made but it is certain that Vincent's incarceration supplied the spark that lit the fuse of revolution!

The final chapters were written in meetings that took place as, autumn turned to winter, in the chief Chartist public houses - The Bush at Newport, The Coach and Horses at Blackwood, The Bristol Beer House at Pontypool and The Red Lion at Tredegar. The pieces of the great plan were put together; individual tasks and duties were detailed, strategy and timing worked out and targets defined. But what did it all add up to? No one afterwards owned that he knew precisely what those targets were nor that he was sufficiently informed to have been able, in an emergency, to undertake the responsibility of his immediate superior. The leaders were notorious for not sharing confidences with the rank and file, and anything committed to writing was destroyed before it could be used in evidence.

Certainly a grand march on Newport was favourite - but what then? If a successful occupation took place the full wrath of the Government would fall upon the insurgents and then there would be no hope of reaching Monmouth to free Vincent. If that act were to be done it should be done first, but no move was made in that direction.

There was talk of stopping the mail leaving Newport so that its non-arrival in Birmingham would signal a successful Welsh uprising and cause the Midlands to follow suit: this was fantasy and John Frost, Newport born and bred, was sure to have known it.

The coach carrying the mails only went as far as The Passage at Beachley where its contents were transferred to a ferry crossing to Aust. The non-arrival in Bristol of the Welsh mails would not have delayed the departure of the Midlands mail coach! In any case, there was not so much evidence that the Midlands Chartists were as keen on outright rebellion as their Welsh counterparts, and were often heard to say at their lodge meetings that it was far too early for such drastic methods!

The destruction of Newport Bridge? To what purpose? To trap the Chartists in their own fortress and so frustrate the other suggestion of a march on London? Or did they intend to make the march, 'burn their bridges behind them', and so cut off their retreat should it be necessary? Then again, who would feed such a multitude once the cheese sandwiches that they carried in their pockets were gone?

Of all the alternatives the last was the most preposterous. If the intention had been to head for the Capital recruiting support along the way, Henry Vincent could testify to the fact that there was little sympathy for Chartism in Somerset, Gloucester or the Home Counties because only the previous year he had made an unsuccessful tour of those areas!

It must not be forgotten however that the Monmouthshire Chartists were counting on starting out with at least 20,000 men! Their ultimate aim was, to say the least, very vague. The moderates like John Frost and Samuel Etheridge probably agreed that a massive, shoulder-to-shoulder demonstration of the working man s need - nay demand - for reform, would further the Chartist cause as nothing ever had before - but it had to be, above all, reasonable and peaceful. It was the basis of real Chartism that cool and calculating petitioning would carry the day!

Zephania Williams even pleaded with his followers, the men of Dowlais, Tredegar and Ebbw Vale, that when the time came they should not carry weapons, but he was overruled and had to settle for a promise that arms would be for defence only.

John Frost was now regarded as the principal Chartist leader in Monmouthshire, but he must have realised that it was fast becoming a position of doubtful authority as the moral force faction started to be outnumbered by the disciples of physical force. He still held doggedly to the misguided belief that in his hands had been placed the means to lead the poor man out of his humiliation and the working classes to a higher plane where they would have a greater share in deciding their own destinies. However, his time was running out; control was slipping away; it was nearly the time of reckoning for the fiery dragon that he and Henry Vincent had unwittingly let loose. The fateful first weekend in November 1839 drew nigh!

At one last secret meeting in the Coach and Horses at Blackwood, the Chartist leaders put the finishing touches to the great plan of action which they felt would sound the clarion call to Chartists everywhere and would administer such a shock to the Government that it would have to take more seriously the complaints and grievances of the working classes.

It was decided that Newport should be marched upon by a mighty show of (it was confidently hoped) some 20,000 protesters. The date originally set for starting out was Monday 4th November but for some reason it was brought forward one day. In any case, a steady stream of information gave Newport's mayor the knowledge that the invasion could be expected at any time. Now it was only a question of when his forward patrols sighted the vanguard of the approaching host.

The Chartist army was trained to advance with almost military precision, in columns down the valleys, disciplined by training officers who had served in the British Army and one who had fought with the Texan Army in the war against Mexico. The columns consisted of brigades of 500 men, companies of 165 men each with its own company commander, and sections of 10 men with their own captains in charge. The first companies, leaving Blackwood and comprising men of the Sirhowy Valley were led by John Frost, draper, ex-mayor and ex- JP of Newport. At Newbridge they should have been joined by the men of Brynmawr, Nantyglo and Ebbw Vale under the leadership of Zephania Williams, Chartist moderate, eschewer of violence, ex-mineral agent of the Sirhowy Ironworks and landlord of the Royal Oak Beerhouse – or was it the King Crispin of Brynmawr as mentioned in the reward notice which later appeared in the Monmouthshire Merlin?

Leaving Pontypool, heading the men of Blaenavon and the Eastern Valley, was William Lloyd Jones, watchmaker, tub thumper extra-ordinaire, stirrer of passion and erstwhile actor who made every entrance and affected every gesture as if he were still on the theatre stage.

Sunday, 3rd November 1839 dawned grey, heavily overcast and, as evening approached, settled in to continuous rain that emptied down in torrents. Some were to say that it was the worst weather of the year and that, in itself, portented evil for the events of the night. To begin with, thousands of expected supporters did not turn out, preferring to remain in the secure warmth of their little cottages, no doubt reassuring themselves that they would hardly be missed. During that Sunday afternoon and evening, impress parties roamed the towns retrieving less enthusiastic Chartists from under beds, inside cupboards, from attics, from cellars, out of church and chapel and even from the arms of spouses! Many refugees fled up the hillsides and across the moors, intending to return after the march started, although they had been left in no doubt of the dire consequences that they risked.

What was more, the quality and determination of a large portion of those who did march needed to be called into question. By all accounts the small nucleus of dedicated, politically minded men who made up the marshals, captains and section leaders had extreme difficulty in exercising discipline over a large number who, despite the appalling weather, appeared to set out as if on an outing. A large number were drunk at the start and continued to drink through the night by forcing every inn along the route to open its doors; just as numerous were those who confessed sheepishly to researchers in later life that they were 'only along for the fun of it and any loot that was going!' Not one man among them then imagined that within a few hours he might be dead, badly injured or faced with a charge of high treason!

The innocents along the way came in for some rough treatment; ladies silently watching the procession from cottage windows or doorways were subjected to embarrassing remarks and rude gestures. Any able-bodied men who chanced by, on their way home from chapel or tavern, were seized and frog-marched away within a circle of pikes. Those who protested most and struggled hardest were beaten, stripped and tossed into the canal!

All through that black, tempestuous night the rain was relentless but the columns kept moving down valley road, tramroad and towpath, the men like drowned rats, fatigue taking its toll in every step and morale sinking fast. It was only the shouts of encouragement and the urging onwards by the stoutest hearts that kept many of them on their feet. Sheer courage, stamina and comradeship were in ample evidence that night, but it was not enough!

Dreadful mistakes were made by the leaders; on-the-spot decisions, unforeseen in the forward planning, drastically altered the course of events and, above all, the atrocious weather played havoc with time schedules and rendezvous agreements.

In Newport, preparations were being made to meet the growing menace to law and order. The plans of the Chartists were not known for a certainty but it was obvious that the town's tiny police force of one superintendent and three constables was pitiful in the face of the expected horde. Therefore, 500 special constables were sworn in by magistrates and issued with truncheons. At first only 150 were called out; 50 were placed in the Westgate, 50 at the Kings Head and 50 at the Parrot which was serving as a temporary police station. No call was yet made on the military.

During the course of the day and evening, the specials were active in challenging groups and individuals who appeared suspiciously on the dripping streets when most stayed indoors. It was no secret that there were already many Chartists in the town and anyone who could not give good account of himself was detained in the Westgate. It was among the specials that the first casualty of the day occurred, hours before the marchers crossed the borough boundary. Mayor Phillips, anxious for more up to date information, dispatched two volunteer constables on horseback towards Risca. They were ambushed by a Chartist forward patrol but managed to escape; one of the two men, Thomas Walker, licensee of the Parrot Inn, sustained a stab wound of such severity that he was lucky to stay in his saddle until he reached safety!

Walker himself presented one of the many imponderables for which this conflict was noted: why, if he was the landlord of a public house and meeting place used by the Chartists, was he a volunteer risking his life in a force hell-bent on their defeat? Could he have been one of the double agents who kept the authorities supplied with up-to-date information on the Chartists' latest moves?

Things were not going too well for the men from the mountains. Timing was now badly amiss. Zephania Williams and about 2,000 of his Blaina men had been kept on the slopes of Mynydd Carn-y-cefn in a steady downpour for over three hours, waiting for the men from Ebbw Vale. At 2 am he was only at Llanhilleth when John Frost's columns were already at the Welsh Oak in Pontymister. They all should have been there at midnight, preparing for an assault on Newport while the town slept.

Far too much time was wasted by hundreds of trained men in scouring for deserters and shirkers - there were far more of these than staunch Chartists would admit; the weather made it doubly difficult to clear each tavern when a halt was made; and then there were the fatal errors of judgement made by the leaders in order to deal with the changing conditions.

John Frost was responsible for the most damaging of them but he was, at 1 am on that dreadful Monday morning, clearly out of his depth in the role of a general commanding somewhere in the region of 5,000 troops, many of whom were still miles away, struggling down pitch black valleys in severe storm conditions!

Just after midnight he was in position at the Welsh Oak with enough men to have surrounded the St Woolos workhouse-cum-barracks, effectively bottling up the whole of the 45th Regiment, and then to have taken the town and held it until his main force arrived. Instead. he chose to wait for six hours.

Zephania Williams arrived at about 4 am but only a small contingent from Pontypool put in an appearance.

It seems that William Jones had reached Malpas Court in good time to find that Thomas Prothero and his family (proposed kidnap victims) had flown. From this point Jones sent his first company on to the Marshes Tollgate, up Penylan Lane (Barrack Hill) to rendezvous with the Western Valley men at the Cefn. The rest of the advance Pontypool companies were ordered by Jones to remain at the Marshes Gate while he went back to Croesyceiliog to hurry along another brigade of 500 men. None of these men took any further part in the rising, and were still at Malpas at 10.am when the first fugitives from the battle fled through their ranks.

At 8.30 am on Monday 4th November 1839, Mayor Thomas Phillips finally felt that the position was so serious that the intervention of the military was called for and he sent an urgent message to the Workhouse. Within minutes, Lieutenant Basil Gray, two sergeants and twenty eight other ranks quick-marched down Stow Hill and were hidden in the front rooms of the Westgate Hotel behind closed shutters.

At 6 am John Frost gave the order to advance, and hundreds of cold, sodden, bedraggled miners and ironworkers dragged themselves from rooms and outbuildings of the Welsh Oak, barns, ditches, hedges and anywhere that gave the slightest shelter. They were cheered at once to find that the weather was improving and the sun making spasmodic appearances. As they made their way from the Cefn to Bassaleg many of them presented sorry sights. The men from Dowlais for instance, had been on the road for as long as 13 hours and those among them who were over 70 years of age had to be supported by the young!

They were running so late now that the important 'underground' Pillgwenlly group, whose job it was to capture a dockside warehouse filled with gunpowder and who failed to receive a prearranged signal, all went home to bed under the impression that the march was postponed. By the time they rose in the morning all was lost!

The Chartist attack on the Westgate Hotel, November 4th 1839

The packed ranks of John Frost's brigades moved across Tredegar Park, following the tramroad, under a forest of pikes, scythes, iron bars, axes and long barrelled guns. At Courtybella, by way of the steep inclines of the Waterloo trip and Belle Vue Lane, they finally reached the top of Stow Hill where they made their way warily past the St Woolos Workhouse, recently built in Bull Field, with the occupying soldiers watching in silence. John Frost had often made speeches in which he optimistically assured his audiences that the Chartists had nothing to fear from the military because they were sympathetic to the Cause.

It was this misplaced faith that made some of the braver elements in the passing mob invite the soldiers to join them!

Near St Woolos Church, the march halted for the platoon leaders to organise the ranks into some semblance of order, pikes in the centre, guns on the outside, and then the descent began.

Meanwhile, Mayor Phillips had already read the Riot Act from the steps of the Westgate Hotel, but at 9.10 am, when the first massed ranks of the marchers swung round to face the hotel, all was locked, barred and shuttered. The troops were well hidden although by this time it seems certain that the Chartists had learned that they were there and were not over-awed by such a small presence.

They had also found out about the prisoners held in the hotel's cellars and a shout of 'Yield up the prisoners!' echoed around the square. No satisfaction being given to this demand, a party of men with axes began hacking at the doors and during these ugly moments a gun was fired outside. No one is sure who pulled the trigger or why, but there is a favourite story of an over-zealous special constable making a lunge for a Chartist musket which was accidentally discharged in the struggle. Whatever the cause, it had the effect of inflaming the situation and in minutes a cursing, heaving melee filled the hotel's hallway and passages.

More shots were fired, the special constables retreated up the stairs and Mayor Phillips, standing his ground, received wounds to his arm and hip. He was dragged through the open door from the hallway by the soldiers who fired a volley into the passage, killing several intruders and blowing off the finger of one of the axemen!

Some say that the Mayor over-reacted, but in his painful, blood-soaked condition it does not seem surprising; he had after all only just been saved from receiving a death thrust when a soldier shot the pikeman dead. If that were not enough, in the murky, smoke-filled hallway, another soldier had mistaken him for a rioter and had been prevented at the last moment from shooting him by a sudden shout from a sergeant!

Say what one will, the Mayor's order to the soldiers to open fire was given under the most extreme and bloody provocation, and what followed is generally accepted as the saddest event in Newport's history. Today, opposing factions regard it either as the most glorious or the most shameful!

The shutters were raised on the front bay windows and the crowds in the square were raked with a devastating fusillade of rifle fire. Lieutenant Gray afterwards affirmed that of the 22 rounds issued to each man, an average of three each were fired. The result was instantaneous stupefaction and incredulous anger. The pikemen were still fighting furiously in the passage-way when those outside recovered from their confusion and horror sufficiently to press home another attack; this wavered and broke before a further withering volley from the windows. About 25 minutes had passed since the fighting started and now, as though at a given signal, a great cry arose all around Westgate Square and the assault party of two or three hundred men scattered and ran in any direction that offered escape, leaving the roads littered with their weapons! Some raced back up Stow Hill, meeting Zephania Williams and his men on the way down. He was difficult to persuade that the Chartists had been defeated in such a short time and he tried to rally the running-scared rebels but was forced to retreat with them.

At the Marshes Gate the Pontypool men, still in fixed position, met groups of the fleeing rioters and turned with them to make a speedy exit from the town.

Back in Westgate Square, when the gun-smoke cleared, a most ghastly spectacle was revealed. Dead and dying rebels lay in widening pools of blood all round the front of the hotel and in the hall and doorway. Some were hideously wounded and as they crawled about, crying pitifully for assistance, they shocked the small groups of onlookers who, ghoulishly, had gathered to see some boisterous action never bargaining for the cruel scene of slaughter that materialised!

The soldiers emerged from the hotel and combining with the rest of the regiment and the special constables, commenced a systematic search for and pursuit of everyone involved in the insurrection.

Some were hidden in the town by Chartist sympathisers who took in wounded and able-bodied alike. Many were struggling back the way they had come but keeping off the beaten track which was alive with their hunters. Dozens were apprehended cowering in barns, beast-houses, garden sheds and outside bog-houses as far afield as Bassaleg and Caerleon. Two at least managed to reach America, but most arrived back at their homes either the next evening, later in the week or even months afterwards, as in the case of those who, undetected, took passage to Bristol on one of the regular packet boats.

Despite earning the reputation of the worst riot of the 19th or 20th centuries in terms of violence and number of fatalities, the defence force of Newport suffered remarkably few casualties. Besides the Mayor, several soldiers were wounded; Mr Samuel Hallam, the owner and keeper of the Westgate Hotel was slightly hurt together with some of the special constables - three of them suffered so badly that they were granted pensions of £20 per annum. for life!

Mr Mullock, the eminent Newport artist and brother of the founder of the printing business, had set himself up in a room over a shop on the corner of Skinner Street, overlooking Westgate Square. He was hoping to catch the action on his sketch pads but from the first volley of shots a stray ball ricocheted around the room and grazed his top hat. He beat a hasty retreat!

Nine men lay dead in Westgate Square and another was found nearby. They lay there all that day, the soldiers not allowing anyone to approach, but at nightfall the bodies were spirited away to St Woolos Churchyard and buried in an unmarked grave.

It was impossible to calculate the total fatalities but a conservative estimate at the time was that another ten or twelve Chartists died on their way home or in their homes. At least fifty wounded were scattered around Beaufort, Tredegar and Ebbw Vale. Samuel Homfray learned the names of several but there is no evidence that he divulged his knowledge to the authorities. Other reports indicated that at least a dozen backroom amputations took place.

John Frost was in the leading rank as it wheeled round in front of the Westgate, but as the first shots cut down the assault leaders he was quick to make a bolt for the side streets. As already pointed out, Frost was essentially a man of peace, and to find himself in the front line of a bloody battle was more than he could bear. For a short while he hid in a tram on the outskirts of the town but after ten hours he was captured.

Acting on information, a squad of special constables under the leadership of Mr T J Phillips, magistrates clerk, went to Gold Tops, to the house of Thomas Partridge the Chartist printer (Samuel Etheridge s assistant). There they found John Frost, as one account put it: 'a weeping wreck,' or in the words of another: 'eating a hearty breakfast,' but nevertheless armed with three pistols, a flask of powder and a large quantity of balls and percussion caps.

William Jones of Pontypool was arrested in a wood at Crumlin a week later after holding off his pursuers with a pistol.

MR JOHN FROST,
CONDEMNED TO DEATH FOR HIGH TREASON,
Jany 8th 1840

John Frost in Monmouth Jail, January 8th 1840

Zephaniah Williams, who had last been seen in Tredegar Park 'weeping like a child', managed to evade capture for three weeks, hiding in the woods around Caerphilly. He was finally caught in Cardiff at 3 am on 23rd November, asleep in a berth on a ship just about to sail to Portugal.

On 13th January 1840, at Monmouth Assizes, the three principal leaders of the armed rebellion were found guilty of high treason and three days later were sentenced to death by hanging, drawing and quartering.

A doubt was raised as to whether a list of witnesses for the prosecution had been delivered to the defendants' counsel within the legal time limit of ten days, and indecision on this point caused the sentences to be commuted to transportation for life. This was probably the wisest course for the authorities to take, after being persuaded that the execution of such prominent Chartists would be likely to lead to more widespread outbreaks of violence, or even a general uprising.

At the preliminary examination of prisoners in the Westgate Hotel ten days after the bloody affray, many outraged citizens of the town and from along the route of the march, came forward to identify and to give evidence against the rioters. Among the accused were John Frost's 16 year old son, Henry (discharged because he was not carrying arms), and John's uncle, Edward Frost (bound over to keep the peace). Many others who were positively identified as having taken part, received varying terms of hard labour, and even those who could not be implicated but who could give no satisfactory explanation for their presence in the town, were given sentences for vagrancy.

Without being given a last meeting with their families, the three leaders were smuggled out of Monmouth Jail at midnight on the Sunday following sentencing, and escorted by six Metropolitan Policemen and 24 soldiers of the 24th Lancers, were driven to Chepstow to take ship for Portsmouth. There, the sailing ship 'Mandarin' was waiting to carry them to Van Diemen's Land.

Over the years, several huge petitions were presented on their behalf but it was not until 1854 that they received conditional pardons, whereupon John Frost went to America. In 1856, when full pardons were granted, he returned to his homeland and as he set foot on Rodney Wharf he found a tumultuous welcome awaiting him. Horses were unhitched from his carriage and he was drawn through the streets by his old comrades.

The Mayor at that time, Mr Charles Lyne, informed his Council that on 25th May 1857, John Frost had presented to him his full pardon signed by Queen Victoria and had requested that his name be replaced on Newport's list of freemen who could vote in parliamentary elections. Mr Lyne said that on investigation it was found that the old rebel's name had never been erased from the list. The Council's instructions were that John Frost should be told that provided he spent the requisite amount of time in the town, his name would be retained on the list.

He was last seen on the streets of Newport on Election Day 1868, and by sheer mischance his appearance coincided with another entirely unconnected, localised riot .in which the military was involved. On July 28th 1877, in Bristol at his daughter's home (and he had had seven children) he died at the ripe old age of 93. For all his actions and the vicissitudes in his life, he must have obtained the utmost satisfaction in the knowledge that he had outlived all those who had contrived his downfall, especially his arch adversaries Thomas Prothero, Thomas Phillips and Mr Justice Tindal who presided at his trial.

On 23rd November 1839 the Monmouthshire Merlin carried the news of the conferral of a knighthood on Mayor Phillips, and very soon after that, quickly recovered from his wounds, he was called to Windsor to receive the honour from Queen Victoria for the courageous part he had played in the defence of Newport and, by implication, of the Realm.

A letter dated 19th February 1840, conspicuously bearing his signature on behalf of the Corporation, was sent to Queen Victoria offering congratulations on the occasion of her wedding to Prince Albert. In highly ingratiating fashion, it contained paragraphs like the following:-

'When menaced by a recent insurrection directed to the subversion of your Majestys lawful authority, that authority was supported by the inhabitants of this Borough with a zeal and loyal devotion which in every period of our history has characterised the affection for their princes of the natives of this portion of your Majesty's dominions . . .'

Of course, when the letter talked of 'the inhabitants of this Borough', those self same inhabitants knew that most of them were receiving credit for something in which only the Mayor, thirty soldiers and a handful of policemen had taken part.

Charles Cavendish Fulke Greville was the Court Diarist of the time, and in his celebrated 'Memoirs', he was quite specific about the treatment of Charles Phillips when he went to his investiture. Apparently it was the intention of the Queen's closest advisers to let him collect his knighthood and then hurry him off back to Newport as a mark of the little regard they had for his low station and the treason in which his town had been involved. Wiser judgement prevailed however, and the doubters were persuaded that it would be good for the Queen to be seen encouraging others to do their duty, by heaping Sir Thomas Phillips with civilities and sending him home in triumph.

Even Thomas Phillips himself admitted that there seemed to be some confusion and unpreparedness for his reception. In letters written by him afterwards, he states that he was informed that the sword used in his investiture was the Coronation Sword of George IV - never before used for such a purpose! The traditional sword was the Sword of the Gold Stick in Waiting, but someone had forgotten to procure it for this occasion. Hurried consultation obtained Her Majesty's concurrence to the substitution of the Coronation Sword from the Regalia.

Neither Zephaniah Williams nor William Lloyd Jones ever left Australia. The former, with his knowledge of coalmining, became a very wealthy man from pursuing that line; of the latter little is known except that he died a pauper in 1873. Williams followed him a year later - both in Tasmania.

One who did not fair so well in spite of being on the winning side, was Stephen Rogers, a prominent grocer and provision merchant. His sin was that having volunteered himself as a special constable, he had stood alongside the soldiers in the Westgate Hotel and had been a member of the party which had arrested John Frost. By 1845, vindictive tongues had so defamed and humiliated him, and so coerced his customers into deserting him, that he became bankrupt. For his past loyalty however, he was awarded a post as second clerk in the Custom House, and later he was promoted on the recommendations of Sir Thomas Phillips, R J Blewitt MP, Octavius Morgan and other magistrates.

It would appear that the way in which the business of Stephen Rogers suffered was not uncommon where an owner had shown outright opposition to the Chartists. Several others who gave evidence against the three leaders at Monmouth Assizes, were placed on a black list leading to heavy trade sanctions that took years to overcome.

Many and varied are the accounts given of some aspects of this calamitous rebellion, and one that lends itself admirably to conjecture is that of the bullet-holes in the cast iron pillars of the Westgate Hotel portico.

These pillars purportedly still survive having been preserved and transferred into the new Westgate Hotel when built in 1886. They continue to do their original duty but now inside the entrance instead of outside. Each one has a set of 'bullet' holes, credited to the ragged firing of the rioters into the front door. It is remarkable therefore that some of those rioters appear to have been excellent marksmen who, in a heaving, panicky mob were able to take their time as in a shooting gallery, and carefully place a small group of shots at approximately the same height on each pillar and within a hand-span of each other! It is also noteworthy that all the holes seem to have been made by the same calibre of firearm - puzzling indeed given the hotchpotch of shotguns, muskets, fowling pieces and the like which were loosed off in such a short space of time!

If these were genuine bullet-holes it is hardly likely that they would have been so neatly grouped in the heat of battle, just as it is even less likely that those riflemen outside the hotel would have fired into the backs of their own comrades who filled the passage-way. Could it be that the bullets were fired into these pillars from the same gun at a later date, by some shrewd person with the tourist trade in mind? Or indeed are they bullet holes at all in view of the evidence unearthed much later on?

The truth of the matter appears to be that there was no knowledge in the town of any bullet-holes until 45 years after the battle in Westgate Square! It was then reported that, on 17th September 1884, workmen who were demolishing the old Westgate Hotel prior to its rebuilding, discovered four small, leaden 'slugs' embedded in the original pair of *wooden* pillars (not cast iron!) that they were replacing!

There are many other questions that will never be satisfactorily resolved, in no small measure due to the Chartists themselves.

It has already been established that the leaders kept the rank and file ignorant of long term plans, and the contradictory statements afterwards volunteered by a rare few of the Monmouthshire Chartist hierarchy would appear to confirm that little thought had been given to what lay beyond the immediate future. When the hue and cry was on, the lodges burned all incriminating records and what is not generally realised is that for the lifetimes of those who took part, a stony wall of silence was maintained between father, son or grandson. For this reason there are few wholly reliable accounts.

Why, for instance, did Zephaniah Williams wait for three hours for the men of Dowlais when he already had a sizeable army with which to proceed from Ebbw Vale? And why did John Frost decide to wait for six hours at the Welsh Oak Pontymister, and so lose the element of surprise on a town where the majority slept? Why, also, if he was so against violence and sickened by the sight of blood, did he carry three pistols and ammunition?

What instructions were given to the leading brigade to carry out? Not to proceed beyond the Westgate Hotel? Was its single intention to pack the square and to demonstrate 'peacefully' whilst the watery, morning sun glistened on a thousand intimidating pike, axe and scythe blades? Or were the carefully planned orders changed by those in the front ranks at the last moment?

Why did William Jones prevent the men of Pontypool from proceeding beyond the Marshes Gate and so effectively deprive the rising of a considerable part of its force?

Why was it planned for everyone to rendezvous in one place instead of entering the town centre from three different directions (Pillgwenlly, Stow Hill and Marshes Road) and to ignore the Westgate until all other strongpoints had been secured?

There has always been tremendous room for doubt. Any decisions made, for instance, on that last mile of the march would have been known only to four men in the front rank.

John Rees (Jack the Fifer) who led the final assault, and David Jones (the Tinker) both managed an incredible escape to America and were therefore unable to be interrogated. Williams, the army deserter and Chartist drill instructor, was killed by a shot from Lieutenant Gray's pistol. John Frost was alongside these men until the shooting started and for the rest of his life remained firmly reticent about those final moments.

In 1938, Mr Ness Edwards who was soon to become MP for Caerphilly, produced a document from an anonymous archive, supposedly a letter dictated by Zephaniah Williams to Doctor A McKichnie on board the prison ship Mandarin en route to Tasmania. In this unlikely version of the great rebellion it was stated that the capture of Newport and the announcement of the victory was to be the signal for a mass attack on Cardiff, and for hundreds of thousands of waiting English Chartists to overthrow the Government. The resulting new republic was to have John Frost as its first president!

It can only be construed that this was an example of Zephaniah Williams in cloud cuckoo-land for it was demonstrated immediately after the failed coup that very few English Chartists shared this fantasy.

There are those today who grasp at any straw in order to transform this rashly brave but doomed-from-the-start undertaking into one of the great incidents in Newport's somewhat chequered history, when in actual fact it blackened the town's reputation and caused its innocent citizens to suffer a stigma for many years to come. It is not just coincidence that no occasion could be found for a royal visit for the rest of the century - there was ample opportunity in 1875 but the Prince of Wales rejected an invitation to open the Alexandra Dock, named in his wife's honour!

There is absolutely no doubt in anyone's mind that the concept of Chartism was morally right, but the Monmouthshire insurrection was ill-advised and premature - an opinion in which all the Chartist lodges in Britain were unanimous. The national leaders must have thrown up their hands in despair when the news broke of the rebellion and its terrible ending, for it destroyed overnight any goodwill that was slowly building by passive means.

Sir Edmund Head, Assistant Poor Law Commissioner, toured the district after the rising; he was examining the setting of Monmouthshire Chartism and seeking the deeper reasons that sparked the riot. One of his conclusions from enquiries made in the Forest of Dean, where many rebels sought refuge, was that they received very little sympathy from the colliers of the Forest. The same feelings were encountered among the thousands of Chartists of the Merthyr Valley who were asked to join the great march but refused partly because they were still smarting from the failure of their own bloody riot in 1831 and partly because the Monmouthshire men had at that time failed to come to their aid.

Historians in general award little prominence to the Chartist Riot. Most of them, discussing the movement in depth, give no more perhaps than a paragraph in passing to mention what they refer to as 'the Newport riot' and attach no importance to the incident against the greater background of national Chartism.

Indeed, most of the reference books concentrate on the brutal, infinitely more determined, bloody rioting that took place in Merthyr eight years earlier. More importance even seems to be attached to a more low key disturbance in Birmingham in 1839, when William Lovett was arrested and sentenced to 12 months imprisonment for addressing a rowdy convention!

On the other hand, a few local historians and modern pro-Chartists in particular argue that the vital point of the Charter, concerning the franchise for all men over the age of twenty one, was conceded in the next forty years, and five of the six points in seventy years. This they put down entirely to the stimulus given by the Riots. But the assertion can be made with greater justification that, in a slowly enlightening world, these reforms would have come about in only one generation. The reason why this was not the case can only be explained by this terrible error of human judgement causing authority to close ranks and to become more deeply entrenched against the Movement.

Chartism persisted for at least another decade, proceeding more in accordance with the wishes of the moderates, but in 1848 it received another self-inflicted injury from which it never recovered!

A great petition was again presented to Parliament ostensibly bearing nearly six million signatures. However, close scrutiny revealed that it contained no more than two million signatures and many of these were forgeries! The doubt that this cast on the integrity of the Chartists proved to be as great an 'own goal' as the rebellion itself had been, and the Movement was ridiculed into oblivion!

And at the time that was that!

Succeeding generations were happy and relieved to let the whole unfortunate episode fade from memory. Consensus of opinion for long afterwards was that the rebellion had been a violent intrusion by strangers into the borough, many of them in various stages of drunkenness and with the infernal cheek of not even being Welsh!

It is not without significance that so many eye-witnesses to the passage of the marching men, mention the pillaging of taverns and inebriation that led to unwonted thuggery against dissenters and innocent bystanders along the way. Neither is it a well advertised fact that, in addition to representatives of the dreaded marauding bands of oddly-named 'Scotch Cattle', a high proportion of the rest were English or Irish immigrants and their sons who owed little allegiance to the area and only thinly disguised their contempt for their Welsh neighbours!

Edward Royle in his book 'Chartism' has written:-

'Where the Chartists did resort to violence as at Newport in 1839 and Bradford in 1848, it did little to further their cause. The quest to show Chartist achievement has also led to sometimes a listing of enactments of the later 19th and 20th centuries by which many points of the Charter were granted, but this is fallacious. Those Acts <u>cannot even remotely be attributed to Chartist pressure</u> and the real spirit of democracy which lay behind the points of the Charter remains unrealised even in the later 20th century.'

These sentiments have been echoed over and over again by almost every leading authority on Chartism but to no avail where the die-hards are concerned. It is most difficult to convince them that the Chartists of Monmouthshire were their own worst enemies who played a leading part in the demise of the national cause.

In more recent years, the repugnance and shame felt by Newport's 19th century citizenry has seen a cooling off, and the emergence of a new optimistic view that the Chartist rising was a legitimate part of the town's history, which it undoubtedly was - but for all the wrong reasons! A possible cause for this is that such feelings are born out of a yearning to 'liven up' a lacklustre, historic image in an age where civic pride and a colourful background have become more important than ever to attract attention to the town. A dearth of celebrated occasions simply will not do! A complete absence is catastrophic! Another modern writer in a passing reference to Newport, has called this attitude 'invented tradition' - the gradual acceptance of notoriety as celebrity; the creation of a festival from a funeral!

So, this being the case, what is wrong with choosing the most inglorious episode - the one that briefly put Newport in the national limelight all those years ago - the one that bestowed upon the town the dubious but nevertheless unique honour of hosting the last, great, bloody rebellion to take place on British soil?

One direct result of the Chartist Riot was the decision to make Newport a garrison town, and so the Barracks were built near the top of Penylan Hill which naturally was renamed Barrack Hill. The Barracks were opened on 22nd May 1845 and the 75th Regiment moved from their temporary abode, in a warehouse at Pillgwenlly, 'dressed in their clean summer attire, to the capacious and admirably suited barracks overlooking the town, and apparently pleased at the prospect of country lodgings!'

At about the same time, the Mayor and Corporation took steps to strengthen the town's defences by instructing the Watch Committee to create a permanent special constabulary.

Chapter Nine

The Nineteenth Century

New markets and the Town Hall,
Poverty, Education, Public Health
The Water Supply and the Police Force

In relation to the Chartist attack on the Westgate Hotel, it has been revealed that Mr Mullock was fortunate to escape a close encounter with a musket ball. This was not Henry Mullock who founded the well known printing firm, but his brother, James Flewitt Mullock a talented artist whose work became a valuable chronicle of his times. The Mullock brothers were the sons of Richard Mullock, pipe-maker, and china and glassware dealer, who was to become Mayor of Newport in 1842. He operated a small pottery at the lower end of Corn Street.

James Mullock's paintings, drawings and lithographs have done much to fill in vital details of everyday life in the middle of the 19th century. From them it has been possible to obtain a fair idea of the likenesses of dignitaries, their families, their clothing styles, houses, pets and even the flowers that they favoured in their gardens. His landscapes were useful in showing how Newport was developing - all in all a rich source of historic information.

But James Mullock's creativity was more prolific than was generally realised and it was largely as a result of later 20th century research by Robert Cucksey, Newport Museum's Keeper of Art, that the true extent of the man's industry is becoming known.

Besides his illustrations for newspapers and periodicals which are well documented, the artist was responsible for many grander works in oils and water-colour, and in many cases they depicted something of his native scene. Several of his canvases have been traced to far-flung corners of the British Isles, and one or two much farther afield. Invariably, the owners had only superficial knowledge of the painter or his subject but to the practised eye, background glimpses of Trinity Church, Christchurch, St Woolos Church and other landmarks, were telltale enough.

The talent of James Flewitt Mullock, born 1815 and died 1892, lost its demand with the progress of photography, but while he was flourishing he captured for posterity dimensions of the town that would otherwise never have been recorded.

Surprisingly, one thing that was badly lacking in this busy market town was a market building! Remember that the only place with any such pretensions had been demolished in 1793 and ever since then all market trading had been carried out in the streets, accompanied by the nuisances already described. The Lord of the Manor in 1817 was the Duke of Beaufort and he was apparently much more approachable on the subject of markets than his predecessors had been, for he offered or was prevailed upon to build a new covered market for the town.

The site, purchased for £100, was a piece of land reclaimed by the filling-in of the Town Pill where it neared High Street. It was at one end of the larger site where the present market stands (the High Street end). Constructed in stone, single storied, it was rectangular, measuring approximately 60 feet by 125 feet internally, with entrances from High Street, Market Street and Griffin Street. On the river side it was hemmed in by buildings that precluded the making of another doorway.

Dock Street was not then in existence; Market Street ran into the Old Green and Griffin Street into Upper Merchant Street which disappeared when eventually Dock Street overran it.

By 1850 this market hall had become too small and business once more began to spill over into High Street with recurrence of the old annoyance and aggravation to the permanent shopkeepers. There was also great controversy when the Duke of Beaufort's toll collector tried to insist on market tolls from the street traders on market days.

Both Market Street and Griffin Street emerged into the new Dock Street in 1865 and the Duke extended his market down to this point. It now occupied almost the same site that it does today and had entrances into four streets. This, Newport's third market hall, was purchased by the Corporation in 1885 for £16,500 on condition that a ban was placed on all sales elsewhere than in the market building. Whereas the Duke had never had the power to enforce such a regulation, he knew that the Corporation was able to do so.

Immediate steps were taken to rebuild the old unsightly structure. Surrounding land and buildings were purchased for £8,500; a tender was accepted from a local builder, John Linton, for £13,000 and eventually, at a total cost of £42,000 the fine market that has served the town ever since, was opened on 1st May 1889.

The building was magnificent by comparison with any other in the town except possibly the town hall, and its splendid mien utterly befitted its role as the commercial hub of a thriving municipality. The main frontage to Dock Street in handsome dressed stone, was four storeys high with in-built shops on either side of the grand entrance arch. Above the arch rose an imposing tower of another three storeys, topped by a lead covered, square spire. Similar spires (without towers) finished off the Market and Griffin Street corners.

The central hall was 192 feet long by 145 feet wide, flanked by galleries on three sides and a central one running from end to end. The lofty, glass, barrel-vaulted roof, 53 feet high, was supported on cast iron columns and a network of cast iron trusses. As far as external aesthetics were concerned, the Victorians of Newport never had the full opportunity to understand what an architectural treasure they possessed. Dock Street was not the broadest of streets, and opposite the market stood buildings backed by a miscellany of obstructions to viewing (ships' masts, rigging, wharf sheds etc). Under these conditions the general public were never able to stand far enough back to appreciate the jewel in their crown! The 20th century has considerably enhanced the 19th in this respect. Now, with all the aforesaid impedimenta removed, Newport Market presents an outstanding view from almost any angle that no Victorian eyes could ever have enjoyed. By night, floodlights on the roof add another dimension to the majesty of the old building.

As they wend their way through the well-stocked stalls, modern shoppers, mentally ticking the prices, should spare a thought for their counterparts who, in the brand new market, had to contend with prices like these:

Beef 2½d to 4d lb.		Mutton, Pork Veal	3d to 4d lb.
Geese	1/3d each	Ducks	1/6d a pair
Fowls	1/0d a pair	Potatoes	10d a bushel
Eggs 7 for 3d..		Butter	7d lb.

Apply the modern equivalent of five pence to the shilling, allow for a century of inflation and it is easy to see how hard done by the old Newport housewives considered themselves to be!

Paralleling the problems of the general produce market were those of the monthly cattle market, which for centuries had never had a home of its own. It was held in High Street and stretched from the Heathcock Inn yard (sheep market) by the bridge, to the Westgate, completely filling the roadway with tethered animals, their food and their defecations. For

154

one whole day the area was made most uncomfortable for passers-by; shopkeepers, whose premises fronted the street, objected most forcefully at having to clean the filth from their pavements and gutters under threat of heavy fines.

For years discussions had been frequent on the subject of countering this disgraceful state of affairs. One powerful lobby was in favour of a new cattle market on the town marshes so that very little livestock would have to pass through the main street. Ultimately, the solution was supplied by the Tredegar Wharf Company and an announcement was made by the Mayor to a meeting of the town council on 16th February 1844. A letter from Mr Samuel Homfray, Chairman of the Company, stated that on behalf of the town it was his firm's intention to build a cattle market on company land at Pillgwenlly.

The site is well known today, but in 1844 it was one of those sunken portions of land between Pill Road (the unfinished Commercial Road) and Dock Road. The northern end was to front the newly built Ruperra Street. The perfectly square, 4½ acre site needed many thousands of tons of ballast from ships and other sources to raise the nine feet deep depression to the level of the adjoining roads.

It was remarkable how quickly the primitive but slowly emerging technology of the 19th century achieved its objects - bolstered by thousands of willing hands and strong backs! The laying of the foundation stone by Sir Charles Morgan in March 1844 was soon followed by the opening of the finished market on October 16th of the same year! So Newport acquired one of the finest cattle markets in the British Isles and local people, viewing it for the first time, were lost in wonder that such a transformation from 'barren marsh' (Monmouthshire Merlin 19th October 1844) could have taken place in only eight months!

Several new streets quickly appeared as essential access to the market. There were entrances on each side through Tredegar Street, East Market Street and West Market Street; in the new South Market Street, the old Union Inn was incorporated and thereby ended its long isolation on the canal towpath.

The finely appointed market contained extensive covered accommodation for cattle, with 120 stalls, pens capable of containing 1,500 sheep and 1,000 pigs. In the open air there were pens for 2,000 sheep, 500 pigs and 1,000 cattle. Another generous covered stable, measuring 23 feet by 130 feet, held 18 stalls for horses in conditions befitting the best equine establishments.

In the market's heyday the weekly livestock sales, cheese markets and wool fairs were rated as among the most successful in the land, whilst grand cattle shows drew the attention of agricultural society from far and wide. Even after half a century's wear and tear, the premises were adjudged to be an excellent arena in which to stage the greatest festival of Welsh art and culture. For a week in August 1897, the market was host to the Royal National Eisteddfod under a gigantic canvas pavilion holding 13,000 people - packed to capacity every day!

The market ground also became the regular venue for the great commercial fairs that were held on the second Wednesday in April and August, Whit Wednesday (wool) and Lord Tredegar's annual cattle and poultry shows, reputed to be the largest of their kind in the British Isles.

~ 0 ~

In the first quarter of the 19th century, with all the dramatic upheavals that set the quiet little haven throbbing with energy and equipped it to rival the greatest ports in the world, it is incredible to think that all the great decisions were made in a series of makeshift meeting places.

If one cares to recall the early days of municipal administration, the small councils of Newport were seen gathering in the exchequer chamber, a small room over the South Gate of the castle. Forced by the attentions of Owain Glyndwr to move headquarters to the West Gate Tollbooth, it was not very long before this too became unsuitable; then it was found that the only other rooms large enough to accommodate a full council meeting were in public houses! Thus it was that use came to be made of the Westgate, the Kings Head, the Parrot and the Carpenters Arms ~ the latter becoming the favourite.

Newport Town Hall, Commercial Street 1842 ~ 1884

In later years there was a council room in Commercial Street opposite St Pauls Church, but this was very inconvenient when used as a courtroom because of the distance that prisoners had to be conveyed from the Mill Street Clockhouse.

The whole situation was most unsatisfactory and demeaning when the corporate body of a thriving town had to meet like conspirators in the back rooms of taverns, so at last it was decided that the Corporation should have permanent premises more becoming of its status. Plans for a town hall and police station were accepted: a site was chosen in Commercial Street; building had no sooner commenced in 1838 when the unexpected occurred!

The Home Office stepped in and questioned Newport's right to build a town hall. Counsel's opinion was sought and the verdict was that Newport did not have the right and so building was suspended, leaving the structure, in the words of Alderman H J Davies: 'with bare walls, beams and joists green from exposure to the weather!'

It took four years to sort out the problem but finally, in 1842, for the first time in its history the town possessed its own, purpose-built, seat of local government. The 1850 Directory of the town described it as 'a neat and chaste edifice'.

This would probably have served the needs of a normal community for generations to come, but Newport was not normal. It continued to grow rapidly and by the 1880s, after the opening of the Alexandra Dock, and with its population standing around the 35,000 mark (increasing to 51,000 in the subsequent ten years), it became obvious that the old town hall was too small. The point was driven home when the Home Office threatened to withhold the police grant of £2,000 per annum because of the inadequacy of the police cells and accommodation. There were suggestions that a completely new town hall should be erected on the Friars Fields (purchased in 1860 and cleaned up by the Corporation), but this was rejected on the grounds that it would be unbecoming to the dignity of the town for its civic buildings to be situated in a back street.

The Council finally opted for acquiring additional land at the rear of the existing town hall so that the finished building would have an imposing 61 feet frontage to Commercial Street for the municipal portion, a depth of 106 feet and an equally broad expanse on Dock Street as the police station.

Built of tooled stone blocks in Italian Renaissance style, the town hall, surmounted by its handsome high clock-tower, stood out proud against the skyline that had previously remained unaltered for centuries. Opened by the Mayor, Colonel Lyne, in 1885, it was a credit to its designers and eminently worthy of the town of the future.

For a building of such importance, architectural interest and prominence in the town centre, it became redundant in a surprisingly short time. How values have changed! Its planners would have been shocked to learn that in a mere eighty years or so, their proud showpiece would give way to a block of shops and offices, and would be replaced by a resplendent Civic Centre in what they would have looked upon as a 'back street'.

~ 0 ~

One of the nation's more execrable problems, to its shame increasing despite the vast wealth that the working classes were helping to pour into their masters' pockets, was that of poverty. The situation was mirrored in every community and Newport had more than its fair share.

The great majority of the population was poor, and an unacceptable percentage of this majority was destitute with no other way of staying alive than by begging or thieving. Any relief that these unfortunates received was as much a question of luck in avoiding the stocks, the whipping post or prison, as of finding themselves living under an authority that cared enough to supply even the most rudimentary and primitive succour.

Passing the buck was the order of the day. Reluctantly it seems the town would look after its own from a fund which was supervised and eked out in the most niggardly fashion; anyone who could not prove entitlement by reason of being or having become a burgess, would not be accepted as a liability on the poor rate and, under the harsh Settlement Acts, could be ordered back to his original place of settlement to become its responsibility. This method of shunting from parish to parish has already been described and there is a record of the Newport magistrates ordering one poor individual to be frog-marched all the way back to Blyth, Northumberland!

The title given to the person responsible for the collection and dispensation of the poor rate was the Overseer of the Poor. In Newport prior to 1801 the position was considered to be so lacking in esteem that it was unpaid and consequently, being such a burdensome and thankless task, was inefficiently performed. Besides the relief of destitution, it included the suppression of vagrancy, mending roads, destruction of vermin and the 'furnishing of soldiers and sailors!'

Nobody would volunteer for such a job but no option was given. Overseers were elected by rotation of the 'best' housekeepers or inhabitants, and none was allowed to do it again until the full rotation was completed. Unpaid the job might have been, but it was still possible to profit from it in small but devious ways. Apparently for some time, someone was

157

subsidising his drinking habits because, on 20th October 1794, the Council made an order forbidding the supply of free liquor on the occasions when the overseer was working on his books; only the rent of the room used as an office was allowed as an expense.

In 1819, an act of Parliament made mandatory the appointment of salaried overseers of the poor, although Newport had been paying one voluntarily since 1801 when William James was hired at ten guineas per annum.

Bookkeeping it appears was not a qualification too highly demanded of the early overseers. The poor relief books were supposed to contain complete lists of those paying and those receiving, but prior to 1800 were sometimes non-existent or else poorly kept and seldom audited. In 1806 the overseer, Mr Bird, could not be made to present proper accounts, was judged to have misapplied the funds and was sacked.

Some time between 1784 and 1805 the old free school building in Commercial Street was converted for use as a poorhouse to be maintained by the parish. Several rooms and apartments were added to it. Most of its inmates were paupers but it was also quite common practice to included a few idiots and lunatics. They were expected to work when they could, and several prominent business men profited from the very cheap labour supply. In later years many were employed by Samuel Etheridge, the Chartist printer, in the printing and distribution of propaganda leaflets.

The Poorhouse became so overcrowded in 1810 that it was necessary to evict many of the inmates. How they fared is not recorded.

If it was not degrading enough just to be a pauper, the authorities heaped on the indignity by insisting that all those on relief should wear a badge of scarlet cloth to broadcast their humiliation. Needless to say, this shameful rule was too much to bear by many who continued to ignore it.

Duties of overseers included the award of monies for clothing, medical attention, tools of the trade and the five pounds fee for apprenticeship. Many of these payments were considered to be money well spent as they enabled paupers to carry on or take up a trade, and to go back to work when cured of illness, thus ceasing to be a drain on parish relief.

It was recorded in 1782 that William Mathews was set up in business by the provision of a basic kit of tools (trade unspecified), and in 1793, Mrs Roswall was able to hold up her head again when she was given a new spinning wheel. The reason why these two examples survived in writing when there must have been numerous other like entries in various poor rate registers, might owe something to the aforesaid doubtful quality of the early 19th century bookkeepers!

Three doctors, Hawkins, Brewer and Fox did well out of the poor rate as later entries in the accounts for referrals would appear to indicate.

There was a long register of the occupiers of tenements in the Friars Fields slum, and one whose name appears there was Evan Ricketts with a pencilled footnote, 'the bully with the broken beak!' What success the overseer had in his collection here can only be left to the imagination!

After 1835, the newly created Municipal Corporations had to take the subject of poverty much more seriously and were given statutory powers to raise the necessary taxes. The first direct sign of this in Newport was the large, new, purpose-built workhouse opened in 1838 near St Woolos Church. We have already learned that its first inmates were the soldiers brought in to quell the Chartist Riot.

A world apart, at the other end of the social scale, an entirely different life was experienced, and the Newport Reference Library archives contain an illuminating example of this.

A workman, renovating an old building in Commercial Street in 1950, uncovered a bundle of papers which proved to be a small selection of bills and accounts for the household of Joseph Latch, wealthy business man, owner of ships and coal mines, and twice mayor of Newport.

Mrs Latch's haberdashery bill with the Cambrian House from August to December 1835 was £16-9s-3d and for the same period in 1836 £20-2s-7½d. For these very substantial amounts the good lady purchased: 2 tuscan bonnets at 25 shillings each, 36 pairs of white cotton hose for a total of 4 shillings and 3 pence, 2 to 3 pairs of shoes each month, dozens of yards of silk, velvet, bombazine, linen, crepe, muslin, cambric, cotton, ribbon, flannel, chinchilla boas, pelisses, handkerchiefs, buttons, pins and hooks-and-eyes!

For the same period, Mr Latch's accounts seem to have been restricted to his tailor only, and amounted to the grand total of 8 shillings and 2 pence for repairs to cloak, trousers and waistcoat!

Before departing completely from the subject of Newport's have-and-have-nots, it is worth mentioning another intriguing piece of historic chicanery, not entirely unconnected, and in this case linking the 15th century with the 20th when it was finally laid to rest with no hope of resolution and entirely to the advantage of the rich and privileged.

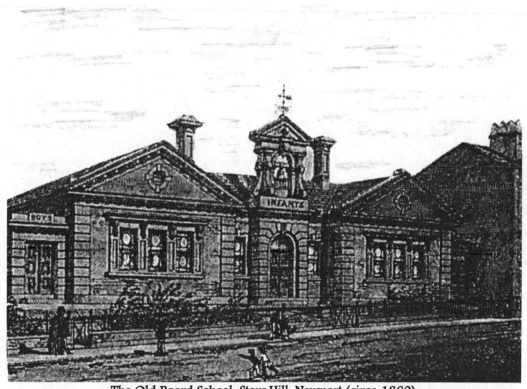

The Old Board School, Stow Hill, Newport (circa 1860)

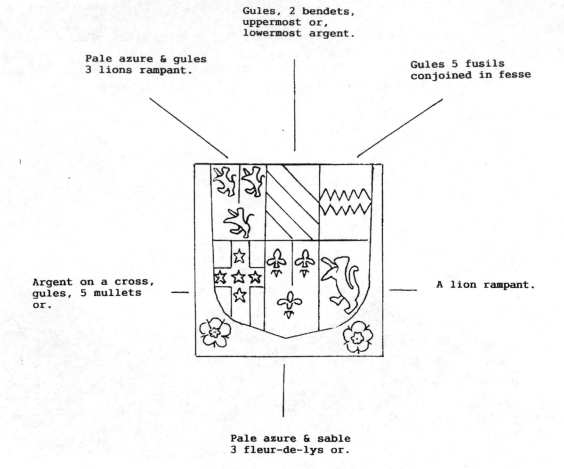

Gules, 2 bendets,
uppermost or,
lowermost argent.

Pale azure & gules
3 lions rampant.

Gules 5 fusils
conjoined in fesse

Argent on a cross,
gules, 5 mullets
or.

A lion rampant.

Pale azure & sable
3 fleur-de-lys or.

The Herbert Shield of Arms

In the year 1410, with Newport still shocked and floundering in the wake of the mindless damage inflicted by Owain Glyndwr, the Earl of Pembroke (the original De Clare title) made a substantial gift to the poor, bewildered inhabitants. Half way up Stow Hill he caused to be built a House of Refuge for the poor and homeless, and a free school for their children. The building itself was a fact although there must be some doubt about its use as a school at a time when education for the extreme lower class was unheard of and , in Newport, was to be nearly four hundred years before other philanthropic gentlemen began to think along these lines.

The Earl's arrangement was that his Poor House should be maintained out of income received from the adjoining land which he donated in perpetuity to the burgesses of the town.

In those days, Newport was divided into individually named areas all of which were specified in the 6th Earl of Stafford's Charter of 1427 when the town boundaries were first prescribed. Kyngeshull was the one involved in this case, known in the 17th and 18th centuries as Kensal Lands and ultimately bequeathing the name to the large old house, Kingshill, which now shares its ground with Bishopstowe, 91 Stow Hill. The early history of the old house is shrouded in mystery - even the Church in Wales who owned it for most of the 20th century, never found out, but it is known that for a time in the very early years of the 19th century, it was occupied by Jeremiah Homfray, brother of Samuel and owner of the Ebbw Vale Ironworks.

Anyway, the old Earl's gift did not offer all that much because the land consisted mostly of open fields, although today it is some of the most valuable real estate in the town centre. A document held in the National Public Records Office refers to 'My lands called Kyngeshull' and records an area of between 180 and 210 acres. This is now partly contained within the circle of roads from Charles Street to St Woolos Church, down Vicarage Lane, through Clytha Square to Mountjoy and thence along Commercial Street back to Charles Street.

By the 18th century, the income from Kingshill was so small that there was a real danger of the House of Refuge ceasing exist, so in 1762 the Morgan family of Tredegar offered to defray its costs in exchange for whatever returns the land gave. There was never any suggestion of the land being sold or legally transferred to Charles Morgan, but by 1794 Tredegar Estate records were claiming outright ownership.

The 1800 report of the Newport Overseers included an invoice for £111-9s-5d paid to several contractors for repairs to the old building and this caused a heavy rate of six pence in the pound to be levied on the town's inhabitants - proof positive that at that time the Tredegar Estate was no longer honouring its obligations under the agreement made with the borough in 1762.

John Frost was constantly at odds with the Morgans, regarding them as archetypal of the rich landowning classes that he disliked so intensely, and in 1836, the year of his mayoralty, he made a bitter speech in the council chamber on the subject of the Kingshill enigma, accusing the Estate of acquiring by stealth, land which belonged to the people of Newport by right of the Pembroke bestowal of 1410.

Unfortunately the investigation was not followed through, either by John Frost's Corporation nor for that matter by any of its successors over the next 70 years. It was not until 1912 that a more enlightened town council, less hamstrung by feelings of awe towards the local aristocracy, ordered a new enquiry. But it was too late! The Town Clerk's report of 9th December 1913 concluded that by allowing so much time to elapse since the original accusations without any action being taken, the town's right to the land remained unproven and that 'laws come to the acceptance of the vigilant not of the sleepy' was the lesson to be learned from this episode!

The old House of Refuge remained on 'the site at 69 Stow Hill until well into the 20th century, serving several purposes but latterly as a reception centre. Today, the cleared plot of ground is a private car park but entry is still by way of an ancient, walled archway, above which can be seen the time-worn, badly eroded stone crest of the 1st Earl of Pembroke.

- 0 -

Until the first decades of the 19th century, education of the young in Newport was hardly considered to be worthwhile, except in wealthy families who could afford private tutorship. Buildings to which children of the lower classes could resort for lessons were almost unheard of, although here and there a few learned men possessed of rare humanitarian spirit, offered to share their knowledge without thought of reward for their trouble.

The story has already been told of Newport's gift from the Earl of Pembroke in 1410, of the building on Stow Hill to be used as a house of refuge and a free school. No more was heard of such an educational establishment until 1650 when the Commonwealth Parliament's Act of Propagation made provision for a free school in the town. This is probably the one next mentioned in 1711 when the great overhaul of Newport's by-laws took place, and arrangements were made for the school's maintenance out of local taxation; fifty years later an old town map was still showing the building on Stow Hill designated as a free school.

In 1774 the Overseers received an order to execute a warrant 'to levy the same for rent due to the tenement belonging to the Freemen of Newport commonly called the Free Schools'. Sometime after 1784, the Stow Hill property reverted to its original use as a poor house and the last known home of a free school was a building opposite St Pauls Church in Commercial Street. This too was eventually converted back for use as a refuge for the poor.

Ignorance and illiteracy were widespread and, all through the ages, maintaining this situation had been one way in which the rich held sway over the poor, believing as they did that educating the masses was as good as sewing the seeds of revolution against themselves.

The skills of reading, writing and especially numeration had for long been those for only the clergy or the nobility to acquire, and anyone else showing such talent was viewed with deep suspicion. After all, not so much time had passed since literacy was used as evidence against women in witchcraft trials!

It was however Newport's great benefactor, Sir Charles Morgan of Tredegar who once again displayed his family's munificence and, turning his attention to this problem, he decided that the time had come for those of his class to help spread knowledge among the poor of future generations.

A movement had been growing, fostered in the North and Midlands, to provide 'Boys British Schools' wherever the need was shown to exist, and where the desire of the populace was strong enough to presuppose the success of such ventures. When Sir Charles gave his patronage and a subscription of £100 to such a school in the town, suitable premises were found at the Old Green and the first Newport Boys British School opened its doors on 28th March 1815, just as armies were gathering all over Europe to begin their fateful marches to a tiny village in Belgium named Waterloo.

Initially, 133 boys of all religious persuasions were accepted, from six to twelve years of age, and they were taught the three basic 'Rs' together with a fourth - religious instruction. By 1831 this school had admitted 1136 pupils.

The school's upkeep depended upon the generosity of its wealthy patrons and on the children's fees, but it was a sign of the times that parents were either very apathetic towards their children's education or else found the fees difficult to maintain for any length of time.

162

This sorry state of affairs can be illustrated in the fact that from the 1830s to the 1880s a child's total attendance at school varied from only three months to twelve months, the latter period being a rarity!

It was the custom for patrons to make an annual examination of the boys - a wise, monitoring move but probably with the underlying motive of making sure that donations were not being wasted. On such occasions, Sir Charles Morgan together with representatives of the local gentry and their good ladies, gathered in the schoolroom to carry out the tests. More often than not they were complimentary about the children's progress, their cleanliness and the neatness of their clothing. At the end of the session, a mountain of mince pies would be produced as a reward for the boys' efforts and they would proceed to demolish it with gusto!

The first girls school presents something of a mystery. In the minutes of a council meeting dated 19th July 1819 a grant of £20 was recommended for this school 'in honour of the coronation of King George IV'; but King George III did not die until 29th January 1820! Details of this school, its premises and where situated are not recorded.

It was in 1828 that a British School for Girls opened in Llanarth Street, run on the same financial terms as the Boys School and redressing the unfair prejudice towards the education of young working class females. In charge was a highly skilled teacher from the well respected Borough Road School in London. The school premises were not ideally situated for young ladies, finding itself hemmed in by beerhouses and standing on the edge of the 'Devil's Half Acre' of the Friars Fields, but the school examiners were highly satisfied and caused a doubling of orders for mince pies from Peter Napper's Bakeshop on the corner of Thomas Street.

Another early Newport school, promoted by the National Society for Promoting Education of the Poor (founder, the Reverend Dr Bell), was the National School. The Town had one each for boys and girls. However, in contrast to the British Schools, the situation of their buildings was a matter of uncertainty until they found permanent homes in 1840.

The opening of the new Workhouse at St Woolos in 1838 made redundant the poor house in Commercial Street; Sir Charles Morgan purchased it for £550 and presented it for use as a combined National School for Boys, Girls and Infants. Following some adaptation and refurbishment, the 190 feet long building accepted its first pupils in 1840 and served the town well until its final closure in 1897.

A Commission of Enquiry into the state of education in Wales, set up in 1847, found conditions in Newport's National School far from satisfactory, due mainly, it was said, to the soft approach of the master. Of him the report stated scathingly:-

'He was unable to cope with the ruffian class of children who seemed to come and go as they pleased, learned next to nothing and kept up a constant counteraction to discipline. They chalked all over the doors, threw their caps about and fell into scuffles whenever the master's back was turned.'

The Old Ragged School, Mellon Street 1863

The Old Ragged School, Mellon Street, 1970

By this time, according to Scott's History of Newport, other schools in existence were a Catholic Day School, a Lancastrian (British?) Boys School at Canalside, and eleven private schools including several boarding schools. In addition there was the small Poor Law School on Stow Hill and a Church of England Middle Training School for more advanced scholars in Dock Road.

Sometime later, groups of employers began to think along similar lines in regard to their own workers' children, and they set about providing schools, usually inside the factories. Cordes Dos Works was a typical example and its school is discussed in a later chapter. In 1857, a prize-giving system was introduced by these industrialists with awards for good attendance and progress in learning. A total of £70 was allotted to be distributed in annual prizes of £2, £1 and 5 shillings.

There were still however, hundreds of children in Newport who, because of their parents' abject poverty, received no schooling at all, and it was for these unfortunate little mites that the 'Ragged School' was created. Another group of philanthropic gentlemen, and one in particular - Mr James Jones, teacher - opened the school in a large room at the rear of the Sunderland Inn, 31 Llanarth Street, although according to the 1861 Census it was in Union Street. It catered for about 300 boys and girls and sometimes as many as 450. Even allowing for a high incidence of absence through sickness and truancy it must have been a large room indeed!

In only two years this school was in trouble due to lack of financial support, but a public appeal resulted in the building of new premises in Mellon Street at a cost of £450. A separate ragged school for girls which opened in 1860 in Queens Street, off Cardiff Road, was integrated with the boys school and they all moved to the new building in 1864. The original school building still stands on the corner of Dock Street and Mellon Street in a smart livery of painted cement rendering and large plate glass windows more in keeping with its modern use as offices. If it were not for the inevitable external wall plaque it would not be possible to identify it as having such a place in the town's history.

The superlative moment for these poor, sad youngsters was on the magical day at Christmas time when they attended their classroom to find awaiting them, large helpings of roast beef, plum pudding, the inescapable mince pies and bags full of sweets to carry home!

All these establishments and the new Maindee British School which opened in 1867, together with several church and dissenters' schools that had been formed along the way, formed the basis for Newport's educational system until the Education Act of 1870 swept away dependence on charity and gave the Government the responsibility for providing free primary school education. It was from that time forward that the typical Victorian brick, stone and slate school buildings with their distinctive little bell-towers and open-air toilet blocks, started to make their appearance all over the town. Many have now gone, but of those that remain, some are derelict awaiting demolition, some given to other uses but one or two can be found still performing their original function.

- 0 -

'When typhus or cholera breaks out, they tell us that nobody is to blame. That terrible Nobody! Nobody adulterates our food, nobody supplies us with foul water. Nobody spreads fever in blind alleys and unswept lanes. Nobody leaves towns undrained . . .'

Samuel Smiles 1889

Over the centuries, scant regard had ever been given to the organised treatment of illness. The first suggestion of any building provided in Newport specifically for this purpose was that of a 'spittehouse' in Corn Street. This appeared in King Henry VIII's 1547 Survey of Newport and it may have been referring to an outlying building of the Austin Friars where the monks cared for the poor, the starving and the sick.

Heavy reliance was placed on the monasteries in this respect; they absolved the town authorities of the responsibilities and the cost of any form of health service. This of course all ended with the dissolution of the monasteries and from then on, ill health was a matter of the utmost gravity.

It was not until 1839 that the first voluntary movement was started in Newport. It took the form of a dispensary for the treatment of those who were too poor to pay and who were not eligible for poor relief. At a time when infected filth lay about the streets , drinking water was heavily polluted and vermin and rabid dogs roamed freely, the need for some form of improved health care was becoming absolutely essential.

A clearer idea of the horrifying conditions that were the root cause of the town's unspeakable sanitary and health problems can be gained from examples given in a report for the year 1850.

Not one of the houses on the east side of Commercial Street had a sewage connection but merely drained all types of effluent into the low ground alongside the canal to form a permanent, foul-smelling mire. Properties on Stow Hill poured their sewage under raised pavements into open roadside gutters. The thirty tenements of Charles Street included several poor lodging houses, sublet into terribly overcrowded apartments - one of five rooms held thirty persons! Many of the lodgers were rag-and-bone merchants who kept piles of their unsavoury stock in their rooms! There were at least forty-four similar lodging houses in Newport, housing from four to forty-nine persons!

The Friars Fields needs no further comment having already been more than adequately dealt with!

Seventeen slaughter houses helped to enrich this over-ripe atmosphere and, over one short period, the so-called Sanitary Committee made a concerted effort to effect the removal from one part of the town, of the accumulated filth of over 9,000 people!

166

Makeshift premises for healthcare in Llanarth Street were used until 1847 when the Dispensary transferred to 17 Dock Street where it remained until 1857. Then it moved to The Mount, 11 Park Square (for many years since World War II the Royal Air Force Association Club) following the benevolent Dr Woollett as he moved his residence from time to time.

On 14th August 1856, Dr Williams, the Medical officer of Health, gave his quarterly report to Newport Corporation. The recent outbreak of typhus had caused 51 deaths, considerably more than the average number who usually succumbed when cholera struck. The chief causes were given as overcrowded housing and the water supply which despite recent improvements was still teeming with bacteria. The Medical Officer stated that a bottle of clear water taken from any tap in the town and exposed to sunlight would, within three days, become brown and murky!

The main concern of some of the councillors and especially Samuel Homfray, did not appear to be for those who were suffering but more for the effect that too much publicity of the epidemic would have on the town's sea trade!

More anxiety was expressed in the 1866 report of the Inspector of the Board of Guardians, about a place named as 'The Old Barn'. This could only refer to the old Chadwick's Theatre, the large wooden building between Lewis Street and William Street which was known to have been converted into an isolation hospital. The report stated that it was 'a perfect pest-house and a source of disease, so full that the beds of both female and male patients were touching each other!' The Council was further informed that 'the Inspector had visited the Old Barn and although his olfactory nerves were pretty well used to disagreeable effluvia, he was aghast at the stench that rose from it!'

In contrast to this report, the Medical Officer was much more optimistic in February 1869 when he stated that there had been no epidemics and that the last quarter of 1868 had seen the mortality rate drop to 1.7% per thousand of the population - the lowest ever reported. At the conclusion of this welcome news, he added: 'We are indebted to the extreme mildness of the season, as there is no greater fallacy than to suppose that cold weather is healthy'.

Regular MO's reports such as this gave a valuable picture of a Victorian community's health and sanitary problems; even weather reports paint in essential background. The winter of 1868 was obviously one of uncommon temperateness.

Of course, by this time many more precautions were being encouraged against the spread of the all too common, virulent and deadly infections that loomed overall. For instance, it was generally believed that some degree of protection was afforded by a coating of white-lime applied liberally to the walls of houses, passage-ways, back-yards and outdoor privies. To this end, the council supplied the necessary tools on hire and lime brushes were in constant demand, so much so that in July 1870, when 43 brushes were already let out, more had to be ordered to replenish the dwindling, worn-out stocks.

In 1858, Sir Charles Morgan, Lord Tredegar, offered a site on Stow Hill (no doubt once part of the Pembroke endowment to the town), and after acceptance, a new Dispensary was built, opening in 1860 with the address of 34 Stow Hill. A few years later these premises were re-equipped and styled as 'The Infirmary', but as yet with no provision for indoor patients. In 1862, the generosity of some local gentlemen provided six beds in two wards, but it was another twenty years before the accommodation was increased by five more wards, twenty beds and a children's ward. By this time however, the huge population of Newport was making the infirmary totally inadequate. Even by the year 1900 there was room for only fifty adults and fifteen children!

Newport Infirmary, Stow Hill 1893

A magnificent offer of £5,000 was made by Dr Garrod Thomas on condition that a further £15,000 should be raised within three years, for the provision of a new hospital to satisfy the town's requirements. Almost immediately, Sir Charles Morgan, now 2nd Baron Tredegar, placed a four-and-a-half acre site on Cardiff Road at the disposal of the Infirmary directors. The new Royal Gwent Hospital was officially opened by Lord Tredegar in 1901 and the health of the town began to be cared for by medical standards previously undreamed of!

This building was another of impressive aspect to add to those already acquired by the town. The Renaissance style architecture designed on the pavilion principle, had a tall administration block in the centre, facings of deep red brickwork with dressings of bath stone. Accommodation was provided for 150 patients with operating theatre, post-mortem room, mortuary, telephone exchange, lift, boardroom, nurses' dining room, sitting room, bedroom and kitchen. A separate block held the out-patients department. The total cost was £40,000.

The Royal Gwent Hospital Cardiff Road

Today, vastly extended, with a small part of the original building cleverly included but still open to view, the Royal Gwent is one of the most modern, up-to-date, efficient hospitals in the country - a far cry from the humble 'Dispensary' from which it arose.

Alltyryn Hospital for Infectious Diseases was a little older than the Royal Gwent, having opened in 1896 with extensions in 1903. Beautifully situated in Alltyryn View near the Barracks, overlooking the Little Switzerland panorama, it had accommodation for fifty-seven beds in three ward pavilions, one of which was isolated for consumptives. It was demolished in 1994 to make way for a small housing development.

It was a little known fact that Cardiff Corporation had established an isolation hospital on Flat Holm Island out in the Bristol Channel and in 1900 Newport Health Committee was allowed to lease places in this hospital for a period of three years.

Newport had always depended for its fresh water supplies on springs and wells. It now seems unbelievable that up until 1846, a population approaching 19,000 relied upon six town wells and often resorted to the polluted canal for drinking water!

The town wells were those at Baneswell, Mill Street, Corn Street, Stow Hill, the Salutation and Pill End. Two of these wells received regular mentions in the council minutes under the names of Anne's Well and St Thomas's Well. It was never specified which was which, but St Thomas's Well was probably the one that stood in Corn Street - the well of the Austin Friars near the Benedictine Chapel of St Thomas, and now approximately where stands the Potters Arms. Between 1854 and 1857, new pumps were fitted to the Pentonville, Salutation and Corn Street Wells, and all the others were cleaned and repaired by a contractor for a fee of £8 a year. The well at Baneswell was reputed to be contaminated by springs draining from beneath St Woolos Churchyard, the condition of which was described as being atrocious and shameful.

The cemetery had been full for years but burials were still being carried out and coffins piled in although there was little soil left to cover them. The place represented a ghoulish aspect with coffins protruding from the ground, many broken open with the grisly contents spilling out. 'The smell at certain states of the weather on passing through the churchyard was so pungent as to be offensive and injurious' (Local Government in Newport 1835 to 1935: J Warner). This had been the cause of distress for a long time and few issues of the Monmouthshire Merlin failed to include some bitter comment.

There were other burial places in Newport, all close to the centre. Six chapels had their own chapelyards but they too were filling rapidly! The problem was only slightly alleviated when, in 1842, a group of business men calling themselves the Newport Cemetery Company, converted a piece of land fronting Clifton Road, opposite St Woolos Church, into a private cemetery. By the time this became full 250 interments had taken place.

The distasteful problem at the top of Stow Hill was believed by many to be affecting the purity of the water at the foot, but if simple logic had prevailed the reverse would have been seen to be the case.

Newport was, as ever, an incredibly dirty town; the state of its streets defied description. They were inches deep in unimaginable filth against which the efforts of the town's single scavenger were useless. This made all six wells more open to pollution from the streets above them than from the springs of St Woolos, which would have received some degree of filtering in their long passage down the hill.

In 1811, it was resolved to employ a mason to clean out the wells, close some of them with masonry and fit two-inch-bore cocks and handpumps. At the same time, a small reservoir was ordered to be built underground near the Mill Street well, enclosed in masonry, 12 feet long, six feet wide and 10 feet deep. If this pathetic little tank made any impression at all it was kept very quiet!

There was no doubt about the extent or the intensity of the fouling of the town's water supply, and the recurring outbreaks of cholera and typhoid went a long way to making up the Corporation's mind to tap other sources. Even so, there was always a hard-line group of blinkered councillors who insisted against all the evidence that the town did not need a new water supply.

On 16th June 1846, parliamentary powers were obtained to form the Newport and Pillgwenlly Waterworks. In the preamble to the Act it was stated that it was for the purpose of 'giving powers to the Company to supply the town and borough and shipping of Newport and Pillgwenlly with pure and wholesome water'. The first directors were Joseph Beaumont,

James Jamieson, James Cordes, Philip Jones, Samuel Homfray, Thomas Powell, Joseph Latch, Jeremiah Cairns, Thomas Cooke and John Lawrence.

The Act provided for the forming of a reservoir from the springs of Ynysfro, Cwrtymynys and Pensarn in the Parish of Rogerstone, the water to be piped into Newport at a point near the Marshes Tollgate.

Other provisions of the Act covered penalties for failure to lay on supplies within 28 days of householders requests, wasting water, allowing non-payers to use water, fouling water supplies and damaging equipment. The first Waterworks Offices were on Stow Hill and when they were dispensed with the site was used to build the public baths in 1890. In those days, a small waterworks reservoir stood on the rear of this site with return frontages to North Street and Wesley Place; its object was to act as a halfway 'rest area' for water to be pumped to the properties at the top of the hill. Today, a small modern courtyard of pretty, redbrick houses called Baneswell Court takes up the area.

Although the first piped water came late for most people, it was just in time for those in the big houses over the railway tunnel, the digging of which caused their personal wells to run dry.

Ynysfro Reservoir, completed in 1847 and visible in the Little Switzerland panorama from Ridgeway, had an area of 15 acres, a mean depth of 37 feet and a capacity of 82 million gallons. It cost £20,447 but at first was connected to only 220 houses. By 1851, 1,284 houses were connected out of 2,908.

The first fresh water made its appearance on the streets of the town in 1859, through the medium of drinking fountains at Station Approach and St Pauls Church. Within a few years water was rather more widely distributed through a series of 157 standposts, plugs, Lamberts hydrants and bore hydrants for fire-fighting purposes. Each type had a different method for connecting the hoses and whilst some were owned by the Waterworks Company, the majority were provided by the Local Board of Health.

Demand continued to outstrip supply, so, in 1872, another Act of Parliament was sought to enable the building of Pantyrheos Reservoir on the slopes of Twynbarlym, using water from the Pantyrheos and Henllys Brooks. This added a further store of 145 million gallons, capable of supplying 150,000 gallons a day. With a depth of 90 feet this was at the time the deepest reservoir in Great Britain.

Two years later, Ynysfro was enlarged by the addition of an upper pond making its new capacity 118 million gallons.

Strange to relate, there was still opposition to any further improvement to Newport's water supply, although it was patently obvious that the population explosion that the town was experiencing could not be sustained by even the excellent facilities that had already been provided. The expansion of Maindee as a suburb was advancing rapidly and hundreds of new connections were being demanded. In these circumstances, and in opposition to the negative, heads-in-the-sand stance from both members of the Corporation and from public opinion, the Company obtained further powers to build another reservoir to the east of the town at Wentwood.

Opening in 1894, this great pond was placed above Llanvaches using the watersheds of Pencaemawr, Mynydd Llwyd (Grey Hill) and Mynydd Allt-Tir-fach (Turvey). It cost over £250,000 and held 300 million gallons. The private water company was taken over in 1888 by Newport Corporation at a cost of £278,000.

There were no sophisticated filtering processes in any of those early reservoirs - only water running through reasonably clean sand -but some effectiveness was shown in the swift decrease of cholera and typhoid in the town.

The whole of Newport's supply system was in serious trouble in 1895 when from

January 26th to March 18th a great frost descended on the town. During this fiercely cold, eight week period there were bursts in 106 mains, 1,000 household pipes and 194 service pipes under the pavements!

The wells continued to be used for some time. The last of them, Baneswell, was closed and sealed in 1901 but until then its water was known to have been distributed by Solomon Meaker and his donkey cart, carrying barrels which cost their owner a half-penny to fill. This enterprising tradesman transported water to the docks but on many occasions he got only part way there when he discovered that his casks had been emptied by mischievous urchins who crept up behind the cart and turned on the taps! The Baneswell pump, on the corner of Bailey Street and Pump Street (site marked with an appropriate plaque), was eventually found to have its outlets choked with dead rats!

Wentwood Reservoir was later enlarged to hold 410 million gallons by means of a tunnel from the Castroggy Valley.

It is interesting to note that Newport's water apparently travelled well and played a small but important part in the First World War. Two ships, the 'Winifredian' and an unnamed vessel, left the Alexandra Dock in 1915, carrying 2,000 tons of drinking water for the troops fighting in the Gallipoli Campaign.

The people of Newport in 1919, were presented with overwhelming evidence that their water supply was once again in serious danger. From the year 1888 consumption had trebled and was estimated to double again in the next twenty years. The existing reservoirs, as extensive as they were, were simply not enough! On January 24th 1919 the ratepayers were given the opportunity to show their opinions on a gigantic new scheme to obtain water from Talybont on the fringe of the Brecon Beacons. They were told that the Corporation had an option to purchase 1,450 acres of land at a very reasonable cost. Damming the Caerfanell Stream was intended to produce a lake over two miles long with a surface area of 323 acres. Its capacity would be 2,567 million gallons with a yield of 75 million gallons a day. The total cost with one pipeline carrying 4 million gallons was given as £733,000.

As with all previous attempts at improving the water supply, this news was received with the same apathy and resistance. The ratepayers turned down the idea. Voting showed 1,425 in favour with 3,795 against, In January 1920 however, just one year later, a much more representative poll reversed the previous result and the ayes narrowly won the day. The voting this time was: for 5,331, against 4,522, a majority in favour of 809.

It would appear that many inhabitants were still voting with their pockets and not their heads but at least the fact that they were allowed a referendum at all showed the Corporation's willingness to demonstrate its accountability where public money was at stake, an example that not all succeeding councils have been over-eager to follow!

Early work on the Talybont Reservoir in its 6,000 acre catchment area commenced in 1923 and went on for sixteen years until final completion in 1939, giving welcome relief to the severe unemployment suffered in the Monmouthshire valleys. Twenty years later there was said of it:

'Those who planned and built it could have had little idea of the vast projects that it would render possible in the years to come.'
Editorial Comment, South Wales Argus
September 1959.

~ 0 ~

Up until 1836, Newport , like every other town outside of London, had no regular police force. The Newport Improvement Act of 1826 catered in a small way for this deficiency by giving power to the town council to employ watchmen and night patrols:-

'To exert themselves in the prevention of fires, murders, burglaries, robberies and other outrages, disorders and breaches of the peace, and they are empowered to apprehend all felons, malefactors, vagrants, nightwalkers, disorderly persons and disturbers of the peace who shall be found wandering or misbehaving themselves within the town during the hours of keeping watch . . .'

These watchmen had no experience whatsoever in law enforcement and the job was only part time augmentation of their regular callings. The first four watchmen to be employed under the Act were Richard Davies, hatter, Samuel Watkins, shoemaker, Rosser Lewis and William Jones, labourers.

In addition, the Mayor appointed up to a dozen petty constables selected from tradesmen and labourers, unpaid and therefore unreliable, lacking in inducement to perform their duties conscientiously. This was at a time when Newport was entering what was probably the most lawless period in its history, with the criminal element becoming an increasing problem as the number of bolt-holes grew in the Friars Fields and other dark alley-ways.

The Municipal Corporations Act 1835 revolutionised local government in England and Wales. For the first time mayors and their councillors were to be elected by, and accountable to the local ratepayers but besides these provisions the Act created watch committees with powers to form and manage police forces. On 12th January 1836, Newport's Watch Committee of nine members was elected. John Frost was one and he was appointed a magistrate at the same time. The Committee wasted no time!

Sergeant Redman of the Metropolitan Police, said to be 'a fine young fellow' was appointed to be the first Chief Constable, and the Newport force was created in two divisions. The Town and Pillgwenlly Divisions had just two or three constables in each. About twenty-four petty constables were appointed to form a reserve - all recruited from numerous other walks of life.

The police stations developed as follows

Pillgwenlly	1838	A constable's house in Church Street
	1859	Temple Street
	1905	Alexandra Road
Town	1838	The Superintendent's house near the Red Lion Inn, Stow Hill
	1839	Rear of the Parrot Hotel
	1840	Opposite St Pauls Church
	1842	The Town Hall Maindee
	1889	Speke Street
	1898	81 Chepstow Road

The early years of the Borough Force were fraught with complication and difficulty. To use a modern expression, it took a long time 'to shake the bugs from the system!'

The Watch Committee sacked Superintendent Redman while he was recovering from an injury sustained in a big fight in Commercial Street. His replacement, Edward Hopkins from the Bristol Force, was soon in trouble when all of his constables resigned, and he himself was reprimanded for improprieties in police procedures. Sometime later he was accused of being drunk on duty and a constable reported him for not taking action on matters referred to him.

The Watch Committee's remedy for this complaint was to issue the offended constable with a notebook so that his reports could be reported in writing. This apparently corrected the one detail omitted by the Committee when it issued a constable's standard equipment: greatcoat, dress coat, trousers, cape, truncheon, rattle, armlet, cutlass (night duty only), belt, hat, boots, handcuffs and lantern.

When this equipment order was being discussed by the Watch Committee on 6th June 1838, John Frost proposed an amendment to omit cutlasses from the list because 'the staves of the constables are sufficient to protect them, that to arm constables with deadly weapons by which life might so easily be taken away, would be improper and would in all probability lead to serious consequences,' - this from the man who a year later led the greatest show of cold steel that the town was ever to witness. The motion was lost!

Numerous were the occasions when policemen were reported for drinking on duty or for being found in public houses after hours. They were reprimanded for not paying respect to strangers in the street, one for playing a fiddle in the street whilst on duty, one for being found in a brothel when on duty and one for arresting a woman and keeping her in his house all night before delivering her to the police station.

The force set up its original 'Lost Property Department' in 1845, and the first object to come into its safekeeping was 'a barrowload of muck!' Despite the placing of notices about the town, nobody it seems came forward to claim this desirable item!

Even a condition for the payment of the constables' twelve shillings a week wages had a ring of humour, saying: 'constables must be paid on a Friday so that they may take advantage of going to market on Saturday with their wages in their pockets.'

These were the lighter moments in the life of the early Newport bobby, but obviously in a career given over to law enforcement in such violent times, the serious side was bound to predominate and often reflected the sad and scamier conditions of the day. For instance, one constable, having previous experience, was put in charge of the newly built (1838) Workhouse on Stow Hill, with his wife as matron. The figures for the period from January to May 1845 show that no fewer then 12,872 Irish immigrants, fugitives from the potato famine, were given refuge by the Board of Guardians - and this was in addition to Newport's own poor and destitute!

Dealing with drunken mobs was a common and highly dangerous duty in a town which possessed 60 inns and 300 beerhouses (one for every 39 inhabitants!) Many constables received severe injuries at the hands of marauding ruffians, and at least two were known to have died. Election nights and Squib (Guy Fawkes) nights were the excuses for the most drunken, violent and bloody affrays. One of the worst localised riots in Newport's history took place on Election Day in October 1868. This was the election occasioned by the standing down of Crawshay Bailey after three terms as the Conservative member for the boroughs of Newport, Monmouth and Usk. Campaigning to win the seat were Samuel Homfray (Blue) against Liberal, Sir John Ramsden (Red), and the latter was successful by 1,618 votes to 1,449 which gives some indication of the number of men in *three boroughs* who were entitled to vote!

All that day the town filled with a very rough element from the valleys and by evening the majority of them, hopelessly drunk, were forming themselves into groups representing the Blue or Red parties. Soon they were fighting furiously up and down the town, battering each other with sticks and clubs and hurling huge stones. The police made attempts to intervene but their small numbers were powerless against the great tide of violence that washed over them and finally headed for a showdown at the Town Hall.

On arrival at that building, the crowd vented its fury in a hail of stones, breaking most of the windows. The situation was completely out of hand so the Mayor called out a detachment of the Royal Welsh Fusiliers and from behind their ranks of fixed bayonets he read the Riot Act. When this failed to stop the bombardment, the soldiers charged the rampaging mob and drove it around into Baneswell. Here in the general confusion, an innocent lady, Mrs Grant, who was standing on her own doorstep, received a bayonet, thrust from which she died. Her son, trying to protect his mother, also received five severe wounds and he died from them a year later. Several other men were badly wounded in front of the Queens Hotel and when the day was over there were broken heads all over the town.

Newport Police, the squad that captured the 'Belgia' 1914

There was almost a repetition of this riot at the next election in 1874. A similar drink-sodden mob again stoned the Town Hall and this time the Mayor was assaulted and robbed. The military were called out and the sight of their fixed bayonets caused the crowd to disperse; the police force was then able to take control for the rest of the day.

Another sign of the times which highlighted other problems facing the police, was given in the Superintendent's report for 1858. It stated that the town was then the possessor of 55 brothels containing 282 prostitutes, in addition to the 38 beerhouses where another 55 lived. If the court records are to be believed over the next forty years, it would appear that there were brothels in every part of the town, particularly in the haunts of the seagoing fraternity along and off Commercial Road.

Since their inception, members of Newport's Police Force have been called upon to perform all sorts of duties, including some not usually associated with their profession. In the early days it was their responsibility to ensure that street lights were lit, that the town's pump handles were locked in the evening and unlocked each morning, and in the absence of a fire brigade, to fight fires.

The presence of a fire engine in the town cannot be confirmed before 1826 because that

175

is the year in which first reference was made in the Improvement Commission's minutes to payments for the repair of such a machine. This was before the formation of a police force so it must be assumed that the watchmen had to place their trust in any voluntary help that came to hand in the vicinity of a fire. By 1845, the old engine seems to have come to the end of its useful life and the Commission bought a new one for £120.

When the Town Hall and Police Station was built in Commercial Street, the Superintendent was ordered to live there and look after the fire engine which was moved from its previous shelter, the Old Engine House at the Castle Green.

On 16th October 1849, the Sanitary Committee sent a letter to the Watch Committee congratulating the police for their unstinting services during the cholera epidemic. Their efforts had included door to door visits to ascertain the prevalence of the infection, reporting their findings to medical officers, and the display of 'extraordinary fortitude and indifference of self security in being obliged to place diseased corpses in coffins'.

There was however the one occasion at the start of the First World War when Newport's bobbies were involved in an incident that must rank as the most bizarre in the history of any police force.

It so happened that just after 6 pm on August 3rd 1914, the 9,000 ton German freighter, 'Belgia', was refused entry to Newport Docks on Admiralty instructions, so she steamed away and anchored in the Barry Roads. War was declared next day and there being no military assistance to hand, the Chief Constable, Mr C E Gower, hurriedly armed two of his sergeants and eight constables with rifles borrowed from the Territorial Army and led them aboard a tugboat commandeered by the Deputy Dockmaster, Captain F W Cutcliffe. Post-haste, the small contingent of amateur soldier/sailors, totally untrained in what they had to do, sailed down channel and on 4th August 1914 boarded and captured the ship. They were more than a little surprised when they got their prisoners back to Pill Police Station and found that in addition to the twenty members of the normal crew, there were also seventy-five German Navy reservists who, if they had not felt like surrendering, could have made things really difficult for the eleven stout-hearted policemen!

Chapter Ten

The Nineteenth Century

The growth of Pillgwenlly and Maindee.
Brynglas and the Dos Works
The Railway.
Solution to the Marshes problem.

The opening of the Town Dock and the Cattle Market really breathed life into Pillgwenlly and triggered a building boom that soon raised streets of houses on both sides and the full length of Commercial Road, which was given a new surface, a few gas lights at the town end and a privately owned horse-drawn omnibus service from the Westgate. The construction work was so rapid that the ballasting of the depressions could not keep pace, and the foundations of many houses were made to stand directly on the original Pillgwenlly levels, being given basement rooms that flooded when the tides were high. The resulting degree of structural instability became so great that many streets of 1840 vintage had to be pulled down, realigned, rebuilt and often renamed before the century was out.

Linton Street and Wallis Street were created out of original, poor little back-to-back terraces at the bottom ends of Kings Parade and Castle Street. Wilson Street stands exactly on the site of Protheros Row but faces in the opposite direction. Speedwell Street disappeared inside the western boundary of the Uskside Engineering Works whilst St Michael Street once carried the name of High Street which could not be justified once Pillgwenlly was absorbed into a town which already owned a street of that name.

Other now departed names, suggestive of quiet suburbia rather than busy dockland, were : Globe Cottages, Garden Lane, Constables Lane, Wedlocks Court and Pyne Court (later part of Pottery Road). The most intriguing however was surely 'Quiet Womans Row', a terrace of small cottages standing at the extreme end of Dock Parade, right alongside the entrance lock of the Town Dock. Built integrally into its centre was a tavern called 'The Quiet Woman'. Which gave name to which only the mysterious lady herself would know, but it is said that the sign which hung over the front door, depicted a woman, headless, and therefore incapable of speaking!

After the passing of these houses the site was never residentially redeveloped and so far remains a far from prepossessing area of minor industry.

The Old Town Dock has long gone, filled in, its surface to be gradually developed as the Corporation thinks fit, but at the time of writing the great entrance lock still remains for anyone who has the inclination to stand, stare and reminisce on the town's former glory as a leader among the world's centres of maritime trading. Clogged up with silt and the flotsam of many years, overgrown with rough weeds and grasses, it can nevertheless still be easily identified as the passageway that, in its time, admitted the world's largest ships into a safe, tideless haven.

As the old town warmed in the glow of Pillgwenlly's good fortune, the bare patches within the borough boundaries began to be covered as new buildings followed bodies in pursuit of the new-found wealth. The population rose more quickly than ever before. Between the two National Censuses of 1841 and 1851 it nearly doubled from 10,492 to 19,328; the number of houses was 2,230 - ten times more than forty years earlier!

These censuses contained further meat to coat the bones of the growing town and a quiet browse through the returns for High Street, Baneswell and Commercial Street is almost as effective as having been able to accompany the census enumerator on his rounds.

Besides the trades and occupations which are still familiar a century and a half later, the commercial centre housed individuals whose self-styled titles read like a Dickensian catalogue. Take for example:-

Currier, millwright, ostler, weaver, druggist, hatter, straw-bonnet maker, brightsmith, barber, haulier, pipe-maker, sawyer, stone-cutter, stenciller, compositor, shoemaker and binder, clock and watch maker, umbrella maker, tallow chandler, cheese factor, tog maker, hobbler, book-binder, basket maker, washer woman and *chirophagist!*

Doctors, surgeons, accountants, architects, 'attorneys' and all other manner of professional gentlemen were abundantly represented.

High Street alone had fifteen public houses, ten grocers and numerous tanners, saddlers, maltsters and corn merchants. Many of these traders described themselves as journeymen; there was a surprising number of schoolmasters and governesses, and a glut of dressmakers, seamstresses and errand boys. Here and there were notes describing the occupier as 'pauper' or 'deranged'. Lodging house keepers cropped up everywhere, as did a remarkable number of those who considered themselves to be 'scholars' and 'of independent means'.

By the 1851 Census, the recently arrived railway was making its presence felt with the appearance of porters, engineers, firemen and plate-layers.

Both censuses were important barometers reflecting the town's increased prosperity and the growth of its business and industry, but there was a further significant pointer in the fact that so many heads of families gave their birthplaces as elsewhere in Wales and more often than not in the adjacent English counties.

Another of the town's industries, little known but thriving from 1840 onwards, was pottery making which must have had some impact on the employment situation if the number of busy potteries was anything to judge by. In their earlier years it was known for them to employ children as young as eight years of age!

There were potteries at Pill and Maindee (the Alexander Potteries), Crindau (Albany Street), Courtybella, St Julians and a clay pipe factory in Corn Street (Mr Richard Mullock). This wide-spread and obviously popular trade was commemorated in place names such as Potter Street, Potters Parade, Pottery Road, Pottery Terrace and the Potters Arms public house near the aforesaid clay pipe factory.

These were not ambitious potteries; the intention was never to rival the fine ware and ceramics produced in the Midland factories, but there was great demand for the more practical items such as jars, pans, basins, brown and white stoneware crocks and bottles. Unfortunately, only too few of these articles have survived; whilst not being of great value, any such item bearing a Newport potter's mark and turning up in respectable condition will always be welcome to add a little more colour to the town canvas.

One of the two Alexander potteries - the one in Dudley Street, off Corporation Road - survived all the rest and carried on production right up to 1950. The interesting fact about this establishment was that for most of its life its unlikely owner was G F Lovell & Co. the confectionery manufacturer of Toffee Rex fame.

The beginnings of Great Dock Street were first prescribed in 1837. The original length of the road which one day was to extend from the bridge to Cardiff Road (it did not at that time envisage the inclusion of the artificially created Dock Road which became Lower Dock Street) started at the junction of Popular Row and Club Row (Ebenezer Terrace) and dead-

178

ended at Llanarth Street, at the back of the Tabernacle Chapel.

Houses of good class were built at the lower end of Dock Street and by 1846 there were 19 of them, evidence that this area was considered by the better-off citizens to be eminently suitable to their status. Not for another twenty years was this allegiance transferred to the houses constructed after 1856 on the Gold Tops fields.

The year 1844 saw the building of Newport's first High Street Post Office, and of Victoria Place, another residential street off Stow Hill. These 'gentlemen's' tenements are still in existence today, a hundred and fifty years on, having been raised from a state of near-dilapidation and converted into well appointed apartments.

Across the river, in the as yet unknown and undefined suburb of Maindee, there appeared to be nothing but green fields and meadows.

In 1832, the Boundary Commission caused the transfer to the Borough of Newport of a strip of land averaging 400 yards wide and extending from just above the bridge southwards to Liswerry Pill. Using present day topography as a guide, this represents an area stretching from East Usk Road in the north to Lysaghts' Institute in the south, and eastwards from the River Usk to the junction of Caerleon and Church Roads at the upper end and at the lower end across to Colston Avenue off Corporation Road.

The survey map of 1836 shows that after crossing the bridge, immediately on the right, was a wharf and a house called Rodney House. The wharf itself became known as Rodney Wharf (now London Wharf) and the house survived as the home of the landing stage superintendent until it had to make way in the 1930s for a commercial garage and the new Labour Exchange.

From Rodney Wharf in 1823, the old steampacket 'Lady Rodney', commenced a regular passage service to Bristol, a journey of from four to six hours according to the tides, and costing two shillings for fore cabins and four shillings for after cabins.

Clarence Place (not then named) was a short length of road fronted by a small terrace of cottages and gardens called Clarence Cottages. The only other building in sight was the Turnpike at the junction of Caerleon and Chepstow Roads. Opposite the Turnpike was a straight lane leading to the riverbank (the future East Usk Road). At the end of this lane a long narrow pill having its mouth just above the bridge, cut inland approximately along the line of the future Tregare Street and the old 'Muxon' to its source at the Duck Pool, hence its name - Duckpool Pill - which ceased to exist when filled in with spoil from the now railway embankment. This was the main reason why the north side of Clarence Place took much longer to develop than the south side - because the made-up ground could only take the weight of wooden sheds and store houses.

An old resident of the area, in whose boyhood all this happened, remembered the Muxon as: 'a dark and dangerous tarn - a villainous, deep pool albeit inhabited by the most gorgeous minnows, both red and silver breasted'.

The origin of the name has never been revealed but many of the children of the 1920s, 30s and 40s, who continually traversed this short, ever muddy stretch of track connecting Tregare Street with Turner Street, firmly believe that it was somehow derived 'from muck!'.

This might be the opportune moment to explain how the Clarence of Clarence Place originated, and how it was bestowed on the track 'just over the bridge'.

The truth of the matter is that it did not relate to any of the Dukes of Clarence of later history, but to their predecessors, the Earls of Clare, five generations of whom had once owned Newport from the 12th century onwards. Clarence was a derivative of Clare. Once therefore, this land had been Clare's place.

The early 19th century knew no parish of Maindee. All the land transferred to the borough on that side of the River Usk was in the parish of Christchurch. A large, stone house called Maendy had existed since 1615 in the area to which it eventually gave its name. In 1807, it was left by William Kemys to Charles Kemys Tynte. When the new Chepstow Road opened in 1817, Maendy House found itself at the end of a 100 yard long driveway, behind handsome wrought iron gates, just on the south side approximately where Hawarden Road faces Coleridge Road today. Extreme dilapidation in 1859 caused the house to be almost entirely rebuilt in excellent style, but even in this condition it survived only another 54 years when its extensive parkland was required for the creation of the Balmoral and Conway Road housing estates. If the decision had been made to preserve Maendy House, it would now be standing proudly at the junction of Wyeverne and Blenheim Roads.

Other than this house and a few cottages near the bridge there were only Duckpool Farm, St Julians House, Fairoak Farm, Etheridge's Cottage (on the corner of Caerleon and Duckpool Roads), Penylan Farm and Somerton Farm, within miles of the town, but in 1848 the first houses began to appear on the lower slope of Christchurch Hill. At the same time, Mr Willmett, a ship-owner, built his house, Fair Oak Villa, a small, unpretentious mansion, in an orchard in Maindee on the corner of the lane that eventually became Wharf Road.

Maendy House was sold in 1850 by Kemys Tynte to Rennie and Logan, the railway contractors, who divided the estate up amongst themselves. John Logan took the house, a 30 acre park and Somerton Farm - all on the south side of Chepstow Road. Rennie's share was all on the north side - Penylan Farm and 155 acres of land. He promptly built the mansion, Maindy Park in 55 acres; this was sold in 1870 to two ship-owning brothers, one of whom took the house and the other built Maindy Hall nearby.

Both houses were positioned on the Eveswell slope, approximately along the line of the present-day Wordsworth Road. Their communal driveway was the track that would one day form Tennyson Road and their shared lodge stood at a wide gateway giving on to Chepstow Road. It is a popular belief that the old stone house known as 2 St Johns Road is the original gate-house to the mansions; this is understandable because it certainly has a lodge-like appearance, but all the evidence is to the contrary. The ordnance survey map of 1880 shows the real lodge, in splendid isolation, a little farther eastwards on the site now occupied by numbers 237 and 239 Chepstow Road. At that time the mystery house was not shown to have been built, but by 1896 it was being offered for sale under the name 'St Johns Lodge'. Reference to Johns Directories for the years 1928 and 1929 points to the fact that Maindy Park Lodge was pulled down between these years.

High above the two stately mansions, at the top of the steep hillside, was a much more ancient creation in the shape of a small, circular, earth tumulus or mound, described on old maps as 'The Camp'. Its history is open to question and although its presence has been ascribed to the Romans it could be much older. Military use has been suggested and there are tales of it being a cattle shelter in mediaeval times. Its outstanding position and command of glorious views in all directions made it an obvious choice of situation for William Kemys of Maindy to build his summerhouse. However, once the top of the hillside began to collect its cloak of 20th century houses, the tump was surmounted by two pairs of large, semi-detached, Edwardian villas now known as 50 to 56 Clevedon Road.

Far below these properties, down on the main Chepstow Road and almost opposite the gates of Maendy House, was the imposing entrance to Beechwood House which was the next door neighbour to Maindy Park. Set in a further 30 acres of the former Kemys Tynte Estate, it was built by George Fothergill, the Newport tobacco manufacturer. Fortunately for the town, in 1900, the house together with its grounds was dedicated for use as a public park. Hopefully it will remain not only a delightful haven of quiet greenery amidst the sprawl of urban concrete but also a reminder of long gone days of elegant living. Such desirable aspirations for the house itself are in jeopardy at the time of writing as a result of a disastrous fire; it is every Newport citizen's fervent wish that something - anything - may prevent the loss of another vital piece of Newport's pitiful little stockpile of links with the past!

The remainder of the Kemys Tynte Estate was acquired in 1849 by the Freehold Land Society and full scale building of the new suburb commenced but even as late as 1880 Maindee consisted only of a concentration of cottages along the main road and some in the commencement of the side streets. Little existed from Kensington Place onwards except the four mansion houses already referred to and a few not so large, but equally resplendent, gentlemen's villas standing in gardens which resembled small, classically landscaped parks. Of these, Ffrwd Vale disappeared as part of the rebuilding of Eveswell Nursery and Primary Schools between 1987 and 1989, but still standing today are The Lawn(derelict), Eveswell House and Cambrian House, all having been converted to various commercial uses.

Even Clarence Place, as near as it was to the town centre, was then still regarded as a rural retreat for town families. It was customary for street directories of the period to carry a separate register of those persons considered to be gentry, and a surprising number were shown to be living in Clarence Place; by 1907, the district was looked upon as one of the best shopping areas in Newport.

- 0 -

Brynglas House was another landmark for which Newport was noted, although it was well outside the borough boundary, in the parish of Malpas. It was built in 1832 by Alderman Allfrey who had converted the tannery portion of Newport Castle into his family brewery.

The house stood on one side of the old Crindau Pitch, near its highest point just as Crindau House occupied a similar position at the foot of the hill; the latter property however was placed in the separate parish of St Woolos by the strange meandering of the boundary. The steep roadway had by now lost its role as the stagecoach route to the north and had reverted to the peaceful serenity of a country lane curling up from the main Malpas Road.

Mr Allfrey died in 1853 and Brynglas was sold to James Brown, an esteemed local councillor whose tireless work for the town and his unceasing fight against corruption earned him election to the mayoralty no less than three times! He has been described as 'a pugnacious, sturdy and far-seeing man who revelled in controversy.'

He was also the founder of the Star of Gwent newspaper. Unfortunately, his love of lavish entertaining at Brynglas and the cost of his constant legal battles, drove him to bankruptcy and in 1857 he was compelled to sell the house to James Cordes, a wealthy Midlands industrialist. Cordes, of Spanish/American descent, was opening a new factory at the rear of the Mill Street Gasworks. In his view it was most desirable to have a nice house in picturesque surroundings but within easy reach of his work-place.

The factory became known as the Dos Works meaning in Spanish, Cordes second works after the first one which he had built in the Midlands, and for a century and a quarter it dominated the site that is now occupied by the GPO Building and several other industrial units. Only one vestige of the old buildings remains. The Cordes were a very religious family, deeply aware of their good fortune in relation to the poverty that surrounded them. Therefore they treated their employees extremely well for that day and age and were especially concerned for the children of their workers, particularly those that laboured alongside the adults. To ensure that their education did not suffer, James Cordes built a school within the factory precincts and insisted that all 'his children', as he called them, spent part of each day improving their knowledge and obtaining a Christian upbringing.

181

Old Dos Works School 1959

The Dos Works employed 320 young boys in 1867 and many of them, educated on the premises, went on to become leading citizens of Newport. Even so, despite the school being born from the most charitable of motives, the headmaster found that he could not dispense with the traditional methods of maintaining discipline. There was a thin strap for minor offenders, a thick strap for the more obstreperous and a 'dark hole' for the temporary incarceration of the really bad boys.

If the modern visitor cares to turn the corner at the Royal Mail public house (the Old White Lion) in Mill Street, he or she would be in Factory Road. This road was originally the lane that gave access to the first gasworks, but with the arrival of the Dos Nail Works, it was lengthened as far as the factory gates and given its appropriate name. A similar access was created at the rear from Barrack Hill and named Dos Road.

A short distance along Factory Road stands the only portion of the old works spared by a ruthless redevelopment project in the 1970s. This two-storeyed, greystone and slate example of mid-19th century office architecture presents an air of loneliness and incongruity among its modern counterparts. At its entrance it displays Newport Civic Society's plaque advising of the building's place in the town's history and paying tribute to the Cordes family for its benefaction and concern for the poorer classes.

It is now all that is left of the grimy, derelict sprawl that started life in 1835 as the very first, large factory within the Borough of Newport, close enough to the town centre for its tall chimneys to waft sooty pollution over High Street.

The building that would have been by far the more interesting as a standing relic of times gone by, would surely have been the old Dos School; it was, however, highly predictable that its unique, historical significance - it was the oldest school building in the town - would put it top of the list as a target for the purblind axe-men of the planning committees.

It stood a little further on past the main factory entrance, through a side gate and on the crest of a slight incline. The street directory of 1880 places it in a long forgotten, little byway named Maddox Close.

Towards the end of their life, for many years during the 1930s, 40s and 50s, the old school buildings found use as the headquarters of the Newport Sea Cadets. The main schoolroom was a large hall, raftered and open-ceilinged high into the pitch of the roof. One fireplace, grossly inadequate for its purpose, was the sole source of heat in winter. Off to one side were the master's room, another small classroom and, at the rear, the open-air privy or 'dubs'. Right up to demolition day, high on the gable end wall, hung two large honours boards carrying, in faded gold leaf paint,the names of workers' children who over the previous century had excelled in their studies. Treading in their footsteps across the ancient, splintered, timber floor, a host of 20th century youngsters (your author among them), drilled, marched and learned nautical skills in the shadows of those boards, the whole time in complete ignorance of their important historical surroundings! Mysteriously, throughout the buildings for as long as anyone could remember, a dank, musty, all-pervading odour had persisted - as if the walls were giving up an atmosphere trapped from a bygone age!

A popular story told of Brynglas House is that from its balcony Mr Cordes could not only see his works but clearly hear its maroon. An arrangement was made with the factory manager so that Mr Cordes could tell each morning if his early presence was required. One firing of the maroon signified that everything was running smoothly; two blasts warned of some emergency! This was the story handed down by Victorian scribes, but it would appear that they confused the signalling apparatus. In 1946, a blunderbuss was on display at Newport Museum and this, it was said, was the gun which was fired at the Dos Works for the reasons stated.

Following the deaths of James Cordes and his wife, their son Thomas, now Newport's member of Parliament, in 1877 rebuilt and extended the mansion in a most luxurious fashion, lavishing a fortune on its furnishings, fittings and landscaping. The result was a splendid residence containing ground floor library, drawing, dining, morning and billiard rooms of enormous proportions, and a first floor comprising eleven main bedrooms, four dressing rooms, a bathroom and eight servants' bedrooms. The mind can do no other than boggle at the thought of that solitary bathroom on the occasions when the house was full!

There was a wing containing extensive kitchen, larder and storeroom accommodation, whilst the 21 acres of ground were equipped with stabling, tennis courts, kitchen garden and a wood. Standing nearly 300 feet above the River Usk, the house commanded panoramic views in all directions except the west which was screened by a grove of trees.

Brynglas had only one more private owner, a Colonel Williamson who purchased from Thomas Cordes in 1892. After her husband's death, Mrs Williamson remained in residence and the only notable thing known about her stay is that she allowed the house to be used as a military hospital with over 40 beds, during the First World War.

In 1922, Newport Borough Council purchased Brynglas House and it became very well known as one of the town's secondary schools (for some time known as central schools) until 1972.

Thousands of Newport's senior citizens - and many not quite so senior - remember with great nostalgia those few years spent preparing themselves for the future in this stately old building. Again fortune has smiled one of its rare architectural smiles and decreed the preservation of Brynglas to serve as a community centre, outwardly revealing much of the elegance and character of a bygone age but, sadly, remaining one of the last reminders of Newport's wealthy Victorians.

Burning of the first Railway Bridge over the River Usk at Newport.

- 0 -

Then one day, the railway came to town.

By 1845,the Great Western Railway had reached Gloucester from London and a connection was proposed to be made with the mineral producing districts of South Wales, the manufacturing areas of the Midlands, and Ireland by way of a ferry from Fishguard to Wexford.

There had been a surprising amount of resentment against the entry of the railway into Monmouthshire. The 'Merlin', in an issue from 1837 had this to say:-

'The proposed railway is uncalled for and unnecessary, there being for its maintenance merely the travelling and carrying which is barely sufficient to support on the road two mail coaches, two stagecoaches and four stage wagons.'

This criticism continued in a tirade against the connection with Ireland, suggesting that it would be the cause of an influx of Irish peasants who would put up the poor rate, increase unemployment among English and Welsh farmers and flood the country with Irish corn, butter, pigs etc. The farmers argument was further reinforced by advancing the theory that 'the iron horse steaming across its pastures' would lead to a drop in the demand for live horses, and that its belching smoke-stack would discolour the wool of the grazing sheep!

However, Parliamentary sanction was given in 1845 and in 1846 Contract 1 was granted to Messrs Rennie and Logan for the section of line between Maindee and the River Ebbw. Operations commenced with the simultaneous construction of the tunnel under Stow Hill and the bridge over the River Usk.

There were several open fields between Mill Street and the northern slope of Stow Hill. These were the Saxon fields of old, the 'brendekyrg' and 'beneweork' fields, and it was through them that the railway had to pass.

First came Gold Tops, then Dragon Field and Six Acre Field which were used for many years to stage displays by the local militia. It was across these last two fields that High Street railway station was to spread. Finally there were two smaller fields acoss Baneswell and up the side of Stow Hill - Cae Croch and Hill Field - the latter to contain the opening cutting for the tunnel. It was also in these fields that Clytha Park Road, Faulkner Road, Devon Place and the far end of Bridge Street were to be the forerunners of a mass building programme that covered the ground all the way up to Ridgeway and Risca Road.

The tunnel emerged again on the other side of Stow Hill near Waterloo Road, or The Trip as it was still then known. Its great depth (75 feet on the town side and 65 feet on the other) had the unfortunate effect of draining the springs and emptying the wells of the better class houses on the surface; thus ,the bathroom and kitchen pumps of the large residences such as Brynhyfryd and Springfield, ran dry! Even a newly discovered spring well in Clifton Road became useless and was not heard of again until uncovered some fifty years later during excavations for the electric tramway.

Two great shafts were sunk at each end, and with over 400 labourers and 50 horses working round the clock, the many thousands of tons of excavated spoil were at first spread about the surface immediately adjacent to the mouths of the shafts, almost inundating the reputed site of Newport's first castle (see the appropriate chapter). When, however, the new railway bridge over the Usk was sufficiently completed for track to be laid, the tunnel earth was transported in horse-drawn trains across the river to form the embankments on Maindee Common.

This bridge was another fine example of Victorian engineering. Designed by Robert Brunel, it was 700 feet long from bank to bank, piled into the river bed and supported on 11 arches of 50 feet and a central span of 100 feet. Costing £20,000. it contained 80,000 cubic feet of timber, every beam of which having been immersed in creosote for 12 hours at 120 lbs pressure per square inch. It was spoken of as the finest bridge of its kind ever produced.

The finishing touches were being applied in May 1848.

Early on the morning of the 30th of that month, a workman was using a heated rymer to clean out a hole preparatory to driving one of the last bolts in the central arch. The rymer was too hot and in his carelessness the workman had neglected to keep a supply of water close by in accordance with instructions. The timber, impregnated with the highly inflammable oil, instantly burst into flames which raced in seconds along the whole length of the bridge. In six minutes the structure was ablaze from end to end, fanned by a stiff breeze. Fire-fighting was out of the question although valiant efforts were made by the tiny police contingent and a solitary engine brought much too late by soldiers from the barracks.

The people of Newport watched in horror as the brand new bridge went up like a torch and, at 9 am, slowly collapsed in on itself in a dense cloud of oily smoke and spitting steam, sending a great log-jam of burning timbers swirling away on the river currents. When the tide receded, it left behind a mass of blackened, charred debris, making both banks of the river look as though a series of terrible wrecks had taken place!

Once the shock of this calamity was over - and the period of mourning was not unduly protracted - there was some idea of rebuilding in stone out of the ample insurance compensation, but it was finally designed in timber soaked in a much less volatile 'pickle' by means of a newer process called 'kyanizing'. Rebuilding commenced immediately and this time pipes were laid from the local waterworks across the full length of the bridge so that in the event of another fire, plugs could be pulled to cause a vast amount of water to soak the whole span. The huge central arch was in any case constructed of iron!

The whole structure was solidly rebuilt in stone and iron in 1880.

During the replacement of the burnt bridge, the main railway station was rising alongside the tracks between High Street and Mill Street. To gain access to it from the town centre, a gap had to be provided with a short stretch of new road, so two properties on the north side of High Street were demolished for this purpose; they were the 'Red House' of Llewellyn Morgan, apothecary, and the house where John Frost had resided before his enforced exile. With their removal, Station Approach was created and although the original idea was to make the access through an imposing stone archway from High Street, for some reason the plan was not carried out.

The South Wales Railway officially opened on 18th June 1850 in a way likely to be remembered throughout people's lifetimes. On that day, the first ever train made the return journey from Chepstow to Swansea; passenger fares were 12/6d for gentlemen and 7/6d for ladies. At the controls, on the platform of the engine, was the irrepressible Mr Isambard Kingdom Brunel, creator of more engineering wonders, ships, bridges, railways than any man before or since!

No matter how remote the area through which the train passed, there were knots of locals lining the track to wave and cheer. They even brought out the sick and disabled on stretchers to marvel at the sight of the little locomotive with its barrel-shaped boiler, hissing steam governor and tall, iron chimney that belched black smoke and showers of sparks!

In Newport, the welcome was ecstatic. It seemed as if the whole population was in the flag-bedecked streets, lining the road-bridge and waiting at each end of the tunnel. As the train crossed the River Usk, Mr Brunel gave several piercing blasts on the steam whistle, to be answered by a barrage of gunfire from the Barracks and in the words of an over zealous newspaper correspondent: 'thunderous cheering from a hundred thousand throats!'

After a short stop at Newport Station for the Mayor and his Corporation to give greetings and congratulations, the train continued its historic journey, first for a stop at Cardiff, and then on to Swansea where the dignitaries were treated to a civic breakfast. From then on, events on the South Wales railroad unfolded with great rapidity.

Within a few years Newport became the fulcrum of a half-circle with railways radiating east, north and west. In 1852, the Monmouthshire Railway opened its Eastern Valley line to Nantyglo and Blaina through Pontypool, then a line to Monmouth via Usk, and another to Ebbw Vale. The northern line via Abergavenny and Hereford was opened in 1853.

The year 1863 brought the Brecon and Merthyr Railway via Dowlais Top and Bargoed, and in the following year the London And North Western opened a line from Nantybwch, Tredegar, via Nine Mile Point to Newport. Then came a lull of 22 years until, in 1885, the Pontypridd and Caerphilly line connected the mineral-rich Glamorgan valleys to Newport's eager docks.

In Mill Street it will be remembered that the town's second Clock House jail had stood since 1799 but had been redundant since the opening of the new Town Hall and Police Station in Commercial Street. This quaint, circular, stone building, without a clock but so named because its predecessor had one, was finally demolished in 1848 because it encroached into the line of the railway. Some ill-informed students of the town's history for a while toyed with the theory that the Pentonville area of Mill Street owed its name to the presence of this insignificant little jail as though it had some relation to its mighty London cousin, but the ancient villeins of Pyndanville would have known better!

The High Street Station was a low, single-storey building with a booking office on each of its two platforms. It remained thus, virtually unaltered, until the present, brick, multi-storeyed edifice replaced it in the early 1930s. Within three years of its original opening a further four stations were built in Newport although they were never all in use at the same time.

On 21st December 1850, a station was opened at Courtybella near the present Whitehead Iron Works. This was a temporary terminus for trains from Blaina; it became disused eight months later when a new station was erected at Lower Dock Street.

On 1st July 1852, another temporary station appeared at the Marshes Turnpike, near the bottom of Barrack Hill, for passenger trains to Pontypool Crane Street. A horse-drawn omnibus service carried travellers from the town centre and they had to climb a steep flight of steps up to the station platform.

Finally, on 9th March 1853, a station opened in Mill Street (adjoining High Street Station) to replace the temporary halt at Barrack Hill.

Mill Street and Dock Street Stations closed to passengers in 1880 and all traces of both have now disappeared. The fact that the only station in the modern town is still officially addressed as 'Newport High Street', shows that there was a time when it was necessary to identify it from the others.

The goods lines of these stations were in many cases laid over the old tramroads which ran through the streets of the town from Courtybella to the Old Town Dock, from Pillbank Junction to Dock Street and from Llanarth Street to Salutation Junction. Very little remains of this network but if one knows where to look, short sections of rusting and overgrown rails, empty railway 'avenues' and tell-tale signs of level crossings in main streets can still be found.

As a footnote to the story of Newport's railways, it only needs to be said that the tracks in the early days would have presented a strange sight to the modern beholder. They were laid to Brunel's broad gauge of 7 feet 0.¼inches and were only replaced by the much narrower standard gauge of 4 feet 8 ½ inches in 1872. Three years after this, the Monmouthshire Railway was absorbed into the Great Western Railway.

In order for the railway to reach High Street Station after crossing the River Usk, it was necessary to lay track across the end of Thomas Street, and this was achieved by means of a level crossing with gates, effectively closing this narrow but vital roadway every time a train was due.

The Railway Company suggested to Newport Corporation as early as 4th August 1846 that Thomas Street be permanently closed and a new opening made through the castle precincts into Marshes Road, but this was too controversial to contemplate in the case of the thousand year old thoroughfare. Such action had to wait another forty years before it was seriously considered.

Thomas Street was still the only access from the town centre into Mill Street, and on to Malpas. For a time the level crossing was not too troublesome but when the arrival of trains became more frequent the resulting closing of the gates caused much frustration and inconvenience. In 1873 therefore, the Corporation agreed with the Great Western Railway that the crossing should be closed, Thomas Street was permanently blocked off except for a pedestrian subway and an overbridge provided for the use of the residents of Pentonville. A new opening was to be formed from the castle precincts into Marshes Road.

187

Newport 1829 as seen from Duckpool Pill

A brewery was then in possession of the castle and negotiations for its land were protracted, but eventually everything was settled amicably, the Council and the GWR sharing costs.

An opening was excavated in the railway embankment where it crossed the Castle Green, an iron bridge was inserted and , in 1875, the new road access from High Street was created. It required but a name and popular opinion was for 'New Entrance' (ie into Marshes Road) but, confounding everyone, the Corporation, in 1875, chose 'Shaftesbury Street', after the 7th Earl, who whilst being renowned for his great sympathy and help for the poor, had no connection in any shape or form with the town of Newport! Resistance to the new name remained fairly solid among at least two further generations of citizens who insisted on sticking to Marshes Road!

~ 0 ~

In the town centre several improvements were deemed necessary
- two of them very urgently!

The first, taking place on Stow Hill in 1862, was to the footpath on the right hand side ascending. As today, it stood high above the roadway and was obviously the original level of the surface from which the road had been scoured by centuries of travellers. It was unpaved, uneven and had a sheer drop at the side with no parapet. Over the years there had been many accidents, some serious, and although most involved homeward bound roisterers the worse for drink, the path was highly dangerous to anyone during the hours of darkness. The embankment was therefore shored up and contained in stone, the surface was paved and a parapet raised. At intervals, railed ramps were placed to give access to the roadway and, but for one major overhaul, it subsists today pretty much as it did then.

Set into the stone retaining walls were the doors of cellars belonging to the houses on that side of Stow Hill. They were in very dilapidated condition in 1862 and at a Council meeting, were described as presenting the appearance of 'a gentleman in clean linen with a black eye!' No action was proposed as the doors were privately owned.

The second serious problem was with the river bridge - 'the fine stone bridge' built in 1800 when the population was about 1,087. Over half a century later, it was doing its best to cope with something in the neighbourhood of 25,000, in addition to the vastly increased numbers of outsiders who wished to cross from Maindee in order to take advantage of trade in the town.

The bridge was too narrow and nose-to-tail traffic jams of horse-drawn wagons, coaches and handcarts, trying to pass each other, mounted the narrow footways making urgent action imperative.

In January 1865, a meeting of the Highways Committee was held to discuss a widening scheme. A design by T Dyne Steel, the Borough Engineer, at a cost of £1,575, was approved and work commenced.

Additional new pedestrian walkways were added on either side, projecting out over the river, supported on lattice girders cantilevered up from the existing sides of the bridge and surfaced in tarmacadam. The old footways were absorbed into the carriageway to increase its width to 23 feet. The improvements were finished in 1866 and in conjunction with the strange non-obligatory by-law which for some time had required pedestrians to keep to the right, the jostling on the pavements was somewhat eased.

The mounting problem of disposal of the dead was also being resolved. Burials continued in the St Woolos Churchyard until its final closure in 1866, but they were mainly in family graves and all other interments were placed in Newport Cemetery, opened in 1854 on land obtained from the Tredegar Estate between the Risca and Bassaleg Roads - the first municipally-owned burial ground in Great Britain.

The chapel cemeteries in regular use around the town were those of Mill Street Chapel (next oldest to St Woolos), the Tabernacle and English Baptist both in Commercial Street, Mount Zion, Hill Street, the Welsh Baptist, Charles Street and the Ebenezer Chapel opposite the Salutation Inn. Their burial grounds were all closed in 1869. Another new cemetery was consecrated at Christchurch in 1883.

It does seem that in the latter half of the 19th centuary, the attitudes of Newport's town councils had changed from those that had prevailed in the years before and immediately following the introduction of the 1835 Municipal Corporations Act.

In those days, to hold a council meeting was to hold a 'hall' and the minute books recording the halls of the Corporation up to 1805 cannot be said to make interesting reading as there is little to read. At the top of each foolscap page appears the names of all those who attended the first meeting and then below, *on the same page*, are details of the next six or seven meetings, with the unlikely implication that there was never any alteration to the numbers or identities of those in attendance. The 'details' consisted of the date of the meeting, the place and usually a short list of newly sworn-in burgesses. Apparently no town business came up for discussion.

Then, after 1805, a change occurs and each meeting acquires a whole page or even two to itself, each commencing with a full list of those actually present.

It may be of relevance to the improved record keeping to mention the fact that on 9th November 1805, before the Mayor and seven aldermen, a new recorder was sworn in - none other than Sir Charles Morgan of Tredegar! At the same meeting, Rowley Lascelles was sworn in as a burgess and immediately afterwards as an alderman of the borough - at the beginning of the meeting he was not even a member of the town, but at the end he was a member of its ruling hierarchy! Exactly the same thing happened to Samuel Homfray senior and, by the time Commercial Street opened in 1812, Richard Fothergill had also received these honours. The whole of the Board of Directors of the Tredegar Wharf Company had therefore become members of Newport Corporation!

This partial handing-over of the running of the town to a small but very powerful clique in the aldermanic lobby can only suggest that Newport was paying a higher price for the Pillgwenlly concessions than history has popularly been led to believe.

Those early corporations were composed in the main of self-made, unscrupulous men who were often accused of using their positions to feather their own nests, and to whom accountability was a dirty word. Many were the libel cases in which they were involved and fierce were the verbal battles in the council chamber which were usually won for them by the simple expedient of closing ranks against their accusers.

Men like John Frost and James Brown, a generation apart, were both highly respected Mayors of Newport, both spent their political careers fighting hypocrisy and corruption, and both paid dearly in financial terms for their integrity.

All the improvements in the town, carried out under the auspices of those early councils, were mostly on the grander scale, smacking somewhat of empire building. Many thousands of pounds were expended on necessary but over-lavish municipal buildings and extensive improvement to the port facilities - all guaranteed to add prestige to those mayors, aldermen and council members who presided over them.

Meanwhile the cemetery became a charnel house, the canal a sewer, the water supply badly tainted and the streets permanently filthy and odorous. To make matters worse, there was no place for the treatment of the sick, the poor were kept just above starvation level and everywhere could be seen bare-footed, begging children for whom there was no hope of even the most basic schooling.

No attempt was made to tackle the problem of Newport's 'festering sore' , Friars Fields, and possibly the fact that for a long period it was owned by the Town Clerk, Thomas Prothero, had something to do with this!

This was the scenario against which John Frost made his debut when he set up his drapery business in High Street in 1811, and he immediately began to campaign for reform. He was known as an avid pamphleteer and continually flooded the town with his broadsheets, bitterly criticizing conditions imposed on and suffered by the working classes; he was also prepared to mount any rostrum to give vent to his feelings in powerful, inflammatory rhetoric, probably learned during his apprenticeship in London where he had spent much of his time in the coffee shops and taverns frequented by militants and revolutionaries who were deeply influenced by recent events across the English Channel in the shadow of Madame Guillotine.

What all this led to, and the disastrous consequences to be seen in the years to come, have been reviewed in another chapter but undoubtedly much of John Frost's wrath was fuelled by the profligate examples, witnessed in his early years, of the actions of those councils interested more in their self-esteem than the welfare of those they were elected to protect.

An end was at least put to the contentious question of the Town Marshes over which many successive corporations had cast covetous eyes whilst trying to forget that they were only trustees for the freemen shareholders and not outright owners. It had been one of John Frost's oft-repeated claims that much of the freeholders' income from the Marshes was used to pay for municipal banquets!

The original number of freemen having shares in the income from the Marshes had once been well over a hundred. This income was made up from sales of hay, grazing leases, lettings for other purposes and occasional use as a race-course. The number of shareholders gradually diminished as members died but widows were allowed to take over their late husbands' portions until they too died or remarried. By 1868 there were only 35 valid shares remaining, 20 in 1878, only 3 in 1880 and in 1905, just a solitary widow; this was the widow of Abraham Clements and, living into very old age, she received the last payment of all, remarkably, in 1924! The last full freeman was William Williams, the town cryer, who died in 1891.

For the six years prior to 1855, the income from the Marshes averaged a mere £60 a year, which shared out in paltry amounts when apportioned to those entitled.

The Newport Corporation Act of 1855 presented a very satisfactory solution to the problem. It enabled the Corporation to purchase the interests of the remaining freemen on generous terms that provided more profitable shares in the sum of £200 a year for the first five years, £140 for the next five years and £100 thereafter. These amounts ensured that each freeholder or widow would be two to three times better off, and their share of the income would increase proportionately as numbers grew less.

The 44 acres of the Marshes finally became fully vested in the Corporation with no encumbrances on 26th May 1896, and by 1901 about 500 houses were erected, bringing in £900 a year in ground rents. The 16 acres that remained after this development were dedicated as a public open space, becoming known as Shaftesbury Park, taking its name from the the nearby main road to the town centre.

The Corporation's penchant for naming streets after recent mayors of the town was now exercised more vigorously than ever. As always, the public was not consulted; if they had been, the choices would certainly have reflected more lively and imaginative tastes!

In the case of the Marshes Estate, the names Pugsley, Evans and Hoskins were well to the fore. Less obvious were Wyndham (Wyndham Jones, Mayor in 1872), and Nelson Street after Nelson Hewertson who was Mayor in 1873. One would have to delve deeply into council minutes to discover why, several years after its christening, this latter street was re-endowed with that same gentleman's surname. One might only suspect that this was at the instigation of of those closest to Mr Hewertson who feared that to future generations his eminence would be erroneously attributed to the country's most illustrious naval hero!

Chapter Eleven

The Nineteenth Century

New Dock Street and a Free Library
A great day of inauguration
Public Transport - The Tramways.

W A Baker's Westgate Foundry, Dock Street and Skinner Street, 1900

Any one of Newport's current, younger generation who knows only the short length of what today passes for Dock Street, must find it hard to believe that this was once a bustling, half-mile long artery that geographically divided the town, but at the same time formed an inseparable umbilicus pumping lifeblood from the docks to the commercial centres. From north to south it maintained a strict boundary between the major areas of shopping and river wharfage with its maritime trade. Even its name was not then anomalous for it *really* did lead all the way to the docks, and every aspect of the town's life and culture was reflected along its length.

At the High Street end was the General Market with its appurtenant wholesale warehouses for fruit, vegetables, meat and fish. Opposite was a cobbled, open-air market where travelling traders displayed their wares and shouted humorous spiels, often by the light of naked acetylene lamps. On the 22nd August 1949, this spot became the town's first central omnibus station, then a car park and currently a pleasantly paved and landscaped area.

Lower down, where Skinner Street and Corn Street crossed, were the corn merchants, more wholesale fruit and vegetable warehouses, the Windsor Castle and Potters Arms public houses and the Olympia Cinema (the largest of ten in the town, built upon the site of the old Westgate Iron Foundry). Beyond were to be found Police Headquarters, Capitol Car Park, Capitol Cinema, Central Fire Station, Public Museum and Art Gallery and Newport Playgoers Little Theatre. This comprised most of the 'lost' portion of Dock Street, now buried under the

Kingway Shopping Centre and Central Bus Station.

Up to this point, the nature of the buildings indicated that here was the locality that catered whole-heartedly for the town's cultural, educational and entertainment needs.

Crossing over Ebenezer Terrace as it curled round towards its convergence with Commercial Street and Cardiff Road at the Salutation Inn, was equivalent to taking a step back in time and this is still possible today for Lower Dock Street exists virtually unchanged.

This is the Great Dock Road of old, the road unintentionally hammered out by the army of navvies taking a short cut across the nine feet deep hollow of Pillgwenlly marshland to their work of building the Town Dock. From Ebenezer Terrace to George Street and beyond, the commercial heart of Newport pulsated. Now a shabby, run-down area, many of its buildings still show in their architecture, evidence of an opulence to match their former status.

Here were the offices and apartments of the wealthy shipowners, agents, brokers and chandlers; colliery proprietors and coal merchants abounded; docks administration was represented by the Harbour Commissioners, the Board of Trade and the Custom House, still standing proud since its removal from Skinner Street in 1858, and joining the ranks of the few Newport buildings privileged to wear a blue commemorative plaque.

There were nearly two dozen foreign consulates and vice consulates, two army drill-halls, the Masonic Hall and eight large public houses. The place teemed with a vigour that any of Newport's present day streets would have been hard put to rival.

Continuing across the George Street intersection, on the left, was the old Western Valley Freight Railway Station and beyond it the Octopus Bridge, entrance to the Town Dock. Opposite, on the corner of South Market Street, stood the Richmond Hotel which in its previous incarnation as the Union Inn, provided refreshment and guidance for the owners of the hundreds of tramping boots; returning, next was John Street, one of the entrances to the great Cattle Market.

All this is within living memory in a truly historic but nevertheless fledgeling street. So how did Dock Street materialise so quickly in a town whose other basic thoroughfares took centuries to develop?

The completion of the Town Dock in 1842 exacerbated the problem of passage through the narrow streets by the sudden change of direction of the bulk of the labour force to the southern end of the town. It had been bad enough at the commencement of operations, but the workmen themselves had achieved a partial solution from Club Row onwards. But to get to this point, where Cross Street and Cross Lane intersected, the main route was by way of Skinner or Corn Streets and the canal bank. Local people knew this and avoided it whenever possible as it was not a pleasant path by any means, taking into consideration that it skirted the 'mantrap' of Friars Fields and was unlit and dangerous along the towpath. In addition, the highway through Club and Poplar Rows was usually disgusting with the ordures cast out by the inhabitants!

The majority of the dock workers were strangers to the town, and being unfamiliar with the terrain, sought out safer alternatives to their destination along byways previously considered inviolable by the locals.

Commercial Street led only to Pill Road (Commercial Road) which even then, twenty years after its laying down, was still an unmade, dangerous route to negotiate. The more popular course chosen by the men was down the narrow lane from Commercial Street, at the side of the Tabernacle Chapel, across the gardens of Jayne's Buildings and Union Street at the rear, to the junction of Cross Street and Club Row. Here was Mellons Bank (Mellon Street) and here commenced the unofficial, artificial, Great Dock Road trodden out across the wetlands.

The Tabernacle, Commercial Street 1906

194

Someone must have thought this to be a good idea and it was not actively discouraged. Rather was the stretch officially acknowledged by 1839 as the regular route for vehicular traffic to the docks. However, this built up so rapidly that Tabernacle Lane soon became a bottleneck of immense inconvenience.

The newly formed Great Dock Street crossed an ancient division of Newport formerly known as Caer Fitchog, and at a sharp left hand turn into Tabernacle Lane, came up against the end of the Tabernacle Burial Ground and the back wall of a carpenter and coffin maker's workshop in Llanarth Street. In December 1839 the latter was removed to give a new entrance (just as narrow but without the sharp bend) into Llanarth Street. Also in 1839, Newport for the first time allotted numbers or names to every property in the town and shortly afterwards the first mentions in writing of Dock Street addresses began to appear, thus planting the official seal of approval on the name.

On 26th May 1840, Sarah Williams advertised in the Merlin that she was opening a millinery shop at No 4. By 1846 there were nineteen three-storied houses and in one of them, No 17, Doctor Woollett opened the Newport Dispensary.

By 1850, the narrowness of the entrance from Llanarth Street was causing great problems. The solution was obvious - the Tabernacle's graveyard had to go!

This piece of ground extending across the end of Dock Street suddenly caused the normal carriageway to become funnelled into half its breadth. Another Newport Improvement Act allowed the widening to take place by the removal of much of the burial ground, and this was done by the exhumation of bodies resulting from twenty eight years of interments, and reburial in old St Woolos Cemetery.

Dock Street was now an important addition to town centre topography although it extended only from the docks as far as Llanarth Street - important enough nevertheless to come in for a spate of building such as the town had not seen for some time. The speed with which houses were erected caused the immediate neighbourhood to deteriorate rapidly by reason of the untidiness of the contractors and the excessive debris of the trade.

When the pattern of streets remains unchanged long term, it is much easier to convey some idea of what a town looked like a century earlier. It is in cases such as Newport's, where modern development has obliterated or changed the course of many of those streets, that describing them becomes much more difficult. Dock Street is a particular illustration.

In old Newport - and here is only meant pre 1970 - the Tabernacle Chapel was a fine example of early, 19th century chapel architecture. Its handsome, 45 feet wide, dark red brick facade had dominated Commercial Street since 1822 and it has been used in this piece of narrative as a guide to the position of adjacent streets and buildings. But where was the Tabernacle itself situated?

The reader is requested to imagine himself/herself to be standing outside Lloyds Bank, 42 Commercial Street, on the corner of Llanarth Street. Here in 1850 was the printing works of George Corner and next to it, along Commercial Street, was the 700 seater Tabernacle Chapel. It was never the custom to include churches or chapels in street numbering sequences, but today it has been necessary to address the two shops that now occupy the site, as numbers 42A and 42B.

Tabernacle Lane ran down the northern side of the chapel but the building of the printing works completely sealed its Commercial Street entrance.

On the right, proceeding down Llanarth Street towards John Frost Square, are to be found numbers 42 to 39 consecutive, all now modern shops. Here at number 40 was Newport's original ' Dispensary' which in 1847 became the Volunteer Tavern and in 1882, the Borough Arms. The large shop on the corner of Llanarth Street and John Frost Square stands just about on the spot where the old carpenter's shop was broken through to give

Dock Street's new entrance, and more recently was the site of Phillips' second hand shop, 164 to 166 Dock Street. Right in that corner of the Square would have been the lower end of Tabernacle Lane, and the Borough Library, Art Gallery and Museum occupy, almost exactly, the old Tabernacle Burial Ground which was removed to widen Dock Street.

So it was here that the original street ended and immediately opposite, on the other side of Llanarth Street, was a gap between two properties entrance into Friars Fields, a no-go area for any respectable citizen.

In 1860 the Fields, extending to 12,000 square yards and incorporating 169 mean tenements, were purchased by Newport Corporation and the long-awaited demolition and clean-up began.

First proposals for the future use of this land were as a public park, but sites for light industry and warehousing, with a sprinkling of dwelling houses, finally won the day. At the same time, the Borough Engineer put forth a proposal to extend Great Dock Street through to Corn Street but this suggestion was not then acted upon. It was not until a council meeting on 22nd February 1881 that a firm decision was taken to push Dock Street through to High Street, to emerge near the bridge opposite the new entrance made into Shaftesbury Street in 1875.

Newport Free Library, as first established 1870

It seems that no sooner was it said than it was done. Only eighteen months and £30,000 expenditure later the work was finished, Newport had acquired its first town centre by-pass and a direct link had been forged with the docks, a link that generated a new vibrant efficiency - something in which the old town had recently been flagging.

From its old terminus in Llanarth Street the extension crossed Friars Fields, eradicated Union Row, took a strip off the top of Batchelors Timber Yard, cut across Skinner Street, Upper Merchant Street (across the front entrance of the Provision Market) and on to the Old Green. Making way for it required the demolition of dozens of houses, shops, warehouses, stores and stables, not to mention several well known public houses.

Newport Library and Art Gallery, Dock Street (rebuilt 1882)

The Free Libraries Act 1870 gave local authorities the option of providing their communities with places where books were available to everyone at no cost. Newport's altruistic Corporation opened its first free library on 1st February 1871 in the old Diocesan Schoolroom, Dock Street. It started out with 3,064 volumes and in the first year there were 27,992 borrowings, proving the wisdom of the Council's quick implementation of the Act!

Lord Tredegar made a gift of the school site in order for the Corporation to build a new library. While this was going on, the books were temporarily housed in the Ragged School.

By 1882, another grand building graced the town. At a cost of £3,500, George Thomas, a Pembroke Builder, erected the library in architecture of the Free Style Renaissance. Constructed in blue pennant stone with freestone dressings, it had a frontage to Dock Street of 66 feet, a depth of 108 feet and was addressed as No 158. It was shelved to accommodate 40,000 books. It also contained a museum and art gallery that almost immediately proved to be too small. In 1895, at a cost of £1,138, an extension at the rear made good this deficiency.

Demand for the use of the library became so overwhelming that it was necessary to open further branches at Temple Street (1890), Maindee (1898) and Lyne Road (1899).

In those days there was nothing that Newport liked better than a great show of parading and partying in the streets, and on many occasions past it had found good reason for such celebration. When it happened no expense was spared in the decoration of the streets, entertainment of the public or fêting of the dignitaries. This latter aspect was not so strange as it appears, for one of the more unusual habits of the Victorian working classes was to make a fuss of their betters, creating much jollification on the uncommon occasions when the local aristocracy appeared among them. One such day was 7th November 1882 when not only one, but five memorable events were the reason for festivity!

When Park Square was formed in 1860, the central area of verdure was closed to the public. Later that same year, the statue of Sir Charles Morgan, 1st Baron Tredegar, was removed from its site in High Street where it had languished for ten years, and was re-erected in the Square. The workmen who safely accomplished this task were Messrs Clarke and Wynn, the latter being the grandfather of Robert Wynn the well known, national heavy haulage contractor. The small park still remained an inaccessible, railed-in shrine to the noble lord for the next 22 years. Its first inauguration as a public park was part of the wonderful package opened on that November day in 1882.

Following hard in its footsteps, came a most unusual cause for rejoicing - the return of the silver mace missing for over two hundred years from Newport's civic regalia. It had not been seen since 1655 when Walter Nichols was mayor. The mace even bore the Nichol 's family crest and Walter's name was mentioned in the charter of James I. Now, a Mrs Nichols, descendant of Walter and still resident in the town, had found the mace in a long un-opened family chest and presented it back to the town with suitable pomp and ceremony.

The same day was chosen for the official opening of the new wards for twenty patients at the Stow Hill Infirmary, and the resplendent Municipal Library, Museum and Art Gallery in Dock Street. The icing on the cake came with the cutting of the ribbon to accept the new, extended Dock Street as one of the town's main thoroughfares.

The noted Newport historian and former borough librarian, Mr James Matthews, wrote of the occasion as if he was an eye witness which, as a young man, he might well have been. Certainly no more graphic account of the celebrations exists than his, and it is therefore deemed appropriate to borrow this extract from 'Historic Newport' -

'In years gone by the people of Newport had celebrated the various events of local interest by demonstrations which were regarded as being of credit to the town, but the great pageantry of November 7th 1882, in honour of these undertakings threw all previous efforts into the shade. Throughout the entire length of new Dock Street, Venetian masts were placed, prettily decorated with thousands of flags, banners and shields . . . while at High Street a reception pavilion was erected, richly draped in crimson cloth and bullion fringe, and profusely set off at the top with banners and flags. Over the entrance to the Town Hall a massive coat-of-arms was placed, backed with flags of all nations. Other streets along the line of the route were also decorated with arches, Venetian masts, flags and devices.

The procession consisted of the Corporation, Magistrates, Clergy and Ministers, Consuls, Directors and representatives of all public bodies in the Borough . . . After passing through the public streets the procession passed through the new thoroughfare and broke off at the Free Library. From that moment the old name of 'Great' Dock Street sank into oblivion!

The story of public transport in Newport began many years in advance of the first tramcar making its appearance on the streets.

Several entrepreneurs took the opportunity during this period to provide horse-drawn passenger carriages over various routes, with varying degrees of success. George Masters was the first. He was licensee of the Parrot Inn and like most publicans of that era, he went in for sidelines; for a while, public transport was his.

Newport Corporation Horse Bus 1880

In 1845, he commenced running a twenty seater carriage from his wine vaults in Bridge Street to Church Street Pillgwenlly, making four return journeys a day at what was then a hefty fare of four pence.

From then on, others introduced services throughout the town and to destinations as far afield as Pontypool, Monmouth, Abergavenny and Chepstow. The omnibuses of Messrs Pobjoy, Wilton and Williams were also well known on Newport's streets. Within the borough however, the passenger trade mostly favoured the routes between the railway stations. Samuel T Hallan, the long term licensee of the Westgate Hotel, was also an interested party in such ventures, and he eventually handed over the running of the hotel to his wife so that he could concentrate fully on his horse buses.

In 1870, Parliament, bowing to pressure all over the country from towns eager for this kind of public transport, introduced the Tramways Act, 'to facilitate the construction and regulate the working of tramways'. The first steps in this direction were to be the obtaining of a provisional order from the Board of Trade, followed by a confirmatory local Act of Parliament.

One would think that with so many other towns setting the example, that Newport's hitherto progressive ruling body would have been quick to follow suit but curiously, although not altogether unpredictably, such was not the case.

At a meeting of the Council on 22nd November 1870, a small group of supporters raised the question of installing a tramway system; the proposal was not well received!

At successive meetings extending over the next two and a half years, the short-sighted majority imposed its will with excuse after excuse as to why the idea was untenable. It was insisted that the cost would be insupportable, that the narrowness of the streets would not allow easy passage to the tramcars, that it was totally unfair for publicly-owned land to be used for private profit, and some councillors persisted with the uncorroborated opinion that the scheme did not find favour with the general public.

Uncharacteristically, one of the most vociferous leaders of the anti-tramway faction was the ageing Alderman Samuel Homfray who in his younger days had vigorously supported anything and everything that held promise of improving Newport's stature. His father (also Samuel) and his uncle, the late Baronet Sir Charles Morgan of Tredegar, nearly seventy years earlier, had been responsible for the formation of the Tredegar Wharf Company which had given the new suburb of Pillgwenlly to the town. Now, Samuel Homfray's objection was based upon the fact that the tram rails would have to be laid over land the freehold of which was still owned by the Company. His son, Lorenzo Augustus, also an alderman, firmly backed him in his inconsistent stand.

It was 1873 before the project received sufficient support to override the objections, and the granting of the Board of Trade Order was quickly followed by the appropriate enabling Act.

By late 1874 a single line with passing sidings ran from the Queens Hotel, Tredegar Place (Queens Square), along Commercial Street and Commercial Road to Temple Street with a loop through Ruperra Street, Dock Street, and Bolt Street serving Dock Street Railway Station. Shortly afterwards the line reached the end of Commercial Road.

The official opening took place on 1st February 1875, running two cars only, but on the next day nearly 1,000 passengers were carried at the standard fare of 2d. Three years later this was reduced to 1d and immediately the number of passengers doubled!

For a short while two independent companies shared the rails in Newport's streets and there was bitter rivalry between them. The years 1884 and 1885 were notable as a period when opposing drivers obstructed, abused, raced and even fought each other to obtain custom!

In March 1885, the Newport Transport Company was formed to run the whole undertaking, and in December 1893 the Corporation decided to acquire the Company but to leave its management in the hands of private enterprise. At this time and for the first time, track was laid across the bridge to serve Maindee.

The year 1894 saw the service running the full length of the town to Pillgwenlly and by the end of that year there were termini on the other side of the river along Chepstow Road at Kensington Place, and on Caerleon and Church Roads at the foot of Christchurch Hill. Twelve months later, the Chepstow Road line had reached the Cross Hands at Somerton and by 1901 the Corporation Road terminus was at Lysaghts Works. It was at this point that Newport Corporation took over full management of the horse-tramway. Electrification was just around the corner.

Newport's first Power Station, Llanarth Street 1900

The town itself had received mains electricity in 1895.

The Board of Trade made the Newport (Monmouthshire) Electric Lighting Order 1891, an Act confirmed it and on 14th October 1895 Newport's first power station was opened between 21 and 22 Llanarth Street. Positioned across the entrance of old Union Court, this would have placed it on the eastern side of John Frost Square close to the main entrance into the modern Kingsway Shopping Centre.

The sum of £28,000 was borrowed to finance the laying down of 12,300 yards of mains

201

for private supply and 4,850 yards for street lighting. A local government enquiry held at the Town Hall on 3rd January 1894, accepted a tender of £23,384 from Messrs Fowler & Co of Leeds. A deduction of £3,828 was made from the tender to cover the cost of the power station's generating engines which were made locally by the Uskside Engineering Works. The plant had the capacity to keep 7,500 lights burning at any one time.

Initially, 40 arc lamps each of 2,000 candle-power, were erected along Llanarth Street, Commercial Street, Commercial Road, Dock Street and Bridge Street. The first building of any size to receive illumination was the Empire Theatre in Charles Street.

In 1900, the single building that comprised the power station was enlarged by the addition of new boilers, workshops and cable stores. At the same time, 36 new lamps were erected in Alexandra Road, Caerleon Road and Shaftesbury Street. Come the year 1906 and Newport possessed more electrical connections than any other town of comparable size in the country!

The Llanarth Street power station continued to be used for generating up to 1928 and was retained as a substation into the late 1960s. It was made inadequate by the electrification of the tramways in 1903, so a new East Power Station was built on Corporation Road with a tramway depot accommodating up to 50 tramcars.

The new tracks for these more sophisticated trams were bedded into mixed panels of granite setts and Jarrah hardwood blocks from a species of Western Australian eucalyptus tree. In the ensuing years, and long after the tracks were removed, roadworks which broke through the tarmac surface, often revealed the wooden blocks in High Street and Commercial Street.

The first electrified trams trundled over the bridge to Maindee in 1904, and by the end of that first year of operation the undertaking had carried 5,010,174 passengers. In 1937, their last year before being phased out, the trams carried 7,832,983 passengers but to this total must be added the 9,961,924 carried that year by the rapidly expanding, petrol driven omnibus service.

Chapter Twelve

The Nineteenth Century

Town Trivia, Crime and Punishment,
Entertainment, The Fire Brigade,
The further development of Maindee,
The Transporter Bridge, A Great Champion.

While the face of Newport was undergoing dramatic changes, and innovatory services were following each other in quick succession, ordinary life in the town went on much as it had for ages past - human nature was little affected by advances in Victorian technology.

For thirteen years, from 1857 to 1870, a weekly newspaper 'The Newport Gazette' among others, reported the ebb and flow of the town's tide of events, giving an excellent perception of the sort of place in which it was to live. The advertisement pages themselves throw plenty of light on the life-style and to a great extent the gullibility of the general public.

The Newport Lozenge House, 36 High Street, stated that their quality sweets included the celebrated pectoral cough candy, Everton (Toffy), and 'horehound' candy.

James Homer proclaimed 'Boots! Boots!' - an immense stock at 124 Commercial Street.

The Patent Vulcanised Coat was the best in waterproof clothes and 'absolutely free from smell!'

On 8th May 1858, James Cox of 31 Lower Cross Street was boasting a cargo of prime, sweet Devonshire Cider, and of first quality, Irish, 'Protestant' potatoes! No hint was given as to how one should recognise the odd Catholic 'spud' that might have infiltrated the consignment!

To take the patent medicine advertisements seriously, was to concede that medical science could go no farther.

Holloways Pills were truly 'amazing' and the list of ailments in which they were said to be efficacious was endless. What is more astonishing is that the editorial comment in one edition carried devout testimony that the pills were genuinely capable of achieving all that was claimed for them.

'Quackery unmasked and defeated!' was another slogan that continually assaulted the eye, and Doctor De Roos regularly broadcast that his 'Guttae Vitae' life pills cured everything that Holloways could not.

By 1860, a Doctor Buchan was enrapturing with stories of his vegetable skin ointment and concentrated vegetable essences as recommended by the Lord Mayor of London and the entire membership of the City Guildhall. Obviously too many late night sittings on cold hard benches were responsible for their devotion.

The Comtesse de Brissac in 1748 had discovered an infallible remedy for the removal of disfiguring smallpox scars. For a small charge Doctor Stanway was willing to divulge the secret.

Mr Blake's Peruvian Drops and Neurosian Extract were invaluable for 'those who were prevented from entering the married state by the results of early errors or youthful imprudence.'

There was a hair restorer on the market that was the 'miracle of the age'. Rosealie Coupelle's Crinutriar was sworn to by several anonymous gentlemen who, previously as bald as eggs, now sported luxuriant thatches both above and below the ears! Two years later,

Miss Coupelle had turned her attention to character reading from handwriting, and by 1866 she was an expert in perfumery.

During this newspaper's informative but limited lifetime, its pages first broke the news to its Newport readers of such momentous events as the death of Albert the Prince Consort, and the liberation of 23 million serfs in Russia by Tsar Alexander II (1861). From across the Atlantic in 1859 came news of Charles Blondin's tightrope walk across Niagara Falls and of the assassination of Abraham Lincoln (1865). From this same source Newport learned of the original Siamese Twins who, in America, had married two sisters, fathered families and despite their physical inseparability, had not spoken to each other for years because of some domestic difference! Only four years later, on 12th July 1869, those same twins visited Newport as part of their British tour.

The Suez Canal opened in 1868.

From the world's battlefronts came weekly bulletins of the Indian Mutiny (1857-1858), the American Civil War (1861-1865), the Prusso-Danish War (1864), the Austro-Prussian War (1868), the Franco-Prussian War and the Italian Wars of Unification (1870).

It was however in news closer to home - one might say from the hearth - that the heart and soul of 19th century Newport was fully exposed.

The death was reported on 30th September 1857 of George Masters, owner of the Wine Vaults in Bridge Street and pioneer of the town's first passenger omnibus service. Tragically and somewhat ironically it was an accident involving two horse-drawn vehicles that caused Mr Masters' sad demise. Returning from a visit to Caerleon late in the evening, his carriage was in collision in the pitch darkness of Maindee, with a coal cart driven by Levi Leonard. Mr Masters was thrown into a hedge and died shortly afterwards. At the subsequent enquiry, Leonard was *admonished* for his statement that he had not been drunk - 'only a little fresh from imbibing several pints of ale!'.

A few weeks later, Newport policemen broke up an illegal prize- fight in the early hours of the morning at Malpas, between 'Lewis, the Newport Mouse' and 'a Bridgewater fellow'. The attendant rabble was put to flight but it reassembled elsewhere, at a greater distance from the town, and concluded the affair.

The continuing, dreadful state of the town's streets caused a correspondent's anger and he gave vent to it by writing that he 'was never clean about the legs', and suggesting that the hordes of street urchins should be conscripted into a 'sweeping brigade' and the ragged classes into a 'bootblack Brigade!'

On February 26th 1858, Doctor Hawkins performed a caesarean operation on a Baneswell woman who was deformed and only between three and four feet tall. Under chloroform the patient 'remained unconscious to the very last stitch', and produced a healthy baby girl.

One reader's letter, printed in 1862, gave firm views on the gas meter installed in his home and the outrageous charge of two shillings a quarter made for its rental. It was, he said, 'a pretty little box with three watches on it that don't tell the time to nobody!' His contention was that the Gas Company should pay for its own tools!

The 5th November 1865 fell on a Sunday so 'squib night' was celebrated on Monday the 6th. Minutes of the next Council meeting were scathing on the subject and revealed that once again, 'Big boys and little boys were vying with each other in frightening little girls and protected females generally. The whole affair was a repetition of a nuisance which we hope and believe the next generation will never witness!' As it turned out, this was a vain hope and the flaming tar barrels continued to roll for many a squib night to come!

Another Council meeting discussed the shortcomings of Carpenters Arms Lane as a thoroughfare and possible ways of improving its ingress and egress. Apparently through this narrow alleyway, connecting High Street to Market Street, poured the whole of the traffic from the Eastern Valleys and South Wales Railway Stations, on market days especially. This avalanche of humanity would be very hard to imagine today by the occasional pedestrian who chances to use this shabby and often smelly passage.

The reporting of criminal court proceedings threw up many pithy examples of both the drama and humour of the times. Some accounts were rendered all the more entertaining by the curious way in which 19th century journalists reported, strictly verbatim, the courtroom crosstalk thus introducing a whimsical element into cases which should have remained wholly serious. An instance of this appeared in November 1857, in a case of affiliation where farmer Jonathan Leonard was summoned to show why he should not pay for the support of Ann Driscoll's illegitimate, male child.

The complainant (actually reported as a good looking, Irish serving girl) had been employed at the house of the defendant's mother and she swore that Leonard was the father of her child. She also stated that he had offered her £7 to swear the child on to someone else! A fellow servant gave evidence that he had seen the defendant and the complainant lying down side by side in a shed near the house at 6 o'clock in the morning, in January last.

'Holloa', said he, 'what be a-doing there?'

'Hoisht!' said Ann, and then it was that the servant ascertained that both had been in the shed all night - in mid-winter!

Jonathan (note the friendly use of the Christian name by the reporter) was ordered to pay two shillings a week and costs.

January 1859. Mary Croxton was charged with assaulting Mary Barry. Both made statements that were totally unintelligible to the court. Both were discharged.

August 1859. 'The murder at Newport'.

The galleries and benches of the court were packed full of ladies, all straining to catch a glimpse of Matthew Francis, 'the murderous beast' who had cut his wife's throat after a day of abusive argument started by his inefficient cooking of the breakfast bloater!

November 1859. Joanna McGrath was charged with being drunk and disorderly, in the words of the Chief Constable, 'for about the hundredth time!' The Mayor said that she seemed to have done a little better since her last appearance when he had excused her, so he excused her again. Over the next few years, she appeared at regular intervals on the same charge and received prison sentences of from two to three months on several of those occasions. By strange chance, on the night of the 1861 Census, she was listed among other women prisoners occupying cells in the Town Hall Police Station; her age was given as twenty five years and her occupation boldly inscribed as 'prostitute!' Most of the other females locked up with her were favoured with the description, 'women on ships!'

April 1862. Caroline Davies was charged with soliciting in High Street, and with being indecently dressed. She was fined twenty shillings with the option of six months in prison. The magistrate stated that he was thinking in future of displaying such offenders on a high platform in the courtroom so that everyone could see their disgraceful manner of dressing!

There were certain types of transgressions which led the field in Newport and kept the courts at their busiest. Horse, cattle and sheep stealing were very common but wife-beating was a close runner-up. As a matter of fact, there was almost a conveyor-belt quality in the courtroom appearance of men who assaulted women (wives or otherwise), only matched by the number of drunken slatterns and prostitutes involved in street brawls, who then turned their venom on to the policemen who intervened, inviting further charges against themselves by the use of obscene language screamed out to the offence of passers-by!

Violence apart however, other common misdemeanours were the making and passing of counterfeit coins, the evasion of public transport fares, the driving of horses 'frantically' and without reins, and allowing the consumption of alcohol after hours. This last offence seemed to apply to every other publican in the town, and on one notable occasion the police found that the guilty premises contained fifty men, sixteen of whom had women of ill-repute seated on their laps!

Petitions for bastardy were rife at that time, and even graffiti (a word then unknown) was obviously becoming a problem because it was discussed at another meeting of the Corporation where concern was expressed at the number defacements occurring to new and renovated buildings or anything that received a fresh coat of paint!

Even the clergy were not above reproach, and one edition of the South Wales Telegram in May 1877, was filled with criticism of the Reverend Canon Hawkins who allowed sheep to graze in St Woolos Churchyard among the graves. Apparently, in keeping down the grass they also chewed their way through all the floral tributes. One correspondent wrote: 'I'd rather eat American mutton till wool growed on me than fancy I was a-scrunching of a poor Chartists essence, or a-digesting of the remains of they poor cholera patients as was interred in the parson's sheepfold!'

Such was the way in which a portion of the town conducted its affairs - a way that the remainder, comprising the decent, honest working classes and the gentry, had to learn to live with. This was no hard matter provided a wide berth was given to the areas abutting the canal and the river wharves.

Some readers will have had great-grandparents or grandparents who knew the town under such circumstances, and even your author can claim some affinity with the period, having had a grandfather who was employed by Mr Fennell, the well known fishmonger, who in 1868 appeared several times before the magistrates on charges of poaching salmon at Goldcliff from fisheries that he eventually came to own.

A further. very odd example of conditions prevailing, was given in an article printed in 1870 by the editor of the Food Journal. The subject written of was 'food additives' but certainly not in the sense they are thought of today. The grievance was against cheap food being deliberately doctored with foreign substances to make up bulk. The writer maintained that 'food manufacturers should be compelled to state the real ingredients such as: best butter with starch, mashed potatoes and horsebone oil, coffee with breadcrumbs and sand, tea with iron filings, sugar with chromate of lead and beer with salt and cocculus indicus!'

In the town's defence however, it must be said that with all its faults it was no better and no worse than any other similar community wherein the best of the Victorian era's virtues endured an uneasy existence alongside the worst of its vices.

Nothing so far has been said of the way in which the more dilettante residents filled their leisure hours, and yet not to do so would be to omit some of the more essential ingredients that gave soul and character to the town.

There had been a time, not long departed, when entertainment consisted only of whatever people could create for themselves, or when strolling players, minstrels or mummers chanced along to give alfresco performances in the yards of public houses or in the Dragon Field. The latter flat open space near the town centre was also a popular place for displays by the military with their marching bands and refought battles of the Napoleonic Wars; it is now part of the site of High Street Railway Station.

Purpose built theatres were rarely found in small towns like Newport, and covered auditoriums, where they existed, were merely any large rooms where several rows of benches could be arranged. Certain public houses possessed such accommodation but occasionally, separate buildings were adapted for use.

Probably the first building used regularly for a theatre in Newport was the Old Tythe Barn, already mentioned in relation to the Stowe Fairs. It adjoined the old St Woolos

Vicarage which later became the thatched-roofed Six Bells Inn. Little did this historic old hostelry suspect that one day (1995) it was to have its character completely stripped away and its reputation emasculated by having its hallowed name replaced by one so insensitive and puerile that it will not be dignified here by repetition!

The Barn must have been totally adequate for its purpose because, in the later 18th and early 19th centuries, many famous actors and actresses of the day gave performances there. John Kemble, his sister Sarah Siddons and their niece Fanny Kemble, appeared several times.

Over the succeeding years several small theatres opened, flourished and died in the town. In 1821, there was a theatre on the corner of Commercial Street and the lane leading into Friars Fields (Friars Street). This was immediately opposite the opening to McCarthys Court named after Mr McCarthy the baker, whose premises were at No 6. This small cul-de-sac still exists, giving access to the service areas of adjoining shops.

This theatre, chapel-like in its construction, was known as the New Theatre and later in its career as the Old Theatre. Its owner/manager was Mr Potter, every member of whose family seemed to be possessed of acting talent and appeared regularly in their own productions.

An old playbill dated 3rd September 1821 describes the feast of entertainment offered that week. 'Ivanhoe or the Jew and his daughter' was a drama during the course of which was presented a superb view of Brian's castle on fire, the banquet hall and tower in Cedric's castle and the awful preparation for the burning alive of Rebecca. Heady stuff indeed, rounded off in appropriate style with a comic song by Master Potter and a fancy dance by Madam Grose!

The first Town Hall, opening in 1842, contained an assembly room that was eminently suitable for the seating of fair-sized audiences. After a while it became a popular venue for lectures and musical evenings. The entertainment provided was not ostentatious, noisy or over-vigorous as one came to expect in later years, but it was novel for the times and grew ever more appealing as aestheticism in taste was stimulated.

A typical night out in the Newport of 1846 might have involved a visit to the Assembly Rooms to see Mr Charles Kemble (younger brother of John). Although the weather on that evening in May was not conducive to leaving home, Mr Kemble found himself playing to a packed audience when he gave his 'Readings from Shakspere' as the show was billboarded. This was the way that the Immortal Bard's name was ordinarily spelled in those days. Later that same year, for three nights in November, the Assembly Rooms overflowed to hear the lectures of Mr Joseph Wolff, 'the renowned Eastern traveller'. His stories embraced journeys that he had made from 1821 to 1845 and were interwoven with accounts of 'perilous adventures and hairs breadth escapes which inspired thrills and horror among the audience.

At regular intervals they came to Newport to transport their ecstatic audiences for a few short hours out of their humdrum existence into worlds of magic and make-believe. Explorers, theologians, actors and actresses, poets and politicians - all brought their own brands of escapism guaranteed to send their devotees home to their beds with their heads in the clouds.

Unusually for those days, a huge band of musicians, the Julien Symphony Orchestra was touring the country. It was notable for its fifteen French drummers and drum major. They appeared at the Town Hall in 1847 and 1850.

By 1854 however, all the evidence pointed to the fact that a proper theatre was required. There was no serious complaint about the Assembly Rooms, only that they were not always available.

On 28th March, work commenced on a prime site at the corner of Great Dock Street and Caroline Street where the old castle-like, ex-drillhall now stands. Here soon afterwards,

Newport's 'Theatre Royal' was opened by a one-armed actor/manager named Chadwick. His missing hand was apparently replaced by a large metal hook! From all accounts this elegant theatre bore an uncanny resemblance to Shakespeare's 'Globe'.

Chadwick's wife was also an actress, a rather large handsome lady, quite talented and popular with all the local 'stage door Johnnies' who in those days were very appreciative of ample proportions. 'House full' notices were a regular feature in the foyer.

For three years the Theatre Royal delighted the citizens of Newport and then, early in 1857, disaster struck. James Chadwick, appearing in a show with some nautical connection, had just finished a spirited clog and hornpipe dance and was about to enter the finale wherein a ship was to go up in flames. Incommoded by his one arm, Chadwick was helped in the pyrotechnics by a ship's chandler, Captain George Williams, and young George Hoskins who was destined to be a future mayor of the town. Something exploded prematurely, all the fireworks went off together and flames ran up the curtains. The audience escaped unharmed but the theatre burned to the ground. No one showed any interest in its restoration so the ruin was abandoned.

The Chadwicks however, were a forceful enterprising couple and without ado they opened another theatre on the ballast bank at the Capel Crescent end of Lewis Street. Although only a timber structure, it must have been substantial for it had seating for between 800 and 1,000 patrons.

Opposition soon arrived in the shape of another actor/manager, Mr Lovegrove, who opened a theatre in George Street, the site of which has since been occupied by another drillhall, a clothing factory, a builders merchant and currently a furniture superstore.

Chadwicks theatre survived the competition because it was fortunate enough to receive the patronage of the iron magnate, Samuel Homfray, his brother-in-law Viscount Tredegar and several other wealthy county families. When the building finally ceased its theatrical career it was used until its demolition as a totally ineffectual isolation hospital for infectious diseases.

The Parrot Inn now stepped into the breach. By 1840 it had been extended at the rear by a bar-like room with rows of bare benches on flooring raised from the aisles along which passed waiters with such beverages as the patrons desired. The position of this little theatre, known for a while as 'The Gaiety' and later as 'Morella's Palace of Varieties', earmarked the spot for future histrionics being as it was almost exactly where in Charles Street the New Theatre (afterwards renamed The Empire Theatre) was built in 1888. Shortly after the building of the Parrot Gaiety, Howard Johnson of the Theatre Royal, Haymarket, fitted it out in a way suitable for dramatic presentation. This 'petite salle' as it was then described opened with Tobin's 'The Honeymoon' followed by 'George Barnwell' and 'Raising the Wind'.

A population of over 23,000, steadily increasing in 1861, made it abundantly clear that another, larger venue for public diversion and amusement was a matter of the greatest urgency. Emerging to fill this need was the great Victoria Hall.

The new Bridge Street was opened in 1863. It led from High Street (Westgate Square) into Baneswell and out again towards the higher ground where the trains emerged from the tunnel, slowing on their short, final run into High Street Station. At this point a bridge carried the road over the tunnel to its junction with Devon Place. At the western end of Baneswell Square, on either side of Bridge Street, there arose two fine buildings that were to become town landmarks to at least four generations of Newport residents.

Mr H Pearce Bolt was not a native of Newport but arrived as a young stonemason from his birthplace in Hatherleigh in Devon. Gradually winning a reputation for quality building, he was responsible for his own home, Hatherleigh House Christchurch, and gave his name to Bolt Street Pillgwenlly, and Bolts Row Chepstow Road. His finest achievements were the

Queens Hotel and the Victoria Hall Assembly Rooms.

The hotel stood centrally dominating the Square. It opened in 1863, and from that day forward that portion of Bridge Street became familiarly known as Queens Square. The Assembly Rooms were immediately opposite to the hotel on the other side of Bridge Street although the main entrance was in Station Street. The site is now that of the Cannon Cinema.

An article in the illustrated London News on 1st February 1868, gave a glowing description of this splendid new home of the live arts, and likened it to the best of its kind in the country. A résumé of this report is as follows:-

'Costing £12,000 the building has a seating capacity of 2,500 in its galleried auditorium, measuring 56 feet by 77 feet. The stage measures 30 feet by 43 feet. In the great vaulted basement are Turkish and swimming baths, a reading room and a room used by the County Court. Externally, a wide flight of steps commands the entrance.

Noble porticos are carried up to the extreme height of the building, supported on six Corinthian columns with well carved capitals surmounted by a prominent and excellently executed figure of Her Majesty with leonine supports'.

It proudly opened its doors to Newport on 28th February 1867 with a performance of 'The Messiah', and from then onwards it never looked back. Listed among its steady stream of popular plays were Rob Roy, The Man in the Iron Mask, The Corsican Brothers, The Three Musketeers, Rip Van Winkle and Dick Turpin. Many productions of Shakespeare and Gilbert and Sullivan followed.

May 1869. Lady Don, a leading actress, performed in 'The Daughter of the Regiment', 'The Maid with the Milking Pail', 'Sweethearts and Wives' and 'Simpson and Co'.

March 1870. Messrs Pool and Young exhibited their 'Phantoscope'. displaying special tableaux and illusionary scenes being 'wondrous, interesting, beautifully amusing and instructive'.

May 1870, The Great Vance filled the evening with a selection of comic songs and impersonations.

June 1870. Ada Warren, a clever and accomplished actress, gave the closing performance of the theatrical season in 'Time and the Hour' and 'Mr & Mrs White.'

Probably the most famous of all personalities to grace this stage was the world renowned author, Charles Dickens, who appeared on Thursday, January 21st 1869. During the course of that memorable evening he steered an enthralled audience through tears and laughter with his emotional readings from 'A Christmas Carol' and 'Pickwick'. A tumultuous standing ovation was his reward.

Sadly, this was the one and only time that he was to be seen in the town, because he died the following year on June 9th, with one book unfinished.

Imagine then, the enterprise of the Newport printer and bookseller who was offering this book, 'The Mystery of Edwin Drood', in a serialised form, only one month after the great man's death! (Newport Gazette July 9th 1870).

Novelty acts there were in abundance, and one of the most popular was 'Alvo, Emperor of the Air' doing double somersaults and a great evolution and flight from ceiling to stage!" His last appearance was on February 12th 1883, and for a few months afterwards the Assembly Rooms were closed.

The Lyceum Theatre, Bridge Street Newport

Some renovation and refurbishment took place, and on August 27th 1883 'The Royal Victoria Theatre' opened its doors.

The occasion was marked in performances of 'HMS Pinafore' and 'The Pirates of Penzance' by the Company of Mr D'Oyly Carte. The year ended with the pantomime 'Aladdin and his Wonderful Lamp' with placards proclaiming that 'it is produced in a magnificence never before attempted in this town!'

On the night of 27th May 1896, history repeated itself. The Royal Victoria Theatre caught fire and like the Theatre Royal forty years earlier, was completely gutted despite all the efforts of the town's fairly new fire brigade. At one o'clock in the morning, the great roof fell in and all was lost.

For a short time afterwards, Newport had only one place for large gatherings of a serious nature and this was the Royal Albert Hall, built in 1875, but not the stately edifice that its august name suggested.

Completely hemmed in by buildings fronting Commercial Street and Stow Hill, it had no adequate facade to either, although there was an insignificant entrance from each. Internally however, it was large and well furnished. In later life it became Stow Hill Territorial Army Drill Hall, well known during the Second World War, and for some years afterwards for its Saturday night 'hops'. It was demolished in the 1970s, but its site has been preserved in the form of a new service road to the rear of the large Commercial Street shops, creating a throughway from Stow Hill via the old School Road to Charles Street.

An ornamental flowerbed and a commemorative plaque marks the old Stow Hill entrance to the Albert Hall, the peculiar situation of which is easy to imagine from the unlovely rear aspect of the surrounding buildings.

Early examination of the burned out shell of the Victoria Theatre gave rise to some optimism as the external walls remained firm and tall, with the statue of Queen Victoria still erect on her lofty perch at the front gable end, smoke-blackened but sound. It was therefore considered worthwhile to rebuild in its original form and, at a cost of £20,000, the phoenix rose from the ashes.

On 4th October 1897, the noble theatre renamed the 'Lyceum' opened with the musical show, 'The Geisha'. Prices were: stalls and circle four shillings, balcony three shillings, pit one shilling and six pence, pit stalls one shilling, and gallery (the gods) six pence.

The Lyceum's seating capacity was 1,000 less than the old Royal Victoria of which it had been said that two circus rings could be set up in the auditorium and still leave room for a huge audience. Nevertheless, the Lyceum Theatre became no less rich in its traditions, and the most illustrious names in the entertainment world were pleased to walk its boards. In quick succession and at regular intervals came Sir Henry Irving, Ellen Terry, Sarah Bernhardt, the Garrick Company, the Carl Rosa Opera Company and John Philip Sousa and his fifty strong brass band. For one week in April 1905, the great magician and escapologist, Harry Houdini, thrilled the crowds and also added to his prestige by making a spectacular escape from a cell in Newport Police Station.

So the shows went on, well into the 20th century, until eventually, a reluctant management had to concede that live entertainment in Newport could no longer compete with that offered by the cinema screen. After the Second World War, the beautiful old theatre joined the ranks of the nine picture palaces in the town (the Maindee, Coliseum, Odeon, Olympia, Capitol, Tredegar Hall, Pavilion, Plaza (ex Tivoli) and the Gem).

Occasionally, a live show was still presented, and that usually did well because it had now become a novelty; Christmas pantomime attracted crowds large enough to make the break away financially worthwhile. The time came however when all efforts to preserve the theatre as a vital reminder of the town's heritage, proved unsuccessful and the end came a remarkably short 64 years after its opening. On Saturday 18th February 1961, the pantomime 'Little Miss Muffet' took the last curtain calls and encores ever to be heard in the Lyceum Theatre.

There was one other place to which the townsfolk could resort for evenings of bright lights and colourful charivari; this was the Empire Theatre in Charles Street, built in 1888 to satisfy the trend towards noisier, more vulgar tastes. The Lyceum still remained a sanctuary for the aesthetic, but for those who preferred the brash atmosphere of the music hall with its jugglers, red-nosed comedians and earthy humour, the Empire was the place to go. The early shows were vintage, old-time music hall with as many as three different chairmen each night. The theatre manager sat at the front of the audience and encouraged applause with a wooden gavel. Most of the best known variety acts of the next fifty years topped the bill here, and the long queues of theatre-goers up and down Charles Street were a common feature of the town on Saturday nights.

For a while after the First World War, the Empire was a repertory theatre where the Terence Byron Company presented many memorable plays.

It all ended however in what seemed to be the traditional way for Newport theatres - it burned down in 1942!

Theatre-going was by no means the only pursuit of the fun-loving Victorians of Newport. Many preferred more active and participatory forms of amusement, and found them in outdoor distractions. Of these there is not much recorded for the first half of the 19th century except for the Stowe Fairs, but they were more in the nature of menageries, side-shows and general tomfoolery than athletic or competitive.

The largest, open, level area of land in the borough was that of the Town Marshes and despite an inclination to wetness, was the ideal choice for open-air pursuits. For a period, Newport Races were a popular diversion. A meeting on 3rd September 1832, reported in the Merlin, had seats in the grandstand at two shillings and sixpence and elsewhere at one shilling. Most of the riders owned their own horses which suggested that they were gentry or middle-class farmers who wagered heavily on themselves.

A good day's racing was usually succeeded by a dinner at the Westgate Hotel and a grand Race Ball at the Town Hall Assembly Rooms; present would be everyone of note in the town including guests such as Sir Charles Morgan, Mr Crawshay-Bailey and Captain West, commanding officer of the 48th Regiment.

Private race meetings were also held in the grounds of Tredegar House and these were by invitation only. One such occasion was reported in 1839 when twelve gentlemen's coaches lined the course and a colourful bevy of gentry with their ladies, cheered on the contestants in three races. During the evening that followed, Tredegar House was ablaze with light for the feasting and dancing enjoyed by the race-going visitors.

A town cricket team was known to have been established as early as 1834, playing all its home games on various, unspecified fields rented from farmers for £4 to £5 a year. Another report in the Monmouthshire Merlin announced that this inexperienced side had defeated Pontypool by 92 runs to 81.

By 1856, Newport Cricket Club had been formed and a very select fraternity it seems to have been, with all 70 of its members representing much of the wealth of the town, and drawn from the most prominent men in business and local government; even the local member of Parliament was a player-member!

The president was Alderman Samuel Homfray, and his son, Lorenzo, was captain. Members were Alderman E J Allfrey of the Castle Brewery, Crawshay-Bailey MP and ex-mayors or mayors-to-be David Harrhy, James Brown, Thomas Cordes and George Gethin to name but a few.

Alderman Samuel Homfray - Mayor of Newport 1854 - 1855

There were also the sons of fathers who had once been a power in the town - Henry and Thomas Latch, and Charles Prothero of Malpas Court.

The club rule book for 1856 makes interesting reading. Selection for membership was very formal and was carried out by one black ball in three for exclusion: the annual fee was ten shillings and sixpence; teams were to be selected from the first 22 members to turn up at the ground; there was a fine of one shilling for any non-playing member leaving a bat, any part of his dress or indeed any part of himself within forty yards of the wicket! The balance sheet for the same year shows that the score-book cost twelve shillings, bats and balls £4, the rent of the Marshes was £17-0s-0d and the fees of a professional bowler were £15-12s-0d, partly paid for by an on-the-spot 'whip round' of £4-3s-0d (there was no shame in shamateurism in those days!)

By 1859, the club was paying £91 for its portion of the Marshes, but even this did not guarantee the privacy needed by concentrating batsmen and fielders, because the Newport Rifle Club was using a range right alongside the cricket ground and shooting competitions were often in progress at the same time as cricket matches!

A grand day out in summer for all to enjoy, started as an experiment in 1867 and proved so successful as to become a permanent annual feature for many years afterwards. This was the Newport Regatta, held on the Marshes and the adjacent reach of the River Usk; admittance was sixpence for adults and threepence for children.

The press announcement for the regatta to be held on 3rd July 1869 forecast the attendance of Lord Tredegar and family, the Regatta Committee and the Mayor and his Corporation. During the course of the day there were to be:-

Boat, yacht and rowing boat events, on the river,
Horse, pony, donkey and bicycle races on the Marshes,
Athletic contests.
Refreshment stalls, and a grand finale in a brilliant
display of fireworks.

At the fair held on the 11th September 1871, great crowds attended to see the world famous highwire walker, Charles Blondin, who had already crossed Niagara Falls three times in 1855, 1859 and 1860, the last time on stilts. Blondin whose real name was Jean Francois Grevelet, performed many daredevil tricks on a 300 feet long rope at a height of 50 feet.

It was not long before these aquatic activities created sufficient interest to make this stretch of the River Usk come alive with boats in competition with one another, and it was only a matter of time before Newport Rowing Club was formed with headquarters, boathouse, and slipway on the river bank near the Marshes.

When interest in holding town regattas had waned to the point of an occasional fair and ox-roasting on what was to become Shaftesbury Park, the Rowing Club still held its own mini-regattas until well into the 1920s, and 'gave opportunities to its members of enjoying 12 to 15 miles of rowing amidst beautiful scenery' (the Borough Guide Book 1907).

That first, exclusive cricket club seems to have disbanded by 1870 but it was to undergo a revival which was followed by a long history of success, promising a reputation as one of the most formidable town cricket clubs in the country.

The year 1875 saw the formation of Newport Cricket, Athletic and Football Club. Two years later the club took a lease of land at Rodney Parade. Playing football for Newport at that time was a gentleman named Thomas Baker Jones who afterwards became a well known solicitor in the town. He held the record of scoring a try for Wales against Ireland - the first ever scored by Wales in international rugby! Tom Jones was 96 years old when he died in 1959.

In the earliest days, the absence of a gymnasium necessitated the use of a shed belonging to Samuel Homfray in the Cattle Market, and after 1882, buildings in the Castle precincts and in Cross Street. By 1891, a new gymnasium was built on the club's own ground and Lord Tredegar followed this up by granting an adjoining four to five acres at a nominal rent for the laying out of a splendid cricket pitch - no mean feat when the ordnance map for

1881 shows the best part of this land to be a 'great salt pond'.

In 1894, the club changed its name to Newport Athletic Club. By this time its rugby union football team had been playing for twenty years. The club went on to achieve a reputation of great renown in all forms of its sporting activities - world-wide in the case of the football section which took great honours and popularised the name of Newport wherever the game of rugby was played. Fortunately for the town this is one of the rare traditions that it seems will not be allowed to fall at the wayside by a populace that has proved to be so capricious in the past. Even the 'finest cycle track in the country', laid round the original club ground with its own grandstand, fell into disuse in the early 1930s, although the tarmac track survived to provide local children with a wonderful place to tear around on their old 'bikes' and compete for the greatest number of circuits before being chased away by a sorely tried groundsman.

The centenary of this illustrious club was celebrated in 1975, and for an interesting and detailed history the club's own centenary handbook is recommended as engrossing reading.

If there was one pursuit left to complete the sporting itinerary of the town, it was the game of golf, a pastime that was becoming fashionable among the slightly better off working classes. Sometime soon after 1900, parts of Somerton and Ladyhill Farms were converted into an eighteen hole course. 'The Golf Links', as they were commonly known, were advertised as being 'within 250 yards of Chepstow Road's electric cars', a short distance along a sandy lane which is today Aberthaw Road. It was another popular excursion for the townsfolk to dismount from the tramcar and stroll across the Links to the village of Liswerry to take refreshment at the Liswerry Hotel. One of the hazards of this golf course was Liswerry Pond which, during a succession of surprisingly hard winters, was frozen over and invaded by dozens of unflinching but foolhardy skaters. Newport Golf Club used this course until 1912 when it found a new permanent home at Great Oak Rogerstone

Anyone wishing to inspect the great oak tree that gave its name to the area in the immediate vicinity of Newport Golf clubhouse at Rogerstone, would have a wasted journey. There *was* such a tree there once, and it was reputed to be the largest oak in Great Britain. Known both as the Golynos Oak and Derwen Fawr (Great Oak), it was cut down as long ago as 1810 to supply the Royal Navy with ship-building material. Its girth was over 30 feet and several of its main branches were as large as ordinary oaks. Said to be well over 500 years old, it was reduced by five men working for three weeks to 2,920 cubic feet of quality timber and over three tons of bark! Much of the extensive root material was used to fashion exquisite furniture items.

~ O ~

Harking back to the story of the Newport Borough Police Force, it may be recalled that one of the functions of this small body of men was that of fighting fire, and in this duty it had no supplementary help for fully half a century.

On the night of Maundy Thursday 1884, a serious fire broke out in a house in Caroline Street and two young children were trapped in an upstairs room. By the time the police had arrived with their pathetic, forty year old engine, the situation was hopelessly out of control.

Working nearby in his Dock Street yard, was Mr Cox the coachbuilder, and when he heard of the tragedy that was being enacted, he ran to the scene carrying one of his ladders which he placed against the wall of the doomed building. While the police watched helplessly, he scaled it, entered a window and brought out one child which unfortunately died soon afterwards: the second child perished in the flames. Mr Cox was so troubled by this that he was motivated into gathering twenty friends about him to form the town's first voluntary, unpaid, fire-fighting force. The idea was not too brilliantly conceived because other towns had already gone down this road, and it was to Cardiff's Fire Captain that Mr Cox turned for second-hand uniforms to be washed and repaired by Mrs Cox before issue to the small band of volunteers.

Although proud to accept credit for being the founder of the brigade, Cox never looked for further responsibility and was content to remain an ordinary fireman for the rest of his days. The first elected captain was Mr Whitehall, a Commercial Street jeweller, but he soon relinquished this post to his lieutenant, Mr H S Lyne, who remained Brigade Chief for many years afterwards.

To support the volunteers in their first year, public subscriptions raised £108-3s-0d plus a grant of £50 from the Corporation. Uniforms cost £107-16s-3d and boots £26-9s-0d. They had no hose wagon so Mr Cox built them a brake, and each time an alarm was given, someone had to run to borrow a horse from Mr Sheppard, a market fishmonger!

The brigade's first ever call-out was to a parlour fire at Claremont, Herbert Street, the home of Mr Mark Mordey another future mayor of the town. The outbreak was dealt with efficiently and little damage resulted.

By the end of 1885 the volunteers were provided with a new steam engine and soon had cramped, makeshift but adequate premises in Dock Street. The Corporation Fire Brigade Committee, in September 1889, authorised the purchase of four ladders from J Stone for £7-12s-0d, just beating E Truman's tender of £7-16s-0d (one shilling per rung). The original fire engine, obtained by the police in 1845, was sold for £12 to Shand Mason & Co who in turn supplied a telescopic ladder for £45.

It has already been established that the local authority and the Water Company had, over 20 years before, developed a system of primitive cocks and hydrants for police fire-fighting purposes, but at that time the town was contained within much narrower boundaries than those for which the fire brigade was now responsible. For this reason, in 1891, new Stone's Patent Hydrants were added.

The Council also thought it prudent to equip 22 firemen's houses with electric bells connected to the Central Police Station. Up until then, the alarm call-out system had been far from satisfactory. A few firemen's houses were connected by telephone wire (Western Counties Telephone Co) to the Police Station; those living nearest were summoned by messengers on foot!

As time went by, more equipment (hoses, hose carts, ladders, 'tomahawks' and steam engines) were obtained, and the brigade acquired greater skills. Fireman Cox and a few others attended the Exhibition of the Fire Brigade Union in London in 1893, and they returned with several efficiency medals and certificates.

Sadly it was Fireman Cox's devotion to his brainchild that brought about his untimely end.

A brigade practice was taking place in the use of a sheet for catching jumpers from burning buildings and as the rehearsal 'victim' on that day proved to be an absentee, Cox took his place. Although by now having become a trifle ungainly for such athleticism, he made the jump from a high building in Dock Street only for something to go terribly wrong. He died soon afterwards of severe internal injuries. This happened in 1903 and 30 years later his widow recounted these reminisces at the behest of the South Wales Argus, probably not realising as she did so the valuable contribution that she was making to the somewhat sketchy, early annals of the Newport Fire Brigade.

The Old Fire Station, Dock Street, Newport

A man died in a fire at Pillgwenlly in 1894. There were unusual circumstances surrounding this incident although there is no saying had they not existed that the outcome would have been any different. It was the custom every so often for the Water Company to turn on a fast flow of water in the town drains to scour and clean them. This was normally a nocturnal happening but no warning was given to the police or fire service. It was during one of these periods that the Pillgwenlly fire occurred, and it caused such a lowering of water pressure in the mains that there was insufficient available to fight a powerful fire. To prevent such tragedies recurring, an agreement was reached with the Water Company on regular times for sluicing the drains and the means to stop it in emergencies.

A letter from Fire Captain Lyne to the Council in 1893, made strong representations on the shortcomings in the fire-fighting capacity of the town. By far the greatest criticism was directed at the alarm system which was neither adequate nor always in full working order. Newport, it appeared, compared very unfavourably with many other towns of over 50,000 population (all listed in the letter). When fire broke out in outlying districts of the borough, it was often necessary for a patrolling policeman to run nearly half a mile to his station in order to telephone the Central Station, which then had to send a messenger to the Fire Station! Furthermore, because of the lack of horses, the firemen might well arrive at the blaze exhausted from manually dragging the hose carts! Finally, Captain Lyne's letter poured

217

scorn on the building that served as the Central Fire Station, stating its unsuitability in size, state of repair and lack of accommodation for horses or men.

This jolted the Corporation into speedy action. One alarm system that had been tested in other towns was discussed and discarded as impracticable. This was one where it was only necessary to break a glass panel set in the top of a post and pull a handle. The simplicity of this would encourage drunks and practical jokers to make false alarms 'whereas' said the report 'it requires a certain amount of sobriety to use a telephone!' For this reason the Saunders and Brown system with telephone handset was adopted - at four points on the Maindee side and five from Pill to Shaftesbury Street. The capital cost was quoted as £236 or £44 a year over five years.

Plans were also approved for the building of a new Central Fire Station costing £2,000, on land next to the Temperance Hall (later to become the Capitol Cinema) in Dock Street. There was accommodation for two steam engines, stabling for two horses and rooms for two residential firemen who would relieve each other in shifts. For the first time there was a direct telephone link with the Police Station and, should it develop a fault at a crucial moment, the added advantage of a mere seventy-five yard dash from one to the other. January 30th 1896 was arranged as the official opening day.

Almost as if in defiance of these proud, improved defences, and only four months later, the town suffered what was probably the most devastating fire in its history - when its most prestigious building, the architecturally beautiful Victoria Hall, Bridge Street, was reduced to a blackened ruin!

A year later an incident illustrated how much co-operation the brigade could expect from members of the public and if it were not so serious it would have been funny. A large fire broke out at Cwmbran Patent Nut and Bolt Works and a call for help went out to the Newport Brigade. Two horses were procured from the Kings Head and an engine set out poste-haste. On arrival help was requested from a large crowd of men gathering to watch, but offers were not forthcoming without the promise of a supply of beer! A great deal of damage was the result!

At Maindee in 1898 a block of Community Buildings appeared on the corner of London Street and Chepstow Road. Housed within were a new district police station, a fire station and a reading room. For many years afterwards, Maindee echoed to the clamour of bells and the clatter of hoofs on cobbles whenever an alarm was raised and the new generation of 'steamers' took to the streets.

It was in 1930, when steel wheel-rims had long given way to pneumatics and a much more powerful form of horsepower was the driving force, that Maindee Fire Station was closed down. Obviously the Central Station in Dock Street was considered fully capable of administering to all the town's fire-fighting requirements, even allowing for the fact that there was only one road bridge over the River Usk. The main double doorways that had so often disgorged their two, noisy, bright red engines, swaying madly and doing their level best to dislodge the riders who hung on like grim death, were converted into the more sedate, arched windows that ever since have graced the facade of Maindee Library.

For a while the living accommodation was retained for two firemen, and the alarm bell still told them when to telephone Dock Street. However, this was not the last to be heard of a fire station in this area.

In 1960, a new fire station was built at a cost of £58,000 on the cleared site of the houses in Eveswell and Archibald Streets that were destroyed by wartime bombing. With only one, highly congested road bridge serving the town, the eastern bank had once again become an area that on occasions might be dangerously inaccessible to centrally based appliances.

The whole picture was eventually destined to change again. Three good road bridges now span the Usk (and more are said to be on the drawing board); the main fire station stands at Malpas on part of the old derelict brickworks, right alongside Junction 26 of the M4 Motorway, giving fast access to eastern Newport. The 73 year old, Dock Street Fire Station closed its doors for the last time on Sunday 5th October 1969 and, accompanied by its near neighbour the Central Library and Art Gallery, sank into the foundations of the new shopping centre!

~ 0 ~

During the 19th century, a series of Improvement Acts were instrumental in considerably extending the town boundaries from those that had enclosed the tiny area since the 15th century Charters.

In 1832, that part of St Woolos parish comprising the Pillgwenlly suburb was absorbed. At the same time, a strip of undeveloped land in Christchurch parish, fronting the eastern bank of the River Usk, was brought in. Nothing was done with this land for many years although the adjoining green fields of Maindee were stirring in the hands of private enterprise.

The area of the borough before 1832 was a mere 239 acres; afterwards it was 938.

By 1876 the borough was contemplating the addition of a very large area of Christchurch including Maindee, but due to public resistance in the fear of high rate increases, and a dispute with the Christchurch Local Board of Health over sewage disposal, only the smaller area of Barnard Town at the foot of Christchurch Hill was obtained; a much larger portion of St Woolos accompanied it.

The 1889 Act finalised the great plan for Newport for the next 44 years, almost doubling the total land area within the borough boundaries. The stages leading up to this moment were:-

		Acres	Acres
Prior to 1832	Newport	239	
After 1832	Newport	239	
	St Woolos & Christchurch	699	938
After 1876	Newport	239	
	St Woolos	2192	
	Christchurch (Barnardtown)	303	2734
After 1889	Newport	239	
	St Woolos	2225	
	Christchurch (incl. Maindee)	2234	
	Nash	217	4924
After 1904	St Woolos (Alexandra, Newport& South Wales Docks & Railway Act.) Diverting and straightening River Ebbw.	96	5020

After this, the people had a rule of thumb method for determining the extent of their town: 'One step beyond the end of the tramlines was to stand outside the town!' Indeed, this remained an adventure into the late 1930s when a popular Sunday afternoon jaunt was to take a tram to the Bishpool Lane terminus, step out on to 'foreign' soil and walk the 'Seven Stiles' to Llanwern.

How the district described as Barnardtown received its widely known, but never officially recognised name is deserving of explanation. It is a name that is fast falling into disuse and is now only familiar to members of the older generation. One still hears the occasional remark from the senior citizen that he or she attended Barnardtown (Church Road) School, but rarely, if ever, can this person explain how the name entered the town's vocabulary.

It seems that in the mid 19th century, this small, developing appendage of Maindee, from Caerleon Road to the foot of Christchurch Hill, was acquiring something of a poor reputation; until, that is, a man with a mission, Philip Barnard, appeared on the scene. He collected together a group of decent dedicated, god-fearing men who between them, caused the building of respectable homes in streets named Lord, Bishop, Dean and Canon, which testified to their Christian origins.

Just along the road from Barnardtown, on the short stretch approaching Newport Bridge, was Clarence Place. This area has already been described as it was when the 1832 Improvement Act first added it to the borough. Forty-four years later, when Barnardtown was included, Clarence Place was just beginning to look like a suburb.

The north side was to remain sparsely developed for some time to come. Most of it was industrialised with a large timber yard and several stable blocks housing 60 to 80 horses belonging to the horse bus proprietors. On one corner of the lane due to become East Usk Road was a cooperage making sugar barrels and on the other, a tar works. Among these buildings, the Isca and the Ivy Bush public houses were about to appear.

On the south side, nearest the bridge, there was a track leading to Rodney Wharf and alongside it a drill hall with a piece of land used as a parade ground by the militia (hence Rodney Parade). Adjoining, was the cottage, nursery garden and orchard of Mr Dicks (now the site of the old Newport Technical College). Next along the main road was a terrace of eight large imposing houses with short forecourts; behind these was a ropeworks extending back to the Athletic Ground. Taking Clarence Place to its junction with the proposed Corporation Road were two more terraces of similar gentlemen's residences with front gardens of from 30 to 80 feet long.

All this altered on August 3rd 1897 when a great fire consumed the ropeworks, Dicks' nursery, most of the big houses and at the height of its severity, reached the Athletic Club railings which twisted with the intense heat.

In 1887, Corporation Road was laid out over the full length of that first strip of Christchurch parish that had remained as green riverside fields since its acquisition 55 years earlier. In no time at all, the following description of the effects of the new road appeared in the local papers:-

The district through which it passes has marvellously developed by the erection of street upon street of houses at right angles to it, and of huge industries upon it.'

When it became established in 1880, the East Usk Chemical Works at the end of Coverack Road, was in the forefront of industrial development on the east bank of the River Usk. It made its presence felt ever after with the pungent odour (known locally as 'The Chem'.) that wrinkled the nostrils of several generations of Newportonians, and cleared the bronchia of the many children who were made to stand and inhale deeply in the shadow of the bubbling glue vats.

It soon became realised however, that if more concentrated industry were to come on the eastern bank, an obvious attraction would be a second river crossing, and indeed, when Lysaghts were showing interest in building a steelworks, the Company was given to understand that this was a firm consideration.

In 1889, Newport Corporation received Parliamentary sanction to build a subway under the river from Alexandra Road Pillgwenlly to the newly constructed Corporation Road. Seven years were allowed for the project which was held over for the full term and, when reconsidered in 1896, was dropped due to the estimated, prohibitive cost of £715,000.

A ferry service was the next suggestion as an alternative, and in 1897 the Corporation actually obtained powers for such a scheme, but although several operators showed interest it was not proceeded with because the great rise and fall of the tides and the vast amount of mud exposed at low ebb, created dangerous problems.

When after two years of negotiation, Lysaghts commenced the construction of the huge 'Orb' sheet rolling works, Newport Corporation had to take action on its promise 'to provide better communication between the two banks of the river'. The Borough Engineer, Robert Haynes, favoured a bridge that would not hinder the passage of shipping, much of which still carried lofty masts and rigging.

A conventional bridge such as already existed was out of the question because the high level necessary would require approach roads three quarters of a mile long with gradients of 1 in 20. Enormous costs and engineering problems would have been involved.

Other types of bridge, designed to open either by lifting (bascule) or swinging, were also considered inappropriate because of the number of piers required which would be obstructive and hazardous to navigation not to mention once again the huge cost.

A French engineer, Ferdinand Arnodin had designed and built bridges known in France as 'transbordeurs' which worked on the principle of overhead ferries, leaving rivers and channels free for the passage of the largest ships. In 1899, a deputation formed from the Newport Harbour Board and the town Corporation, and headed by the Borough Engineer, visited Rouen to inspect M. Arnodin's most recent masterpiece and to judge its practicability in Newport's case. What they saw must have impressed them, and on their return they immediately sought and were granted, powers to build a transporter bridge.

Among several designs which were considered and rejected was one which, because of its unusual qualities should not be allowed to remain buried in the archives. At first sight the elevation of this particular bridge was almost identical to that which was eventually adopted. However, closer inspection reveals at each end, a long stretch of road decking raised like a drawbridge. The idea was that the gondola should be drawn to the centre of the span and the two drawbridges lowered to rest on each of its ends, thus creating a conventional carriageway to be raised when ever a ship required to pass.

Robert Haynes and Ferdinand Arnodin were appointed joint engineers; the construction was put in the hands of the civil engineering firm of Alfred Thorne, and in 1902 work commenced.

Massive, two-legged, steel, lattice-work towers reaching 242 feet above road level, were erected on each river bank. Over the top of each tower were carried eight enormous cables, each weighing 3½ tons and anchored to the ground by 2,000 ton blocks of dense masonry. From these great main cables, dozens of suspension cables of varying lengths supported the horizontal girders bridging the 645 feet span, and carrying the track across which the multi-wheeled gondola trolley was drawn back and forwards by electrical power.

The trolley track was positioned 177 feet above the high water mark and carried the

221

gondola on 30 cables within a few feet of the highest tides. This travelling section of roadway, 33 feet long by 40 feet wide, had a pagoda-roofed control cabin on one side and took no more than a minute to make the crossing with its maximum load of six vehicles and a hundred foot-passengers.

Building of the Transporter Bridge

In four years and at a cost of £98,000, the bridge stood completed, and at 11 am on a very wet 12th September 1906, it was declared open by Viscount Lord Tredegar in the presence of the Mayor, John Liscombe, the Corporation and a crowd of about 600 hardy individuals who braved the elements on a very exposed river bank to see local history in the making.

Public opinion was sharply divided as to the merits of the Transporter Bridge. There had been strong opposition to its very idea, and once it became fact this was no less reduced. Arguably it was out of date almost as soon as it began operating, and it certainly never lived up to its creators' expectations despite a sustained propaganda campaign. An article in the Newport Christmas Annual of 1906 had this to say:-

'The Transporter Bridge has done and will do much to bring Newport before the public, in that it is only one of the two at present constructed in this country (Runcorn Bridge built 1905, demolished 1961). A representation of this masterpiece of engineering skill is being thrown upon the screen by means of the cinematograph in places of amusement all over the country.'

An entirely different opinion was expressed at about the same time by a spokesman for the Newport Chamber of Commerce in a publication entitled 'Commercial Newport':- 'The saying of a celebrated general, 'It is magnificent but it is not war', may be paraphrased to read 'it is magnificent but it is a white elephant', that is in the opinion of many of the townspeople, and although expensive to maintain, and falling far short of being that popular convenience that it was meant to be, it serves a large purpose if it did no more than form a factor in bringing Lysaghts Works to Newport.'

Similar views have been aired in the town's meeting places, taverns and private parlours from that time forward. A Newport Library publication in 1980 describes the bridge as 'quite unique amongst the few transporters still in use.' Only five years later the transporter ceased to transport and was closed to the public due to structural defects. At the time of writing, the sleeping giant has been awakened by a £3 million refit and only time will tell if this enormous expenditure will bring success as a tourist attraction where it once failed as a practical answer to a particular problem of a past generation!

During the first half, or thereabouts, of its lifetime, the Transporter was a toll bridge and up until September 30th 1946 the charges were one penny on the gondola and threepence to make the challenging climb up a tower and cross by foot on the catwalks alongside the trolley tracks. The latter route provided an unforgettable experience for those seeking a breath-taking aspect, but it was not to be lightly undertaken by the timid, the vertiginous or for that matter by anyone in decent clothes which would attract the layers of grime and soot deposited on the handrails from the chimneys of the industrial docklands and the funnels of the many ships that had passed beneath.

In the 1990s, only one transporter bridge in Britain, other than Newport's, remains in working order and fully used by the public at large. This bridge, five years the junior of its Newport counterpart, spans the River Tees in Middlesborough, the town where, coincidentally, the firm of Dorman Long fabricated the steelwork of the Newport bridge! Although strongly resembling the Newport transporter in dimensions, it was British designed and not French; it is also of cantilever construction instead of cable suspension. Another odd coincidence - two miles upstream from the Middlesborough bridge, a second crossing of the River Tees is called Newport Bridge!

Of the world's original fifteen transporter bridges, only seven now remain, and of these only three are working as their makers intended. Technical information is scarce for the bridges which have gone but it would appear that Newport's was one of the largest due to the great span required and the enormous fluctuations in tide. Only one of the survivors has more steel in it, and that is the Osterronfeld Bridge at Rendsburg in Germany, which has a main railway line running over its top.

The full story of the Transporter Bridge did not end with its opening. There were two somewhat unfortunate sequels which, possibly because of their embarrassing overtones, were kept in low profile from then on.

A claim was received from Lysaghts, Orb Works, Corporation Road for damages in respect of the bridge being made subject to tolls. This apparently had not been part of the deal when the incentives for building a factory in Newport were being discussed. The original claim of £7,000 was reduced to £2,000 in an out-of-court settlement. An announcement was made at a council meeting on 17th December 1907, stating that the agreement was: 'in settlement of all claims and demands against the Corporation in respect of their action with the charging of tolls over the Transporter Bridge or under Clause 5 of the Agreement dated 9th December 1906'.

Next, Monsieur Arnodin respectfully requested a further £200 to cover additional visits made with his resident engineer in order to inspect various phases of work on the bridge. Before any decision was made the Frenchman was asked if he would agree to remitting £150 of his fees to Mr RH Haynes (Newport's Borough Engineer) who had worked jointly with M. Arnodin on the project. The latter readily agreed to this suggestion - no doubt assuming that it would be deducted from the £200 of his additional claim.

A letter was promptly sent to him turning down his request; Mr Haynes was granted his £150 by reduction in M. Arnodin's original fees *plus* an extra £150 from the Corporation!

M. Arnodin was extremely gracious in his disappointment. His letter of reply, read out in Council, stated that he would abide by the decision although he felt that it would be only justice to repay him the extra expenses: 'A small question of money does not alter the feeling respect that I have for your Council, which is based on the more elevated sentiment of material esteem'.

Shabby treatment of the man who had been fêted in the town right up until the last rivet was driven? Or was it just a case of the public purse making a bumbling and, on the face of it, an extremely ungrateful show of honouring its duties to the town's rate payers?

- 0 -

It was an undeniable fact that for a town of its size Newport was not well blessed with impressive public buildings. The few that have been discussed already were the town's sum total and visits to other town centres immediately revealed their superiority in this matter. An upheaval of piety had taken place in the mid 19th century and this had resulted in the appearance of many new churches and chapels but lately this religious fervour had begun to decline. By the final decade, Newport was booming in every way but spiritual, and fewer than one person in seven belonged to any religious house.

The Forward Movement of the Presbyterian Church was quick to notice this dearth of godliness, having sought it out and conquered it in Cardiff and elsewhere.

In 1895, the challenge was taken up by the Reverend Seth Joshua and his brother Frank, who with their crusading parties moved into Newport, holding meetings wherever a few or a few hundred could gather. The effects were almost immediate and very startling!

People flocked to hear the new 'barn storming' preachers. The 1,200 seats of the Tredegar Hall were regularly filled, and in the Corn Exchange congregations had to be turned out every hour to make room for second and third sittings!

Following hundreds of conversions in 1901, the Church was constituted and it grew rapidly with the formation of Bible classes, a Christian Endeavour Society, a boys brigade group and other cultural and social activities. Finally, a site in Commercial Street, backing on to Fothergill Street, was obtained from the Tredegar Estate at a low ground rent and at an eventual cost of £10,000, a church was built to be known thereafter as the Great Central Hall. On 4th October 1906, it was officially opened.

Internally it could only be described as splendid and inspiring, with its high, vaulted ceiling arched over a majestic, unprosceniumed stage, backed by a magnificent organ and with floor and balconies seating well over 2,000.

In direct contrast, its outside appearance was not what one would have expected after viewing the imposing interior. The frontage was part of a grimy facade of shop fronts from which it was hardly distinguishable on the approach from either side.

The great hall soon became the envy of lesser religious and non-religious bodies, and when it was realised just how considerable was its appeal, it was decided to grant lettings to suitable applicants. Anything smacking of light entertainment was rejected, but warm welcome was given to lectures, serious musical concerts and grand choral festivals. In the 1950s, the stage and its surrounds used to disappear beneath massed choirs numbering 600 or more singers at concerts given by the Federation of Music Societies. No better recommendation for the building's excellent acoustics could have been than its use by the BBC for the broadcasting of concerts and religious services.

In the earliest days of diversification, weekly 'bioscope' shows were given; for these, admission charges were 2d in the balcony and 1d downstairs. Such entertainment was believed to be the town's first introduction to moving pictures.

As time went by, use of the Central Hall for such purposes became less requested. The great crowds were more eager for other forms of amusement in buildings being purpose-built. The new picture palaces were packed every night and all the diversion needed to quench the thirst of the homespun majority was to be found on a few reels of silent celluloid or in the more convivial atmosphere of the town's two theatres. There was still support by the purists for things classical but their numbers were growing too few for practicality and even the church stalwarts became reduced to a few dozen at Sunday services.

The struggle for survival ended in September 1960 with a concert given by Sir John Barbirolli and the Hallé Orchestra. Just before taking up his baton, Sir John said: 'Tonight it is the sombre privilege of my orchestra and I to play the last notes of orchestral music that will ever be heard in this hall'.

Those last notes were contained in Elgar's 'Enigma Variations' and they were heard by that last, rapt, capacity audience in the sad knowledge that they were present at another historic milestone. The last religious services had been held on Whit Sunday 21st May.

The ostentation of modern shopfitting made it impossible to imagine what had gone before. Fortunately however, it is still possible to get some idea as to the nature of the old building. Contrary to the impression given at the front by No 82 Commercial Street, a large portion of the original survives at the back. Off Kingsway, opposite Ebenezer Terrace, is Fothergill Court (once Fothergill Street). Now a nondescript parking and loading area for the main street shops, its prominent feature is the rear end of the great hall, very difficult to imagine as once being one of the town's more pretentious buildings. The stark, grey stone walls inset with large, arched, boarded-up windows, are more reminiscent of an old warehouse.

Time now to take further stock of the town as it stood poised on the threshold of the present century. Its growth during the 19th had been truly meteoric and in the words of Mr Kyrle Fletcher: 'the changes and progress of a thousand years seem to have been forced into this one century'.

An apt illustration is given in the following table:-

Year	Population	Year	Population
1801	1,135	1861	23,249
1811	1,346	1871	26,957 (3,970)
1821	4,000	1881	35,313 (5,447)

1831	7,062	1888	45,769 (8,000)
1841	10,492 (1,767)	1891	54,707 (8,300)
1851	19,323 (2,908)	1901	67,279 (11,801)

The figures in parentheses show inhabited houses where known.

The rateable value rose from £97,000 in 1873 to £280,000 in 1896.

The 1888 population figure of 45,769 meant that Newport was still over 4,000 short of the number required to attain county borough status, but this little matter was remedied a year later when the Newport Corporation Act 1889 extended the town's boundaries, causing the absorption of Maindee's 7,000 inhabitants. When the Chairman of the Committee was giving Parliament's decision on the Bill, he made the following very interesting remarks -

'We have necessarily gone into this matter with some pains and care, and we have clearly in our minds the unwritten law of this Committee that we should not include in an urban district an agricultural district, not yet the seat of population either of a residential or of a manufacturing or industrial character. But no rules are of such general application that they are not subject to modification according to the circumstances of any special case, and we think there are circumstances of a somewhat remarkable character in the case of Newport.'

We have here a rising town which is evidently making considerable progress, and which seeks expansion. The natural course of expansion does not appear to be westward, but rather eastward; but this community in endeavouring to move eastward, is met by the barrier of the river, and the river appears to be not so much really a barrier as a connection, and there seems to us to be strong reasons why we should take this river rather as a connection and as a union than as a line of separation, and we think we ought to give the community of Newport advantages and facilities for moving eastward by giving the extension of the borough in that direction. We think it desirable that the river should be regarded, as I said a moment since, rather as a connection than as a barrier, and we think it important that both banks of the river should be under the same jurisdiction and the same authority'.

Amidst this and other marvellous examples of pompous, Victorian verbosity the County Borough of Newport was born, and its first Mayor was a very remarkable man indeed.

Alderman Henry John Davis was another well known researcher into town antiquities, and in this capacity he held the highest qualifications, having himself been an eye witness to all the important happenings in Newport for the previous half a century. Arriving in the town in 1838 at the age of twenty five, he was just in time for the Chartist Riots and actually took part in the arrest of John Frost. He became a town councillor in 1848 and Mayor in 1851. Exactly forty years later, at the age of seventy eight, Alderman Davis became Mayor of Newport for a second time, having outlived every other member of his first corporation - an unparalleled record of municipal service.

In 1896, the docks dealt with 4,564,947 tons register inwards and outwards, compared with 22,929 a century earlier. Total imports and exports including bunker coal were 5,291,053 tons, and the port was recorded as the third largest in the world for foreign coal shipments and exports of iron and steel - greater than all the other Bristol Channel ports combined. The revenue collected at Newport's Custom House surpassed the sum of Cardiff and Swansea in total. It was selected by the Board of Trade for statistical purposes as 8th in the list of Britain's 14 great ports.

By 1901, in addition to the main floating docks, the harbour complex had acquired graving (dry) docks capable of receiving the largest ships, and 35 miles of railway sidings which were steadily building towards their eventual total of 100 miles.

Adjoining Jack's Pill were the Edith Dock (220 feet long), Alice Dock (289 feet long) and Mary Dock (350 feet long). All were accessed by water gates from the river. In the Pill itself was a repairing berth 350 feet in length. The Alexandra Graving Dock (532 feet long) had an entrance only from the dock.

Largest of all, the Tredegar Dry Dock filled the ancient Pill Gwenlly at the end of Commercial Road, with its 708 feet long box of stone and concrete.

On the eastern bank of the River Usk, almost opposite the Alexandra Dock entrance, the Union Dry Docks were constructed, 357 and 530 feet in length respectively.

If all this were not enough to satisfy ships awaiting repair and requiring to be clear of the water for this purpose, there was the 'grid-iron' at London Wharf, Rodney Parade. This comprised a set of heavy, timber rails laid in the river bed at right angles to the quay, on which vessels up to 246 feet in length would be completely exposed at low tide. The grid-iron is probably still there, buried under siltage that has built up over the years since the practice of pressure-hosing it was discontinued.

All these facilities were backed up by the most up-to-date fitting shops, forges, foundries, carpenters' and boiler-makers' shops and ship-building yards - making Newport's class of docking second to none in the country.

This was now a town with nearly a hundred miles of streets and immense commercial substance. Some degree of this affluence can be gauged from the business conducted through the postal services. The Central Post Office was about to be rebuilt in grand style; there were 60 sub post offices and 80 wall or pillar boxes; £50,000 worth of stamps were being purchased annually and £84,000 worth of telegrams sent. There were two telephone exchanges with 500 subscribers.

Another aspect of this early Edwardian period, pointing to life-style and behaviour could be found in a price list displayed in 1903 at the Grosvenor Hotel, 51 Commercial Street

Quality Pale Ale	**10 shillings per 6 gallon cask**
Quality Mild Ale	**9 shillings per 6 gallon cask**
Edinburgh Porter	**7 shillings per 6 gallon cask**
Flor de Mexico Cigars	**18 shillings per 1,000**
Kings Whiffs	**5 shillings per 100**
Players Gainsborough	
Cigarettes	**19 shillings per 1,000**

Other popular brands of cigarettes listed were : Woodbines, Tabs, Cousin Tom, Luck and Regalia - all sold in penny packets of five!

A guidebook of 1905 carries this description of the town:-

The private residences are built on the slopes and crests of the small hills which form its background from the river; and , in fact, the town for this reason boasts of the most charming suburbs of any place in this part of the country, affording as it does extensive and interesting views of

mountain scenery on the one hand and on the other hand, of the river and docks, the waters of the Channel, the Somersetshire coast and towns in the distance beyond. This contributes largely to its having become a very desirable place of residence and health resort.'

What a contrast in terms to those expressed by visitors a hundred years earlier, and how fortunate for the town that no laws yet existed to penalise publicity agents who were this economical with the truth!

- 0 -

At about this time a bright star was in the ascendant.

Born September 13th 1890, John Michael Basham was a poor boy, but as so often happens when fate chooses to endow a rare talent, it also adds the coalescent ingredients required to overcome adversity of background. This was only too true in Johnny Basham's case.

While he was still a young newspaper boy in ragged clothes, he began to display some of the skills that were to lead him to a world of riches and nation-wide acclaim. Larking about with his street pals and sparring playfully with subsequent work-mates, proved to the astonished youngster that that he could beat everyone who squared up to him. It was only a matter of a very short time before he was looking for stronger opposition, and he found it initially in fairground boxing booths where he collected numerous bruises, a few shillings and, what was most important, a lot of valuable ring-craft.

His physical appearance could not be said to be impressive, medium height, slim, spindly-armed and ribby might have been an apt description, but hidden away in that innocuous looking frame was the most amazing agility and lightning punching power. No wonder then that he could produce a showy, entertaining style, drawing large, admiring crowds at all his exhibitions and prize fights

At age twenty-four the First World War claimed him for the Army and by then he had become a nationally recognised boxer with a long string of impressive successes behind him.

On December 14th 1914, at the National Sporting Club, Johnny Basham took the British Welterweight title from Johnny Summers. In 1915 he was victorious in defence of his title, and the following year he defeated another challenger to retain the title and to become the first British boxer at his weight to win a Lonsdale Belt outright.

There was no doubt whatsoever in the minds of the boxing fraternity that but for the war Johnny Basham would have won far greater laurels, becoming well known in the United States and seriously contending for world titles. As it was, his career had to take second place to his job as sergeant physical training officer in the British Expeditionary Force in France. Having fulfilled that duty, his return to civilian life was marked by a long run of successes leading up to May 24th 1921 when he became British and European Middleweight Champion by beating Gus Platts in a 20 round thriller.

This should have been the zenith of the Basham career but the cheering had hardly died away when Johnny came up against the man he was never able to beat in several meetings, and the jinx lived on! On October 14th 1921 he was stopped by Ted Kid Lewis and his titles taken away from him.

From that time on, the Basham story continued in a much more subdued manner, but even if the bright lights dimmed somewhat, the magic of his flashing fists and dancing feet remained in sufficient measure to give lessons to up-and-coming youngsters and to delight the crowds who for years afterwards flocked to see this boxing legend.

Sadly, the story did not end in rich rewards. Johnny had earned a fortune in his time but lack of sound financial advice and an extremely over-generous nature combined to drain away his resources. Charities benefited extensively from his donations and he was the softest of touches for anyone who professed to have a problem curable only by the immediate handing over of pound notes!

Despite the rough nature of his calling and the tough implication of his surname, Johnny Basham was ever the gentleman of the mischievous sense of humour, and the darling of the people of Newport. Who of those who were privileged to be present, will ever fail to remember the scene on Newport Athletic's rugby ground towards the end of the Second World War?

The Heavyweight Champion of the World, 'the Brown Bomber', Joe Louis, then a member of the United States Army, had just finished an exhibition bout when a small cloth-capped figure clambered into the ring. It took but a second or two for recognition to dawn but as the glistening Lonsdale Belt was held aloft a huge roar rose from the packed crowds. This was one of those all-time, unforgettable, show-stopping moments and it was etched for posterity by the sight of the giant American holding aloft the hand of the aging, diminutive Newport boxer as a tribute from one great champion to another!

The pity of it is that the most important, visible sign of the Basham triumphs - that Lonsdale Belt that he owned for 33 years - had to be sold and was allowed to leave the town for some unknown destination instead of remaining as a permanent monument to one of Newport's finest ambassadors!

He died on June 7th 1947.

Chapter Thirteen

The First World War

Post War Problems
A New Bridge
The 1920s

It is almost impossible to think of the First World War in terms other than of a mindless attempt at mass genocide with two gigantic, static armies cutting each other to pieces and wasting the flower of Europe's youth across vast, featureless seas of mud and rusty barbed wire. This is a fair and natural reaction, very difficult to associate with any activity taking place at home. It must be remembered however, that it was mainly due to the sterling efforts of those left behind that the frightful carnage was finally brought to a sad but victorious end. In this, Newport and its citizens played a vital part, above and beyond just being the inhabitants of a port that was to become one of the more important links in the nation's lifeline.

On the 14th July 1914, with the opening of the final phase of the Alexandra Docks, the town became custodian of one of the most valuable of the country's wartime assets; here was one of the world's largest and safest areas of artificially enclosed, deep water with the world's biggest entrance locks, capable of admitting the largest ocean-going ships. Three weeks to the day after its opening, on 4th August 1914, it began what was probably the most testing time that ever a new dock would be required to undergo.

On that day, Britain declared war on Germany and, before the day was out, the town and its great dock had become fully involved by the capture in Mid Channel of the German steamship 'Belgia' (see under 'Police'). From that moment on Newport went to war!

The conversion from peacetime routines to those geared to the conduct of a bitter conflict, was the subject of immediate action although it was nearly a year before the effects began to show. No one, for instance, could foresee how great was to be the drain of labour from the industries whose employees were by tradition regarded as exclusively male and where the physical requirements and rough nature of the work would never have been considered suitable for the opposite sex.

The original rush of starry-eyed, young volunteers to the trenches, and the further half million called for by the Government, seemed as if the armed forces were well served, but no one in his wildest dreams could have imagined that this was to be a war such as no other war had ever been! The unspeakable horrors and battles of annihilation had yet to come and the unimaginable compulsory military service that was to feed further millions to the cannon, was not then considered necessary.

By the time it became universally acknowledged that the war would definitely _not_ be over by Christmas, the shortfall in manpower was such that it could only be made up by introducing females into the manufactories - an unprecedented and momentous development which was to have dramatic effect long after wartime exigencies were satisfied.

Early in 1915, the Uskside Engineering Works commenced production of large projectiles for naval guns. The Ministry of Munitions designated the factory as a National Training Centre and in July, 230 women were engaged in the turning of shells. Other products were heavy, ship's forgings such as shaftings and rudder mechanisms.

Shortly afterwards, the new Great Western Railway fitting shops at Maesglas were converted to the manufacture of 60 pounder, high explosive shells. Many females were trained here as machinists and turners. They worked three, eight hour shifts whilst the men worked two shifts of twelve hours each. As time went on, the number of women employed here became four times that of the men.

March 1916 saw the opening of the United Tube Works Ltd (afterwards the Mannesmann Tube Works and later Stewarts & Lloyds Ltd) in a new factory at the end of Corporation Road. Starting with 250 employees, its first productions were forgings for shells and gas cylinders.

The Ministry of Munitions set up a National Cartridge and Box Repair Factory in April 1916. These premises were situated on 13 acres of ground alongside the entrance lock of the Alexandra Dock. The building was a salvage depot for the sorting and reclamation of shell boxes and shell cases, and 85% of its work-force was female. For the next half a century Newport knew these premises as 'The Box Factory' no matter who was in occupation.

Lysaghts did not make finished articles of war, but its steel plate was used extensively elsewhere in the manufacture of munitions.

The East Usk Chemical Works, Corporation Road, was taken over in 1916 and new plant installed for the increased production of the sulphuric acid used in fertilisers. Bones and fat gave up the very important glycerine, and the glue that was needed for the making and repair of aeroplanes. A very large number of women were employed.

Braithewaite & Co Ltd made trench covers, railway points, water tanks and skin and deck plating for ships. Here too large numbers of women were employed.

Due to a severe shortage of sugar and other raw materials, Lovells Confectionery Works turned a large part of the factory over to war work, manufacturing mine sinkers and tank tracks, and repairing over 6,000 ammunition boxes a week.

Nearly half the men who worked at the Newport Gas Works had gone into his Majesty's Forces and as their work was almost entirely unsuitable for women it was a credit to the older and unfit men and the boys that the undertaking was kept in full operation.

It was not generally realised how important the by-products of gas manufacture were in the conduct of modern warfare. Toluene for instance, was a vital ingredient of trinitrotoluene (TNT) and with the appropriate extra plant installed, all the gas works in the country produced large amounts. In addition, the Newport works produced large quantities of benzol, and many other explosive substances were obtained from cold tar such as carbolic acid, benzene, ammonia, sulphur and naptha.

In the great dockyard complex, the shipyards of C H Bailey and the Tredegar Dry Dock & Wharf Company repaired or refitted no less than 1,974 warships and merchantmen, equipping the latter with 172 gun platforms and many Marconi wireless telegraphy cabins and masts. Even small corners of these yards were given over to the manufacture of shell parts by women.

When peace finally returned, Newport like everywhere else, tried to resume the life which it had forsaken four years earlier. Then had been a time when Edwardianism had hardly faded away and strong overtones of the Victorian era were still in evidence. By 1918 however, such a life and all its traditions had received a jolt from which it was never to recover.

Consider for instance the case of the ladies. This was the way in which a local writer had described them in 1907:-

'Ladies of Newport - the loveliest in the land; loyal in love; light-hearted and footed; limpid in language; lively in laughter; not lazy lackadaisical lasses, but labouring to lighten our loads or lessen our losses!'

231

Little did this anonymous correspondent realise how prophetic were the last two statements in his dissertation - although obviously not in the way they were meant. For what it was worth, he also said:

'The manners of Newport men are a model for the world', but the less said about that the better!

The fact remains that the ladies so described in 1907 were, only eight years later, up to their elbows in the grease and oil of the wartime factories, replacing men as tram drivers and conductors, and generally performing many other inveterately male tasks.

It was unanimously agreed that these pioneering feminists did nothing but good for the reputation of their sex. Although it had been necessary to employ them in the ratio of 3 women to do the jobs of two men (remember that much of the work was quite arduous), their punctuality was very good, sick absence normal, output excellent and their whole attitude unquestionably cheerful and loyal. Of course the incentives had never been better, apart from the overwhelming priority of winning the war. There was the breaking of new ground and the almost child-like, daring intrusion of girls into boys' games. Previously unheard-of opportunities presented themselves in a wider range of activities, many of which were out of doors and, last but not least, the wages were good!

When the war ended, it was with great reluctance that these jobs had to be handed back to returning service men - but not all! There were those enlightened employers who fully realised the worth of their female workers, and who made room for a few retentions. The Post Office, banks and building societies were leading examples of the changing order. The war had given the first nudge to this thin edge of the wedge!

Whereas in Newport at the height of hostilities, women made up 83% of those employed on work of national importance, after 1918 the figures returned to those shown below:-

Male		Female	
Transport	40%	Domestic Service	30%
Iron & Steel	25%	Distributive Trades	18%
Distributive Trades	15%	Tailoring & Dressmaking	15%
Building & Allied Trades	10%	Educational & Secretarial	12%
Glass, Rubber & Chemical	1%	Food Manufacture	5%
		Laundry Work	5%

Shortly after the cessation of hostilities it was realised that no satisfactory record was available of those of the town who had made the ultimate sacrifice in the defence of their country. To remedy this and to provide an everlasting memorial the teachers of Newport set out to create a comprehensive Roll of Honour. Completed in 1923 and presented to the Corporation in 1924, it contained the names of 4 women and 1,511 men of the Merchant Marine, Royal Navy, Royal Flying Corps and the Army.

The period following the Armistice was a time for soul-searching and recrimination. Many took the opportunity to take a good look at their town and, not liking what they saw, voiced firm opinions of the best way to go forward. It was alleged for instance that for the previous 30 years or so, Newport had suffered from a severe lack of the exciting, stimulating leadership that had formerly been its proud boast.

One of the sterner critics was the much respected W J L Collins ('Dromio') of the South Wales Argus who, in 1919, wrote a series of articles that painted a gloomy picture of an uninspiring community. Newport was said to be : 'a higgledy piggledy, haphazard, crowded conglomeration of houses, shops, churches, chapels and cinemas with surroundings drab, mean and sordid. It was crowded and commonplace, the architecture bland and the public institutions feeble in influence. No more than three generations could claim to be native born of Newport and the fire of civic enthusiasm burned low!'

The captains of industry were accused of 'a blind pursuit of wealth and prosperity with little concern for the well-being of those who toiled to this end!'

The articles recognised the necessity for many Newport men and women to earn their bread by hard, dirty and soul-destroying work, in conditions far removed from comfort beauty or pleasure. This was the price to be paid for industrial achievement but it did not mean that working life had to be so drab, and it should have been the duty of the municipality to see that the colour, beauty, comfort and inspiration should be available outside that working environment.

This was one view of the Newport of 1919 and, as it happened, it was one with which the majority of South Wales Argus readers could easily identify. The end of hostilities had promised so much. No sooner had the shadow of death and destruction been dispelled so that people could begin to reshape shattered lives and plan for a hopeful future, than the frantic burst of post-war parliamentary activity passed long awaited legislation intended to enhance those prospects.

Nearly 400 years earlier (1536), King Henry VIII had allowed the first Welsh representatives to enter Parliament. Twenty-four members were returned for the Principality and Newport was combined with Monmouth and Usk as a tripartite constituency sending one member. So the position remained until the Representation of the People Act 1918 made dramatic changes.

The gain of the country as a whole was the granting of the vote to six million women over the age of 30; Newport profited by becoming a single parliamentary constituency in its own right.

This was Lewis Haslam's last period as Newport's MP, a position he had held since 1906. In 1922, the Conservative Party withdrew from the Coalition and in the general election that followed, Reginald George Clarry became the town's Conservative MP by 19,019 votes to the Labour Candidate's 16,000; but for a short break during the reign of the ill-fated Labour Government from 1928 to 1931, Mr Clarry remained Newport's MP until 1945.

On a more domestic issue, this was the time when the ancient Church of St Woolos won back some of its long lost limelight after languishing in the background for so many years. On 29th September 1921, the Governing Body of the Church in Wales ordered the creation of the new Diocese of Monmouth from the territory contained within the Archdeaconry of Monmouth - originally part of the Diocese of Llandaff.

Newport was declared the seat of the Bishop with residence at Kingshill House, Stow Hill, donated by Lord Tredegar and renamed Bishopstowe for the purpose. It remained under this title until the building of a new Bishopstowe in the grounds, at which time the old house was sold under its old name to become an annexe of Rougemont School which stood on its Stow Hill frontage.

St Woolos was designated the pro-Cathedral of the Monmouth Diocese. The first Lord Bishop was the Right Reverend Charles Alfred Howell Green, elected 18th November 1921 and enthroned in the Cathedral 3rd January 1922. It was not until 1949 that St Woolos was confirmed as the permanent diocesan cathedral, possession of which gave Newport cause for much pride in the light of this prestigious enhancement.

Within a few years of the aforementioned events, a new guidebook emanating from a private source, gave a description of the town which contrasted starkly with the unkind remarks of the South Wales Argus in 1919. Of course it is acknowledged that by its very nature a guidebook would hardly say otherwise.

In a startling catalogue that read like an encyclopaedia of commercial assets, Newport was shown to possess sheet iron rolling mills, nail and rivet works, brattice cloth, India rubber and chemical works, engineering works, shipbuilding yards, iron and brass foundries, cast iron pipe manufacturers, dry docks, saw mills, creosoting works, brick and tile makers, lime kilns, flour mills, clothing factories, tobacco and confectionery manufacturers - all trading to increase the prosperity of the town and to increase the large export shipping trade.

This 1928 publication went on to state:-

'The tremendous wave of commercial activity which swept over Newport 50 years ago, was responsible for much hurried town planning and building, hardly in keeping with the heights to which the town was destined to rise. The last 20 years has seen much of this original and inartistic work replaced by structures worthy of the commercial glory with which Newport has literally covered itself.

Since the advent of the 20th century, art has done much to beautify the exterior of industry, and the principal thoroughfares are now as pleasing to the eye as long stretches of business premises well can be. in spite of its enviable position in the forefront of our great commercial towns, Newport is exceptionally healthy. Its remarkably low death rate of 10.2 per 1,000 is well below the all-England average of 11.6 and the cost of living here is rather lower owing to the extraordinary transport facilities which the town enjoys!'

In 1920, Newport Bridge was giving cause for concern. A hundred and twenty years old, it had been drastically altered and widened in 1866 to cope with the huge increase in population that the town had by then sustained; in 1920 with another fourfold increase added to the tremendous wear and tear of time and tide, the Corporation felt that it was right to look into the question of replacing the bridge entirely.

Figures taken from two censuses on separate days, 60 years apart, give some idea of the increased traffic flow:

23rd December 1864		15th August 1925	
(7 am to 7 pm)		(6 am to 10 pm)	
Carriages and gigs	109	Motor vehicles	6,131˙
Saddle horses	98	Tramcars	1,447
Wagons and carts	444	Cycles	6,951
Asses and carts	20	Horsed vehicles	1,133
Handcarts	74	Horses	81
Cattle	7	Handcarts	241
Total	752	Total	15,984
Pedestrians	3,725	Pedestrians: too numerous to count.	
Population	25,103	Population	97,751

˙ This figure trebled in the next 25 years.

Newport Bridge and the Old Green 1893

Further proof of the urgency of the situation had been provided by a series of ominous discoveries made on each occasion that the bridge required attention. For example, the eradication of the 'Dip' in 1893 had exposed eroding weaknesses in the town-end piers, and it cost £19,706 for repairs to the stonework. Hundreds of tons of reinforcing stone had to be deposited in the immediate upstream and downstream riverbed to prevent tidal scour.

In 1913, a very concerned Borough Council sought expert advice and in so doing displayed amazing presentiment. The firm of leading civil engineers, Sir John Wolfe Berry Lister and Partners, was engaged to look into the problem and in addition to draw up plans for a second river crossing. The result was a choice of seven bridge sites, four north and three south of the existing bridge, with preference stated for the southern suggestions, one of which was almost exactly where the George Street Bridge was to cross half a century later.

The report also advised that in the light of the single existing bridge's doubtful reliability, a relief crossing should be provided - and the sooner the better !

The First World War put paid to any further bridge activity at that time but as soon as it was over Parliamentary powers were obtained forthwith and immediate action carried out to furnish a supplementary structure.

In 1920, a temporary bridge which had been used on the River Thames at Southwark, was brought to Newport and erected alongside the old stone bridge, with an angled access from Clarence Place and the other end in the Castle grounds.

With the Ministry of Transport guaranteeing 65% of all costs, the tender of £140,275-10s of Sir William Arrol & Co Ltd, was accepted, and on 10th June 1924 work commenced on the new bridge. All traffic, including the electric trams, was diverted on to the wooden relief bridge - a far cry from the rerouting via Caerleon and Malpas that had been necessary on the occasion of the previous bridge-building in 1800.

Preliminary operations identified some predictable problems. A large amount of debris had to be cleared from the riverbed on both sides of the old bridge's pier foundations, all of which were to be used again after heavy reinforcement. This debris consisted of large stones and solidified cement bags used in previous bridge maintenance. There were also many water-logged tree trunks and old timber members. One very interesting relic that the riverbed surrendered, was a carved stone believed to be part of the mediaeval cross that once stood on Stow Hill (see under Crusades).

Built into the finished bridge there had to be the means of fulfilling its other important functions - that of carrying public utilities across the river. Beneath its busy road surface and pavements were ducts containing dozens of electrical and telephone cables, gas and water mains.

On the 2nd June 1927 at a final cost of £250,000 the new Newport Bridge was opened by the Minister of Transport accompanied by the Mayor, Mr A T W James.

The extra width and strength of the new bridge eased the congestion for a while but in a town of Newport's size, where for a long time it had been felt that one bridge would be insufficient, the measures taken were soon seen to be of a palliative nature only. Once again it was necessary to resort to playing with traffic circulation and creating one-way systems. A very critical speaker at a Rotary Club dinner blamed successive councils for 'frittering away money on half-hearted schemes which proved no solution at all. Most council members had been business people, which more or less proves that control of councils by business people is not always a good thing!'.

One cannot be sure if this gentleman was advocating that the multi-million pound commercial empire controlled from the Town Hall should be in the hands of a board that had no head for business!

- 0 -

The stage has now been reached which is within the living memory of many, and for this reason it may not yet be regarded as having true historical significance. Such treatment is usually reserved for times deep past where all the players have 'shuffled off this mortal coil' and only second-hand account is available. However it would not be equitable to terminate the story of a town simply because it has reached a point of contemporaneity. Even for those who have survived, memories dim and the period becomes a partly closed book; nevertheless, if the trouble is taken to dust off the covers and turn a few pages it is surprising how near-non-events can be made to supply a little colour and meaning.

The quarter century following the 1914-18 War was not noted for unusual memorability nor for the emergence of any one outstanding personality at whom future generations might point and say proudly: 'He or she was born in Newport!' Even so, this period is not deserving of being entirely passed over, acting as it did as a vital link between two eras that, whilst having nothing in common, had equal parts to play in changing the face of the town. To put some substance into what would otherwise be a dull, uninspiring, almost blank space, it is necessary to study the gleanings from council minutes, newspapers, and other journals such as the Newport Year Books, town guides, directories and almanacs.

The 1920s had very little to recommend them. In comparison with the cataclysmic events of the previous decade, it would not be much of an exaggeration to say that the clock would have had to have been turned back as far as the 18th century to find a period of similar quiescence. Information throwing light on the happenings in Newport at this time is plentiful in total, but rather more thin on the ground when the imaginative is separated from the commonplace:-

1920

The Right Honourable Viscount Churchill, Chairman of the Great Western Railway Company, visiting Newport, spoke of the serious need for a Severn Bridge.

Several cases of rabies were diagnosed in the town.

Serious race riots broke out.

In September, the railway workers went on strike and 4,000 troops entered the town in case of disorder.

The Council was informed that in the 20 weeks ending 26th September, Newport schoolchildren had killed 16,000 rats!

1921

Drug smuggling was not unknown; a raid by Newport Police and Customs Officials uncovered 2,000 morphine pills on a ship in the Alexandra Dock.

The Prince of Wales visited the town in June. He inspected troops on the Athletic Ground, travelled over the Transporter Bridge and carried out a tour of the docks.

Lord Tredegar presented Kingshill House, Stow Hill, as residence for the Bishops of Monmouth.

Violence flared the length of Dock Street with running battles between foreign and British seamen; pistols, knives, clubs and stones were used. At a time of very high unemployment there was great bitterness, caused by the cheap, foreign labour on British ships.

Police Sergeant Nancarrow died 26 years later and it was confirmed that injuries received in these riots, although not restricting his police duties, almost certainly contributed to his death.

At midnight on 17th October, the new Diocese of Monmouth came into being.

A few days before Christmas, the Newport Christian Hot Pot Fund gave its 22nd annual distribution to the poor.

The annual report of the Chief Constable was notable if only for the cognisance that it gave into the attitude of the townsfolk to their own security. It seems that they either had remarkably trusting natures or else suffered from the most incredible carelessness. The report stated that between the hours of midnight and 6 am over the course of the whole year, patrolling constables had discovered premises unsecured and doors left open to the extent of : 266 dwelling-houses, 215 shops, 246 offices, 64 warehouses, 89 outbuildings, 34 places of worship, 13 schools, 23 stables, 14 cellars and 106 workshops! All the occupiers were informed. The figures for succeeding years proved to be very similar.

1922

The report of Newport's Medical Officer of Health revealed that many virulent infections were abroad although none had reached epidemic level. Those that topped the list were: diphtheria, scarlet fever, whooping cough, measles, pulmonary tuberculosis, typhoid, encephalitis-lethargica (sleepy sickness) and puerperal fever.

During the course of the year the town received a surprising amount of adulation from the national press. A typical example was:

I came, I saw, Newport conquered. To see Newport is to be convinced of its potentialities. Newport has the finest coal fields at its back door and the ocean at its front door, and giving the most rapid dispatch to loading and unloading steamers of any port in the kingdom. It is the Western Watergate of Britain'.

It was a fact that practically every week records were broken in the docks for the quick turn-round in shipping.

However a record of a different kind was about to be made. On October 5th 1922, the temperature recorded in Newport was 80 degrees Fahrenheit (26.5 Celsius) and, for so late in the year, this had not been surpassed 70 years later as the century drew near its end!

There was a tremendous blizzard on the night of April 1st. Next day the unemployed commenced moving 960 tons of snow from the streets.

At this time, attendance at meetings of the Town Council was guaranteed to supply a little light relief.

Certain aldermen and councillors were noted for their ability to talk at great length without making any clear point. Often, as soon as these filibustering members were perceived as about to rise to their feet, their colleagues started leaving the chamber on all sorts of pretexts and, if the time was propitious, the Mayor would hastily call an adjournment for lunch!

Many councillors had special interests or pet projects that were trotted out, pontificated upon and then replaced on the shelf until a further opportunity presented itself. These subjects rarely had any bearing on the running of the town but served to fill a quiet half hour when council business was flagging. It was not unusual for non-participating members to be lulled into somnolence whilst others could exhibit petulance bordering on puerility. Doubt could even be cast on the discernment of some, as in the case of one who, in a debate on Newport Castle, exclaimed: 'It is impossible to think that this is where King Charles and his knights sat round the Round Table!'

The Transporter Bridge was a recurring subject of discussion. It was drastically under-used, running at great loss and, in March 1923, out of order! The nickname 'White Elephant' seemed well earned and was never more widely used than in the council chamber. To save some expense, a motion was passed to reduce the foreman's wages; it was also decided to close the bridge at night to cut overtime costs, and vigorous debate continued on the possibility of making the bridge toll-free which, ironically, would also have created savings! In the course of these deliberations it came as a great surprise to many councillors to learn that their predecessors had been obliged to make a considerable, lump sum payment to Lysaghts Works as compensation for the Transporter Bridge _not being_ toll-free from the beginning!

Vermin infestation was still a great problem, with the black rat being a particular menace; there were several instances of babies being bitten in their cots or prams. Despite the laying of 17,000 baits, the rat-catchers reported that not one had been taken!

A proposal was made that bands should be invited to give regular concerts in Newport parks (Belle Vue and Beechwood) and paid for out of the rates. The unanimous assent that this received was so unprecedented in the life of that corporation that the proposer sat stunned in his seat!

An ill-fated project was the setting up of a municipal piggery on the refuse destructor site in Soho Street, between Conway and Corporation Roads. This venture was expected to give a reasonable profit, and a figure of £200 a year was hopefully bandied about. One councillor, in whose bonnet this bee had lodged, was said to have 'hogged' council time with an unremitting barrage of enquiries on porcine welfare. As things turned out he might as well have saved his breath because by July 1923 all the occupants of the council sty had succumbed to swine fever!

Temperatures were again raised when it was suggested that all female clerks earning pin money in council employment should be sacked to provide work for ex-servicemen. One defender of the fair sex said: 'It is somewhat difficult to see how the position of a girl earning £50 a year could be coveted by the class of man whom it is desired to help'.

In early summer, the whole of the Corporation had a jolly junket to Talybont for the cutting of the first sod of the water scheme. This prompted a certain reporter, noted for his humorous treatment of civic business, to wax lyrical in the South Wales Argus:-

For expense of course we cared not a hang.
So we left the Town Hall in some chars~a~banc.
At Caerleon Asylum the inmates cried:
Here's a fresh batch ~ pray come inside!

Before the year was out there had been another discussion on the need for a Severn Bridge crossing, the defeat of a motion to build a town crematorium because the disposal of corpses by burning was considered to be 'pre-Christian', and complaints were heard of the digging-up of Clarence Place by Post Office cable layers only one week after it was newly resurfaced with Trinidad Asphalt at fifteen shillings a square yard'. It might have been only yesterday!

1924

The foundation stone of the Cenotaph was laid in Clarence Place, and two months later in June, the completed monument was unveiled by Major General Lord Treowen in the presence of a huge crowd and a massed parade of troops.

Temperatures in Newport soared to 93 degrees Fahrenheit.

Outbreaks of smallpox were still too frequent for comfort and concern was expressed about the laxity seen in some quarters in containing the disease. The example was quoted of the Gloucester hospital where several isolated patients went missing and were found having a party in a nearby public house!

Eight members of the council came in for heavy criticism for taking an all-expenses-paid trip to Wembley to inspect some new building blocks of 'ferro-concrete'. The question was asked why one of the blocks could not have been sent by train to Newport. This obviously involved one of the countless committees or sub-committees to which matters were constantly being 'referred back' to obtain further information - only a small proportion ever seemed to reach satisfactory conclusions!

The year ended in more heated debate on a subject that was a particular thorn in Newport's side.

In 1917, a Mr Brooks took a lease on a field at Liswerry and thereafter allowed it to fill up with the makeshift shelters of homeless people so that it soon resembled the worst slums to be found in poorest parts of the Third World. By 1924, Brooks Field had been christened 'Bacon Box Avenue' by one councillor and it comprised dozens of appalling shanties made out of old tarpaulins, scrap timber and rusty, corrugated iron sheets. Some of the hovels were no more than a few poles stuck in the ground and draped in sacking!

This awful, insanitary place, set in a soggy patch surrounded by reens, not far from the Corporation Road tram terminus, was even discovered by the national press, much to the shame and embarrassment of a town council that was just beginning to pride itself on coming to terms with its housing problems.

1925

This year saw the breaking down of one of the last great bastions of Victorianism when the Baths Committee courageously introduced limited mixed bathing sessions at Stow Hill Baths.

Brynglas House was reopened as one of the new central schools.

A cable was laid from the town power station to Malpas and Caerleon. A debate on St Cadocs Hospital revealed that all the machinery at the hospital farm was now driven by electricity. The question was asked: 'Shall we ever see the day when Newport Corporation will supply power to farms for miles around?'

1926

This was an exceptionally quiet year if the short-lived General Strike and its repercussions are left out of the reckoning. However it did provide the swan-song for the refuse destructor which had been purchased in 1910 following 'expert' advice indicating that it would be much cheaper than tipping. Now it was estimated that tipping would be cheaper to the tune of £10,000 a year!

On 2nd June the new river bridge was officially opened.

Only one other fact worth noting emerged this year : Newport was a town possessed of 80 inns, 50 beerhouses and 34 drinking clubs. There was one licence for every 588 of the population and 200 prosecutions for drunkenness in the year.

1927

One period of 24 hours in January produced 1.94 inches of rain; it was estimated that 878,000 tons of water fell on the town!

The Chief Constable (proudly?) reported that *no* methylated spirit drinking had taken place in the town during the previous twelve months!

The Health Department made chicken pox a notifiable disease as a precaution against the greater scourge of smallpox which was still prevalent in the county districts.

Housing development on 120 acres of farmland at the Coldra had been present in the minds of Town Councils for several years. It was now decided not to proceed and thus the Ringland Housing Site was to remain in abeyance for another 30 years!

1928

A plan to build a new cathedral on land at Bassaleg was abandoned when it was learned that the cost would exceed half a million pounds.

Lord Tredegar gave 61 acres of his deer park at Cardiff Road to Newport Corporation at a nominal rent of £2 a year, for the purposes of a public park and recreation ground.

1929

The year was notable only for the fact that the town had more smallpox cases than for many years.

Thus, ingloriously, unhealthily and uneventfully, passed the third decade of Newport's 20th century. Of the brave, new world sought for so hungrily after the end of the Great War, there was still no sign and another generation would have to pass before the first glimmerings of hope in this direction.

Chapter Fourteen

The 1930s

This era began much as the 1920s had ended although contemporaries of those days, who are still very much in evidence as this writing takes place, would say that life had become that much more relaxed and 'modern' with the acquisition by every cinema of talking pictures, wireless in many homes (mostly rented -Rediffusion- 2/6d (12½p) a week), and gramophones in the majority of parlours.

Having said this however, it was freely admitted that the existence of such things in no way balanced the scales against poverty and the large, squalid slum areas that blighted the town.

Whatever else may be said of the town councils of those days and, in spite of their occasional excesses, they could not be accused of poor housekeeping. For several years in succession they managed rate reductions and, in the first year of the decade, brought about a mammoth reduction of one shilling and tenpence!

They would also readily admit to the fact that the town's ratepayers could not afford some projected scheme or other and would cheerfully postpone it until a more propitious time. This was the kind of accountability that the town had struggled for over hundreds of years to achieve and it was inconceivable that there might ever be another time when its administration would not be quite so mindful of the wishes or the depth of the pockets of its inhabitants!

The first feelers were put out on the subject of a municipal airport.

The total enfranchisement of women (1928) had added 9841 females over the age of 21 to the borough's voting lists.

Having outlived its useful life, the Old Town Dock was filled in - 88 years after its triumphal opening.

The charge for sending a letter inland rate and to the United States or the Dominions was 1½d. (just over ½p) for the first ounce and 1d for every additional ounce. The number of parcels handled by Newport General Post Office was 63,540,828.

The trade figures had been deteriorating for some time and reflected the national trend. In 1930, Newport docks and river wharves dealt with over 2 million tons less than in 1913!

1931

The year started savagely. On its second day, 22 degrees of frost were registered in the town!

Slow recovery was being made from 19 cases of mild smallpox and an epidemic of 227 cases of diphtheria - the worst for ten years. Fortunately there were no fatalities.

Double-decker buses were seen on Newport streets for the first time.

The police became mobile - on four wheels instead of two. Two 15 horsepower four-seater, open touring cars were purchased for the sum of £630-10s. Their occupiers were referred to as 'speed police!'

The night of 27th and 28th May brought 'Lightning, wind, deluge and cloudburst - swimming pigs, hysterical women and marooned families' (South Wales Argus headline). It was described as the worst storm ever to hit Monmouthshire, and the unprecedented volume of rain falling on the town in such a short space of time, created untold havoc.

Malpas Brook overflowed, drain covers everywhere were forced up, Kimberley Park became a lake and Malpas, from Goodrich Crescent to the Rising Sun, became a mini-Venice. Caerleon Road from Duckpool Road to Richmond Road was a swirling torrent, and on Chepstow Road a culvert burst through the pavement near Kensington Place. Elsewhere, the River Ebbw burst its banks and submerged Tredegar Park, Forge Lane and Lighthouse Road.

Obviously, to prevent the recurrence of such a catastrophe, urgent measures were called for. A few weeks afterwards, for just such reasons, councillors spent many hours in inconclusive debate. At the same meeting it took just five minutes to vote a substantial rise in salary for the Mayor!

The South Wales Argus ran a series of articles to explain the theory behind a new invention which it was hoped would catch on; it was entitled 'Television - how it works'.

Giant, skeletal pylons started their march from Newport across the moors in a south easterly direction to Severnside, opposite Bristol, where linkage with the National Grid was to be effected. Digging of the foundations for one of them uncovered human remains at a depth of nine feet. They were not old by archaeological standards -possibly those of a victim of the great flood of 1603. By contrast, a human skull was discovered at the turn of the century, when the great entrance lock to the Alexandra Dock was being excavated across the old, winding estuary of the River Ebbw. Lying 42 feet below the surface, its original owner was estimated to have lived over 4,000 years ago.

The assumption that both sets of remains were lying at their original surface levels (and this is borne out in the older case by the presence of tree roots) has convinced the experts that the coastal belt of Gwent has been subsiding for millennia, and was once standing at least 30 feet above sea level which itself only then came up to the present 5 fathom line. The substance of this theory received added weight when, in 1961, a human skull was uncovered 40 feet deep in an excavation of the floor of a mill at the Orb Works Corporation Road. Its age was initially set at over 2,000 years.

The publication of wills revealed the astonishing fact the two local residents had each left over £1,000!

Newport had its own pleasure beach or lido, as the press was fancifully inclined to describe it. Known to one and all more generally as 'The Lighthouse', it provided a very popular day out for all the family at a modest fare on one of the Red and White omnibuses which left at regular intervals on summer Saturdays and Sundays, from the Rodney Road terminus.

A publicity write-up of the time offered the following:-

'Just below St Brides on the Wentloog Level, a number of tradesmen's premises rise out of the mud and grass. The Lido will bask in the singeing haze of May days and June, with happy days by the briny, hurdy-gurdies, swings, roundabouts, ice-cream swallowing, leisurely lunches spread on napkins, deep breaths of ozone, hastily improvised cricket, and crab-hunting among the boulders, paddling and bathing'.

Nowhere in this idyllic picture was warning given that at low tide the sea would retreat almost out of sight, leaving crab-hunters and bathers coated in glutinous mud that had to be laboriously removed before dressing to go home!

Those who never joined this throng, or indeed who were not born to see it, need the strongest of imaginations to picture this now-desolate stretch of scrub-covered seashore as a once noisy, colourful, bustling place capable of giving many of the smaller, more fashionable, Welsh resorts a healthy run for their money.

242

This was the year that sounded the death knell for Newport's once famous Wool Fair. No buyers turned up at the Cattle Market because of a record importation of cheaper foreign wool. The days were just a memory when shrewd farmers did brisk business from morning to night with keen wool buyers from all over the country.

Greyhound racing was about to make its debut in the town but at first there was indecision as to where its home should be. Three sites were considered - at Somerton Park, on land near Lysaghts Works, and in the Durham Road area. The Cardiff Arms Park Company settled the issue when it purchased Somerton Park, and the first greyhound race meeting open the track on November 17th.

A tenancy of the ground was granted to Newport County Association Football Club and the first match was played against Clapton (Leyton) Orient on August 27th.

Fox-hunting was never so popular, and weekly accounts were published of every twist and turn made either by Lord Tredegar's hounds or those of the Llangibby Hunt - as often as not with disappointing results, although even the frequent occasions when no fox was sighted were always reported as 'a good days hunting!'

This primarily rural sport was found taking place several times within the borough of Newport itself.

In Pillgwenlly, there had been numerous signs of a fox being active among the back garden and allotment chicken runs. In the end, a large hunt was organised on foot by hundreds of participants armed with sticks. Reynard was eventually run to earth in W A Baker's Foundry, but he dived into the River Usk and swam gamely across to safety on the Liswerry shore.

The second fox was not so lucky. Chased for miles from Magor by the Llangibby Hunt, it passed over Christchurch and took refuge in the bedroom of an empty house at St Julians where it was killed. Sometime afterwards, a third fox received the ultimate humiliation when, at Rhymney House on the Old Town Dock, it went for a goose that was protecting its young. In the ensuing flurry of fur and feathers, the fox was pecked to death!

Sightings of urban foxes became regular occurrences throughout the 1930s.

On Sunday July 3rd, the inhabitants of the town craned their necks skywards to witness one of the wonders of the modern world as the Graf Zeppelin passed over at a height of about 1,500 feet. It was part way through a 'showing the flag' tour of Britain, and among its invited passengers was a native-born Newportonian, Mr P Eric Rees, who persuaded the Captain to make a slight detour so that the mighty airship could see, and be seen by his town.

As the 700 feet long, silver cigar slid across the rooftops, pushed by its noisy droning engines, Mr Rees was privileged to behold what was probably the first ever great panoramic aerial view of the town, made all the more breath-taking by unfolding in slow motion. A week later, readers of the South Wales Argus were able to marvel for themselves at the written, eye-witness account.

The idea of a local airport had not yet been laid to rest. The initiation of the final stage of the Talybont Water Scheme brought many VIPs to the ceremony. One, flying his own aeroplane, made a clever, three-point landing in a field on the eastern side of the Transporter Bridge (probably on the future Coronation Park). In an after dinner speech later that evening, this gentleman-aviator hinted that the Corporation need look no further for a more suitable airport site than where he had landed. His take-off was just as competent as his arrival had been and he arrived back in London just over an hour later.

The good nature of the general public was apparently doing a disservice to the campaign against vermin, especially in the Castle Grounds where rats abounded. People were taking their children, armed with bags of corn and bread-crumbs, to feed the pigeons from the bridge, but at the same time they were unintentionally creating a harvest that attracted rats from far and wide. Besides regular appeals to the townsfolk to desist from feeding the birds, an annual cull was mounted against the growing menace. The 1932 tally was 120 rats.

In an attempt to rejuvenate the fortunes of the town, the Corporation put Newport on exhibit at the Birmingham Industries Fair and a publicity film was being shown at over a hundred cinemas. Someone, somewhere, had blundered however, because all enquiries at the Fair were being directed to the Great Western Railway Department at Cardiff! When this little matter had been corrected, the enterprise was maintained to have been well worth while.

The penny (go anywhere) tram fare was increased to three half pence.

Salmon of 30 lbs and over were being caught regularly in reaches of the River Usk, just above the town.

An order was finally made to clear the 40 or so decrepit vans, shanties and tents from the notorious Brooks Field at Liswerry.

Ever mindful of its duty to the ratepayers of Newport, the Council cut £371,000 from its capital expenditure programme.

The annual mile and half mile swims in the muddy waters of the River Usk were, as ever, proving to be great entertainment and attracted huge crowds of onlookers along both river banks. Viewing the river today - and it has hardly changed in 50 years - it must be hard to convince the younger generation that a large number of apparently intelligent people , all at the same time, actually took pleasure in plunging into the Usk's brown opacity!

First conceived in 1912, the race consisted of two legs starting from a rope strung across the river at Rexville (Lovells Confectionery Works) near the mouth of Crindau Pill, upstream for half a mile, round the right hand bend at Pillmawr to the turning point a little distance before the St Julians railway bridge. One half of the swim was always against whatever tide was running and therefore it was not a contest for the faint-hearted. Nevertheless, the entrants were numerous in both male and female sections and the fastest competitor this year was home in 26 minutes.

The Hotpot Fund was still a going concern although the hotpots themselves had died out during the Great War. Now in its 33rd year, 700 ticket holders flocked to East Usk Road. For several hours of one day, shortly before Christmas, the lane leading to the Williams Press Printing Works was filled as the lucky recipients took away their joints of beef and over 1,000 loaves of bread.

The year ended with the publication of the gloomiest trade figures so far. Hardly any ore was imported, pitwood was down from 358,000 to 136,000 tons and iron and steel exports from 446,000 to 110,000 tons.

1933

The football season ended dismally on May 6th with Newport's rugby team unbelievably having lost 25 matches - the last 6 home games in succession - and many were defeats at the hands of teams that in later years would often be considered mediocre.

Publication of the 1931 Census figures showed that Newport's population had suffered a substantial decrease. The 1930 figure of 97,220 was reduced to 89,918, although the number of houses had risen by nearly 300. The reason for this unusual change was given as the huge swing of borough residents to houses being built in the Magor and St Mellons rural areas where they touched the borough boundaries. This was seen as further evidence to support the town's urgent demands for boundary extensions.

A strange and seemingly unfair rule had been enforced for some years by the Education Committee. It had been made a condition of employment of teachers at schools within the borough that they could not live outside the borough. This was a condition that applied to no other class especially that including members of the town council who would have been decimated by its application. The rule was altered to allow residence within six miles of the town centre even if outside the borough.

A quart of milk was costing 5d (2 pence) in the town - the cheapest since the end of the Great War.

The price of petrol at the town's pumps went down from 1/8d (7 pence) to 1/3d (6½ pence) a gallon due to over-production in the United States and the fall in the value of the dollar.

The famous peacocks and other exotic birds in the Belle Vue Park aviaries commenced to be run down when it was decided that their maintenance was becoming too difficult. Apparently the larger birds were not being properly looked after, were fighting amongst themselves, and the parrots and parakeets were escaping to fly wild in the park. At about the same time, entertainment by public radio broadcasting in Belle Vue, Beechwood and Shaftesbury Parks was discontinued in order to make a saving of £400 a year.

There were 10,000 unemployed in the town.

Newport Civil Service Sports Club was opened in the very rural and sparsely populated parish of Bettws. Cutting the ribbon on 11 acres of football, hockey and cricket pitches together with several fine tennis courts and a pavilion, was Sir Noel Curtis Bennet CVO, Chairman of the National Playing Fields Association.

For the first time in Newport's history all three of the magistrates who sat on the bench and conducted the entire business of the Court, were women!

A meeting of the Newport Harbour Commissioners again discussed the very controversial subject of a Severn Barrage. This had been a popular debate since 1926, and now seemed to be approached much more seriously judging by the intense research which had obviously gone into the facts presented.

The finished engineering wonder was to consist of a barrage built across the English Stones (site later chosen for the Second Severn Bridge) in which would be set a series of electrically operated lock-gates and lift-up bridges. A turbine dam, 4,500 feet long, would contain 72 turbines and electric generator units. The total cost was estimated at £37,726,749 with another £650,000 for the approach roads on both sides. The water flowing seawards would be reduced by 50% at spring tides and 40% at neaps.

Extension to the borough boundaries was becoming urgent business and for this purpose the Parliamentary and Improvement Committee decided to promote a Bill in the next session of Parliament.

In June, the Newport Sea Cadet Corps gave a display at Stelvio House for the Ladies Guild of Newport Navy League. 'Under the command of Chief Instructor Strath, the boys moved smartly and gave a fine display of physical training, field gun training and arms drill' (South Wales Argus). This item is included as a means of introducing another very remarkable man without mention of whom any modern history of Newport would be incomplete.

Jack Strath earned this accolade without the usual ingredients deemed necessary - the attainment of wealth or high office. He was 49 years old when the above newspaper report appeared, and just a few years afterwards your author made his acquaintance as a very young, easily intimidated cadet in the presence of a formidable chief petty officer. Six years under this highly motivated and dedicated man who could, nevertheless, display a razor-sharp wit when the occasion demanded, were more than enough to prepare any youngster for the rigours of whatever life destiny was to choose for him.

This particular youngster in fact grew into the man who eventually was given the utmost pleasure and privilege of obtaining a most illuminating interview from the grand old sea-dog a short while after he celebrated his 107th birthday, but also, sadly, only a few months before his death.

Jack Strath and his Field Gun Team, 1946.

Born in Plymouth on April 2nd 1884, both his father and grandfather had been Royal Marines. He was orphaned at the age of thirteen, and in 1899 was accepted into a training school for naval orphans at Greenwich. By the tender age of fifteen he was serving an extremely harsh and oppressive regime aboard the training ship 'HMS Impregnable', a 110 gun, wooden battleship-of-the-line, of the same design as but even bigger than Nelson's 'Victory'. Flogging with the birch was the common form of punishment for young offenders!

February 1915 found a 31 year old Jack Strath aboard the ironclad battleship 'Albion', taking part in the massive bombardment of the Dardanelles at the commencement of the ill-fated Gallipoli Campaign. The rest of his war was spent on convoy duty in the North Atlantic.

During the whole of his naval service he confessed to having visited every part of the world except the China Station, but it was at the very last place to which his Royal Navy duties brought him that he made the home in which to start a long new career - devoting all his efforts to the task of building character into the youth of his adopted town.

In 1924, the Admiralty decided that Newport was eminently suitable as a place in which to establish a training depot of the Royal Naval Volunteer Reserve. In furtherance of this project, the sailing ship, HMS Dahlia, was ordered from Plymouth to the Alexandra Dock at Newport to be used for training purposes. The man mainly responsible for the intricate seamanship necessary for its safe passage under full sail was none other than Chief Petty Officer Jack Strath.

The RNVR contingent was formed but it was soon found that HMS Dahlia was not suitable and so she was replaced by a larger, steam-driven vessel, the survey ship HMS Mutine, which was permanently moored in the Alexandra North Dock. From this moment on, many were the youthful volunteers who quailed but thrived under Jack's rigid instruction.

He retired from active service in 1928 and settled down in the town which was to be his home almost to the end of the century. However, he soon found that enforced inactivity was alien to him. All that vital, hard-earned knowledge much of it probably unique in the eyes of modern seafarers, was just begging to be shared.

Along came the perfect vehicle in the shape of the Sea Cadet Corps into which he could channel his boundless energy. From 1932 to 1954 he was to put many hundreds of Newport youngsters through their paces, preparing them if they were so inclined for a life on the ocean wave, but what was more important, instilling into them the dignity, sense of fair play and citizenship that he himself had lived by all his life. It was not surprising to learn of the successful men who had received part of their early education at his hands - there was even a mayor of Newport among them.

On public recreation grounds, at fairs and fetes, and at charitable functions far and wide, CPO (later Sublieutenant) Strath's field-gun team was a star attraction. Everyone waited with bated breath for the finale when the little muzzle-loader roared, belched flame and enveloped itself in a cloud of white smoke. When questioned about these occasions, the 107 year old eyes twinkled in fond remembrance as he recalled that every time the gun fired the law was being broken. Apparently it was illegal for junior organisations to load and discharge fire-arms even with blank ammunition. 'We were the only cadet force in the British Isles that fired a field gun during a public display', he chuckled, 'and I used to obtain the cordite from a secret supplier in Pontypool, and made up the charges at home!' No one ever noticed this well advertised infringement of the law or, if they did, they always turned a blind eye!

At the age of 107, Jack Strath, a man with a life bridging two centuries given to the service of his country and his fellow men, held several records that will likely never again all be held by one man. He was the longest recipient ever of a Royal Navy pension, having drawn it for 63 years; he was almost certainly the last man alive who had served both on a great, Trafalgar-like, wooden battleship and in the steel plated monsters of later years; he was the oldest man in Wales and was only pipped by a few months for the Great Britain title!

He of the ramrod back, who only buckled slightly when seriously hurt after being hit by a motor-cycle at the age of 92, deserves all that same adulation awarded to those other town benefactors who strutted centre-stage while he worked unassumingly in the wings.

As a footnote to the story of Jack Strath's consuming passion for the welfare of young people, it is felt that his great friend and senior officer for nearly a quarter of a century, clearly rates a mention.

Under the auspices of the Navy League, the Newport Sea Cadet Corps was in the charge of Lieutenant Commander Alfred Searle, partner in a local firm of solicitors, who had been founder of the Corps in 1900. He too was a remarkable man who often astounded his young proteges, in his 80th year, by demonstrating the correct way to turn a somersault on a gymnast's trapeze!

The partnership was broken in July 1941 when Commander Searle's house, 'Gaerwood' Kensington Place, received a direct hit from a parachuted German land-mine, and the long time leader of Newport Sea Cadets was killed.

Solemn and soul-stirring was the occasion when Jack Strath led his cadets in a slow march as they drew the field gun carriage bearing the coffin of their Commanding Officer to its final resting place.

The last big event of 1933 was the town's first military tattoo, taking place at the Athletic Grounds in October. For two days, thousands flocked to see military displays, superb gymnastic and athletic competitions, brass bands and old battles expertly recreated by local regiments dressed in the appropriate period uniforms, with flaming cannon, thundering explosions and burning castle backcloths. As night fell, the whole pageant was lit by powerful searchlights, skimmed by low flying aircraft. It was outdoor entertainment and spectacle of a magnificence rarely before seen.

1934

For many years, the town centre had suffered through a short section of the High Street being narrowed to half its width by a protruding block of buildings. At this point large vehicles had to pass each other quite gingerly and at busy periods the whole main street was held to ransom.

The offending buildings were those between Market Street and Griffin Street, and in January their demolition was set in motion, exposing the rear wall of the Market Hall for the first time in half a century. The project was the source of grand entertainment for passers-by or those with time on their hands, and the obliging builders provided viewing panels in the high wooden hoardings that surrounded the site.

The replacement structure (set well back from the original building line), comprised a row of shops with offices over, a new arcade entrance to the Market and a sizeable department store first known as Hills and Steele. As the years went by, the latter in turn became the Universal Stores, the British Home Stores, Newport GPO and, most recently, a modern extension to the Market.

A grand new road, 50 feet wide, was commenced at the Old Green between Dock Street and Screw Packet Lane. Due to the drop to the canal and railway below, this road negotiated the decline on concrete stilts, decreasing in height until it met the ends of Skinner Street, Corn Street and Canal Parade at the lower level. In its infancy it was optimistically called 'the Newport Bypass', although no one thought it strange that it was first necessary to travel into the town centre in order to get on to it! Soon afterwards, the road was officially christened 'Kingsway' but not for another 40 years was it to take on some semblance of a town centre bypass, and then only after complete demolition and rebuilding in conjunction with the other great transformations that were taking place.

The Mannesman Tube Works Corporation Road (afterwards Stewarts & Lloyds Ltd) made history when, as an experiment, it produced the longest, weldless, steel tube ever achieved anywhere in the world in one rolling. It was 178 feet long, 8½ inches outside diameter with a shell thickness of 0.212 inches.

In March, the Newport Borough Boundary Extension Bill was passed by the Special Committee of the House of Lords with a few amendments. Designed to absorb the whole of St Woolos parish (including Maesglas), and parts of Christchurch, Malpas and Bettws, the original area applied for was 3,808 acres but the Lords reduced it by 955 acres to 2,853 acres.

A severe period of drought was experienced in the spring season and by April Wentwood Reservoir was reduced to almost a quarter of its capacity - from 410 million to 113 million gallons: Pantyreos was similarly effected and lost well over half of its 145 million gallons. These were the reservoirs that supplied most of the people living on higher levels and so they became subject to the most stringent restrictions.

Courtenay, 3rd Baron, Viscount Tredegar, died on May 3rd at the age of 67. His extravagant lifestyle in the 30 years since he inherited the title had gnawed deeply into his capital and he seems to have given little regard to the example set by his forebears in the exercise of astute financial management and investment. His son, Evan, became 4th Baron, 2nd Viscount, continuing his father's love of lavish entertaining and extensive foreign travel.

In July, the town celebrated its own Navy Week. Four destroyers of the 12th Flotilla, the Valentine, Vidette, Windsor and Westminster, entered the Alexandra Dock for a visit of one week. To entertain the 24 officers and 400 ratings, there were massed parades, dances, guided tours around Monmouthshire and, not unexpectedly, extended licensing hours. A grand regatta was held in the Alexandra Dock and 10,000 visitors were attracted to see the programme of aquatic sports both serious and comic, and to be conducted over the warships.

Further additions were made to Newport's outdoor leisure attractions in the summer.

A private company acquired land part of Bullmoor Farm Caerleon, on which to build an open air swimming pool, cafe and restaurant. Bullmoor Lido as it became well known, opened to members of the public in July and they flocked there in hundreds on clement days, travelling by specially timed omnibuses, on foot and by bicycle (motor cars were then very thin on the ground as family transport). Situated alongside a pleasant, non-tidal reach of the River Usk, the 8½ acre complex comprising large adult pool and smaller children's pool with adjoining lawns, became Newport's favourite out-of-town resort, gradually relieving St Brides Lighthouse foreshore of its dubious hold on this honour. Bullmoor's popularity held in varying degrees for the next 55 years until its waning fortunes finally fell victim to the changing tastes of a much more affluent, adventurous and wide-ranging society.

A few weeks after the opening of Bullmoor Lido, another open air swimming pool made its debut, but although it too could be described as having similar rural aspect, it could almost be said to be within the town. Situated on the side of a wooded slope in the grounds of Alltyryn House, it was approached down a long winding path from the junction of Barrack Hill and Alltyryn View. The entrance gate was not far from the Barrack Hill omnibus terminus.

The pool, measuring 100 feet by 35 feet was placed in a dingle where the house's original spring and ornamental pools had been situated, and well may be remembered for having a very uneven (if not rocky) bottom. Fine weather at Alltyryn always seemed to bring out a permanent population of biting midges. The Lido did not survive the 1960s and is now part of Newport Borough Council's Alltyryn Wildlife Nature Footpath.

In September, a meeting of the Parliamentary and Improvement Committee, discussing the House of Lords' findings, decided to promote a Bill in the next session of Parliament to extend the borough boundaries. The cost of £7,035 was considered to be very reasonable. Over the next two years the move was to cause much argument and objection from the surrounding parish and rural authorities who stood to lose some part of their areas.

Rising flour prices forced up the price of a 1 lb loaf of bread in the town, to twopence farthing (just under one new penny).

Newport Castle was in a dreadful condition and had become an eyesore of crumbling masonry. Its owner, Lord Tredegar, handed it over to His Majesty's Office of Works for restoration.

The Medical Officer of Health's annual report revealed that the town's infant mortality rate was the highest ever, at 93.7 per 1,000; this was 34% above the national average and was stated to be the result of influenzal and diarrhoeal diseases and prematurity. The town death rate was 13.18 per 1,000. Pulmonary tuberculosis was considerably reduced, but cancer was on the increase especially among females. Only one case of smallpox was diagnosed and this in a foreign seaman at the docks; he was quickly whisked away to Crick House which for some years had been Newport Borough's isolation hospital for the more virulent diseases.

Sixty seven houses were scheduled for slum clearance. Their demolition resulted in the loss of such quaint sounding, 19th century byways as: Stow Passage, Providence Place (Baneswell), Fulfords Cottages (Victoria Avenue), White Lion Court (Mill Street), Severn View (Stow Hill), Victoria Square (Baneswell) and Somerton Cottages.

The daily issue of milk to Newport's schoolchildren commenced in October; by the end of the first twelve months nearly two million bottles (approximately one third of a pint) had been issued - one and a half million at the parents' expense. and half a million at the expense of Newport Education Committee.

Like many other towns up and down the country, Newport still admitted to the shameful necessity of a 'boot fund' for the purpose of supplying footwear to the children of the very poor. In 1934 the fund distributed 1,051 pairs of boots to the value of £216-18s to:-

'small boys and girls who, shiveringly, wend their way through snow, ice and rain, clad in well worn garments and boots that had long allowed their toes and feet to be exposed!'
(South Wales Argus).

A Newport Rotarian, returning from a visit of observation in Germany, revealed by his own gullibility just how easily the outside world was being taken in by the emerging Nazi regime. His report to the local press was complimentary on the subject of Hitler's 'labour camps' provided by a benevolent dictator as a measure to help the 'unemployed!'

1935

First, a few pertinent facts about the Newport of this particular year:-

As of June 30th there were 21,734 houses in the borough (including the areas added on 1st April) of which 395 were void.

The unemployment figure was 10,227 - over double that of ten years earlier.

The number of motor vehicles registered in the town during the whole year was 9,647, an increase of 93.87% over the figure for 1921. The same period saw an increase of 157% in the issue of driving licences. There was now one vehicle for every 25 residents.

A request was made to the Office of Works to expedite work on preservation of the Castle in consideration of the council removing Shaftesbury Buildings which for many years had masked all sight of the Castle from the High Street.

A 13 year old boy, convicted of stealing, became the first to be sentenced to be birched under the Children's Act 1933. Following a 1,000 signature petition and an appeal to the Home Secretary, the whipping was suspended but it required the King's signature to give final remission. For some time afterwards it was the practice in courtrooms to leave birches lying in full view on tables to give young offenders a reminder of the fate that could be awaiting them.

The 1st April was the appointed day for the coming into force of the Newport Corporation Act, the main provisions of which were to bring about another large boundary change. The previous Corporation Act of 1889 had added nearly all that part of the town on the eastern-side of the River Usk, bringing the total area of the borough to 4,924 acres.

In the course of construction of the new entrance lock to the Alexandra Dock, it had been necessary to divert and straighten the serpentine wandering of the River Ebbw estuary. For this purpose the Alexandra Dock (Newport and South Wales) Docks and Railway Act 1904 had added another 96 acres to the borough, bringing the total area to 5,020 acres. This was increased in 1935 by 2,853 to make 7,873 acres. The boundaries were pushed out as follows:-

In Christchurch parish, as far as Bishpool; Ladyhill and Farmwood, including Liswerry; the whole of St Julians to the River Usk; at Malpas from Crindau to the Three Blackbirds; in St Woolos parish the Gaer, Maesglas, Alltyryn, Tredegar Park, Pye Corner and High Cross.

The population of Newport for the first time exceeded 100,000.

Discussion on the site for the new civic centre was a regular feature of Newport Council meetings. At first, the popular choice seemed to be for the area occupied by the existing Town Hall, the Police Station and the Capitol Car Park at the rear, together with land between Corn Street and Merchant Street. However, before the year was out a firm decision was taken to build the new seat of local government at Clytha Park. This comprised an area of 41,914 square yards bounded by Clytha Park Road, Fields Road, Godfrey Road and Faulkner Road. The price being only the product of a 3.2224 d rate, was considered to be a bargain. In one way this was a fortunate selection because otherwise the town might have lost another of its most popular taverns - the Potters Arms was included in the original scheme!

Health-wise, measles was the scourge of 1935. There were 925 cases in eight months, including 25 that were fatal!

The subject of the Severn Bridge was never far from the agenda. The estimated cost of a crossing from Beachley to Aust was now given as £5 million - £2 million for the bridge and £3 million for the approach roads. By August the National Council of Road Improvements had instructed Sir Alexander Gibb and Partners to prepare figures to be placed before the Gloucester County Council and the Ministry of Transport.

Throughout the ages Newport had always known how to put on a show when there was something worth celebrating and on May 6th the town commenced a week in which it excelled itself.

This was the day when the whole country rejoiced and showed its undying loyalty to King George V and Queen Mary on the occasion of their Silver Jubilee. The contribution of Newport, and indeed the whole county, was a never to be repeated experience, even allowing for the great displays that were to come at the end of the Second World War and the future Queen Elizabeth's Coronation! For that matter, the present Queen's own Silver Jubilee in 1977, could not match her grandfather's for the sheer intensity and magnitude of joyous feeling for the Royal Family by their subjects, many of whom had lived through some of the most cheerless years in history. Future, better-off generations were to show themselves much more restrained in their indication of such regard.

On Silver Jubilee Day 1935, nothing was spared in efforts to commemorate it!

The Athletic Grounds were open all day for a great variety of events and entertainments, the best remembered of which was the issue to every schoolchild of a half pound of chocolates in a flat, rectangular, silver-painted, tin box bearing miniature coloured portraits of their Majesties. Thousands were given away and the day saw a constant stream of boys and girls leaving the grounds with their prizes clutched tightly in their hands. Many of these distinctive little tins with their hinged lids, are still to be found in households around the town, some battered and chipped, used as pencil cases or trinket boxes; others are still in the possession of their original recipients and proudly kept in pristine condition.

But it was the evening of that Monday when the celebrations reached fever pitch and new heights of glorious spectacle. It was as if the whole of the British Isles suddenly burst into flames as thousands of beacons were torched. The best viewing point in Newport was at Christchurch where many gathered to see the great bonfire on Lawrence Hill blazing into life and as it did, 'a ring of fire enclosed Newport and Monmouthshire. Beacon after beacon started as mere pin pricks of light in the distance and sparkled along the whole of the Bristol

Channel's Somerset coast. Great fires blazed on the heights of Cwmcarn, Ebbw Vale, Blaenavon and Pontypool. Residents of Abergavenny saw the crest of the Sugar Loaf (Mynydd Pen-y-Fal) through a halo of flames and wherever the eye chanced there were to be seen a hundred flickering lights' (South Wales Argus 15th May 1935).

For many centuries, Twyn Barlym had been the greatest of all beacons on such occasions and this was no exception. A huge bonfire was built here by Risca Boy Scouts and when the signal came for ignition: 'high up on Twyn Barlym gleamed one of the best situated fires in the county, while the broad back of the hill range was sprinkled and flecked with fire!'

In the town, searchlights mounted on the Transporter Bridge swept back and forth over the rooftops, and major public buildings such as the Town Hall, the Market, St Woolos Cathedral, the Castle and the Cenotaph were bathed in floodlight.

The rest of the week saw Silver Jubilee parties taking place in many of the working class streets which were closed to traffic, and every inch of house frontages were covered in a profusion of coloured bunting, Union Jacks and portraits of their Majesties. Prizes were awarded for the best, and one of the front runners was tiny Lord Street in Barnardtown. Typical of the humour of those days was the notice displayed at the end of one such street which read: 'Landlords not admitted – rent spent!'

Then life returned to normal.

The County Officer for Health, reporting on the continuing menace of pulmonary tuberculosis, apportioned much of the blame for its obstinacy on 'indulgence by the young in the popular craze for sunbathing!'

A lady who pleaded guilty to a minor misdemeanour in Newport Police Court, was admonished by the Clerk for having the temerity to wear her beret at a jaunty angle!

Newport housewives apparently put their faith in 'Soako' for their weekly wash. A large advertisement appearing regularly in all local newspapers exhorted them to buy this detergent at 3½d or 6d a packet because 'the rich Soako suds loosen every scrap of grease and grime completely'.

Sir Alexander Gibb and Partners produced the eagerly awaited feasibility study for the Severn Bridge. Two alternative sites were suggested – from Aust to Chepstow and a slightly longer one crossing over the English Stones. The latter was the route recommended at a cost of £1,554,000 – the cheaper of the two by £10,000.

Paradoxically, the same two sites were selected when the building of each bridge eventually took place in the 1960s and 1990s but by then the consulting engineers had undergone a change of heart in their opinions as to the order of preference.

Within a short period of time proposals for this venture took a new turn when Newport Corporation voted 34 to 2 against acceptance because of a lingering doubt about the detrimental effect that the positioning of the bridge's 85 piers might have on siltage at the entrance to the Alexandra Dock. This was openly avowed to be a delaying tactic only. Basically, the Corporation was in favour of the bridge but needed to gain time to obtain the necessary safeguards against the possible damage that changing the course of nature might produce.

It would have been very interesting to see the repercussions on today's travel situation if the bridge had been built at that time, for it was intended that it should be accessible to everyone. Note some of the suggested tolls:-

Bicycles	4d
Horse-drawn vehicles	2s to 2/6d
Cars	2s to 4s according to horsepower
Steamrollers!	10s

The intention was that the bridge should be toll-free in eight years!

On 14th September, the most catastrophic traffic jam in the town's history occurred when Newport County Football Club was playing at home to Cardiff City in the seventh clash between the two third division clubs. The result was a goal-less draw which meant that for the seventh time Cardiff had failed to beat Newport.

There were 16,500 fans crammed inside Somerton Park and the problem started when they all, simultaneously and in a well-behaved manner, began to wend their way homewards. The situation was made worse by the fact that Newport Rugby Club was at home to Abertillery, and the Athletic Ground's substantial crowd began to decant into Corporation Road to swell the mass moving ever more slowly toward the bottleneck of the River Bridge.

All roads on the Maindee side were totally jammed with humanity on foot, bus and tramcar (Newport Corporation Transport had pressed every available vehicle into service). It took some of these vehicles an hour to travel from Maindee Square to Clarence Place and by then most of their passengers had dismounted to take the easier option. Two men who had walked from Somerton Park to Clarence Place, entered a cafe for a meal and when they re-emerged, the same buses were stranded outside as when they went in!

The River Usk bridge was the obvious culprit in this appalling situation, followed closely by the failure of the new Kingsway bypass to give the relief for which it was intended. Journalistic comment was emphatic:-

'It can never be the solution to the traffic problem any more than its unblushing sister, the Transporter Bridge, has any potential value other than as a landmark!'

Newport Bridge was then only eight years old and already the clamour was on for another, although the Corporation's token quota of heads-in-the-sands councillors (one a future mayor) objected to a second crossing down-river because 'only Cardiff would benefit by the passing of traffic more speedily through Newport'

A few months later it was revealed that although the bridge had been the major contributor to the mighty traffic jam it was not the only one. Mr Nocivelli, a member of Newport's popular and well respected ice-cream family, had set up a stationery handcart in Somerton Road just before the great exodus began. The charge of obstruction brought against him in Newport Police Court disclosed that for ten minutes he had been instrumental in holding up over three hundred vehicles!

Another violent storm rocked the town on 22nd September. All was quiet until 1.15 am when, with the town sleeping, great flashes of lightning and deafening bursts of thunder preceded what was to prove to be the third highest night's rainfall (2.09 inches) since records began in 1875. A fearsome storm lasting all night brought down hailstones the size of walnuts and left a scene of devastation in its wake.

Many large town centre shops were flooded. The basement boiler room of the Royal Gwent Hospital was under 10 feet of water caused by the sudden discharge from the turgescence of the giant sponge that the Friars gardens at the rear had become. The Town Hall police cells had to be cleared of prisoners, and a 50 feet long wall crashed down in Baneswell. The force of the rivers of storm-water which appeared here and there as if by magic, tore large holes in Cardiff Road near Tredegar Park, blocked Chepstow Road with mud and rocks sluiced down from Lawrence Hill, and submerged Somerton Park.

As the water subsided over the next twenty four hours the police were issued with tools and sent out to augment the workmen replacing hundreds of heavy drain-covers which had lifted and in some cases had been thrown long distances by the sheer force that had spouted beneath them.

Newport Playgoers Society resolved to buy St James Church, adjacent to the Public Library and Art Gallery in Dock Street, for conversion into a 'Little Theatre'. A Little Theatre Company was formed with capital of £4,000 and work was quickly commenced in transforming the church into a comfortable, 450 seat theatre with a 45 feet wide by 26 feet deep stage and rehearsal rooms.

Many times during the previous two centuries, ships entering the River Usk had been described as 'the largest ever', but on 9th November this was a positively incontrovertible fact as with a series of complicated manoeuvres, the 600 feet long, 16,000 ton bulk of the ocean liner 'SS Doric Star' was gently eased around the bend near the Old Town Dock and into its final berth at Blaina Wharf. On a grey day drizzling rain, hundreds of spectators turned out along the river banks and across the top of the Transporter Bridge to witness the tricky operation.

The Doric had been purchased for breaking by John Cashmore Ltd for £50,000. Only 12 years old, the luxury liner was a victim of a recession which had caused the original 1,500 complement of free-spending cruise passengers to dwindle alarmingly.

Before the actual dismantling began, a grand sale was held aboard the ship with much of the proceeds intended for charity - the Royal Gwent Hospital in particular. Equipment and furnishings were avidly sought by collectors, souvenir hunters, tradesmen, bargain chasers and ordinary householders alike. Sections of beautiful walnut panelling went for £8-10s, mahogany wardrobes and sideboards for 18s to £1; there were dozens of Queen Anne style oak tables with leather tops, and satinwood tub chairs. The massive, white marble fireplace from the sumptuous lounge caused enthusiastic bidding, and life-belts and ashtrays bearing the ship's name were in great demand as mementoes.

1936

The highest tide for over 40 years swelled the Usk on 16th January; the rise was almost 50 feet along parts of the town reach. A large breach was made in the sea defences at Goldcliff and, whipped by a tremendous gale, the pounding waters of the River Severn poured through and over to cover the moors in a reduced semblance of the 1607 inundation. There had been more recent, similar encroachments in 1903 and 1910 but this was by far the most serious.

In Newport, all the riverside streets above the bridge and many on the Maindee side along Corporation Road, received ground floor flooding to a depth of several inches. Lovells factory, workshops, sports club and playing fields were similarly immersed.

The first stretch of dual carriage highway with cycle tracks in Monmouthshire was introduced to deal with the huge increase in road traffic between the Western Valleys and Cardiff. The narrow, mile-long Forge Lane and its pretty avenue of trees, running alongside Tredegar Park from Bassaleg, was improved to this standard. It remained for many years a short, curious, futuristic section of modern highway whilst all roads around it languished in a period of repairing and widening schemes leading up to the eventual arrival of the motorways. One of the last toll-gates in the county - the Bassaleg Turnpike - was demolished during these works.

In February, another celebrated landmark disappeared from the Newport streets when the Eveswell fountain and water trough at the bottom of Batchelor Road, was demolished by an errant cattle truck. Whilst never having been claimed to be on the exact site of the legendary ancient well, the trough almost certainly had once shared the same spring, but this had been replaced by piped water for the purpose of hygiene. After this accident the circular trough was not rebuilt.

254

The legend that goes with this well has it that in a small cottage at Whitson there lived a girl named Eva; she died but reappeared as a ghost which, when being exorcised, made off across the moors. Arriving at the well in Maindee she escaped her pursuers by diving into it and was seen no more. Ever after, the spot was described as Ffynon Eva - Eve's Well!

A modern innovation leading hopefully to the improvement of law enforcement, was the installation at strategic points around the town of 38 police emergency call-boxes. Resembling ordinary telephone kiosks in shape, but painted blue, windowless, and having a beacon on top which flashed when the nearest patrolling constable was required, these boxes soon proved their worth.

Figures published in 1936, a year after their introduction, showed that 98,847 calls were made by the police and 382 by members of the public. The resulting acceleration in the reporting of crimes, accidents and fires, and the apprehension of offenders was truly astonishing.

Police Box, Alltyryn Road, Newport, 1935

This closed circuit telephone system was gradually made redundant by the introduction of the 999 emergency call service in Newport's 117 public telephone boxes, and the technology that eventually provided each constable with his own two-way radio. When in 1969 it was discovered that the vastly reduced number of calls had led to each costing approximately £7, it was decided to remove all the familiar blue boxes except one. Situated quite distinctively at the junction of Somerton Crescent, Hawthorn Avenue and Chepstow Road, it stands a very good chance of extending its half century of existence in the care and ownership of Newport Borough Council. It is after all, well on the way to becoming an ancient monument representing an almost forgotten aspect of earlier 20th century life.

The centenary of Newport's achievement of its democratic borough status was celebrated by a body of administrators whose actions and decisions often suggested that its members were reincarnations of their ancient predecessors. At least the Mayor was of this opinion and he made it quite clear in a speech given at a private function. He was particularly vitriolic on the subject of some of his fellow councillors.

'Some men' he said, 'seek election for their own aggrandisement. Some have no ability and through a period of years have not improved, and have been unable to do the town any good. Through them, Newport has been allowed to drift and is not what it should be'. Then, as if to defend a suddenly realised indiscretion, he hastily added the contradictory and hackneyed comment that: 'Newport is second to no other town in Britain!'

This came from the leader of the faction that was convinced that a second river road bridge would be bad for the town, and was a typical attitude in local government where a community was 'allowed to drift' because of conflict among its navigators. Following close on the heels of this example of forward-looking retrogression was another.

There were no women police officers in the Newport Borough Force, although they were not unknown in other towns and had existed in the Metropolitan Police since 1914. Occasions when they would have been useful were becoming more readily recognised, but in spite of only two women constables at first being contemplated, heated debate culminated in a council vote against this modern trend. The case was positively inarguable but even in the face of the evidence that nowhere else had the experiment proved a failure and that most authorities which had taken the plunge had increased their quota of women police constables, Newport Corporation remained obdurate.

The month of April saw the possibility of a great evil about to be lifted from the British Isles. Parliament was debating the prohibition of football pools, and forces were being mobilised in anti-gambling circles to add weight to the move.

At Victoria Avenue Church Maindee, the annual assembly of Monmouthshire Congregationalists put down a strongly worded resolution in support of the Bill. If any prayers were offered in addition they remained unanswered for, shortly afterwards, the Commons voted decisively against prohibition, and football pools went on to become a most popular and indeed harmless national pastime. As a matter of fact, in Newport their sheer bulk in the sorting office was used as a partial excuse for the new General Post Office extension which was soon to rise on the site of the old Savoy Buildings at the corner of Station Approach.

Another of Newport's sons had been destined to reach heights far beyond the expectation of anyone born of humble origins. Like Johnny Basham, his contemporary although fourteen years his junior, he too was a Pill boy and knew the feel of cobbled paving under his bare feet. However, his achievement of fame and fortune came by following an entirely different route.

James Henry Thomas was born at 51 George Street on October 3rd 1875. At the age of five it cost a penny a week to send him to St Pauls National School, the fee rising to tuppence on his seventh birthday. Little Jimmy, so-called because of his lack of height and weedy build, was one of the poorer children, easily identified by his worn-out, multi-patched clothing and almost non-existent boots.

At the age of nine, he obtained a job as a part-time errand boy and sweeper-up at a chemist's shop in Commercial Street where he worked from 7 am to 9 am, attending school until lunch time, doing another stint at the shop and then working again after afternoon school until 6.30 pm. On Saturdays, he often worked a sixteen hour day - all for four shillings a week!

Leaving school when he was twelve, young Jimmy carried on for two years as general dogsbody in a draper's shop.

His father was a railwayman and, as the family lived in a concentrated railway area (just across the tracks from Dock Street Station, engine sheds and freight yards), it was a natural progression for a fourteen year old Pill lad to follow.

Small and puny he may have been, but what he lacked in stature was more than made up by a powerful voice, unbending determination or stubborn streak, call it what one will, and a modicum of belligerence - common enough traits in those whose size often made them the regular butt of jokes and targets for the bully.

It was only a matter of time before Jimmy's ability to defend himself led to the standing-up fearlessly for others, and at the age of fifteen he brought all the engine cleaners out on a day's strike over a management cut-back in cleaning materials. He won this dispute and was immediately earmarked as a spokesman for the workers, a role that he easily assumed for the rest of his railway career.

James Thomas, active trade unionist and powerful orator, became the first General Secretary of the National Union of Railwaymen when it was founded in 1918. He led the nine day National Railway strike in 1919.

He saw as his ultimate ambition nothing more than becoming an engine driver. Never in his wildest dreams could he have foreseen life beyond that, much less the fairy-tale that was just about to unfold.

A job transfer to Swindon was seen by some as a ploy to remove a thorn from the side of the South Wales management, but it did no more than widen Jimmy Thomas's interest and point him in the direction of local politics. In a very short space of time he was made a Freeman of Newport, Mayor of Swindon and, in 1924, Member of Parliament for Derby, entering the Cabinet as Colonial Secretary. The four shillings-a-week ragamuffin from George Street now held one of the highest positions in the land!

After the 1929 General Election which returned another Labour Government, Jim was once more a Cabinet Minister but now as Lord Privy Seal with special powers for reducing unemployment; in the 1931 National Government that followed, he was Secretary of State for the Dominions and once more Colonial Secretary. His salary was in the region of £5,000 a year and he lived in a £15,000 luxury house at Ferring in Sussex.

His flamboyance, love of entertaining and the many official functions that demanded his attendance in the company of high ranking personages (kings, queens and presidents etc.), meant that most of his public appearances were made in evening dress - hence his nickname 'Boiled Shirt Jimmy'.

By 1936 James H Thomas had reached a pinnacle denied to most men, but almost overnight his world crumbled about him.

A short time before Budget Day (21st April) the Chancellor of the Exchequer briefed the Cabinet on the provisions of the Budget and somehow information was leaked from these top secret meetings.

A Tribunal was set up to seek the source of the leak. At the hearings it was established that two close friends of Jimmy Thomas, Sir Alfred Butt and Mr Alfred Bates, only a short time before had taken out insurances against a rise of 3d in the pound of income tax and 2d on the tax on tea. Furthermore, it emerged during questioning that the Thomas house in Sussex had been purchased outright by means of a huge loan made by millionaire Sir Alfred in circumstances whereby it did not require repayment. No connection was proved between these events but, inevitably, conclusions were drawn.

The Tribunal had not reported by 22nd May, but on that day Jimmy Thomas resigned his post as Colonial Secretary and so ended eight successive years in the Cabinet and his membership of five Cabinets in all.

Ten days later, the Tribunal announced that it had exonerated every member of the Cabinet except Jimmy Thomas. Its findings were 'that unauthorised disclosures on Budget secrets were made by Mr J H Thomas, ex-Colonial Secretary, to both Sir Alfred Butt and Mr Alfred Bates who both made use of the information for their private gain'.

On 11th June 1936 the great dream ended. He who had had within his grasp more power than any other Newport man in history and was looked upon by some as a future Prime Minister, stood and announced to a deathly silent House, his resignation from the Government. His tearful statement included the words: 'I did not consciously give away Budget secrets'. Then, bowing to the Speaker, Jimmy Thomas, his career in ruins, left the floor of the House which for so many years had been the scene of his greatest achievements, and passed quietly into anonymous retirement. At Dulwich in London, James Henry Thomas, Cabinet Minister, Newport born and bred, died in 1949 aged 74.

In August, Newport Cricket Club decided to celebrate the hundredth anniversary of a town cricket team, by playing a match in the style of a century earlier. Players dressed in top hats, wore no pads, sported mutton-chop whiskers and ran every run. Someone however appears to have miscalculated over the years : the match was said to be in commemoration of the first ever played by a Newport team when beaten by 'Ragland' in 1836, but it has already been established from an account in the Monmouthshire Merlin in 1835, that a match played in that year resulted in Newport beating Pontypool!

One last reference to the menace of vermin : the problem was either greater than ever or the forces arrayed against it were much better organised for Newport now had its own official 'Rat Week!' During the year the council rat-catchers laid 27,000 baits which poisoned 1,179 rats, whilst a dog and ferret campaign accounted for 1,028. No figures were released of the number of dogs, cats and ferrets killed by rat-bait!

This was a matter of continuing frustration and embarrassment for the Town Council which continually played down any outside reference to the problem, and when the Clerk to the Pontypool Urban District Council referred derisively to 'the thousands of rats seen swarming in Newport's main streets', there was an emphatic denial. However, the story was not so far from the truth and many local residents of the day would attest to having seen a large migration of rats crossing from one side of Shaftesbury Street to the other! Even the fashionable suburb of Christchurch suffered its own plague at about the same time!

At a fête organised by Newport Boy Scouts Association, the District Scout Commissioner, A L Lloyd said:-

'If Boy Scouts were allowed to introduce a form of knee breeches that would do away with the necessity of showing bare knees, I am sure that we would have a bigger membership. After all, it does take a certain amount of moral courage to walk down Newport High Street with bare knees on a Saturday!'

Whatever may have been the thinking on town life in the few years that remained before the Second World War exploded outdated conventions, it could never have been described as dull. Methods employed to introduce some degree of decorous gaiety were colourful, imaginative and possessed thrusting originality, all characteristics from an injection of which many of today's diversions could profit.

One such event was organised for October 8th when a Dickensian Anniversary Party commenced, the proceeds going to the Royal Gwent Hospital.

During the course of that day, horse-drawn Victorian coaches arrived, one after the other, at the Town Hall steps to disgorge passengers all correctly adorned in the trappings of mid-Victorian ladies and gentlemen. Most of them were amateur actors and actresses who were to take part in the day's revelry. Why this particular year was chosen for the celebration can only be put down to the fact that it was the centenary of the publication of Dickens' first major work: 'The Pickwick Papers'.

Inside the Town Hall, the Assembly Room was the stage for the Trial of Mr Pickwick, presented with much artistic skill by Newport Playgoers Society. The Council Chamber hosted two sketches from David Copperfield and Martin Chuzzlewit, whilst in Number One Committee Room the Brynmawr Playgoers put on The Old Curiosity Shop.

The night was rounded off in some style by a Dickensian Ball in the Assembly Room commencing at 11.30 pm, tickets half-a-guinea each. Of that day it was reported that 'the spirits of 1836 and 1936 were infused!'

The Town Council's final, major decision of the year was to scrap the tramcars in favour of what they peculiarly referred to as 'oil-buses'. One councillor expressed fears in the quaintly Victorian manner that lingered in local politics, that 'vapours emitted by the buses would be detrimental to the health of the town'. The die was cast however, and in less than a year (by September 1937) the last electric tram ever to move through the streets of Newport, made the final journey from the Westgate to the Corporation Road Depot. Hundreds of devoted sightseers lined the route to make their sad farewells, and by the time that No 51 had reached the depot, souvenir hunters had stripped it of destination boards, lamp-shades and time cards!

1937

Newport's Little Theatre, created from St James Church Dock Street, was completed and opened with great acclaim on January 11th with its company giving a most professional interpretation of the saucy, Pepysian, costume comedy 'And so to bed', which, in the words of the billboards, dealt with ' the sprightly diversions of the immortal diarist as well as the dalliances of the Merrie Monarch with the gay ladies of the day'.

Time once again for town celebration on a massive scale only two short years after the last occasion.

The Silver Jubilee of 1935 had been the excuse for a most joyous and glittering display, but hardly had the tumult died away a mere seven months afterwards, when the death of King George V set off a chain of events creating a trauma that rocked the British Constitution to its foundations.

The year following the Proclamation of the Prince of Wales as King Edward VIII dragged on interminably, the world holding its breath waiting for the unprecedented abdication that was to be the settlement of the crisis. When this confusing and very harrowing period was over, a dismal 1936 gave way to a much more promising 1937 with first priority in the crowning of the new monarch. The Coronation was arranged for May 12th and true to its traditions, Newport was an early leader in the field of preparation. It was planned right from the start to swathe the town in patriotic colour, and in some quarters as early as Christmas, local workshops busied themselves in the cutting and stitching of red, white and blue bunting. All together, excluding the side streets which supplied their own decoration, eight miles of flags and three miles of garlands were manufactured in the town. Everywhere people were working to create millions of paper flowers. The lower parts of all the main road lamp standards were encased in red, white and blue pedestals of wood made in the workshops of Messrs Watkins Providers, and even the nails used were all manufactured locally.

The illuminations for the occasion were of a magnificence never before seen in Wales. Six thousand seven hundred yards of cable carrying many thousands of electric bulbs in seven colours connected Clarence Place to Albion Street Pillgwenlly; intermingling with them at intervals were fifty-two set pieces with flashing centres.

The Town Hall itself was a masterpiece of illuminatory wizardry. Over five thousand multicoloured globes and two thousand feet of cable combined to light every angle, corner, nook and cranny of the building's elegant elevation. Just above the balcony a kaleidoscopic series of bulbs formed an ornate rosette which scattered radiance over a wide area. Dominating the whole glorious effect, a beautiful royal crown burst into brightness, true even to the scintillating jewels created by flashing red, white and blue lamps.

Dress rehearsals held on two earlier evenings drew the crowds into the streets, and although the fervour of the real event was yet to come, huge roars of astonished admiration resounded round the town centre as the switch-on revealed the true splendour of the luminous fairyland. What with the night sky being constantly swept by the Transporter Bridge searchlights and all the larger public buildings being floodlit, the attraction was enormous and the Great Western Railway had to put on numerous excursion trains to bring the thousands of sightseers from the Monmouthshire and Glamorgan valleys.

Coronation Week commenced on Sunday 9th May with a grand procession through the town to St Woolos Cathedral. There were eight bands comprising those of the Royal Monmouthshire Royal Engineers, Lysaghts Orb Works, Newport Tramways, Salvation Army and the Youth Organisations. Marching were representatives of many Associations, the Harbour and Pilot Commissioners, Consuls, Government Officials, Magistrates, Aldermen, Councillors, the Town Clerk, the Mayor, Lord Lieutenant and County Court Judges followed by contingents of the Army, Royal Navy, Royal Air Force, Police, Fire Brigade, Ex-service and Youth Organisations.

For the rest of the week, a grand Coronation Fair ran at Shaftesbury Park (admission 3d) with menageries, side-shows, ox-roasting, continuous music, all the fun of the fair and the inevitable 'lost children tent' which did a roaring trade. In a huge marquee, thousands of free dinners and teas were given to old age pensioners and 'poor cripples'.

On Coronation Day itself (May 12th), there was a repeat of Sunday's parade but this time to the Athletic Grounds where the Mayor read the Coronation Proclamation, and a 31 gun salute was thundered out by the guns of the 2nd Brigade of the Royal Horse Artillery. The silver cup for the first baby born on Coronation Day was awarded to little George Albert Avery who weighed in at three minutes past midnight at Herbert Street Maternity Home!

On the following day the Athletic Ground was again the venue for a succession of variety shows and physical training displays by the Secondary Schools and various other organisations, culminating in a grand finale by over two thousand schoolchildren from the elementary and central schools whose mass formation of the Union Jack (a minute portion of which was completed by your author) completely filled the rugby ground.

On two days the town was spectacularly over-flown by Hawker Hart bombers of the City of Gloucester 501 Squadron, and firework displays unceasingly filled the night skies with great starbursts of colour.

Children's parties dominated the side streets which were also ablaze with colour as they vied with each other for the prizes. The residents went to almost unbelievable lengths in their imaginative attempts at decoration, criss-crossing the roads with flags and streamers and filling windows with portraits of King George and Queen Elizabeth. Fairy lights twinkled everywhere after dark and were encouraged by the Council's decision to allow free electricity for three days.

Little did the happy folk of Newport know but they were literally making hay while the sun shone, and the dark clouds of a cruel war were even then gathering just over the horizon, portending long, bitter years before there could be other occasions for such celebration.

The Coronation lighting system had hardly been dismantled and packaged when a large part of it was once again required for use. The reason this time was the annual Royal Gwent Fete, and in order to make it the best ever, the field adjoining The Friars above the hospital was festooned with 10,000 varicoloured bulbs arranged in strips and fiery pillars.

It was only two months after the Coronation anyway when what some would call the greatest day in Newport's history occurred. On 14th July, for the first time ever, a reigning monarch made an official visit to the town. This could have been considered to be the demolition of the theory that the Chartist uprising had caused Newport to be placed on a

Royal blacklist, or else if there were anything in the story, all was now forgiven.

The main intention of the visit was for King George VI to cut the first sod of the new Civic Centre, and when the Royal Couple set foot on the red carpet at High Street Station, they found practically the whole population awaiting them in streets now surely used to brilliant adornment.

The procession passed between massed ranks of cheering, loyal subjects and school children given a special holiday, to assemble at St Mary's Lodge Fields Road, the home of Mrs A B Watson, a lady who had very generously donated the house and garden to Newport as part of the site of the new Civic Centre. Here in its pretty rose garden surrounded by town and county dignitaries, King George expertly cut the first sod with a spade made by Messrs Pleasance and Harper from 35 ounces of silver, which thereafter found pride of place in the Public Museum.

Queen Elizabeth then complimented Mrs Watson on her garden, sympathised over its forthcoming destruction, told the Lord Lieutenant that he had lost a silver buckle from his shoe, pointed out where it lay in the grass and then the Royal Couple were on their way to Cardiff to continue their tour of the Principality.

But what of the workaday Newport of 1937? In the suburbs little had changed since the borough extensions of 1935. Beyond Maindee along Chepstow Road, Alway, Ringland, Bishpool and Treberth were still farms and Aberthaw Road was just starting into construction. Malpas virtually ended at the Graig Park Estate and all the houses beyond forming a strip of ribbon development along the main road, carried grand sounding names instead of numbers; many still depended on cesspits for drainage. Along Caerleon Road, St Julians was a vast, untouched area of open fields, allotments and pleasant walks. The ancient manor house of the Herbert family still stood on the river bank and the other, the more modern one of the Firbank and Cory families, had not long been removed for redevelopment.

Cardiff Road on the other hand, was almost as it is today except that the Maesglas houses still resembled those of the Malpas Graig Park Estate built in the late 1920s by the Allied Building Company, and numbers 202 to 264 (even) Cardiff Road were, somewhat abstrusely, known as numbers 1 to 32 Tre-ap-Gwilym.

Clarence Place however, held a special place in the scheme of things. In contrast to its ultimate fate as the nondescript centre for indecorous, cosmopolitan restaurants and cafes which only came alive at night to the accompaniment of a curry and garlic flavoured atmosphere, this short stretch of main road had by 1937 become one of the town's prime shopping areas - an integral expansion of anything that the other side of the bridge could offer. The locality absolutely throbbed with vitality from the early morning commencement of trading to the late evening passage of revellers from the popular public houses and first class cinemas.

For six days a week the pavements were crowded with shoppers, mothers perambulating their young, little knots in conversation (everyone seemed to know everyone else), and at specific times, groups of permanent day pupils from the Newport Technical College. Even the traffic was as heavy as anywhere else in the town. None of this was surprising in view of what the area had to offer.

The continuous curve of shops with spacious flats over, known as the Clarence Quadrant, possessed practically all the trades required to guarantee self-containment. The list seemed endless. Here there were:-

A furniture store, two dentists, two tobacconists and news-agents, three cleaners and dyers, two drapers, a tailor, a grocer, a motorcycle shop, a baker and confectioner, a wine and spirit merchant, a shoe retailer, a boot and shoe repairer, three butchers, a jeweller and watch repairer, a bank, a sub-post office, a bookshop and stationers, two dairies, a chemist, a greengrocer and a solitary cafe (traditional British cuisine). Not quite so concentrated on the other side of the road were the Transport Workingman's Club, Lucania Billiard Hall, a fish shop, a cycle and pram shop, decorators supplies, another tobacconist and news-agent, a motor garage, a ladies' hairdresser, two gentlemen's hairdressers, a timber merchant, a florist, a gentlemen s outfitter, another draper, an ironmonger and a travel agent.

In addition there were two public houses - the Ivy Bush and the Isca (rebuilt and renamed the Riverside Tavern) and two cinemas - the Coliseum and the Odeon - the latter only recently built and one of the most modern in Europe!

During the summer months, hundreds of people from far and wide streamed into Clarence Place to take trips on the P & A Campbell paddle steamers Glen Avon, Glen Usk and Ravenswood from the floating jetty at Rodney Parade. The most popular destination was always Weston-Super-Mare but the boats also went as far as Ilfracombe, Lundy Island and Tenby; closer to home, excursions might only be round the Uskmouth bell-buoy or the English and Welsh Grounds Lightship.

With a country omnibus terminus (Red & White) in Rodney Road, delivering many more visiting shoppers right into the heart of this thriving little community, it is not hard to conjure up a picture of that long-lost prosperity.

Newport had long been associated with Bristol Channel passenger steamship services, but information is vague about the various vessels that plied these waters throughout the 19th century, although the first paddle steamer made its appearance in the Channel in 1854.

For some time prior to 1886, the only ship making a regular crossing to Bristol was the Black Prince - from Bangor Wharf (the nearest wharf to the bridge). These sailings were terminated after the opening of the Severn Tunnel in 1885.

In 1887, a group of Bristol businessmen chartered the Waverley to start the first real service and from that moment P & A Campbell's White Funnel Fleet was born, In succeeding years this company fought off challenges from competitors, the Red Funnel and the Yellow Funnel Lines. Two of its little steamers were sunk in the First World War and three more in the Second at Dunkirk.

Between the wars, the Rodney Parade jetty received regular summer visits from Devonia, Glen Avon, Ravenswood, Glen Gower, Glen Usk and Britannia, but in 1946 only the last four named were in operation. Fully laden they could carry 900 to 1,500 passengers, and they continued to do so until the summer of 1956 when falling demand and mounting overheads caused the Newport service to be unable to pay its way. The Harbour Commissioners could not accept a drastic cut in the number of sailings and so, after an existence of 60 years, another piece of town history took its final bow.

In 1938, Newport had a population of just over 100,000, with 56,544 electors, and the Town Directory still referred to it as the largest town in the 'English' County of Monmouthshire. Among fifty Justices of the Peace appeared names preserving continuity with leading families of the 19th century - Thomas Spittle, Lionel and Lady Beynon, William Mordey and B Pardoe-Thomas to name but a few.

Market days were Wednesdays and Saturdays, and early closing was rigidly adhered to on Thursdays. A new small, semi-detached house could be purchased for £400 and a large detached for £650! Both transactions could be secured for £50 down! The number of unemployed was 5,000, the lowest for years, showing a reduction of 2,000 in the previous twelve months.

There were 100 miles of streets and in them could be found a variety of sights and characters that added vibrancy and colour that has gradually deteriorated through the years.

Horses were still in great evidence, from the noble shires that pulled brewers' drays and the flat-bed delivery carts of Great Western Railways, the teams that made household coal deliveries, the sturdy work-horses in the shafts of two-wheeled milk floats, down to the sad looking beasts taking rag-and-bone men on their rounds.

Neither was it then unusual to witness a funeral cortege headed by a hearse drawn by four beautifully groomed, black-plumed Belgian Blacks.

They all left their marks on the streets but never for long as little boys with shovels and buckets appeared from nowhere to take away valuable nutriment for their fathers' gardens and allotments.

Another popular visitor in any residential area was the ice-cream vendor, although his business was not the all-year-round affair that it later became. There were many of them, mainly of Italian extraction, who were noted for delicious ice-cream manufactured in their own homes or small backyard factories. Their trading was carried out from handcarts stationed at vantage points popular with members of the public. One of the best known of these families, the Nocivellis, had by now introduced a unique, glass-sided motor-van, complete with chimes, the elegance of which would have put to shame many of those that hunted in packs fifty years later!

The special vendors however, who seemed to be ever present in every street, were those of Walls and Eldorado who rode tricycles on the front of which were mounted large, square, insulated boxes. 'Stop me and buy one' was the motto of the former of these firms although it became nationally associated with all the other manufacturers who used this method of transport.

The cardboard-covered, fruit flavoured, triangular prisms of water ice at one penny or cream ice at tuppence, were sold in thousands and often the salesman would entertain the children by placing a chunk of his 'dry-ice' cooling medium (solid carbon dioxide) on his bicycle bell causing it to ring quite magically without its lever being pressed.

In the matter of Council business, things could not have looked brighter. On the credit side, Corporation assets were valued at £2,798,859 and successful rate collections had reached the amazing figure of 99.278% of the total assessed.

The Borough Treasurer's Office of 1937 issued an informative booklet as a guide to the town's finances and this contained the illuminating but self-disparaging statement that the method of valuing property for rating purposes was a complete mystery to most people; it went on to protest against the widely held belief that rates collectors obtained increases in their wages by increasing the value of properties!

Councillors were still pressing hard for the scrapping of the Transporter Bridge. Costing £6,000 per year (a 2d rate) to maintain, it stilled retained the misplaced loyalty of many who were too young to be aware of the misguided reasons that first brought the bridge to Newport, the conditions unjustly forced upon the town for its building and its all-time, unfulfilled promise.

The second half of the year commenced with one of those tremendous summer storms that were a common feature of Newport's weather in the 1930s. On the night of July 14th, 1.71 inches of rain fell in a continuous, torrential downpour that caused flooding in the town centre and many suburbs. At the same time, bolts of lightning struck properties in every quarter, inflicting the most widespread storm damage within living memory. Strangely, the rural districts closest to the town saw and heard very little of the tempest!

Saturday October 14th brought the largest ever crowd of supporters to Somerton Park when promotion-seeking Cardiff City visited. The gates were closed half an hour before the kick-off with 24,278 fans inside and thousands locked out. Police turned a politic, blind eye to those who swarmed over the roofs of the grandstands and the greyhound tote building. Safety factors had not then achieved the high priority of later years, but in any case the officials were powerless in such a crush. The result of the game was a goal-less draw and match receipts were a ground record £1,342-14s!

In November, the Corporation elected Newport's first lady Mayor, Alderman Mrs M A Hart. A slight controversy arose immediately over her form of address. Turning to the Home Office for advice, the instruction was received that the correct title was still 'Mister Mayor' regardless of sex, but common sense prevailed and with Mrs Hart's blessing it was agreed that thenceforth she should be addressed as 'Madam Mayor'.

1938

On January 3rd there were unusual happenings at Newport High Street Station, centred on a rather unconventional train which was standing at the parcel depot siding. This was the demonstration train of J S Fry & Sons, the famous chocolate manufacturer. It was a great attraction to thousands of children and their parents who paid 2d each to inspect the wonders on view. The Royal Gwent Hospital was given half the proceeds. The three modern coaches contained exhibits, goods and gifts, showed fourteen stages in the manufacture and assembly of a large family Christmas Box and displayed tins of cocoa taken by Captain Scott to the South Pole in 1910. On the first day, 3,743 visitors munched their way through 600 lbs of chocolate and took away hundreds of presentation boxes.

At this time also the Great Western Railway was offering return excursions to Bristol to see a pantomime at from 4/9d to 5/3d. The return fare to Edinburgh for the Scotland-Wales Rugby International was £1-4s!

Later in the month, on the night of January 25th, Newport shared with the whole country the sight of a fantastic, natural phenomenon rarely seen so far south. Unusual sunspot activity disrupted radio communications on a wide scale and, according to the experts, caused the Aurora Borealis, more commonly known as the Northern Lights, to be seen all over Britain's northern horizons. At its height, Newport's night sky was a deep scarlet flecked with orange and occasional searchlight-like rays in shimmering shades of green and mauve. Few ordinary people had ever seen this spectacular manifestation in glowing light, and it was said that villagers in remote hamlets ran from their houses in panic, believing that the world was ending!

Within a week the streets were filled again to greet the famous star of music-hall and films, Gracie Fields. This not-so-young Lancashire comedienne could woo her audiences into enraptured silence with her beautiful rendering of sentimental ballads, and in the next breath, change to an odd, quavering voice, making inane utterances and singing childish lyrics that would drive them into uncontrollable hysterics. Such was the humour of the 1930s, but it is an incontrovertible, if somewhat inexplicable fact that Gracie Fields commanded the same mass idolatry among the mature that is today reserved only for entertainers of the young.

Proof of this was seen in the 6,000 people who completely jammed Commercial Street outside the Town Hall while Gracie was regaled within by the Mayor and Corporation. After a short stay and a quick burst of song from the balcony, she had to make good her escape through a back door into Dock Street where she provided an unexpected bonus for hundreds of football supporters heading for Somerton Park. Then it was on to Mountain Ash for a charity concert in aid of the Boot Fund.

Air raid precautions were now being given much more decisive treatment. After a few years of being regarded with some contempt by the authorities and general public alike, the mounting tension in Europe was causing the subject to assume a much more serious role. Discussions by the Council were well to the fore and acting on Government directives, numerous committees were formed to study the various problems.

Several hundred special constables were recruited and together with groups of voluntary auxiliary firemen, were given training in the actions to be taken in the event of the dropping of high explosive and gas bombs. It was not an uncommon sight on Sunday mornings to come across weird looking figures, gas-masked, oil-skinned, gumbooted and steel helmeted, hosing down closed-off streets in simulation of decontamination after a chemical weapon attack.

Over 200 citizens immediately offered their services as air raid wardens but at least 1,200 were needed to control the 19 ARP sectors into which the town was divided. Anyone with medical or first aid experience was welcomed and classes were held in every available hall or schoolroom to give instruction in dealing with enemy attacks on civilian targets.

One day at Tredegar Park, a realistic mock air raid was staged. Aeroplanes of 614 County of Glamorgan Co-operative Squadron of the Royal Auxiliary Air Force dived repeatedly over the biggest crowd ever seen in the park. No bombs were actually dropped but explosions were created on the ground and a dummy house set on fire. The voluntary services went through a comprehensive programme of exercises intended to save human life, keep damage to a minimum and maintain essential services.

The younger spectators loved it; they were witnessing a new kind of entertainment that in their minds had no application in real life. Those who could remember far enough back, watched in silent trepidation, desperately hoping that they would never face the genuine reason for these rehearsals. They would have had much more cause for concern if they had known then of the secret directive given later to all local authorities to make provision for burial of 10% of their populations!

Apart from such obvious displays, which were intended to sharpen public awareness and to encourage recruitment, preparations were also taking place on an increasing scale behind the scenes, and the man in the street saw little of these. Unknown to most citizens, mock air raids were being simulated two or three times a week when all the volunteer services, collaborating with the regulars, organised such essentials as messenger services, lines of communication, chains of command and fields of responsibility. Plans were drawn up regarding the positioning of warden's posts, air raid shelters, ambulance stations and command posts.

In August, 91,000 gas masks arrived by train from a depot in Blackburn, to be stored temporarily in the old Tivoli Cinema (later renamed The Plaza) Commercial Road, the Premier Hall and at 149A Chepstow Road. They were distributed over the next few months from centres in every part of town. Meanwhile, the first public air raid shelter, capable of holding 50 persons, was completed in Brunel Street adjoining the Transporter Bridge anchorage; the digging of trenches six feet deep commenced in the Capitol Car Park and certain of the public parks.

Step by step, overtly and covertly, Newport was gearing up for another great war!

Figures published by the Education Committee showed that during the previous 12 months the number of schoolchildren in the borough was 13,623. Of these, 12,376 put in full attendance 90.8%.

The Borough Treasurer made the triumphant announcement that at long last Newport was a town without slums and that overcrowding was almost at an end. This statement was accepted in good faith although subsequent events proved it to be far from the truth!

By early summer, several projects intended to bring major benefits to the town were either in the first stages of planning, well advanced in construction or on the verge of opening.

Tenders were being invited for the building of a new boys and girls secondary school (St

Julians High School) on 16½ acres of land at Heather Road.

Demolition commenced of the Savoy Hotel and buildings at the corner of High Street and Station Approach to make way for a £10,000 extension to the General Post Office. Hardly was the roof off when the project was marred by the death of a young lady passer-by who was hit by a lintel falling from a fourth floor window. This very sad misfortune led to a court case based upon an accusation of negligence, and ultimately to a whole new approach to safeguarding the public when in the vicinity of unstable buildings. A well known photograph of the old Savoy in a later stage of demolition (August 1938) clearly shows in the massive timber 'arcade' protecting the pavement below, that the lesson had been well learned.

On July 14th, the new Maindee Swimming Baths were opened by the Mayor, Alderman Mrs Hart. As part of the christening, three councillors undertook to race a length of the main pool in a manner reminiscent of that occurring 48 years earlier when the Mayor of the time, Mr Mark Mordey, and the whole of his police escort took the plunge at the opening of Stow Hill Baths in what was then considered to be an original if not too dignified form of ribbon-cutting.

The new building having cost £40,000, was altogether more resplendent. With its main entrance in Victoria Avenue, it contained an adult pool being 100 feet long by 42 feet wide, and from 4 to 10 feet deep. There were three diving boards at heights of 5 metres, 3 metres and 1 metre above water level, which were removed many years later. A smaller 60 feet by 25 feet, shallow pool catered for children and non-swimmers. Adjoining the upper hall were the slipper baths and a comfortable club room. The overall colour scheme was said to be warm yellow" and underwater floodlighting could be arranged to give colour effects. There was accommodation for 1,000 spectators and a pleasant lounge/buffet was provided on a balcony overlooking the pool.

Newport Athletic Club was undergoing a lean time with regard to membership and at the Annual General Meeting, the Chairman was prompted to remark on the fact that of 60 members present not one was under 33 years of age. He said: 'Our young people want everything done for them; they want to be spoon-fed. Apparently today the boys do not have the keenness which we old men had when we were boys'. This gentleman may well have been an expert in the skills of rugby football, but here he was certainly reading the signs wrongly as events of the next decade were to prove.

The guardians of the town morals were working overtime and their extreme zealousness was often ill-judged smacking as it did of the quaint ethical values more commonly associated with centuries past. It appears that even in 1938 the average citizen did not realise that what he or she regarded as harmless recreation was really thinly disguised, satanic temptation from which outmoded laws made by the pompous and hypocritical, were intended to give protection.

For the first time, Newport's magistrates allowed Sunday concerts in the town's cinemas. Permission was given to the Olympia as long as decorum was observed and programmes gave no offence. To ensure this and to keep the performance up to what was referred to as 'BBC standard', it was ruled that the show should not have a compère or a comedian! In addition, a representative of the Chief Constable had to be present at each performance.

Next, the management of the Empire Theatre appeared before the magistrates charged with allowing the performance of a lewd and indecent act. 'Drina' was a young lady who posed artistically on stage whilst clad only in a layer of grease-paint and the most diaphanous of materials. The charge was brought by the police after three senior officers saw the first house performance and three more went to the second house for confirmation!

Apparently, the show was also seen by a surprising number of aldermen, councillors and gentlemen of the clergy whose enthusiastic evidence obtained dismissal of the case.

Shortly after this, the Empire Theatre was in the news once again when permission to present a circus was refused by the council on the grounds that it might be dangerous. Opponents of this decision pointed out that Cardiff and other towns had allowed circuses in their theatres, and one had appeared at the Empire in previous years. One irate councillor fumed that in view of its record of recent, ridiculous censorship decisions, Newport was already earning the title of 'The Holy City!'

Newport Bridge was once again under discussion. It was already carrying its maximum design load and would therefore soon require supplementation. One encouraging sign was that for the first time the problem had been considered at national level by the Ministry of Transport whereby advice was given to the Corporation that no unwise development should be contemplated in the area of George Street or on the river bank immediate opposite.

Pressure was growing for a town airport. Cardiff and Bristol each had one and one councillor's opinion was that 'a town of Newport's size without an airport is like a similar town of thirty years ago without a railway station!' Two sites were chosen - the less favoured being at Broad Street Common, Nash. The other at Duffryn, had almost unanimous support but the Magor & St Mellons Rural District Council refused to reserve the site, voicing strong objections the main one of which stemmed from fear of another boundary change in Newport's favour.

The building of the new Civic Centre was progressing satisfactorily but concern was expressed at a new estimate revealing an increase in the cost of £14,000 over the original. It emerged that besides increased labour charges of between 6% and 10%, the cubic content of the building had become 579,000 cubic feet larger despite there being no increase in the overall area. The reason for this was that the original plan included large open areas of wasted space that were now being covered or enclosed so as to be more gainfully utilised.

By now, 300,000 bricks and 6,000 cubic feet of Portland Stone had been used by the 60 to 80 strong work-force; but costs continued to mount steadily and in the Council Chamber the question was regularly asked: 'What is going wrong at the Civic Centre?' Speaker after speaker rose to put minds at rest but they only succeeded in involving their colleagues in a welter of ambiguities.

1939

Whilst still clinging to the vain hope that a war could be averted, the town proceeded anew with its air raid precautions. A temporary lull had followed the feverish activity of the previous year but now it was becoming only too apparent that the slope to the edge of the abyss was becoming ever more slippery.

Government directives to local authorities helped to paint a clearer but infinitely more ominous picture.

The existing trenches dug in Newport's parklands were 654 yards long and would accommodate 858 persons seated, with 424 standing. This was nowhere near enough and a Home Office circular decreed that a tenth of a town's population (10,000 in Newport) should be able to share trenches; for this reason the town had to complete a further 2,600 yards and the Government made a grant of £13,500 towards the cost. The town now had nearly two miles of six feet deep entrenchment. Years later an ageing councillor mentioned in debate that he recalled a wartime Home Office circular that directed every local authority to make provision for the burial of 10% of their populations. Could this have been the result of coincidence or merely a failing memory imagining alternative use for the great holes in the ground?

Plans were being drawn up for the evacuation of towns and cities considered likely targets for heavy bombing. Newport was declared a neutral area for evacuation purposes, meaning that whilst no evacuation from the town would be required, it was still not considered to be a safe enough place to be an evacuation reception area.

Fears were being expressed as to the calamitous situation that would arise in the event of Newport Bridge being blown up. It was undoubtedly an important target which if destroyed would sever the A48 trunk road, the main arterial highway between England and South Wales. The Chief ARP Officers referred this up as an argument for a tunnel to be excavated under the River Usk at the earliest possible moment; they were most surprised when the Home Office passed the suggestion on to the Ministry of Transport for serious consideration!

The Borough Constabulary at the beginning of the year comprised : Chief Constable, Deputy Chief, 7 inspectors, 16 sergeants and 198 constables.

Still heavily dependent on charity and public largess, the Royal Gwent Hospital had an overdraft of £91,000 and running costs of £100 a day. There were usually 400 patients in bed at any one time and 11,000 articles in the hospital laundry each week.

A special census was taken in the town to ascertain approximately how many domestic air raid shelters would be needed; the answer produced was 11,500 households. In April, the first two of these 'Anderson' shelters (named after Sir John Anderson, Home Secretary) were put on display in the Capitol Car Park revealing that they were tunnel-shaped and constructed of very heavy, corrugated steel sheets 6 feet 6 inches long by 4 feet wide by 6 feet high. Ideally they were to be sunk halfway into the ground of backyards or gardens - paving, underground pipes or cables permitting.

A month or two later when 2,000 shelters had been installed, many complaints were made that the sunken portions flooded badly after spells of rain; it was decided therefore to line them with concrete which had little or no effect. By one of those strange twists of fate and coincidence, a ship named 'Trelawney' docked at Newport carrying 7,000 tons of Anderson shelters for the town. These had been manufactured at the works of John Lysaght in Newcastle Australia by ex-employees of the Newport works who had emigrated!

Football fever was the current epidemic. Ordinarily a club firmly entrenched in the bottom half of the Football League Third Division and attracting only the moderate interest usual in such cases, Newport County's fortunes had in the 1938/39 season gone from strength to strength.

April 15th, when it dawned, seemed no different to any other typical Saturday but the change became more apparent as the day wore on. A feeling of subdued apprehension hung heavily in the air with tension mounting by the minute, and none of it had anything to do with the worsening international situation! People stood around on street corners or at their front gates watching for the first signs of the many thousands who had packed Somerton Park. Ears were cocked at wireless sets and a large crowd waited outside the High Street offices of the South Wales Argus.

When it came, the lifting of the strange mood started as a distant murmur, growing to a wider hubbub and finally bursting out in crescendos of cheering, shouting and laughing as men everywhere shook hands, slapped each other's backs and made preparations for an evening of hectic celebration. And the cause of it all?

When the final whistle sounded that afternoon, Newport County had beaten Southend United by 3 goals to nil and so clinched promotion to the Second Division! At the same time, Bristol Rovers held Crystal Palace to a draw in London and by so doing destroyed Palace's late challenge.

The County had waited 19 years for this day; their previous best was 6th from the top, and on three occasions they had finished last, lucky that the absence of a Fourth Division in those days saved them from relegation!

Success of a town's football team in the upper echelons of the sport was as good a way as any of putting that town on the map and Newport basked in its team's glory all through the summer of 1939. It could not be known then that the elation was to have such a short life, that a six year war was to play havoc with the Football League and that Newport was never again to see peacetime Second Division football!

On July 1st, the official opening of Talybont Reservoir took place with the Mayor, Alderman J R Wardell, officiating. It was now possible for each person living in Newport to receive 23.17 gallons of water a day. The new reservoir was six times bigger than Wentwood, containing 2,567 million gallons and supplying 67% of Newport's needs. This proved beyond doubt the wisdom of the scheme, and silenced forever the Talybont critics.

The deterioration of the international situation brought about the passing of the Military (Compulsory) Training Act 1939 and under its terms the afternoon of Saturday June 3rd was made a very busy one for the Employment Exchange at Rodney Road. Hundreds of young men between the ages of 20 and 21, many clutching their birth certificates, queued to register and it was sad to see signs of that same euphoria with which their fathers had faced an identical situation in 1914.

The Territorial Army's recruitment appeals had already profited well from the over-eighteen year olds, notable contributors being the High Schools and Newport Rugby Club, whose every eligible member joined up!

By August a general exodus of the town's youth was taking place. Two thousand of the compulsorily registered trainees left to begin their six months introduction to military life, little realising that within a few weeks circumstances were to make them full-time conscripted soldiers, a number of whom would never again see their home town.

At the same time, hundreds of the Territorial Army part-timers went to their 15 day summer camps. The 1st, 2nd, 3rd and 4th battalions of the Monmouthshire Regiment were under canvas at Blackmore Park Malvern, Locking Camp Weston-Super-Mare, Thrapston Northants and Porthcawl.

At 6 am on the morning of August 17th, the town was awakened by the throbbing drone of a squadron of French bombers making a mock attack after a direct flight from France. Several hundred were over Britain at the same time 'attacking' many different towns and cities. They were co-operating with the Royal Air Force whose own bombers were making similar sorties across the Channel.

Chapter Fifteen

A Town at War

'Only the few believed that our boys and girls had lost their grip on life and were blind to the visions of duty - only the few thought that the boys of the 20th century were less capable than their predecessors. Difference of circumstances made different demands upon them but most of their elders knew that they would prove themselves worthy successors of the gallant youths and men who fought in the last war.'

Editorial on the Youth of the Nation
South Wales Argus
1st July 1944

When on 3rd September 1939, Prime Minister Neville Chamberlain made his fatalistic declaration of war on Germany, Newport was as prepared as any town could be - if not more than many - for whatever had to be faced. By the end of September the Borough had spent £49,833 on air raid precautions: slightly less than Cardiff but three times more than Swansea.

It had to be assumed that the town would feature high on the list of principal targets for the enemy bombers because all the ingredients were there. The destruction of the road and rail bridges over the River Usk would cripple all transport systems between England and the important South Wales ports. After all, it was known that a German zeppelin, shot down at Pinner in 1915, had been heading for Newport with this very intention. F J Hando wrote in 1967, that he had actually seen the zeppelin's log with the entry that read: 'Newport river bridge - the only road artery into South Wales'.

Obliteration of the Alexandra Dock sea-gates and the huge entrance lock, would end the town's further maritime participation in the war, and even the Transporter Bridge, lying on the Usk riverbed, a mangled pile of steel cables and girders, would render the channel unnavigable and seal in most of the wharves for a very long period!

Of course, it may well have been that in the case of the Transporter Bridge it was more in the interests of the Luftwaffe to preserve it intact as an important navigational aid, identifying the town conclusively and standing as a unique landmark from which to check positions and to commence bombing runs on other towns. Subsequent events pointed heavily in this direction.

That in the long run, Newport received less attention from the enemy than many towns of less strategic importance was to say the least puzzling - especially so in the light of a rather grim discovery made in a mixture of fate and coincidence when the war had ended. In 1945, a Pontymister man, working on a derelict airfield at Lubeck near Hamburg, discovered some aerial photographs taken by the Luftwaffe in 1941. One was of Ebbw Vale Steel Works and the other a vividly clear, bird's-eye view of Newport Docks, river wharves, Transporter Bridge, Stewarts and Lloyds and Lysaghts. It was indexed in great detail down to the positions of all the barrage balloon sites. The main target seemed to be indicated in the photograph's title - 'Eisenwerk-Lysaghts - Orb Iron Works'.

There is no doubt that Newport's future seemed precarious indeed, so rather than risk being wise after the event, there was nothing else for it but to prepare for the worst.

When the long period of uncertainty was ended by the declaration of war, it was as if a brake had been released and half-heartedness gave way to firm resolution. Changes quickly but imperceptibly took place, and well known features became disguised or hidden by protective material. Sandbags were the new fashion, up the front of public buildings, around the numerous public air raid shelters, wardens' posts, first aid stations - indeed anywhere that needed reinforcement and protection. As time went on, little sandbagged emplacements mushroomed on the flat roofs of many buildings and in these, members of the Observer Corps or the Firewatch Patrols kept their long nightly vigils, the former to give warning of enemy aircraft and the latter to pinpoint the first flickerings of incendiary bombs. Even the immaculate masonry of the new magistrates' courts wing of the unfinished Civic Centre received an unflattering mantle of sand-filled sacks.

All windows and any large area of glass suddenly acquired a criss-cross pattern of adhesive tape, intended to prevent murderous fragments flying when shattered by bomb blast. The latticework effect that this created was not unattractive to look upon but it remained a constant reminder of the ominous reason for its existence.

Wherever there was a piece of ground of sufficient size, a large, usually circular, steel tank was erected, filled with water and allowed to stand as a reserve water supply for fire-fighting in the event that the mains were blown up. Later it was found necessary to cover these 'static' water tanks with wire mesh due to several instances of drowning by children at play.

Tall posts like telegraph poles rose in every part of the town.

At the top of each, high above the ground, was a small platform on which was perched an air raid siren, looking like a small dynamo and operated electrically from a central control station. They were all dismantled at the end of hostilities but in 1952 twenty of them were re-erected as part of a post war civil defence programme.

At night when, as was to be expected, all signs of austerity were cloaked in darkness, another effect became noticeable. The blackout regulations were very strict and rightly so, for the merest chink of light from a carelessly drawn curtain could be seen over great distances from the air!

Every window had to be completely masked by black material, preferably with the edges of the glass banded in black paint. Vehicle headlights were allowed only a two inch slot in a thick padded covering and omnibuses were so ill-lit inside that passengers fell over each other and the passing of foreign coins in fares became a regular sport. Traffic lights were covered in black tape allowing only a tiny cross of coloured light to be seen.

The penalties for breaking the blackout laws could be very heavy - fines of up to £100, although five shillings was the norm. Breaches were frequent and the warden's call of 'put that light out!' resounded regularly in the streets of the town after sundown. Unhappily, besides details of those who appeared in court for blackout infringements, newspapers also carried many accounts of accidents involving both vehicles and pedestrians in the sometimes impenetrable darkness. Unless the journey was absolutely necessary it paid to stay off the streets once night had fallen!

Very soon Newport received its protective screen of barrage balloons, designed not so much to entrap low flying enemy bombers as to drive them to a height where the anti-aircraft guns could fire more safely over the town and make it a little more likely that a crashing aircraft would not come down in the built-up area.

Wide, flat areas were required on which to station the large diesel winches manned by men and women of the RAF Regiment. There were such places in the parks, the docks, factories and fields close to the borough boundaries. Possibly the most central site was in the Athletic Grounds, just inside the cycle track at the rear of the bowling green.

The balloons themselves resembled small bloated airships although they seemed enormous when moored only a few feet from the ground. Their skins of silver-grey, satiny material were filled with hydrogen.

During the months of uncertainty, Newport's balloons took to the air every night when the alerts were sounded and only became visible when a searchlight beam occasionally slid over the canopies. In the early days, during daytime practices, all the balloons would rise in unison like a great herd of tuskless elephants, presenting a forest of cables to the viewers. At first, it was the occasion for the whole town to stop and stare skywards; before long nobody bothered!

The largest Civil Defence Depot in the town was the gymnasium of Newport Athletic Club. Here through each night, a team of wardens and ambulance staff held themselves in readiness for aerial attack, and nursing staff stood by in the event that the building should become a casualty clearing station. In addition, a team of teen-age messenger boys took turns in spending one night a week on camp beds. Their job was to take over should normal communications break down. Many were the nights when in practice they were to be seen in the small hours cycling across town to the Civic Centre Control Room.

Practice it may have been but even if no bombing was taking place, the jagged, red-hot pieces of anti-aircraft shrapnel that rained down were real enough! The lads received six shillings for their night shift and they had to be up very early in the morning to go home for breakfast before starting their day jobs. The shell splinters in all their jagged glory were left in the roads and gutters for small boys to add to their collections of war memorabilia.

It was next to impossible to escape the signs of wartime exigency. The usual head-gear of the police was replaced by blue steel helmets: everyone carried gas masks; at numerous strategic points were placed long-handled shovels, buckets and stirrup pumps for quenching incendiary bombs whilst in a state of minor conflagration. Uniforms predominated : not only those of the armed forces but also the navy blue battle-dress of wardens, rescue and ambulance workers, the varying shades of many other voluntary organisations and last but not least, the bright green jerseys of the Women's Land Army!

This was the overture to Newport's war, and for a considerable time life progressed in an artificial atmosphere to which, surprisingly, adaptation came only too easily. However, before the real horror visited, there were other crosses to bear.

On Friday September 29th, every household had to take part in a census for the purpose of creating a national register of Great Britain's 46 million inhabitants to be used as a basis for security and the issue of ration books and identity cards.

On January 1st 1940, the Government announced that legislation was being enacted to call up 19 to 20 year old males for military service, and if this were not depressing enough, nature took a hand by introducing the coldest spell for over a century! A great frost sent the sheltered thermometer in Friars Street plummeting to 6 degrees Fahrenheit - 26 degrees of frost! This was the lowest temperature recorded in the town since 1815! It was accompanied by a three feet fall of snow and for some time skating on the canal was a popular pastime.

Austerity was now beginning to bite. In addition to rationing, increasing shortages and the demand for each family to register with only one tradesman for foodstuffs, the cost of living shot up by 10% in the first six weeks of the war.

It is far easier to describe conditions in Newport during the 1940s than to chart progress, historic or otherwise. On the one hand most civic activities were suspended, with all energy channelled into the war effort; on the other hand, details of the war itself were indeterminate due to heavy censorship which caused reports to be written in such general terms as to render them vague and of little informative value. In any case they tended to favour more optimistic items : 'A British destroyer with a Newport man on board has sunk a German U-boat!' Artists' impressions of incidents showed only the enemy getting a bloody nose, and in many other ways the propaganda machine intimated that the war was going well when in fact Britain's back was to the wall!

Everything possible was done in the way of saving, conserving, re-using and recycling in order to supplement the raw materials won from overseas at horrific cost to merchant ships and seamen.

Newport's schools and junior organisations made great inroads on the saving of waste paper; halls and yards were loaned as assembly points to which members of the public could bring their paper, cardboard etc and door-to-door collections were commonplace. These methods obtained hundreds of tons to be carted away for pulping. Some individuals made a little profit from private schemes but they were fair game for gangs of enterprising, young collectors whose fees (paid in pennies per pound weight) often included something for a couple of house-bricks, well wrapped up and hidden in the middle of the bundles! One such operator traded from a hut in the timber-yard of Davies Bros in Clarence Place whereon now stands the Clarence House office building. Needless to say, he was not in business for long!

Scrap metal was just about the most important material for recovery and, as in the case of paper, besides those working for no reward there were those who found both a reasonable income and the metallurgical expertise to stand them in very good stead after the war.

Front garden railings were cut away to provide ton after ton of invaluable scrap iron and to this day older properties bear evidence of this necessary vandalism in the sawn-off stumps left in brick pillars and forecourt walls. Old aluminium pots and pans previously consigned to the tip or the bottom of the canal, were now desperately sought as a supplementary source of the metal used chiefly in aircraft construction. Children sacrificed near-new toys, someone brought along a chunk of First World War zeppelin (he said!) and one old gentleman handed in his spare artificial leg!

Wool-gathering became a widespread occupation although far from the derogatory dictionary definition. Dreamy or easily diverted these people definitely were not as they strove long and hard to recover good wool from unwanted or bravely sacrificed, second-hand garments to be re-knitted into cold-weather 'comforters' for the armed forces. The Women's Voluntary Aid Detachment (VAD) were invaluable in the collection, sorting and grading.

Many will remember how, in the middle of a film programme at the Coliseum Cinema, to the accompaniment of good natured groans, the auditorium lights would go up, the stage curtains would part and there, blinking under a spotlight stood the manager. 'Ladies and gentlemen' he would say in a serious tone, and then he would bellow out: 'Woollies for the Navy!' and a hundred wags in the audience would echo his words before he was allowed to get on with his nightly appeal for wool to be brought to the cinema.

All knitters from schoolchildren to the very elderly were united in groups to unpick, dye and re-knit sweaters, scarves and balaclava helmets. There were over 600 knitting circles in Monmouthshire, and as the scheme was extended, free wool was handed out from Newport Town Hall to ensure that there was no shortage for the most needy of all - ie prisoners of war.

The glittering prospects that Newport County AFC had been eagerly anticipating were now well and truly scattered to the four winds. Shortly after the declaration of war, the Football League made its decision about the game. So many professional players were in the forces that the normal competition could not be fairly pursued and it was deemed impracticable and unwise for existing fixtures to be honoured, involving as they did, long distance travel.

Newport County completed only three games in the exalted ranks of the Second Division, beating Southampton 3-1, drawing 1-1 with Tottenham, both at home, and losing 2-1 away at Nottingham Forest (the latter only the day before war was declared), when the leagues were abandoned and replaced by small regional divisions, each containing about eight teams. Newport was placed in the South Western Region together with Cardiff, Swansea, Torquay, Plymouth, Swindon, Bristol City and Bristol Rovers. At the end of April 1940, a humiliated Newport finished at the bottom of the South Western Division. The town had more cause than most to yearn for the downfall of Adolf Hitler!

By February, ration-books had commenced to be used and very soon the people of Newport, in common with everyone else in Britain, shopped for 4 ounces of ham or bacon, 4 ounces of butter, 12 ounces of sugar, 2 ounces of tea, and meat to the value of 1/10d per person per week. Food prices had risen 40% in the first eight months of the war.

In June, the Government called for volunteers to form a reserve fighting force in case of invasion. This second bulwark was to contain men between the ages of 17 and 65 who were otherwise excepted from military service by age, disability or by being in a reserved occupation. Almost at once 25,000 volunteers nationally stepped forward to be known as the Local Defence Volunteers, their only uniform an armband with the letters LDV inscribed and their armament a motley selection of broom-handles, axes, pitchforks and sporting guns. Following a further appeal in July, the number doubled and the name was changed to the Home Guard; by the end of July they numbered a million. Their ranks contained grandfathers who had served in the Boer War and fathers from the Great War. Among them was a wealth of military experience - somewhat rusty but needing only a little training and modernisation to sharpen it up. Once uniforms and proper arms had been issued, backs straightened, chests stuck out a little more proudly and Britain had a second line of defence that was sure to give a good account of itself.

Newport had 336 volunteers for the LDV within a day of the first appeal in May. By June 1st, it was 1,200! They were divided into two companies: Newport East and Newport West, with headquarters at No7 Chepstow Road and the Drill Hall Dock Street respectively. Organised in platoons of up to 30 men, some factories had their own formations. They soon became smart on the parade ground, adroit in the handling of firearms, and the quality of their marksmanship, displayed on the ranges at Severn Tunnel, was excellent. This was truly a force for enemy parachutists to reckon with, and not the rag tag and bobtail lot that good natured disparagement made them out to be.

Unpaid but dedicated, they gave up much of their spare time in standing guard over railways, bridges and the coastline. Members of the public were warned that if challenged they should identify themselves loudly and clearly; they should not on any account take liberties with these part-time sentries whose rifles contained live ammunition.

Ordinary workingmen - clerks, labourers, farmers, shop assistants - found themselves spending one night each week manning the anti-aircraft batteries on the bleak moorland behind the sea walls of Goldcliff and St Brides. One such crew of amateurs was overjoyed when informed that they may have (only may have) been instrumental in dropping at least one German bomber into the Bristol Channel!

Steadfastly they practised the skills that they prayed they would never have cause to use. Sundays were the favourite days on which to see khaki-clad figures, shrubbery sprouting from steel helmets, crawling along the banks of the River Usk, going over the top from the park trenches and lying in the hedgerows. Officers worked out mock battle plans and Blue Platoon's job was to capture Red Platoon's field headquarters or vice versa. Capturing headquarters was the best part, especially when as sometimes was the case, they were based in a public house wherein, after the battle, victor and vanquished could raise a glass to each other before wearily heading home for Sunday lunch!

The townsfolk were under a constant bombardment of appeals both from local and national sources. On all sides the eye was beset by posters urging secrecy: 'Careless talk costs lives', 'Walls have ears', and 'Be like Dad, keep Mum!' Exhortations were made to buy saving certificates and bonds as a mean of loaning money to the Government. Further incentive in this direction was given by a tall coloured indicator on the front of the Town Hall where, by means of an ever rising arrow, people were told each time their National Savings had bought another Spitfire fighter plane. Eventually, there were over 225 savings groups in the town.

Life-style had changed dramatically for a people who had been only too content with the present and more than hopeful of the future. Now, a few short months later, their world had become unrealistic, filled with gnawing doubts and sombre expectancy. Fortunately however it was a passing phase which whilst never absenting itself completely, encouraged the growth of a new cheerfulness. Pre-war reserve melted, the stiff upper lip relaxed and 'we are all in this together' became the aphorism from which all other forms of morale-boosting emanated.

Formerly staid and dour shopkeepers, delivery men, bus conductors and others of that ilk became comedians overnight to their clients; a new generation of sing-along songs caught the imagination as every effort was harnessed to the task of keeping public attention away from the melting pot in which destiny was being decided.

Entertainment and diversion were the keys if the momentum was not to be lost, and with so many professionals conscripted to the forces or to ENSA (Entertainment National Services Association), amateur concert parties came into their own.

Weekly concerts were presented at the Town Hall, the Central YMCA and other suitable venues. Local talent celebrated its moments of glory in front of packed, appreciative audiences the like of which could only previously been dreamed of. It was in such spawning grounds that many future, famous stars received their first ovations.

Some idea of the eventual part played by the Newport Entertainment Service is obtained from figures published at the end of the war. In 2,142 concerts, 300,000 troops and an incalculable number of civilians were entertained by groups bearing such names as Star Variety, Flashlights, Chuckles, Radio Ramblers, Film Follies and the Ajax Concert Party. Much of the music was supplied by the ARP and Police Reserve Orchestras.

On May 27th 1940 it was found necessary to further reduce rations. Sugar came down from 12 to 8 ounces, butter from 8 to 4 ounces per person and Newport's 20,000 housewives were called on to 'man the kitchen front' by waging all-out, war on food wastage, making the most of what little could be obtained and keeping the whole population fit.

In this connection, a statement was issued by the Food Ministry on the subject of bones. It appeared that animal bones were a very valuable weapon of war. If every housewife salvaged 2 ounces each, it would amount to 20,000 tons a year of which every 100 tons would produce 50 tons of fertiliser or 12½ tons of glue!

In the early summer of 1940, the evacuees 'came back'. Seven thousand children from the Medway towns arrived at Newport station on a succession of trains, and they were dispersed to homes in the moorland villages and the valley towns. The reason why they were described as coming back was because they had been before - in late 1939 - but lack of action by the enemy had caused complacent parents to take two thirds of the children home again.

In the aftermath of the great evacuation from Dunkirk came the shock realisation that Britain now stood well and truly alone and it would only be a matter of time before powerful German armies would attempt to sweep across the Channel. Everything that could be done in defence had been done. Two million troops of many nationalities and a million Home Guards were under arms; together with untold numbers of other uniformed but passive defenders and the rest of the population, they watched and waited uneasily.

- 0 -

Preliminary probes by German aircraft began almost immediately and activity in South Wales skies was as vigorous as anywhere. Frequent were the sorties of lone bombers which dropped their loads aimlessly as if not directed at any particular target. Every visit, no matter how casual, drew heavy ground fire and caused large areas to go on alert. Consequently, the wailing of the sirens required bleary-eyed folk to exchange warm beds for cold, hard seats at the end of their gardens when after all no bombs were to fall! These alarms were by no means false but the growing complacency that they tended to create caused them to be more and more ignored , especially by the elderly. Overhead the distinctive engine throb of Heinkel, Junkers and Dornier bombers rose to a threatening crescendo and then receded without giving offence. In the four weeks commencing 19th June 1940, Newport experienced the first 50 alerts of the 480 total for the year to come, but most of the bombs fell harmlessly on farmland in the Rogerstone and Henllys areas.

At 12.48 am on 26th June, the first bombs fell within the borough. Several dropped on open land in industrial areas and some into the River Usk, but one set fire to a tank in an oil depot and only brave and resolute action by Mr W D Riley the manager, stopped the fire spreading to other tanks.

The blazing tank contained 250,000 gallons of petrol; the lone hero, 30 feet above the ground, worked desperately to disconnect it from the others while firemen on the ground played dowsing jets of water over him. He later received the British Empire Medal for this feat and the citation stated that the award was for 'his courage and coolness in climbing the main petrol tank to shut off valves when the plates were already buckling, and the tank might at any time have blown up'.

Mr Riley's comment : 'I was only doing my job!'

During the following four weeks more bombs fell. Some superficial damage occurred in the St Julians area and something - a small bomb or a rogue anti-aircraft shell - ripped a crater in Dewstow Street, the blast shattering hundreds of windows in the neighbourhood. Rural areas close to the town reported narrow misses on village schools, churches and farmhouses. Livestock was killed in the fields and veterinary surgeons were called out to put injured animals out of their misery.

It was all reported in the local press but only in vague terms such as :-

'A South Wales town (or village)' so as to leave the enemy guessing as to where exactly they had been the night before! Sometimes it was as if clues were deliberately released to strain German intelligence to the full 'Last night a bomb fell close to an old manor house occupied by nuns!'
(South Wales Argus).

One night, a shower of leaflets floated down in the outskirts and were picked up in many streets. This was a propaganda ploy which had been used by the RAF months before but the German version carried the speech of Adolf Hitler before the Reichstag on July 19th 1940. Entitled 'A Last Appeal to Reason', these sheets of paper came in for many uses but as collectors' items they were sold in bazaars or roadside stalls with the proceeds going to the Mayor's Spitfire Fund.

A Spitfire fighter plane cost £6,000 and rapidly reaching this target by October 19th 1940, the Fund was soon well on its way to a second aeroplane. A whole squadron became the new goal but so ebullient had the mood become that the town decided to go also for a Royal Navy destroyer costing £750,000! Ambitious as this sounded, the target was reached by March 1st of the following year!

Incendiary bombs fell in hundreds but if they were aimed at Newport, most ended up burning themselves out in the soft soil of the moorland parishes.

A group of school boys acting on information received, cycled furiously to Goldcliff to find a field near the Temperance Hotel (demolished 1967) pock-marked with circles of blackened grass and white magnesium ash. Ignoring the possibility of chemical burning or poisoning, a dig down of two to three feet in each circle uncovered a blunt, cylindrical nose portion of an incendiary bomb. This was about the size of a large can of fruit and unburned because its depth in the soil had starved it of oxygen. There was a fair crop of them in the neighbouring fields but they were not light-weight so just a few were sufficient as souvenirs; the rest were left just below ploughing depth for posterity.

Newport's troubles were not however contained only in threats from above the clouds. Tragedy struck five families 600 miles out in the storm-tossed Atlantic Ocean.

On 11th September 1940, the steamship 'City of Benares', was torpedoed by a U-boat and went down in heavy seas with great loss of life. On board were 90 schoolchildren being evacuated to the safety of Canada and the United States; 77 children were lost, among them seven from Newport.

Previously, 13,000 children had safely crossed the Atlantic; only one other evacuee ship had been sunk but all 320 children that it was carrying were picked up.

In the same week, enemy action took the lives of two more children, but in one of those bizarre accidents that seemed to gain ascendancy during the stupidity of war.

On the night of September 20th, a Heinkel 111 bomber appeared to be in trouble, flying dangerously low over the town. It struck the cable of a Tredegar Park barrage balloon and promptly dived on to the top of Stow Hill. Coming in at a steep angle the plane rammed with fearful force into the rear of a large house in Stow Park Avenue, exploding and engulfing it in a fireball. Mr H D Phillips, a well known business man, his wife and son escaped, but the boy went back into the inferno to save his younger sister and both perished.

Three of the German aircrew died in the plane but the injured pilot landed by parachute in Queen Street where he was arrested and disarmed by Police Constable Doug Cox and a Home Guard officer.

There was another unusual survivor from the crashed aircraft, and many were those who took detours along Grafton Road to the Dogs and Cats Dispensary to stare in awe at 'Tiger', the huge tabby-cat that had suddenly taken to sunning itself in the front window. Little boys were convinced that it pricked up its ears if the word 'achtung!' was shouted at it!

The dead airmen were given a funeral at Newport Cemetery with full military honours and an RAF firing party.

During the remainder of the month of September there were further ineffectual raids on Newport docks, but one raider put in the closest visible appearance that was to be experienced over the town.

At about midday one sunny week day, the sirens gave song and everyone in the busy streets quickened their pace. Daylight raids were uncommon although there had been one alert when Newport's guns had blazed away in daylight at a plane that subsequently proved to be British. In this case however, the alarm was genuine. Within a minute or two, an unfamiliar engine note was detected and flying low southwards along the course of the River Usk, a large aeroplane appeared. Its lines were not immediately recognisable and its markings were strange. Hardly had it roared over Newport bridge and vanished downstream than two RAF Hurricane fighters followed in hot pursuit.

It was at about this time that Mussolini had requested that his Italian Air Force be allowed the honour of joining the attack on Britain, and had based some squadrons of his bombers in northern Europe. The lone aircraft seen that day over Newport, only minutes from its doom, may well have been one of those outmoded Fiat Cigona bombers - at least most of the eye witnesses vouched for the fact that it was not any known German war plane, and several seem to remember a blurred flash of bright colours on the fuselage. Many pundits would say that no Italian aircraft ever ventured so far, but those people of Cwmfelinfach, who saw the plane that bombed their village, were categoric that they were not mistaken about the green, white and red of the Italian flag emblazoned on the fuselage!

October brought to Newport what everyone expected to be the forerunner of the experiences being suffered by London and other cities.

Bomb Damage, The Alexandra Dock Hotel, October 1940

At 7.10 pm on Wednesday, October 9th, a single bomber crossed the town flying low at great speed through a terrific anti-aircraft barrage. Suddenly it loosed a single stick of high explosive bombs and was away!The newspaper report the next day stated baldly that 'bombs were dropped on the working class district of a South Wales town and a hotel a mile from the town centre was damaged'. Of course this was Pillgwenlly!

Falling almost in a straight line, the bombs landed on the Alexandra Dock Hotel, Watchhouse Parade, Pottery Terrace, Baldwin Street, Albion Street, Capel Street and Lewis Street. Extensive damage was done to property but except in the hotel there were no fatalities.

As the attack came just after 7 pm, the Alexandra Dock Hotel was open and dealing with its early evening customers when the building literally blew up and collapsed upon them. Three people including the landlady were killed and several seriously injured customers had to be dug out of the ruins. Off-duty Police Constable Charles Cook risked his life by burrowing deeply into the tottering wreckage to save several lives. For his action that evening he was awarded the George Medal; a police colleague and two civilians received the OBE (Civil Division) and five others were commended for bravery.

Anyone wishing to spend a quiet moment at this scene of both tragedy and great bravery, will find the hotel long gone although it was put back to good repair and operated busily for years afterwards. It is now but a green sward with a few trees where the extreme end of Mendalgief Road has been realigned into Watchhouse Parade.

There were over 600 children in the borough who for one reason or another had special dietetic needs, and this at a time when all foodstuffs were the subject of careful regulation. Good management and careful planning resulted in the provision of wholesome, varied meals of over 800 calories. Following are typical examples of the menus :-

> Lentil soup and steamed fig pudding.
> Liver and bacon and boiled suet pudding,
> Stewed steak and jam tart; raw fruit,
> Roast beef and steamed jam sponge; raw fruit,
> Baked fish with sauce and rice pudding,
> Meat pudding and batter pudding.

Stirrup pumps for fire-fighting were on sale at £1 each, but if six people or more in any one street undertook to share, they could have one free.

On October 26th, after many years of indecision, the Watch Committee agreed to the employment of Newport's first three women police officers. There were already 246 WPCs in other forces.

The town Civil Defence received 60,000 pairs of ear-plugs for issue to the public.

As in the First World War, many suitable factories and workshops were converting to war production. A Royal Ordnance Factory was established in Wednesbury Street (now Standard Telephones and Cables) - another good reason to have expected special attention from the Luftwaffe! Women were taking up work of national importance in increasing numbers although it had not yet become mandatory; the docks and river wharves were more than living up to their peace-time reputation for quick turn-arounds.

At the end of 1940 the town's population was 96,620; there were 23,615 dwellings occupied by an average of 4.09 persons per house. the birth-rate was 16.77 per thousand and the death-rate 15.12 per thousand.

Just before the dawn of the new year there came news of a feat of wartime bravery and endurance that astounded the whole nation and gave a deeply sad but fiercely proud fillip to Newport's maritime heritage!

Floating quietly ashore on one of the smaller islands of the Bahamas, a lifeboat was found to contain two British merchant seamen, barely alive and terribly emaciated. They had been adrift in the Atlantic for 70 days - the last eight without a drop of drinking water! They had drifted for 2,500 miles since August 21st 1940 when a German raider had sunk their ship, the 'Anglo-Saxon' (sailed from Newport July 1940), with shell-fire and then machine-gunned the crew in the lifeboats! These two men, William Widdecombe of Newport and Robert George Tapscott of Cardiff, were the only survivors although up until a week before another shipmate, Leslie Morgan also of Newport, had been in the boat. Thirty-nine men, mostly from South Wales and mainly from Newport, had perished!

However it did not end there! After allowing the men to come through this unmatched ordeal of privation and battle against unbelievable odds, fate took a particularly savage twist and played its cruellest trick. Tapscott joined the Canadian Army but the ship bringing home

Widdecombe after his recuperation was sunk and he was lost!

There is still more of this story to come however, for even as these lines are penned (over 50 years after the event) there remains to be carried out one further solemn act of loyalty to the memories of these selflessly brave men. Languishing miraculously intact in an American naval museum has been found the very same lifeboat that featured in this epic story and determined moves are afoot to bring it back to a place of honour in the town where it rightfully belongs.

- 0 -

William Henry Davies always maintained that he was born on April 20th 1871 at the Church House Inn, 14 Portland Street, but his birth certificate stated July 3rd at the small house addressed as 6 Portland Street, with the birth being registered on July 11th. Of course he could not have known any other home than the Church House where his grandfather, Captain Francis Davies was landlord, and where young William Henry together with his older brother and younger sister were brought up after their widowed mother remarried and left them.

As a boy growing up in the teeming dock and river environs of an outwardly prosperous, but domestically poor Pillgwenlly, he was no better off than most and, if all the stories are to be believed, often considerably worse a denizen of this rough and notorious suburb. He was an habitual truant from school, a ringleader who always had a gang with which to run, a street-fighter of no mean ability and often a thief - not however an exceptionally clever one judging by the number of times he was caught red-handed.

Then, as if this phase had merely been the first of a series of lessons in life, a veil began to be drawn between the erstwhile street gamin and the emerging man of gentler appreciations.

Mundane jobs in ironmongery and picture framing sustained him for a while but he soon realised that his path in life lay elsewhere.

He read many books well into each night, all the time polishing his own eager but rough and ready style. He discovered the art of sketching, proving to himself that he was no mean hand, and this in turn caused him to forsake the grey lacklustre of Pillgwenlly for the green and sunny places with which other suburbs abounded.

He came to love the loneliness of nature and developed a wonderful workshop of word patterns to convey his thoughts to those of lesser perceptions.

Eventually even the horizons of Gwent became too confining so in 1893, at the age of 22, W H Davies set his cap at the world and by way of Bristol commenced the journeying that was to earn him fame as Britain's 'Supertramp' poet.

This did not make him the gentleman of the road that the title suggested and had he not retained some degree of that ruffianly quality from his early youth, he would never have survived in such desperate company and in such desolate regions where his wanderings placed him. He became one of the great tide of down-and-outs that washed back and forth on the North American continent; he was a hobo and a bum and often as uncouth and drunken as any.

'Riding the rails' one day in Canada in 1899, W H made a jump which missed and deposited him on the track with one leg under the moving wheels of a freight train. The loss of his right leg below the knee put paid to his hopes of any further participation in the Klondyke Gold Rush and returned him prematurely to his home pastures. He had not enhanced his fortune one iota but he was enriched by the thousands of thoughts and visions conveyed by stub of pencil to grubby, curled-up notebook, surrounded by the loneliness and splendour of the great North West.

Once home, this dogged little scribbler, a false leg fitted, continued his nomadic way of life, earning his crust by hawking and the door-to-door selling of inconsequential items. Sometimes he achieved the sale of one of his own creations - a sketch here, a piece of verse there.

He came back to Monmouthshire often but rarely did Newport rate a visit as he had apparently offended his relatives, or they him. Each visit was preceded by the news of the sighting 'over the hill' of the small limping figure about to enter town or village.

W H had great confidence in his works and he was tenacious in his efforts to obtain recognition. Using a portion of his sparse savings, he obtained private publication and sent copies of his poems directly to the doorsteps of some of the great literary names of the day. By these methods he became noticed, received encouragement from many notable writers including George Bernard Shaw, and began to feature in ever more complimentary terms in the writings of the leading critics.

He tried to settle down again in his home town and indeed his best known work was commenced in Newport, but for him something was lacking in the chemistry; in 1906 he moved away never to make anything but fleeting return visits.

His most famous book, 'The Autobiography of a Supertramp', published in 1908, was widely acclaimed and was eventually joined by over 700 similarly accepted literary works.

The year 1938 saw his last appearance in Newport at the unveiling of a ceramic plaque on the wall of the Church House Inn, now given the official seal of approval as his birthplace despite the evidence to the contrary. The ceremony was enacted by John Masefield, the Poet Laureate, and on this occasion W H Davies because of illness was little more than an onlooker.

Following several strokes over the next two years which seriously weakened a heart already overburdened by years of dragging a false leg over highway and byway, Newport's famous little tramp-poet W H Davies, died on 26th September 1940 - and hardly anyone noticed!

~ 0 ~

On January 11th 1941, queues once again formed at the Employment Exchange as men up to the age of 37 had to register for service. For the first time since the First World War women were employed by Newport Transport as bus conductresses or clippies as they became known.

At the town's annual Brewsters Sessions the Chief Constable produced a league table for the justices to show that Newport had earned for itself the unenviable reputation of being the town with the most drunkenness in England and Wales in proportion to its size!

Since early on in the war the local newspapers had been including pathetic and distressful columns in which appeared tiny photographs of smiling young men and thumbnail sketches of their connections with Newport and the surrounding areas. This information was inserted as news arrived of casualties, and included killed, missing or prisoners of war. Sometimes, a name was repeated if confirmation was received changing it from one category to another. From time to time, the columns extended to several pages.

Air raid warnings were continuous. Sirens sounded nightly along the South Wales channel coast and the skies were carved by foraging searchlight beams and bursts of gunfire. On occasions night was made into day by parachute flares dropped by bombers to illuminate targets. On the night of January 10th 1941 Cardiff suffered a heavy pounding in which many fires were started across the city; Llandaff Cathedral took a direct hit from a high explosive bomb.

On January 18th and 19th, Swansea received visits and was showered with high explosive and fire bombs but this was only an opening gambit. Four weeks later, for the three nights 19th, 20th and 21st of February, the Luftwaffe was almost a fixture in the Swansea skies and rained down death and destruction with indescribable ferocity.

When the eerie, single tone wail of the all clear finally sounded, the stupefied inhabitants crawled from their shelters into a scene of utter devastation, a crippled town, fires raging, a square mile of the centre levelled and a huge toll of dead and injured! As darkness fell on each of the nights the silent watchers on the coasts of Somerset and North Devon witnessed the fiery glow over the horizon.

Following this up, dozens of German aircraft made return visits to Cardiff on 3rd and 4th March, subjecting the city to what the papers described as 'the greatest fire raid of the war!'

Swansea was probably the prime target because, being a large port nearest to the mouth of the Bristol Channel, it was the first to be reached by French-based bombing formations making turns for their run-in over Lundy Isle. Both Cardiff and Swansea could be hit from east or west.

By March 1941 national statistics showed that 29,000 civilians had been killed and 40,000 injured. The fatalities continued to rise at over 4,000 a month.

Meanwhile, Newport's respite continued. The bombers left the town well alone although they were heard flying over nearly every night. Below the people waited, nerves stretched as they listened for the first screaming bombs to herald hundreds of others in a blitzkreig matching those of the neighbouring towns.

There was still the fear of the Germans using gas. They had not so far but the threat had to be kept fresh in people's minds; sometimes it was necessary to be cruel to be kind and shock treatment was called for.

On May 10th, a mock gas attack was carried out in Westgate Square. No warning was given when teargas was released, and many people were caught out without their gasmasks. Some, badly effected, were given treatment by first aid personnel.

Then on May 31st, the town received a raid of sorts, almost certainly by a solitary aircraft because only one stick of bombs was dropped, falling in a line to cause direct hits on Fields Park Road, Ridgeway Avenue and Glasllwch Crescent. The death toll was 23; 24 were injured and 560 houses received damage in varying degrees.

This indiscriminate, random dropping of single bomb loads suggested to many that the German Air Force was using Newport as a dumping ground for bombs originally intended for elsewhere but which, for whatever reasons, remained undropped and could not for obvious reasons be carried home to Germany. Amazingly, Newport's blitzkreig never came but there was still one horrific night in store for one part of the town.

'Enemy planes which raided a South Wales coastal town did damage to house property and caused some casualties. The planes appeared in a clear sky in the early hours of Tuesday morning and were met by intense anti-aircraft fire. Their stay was of short duration.'

This was the perfunctory and unemotional press statement with which censorship insisted that Newport's worst air raid should be announced.

It was after midnight on the morning of Tuesday July 1st 1941 and the usual alert was keeping those who cared from their beds. Aircraft noise came and went, pulses raced and settled down again until suddenly all hell was let loose in the district of Maindee!

Wardens on duty in the streets caught glimpses of descending parachutes and immediately thought of invasion by paratroops. Others clearly saw huge, cylindrical objects the size of large oil drums, dangling beneath the silken canopies. These were not traditional bombs but parachute landmines each containing hundreds of pounds of high explosive.

Two landed without detonating along the river bank, and were defused later. One exploded on a bungalow at upper Beechwood Road killing the occupant. Another scored a direct hit on a large house known as Gaerwood Kensington Place. Its occupants, 80 year old solicitor Mr Alfred Searle and his housekeeper Mrs Pouncey were never found. The site of the house and garden is now Woodland Park.

Descending relentlessly over Eveswell Street, the last murderous mine plunged on to houses at the Archibald Street end and in a split second the enormous blast transformed the street into a scene of hideous carnage, causing the deaths of 35 and injuring 46.

This was the first big test for Newport's Civil Defence and, whilst not remotely comparable with the terrible raids at Cardiff and Swansea, it brought home the horror in smaller concentration. The ARP services performed magnificently and no praise was too high for their unstinting dedication to the saving of lives of fellow citizens. That night men and women toiled, sweated, burrowed and choked in dust by the light of torches.

Daylight increased the activity, and the search of the ruins continued as feverishly as safety would allow by firemen, doctors, police, wardens and heavy rescue squads who worked until they dropped, sustained by field kitchens in the hands of the WVS and the Salvation Army. Rest centres in churches and chapels, set up for just such an emergency, were filled with those made homeless and those temporarily moved out of the badly distressed area. Willing helpers distributed blankets and made endless cups of tea.

The many months of practice and preparation by the emergency services were now seen to have paid off in full but having said that it was acknowledged that the further lessons learned that night could never have been imagined in rehearsal.

At the final reckoning it was discovered that in one house - the Gimlett household - only Edwin aged fourteen, his sister Louise aged nineteen and their mother were pulled alive from the ruins of 13 Eveswell Street. Father, grandfather, two other sisters, a younger brother and an aunt, all died instantly. Mrs Gimlett's injuries were so severe that she too died shortly afterwards. In No 16 another seven died and at No 15 which took the full force of the blast, the three members of the Garland family were lost.

The old Newport Secondary School on Stow Hill had been in turmoil for the previous week or so as it packed up to move to its new premises in Heather Road. Later, on the morning of the dreadful day just described, hundreds of boys and girls gathered at the splendid new St Julians High School for its opening. Young Edwin Gimlett was not among them and nobody immediately knew why!

The Newport Sea Cadet Corps suffered grievously in this raid. Mr Alfred Searle had been founder and popular commanding officer for 41 years and Mr Albert Garland the bandmaster!

This was the most disastrous 24 hours of Newport's war but the German propaganda machine failed to acknowledge it, broadcasting only that Cardiff, Hull and Lowestoft had been attacked.

Twice more after this German planes opened their bomb hatches over the town. On the night of August 29th houses were damaged in Beaufort Road, Beaufort Place and Badminton Road; in the early hours of September 26th a bomb fell in the garden of St Pauls Vicarage. The only other attack of any significance was just over the north-western boundary of the town. On 7th October 1940 several bombs fell in the Rogerstone area; one in particular, coming down in Park Avenue, almost destroyed the street by rendering 130 houses uninhabitable.

The raids on South Wales continued sporadically until May 1943 when presumably the Luftwaffe was too weakened to penetrate through skies dominated by the Royal Air Force. During the whole attack period it was estimated that between 40,000 and 50,000 incendiary bombs and over 800 high explosive were dropped; of the latter approximately 66 failed to explode.

Cardiff Docks were bombed 17 times, Swansea Docks 16 times and Newport Docks 5 times. The casualty list was:

	Killed	Injured
Swansea	387	412
Cardiff	355	502
Newport	51	159

Materially effected in Newport were 4,533 premises including 11 schools damaged, 36 buildings destroyed and 45 so badly damaged as to result in demolition. The town's last alert was its 544th.

On Sunday August 31st 1943 the 'Battle of Newport' took place. This was the way in which the local press described the most comprehensive and realistic war exercise ever carried out in the town. Nothing was calculated to have been left out; it examined and put to the test every facet of a town under attack and fighting for its life.

The assault began with a mass bombing that devastated large areas of the town and started hundreds of fires which brought out every man and every appliance of the wartime Auxiliary Fire Service, together with innumerable amateurs armed with stirrup pumps. The whole of Newport's Civil Defence Force swarmed in the streets, simulating the digging in ruined buildings for buried casualties to be passed to stretcher-bearers and on to first-aid stations. Rest centres and field kitchens were fully manned, and from midnight onwards the newly-formed messenger service carried dozens of commands between the Civic Centre control room and the outlying posts.

Council officials in the guise of fifth columnists infiltrated defences to plant imaginary explosives and to make misleading telephone calls to command posts. Many were spotted and arrested but over-enthusiasm often caused innocents going about their lawful business to be apprehended and carted off to the lock-up for interrogation!

Parachute troops were pretended to have dropped around the town perimeter and country units of the Home Guard fought pitched battles to keep them at bay. Here and there, where the enemy were reported to have broken in, the town's own units skirmished from street to street in order to expel them. Even the railway bridge and the castle ramparts were not sacrosanct!

That particular Sunday was almost certainly the busiest and the most eventful in Newport's history and the majority of those taking part were giving up their only day off in a 50 or 60 hour working week! In the evening, when the whistles blew to announce that the great battle was over, special constables, firemen, wardens, first-aiders, women's voluntary services, fifth columnists, saboteurs and Home Guards (friend and foe), all began weary journeys to their homes satisfied that the hard slog had been well worth the effort but still keenly aware that soon they might have it all to do again - in deadly earnest!

These were preternatural times. Not for above three centuries had violent warfare inflicted itself directly on the town and as graphically as one tries, it is a near impossibility to transfer the atmosphere of those strange times into adequate written form. Nevertheless, in this topsy-turvy world, whilst awaiting the play of fate's last card, normal life had to go on.

It took several Watch Committee meetings before agreement could be reached to allow a certain film to be shown at the Coliseum Cinema. 'The Birth of a Baby' may have become quite acceptable viewing for all ages 40 years later but in 1941 it was an ultra-controversial subject of medical mystery never before so openly displayed! Sex was a word only to be whispered in mixed company - explicit sex, dare it exist, was for perverts only!

During the six days showing of this film, 10,054 patrons passed through the Coliseum's portals!

The licence of the notorious Steam Packet public house came up for renewal and was strongly opposed by the police. Their spokesman regaled the magistrates with stories of excessive drunkenness, fighting and the continued presence of 'women of a certain type'.

The earliest mention of the Steam Packet was in a Monmouthshire Merlin of 1848, when it was sold for £900, suggesting that in those days it was a desirable business.

Its licence was now refused and the public house ceased to trade for the first time in nearly a century, from its earliest days addressed as Old Green, through the time when it stood in Merchant Street until it finally fronted the new Dock Street. Later converted to a row of shops, the building is now the one starting immediately next to the yard of the King Hotel.

Newport master bakers stated that due to a shortage of raw materials no hot cross buns would be baked for Easter. There was no compulsion about this but if buns were made, other more important things would suffer.

The summer was one of high temperatures. The 88 degrees registered (31 Celsius) was the highest since the record 92 degrees of 1932.

Clothing was now rationed and coupons had to be tendered for various items. The outfitters in High Street and Commercial Street were offering men's 'utility suits' at £3-5s for tweed and £4-5s for worsted. These were cut to the basic requirements - the minimum of cloth, narrowest of hems and lapels, no waistcoats, button-less cuffs and no trouser turn-ups. Shirt tails were cut off, pyjamas lost their pockets and socks were shortened by five inches.

By the end of 1941 there were 6,200 allotment plots occupied, compared with 2,500 pre-war and the Council had plenty more to offer. Portions of the public parks had been requisitioned and altogether an extra 238 acres were made available for cultivation. Parts of the grounds of several schools were divided up among older pupils who also spent their summer holidays at agricultural camps within bicycle ride of the town.

The Parks Superintendent estimated that two thirds of Newport's families were eating their own produce. Inadvertently this gave rise to a new crime wave that filled the magistrates' courts with offenders.

Obviously induced by food shortages and rationing all such horticultural enterprises became the targets for raiders who found easy pickings on the unfenced and unguarded allotments. Most of the thefts were small and were carried out by youngsters, and although the parents who appeared in court showed appropriate remorse, it was often suspected that many of them were the more angry that their offspring had been caught! There were however much more sophisticated and well organised thieves about; in one case it was reported that hundred yard long rows of vegetables were spirited away overnight!

Every miscreant caught red-handed was brought to court. The very young were let off with cautions but the fines that were meted out were derisory and angered the hard-working victims of the crimes who had been breaking all records in digging for victory. They likened the thefts to a form of sabotage, or at the very least, black-marketeering, and felt that the punishment should be made more severe as a deterrent.

The year 1942 was just one week old when the town's worst fire for many years destroyed the Empire Theatre in Charles Street. The cause was never established but it started under the stage and quickly spread to all parts, defeating all efforts to contain it. This again was an incident in which your author can claim more than a passing interest, besides that of being an actual eyewitness. An agreement reached with a kindly stage-door keeper had resulted in a continuous supply of artistes' autographs, many of them quite famous, but on that day autograph album perished alongside the grand piano of Charlie Kunz!

No action was taken to rebuild the theatre but a council sub-committee was informed by Moss Empires Limited that as soon as possible after the end of the war it was intended to build a bigger, better theatre on the site. This promise was sadly never to be fulfilled.

The police reported that in 1941 town drunkenness was 25% less than the appalling figure of 1940. This was probably not so much due to the dawn of the age of enlightenment and self restraint, as to an enforced temperance caused by the early closing of licensed premises on the numerous occasions when beer was in short supply. This situation was further emphasised when the town's Licensed Victuallers made the following pronouncement:- 'That for three months commencing on July 13th 1942, every licensee shall ration his supply of beer to ensure a daily supply, and that all licensed premises shall open every weekday for the sale of intoxicants at the following hours: morning 12 to 2 pm; evening 6 pm until the closing hour or such earlier hour at which the quota of intoxicants is exhausted'.

A last gasp from the Luftwaffe on 5th August 1942 sent bombs crashing down 50 yards from Redwick Church. The blast stripped the roof and destroyed one side causing the closure of the 600 year old building until repairs could be effected seven years later.

The cost of the war was now running at over £14 million a day. Newport's citizens had bought several Spitfires and a destroyer; furthermore, in Wings for Victory Week (May 1943), the sum of £1,211,988 was raised in just over ten days (averaging £12-11s per head of the population) and another £250,000 was smartly donated to buy five Churchill tanks. Meanwhile, incredibly, the Boot Fund for 'necessitous' children had to struggle to raise £350!

Britain had apparently found a new ally. The South Wales Argus was running an advertisement announcing that 'Weetabix is now in battledress!' which should have been enough to cause the Nazis to tremble except that this was an allusion to the famous breakfast cereal's new austerity wrapping, saving 80% material. The large packet retailed at a shilling and the small one at 7½d.

Other bargains were offered in the Candle King stores in Dock Street

Razor blades	1s-0d	(5p)	a dozen
Candles	2s-0d	(10p)	for 3 lbs
Soda	6d	(2½p)	for 6 lbs
New potatoes	1d	(½p)	per lb
Fresh kippers	10d	(4p)	per lb

Another severe wartime budget raised the basic price of cigarettes from 6½d to 10d for ten, and a bottle of whisky from 17/6d to 22/6d. Both these commodities were unofficially rationed by their scarcity.

Another film was the subject of controversy. This time it was banned from being shown at the Olympia Cinema in Dock Street and there was not a lewd scene in it! 'Judas was a Woman' was said by the Chief Constable to be filled with suicides, despair and illegal love. It was far too morbid and depressing to be classed as entertainment at that particular time.

Members of the Watch Committee expressed disapproval at this precipitate move by the Chief Constable without giving them a chance to preview it!

In a speech to Newport Rotarians, the Postmaster made the preposterous suggestion that one day people would be talking to each other on telephones that they carried in their pockets!

During the relatively fine and warm summer, moves were made to dissuade people from travelling away from home especially on holiday. Dancing was to be allowed in the public parks. The experiment began in Beechwood Park on Thursday July 9th when the National Fire Service Orchestra played to 1,400 dancers as they twirled and gyrated around the bandstand on finely mown grass, watched by over 1,000 spectators. It was a huge success, quickly followed up in Belle Vue Park by similar attended dancing to the music of the band of the South Wales Borderers.

The transport undertaking was experiencing problems with schoolchildren who, rather than walk healthily over short distances, were crowding adults off the buses. One councillor recalled that he had counted up to 50 children waiting at the Beechwood bus stop to go to Eveswell School, and suggested that all single stage journeys should be charged at full fare. The matter was held over until a later date.

Sunday cinema-opening was still very much a bone of contention in the summer of 1943, and a fourth attempt at its introduction was again defeated by a council vote of 13 over 12. This decision was seemingly influenced by antediluvian reasoning that, in most other communities, the war had swept aside. When it was pointed out that many towns now permitted Sunday film shows, one councillor fatuously remarked: 'That's their affair'. Another, flying in the face of the fact that on Sundays the town was crammed with servicemen and women with nothing to do, made the absurd statement that 'if a plebiscite of the military were to be taken, it would be wholeheartedly against Sunday cinemas!'

Fortunately this predicament was not to last for much longer and personal, holier-than-thou convictions were soon to be forced aside in fairness to the majority wish of the electorate.

Newport-born Commander J W Linton, grandson of the well known master builder, earned for himself the reputation as the Royal Navy's leading submarine commander and scourge of Axis shipping. For over two years in two submarines, the Pandora and the Turbulent, he had sunk dozens of vessels and even surfaced close enough inshore to successfully engage land targets. Inevitably, in the extremely perilous conditions that it continually operated, H M Submarine Turbulent failed to return from a mission and was presumed lost with all hands.

The truth when it finally emerged was that, returning from a mission, the Turbulent had hit a mine in the Strait of Otranto at the mouth of the Adriatic, and had taken its whole ship's company of 66 officers and men to the bottom!

On May 25th 1943 the London Gazette announced the award to Commander Linton of the Victoria Cross - not posthumously at that time because the submarine was not yet confirmed as lost. The statement added; 'Since the outbreak of war, he sank 1 cruiser, 1 destroyer, 1 U-boat, 28 supply ships - 100,000 tons in all - and destroyed three trains by gunfire.'

At the Buckingham Palace investiture in March 1944, King George VI gave the medal to Commander Linton's eldest son, 14 year old William, smart in the uniform of a Dartmouth Naval College cadet.

Seven years later, history savagely repeated itself.

On April 16th 1951, H M Submarine Affray made a trial dive in the English Channel and failed to surface. It was found two months later with its entombed crew of 75 men. Sublieutenant William Linton, 21 years of age was one of them!

The first three years of the war gave great impetus to the interest in organised dances which provided desirable havens of relaxation in a town bursting with young men and women; in the absence of any alternative at the weekends, recourse could only have been to the public houses with all their adverse implications. Inhibitions about lack of prowess on the ballroom floor were cast to the four winds and everyone sought welcome relief in tripping the light fantastic even if 'tripping' were the operative word! Dance halls suddenly abounded. None of them were built specifically for this purpose but they all possessed good, smooth timber floors which with a scattering of French chalk, were ideal for ballroom dancing. On many Fridays and always on Saturday evenings there were dances at Malpas Pavilion, Clarry Hall Goodrich Crescent, the Palm Court Somerton, the Drill Hall Stow Hill, Bannerman Hall Wharf Road, Lysaghts Institute and, less frequently, Stow Hill Baths (with the removable dance floor). Regularly used were the church halls of St Julians, Durham Road, St Johns, Victoria Avenue and St Davids, Park Crescent.

These were known as the 'hops' but grander balls were held in the Kings Head and Westgate Hotels. Rarely did a weekend go by without seeing the annual staff dance of some commercial organisation, public utility, factory, office or large shop, and these were inclined to be dressy affairs with tickets costing anything from ten shillings to two guineas or more! Ladies invariably dressed in elegant ball gowns, and although evening dress for men was often optional, most felt it incumbent on themselves to fall in with tradition and hire the correct attire. When tickets, taxis, hired suits and rounds of drinks were paid for, many young men found little change from a week's wages!

Woolworths, Marks and Spencers and the British Home Stores contained dozens of separate counters each staffed by three or four assistants. Other substantial shops such as Boots, W H Smith, the London House, E G Taylor and Reynolds all had such a wealth of assistants that together with partners and guests, they could easily fill a large ballroom - as numerous newspaper photographs of such occasions tended to verify.

The rhythm was supplied by many small bands of part-time musicians who, smartly turned out in identical suits or uniforms, performed with decorum, remaining seated throughout the night playing tunes to which everyone knew the words and which were being whistled half a century later. These bands carried names which were stereotyped in every town in Britain, and Newport had its quota in such sober titles as the Mayfair Orchestra, Squadronaires, Orpheans, Pieces of Eight, Arcadians, Georgians, the Astoria Dance Orchestra and the Beachcombers.

A not totally unexpected effect of these volatile times when the town was filled with transient visitors many of them foreign, was the spread of venereal disease, but its extent took the medical authorities by surprise. Much of the trouble was in the reluctance to report cases for this was still an infection, mortifying and shameful in the knowledge of how it was contracted, that invited almost the same, severe vilification once reserved for leprosy. It was suggested that more women police officers were needed with the object of preventing the accosting of members of the Forces by women some as young as fifteen or sixteen. One comment made in the Council Chamber was; 'It has become common practice in the town for young girls to throw themselves at the American Army!' Another, more circumspect, cautioned: 'The United States of America are our allies. We should be careful in that matter'.

This was not the only problem posed by the ladies. Another -although nowhere near as serious - was revolutionary enough nevertheless to cause consternation in the ranks of the righteous. Town officials and all the more upright citizens were appalled at the number of women who now frequented public houses; this was a new phenomenon and many of the town's licensed premises were not designed to accommodate female customers. The Chief

Constable reported that on one evening 114 women had been found in the Rising Sun Shaftesbury Street, and this was a very well conducted house. When questioned about 'the facilities', he remarked that they were adequate - unless the ladies all wished to make use of them at the same time!

The police ordered at least 50 pubs to add ladies toilets where none had been before, and another 18 premises to make drastic improvements.

On the morning of Friday March 31st a great air of expectancy lay over Newport and large crowds gathered in the town centre to await the arrival of some very important personage at High Street Station. Identity not publicised for security reasons, conjecture ran wild and it was not until the very last moment, when the miniature Royal Standards were affixed to the waiting large, black car, that the townsfolk knew for certain that the Royal Family was once more in their midst.

King George and Queen Elizabeth were this time accompanied by their eldest daughter, Princess Elizabeth, on the verge of her 18th birthday. That day a little more town history was being shaped because this was the first official visit ever made by the future queen to a town outside London.

The Allied Invasion of Europe has gone down in the annals as the greatest sea-borne landing of all time and Newport's part in it only came to light gradually, months after the event, when the relaxation of security allowed certain facts to be released. Nevertheless, clues were there especially to anyone who happened to be present in the Alexandra Dock during the two weekends preceding D-Day.

On Sunday May 28th 1944 it seemed almost possible to walk across the docks in any direction over the decks of the closely-packed shipping which included small warships, troop carriers, freighters, escort vessels and a 'Woolworth' aircraft-carrier (a conversion from a merchant ship). On Sunday June 4th the Alexandra Dock was empty!

Half of all the supply ships taking part in this mighty invasion sailed from Bristol Channel ports, carrying two divisions of the United States Army, all their equipment, vehicles, tanks and also 36,000 tons of ammunition that had been secreted around the Alexandra Dock for months. Thirty hours after assembly in the Bristol Channel the armada was lying off the Normandy beaches.

Given this direct participation, it should come as no surprise that Newport's vast facilities played just as important a role in a material sense behind the scenes.

Mulberry Harbour, the great dock that was floated across the English Channel, contained 89,000 tons of steel bars - 90% of the whole - practically all produced by the Whitehead Iron and Steel Company! The same works supplied most of the armoured tape used in the construction of PLUTO, the 'petrol pipe-line under the ocean' that snaked across the sea bed from England to France. No one involved in these manufactures had any idea as to their future use!

Lysaghts made two thirds of the special sheets needed for the motors of tanks, aircraft and ships, and tens of thousands of those for mines. The Corporation Road factory also turned out spare jettison petrol tanks for long range bombers, 180 million brass blanks for 22 mm cannon shells and 6 million for 25 pounder and 6 pounder shells. Many other factories around the town turned out the great variety of accoutrements of war which were used on the highly dangerous convoys to Malta, Russia and in the invasion of North Africa.

Add to this all the men of Newport and Gwent who went back into Europe that second week of June 1944 and the contribution can be seen to have been immense. Somewhere in the great beyond, shadowy figures clad in mediaeval attire and leaning on their longbows were surely nodding approval at the sight of their modern counterparts making for their own Crecys and Agincourts!

In the months following D-Day, dozens of trains arrived at Newport Station bringing hundreds of those wounded in the heavy fighting. Walking wounded and stretcher cases were shared between the Royal Gwent and St Woolos Hospitals; thereafter it became another of the town's benefactions to make these courageous, hurt warriors feel at home. Many of them were not native to the area - not even Welsh for that matter - but long after they returned to their own homes they had cause to remember by word and deed the great kindness that they received and the friends that they made in Newport.

During the same period, other trains were arriving, carrying a different sort of passenger. The evacuation of children from the London area began all over again due to the new threat of Hitler's secret weapon, the V1 robot bomb, a pilot-less plane filled with 750 lbs of explosive that became better known as the 'doodle bug' or 'buzz-bomb'. This and its successor, the even more powerful V2 rocket, were unleashed by the Germans as a last desperate attempt to win the war by terror and large numbers fell indiscriminately on London and South East England.

The dreadful effects of these weapons were not fully realised in the provinces until it was revealed that by the end of 1944, 5,340 flying bombs had killed 4,735 people and injured over 14,000; damage to property was catastrophic! And these figures were to increase by 25% before the Allies finally overran the launching sites!

So the first train rolled into High Street carrying 284 bewildered children, to be quickly followed by others filled with civilian casualties who were to join the wounded soldiers. Station Approach bustled daily with ambulances and omnibuses.

It was a task of the utmost complexity. In nine weeks the arrival figures were:-

1,400 children
1,032 mothers
279 other adults
284 unaccompanied children, privately evacuated.

Bearing in mind that 5,408 war workers had already been found accommodation and that many children of earlier evacuations were still in the area, it was a remarkable feat of co-ordination and organisation. The whole town, its managers and population, had the right to be justly proud of the supremely efficient contribution to the war effort in the way that they responded immediately to the call for help from those who had found themselves to be innocents in the front line.

By September things were going so well that it was considered safe to relax the stringent lighting regulations. As night fell on Friday the 15th, a few street lamps near the Town Hall were lit with low amperage bulbs. The test having proved satisfactory, the first big switch-on came on Sunday the 17th and the main streets were bathed in light of low but adequate intensity.

Crowds turned out just to stroll under the artificial illumination that had been absent for so long; schoolboys on bicycles pedalled excitedly around their new environment; very young children marvelled at sights that they had never before seen. Newport's black-out became a dim-out and road casualty figures began to improve almost immediately.

The last month of the last full year of the war contained two events, the first of which was sadly welcome and the second a misfortune of grievous proportion.

With all fears of a German invasion set aside, a general stand-down of the Home Guard was ordered. Newport, in keeping with all other towns, decided to do this in style in order to give the utmost credit to what had become a formidable, defensive force of part-time soldiers on whom the destiny of the British Isles could well have depended.

A huge parade took place through the streets of the town. Behind the bands of the South Wales Borderers and the 4th Monmouthshire Risca Battalion, the massed town and county battalions marched to the Athletic Grounds where a massive drumhead service was held. When the stand-down was finally ordered and the notes of the Last Post faded away, an era was ended. A slice of life which would never be forgotten was over, but no order no matter from how high received could stand down the great friendships and indomitable spirit of camaraderie that had been forged during the darkest hours under the greatest threat the British people had ever lived through.

Strange to relate, 14 years later a relic was found which was indicative of the primitive lengths to which these old soldiers were prepared to go in order to defeat a ruthless, well armed invader. In February 1958 some young men found a deep, overgrown hole in a Christchurch wood. Packed into it were dozens of bottles filled with petrol. Obviously this cache of 'Molotov Cocktails' had either been overlooked when the stand-down took place, or else some over-zealous members of a local battalion, not entirely satisfied with their official armament, had taken separate measures. The mystery was never solved!

The second incident provided a calamitous end to the year. On December 15th, Newport High School suffered a disastrous fire that destroyed a large part of the buildings. The library filled with valuable books, some irreplaceable, was gutted; honours boards, hundreds of text books, laboratories and all the school's Air Training Corps uniforms and equipment were lost.

Recovery however was remarkable. Help was forthcoming from other schools; classrooms were made available in St Marks Church Hall and lessons resumed almost normally, immediately after the Christmas holiday.

Christmas itself was notable for temperatures giving between 3 and 10 degrees of frost, and for a week when more passengers used Newport Transport buses than ever before in the history of the undertaking!

It is interesting here to note that although a great war had hastened a technological revolution, Newport policemen were still receiving citations for stopping runaway horses!

~ O ~

With the outlook more promising than for many a long day, domestic matters began to come back into their own. The Severn Bridge was once more under discussion together with the new motorway that it would introduce to South Wales. This was the first time that the term "motorway " had been used in preference to "trunk road" . A new Newport bypass was proposed as a link in this major road and the revised plan showed a route commencing at Langstone, passing over Christchurch Hill near the Royal Oak, via Caerleon Road, a bridge over the River Usk from St Julians Recreation Ground to the old Glass Works Albany Street, Brynglas Road, Malpas Road, the Breconshire Canal, Monmouthshire Canal, Risca Road, Bassaleg Road to the junction of Forge Lane with Cardiff Road.

A typical comment from the opposition was that this would create 'a town of ridges and tunnels which will be hideous for generations to come'.

A second town river bridge was contemplated to cross from George Street. Plans were placed before the Divisional Road Engineer of the Ministry of Transport and lists of property for demolition prepared.

The housing problem was given top priority. Already 500 'Portal' prefabricated bungalows had been erected and now a further 250 'American' houses of similar design were to be added. When this was completed the temporary housing stock was as follows:-

Nash 79, Treberth 150, Ridgeway 140, Bishpool Lane 122, Aberthaw Road 40, Maindee

29, Gaer 190.

The temporary nature of these dwellings was gauged in terms of from ten to fifteen years, but little could anyone know that their sturdiness would still be rendering many of them capable of sterling service a half century on. Ironically, at the time of their installation, Newport's MP Mr Peter Freeman described them as 'an abomination!'

On Monday May 7th all the uncertainty ended. Admiral Doenitz the new Fuhrer of Germany, ordered the unconditional surrender of all German troops. Tuesday May 8th was designated VE (Victory in Europe) Day and celebrations commenced. In Newport, VE Day became VE Week in order to fit in all the parades, street parties, dances and other happy demonstrations necessary to diffuse the explosive release of five and a half years of bottled-up fears and anxieties.

Festivities on the grander scale had taken place many times before in the town, some already described, but as splendid as any of them had been, this was the celebration to defy all superlatives, prepared as it was almost on the spur of the moment and disadvantaged by extreme wartime shortages.

VE Day dawned to find many people early on the streets. A large number had not been to bed at all since the announcement of the surrender was broadcast just before midnight, putting all thoughts of sleep right out of the question. Very quickly the town came alive with laughing, joking and singing humanity; red, white and blue burgeoned everywhere in flags, streamers and carnival hats. Total strangers hugged each other like friends of long standing.

Resounding cheers rang out from time to time and wherever music was available impromptu dancing brought the already crawling traffic to a complete standstill. For most of the afternoon and evening a densely packed crowd stood in front of the Town hall and sang their hearts out under the conductorship of a series of soldiers, sailors and airmen.

In the castle grounds, the Civil Defence Orchestra spent the whole afternoon playing and replaying its repertoire of all the popular songs, sentimental or morale-boosting, that had carried Britain through the war; roving microphones picked up goodwill messages from service men and women, civilians, housewives and children, to be relayed in regional broadcasts.

Night time followed day time in unbroken continuity of merrymaking and those public houses that had any beer to sell were filled to capacity, although their customers were not anxious to stay indoors overlong when history was being made outside.

Gradually however, the furore began to die away and in the early hours of May 9th the streets were quiet: 'as most revellers made their way homeward to the peace and quietness for which they had waited throughout the long war years'. (South Wales Argus).

The rest of the week continued in similar but slightly less frenetic vein. People had to go to work although the list of absentees must have been considerable; but the evenings were again given over to unrestrained celebration.

There were dances in every available hall, private parties in most houses and street parties in amazingly decorated surroundings. A fair ran daily in Shaftesbury Park (10,000 attended on the first day) and on Friday a massive carnival paraded through the town with hastily but cleverly constructed floats and hundreds of individual entries. Innovation knew no bounds!

The Grand Finale came on Sunday May 13th in a star-studded concert at the Odeon Cinema, Clarence Place. Appearing on this bill was a twelve year old Petula Clarke, just starting out on a career that was to lead to international stardom.

Either from a fear of not having done enough or a wish to draw attention to the town, a smug questionnaire was sent out to many parts of the country and the replies indicated that nowhere else had towns comparable to Newport celebrated VE Day on such a grand scale!

One thing is very certain. All the grandiloquence in the world and all the skills of gifted writers can never come anywhere near to expressing the true feelings and emotions of those few days. One had to live through it and be part of it to really 'know!'

If evidence was needed that all threat to civilian life and limb was over, it came in July with the standing down of the Civil Defence Volunteers amid similar scenes to those that had accompanied the disbanding of the Home Guard. This was quickly followed in August by VJ (Victory over Japan) Day and once again the town went wild when, at midnight on the 14th, it was announced that Japan had surrendered.

One small item of news was almost lost in the welter of more earth-shattering events. A soldier from Newport, searching for some small souvenir in the ruins of Hitler's Berlin Chancellory, was most surprised to find a dog-eared copy of the South Wales Argus!

During the rest of this memorable year anything else that happened could only be anticlimactic. The weather had the final word. In the early hours of August 29th, the town suffered the heaviest rainfall since 1875! 3.09 inches fell in 24 hours - 2.5 inches in one half hour! Local people said that the horrific thunder and lightning was more frightening than any bombing. Maindee Square, parts of Corporation Road, Malpas and the town centre were under two to three feet of water!

Sometime afterwards, the Harbour Commissioners announced that following the great storm, 10,000 million extra gallons of water had swept down the River Usk to the dock area bringing with them 80,000 tons of debris to settle in the deep-water channel!

As if trying to make amends for this intransigence in the elements, autumn was totally at variance with a most unusual period of mildness and temperatures more appropriate to summertime. Saturday September 29th was the day when the whole town turned out to greet Field Marshal Bernard Montgomery (of El Alamein) when he came to be made the 11th Freeman of Newport. The skies were overcast and a slight drizzle fell. Exactly one week later, on October 6th, the town thermometers registered 70 degrees Fahrenheit (21 Celsius) - not a record but the hottest day since October 5th 1922! Only the town's 1,535 unemployed were in a position to take full advantage of this exceptional Indian summer!

- 0 -

1946. The effects of the war were to linger with the town for many a long day but the unwinding began almost immediately. In early 1946 the Americans began their evacuation; the large US Army camp at Malpas Court was emptied and a train of 14 coaches took the troops from Newport Station to the port of embarkation.

The celebrating was not yet over. The earlier occasions of VE Day and VJ Day had been hastily contrived, spur-of-the-moment affairs as long-awaited news was suddenly broken. On Monday January 10th there began a much more carefully planned Victory Week when the parades, carnivals, bonfires and fireworks said it all over again.

The week had hardly ended when a ship docked at Bristol and unloaded bananas many of which showed up a few days later in Newport shops. Children up to eight years of age had never seen or could not remember such peculiar-looking fruits and viewed them with suspicion until they had taken their first bites!

Streets all over the town rang to the sound of hammers and pneumatic drills as brick air raid shelters were demolished at the rate of ten a week.

Rebuilding for the future was high on the agenda. Already great efforts were being made to attract attention to Newport's eminent suitability as a place for industry in all its forms with ideal sites, plentiful labour and easy communication with the rest of the world. The Severn Bridge was the subject of continuous discussion and artists' impressions of almost photographic quality, near identical with the finished object of 20 years later, appeared in the local press. The route of the proposed Newport Bypass with its new Usk Bridge and Brynglas Tunnels was detailed extremely accurately. It was not then known to be part of the motorway network and the objections voiced by councillors to the Ministry's plans reflected this ignorance. The route, they said, would cause an ugly blot on the Little Switzerland landscape; hundreds of children would be tempted to climb the boundary fences to watch the exciting, fast traffic; it would encroach on many acres of valuable park and allotment land; the lovely, virgin countryside that the road opened up would encourage ramblers to walk and picnic along its verges. Even Newport's MP, Mr Peter Freeman, voiced feelings that 'the Ministry of Transport's ring road through a densely populated area of the town is a serious menace to Newport's future development'.

It is fortunate indeed that these doubting Thomases were not allowed to have their way.

Then came the announcement that a large, chemical engineering works was to be built by Monsanto at Traston Road; Rogerstone Aluminium Works was planning a new rolling mill, and 550 acres of land at Fifoots Point, Nash, were to be developed as a new electricity generating station supplying power to Newport, Monmouthshire and the West of England. Costing an estimated £17 million and possessing six 60,000 kilowatt capacity turbo-generators, it would be the largest generating station in Europe. It was hoped to be operative by 1952. Its eventual cost was nearer £34 million.

This was the first full year of peace since 1938 and in the intervening years many of the town's sons and daughters had given their lives in defence of their country. At the time, the true feelings engendered by their sacrifice were experienced only in those homes where there were empty chairs at tables. The full extent of the town's loss was roughly gauged and further confused by the lack of information regarding the fate of the many reported missing half a world away in the vast Japanese theatre of war. The books were ordered to be closed on the compilation of Newport's Second World War Roll of Honour by 31st December 1947.

The town had to wait another 40 years for the publication of a much more up-to-date Roll which, despite having been painstakingly researched, still admits to the possibility of omissions. The list as it stands numbers exactly 1 , 300 men and women of the Armed Forces made up as follows:-

Royal Navy, Merchant Navy and Royal Marines	719
Army	281
RAF	155
Service unknown	145

The fact that well over half this number were seafarers would seem to be a fair reflection of their hometown's heritage.

In late February, heavy snow fell everywhere in Monmouthshire except in Newport. Up until then the winter had not been unkind so the town was taken by surprise by what happened next!

The first week of March brought two of the heaviest snowstorms in the town's history. The freezing winds that accompanied them caused impenetrable drifting and brought everything to a halt. 100,000 tons of snow clogged the streets and although it was cleared at the rate of 1,000 tons a day, the continuing blizzard made it an almost pointless exercise. The severe frost conditions caused a film of ice to form from bank to bank of the River Usk and at low tide the massive stone piers of the bridge were seen to be encased in thick blocks of ice!

Transport was badly dislocated, at times finding it impossible to function. Bread, milk and coal could not be delivered; bus and train timetables were disrupted and electricity supplies cut off. In such prolonged icy conditions heating was a life or death problem. One solution was found by some enterprising individuals on the Usk riverbank where for years piles of powdery river coal had lain untouched as a legacy of a bygone industry. Digging into the thick snow covering, wheelbarrows and buckets were filled and taken home where the fine dust was packed tightly into old, worn-out shoes which would burn cheerfully for several hours!

Outside the town, drifts stood 20 to 30 feet deep in the fields, and around Henllys and Cwmbran sheep were found after burial for up to six weeks! Severe as any winter has been, before or since, it is the 'white-out' of 1947 that commands most respect.

But, in the midst of all this chaos, a little order of a different kind was being engineered.

The atrocious weather did not prevent a reasonable turn-out to vote in a final referendum on the subject of Sunday cinema opening, and in a 28.6% poll, 13,250 voted for and 7,862 against. At last the town's Sunday entertainment was assured and the overwhelming result of the ballot went to prove, not for the first time, how councillors had often allowed their personal convictions to override the wishes of their electors.

The Transporter Bridge was in the news again. Six months earlier, on 1st October 1946, the charging of tolls had been suspended and figures were now produced to show the result. Apparently the number of pedestrians crossing had doubled, motorists rose by 150%, motorcyclists increased from 3 to 417 and lorries, which had paid the highest toll(6d) went from 23 to 1,116. This looked to be the answer but it was short-lived and the increased use meant increased wear and tear. Savings were made initially but they were almost immediately eaten up in escalating maintenance costs which were seen by the majority to be leading to a situation too damaging for the town's economy to sustain.

For almost as long as there has been public parks in Newport, there had been a by-law on the statute books prohibiting the playing of games on them on Sundays. Now a move was afoot to reverse this rule.

The opposition trotted out the same old objections based upon derogation of the Lord's Day, corruption of morals etc but it was pointed out that on Sundays golf was very popular among the better -off (and not a few councillors) and that a referendum was certain to go the same way as the one on Sunday cinema opening. It was not, it was said, the Council's job to add to the Ten Commandments. The by-law was rejected by a large majority.

This was the year of 'The Boundary Commission of Wales. House of Commons (Redistribution of Seats) Act 1944 and 1947. Parliamentary Borough of Newport and Parliamentary County of Monmouth'. The object of this somewhat elaborate and pompous sounding legislation was simply to alter parliamentary boundaries to coincide with borough boundaries. By its implementation, parts of Maesglas, Gaer, Malpas and Christchurch were to vote in Newport instead of the Monmouth Division. This had the effect of increasing Newport's electorate from 62,904 to 74,709.

The Transport Committee decided to reintroduce penny fares on the buses after many years absence. Return fares were to be abolished (except for workmen) and the price of two singles was not to exceed that of a return.

'We feel that the Newport travelling public should get full value of profit made by the undertaking. It is not fair that the undertaking should be part of the rate collecting unit. We say that the whole should go to the bus users

These admirable sentiments were expressed by the Chairman of the Transport Committee, but when put into practice the result was to wipe out entirely the sum of £30,000 profit made in the previous twelve months. The first two weeks of the new fares showed takings reduced by £1,000 a week, portending a much bigger loss for the ensuing year.

By the end of 1947 the Alexandra Dock collected one more record in the British export market. In December, the largest ever cargo of motor vehicles left for Buenos Aires and Montevideo aboard Houlder Bros' M V Condesa. This was a refrigerated meat ship but on her outward journey she carried 600 vehicles: Morris, Wolseley and Triumph cars and assorted bus and lorry chassis. On the return journey she would bring 6,200 tons of fresh and 2,000 tons of tinned meat.

1948

Police chiefs from other forces, attending a conference in Newport, were most impressed by the cleanliness of the town. At about the same time, a man who had emigrated to America 64 years before, arrived back on a visit. He said : 'I am so glad to see Newport in its present condition with no trash. Everything is so tidy'.

This was a man making comparison with the scruffy, Victorian town that he had last seen in 1884; it would have been very odd indeed if he had noticed no difference!

A great controversy was raging over the most recent acquisition of Newport Art Gallery. The full frontal 'Nude lady smoking a cigarette', a painting in oils by Sir Gerald Kelly RA, was considered by its admirers to be a beautiful work of art by the man who the following year was to become the President of the Royal Academy. Its opponents described it as lewd, disgusting and pornographic, and demanded its removal. A third faction, whilst not wholly in approval, intimated that the picture would be less objectionable if the lady were not seen to be smoking! The hint of pubic hair that was on display appeared not to lift one eyebrow although perhaps in those still not totally unenlightened days it was easier to mention the cigarette than the other!

Art lovers won the day and in the three months that the portrait was hanging 30,000 visitors went to make up their own minds about it!

Four years later (1952), Newport Literary and Debating Society had the final say. The debate was 'The nude lady with the cigarette - a suitable subject for public display or not?'

The 'nots' argument was filled with such disparaging epithets as 'vulgar, abandoned and brazen' It was said that the introduction created an atmosphere of 'insolent defiance and abandonment' and 'It could only be a painting of a Piccadilly prostitute - would any self-respecting Newport woman allow herself to be the subject of such a picture?'

On the credit side its admirers used words and expressions such as beautiful, healthy, eternale femme, artistic and 'a jolly good drawing!' The final vote on the painting's acceptability was 27 for and 7 against!

1949

The fortunes of the town's soccer team, Newport County AFC, had never been so low. Unable to recapture the attractive, intelligent play that had gained promotion in 1939, the club nose-dived as soon as the Second Division was properly reconstituted after the war. Back in the Third Division, the County continued to perform moderately, and by the middle of the 1948/49 season was hovering dangerously low in the league table.

There was some mystery here however, because the team was achieving excellent results in its F A Cup matches against strong opposition. Having won their way to the Third Round and being drawn away to Second Division Leeds United, the end of the road seemed nigh but on January 8th at Elland Road, Newport County beat Leeds by 3 goals to 1 and entered the Fourth Round of the F A Cup for the first time in the club's history.

The draw for this round brought First Division Huddersfield to Somerton Park where a 3 all draw in thick fog meant a replay in Yorkshire. This certainly seemed to be the end of Newport's cup run but to everyone's amazement, Third Division triumphed over First Division on February 5th, away from home, to the tune of 3 goals to 1.

The Fifth Round draw was awaited with great trepidation and when it was announced it was almost as if the whole town was heard to groan!

Portsmouth were leading the First Division and therefore could be said to be the best team in Britain. They had not been beaten at home for more than two years and on February 12th were to welcome a lowly Third Division side to Fratton Park. This had to be the end - but it very nearly was not!

Playing inspired football, Newport County became the first team for several years to score 2 goals against Portsmouth before half time, and one of the few to remain unbeaten at full time. With the score at 2-2, the County survived until five minutes from the end of extra time and then bowed out of the F A Cup when the home side, in a desperate flash of First Division brilliance, scored the winning goal in which all supporters agreed was the finest game of football seen anywhere for years.

A week later, both the County and Newport Rugby teams played at home - the former to Bristol Rovers and the latter to Cardiff. Almost a third of the town's population packed into Somerton Park and the Athletic Grounds. A gate of 24,500 saw the rugby club draw 3 points all with Cardiff, and 20,502 watched the County defeat Bristol Rovers by 2 goals to 1.

During the remaining 30 years of their existence, Newport County were never again to rise to such lofty heights, either in league or cup competition.

For the first post-war condition, report on Newport it is necessary to turn to the South Wales and Monmouthshire Outline Plan of 1949:-

'Newport is one of the best planned towns in South Wales but there is plenty of overcrowding and poor site planning; the road system leaves much to be desired and there has been the usual dispersed residential development in all districts with resulting maldistribution of open space.'

Visiting Newport at about this time, the Minister of Town and Country Planning made the first mention of a new town in Monmouthshire. Speaking at the County Hall Pentonville, he said 'as there is general agreement by Monmouthshire Local Authorities that a new town should be developed in the Cwmbran area, I shall have to make up my mind where it will be situated'.

He was in town again a few months later to announce that a draft order had been made designating a New Town of 35, 000 population, none of whom would be drawn from Newport. The area would extend one mile east and west of Old Cwmbran and Pontnewydd taking in Llantarnam, Croesyceiliog, Pontrhydyrun and parts of Upper Cwmbran and

Llanfrechfa. Later in the year, the seven members of the Cwmbran Development Corporation were elected; Newport Borough was represented by Councillor Percy Jones.

In April the first misgivings were expressed on the future of P & A Campbell's pleasure steamers. They had been carrying an average of 35,000 passengers from the town each year, and in the last year the figure had reached a record 42,000 in 133 sailings. Costs however were soaring but at this stage fears proved to be premature and the service remained undisturbed for the time being.

The South Wales Argus had full columns of advertisements for holiday accommodation. Typical was that of a Bournemouth boarding house:-

'Bed, breakfast and Sunday lunch, 3 guineas a week. Welsh landlady'.

From June 20th to the 29th the average daily temperature was 79 degrees (26 C) the highest registered being 86 (30 C). This very hot weather prompted the same newspaper to comment:-

'Though Newport's Transporter Bridge has long been regarded as a white elephant, there can be no denying that during sunny weather the bridge, working overtime, has been greatly appreciated by harassed parents anxious to temporarily 'lose' their offspring at Coronation Park.'

The decision was made in 1946 by Evan, 4th Baron, 2nd Viscount Tredegar, to give up residence at Tredegar House, the ancestral home of the Morgan family. For the next three years he would live on his Surrey estate at Honeywood House, Dorking.

The fact that Evan was the 2nd Viscount needs some explanation in view of the fact that there had actually been three viscountcies. The first had been given in 1905 to Evan's great-uncle, Godfrey the 2nd Baron who was one of the survivors of the Charge of the Light Brigade in the Crimean War. He never married and therefore on his death in 1913 the viscountcy was extinguished and the baronial estates passed to the son of his brother, Frederick Morgan of Ruperra who had died four years earlier. Thus, Courtenay became 3rd Baron Tredegar and it was he who in 1926 received the honour that created the new first viscountcy.

It could be said that here commenced the break-up of the Tredegar Estate when the long-held tradition of concern for the town that had enriched the family gradually gave way to the use of that wealth for self-indulgence on a grand scale. By the time of the 3rd Baron's death, the estate was valued at £2,300,000, mainly vested in 80,000 acres of land in Monmouthshire, Glamorgan, Brecon, Surrey and Bow in London. Half of this sum was immediately absorbed in death duties!

What remained passed to Courtenay's son, Evan Frederick Morgan, who became 4th Baron, 2nd Viscount, Papal Chamberlain and Ovate of St Mary's Abbey Buckfast, Devon. He continued to emulate his late father s extravagant lifestyle although more in the company of the artistic rather than the country set. On April 27th 1949, aged 56, he succumbed to a virulent strain of continental influenza and died at his Surrey home; he was interred at Buckfast Abbey.

By this time the estate had dwindled to a value of £2,556,221 *in post-war terms* and again estate duty gobbled up a major portion.

Lord Evan had had two childless marriages. His nearest living relative was his father's brother, Frederick George Morgan who now became the 5th Baron. But he was 75 years old and crippled with osteo-arthritis. He was first to realise that in those circumstances it was most likely that the Estate would soon suffer a third, disastrous demand for death duties so, whilst keeping the title, he passed succession of the Estate to his son, the Honourable John

Morgan.

The death of Frederick in 1954 made John the 6th Baron Lord Tredegar, but by now any loyalty to the birthplace of his ancestors and the town that had revered them was eclipsed by the wish to salvage what remained and enjoy it in some tax haven. In 1951, Tredegar House was sold; in 1953, the Honourable John Morgan, heir to the Estate, withdrew his patronages and resigned all presidencies and vice-presidencies of organisations in the area; by 1957, the whole of the ancient Tredegar Estate had been broken up and had passed into other hands.

The death of Lord John, 6th and last Baron Tredegar, in Monte Carlo in 1962, closed down a dynasty which had lasted as a class of gentry for over 500 years in a succession of houses sited in Tredegar Park. For an indeterminate period before that, the family had existed in slightly more humble circumstances - but always in the ascendancy.

Each link in the chain of Newport's development represented a generation of the Tredegar Morgans, with special emphasis on those of the 19th century. By the actions of this family, history of the town had been specially influenced and moulded - not always selflessly in the short term, but there was much in their machinations that had been favourable to the town.

At the highest point on Christchurch Hill stood the parish Church of Holy Trinity. Although the building was Norman, its site had been a Saxon place of worship for much longer. It was a very ancient holy place indeed and in the most remarkable way had survived the ravages of time, the waves of heathen vandals and the native warring factions that were once almost permanent features of the neighbourhood. This record came to an abrupt end in the early hours of Sunday November 6th 1949.

The embers of the last few Guy Fawkes bonfires had hardly ceased to glow around the town when a flame flickered inside the church. By the time the alarm was raised the whole of the roof was blazing furiously. The combined efforts of Newport's Fire Brigade and several out-of-town forces could not contain the conflagration and the morning found a blackened ruin with horrific internal damage.

Twice before, in the 18th century and in 1877, the roof of the church had sustained fire damage but not even in the wake of Owain Glyndwr, the great destroyer himself, had there been a total gutting.

When the roof finally fell in, a mass of ancient records were in ashes, most of the brass ornaments were unrecognisable twisted metal, the organ, furniture, timber-work and the impressive font had all been ruined. The Lady Chapel in which Holy Communion was to have been solemnised later that morning, together with its beautiful altar, had vanished without trace. The tower however survived, and vivid photographs taken from its roof revealed the utter devastation down below. Total damage was estimated at £30,000, an enormous sum by 1949 standards!

If this tragedy were not bad enough, six days later, early in the morning of Saturday November 12th, another great fire engulfed the Church of St John the Evangelist, Maindee. Despite being much younger (opened 1860), it was no less imposing or beautiful than Christchurch. The havoc created was a carbon copy!

Damage this time was about £45,000. Burnt to cinders were the magnificent £12,000 organ, all the oak furnishings, beams and the ornately carved reredos. The war memorials and all the exquisite stained glass were destroyed except for two windows that fortunately had been sent to London a few months earlier for repair to blast damage caused by the land-mine that had dropped in Kensington Place during the war.

Forensic experts were called in from Scotland Yard to examine both fire-blackened ruins but whilst arson was strongly suspected nothing conclusive came from these inspections. The timing, identical targets and the speed of inflammation were all suggestive of something more than accidental coincidence. If fire-raising vandals were to blame, and if they were youthful at the time, it may well be that they are still around even as this account is being written. For their sakes, if such is the case, it is to be hoped that life has treated them no more kindly than their mindless, retarded actions deserve!

On December 17th Newport received its first television signals from the newly opened Sutton Coldfield transmitter. The pictures on some of the early sets possessed by radio shops were encouraging but there were low-lying blackspots where reception ranged from poor to non-existent. Some of the blame was apportioned to interference from windscreen wipers of motor vehicles and to the electric hair clippers of hairdressing salons! Reports from Abergavenny and Brynmawr however were excellent. In this way the curtain was drawn at the end of possibly the most traumatic decade in Newport's history - not suffered alone but full square with every other city, town, village and hamlet in the country, even if its abrasions were not as extensive as many. The times spawned a generation that would forever be unique but at the same time wholeheartedly dedicated to the task of ensuring that inheritors of their town would never again be subject to such experience!

Chapter Sixteen

The 1950s

The days of the live, professional theatre in Newport were numbered but this was far from obvious in early 1950 when the pantomime 'Jack and the Beanstalk' ran for six weeks at the Lyceum Theatre. This was longer than any show in the previous 25 years and altogether 70,000 people saw it!

A Newport night-watchman won a massive £23,000 on the football pools. He did not turn up for work thereafter!

Tredegar House was sold by the Estate to the Trustees of the Sisters of Llantarnam and Newport for use as a Roman Catholic school.

All over Britain thoughts were turning to rehabilitation and rebuilding. Many cities and towns had been at work for years clearing the debris of war from their heavily bomb-damaged commercial centres and replacing lost housing stock. These areas had been given harsh lessons and were left in no doubt as to where their priorities lay. Newport was not in this class, having survived relatively unscathed; nevertheless it was a town that acknowledged its aches and pains but was completely mystified as to where the surgeon's first incision should be made. In such a situation the temptation was to sit back and count one's blessings but that kind of complacency was the sure way to be left behind in the competition for any prizes that would be on offer in post-war Britain.

Over years ancient and modern, successive borough councils had debated endlessly on the town's shortcomings, always harried by a tenacious lobby that argued that there were none - or else if there were they could easily be disguised quite economically by the application of a little plaster over the cracks!

Past actions of vital importance to the town such as the building of the canals, docks, markets and the Talybont Reservoir had been made with equanimity by earlier corporations, but their more recent successors seemed to have shown a marked lack of imagination and decisiveness, due possibly to a surfeit of simpler domestic issues. Now faced with a problem that dwarfed all previous, there came a period of irresolution. The great town re-shapers of the past -Sam Homfray, Sir Charles Morgan, Sir George Elliott and others -would undoubtedly have been champing at the bit in their eagerness to take part!

Many of the less venturesome lived by the Micawberism that 'something will turn up' and clung desperately to the hope that the docks and river wharves were experiencing only a temporary lull in their fortunes; they would soon come alive again with revitalised maritime trade. This air of indecision hanging over the town caused it to remain virtually unchanged and old fashioned with a pattern of narrow congested streets set over a century earlier.

The most recent bridge survey, carried out in 1949, showed that it was carrying over 15,000 motor vehicles daily - nearly three times the traffic of its early years. It was now all too obvious that the days of the cosmetic nip and tuck were over - the patient required a serious operation!

Mayors and councillors at public meetings and private functions were still monotonously reciting the hackneyed cliché that Newport was 'second to none' when it was patently obvious that this was not so. There was however a magnificent, not-quite-yet-finished Civic Centre presiding overall and in it the housing programme was receiving vigorous attention.

In the five years since the end of the war the Corporation had built 1,760 houses; 779 were under construction and another 869 under contract. By comparison, private builders had completed a mere 40 with 51 under construction. The Council's record here may have sounded impressive but it had to be weighed against a waiting list of over 5,000 and the fact that whilst each week four families were allotted, another seventeen were applying. Neither were matters helped by the appalling vandalism which was regularly occurring on the large developing estates of Alway and Ringland where the builders threatened strike action unless their work was better protected.

Finally however, casting aside the equivocation that it had inherited from its predecessors, the town planning committee took the bull by the horns and produced a master plan for the town. From it, a group of local schoolboys built a 1:500 scale model which went on display in the foyer of the Civic Centre.

This first attempt was certainly bold and imaginative, and many of those who remember it would say that it was much more impressive than what the town ended up with twenty or so years later. It was proposed that development should be in five year stages spread over the next century.

No second bridge was indicated although it was acknowledged that there would have to be one if the rest of the plan was to work. An inner ring road was delineated, many ugly old buildings and landmarks were swept away and scruffy streets in the centre were demolished, realigned and rebuilt with tall, clean buildings. Wide new tree-lined roads appeared together with open garden areas, riverside walks and ample car parking facilities. Even a helicopter landing pad was envisaged.

Straight away the proceed-with-extreme-caution brigade massed forces. An inner ring road was said to be unnecessary because a recent survey had shown that of 1,454 vehicles recorded in the outskirts of the town, only 145 would have made use of a by-pass bridge over the River Usk; the cost of implementing the master plan would be astronomical; a new river bridge (if any) should cross at Shaftesury Park (connecting what-with-what unstipulated). The most preposterous suggestion however was that instead of demolishing much of the town's old but most valuable properties and at least six of the loading and unloading wharves, some space should be given to large departmental stores and all the smaller shops moved across the river. There a new commercial area would spread over, of all things, the Athletic Grounds!

The Chamber of Commerce was also a stern critic and put forward its own, much less ambitious plan, obviously aimed at preserving the business status quo with as little upheaval as possible, and 'to remove faults which had arisen through unplanned growth, to remove bottlenecks, traffic congestion and to give detailed proposals for the resiting of certain industries', - in other words to leave well alone except for a touch-up here and there!

The river wharves were said to be totally impracticable along the 'sewer-lined Usk' and it was suggested that light industrial units would be better - this in the same breath as saying that in the master plan there was a 'lack of architectural control and a disregard for harmony!'

Such was the course that the early planning debate followed and the division between the parties made obvious the fact that any compromise would be hard-fought and only achievable by the sacrifice of strongly held convictions on all sides.

1951

In late 1950, the Old Sessions House at Usk had burned down, so until it was rebuilt, a new home had to be found for the Monmouthshire Quarter Sessions. Newport was the choice and on 3rd January ,for the first time since 1788 (except for three improvised sittings in the Monmouthshire County Council Offices at the end of the First World War), the

Quarter Sessions were held in the town.

Before 1788, it was the custom to hold the Sessions at Newport, Chepstow, Abergavenny, Caerleon and Usk with occasional adjourned Sessions at Tredegar and Monmouth. Over the ensuing years Newport made many attempts to obtain the prestigious Court for itself but now hopes were shattered by the announcement that the present arrangement was only temporary until the Usk Sessions House should be rebuilt.

The nationalisation of the coal industry had so far resulted in such a low output from the mines that there was a country-wide shortage. In an effort to save one million tons of coal per annum, a Ministry of Fuel Order, originally ended in 1949, was reimposed on January 8th. The main provision was the prohibition of the use of electricity for advertising. This had the effect of transforming most of the town centre from a glittering miscellany of illuminated shop fronts into a sombre twilight of street lamps and directional signs. One drastic example of the restrictions in action was that of the High Street retailer who had to switch off the 20,000 watts being burned nightly in his ten shop windows!

The Fish Fryers Association announced that due to the rising costs of potatoes, cooking oil, equipment and fuel, it could no longer maintain prices at their present levels. On the other hand it was added that: 'the last thing we wish is to make fish and chips a luxury food'. In Newport's many fish shops the price of a portion of fish rose to 9d (less than 4 pence) and the minimum portion of chips to 4d (just over 1½ pence)!

These were Newport Rugby Club's greatest days and the records show that at that time this was probably the world's finest club rugby team.

In March, they played Cardiff for the fourth time in the season having won the first three encounters. The venue was Cardiff Arms Park and the game was played before a crowd of 48,500 - a world record for any club match, and also outnumbering any Football Association league game played on that Saturday!

The 3 - 3 draw result meant that Newport retained a full year's invincibility with a record of 39 games played, 37 won and 2 drawn with 589 points for and 122 against. Unfortunately this invincibility did not extend to the end of the 1950/51 season for shortly afterwards an injury-stricken side lost to Harlequins.

A baby girl sustained severe burns in a household accident. Following admittance to the Royal Gwent Hospital, she was given an injection of penicillin and on March 21st she died from hypersensitivity to the drug. There had been five other such cases reported in the United States but this was the first known case in Great Britain.

1951 was the year of the Festival of Britain, 100 years after the great Victorian Exhibition. Sponsored by the Government as a fillip to the morale of a country still in the throes of wartime austerity and rationing, it was also intended as a shop window through which the rest of the world could see, by a blatant and unashamed display of self-confidence, that the recuperative period was over and that business as usual signs were appearing everywhere.

In their own ways towns and villages set out to emulate the Capital. Country-wide the Festival of Britain lasted from 1st May to 30th September but Newport chose the fortnight ended 30th June in which to concentrate its own contribution. The town was prettied up in much the same manner adopted for other grand, celebratory occasions and its own festival site opened at Kimberley Park, Malpas Road.

The town transport undertaking had acquired a second-hand aircraft hangar for use as a temporary bus garage and this stood on ground just opposite the park. For two weeks it became Newport's Festival Hall in which to present a picture of life and work in Monmouthshire. Here were given demonstrations of local rural crafts, pottery-making, weaving, furniture-making and fashioning of horse harness in leather and brass. The ill-fated model of the proposed new town centre took pride of place.

In the park a full programme was organised and the days were taken up with gymnastic displays, children's dramatic art exhibitions, show jumping, choral events, amateur boxing and the start and finish of the Argus Road Walk. Bands gave concerts and supplied the accompaniment to dancing, and the traditional fun-fair made the nights gay with music and coloured lighting. As usual there was the competition for the best decorated street and the standard was so high among the twenty-one entrants that the judges had to stay up until midnight to make final decisions based upon illuminatory effects.

Getting people out into the fresh air and keeping their attention for a full fortnight was no problem in those pre-television days and 70,000 visitors to Newport's Festival gave full weight to this argument.

For some time after the Festival ended, there were discussions over the ultimate fate of the hangar/festival hall. There was no further use for it as an omnibus garage, so, while its future was in the balance, it had several temporary lettings. Its site now forms part of Malpas Fire Station.

It was over the next few years that Newport Fire Brigade was kept extremely busy by an unusual number of outbreaks of fire in central locations. The two great church fires in late 1949 more or less represented the beginning of this spate and were undoubtedly deliberately set, but during 1950 and 1951 there was a series of other fires in important town centre properties.

The first incident on November 5th, the anniversary of the Christchurch fire, was a blaze that badly damaged the upper floors of the British Home Stores High Street, and ruined thousands of pounds worth of Christmas toys. In 1951, Abbot and Baker's warehouse and offices suffered an outbreak and a greengrocer in Griffin Street followed suit. The top floor of the Westgate Hotel went up in smoke and in this case a painter's blow-lamp was suspected. By December however it was certain that firebugs were at large; nine cars, each parked in a different part of the town, had been found ablaze in the early hours of several mornings and one obvious attack was made on a private house.

1952

Still to be seen on the streets of the town was the familiar sight of horse-drawn, railway delivery vehicles which mingled uncertainly with the increasing accumulation of motorised traffic. There were the great, wooden, flatbed trucks on their steel-rimmed cartwheels, with dangling chains from which swung metal-bound timber wedges to hold the wheels when parking on slopes. Up front was a small raised seat for the driver and underneath a spare nosebag filled with oats; the merchandise in sacking, cardboard or plywood packaging, was stacked uncovered but with neatly folded tarpaulins nearby just in case. The poor relations of these majestic vehicles were the smaller, rubber-tyred 'covered wagons' used for parcels of lesser proportions and flimsier wrapping.

The gentle, handsome beasts between the shafts knew their places only too well, patiently waiting when the traffic stopped, shrugging off the irritation of exhaust fumes and moving on again without need of a command.

It was now far too noisy to hear the musical jingle of the harness or the rhythmic plod of heavy, steel-shod hoofs, and no longer a safe game for small boys to hitch lifts below the tailboards with only their finger tips showing to any driver who cast a backward glance. Even so, what was left was still a welcome reminder of a more leisurely bygone age.

Progress continued its relentless march. As British Railways put more and more trim little motor vans on the streets it was inevitable that the days of the carter and his horse were numbered. In 1952 therefore it was proposed to replace old fashioned horsepower with the new.

In 1939, the stables in Station Yard Cambrian Road had been occupied by 41 horses; in 1952 they held just 2 valued at £70 each. 'Billy', a children's favourite, was the last to go and there was uproar among the younger generation, spreading to parents, when a story circulated that he was destined for the glueworks! Swift denials were made by the railway authorities to scotch these rumours and Billy found a new home at New Street Station Birmingham. However this story did not have the happy ending that it deserved and in May came news that 17 year old Billy had been put down. Apparently he had found it difficult to settle in his new surroundings, becoming extremely fractious and eventually badly injuring one of his keepers. This was completely at odds with his gentle behaviour during the whole of his long career in Newport.

At The Garw, Croesyceiliog, the first two Cwmbran Development Corporation houses were occupied with rents of £1-16s-0d a week, inclusive of rates! To put such values into their proper perspective, comparison with others might help:-

The price of gas had just risen by 1½d per therm, adding 2½d to the average weekly household bill. Electricity increased from 4½d to 8d a therm; coal went up to £3-7s-10d a ton. A local clothing manufacturer was paying male workers up to £8 a week with bonuses and female machinists up to £5, which they in their own words described as 'good money'.

A newspaper carried advertisements, for a male clerk shorthand typist at from £150 to £425 per annum, or a female clerk shorthand typist at from £120 to £340 per annum (no sexual equality then!) A school groundsman was offered £5-12s-0d a week and a farm foreman could look forward to £6-13s-0d a week.

A bottle of whisky was £1-15s-0d and brandy £1-12s-0d, and even at these prices they were still out of reach of the ordinary pocket. A price list dated 1887 from Lloyd and Yorath's Brewery showed these same two items at 3/6d and 5/- respectively.

A start was made on the massive St Julians Estate, which would eventually house 4,000 persons in 960 houses, flats and old persons bungalows at a total cost of £1,824,000. Construction was by a new method called 'No fines' whereby the walls were moulded in a special concrete mix, meaning that 11 semi-skilled men could complete a pair of houses in 24 hours instead of the 2½ weeks usually taken by two bricklayers working with traditional materials.

On April 12th, the 8 acres of Grove Park Pillmawr Malpas, were opened as a public park. The town now had 24 public open spaces ranging from the large and colourful, through those which were exclusively laid out for sport, down to the small secluded areas intended as havens of peace and quiet. Nevertheless the total area was still deficient of the 2 acres per 1,000 head of population that was recommended by the Ministry of Town and Country Planning.

A rededication service on 25th September reopened St Johns Church Maindee just two years ten months and three weeks after the disastrous fire that had all but caused its extinction. Originally completed in 1865 for under £2,000, restoration costs were over £50,000, a considerable portion of which was raised by public subscription. A new organ was not included in this but fortune was on hand to provide a simple and inexpensive solution.

Pardoeham, a large house in Fields Park Road, had been the home of Mr B Pardoe-Thomas, a Newport shipowner and music lover. Here was one of the very few private houses in Great Britain to have its own, full-sized pipe organ, and it was offered to St Johns at a bargain price. By 1957 it had been dismantled, given renovation in Plymouth and reassembled in the sanctity of its new home.

A one per cent sample was taken of figures derived from the 1951 National Census. Although small, such an enumeration was considered accurate enough to represent the overall picture of Newport in the mid 20th century. A cross section of the results showed that this was now a town of 31,100 households of which 9,600 did not possess exclusive lavatories, 16,700 were without exclusive baths and 8,700 without exclusive use of stoves and sinks.

In the few weeks leading up to Christmas the atmosphere in the neighbourhood of Mitchell and Butlers Brewery Alma Street, took on a distinct change as the rich, mixed odours of beer and Christmas puddings permeated the air. For over 50 years the same ritual had been enacted at Mitchell and Butlers and their predecessor, Thatchers Brewery; long queues of housewives formed outside carrying uncooked Christmas puddings to be expertly steamed by the brewery process. It took ten hours at 8lbs pressure to bring a pudding to full excellence, but at a cost of 6d each, it saved the housewife five times the amount she would have incurred if the operation had been carried out at her own hearth. When the brewery closed down some years later, the queues no longer formed and another town tradition vanished forever.

- 0 -

December 26th 1952 was the date of the passing of another of Newport's regrettably few offspring who in their lifetimes managed to achieve international reputations.

David Llewellyn Harding was born in 1867 at the Church House Inn St Brides - not strictly speaking in Newport but close enough to the western borough boundary to make no matter. When he left the village school he was apprenticed to Robert Little, a Newport draper, and although his performance in that trade must have been adequate it was for his ability at recitation that he became better known. Later he went to work in Cardiff, still in the drapery business, but he was finding better use for his vocal prowess in a dramatic club where he learned enough of basic stage-craft to encourage him, at the age of 23, to become a professional actor with the Bristol Theatre Royal Company. This was in 1890.

Lyn Harding as he chose to become known, went from strength to strength until he was featuring regularly in the famous theatres of the West End. No role was beyond him but he loved to play the better known unsavoury characters and villains to which his bulky physique and deep, resonant delivery ideally lent themselves; his Bill Sykes in Oliver Twist was renowned.

He became a celebrity on both sides of the Atlantic but he never forgot his roots and often took time off from the illustrious circles in which he moved, to return to St Brides where he would give parties for the village children and distribute presents to the poor and elderly.

Lyn Harding's last stage appearance was in 1937.

1953

On 13th January, the Parks and Cemeteries Committee recommended that the public parks and playing fields should be opened on Sundays for games and athletics. The motion was carried by 25 votes to 10 and a spokesman for the losing contingent, with his feet still planted firmly in the age and ethics of Queen Victoria, said: 'It is no wonder that we are all going to hell!'

One had only to give cursory inspection to photographs that appeared in the press at local election times to gain the impression that for the most part the town was in the not overly deft hands of rather elderly ladies and gentlemen whose persuasions must have been sculpted by the spartan upbringing of their childhoods. Most of them were never to change but it is to the eternal credit of the rest that they came round to realising that they now represented a better educated, broader-minded, more widely travelled electorate than at any time in history.

It seemed as if the town had only just found the opportunity to catch its breath after the revels of the Festival of Britain when the time came to start all over again!

It would have been easy to understand if the approach had been a little less warm to another exhausting week of carefree carousal but the opposite was the case, not because of Newport's historic love of dressing-up but this time for a reason uniquely different from any that had gone before. This was after all the year of the crowning of a popular young princess as Queen in her own right - something that had not happened for 116 years and only six times in all out of over sixty monarchs stretching back a thousand years. Huge respect for Princess Elizabeth's father as a brave wartime king, and sympathy over his tragic death which had transferred such enormous responsibility to her young shoulders, demanded the greatest show of loyalty ever seen.

Coronation Day was Tuesday June 2nd but curiously it seemed as if the town was treating it with much less urgency than had been the habit on similar occasions in days gone by. As the streets became aired they took on the semblance of ordinary shopping or working days and, but for colour and decoration, gave no hint of anything out of the ordinary. Midday opening of the public houses and hotels passed with landlords reporting increased business but not unduly so. These were the places noted as barometers of public mood, where revelry always obtained its first nudge, but on this occasion the signs were taking longer to manifest themselves. It was like the taking of a deep breath before the plunge! The answer was in the one great change that had recently overtaken the human race and its name was television!

Television sets were not then the general household item that they were later to become. Reasonable reception of broadcasts had only recently been made possible by the opening of the BBC transmitter at Wenvoe near Cardiff. The early sets were expensive, a 9 inch screen costing £65 to £70 and an 11 inch screen £90 upwards. The cathode-ray tubes were most unreliable and often 'blew' just after the expiry of their two year guarantees - tube insurance was a thriving business in those days! Nevertheless, a substantial number was scattered throughout the town but those who did not possess one had to find one to watch, if not in the homes of friends or relatives, then in the windows of radio and television shops. Several of Newport's dealers loaned sets to village halls in order that rural communities should not miss the historic occasion - and no doubt to be so impressed as to encourage future purchases!

The attraction was immense. This was the first crowning of a non-consort queen for over a century and she a much admired princess who had served her country in wartime as an army driver/mechanic; here was the chance, never before offered, to see her coronation on the day, as it happened. No wonder the streets were quiet for a while!

Everywhere was bright with colour. The versatile improvisation of amateurs combined with the flair and finance of the professionals in a bid to outdo any of the town's previous displays of swank and ostentation. There were however still those older heads who steadfastly maintained that, as good as it was, it had not reached the standard of the 1937 Coronation of King George VI.

The red, white and blue, boxed pedestals reappeared on the lamp standards, the streets were bedecked with flags, streamers, hundreds of flower baskets and tens of thousands of blooms, real and artificial. High winds on several nights brought down some of the best displays but the following mornings found many willing hands to put them back in place.

307

Proceedings commenced at the Civic Centre with a 21 gun salute by 283 Field Regiment, Royal Artillery, Territorial Army. Local residents were asked to leave their windows open in order to avoid possible blast damage.

All the old trappings were there - searchlights on the Transporter Bridge, floodlights on the Castle, Market and Civic Centre, and thousands of multi-coloured lamps in festoons or jewelled crown set-pieces. The great bonfires again blazed on Twm Barllwm, Christchurch and Lawrence Hill to be answered by similar flickerings on the other side of the Bristol Channel.

Shaftesbury Park was host to a huge fair and Bertram Mills Circus; Kimberley Park ran a series of children's parties and variety shows. Large crowds gathered on both banks of the River Usk to be entertained by Newport Sailing Club in a colourful regatta.

One of the biggest crowd-pullers of the week was a game of soccer at the Athletic Grounds between Newport County and Newport Rugby Club, playing the first half with a rugby ball and the second half with the round, association ball. The soccer experts showed surprising control over the unpredictable, oval 'pill' and, by the same token, some of the rugby players looked good enough to play regularly for the County! The result did not matter and the thousands of spectators thoroughly enjoyed themselves.

The week ended with one of the most ambitious carnivals that had ever graced the town's streets, rivalling for colour and spectacle anything that pre-war saturnalia had ever offered. Crowds watching it stretched for miles and in many places stood six deep.

By midnight on Saturday June 6th, the town was already beginning to sink into the kind of torpor not wholly unexpected after the expenditure of so much energy.

There was a most unwelcome aftermath and the reckoning came with receipt of returns that showed a heavy loss to the town of £16,000. Some irrecoverable expense had been anticipated but this sum was more than twice as much! There had been estimates of considerable profits on some of the celebratory endeavours but the sad fact was that nearly every organised event had made a loss; the only places where the tills had jingled loudest were in the private sectors of fairground, circus, public houses and the football match.

An accusatory but totally helpless Council debated the matter and agreed that all the outdoor events had been effected by cold weather, but inept planning and over-optimism on the part of the organisers were chiefly to blame. Recriminations had to be cut short however because the town had only six weeks in which to prepare itself for the new queen, in person, on her first state visit to Wales.

During the night of 15th/16th July, large numbers of men, women and children slept in the streets to ensure the best viewing positions, and balconies and windows overlooking the royal route were fully booked. By the time that the Queen and her husband Prince Philip arrived at High Street Station in bright sunshine, there were 50,000 people waiting.

At the Civic Centre, Queen Elizabeth signed the visitors book that she had previously signed as an eleven year old princess 16 years earlier to the day.

The journey continued up the Western Valley but before the royal party finally entered Glamorgan by way of Bedwas, they were cheered on their way by 10,000 Monmouthshire schoolchildren gathered at Lower Machen.

During this same month, assent was given to a Newport Corporation Act to add a further 309 acres to the borough. This was a much smaller area than had originally been requested, and it was to be used to add 3,000 houses to the developing estates of Bishpool and Alway; 73 acres were allocated from Caerleon and 236 acres from Llanwern; from 1st April 1955, the borough was to comprise 8,182 acres.

If the term 'historic' can be expanded to cover any first time happening, no matter how insignificant, then this was the year of such an occasion. In Commercial Road, a shop opened where customers could wash their own laundry in automatic machines for a small fee. Although the introduction of this revolutionary idea had already started in larger towns and cities, its reception was an unknown factor in Newport where only the better-off owned washing machines, and where kitchen boiler, dolly and rubbing board still reigned supreme. A new word entered the British vocabulary to describe this novelty, and two years later the owner was satisfied enough to open a second 'laundrette' at 167 Chepstow Road whilst looking for a third.

~ 0 ~

Ship repairing and ship breaking were still thriving industries along the banks of the River Usk but the building of new vessels had all but died out by the end of the 19th century leaving sadly wasted areas, rich in the natural features required for putting new keels to water. Many were the vessels making their maiden voyagers from the town but all were built elsewhere. Forces were now at work to remedy this situation.

A group of go-ahead industrialists with shipping interests, mainly from Cardiff and Newport, held meetings to arouse enthusiasm and raise finance aimed at bringing back ship-building, together with its associated boost to employment and a measure of Newport's former maritime glory. When all the problems were overcome, the Atlantic Ship-building Company was born.

A yard containing a new, 300 feet long dry dock was provided on the great river bend convenient to the South Dock entrance and on November 17th 1953 the first phase of Newport's rediscovered ship-building industry began. It was fervently hoped to be capable of holding its own with the old established yards, and of meeting the stiff competition from continental shipyards.

A contract was obtained to supply a 3,000 ton wood-pulp and paper carrier for the Great Lakes of Canada, with the prospect of others to follow. On this day in November, the first steel plates were laid on the stocks of the dry dock.

This vessel was to be unique in several ways. The above-deck work was going to be of all aluminium construction, making for greater weight-saving and bigger load-carrying in canals and shallow waterways where traditional ships often cleared the bottom by only four inches; the bridge superstructure was situated right on the bow. Construction materials were obtained almost entirely from local resources: the aluminium from the Northern Aluminium Company of Rogerstone, machine tools from John Cashmore Ltd of Newport and electrical installations by Brand Electrical and Engineering Co Ltd of Newport.

On August 4th 1954, this ship was christened 'Baie Comeau' (a township on the St Lawrence River) and floated round to the South Dock for fitting out. Work on a sister ship was well under way at this time and on April 28th 1955 the 'Manicougan' was also floated out of the Atlantic dry dock. A third similar ship, the 'Lachinedoc' was immediately laid down. In the meantime it was expected that the yard would supply much of the floating and engineering equipment for the construction of the largest artificial harbour in West Africa, at Tema on the Gold Coast.

It was an auspicious start to a very ambitious enterprise and within a further two years orders were to be received from Cuba for £2,250,000 (4 ships) and the USA for £4,500,000 (3 ships). There was even talk of building 130,000 ton, international class, bulk oil tankers within a few years.

Christmas 1954:-

Chickens	4/ to 4/6d	a lb
Turkeys	5/9d to 6/6d	a lb
Ducks and Geese	4/- to 6/6	a lb
Men's;		
two piece suits	£4-18s-9d	
Sports jackets	£2-8s-9d	
Overcoats	£3-8s-9d	
Ladies' suits	£6-6s-9d	
Men's leather brogue shoes	£2-9s-9d	a pair
Ladies' buckskin wedge shoes	£1-4s-9d	a pair
Children's leather sandals	7/11d to 14/6d	a pair

1955

This was the 80th anniversary of Newport Rugby Club and it was fittingly chosen for the bestowal of honours that any other club might have taken years to gather.

Famous old players, Tommy Vile and Joe Rust were made members of the Order of the British Empire. Jack Hancock was capped for England whilst Trevor Brewer, Bryn Meredith, Garfield Owen and Ken Jones were selected for Wales - the latter becoming the holder of the greatest number of Welsh caps of all time!

In March, the first whisperings were heard of a huge, new steel strip mill, possibly to be built on the moors. A site on the Wentloog Level between Peterstone and St Brides was rumoured.

On Good Friday, Trinity Church Christchurch, restored in glorious style after the disastrous fire 5½ years earlier, was rededicated in a service conducted by the Bishop of Monmouth.

At 1.30 am on the morning of 24th July, St John the Baptist Church Risca Road, was seen to be burning fiercely. By 4.39 am the Fire Brigade was damping down a smouldering ruin. Bad as it was, it might have been worse but for the actions of a group of young men who were returning from a late night dance and who, in their best suits and pristine white shirts, courageously dashed in and out of the blazing building to rescue a large number of valuable vestments and church records.

Once again deliberate fire raising could not be proved but the evidence only just fell short of conclusiveness. Apparently, in each of the town's churches, their fires had started in the organ chamber, spreading upwards to the roof. The investigating authorities commented: 'The means and/or cause of ignition were not present in the church beforehand but was introduced either accidentally or deliberately. Three disastrous fires in churches in six years is inexplicable and above the average for the country as a whole'.

A simple telephone call made on 13th October proved in itself to be a part of the town's historic development. Newport's automatic telephone exchange had just been equipped with the facility of TIM, the speaking clock. At 3.40 pm precisely, the Lady Mayor, Mrs Letitia Bell, raised her telephone and became the first citizen of the town to enquire the time of day.

Guy Fawkes Night loomed nigh. It was now a far cry from Victorian squib nights with their violence and flaming tar barrels but, even if unaccompanied by the original mayhem, some menace was still inherent. The Chief Constable, Mr F H Smeed, announced a clamping down on the indiscriminate throwing of 'jumping jacks, bombers and the like' by which children and adolescents were wont to terrorise their elders. Incidents in crowded cinemas were particularly thoughtless.

Since 1946, the grounds of Malpas Park (the old Malpas Court Estate) had not presented a very pretty Picture. Ugly, rusting Nissan huts which had housed a succession of occupiers - American troops and Italian prisoners of war - were subsequently used for homeless families. By 1955, just eight huts remained standing on an acre of bare earth that turned to quagmire in bad weather. Each hut was divided down the centre by a three inch thick, brick wall and accommodated two families without any cooking, washing or sanitary facilities; these, such as they were, were contained in one other hut situated adjacent to the main Malpas Road. In such primitive conditions lived thirty adults and sixty children and when dysentery, gastro-enteritis and bronchitis began to threaten, urgent moves were made to end this scandal.

P & A Campbell's passenger steamers were still running their popular trips from Rodney Parade, but although the Company's position was known to be precarious, few people realised that this was to be its last year of operation. It seemed unthinkable to most that a summer would ever pass without the familiar white funnels being seen near the River Usk bridge!

Probably the most well known of these vessels was the smallest. The paddle steamer 'Ravenswood' had made its maiden voyage from Bristol to Chepstow on June 3rd 1891. She had been severely damaged in 1941 by incendiary bombs but, restored after the war, she continued her 64 year career plying between the Bristol Channel ports. It was perhaps most fitting that the Usk was the last river she was to navigate when, on 27th October 1955, she made her way to the ship-breaking yard of John Cashmore, and hundreds turned out to catch a last glimpse of an old friend.

The severest road congestion ever experienced now topped the list of Newport's most urgent problems. Difficulties with traffic circulation had been common in the single-bridged town for many years. There was now as large an urban area on the east of the river as on the west and artificially created situations often caused big build-ups. The most well known of previous bridge inspired blockages was that which had followed Newport County's promotion victory in 1939, but the one on Friday December 30th 1955 dwarfed anything that had gone before.

Bearing in mind that these were the days before extended bank holidays and flexible working hours, it followed that everyone went to their places of occupation at approximately the same time. Furthermore, as this was one of the busiest shopping days of the year, the bulk of the non working population would also be in the town centre at some time of the day, and eventually this great mass of humanity would all turn homeward at roughly the same time!

In the words of the Chief Constable: '1955 was traffic jam year'. The number of licensed vehicles had increased by 12% in the previous twelve months and had doubled since the war. Traffic accidents were the highest on record, caused more by frustration than speed. Thus, on the last full working day of the year, conditions were indeed ideal to create a situation in which the town stood still for hours and queues of buses, cars, vans and lorries stretched for miles along every main road converging on the bridge.

Chaos ruled at the Old Green and in Clarence Place. Hundreds of idling exhausts caused poisonous smog to hang in the cold night air, and the police found themselves in the midst of their worst nightmare.

Such conditions had been envisaged 26 years earlier and many times since. In 1930, only four years after the existing bridge was newly opened, Alderman John Moxon was saying: 'We all recognise that another new bridge is the best solution to Newport's through traffic problem'. At that time, 7,500 motor vehicles and tramcars crossed the river each day; now the figure was 2,000 vehicles an hour!

Many were the appeals made over the years to successive governments for the funding of a second River Usk bridge but they all fell on deaf ears. The latest bitter experience when the town centre had been forced to grind to a halt was followed soon afterwards by another when the police had to close the bridge to all traffic for several hours in order to get a 180 ton turbine across to East Usk Power Station. South Wales was effectually closed!

The Ministry of Transport was finally prompted to say that the need was agreed, but it was a question of priority and the Divisional Road Engineer was instructed to undertake a survey of the town's traffic problem. The Minister himself, in Newport for a by-election, was taken to see the bridge's chronic congestion - at 6.30 pm when it had all but cleared!

1956

As the year opened, a scan of the local newspapers gave some indication of the economic climate.

Ford Consul £781, Zephyr Zodiac £968
One year old motor-cycles of 200 to 350 cc - £50 to £85
Loaf of bread 9d (just under 4 pence)
New Main Gas cooker £30-13s-0d
Super Autochange Bureau-type 'Radiogram' £37 guineas
(or £1-2s-0d down and 37 weeks to pay)
Servis washing machine £59-12s-3d,
Axminster rugs £1-6s-0d each,
Wilton carpet £1-7s-6d a yard,
Admission to Billy Smart's Circus for a 2½ hour show 2/6d (18p) to 10/6d (55p)
A 14 day holiday on the Italian Riviera £38-10s-0d
New, semi-detached, 3 bedroomed house (George Wimpey Ltd) £2,575 freehold

March 16th brought the first news of proceedings which were likely to have the most far-reaching effects on the Newport of the future. Mr H F Spencer, Managing Director of Richard Thomas and Baldwins Ltd. announced that his firm was investigating possible sites for a new, £200 million, integrated steel strip mill plant. One of the favoured sites was a flat section of moorland stretching for about five miles to the east of Llanwern with its western tip in the borough.

Test bore-holes, 100 feet deep, drilled in May 1956, gave optimistic results and revealed fairly stable soil at the 40 feet level. It was still early days but hopes ran high enough for estimates to be made of the mammoth work's daily need for water - 14 to 16 million gallons from the River Usk between Llantrissent and Newbridge, and 4 to 6 million gallons from the Severn Tunnel Pumping Station.

The demands on Newport's water supply were phenomenal in any case. Due mainly to the calls of heavy industry, usage averaged 100 gallons a day per head of the population, compared with 35 to 40 gallons per person in towns of similar size. Moreover, Cardiff was also negotiating for the extraction of several million gallons daily from the Usk to augment the new, 5,000 million gallon reservoir proposed for a square mile of the sleepy Sor Valley near Llandegveth.

1957

The very last vestige of the ancient Tredegar Estate was extinguished on 31st January with the sale at Sothebys of the family's fabulous collection of silver plate. Many beautiful and unique items went under the hammer, including the statue of Sir Briggs, the grand old war-horse ridden by Godfrey the 2nd Baron in the Charge of the Light Brigade at Balaclava. The sale realised a total of £18,648.

On 16th February, a 50 feet 8 inch tide rose to the top of the Alexandra Dock sea gate and almost spilled over! At Riverside, East Usk Road, it slowly covered the roadway and lapped at the doorsteps of the terrace of houses facing the river. This time, fortunately, there was no following wind and the flood was just kept at bay by the positioning of a providential supply of tightly-packed sandbags across doorways and the entrances to side-streets. In every passageway occupants stood armed with buckets and mops, watching for breaches in the defences. A boatman patrolled in case of extreme emergency. Officials and engineers of the Usk River Authority came to witness the threat and its messy aftermath,

It now looked as if something might finally be done to counter this age-old menace which left Riverside as practically the last area of the town to suffer in this way.

The passing of Campbell's passenger steamers from the scene left the landing stage at Rodney Parade a useless monument to the town's past recreational activities. First installed on its heavy timber piles in 1896, its upkeep was very costly and it now had no income to set against its expenses. The Corporation proposed to take over the buildings abutting the road as annexe classrooms for the Technical College in Clarence Place but the floating jetty found a new owner when it was sold to a Dutch company.

On June 5th, local tugs, Holman and Dunson, unceremoniously yanked the two 100 feet sections of the jetty and its 65 feet long metal foot-bridge into the river and down to the river-mouth. Here, the 280 ton Dutch tug, Noordzee, took over the tow for the five day voyage to Rotterdam where the jetty was intended to serve the same purpose as it had for the past 60 years. Hundreds of people lined Newport Bridge to witness the nostalgic operation but, remarkably, as little as 30 years afterwards few seem to remember the incident; but the proof remains to this day in the sawn off stumps of the old piles which still stand proud of the river at low tide. They are to be seen immediately in front of the building which never did become Technical College classrooms but instead was converted to an extension of the London Wharf builders merchants warehouse. This has now been demolished and allows anyone across the river in Dock Street an uninterrupted view straight down St Vincent Road into Corporation Road.

It was still fully expected that television would shortly prove to be a passing fancy and its novelty to wear off. It was also the widespread opinion that until this happened it would badly effect people's reading habits but in fact the opposite proved to be the case! The Public Library issued figures to show that, far from the demand falling off, 500,606 books had been borrowed - the first time in the history of the free library that the half million had been surpassed!

By October, both Newport Rugby and Newport County had installed floodlighting on their grounds. As far as the rugby club was concerned, it may have been the start of electrically illuminated evening matches but one game had already been played under artificial light at Rodney Parade 80 years earlier!

In the twilight of December 16th 1878, so the story goes, Newport faced Cardiff on a ground lit by erratic, hissing, acetylene gas flares. The game was played in conditions of intermittent brightness and dimness. Many times running shadows were tackled without having possession of the ball, and tries were scored by lone players at one end of the field when both teams were still mauling at the other!

In the twelve years that had passed since the end of the war, Newport had done wonders with the housing problem and yet the waiting list still stood at 4,000, with the conditions of a minimum of two years wait for couples with two children, four years for couples with one child and six years for childless couples. Since 1946, 4,000 houses had been built and 500 were still under contract; great new estates were in varying degrees of completion. The target populations were:-Gaer 4,327, Malpas 3,157, Brynglas 2,000, Alway and Ringland 12,687 and Bettws (to be started shortly) 11,000 or more.

The Alway and Ringland Estate was bigger than Chepstow and Monmouth put together and had all but exhausted the supply of housing land within the borough. For that reason the Corporation was forced to acquire 350 acres at Bettws in the Magor and St Mellons Rural District, much against the wishes of the rural authority which regarded the move as yet another in the constant threat of boundary extensions.

On November 6th, in a clear night sky, the Russian satellite, Sputnik II, was plainly visible to Newport observers as its third day in orbit took it like a tiny, fiery comet, over South Wales. This was a unique occasion because, gazing down from the capsule, was Laika the dog cosmonaut, and the first living creature to travel in space.

As if touched with a breath of old year puritanism, many dance hall managers frowned on the revolutionary, new and extremely energetic forms of dance which were becoming popular with the younger generation. These were often banned outright but a sign of capitulation came just before the end of the year when it was announced that jiving was to be permitted at two out of every seven dances held at St Julians School.

Four months later, when the new £30,000 Majestic Ballroom (ex-Tredegar Hall Cinema) opened, the management decided to keep an open mind about rock and roll!

1958

Advertised locally
The Majestic Ballroom
Afternoon tea dances 3/- (15p)
Gala balls 7.30 pm to midnight 6/- (30p)
5 dozen bedding plants 6/- (30p)
A family size, jam-filled Swiss roll 1/8d (8.3p)
A pint of Mitchell and Butlers Old Ale 2/2d (10.8p)
A flagon of best Burgundy 13/- (65p)

A packet of 10 Park Drive cigarettes 1/6d (7.5p)
A 12 volt car battery £5
A Vespa motor-cycle £164
A Massey-Ferguson tractor £501
A delightful, modernised, country bungalow. 3 bedrooms, all mod cons 1 acre of ground. £1,850.

A touch of unintended humour introduced the year. As so often in the past, it came during a council debate, this time on police recruitment, where the subject was the 5 feet 9 inch height requirement blamed for precluding keen, young men who were only just under this standard. In all seriousness one councillor suggested that as the height condition was

314

prescribed by the Home Office, one way around it would be to make the helmets of the Borough Force one inch taller!

Newport's leading role as the graveyard of some of the biggest ships that sailed the oceans was slowly being brought to an end but while it lasted it seemed determined to go with anything but a whimper.

During May, one of the world's best known luxury cruise liners, the 17,800 ton Reina del Pacifico, was berthed at a river wharf. She was not the largest passenger ship to end her days at the hands of Newport ship-breakers, but with her white hull and yellow funnel towering above the dockyard buildings, she was certainly the most elegant.

Built in 1931, the Reina spent most of her life cruising between Britain, South America and the Caribbean. Throughout the war she had served as a troopship and in that capacity must have carried to their various war zones many of those who watched her last journey. In more recent years however her record had not been too happy, plagued as she was by a succession of mishaps that almost suggested a jinx!

On her post-war luxury cruises she suffered many bouts of engine trouble, she ran aground, lost her propeller and, worst of all, in an engine room explosion 28 people had died!

Wet weather always seemed to accompany notable happenings in Newport's dock-lands and sure enough on June 2nd a steady drizzle settled over the crowds which gathered to watch the noble ship's final move into the Alexandra Dock.

Aware of the vessel's past liability to accident, the dock-workers and onlookers on the river banks held their breath as the great bulk was eased through the entrance gates but on this occasion its behaviour could not be faulted and it reached its berth without a hitch.

The laying of the foundation stone in June initiated the first phase of the building of the huge Hartridge School complex at Alway and Ringland. The area over which it was to spread was part of the ancient Pwll-pen lands and the farmhouse stood (and still stands) at the rear, on the slope that curved over to Llanwern Village. The school was originally designed to cater for a quarter of all Newport's schoolchildren!

At this time also it came to light that the town had become the source of a most unique export. Italy had not then reached the heights of fashion or classical design in clothing for which it was later to become so well known. For this reason its famous football teams could not find local suppliers of quality sports kit. It was left to Gilesports of Newport to equip Juventus with all their playing kit, boots and tracksuits!

Bordering on the northern side of the Capitol Car Park was the lower end of Friars Street leading into Kingsway. This was now no more than a little-used, cobbled lane noted only for the old, white-washed, stone building which had served for years as the town mortuary. The area was about to be reinstated as part of the central bus station when suddenly in the course of several surveys it was realised that standing here in this little backwater was the last of the town's old gas lamp standards, erected in 1870. This providential identification led to its rescue and removal to safety; the fact was also unearthed that it had originally illuminated the exterior of the 'Ship and Castle Inn', another long-forgotten Victorian tavern, built before 1845 and finally closed down in 1905.

Mid-summer brought a new surge of activity in the continuing saga of the second bridge over the River Usk, and it emerged that much of the delay in allowing a firm decision to be reached had been the result of an objection by the Harbour Commission. The consulting engineer was advising a clearance height of 55 feet above the river's ordinary level, but the Commission was demanding 75 feet. A second objection involved the exact site of the bridge but when both were withdrawn, a favourable forecast was expected from the Minister of Transport who had only recently given the long-awaited go-ahead for the building of the

Severn Bridge to commence within two years.

At this point a quite temporary but convenient deviation from the strict, chronological order of things takes us to 1960 when the South Wales Argus, in conjunction with the Monmouthshire Local History Council, sponsored a competition called 'This was his life', in which entrants were encouraged to write essays on their choices of outstanding, historic, local personalities. Editorial comment lamented that, in all the thousands submitted, not one singled out a worthy female. This, today, would hardly seem surprising in view of the competition's biased title but this appears to have gone unnoticed in the midst of the prevailing male chauvinism of the times!

This shortcoming can to some extent now be rectified by the introduction of Margaret, Baroness Rhondda who died in 1958 aged 75 in a London hospital. Strictly speaking it was not true to describe her as 'of the town' but she lived so long on its outskirts and became deeply enough involved in its affairs to make her worthy of adoption.

Her father, David Alfred Thomas, Welsh colliery owner, industrialist and Liberal MP, was created 1st Baron Rhondda and because he had no male heirs, Lloyd George made special provision for the title to be inherited by a daughter.

In 1908, Margaret Haig Thomas married Sir Humphrey Mackworth. She was becoming a lady of great forcefulness and determination, traits that she soon harnessed to further the aims of the Women's' Suffrage Movement. In 1913, she was arrested in Newport and charged with 'placing a certain explosive substance in a pillar-box at Risca Road' thereby burning all the letters!

Appearing before the magistrates under the name of Mary Haig Mackworth, she admitted the charge and was fined £10 with £10 costs, and on refusing to pay was committed to Usk Jail for a month. She immediately went on hunger strike, after only four days of which she was released in a much weakened state having had the fine paid anonymously.

Two years later, during the Great War, she and her father were returning from a business trip in America on board the luxury liner 'Lusitania'. At 2.12 pm on May 7th 1915, a torpedo from a German submarine sent the vessel to the bottom with the loss of over 1,400 crew and passengers. Lord Rhondda and his daughter survived, although both were in poor condition after spending several hours in the water.

In 1918, Baron Rhondda was elevated to the rank of viscount and, sadly, died only two weeks later. Once again, letters patent awarded the viscountcy to his daughter in default of male heirs.

Having acted as her father's personal secretary for years, she had become an astute business woman. In 1920, she founded the magazine 'Time and Tide' and remained its managing editor for 38 years. At the peak of her career she was a director of 40 companies.

In 1943, Lady Rhondda offered Llanwern House to the National Trust (she had other homes in London and at Shere, near Guildford) but it was refused. The large house was costly and difficult to maintain so gradually became more run-down and decayed. Eventually, years later, the grand old but not historic mansion was demolished with explosives as an exercise for the Territorial Royal Engineers.

After her death, the ashes of Margaret, Baroness Rhondda, were interred in the family vault at Llanwern Church on 29th July 1958.

The rest of the year passed with a selection of events that on the face of it were apparently without historical significance but hopefully this might be an opinion with which future generations might beg to differ.

At Somerton Park, three greyhounds dead heated for first place in a photo finish. The crowds were incredulous and were only convinced when the photograph was displayed. It was a chance in a million and the first time it had happened in the 16,000 races which had taken place in ten years at Newport and Cardiff.

Newport introduced its mobile library service in September. This was the first of any borough in Wales, and the solitary pioneering van carried 2,500 volumes.

A new, £640,000 College of Technology opened at Alltyryn. The old premises at Clarence Place continued to be used as overflow but without advanced engineering and science classes.

October found trade in the docks at its lowest ebb for years. Exports of iron, steel and coal were well down and the only redeeming features were a few cargoes of cars for foreign markets, and a large upturn in the import of iron ore. The largest ore carriers ever seen in a British port were putting ashore individual cargoes of from 17,000 to 23,000 tons intended for the Ebbw Vale Steelworks. During the year, over 880,000 tons came through the Alexandra Dock.

Furthermore, the worsening recession in ship repairing caused Mountstuart Drydock Ltd to close their two Eastern Drydocks after being in business since 1880 and 1905 respectively.

On the 30th of the month came the long-awaited (and oft despaired of) announcement by the Ministry of Transport which put the seal of approval on the second river bridge. It was however included in a much larger package costing £5,500,000 wherein the new by-pass was also specified.

It was a most ambitious plan. New roads of motorway standard were to start from the Usk Road just north of Caerleon, and from Langstone, meeting at Alway and heading via Liswerry and Somerton, through Maindee to the new bridge crossing to George Street. Breaking new ground to the south of the old Cardiff Road it was to end at Forge Lane Bassaleg. For most of the route through the built-up areas the new road was to be carried on fly-overs but for a short distance through Maindee it was to be tunnelled!

An estimated 460 properties of all descriptions would need to be demolished. Half the town rejoiced at these proposals and half near-panicked for obvious reasons but they need not have worried for, as everyone knows, this particular remedy for the town's traffic problems never saw the light of day!

Hardly had the full purport of the ambitious plan been absorbed than ,on November 18th, the Prime Minister, Harold Macmillan, put an end to two years of anxious speculation on the placing of Richard Thomas & Baldwin's giant steelworks. It was to be built on a rectangle of agricultural land, half a mile wide and three miles long, stretching from Llanwern towards Magor, south of and immediately abutting the main London to South Wales railway line. Its initial capability was to be the production of 500,000 tons of sheet steel and tin-plate, rising within a few years to 1,000,000 tons per annum. Construction was expected to commence in the latter half of 1959.

The year ended as it had begun, with levity from the Council Chamber. The motion was that all aldermen and councillors should dress in caps and gowns when carrying out their official duties. The proposer was concerned about the too-informal appearance of members when they gathered in a mélange of variously shaded lounge suits, sports jackets and the occasional top hat and tails!

Probably none of these ladies and gentlemen realised that that they were debating the reinstatement of one of the town's ancient ordinances - indeed it had never been a characteristic of Newport's ruling hierarchy to make a point of learning much about their legislative heritage - but this was not a popular move and over half the council made it clear that even if 'uniforms' were ordered, they would not wear them! The motion was lost by 28 votes to 12 - a truly, earth-shaking debate of major significance to community affairs!

Everyone it seems was enthusing about the new steelworks and forecasting in glowing terms that the town now stood on the threshold of an era of exceptionally good fortune.

Hardly a guest speaker at any function missed a chance to describe the town's rosy future and the following expressions are only a few of those actually reported:-

'The promised land.'
'The most prosperous outlook of any town in Britain.'
'Most promising potential.'
'A very fine future in store.'
'The future is assured.'
and
'The beginning of a great boom.'

Mr H F Spencer, who gave his name to the steelworks, added his weight to every other statement when, at St Julians Boys School Speech day, he prophesied 'an era of fabulous wealth for Newport and Monmouthshire.'

Well over a quarter of a century later, Newport was still awaiting the arrival of this Utopian wonderland!

By June, the Monmouthshire County Council as local planning authority, had received the formal outline planning application for the new steelworks with details much more precise. The proposed site was stated as ' 2,580 acres south of the Western Region railway line, between the Newport Borough boundary near Hartridge Farm and the Bishton—Redwick Road, in the parishes of Llanwern, Bishton, Nash, Whitson, Goldcliff and Redwick - all in the area administered by the Magor and St Mellons Rural District Council.'

The Whitsun Bank Holiday saw a scene that had been re-enacted many times before at Newport Station, but which was now just another dying feature in the pattern of life. The promise of fine weather caused long queues to form at the booking office, extending out into and filling Station Approach as hundreds of people aimed for a short respite at Barry and Porthcawl.

In August, the long period of indecision was ended when the council agreed on Newport's future by-pass. The through-way scheme of Sir Owen Williams was rejected by 43 votes to 2 in favour of the Ministry of Transport's by-pass to the north of the town centre with its motorway river bridge and tunnels under Brynglas. The recommendation was passed to the Ministry accompanied by the strongest of appeals for the second river bridge which was already agreed in principle.

A spokesman for the council housing department was of the opinion that the cost of building the many houses required for the steelworks' employees would force up the average weekly rent of a council house to an all-time high of £2-10s over the next five years!

Weather wise, 1959 was an exceptional year for its lack of rain. The drought lasted for eight months causing huge problems in supply and usage of water. When the heavens finally opened, the Talybont Reservoir had been reduced from three miles to two miles long.

Chapter Seventeen

The 1960s

The building of Spencer Works
Chaos in the town
New bridges
A great frost

The subject of Newport's chronic traffic congestion has recurred so often as to have become almost boring, and despite having apparently arrived at a point where it could not by any stretch of the imagination get worse, it defied all the forecasts and did just that!

As the normal peak hours of confusion were joined by the vehicles involved in the construction of the steelworks, only those who lived and worked in the Newport of 1960 are capable of truly appreciating the outright chaos that followed. To anyone else, mere words are totally inadequate to describe the paralysis that gripped the town!

Preliminary work on the huge industrial site was a massive operation due to the necessity of preparing the low-lying moorland for the immense weight and accompanying vibration that would spread beneath the largest steelworks in Europe. Over 8,500 reinforced concrete piles had to be driven deeply to the stable sub-strata; four million tons of rock and shale substances had to be tamped down over the piles!

Much that was necessary to accomplish this task had to be brought through Newport by way of the strangulating neck which the solitary bridge now represented. The giant derricks and heavy piling equipment were the first to arrive and their great lengths alone caused wholesale disruption when the police stopped all other traffic for up to an hour at a time for these behemoths to negotiate projections and the tighter curves - often by direction the wrong way along one-way streets!

When it put in its first appearance in January, the ballast arrived with a vengeance. Up to 200 tipper lorries each made three to four journeys a day from quarries situated in all directions from Newport up to a 40 mile radius. This had the immediate, horrific effect of causing 1,000 to 1,200 additional vehicles to cross the bridge every day! Very soon afterwards, the number of shale-carriers was increased to 300 working in 24 hour shifts that caused sleepless nights for many Newport citizens. Incredibly, worse was to come from sources other than the steelworks!

The Uskmouth B Power Station was still not finished and some of the equipment being delivered there was enormous. On one occasion, Robert Wynn & Sons Ltd brought a lorry,. 136 feet long, down Malpas Road. It carried a transformer weighing 135 tons and proved too high to go under the Shaftesbury Street railway bridge so, impossible as it must sound to modern ears, it was diverted up Barrack Hill! Following the route of the old stage coaches, the great load finally reached St Woolos via Risca Road where, snail-like, it rounded the Cathedral by way of Clifton Road (the wrong way in those days) and finally, at the foot of Stow Hill, injected itself into the mayhem of High Street. Similar extra-long loads which <u>were</u> able to pass under the bridges, created havoc on the Old Green where they had to negotiate the right angle from Shaftesbury Street to the bridge. Throughout the journeys of all these vehicles, all other traffic had to pull over to allow passage.

One might have thought that supernatural forces were now at work to 'add weight' to Newport's bridge problem but, if such forces there were, they must have been hell-bent on extracting the ultimate sacrifice from the long-suffering town in order for the point to be made. What if anything else could have chosen one of those particular days to bring to the town the longest convoy of heavy army vehicles seen since the war?

Picture the scene. Dozens of crawling, khaki-coloured vehicles travelling westwards; hundreds of shale lorries travelling in all directions; perhaps a gigantic, traffic-stopping load of plant and machinery and, sandwiched between them, the normal heavy, local traffic carrying the simmering natives about their business!

The jams were indescribable, extending up to three miles from the town centre. One Red & White bus driver must have been congratulating himself on getting his passengers from Caldicot to Maindee Square in good time. He then took over an hour for the last mile to the Dock Street omnibus station!

The overwhelming evidence indicated that saturation point had been reached but astoundingly this was not so. By February, 1,400 lorries a day were arriving at the works site and not long after that the figure was over 1,900! On the site, Sir Robert McAlpine now had over 1,000 men employed in construction.

As a knock-on effect of the near impasse situation in the centre, events took a serious turn in the suburbs as desperate drivers sought to find ways around the trouble spots. They were taking shortcuts through side streets never intended for heavy vehicles, mounting pavements, damaging parked cars and endangering the lives of the children whose playgrounds they were invading.

Property suffered vibration damage and eventually residents who could not obtain satisfaction from the hard pressed police, took the law into their own hands by putting up barricades and engaging in ugly confrontations with the guilty drivers.

In February, road accidents in the town increased by 67.7% and personal injuries by 140.9% over the same month a year earlier.

Many extremely reputable contractors were engaged in this haulage marathon but there was so much work to go round that inevitably small operators - even single vehicle owners - vied with each other for slices of the lucrative cake. Among the latter group were those who had invested in small numbers of lorries, snapped up cheaply from bankrupt stocks; they were more concerned in wringing the maximum number of deliveries out of their elderly engines than in taking them off the road for short periods of servicing and repair. Accordingly a very serious question hung over roadworthiness and it was not surprising that brakes failed, engines stalled, exhausts fell off and axles snapped!

The standard of driving also came in for the keenest scrutiny. Never a day went by without a report of lorries overturned in ditches on the moors, teetering over bridge parapets, at the bottoms of embankments or buried in someone's front room or shop front! In the council chamber a remark was made that it would be unusual to find Glasslwch Crescent without a lorry in one of its front gardens! The junction of Charles Street and Commercial Street was a particular black spot for brake failures and anticipation of traffic lights; a young man was eventually killed here. Crashes with other vehicles occurred all over the county. The courts were kept busy with charges of overloading, speeding and dangerous overtaking.

The manager of a local dairy told the Chief Constable that his trainee drivers were leaving as soon as they passed their driving tests to become shale-lorry drivers - days after mastering the controls of a 12 mph milk float, they could be behind the steering wheels of monsters carrying loads of 10 tons or more!

Many cases were cited of drivers who, when challenged over some infringement, could not produce valid driving licence or insurance documents; some were not too proficient in the English language! On several occasions tired drivers accidentally tipped their loads while day-dreaming in traffic jams and deposited mountainous piles of rocks on the public highway. This happened in High Street near the Post Office, in Clarence Place alongside the Cenotaph and outside Eveswell School! A lane closure of several hours was the last thing that was needed in these conditions!

This fatigue was an understandable consequence of the mad race by each driver to complete the maximum four round trips every 24 hours in order to earn the maximum commission for tonnage delivered.

Everyone complained, everyone sympathised with the complainants, and everyone causing the complaints, from government ministers down to the humble tipper drivers, apologised - but always with the reservation that 'if Newport wants the benefits in the future, it must put up with the inconvenience of the present!'

By most people's calculation Newport paid dearly at the time. Compensation _was_ received from Richard Thomas & Baldwin for damage to the borough's roads and pavements but it was vastly under-estimated. It was impossible to reimburse in the hundreds of cases of minor damage to the interior walls of residences let alone the countless cracked window panes, broken mirrors and pictures shaken to the floor.

Nothing could compensate for the intangible for the losses sustained by business through the appalling delays in deliveries, and customers unwillingness to venture out so often into the deadlocked traffic: for the peace and quiet given up to months of noise and dust, and - most distressing of all - the loss of life which now included a police constable doing his duty and crushed by a lorry as he tried to restore order in the daily bedlam at the works entrance!

The other fatalities were among lorry drivers involved in crashes, pedestrians in the heavy traffic and workmen on the site in construction accidents.

By July 1960, the Chief Constable of Monmouthshire, Mr Neil Galbraith, was able to give these accident figures:

-Accidents involving shale lorries.

	Incidents	Injured	Killed
January	13	5	
February	24	5	
March	54	11	
April	50	11	1
May	52	20	1
June	55	14	3
	248	66	5

In the next two months, there were 151 more shale accidents with 5 fatalities, but December was the blackest month of all with 61 personal injuries and 2 fatalities. The surprising thing was however that these were county figures - there were no shale lorry incidents within the borough during December.

When the great ballast haulage was over the records showed that shale lorries were known to have been involved in 545 accidents in 391 of which the drivers were to blame; ten deaths resulted.

At about the same time as the releasing of this catalogue of disaster, the Chief Constable of Newport was addressing an audience of fuel lorry drivers and telling them: 'Newport is tops in road safety. The percentage rise in accidents is less than in the county as a whole'. This statement was true up to a point but only because the town traffic rarely exceeded walking pace! Even so, the month of July saw 8 serious and 38 slight injuries within the borough.

On August 27th, McAlpines announced that the night-time shale trips would end at midnight on Friday September 2nd. The run-down was about to commence!

By this time, the surface level of the huge site had been raised three feet by the importation of over five million tons of stone and shale. At the height of this enormous task, 5,000 lorry trips were being undertaken every day. At the finish, eight million tons of ballast, most of which had crossed Newport Bridge, had raised the surface by 5 to 6 feet.

As if in protest against the partial respite now being granted, fate chose the week preceding to introduce the widest load ever to be seen on the streets of the town. The lattice steel tower made by Tubewrights, Corporation Road, measured 20 feet wide, 58 feet long and weighed 36 tons. Laboriously it inched its way through the main streets en route for Cardiff Docks and the Persian Gulf. Two days later its twin followed!

The shale lorries had the last laugh however. On the very last day of round-the-clock haulage, a tipper dumped a full load - right in the middle of Newport Bridge!

Within the next week, the town witnessed its first multiple crash when *three* shalers piled into each other at Beechwood Park; two others, travelling in opposite directions, hit a car at Graig Park Malpas; another, losing its brakes in Mill Street ploughed into the Aluminium Working Man's Club!

A few months earlier, on May 24th, the retiring mayor, Councillor E Aston had said : 'We have had a wonderful year. A year in which we have everything to remember and nothing to forget', and the bewildered, 'shale-shocked' citizens of Newport, for reasons of their own, were almost heard to say ; 'Amen to that!'

A stronger case for a second bridge over the River Usk had never existed but still the Ministry of Transport dithered. The request by Newport Corporation to be allowed to proceed with forward planning of their own second crossing project remained unanswered.

The onslaught of the shale lorries gradually ground to a halt, being replaced by the more sedate, slow-moving carriers of building materials and items of plant and machinery which, nevertheless made up for their lack of numbers by the sheer bulk of their colossal loads. For almost 12 months contracts worth multi-millions of pounds had continued to be signed with firms both national and international. Now their products were arriving to add strange, new contours to the hitherto flat moorland. Before their erection and the laying of 40 miles of railway track and 25 miles of roads, it was necessary to pour 7,000 cubic yards of concrete into foundation trenches and above-ground shuttering.

In this phase, Newport was spared the further ordeal of an invasion of cement-mixer lorries, although it had to put up with a quota from Aberthaw. Magor Railway Station became the major cement distribution depot, its tall, metal silos making stark profiles against the background of a rural village. Every day several trains of 21 pressurised cement trucks arrived from Erith in Kent. By the end of 1961, 1,000 of these trains had made the 7 hour journey, and the scurrying mixer trucks had become a familiar sight in the country lanes of Redwick, Bishton and Llanwern.

As the most traumatic period in Newport's modern history began to moderate, the domination of the wilder events can not be allowed to smother the fact that there had been life outside the building of Spencer Steelworks!

~ O ~

Stretching almost the full length of Shaftesbury Street, from Mill Street to Barrack Hill, was a terrace of very small cottages built by the Great Western Railway for its employees in the last quarter of the 19th century. These dwellings did not feature in town directories prior to 1880. Known originally as Nos 1 to 12 Browns Buildings and 53 to 193 Marshes Road, the long row included three public houses the Station Inn, the Moulders Arms and the

Winning Horse. The years had long before ceased to treat these properties kindly; they were occupied by respectable families but their appearance of abject shabbiness was very tone-lowering for a town centre approach road.

In 1956, Shaftesbury Street was designated a clearance area; on March 11th 1958 the clearance order was made. By January 1959 all the properties were vacated and by the end of a further 12 months most were demolished.

Now a long drawn out controversy began. The narrow strip, 300 yards long, was left an unsightly mass of rubble by the contractors.

No one viewing this eye-sore could believe that there had ever been room for dwelling houses on the tiny space between the pavement and the railway retaining wall at the rear.

When at last the site was cleared, it was used for some years to carry rows of colourful, three-dimensional advertisement hoardings fronted by their own small, landscaped gardens. In 1963, the Architects Journal seriously suggested that a row of forest trees would have been more suitable for a road 'which was in effect the gateway to Wales!' Most people had for some time regarded it more in the nature of an unprepossessing 'back-door!'

Seven years later, this sorry saga still had one last gasp to give. By September 1970, the Winning Horse Inn had been standing derelict for nine years. One morning at the height of the rush hour, the building collapsed without warning, slightly injuring a lady passer-by and damaging several cars in the crawling traffic!

The Talbot Hotel ceased trading in April 1960. One of the best known public houses in the town, its closure ended nearly a century and a half of licensed premises on the site (starting with the Parrot Inn). It was proposed to demolish the building and merge the plot with that of the old Empire Theatre which had lain burnt-out and derelict in Charles Street for 18 years. Once clearance was effected work was to commence to raise a super-store for Woolworths on what was a prime town centre site. To illustrate the transience of modern buildings even this solid, ultra-modern structure was destined to last for only a little over twenty years before replacement by something of an entirely different design!

Trade in the docks had seen much better days. Shipments of coal were negligible and those of steel and tin-plate were plunging. More or less as an experiment some years before, a few cargoes of new cars had been exported through the Alexandra Dock. The potential exhibited then must have impressed the motor car industry enough to promise the port the handling of 50,000 cars for the South American market over the next five years. This prompted the planned construction of a giant car terminal capable of dealing with 150,000 cars a year by 1961.

Having carried out a survey in and around the town, the NSPCC announced that it had discovered too many cases of overcrowding -families of eight were apparently sharing a room with sanitary facilities several floors below. The town council vehemently denied this. It was not unknown however for unscrupulous landlords who owned larger, dilapidated premises, to fill them with camp beds and suspect gas rings in order to pack in as many as possible of the itinerant, Spencer Works construction workers. There were now 6,000 of them and the number would eventually reach 10,000. Most of them were happy to live as cheaply and as basically as they could, as long as they were not too far removed from the town centre public houses, hotels and drinking clubs which, while the situation lasted, reached undreamed-of heights in their takings!

On November 8th, the Council finally made a firm decision to promote a parliamentary bill to build a new River Usk bridge at George Street. The cost was estimated at £1½ million which, if a 75% grant was forthcoming from the Government, would cost the ratepayers a 3½d rate for 60 years. A revised design was now necessary. Trial borings in the riverbed had revealed subterranean water so in order not to position piers in the river itself, a double cantilever bridge supported by cables was deemed necessary.

In the first week of December, another important town centre store was destroyed by fire. A short sharp conflagration of no more than two hours blazed furiously through Boots the Chemist, ominously numbered 13 Commercial Street, with a return frontage to Corn Street. The ground floor shopping space was ruinously burned out and the top two floors badly damaged by heat, smoke and water.

1961

During February and March, 427 abnormal loads passed through the main streets of Newport bringing heavy items to both Spencer Works and the Uskmouth Power Station. Some were en route to other destinations such as Cardiff and Port Talbot. A few were in the super-enormous class and during one week alone in March everything stopped for 21 such giants.

In May, the Fairfield Engineering Co of Chepstow started to send 120 feet long girders to Warrington to form part of a motorway viaduct. Unable to negotiate Beaufort Square in Chepstow, they were forced to come 16 miles out of their way through Newport! There were 70 of these massive pieces of steel and they travelled only two at a time.

To emphasise this unimaginable situation further, 24 roll housings arrived for Spencer Works. Each weighed 125 tons and the separate lorry loads were so big that they had to take a most circuitous route from Sheffield, travelling 270 miles instead of the normal road distance of 180 miles!

Shades of 30 years into the future - the Royal Gwent Hospital had a waiting list of over 1,000 for general surgery. Hernia cases had to wait for three years and it took three months to see a skin specialist! This was in the palmier days of the National Health Service but in this case the reason for the poor showing was put down to the Royal Gwent being too small for the rapidly expanding community.

The first ripples started to cross the surface of Newport's development pond, driven by a light breeze that was soon to strengthen into a positive hurricane of change. Already the prime sites were being singled out. Davies Bros' builders yard in Clarence Place, the Olympia Cinema and the Town Hall sites were scheduled for multi-storeyed futures.

At the same time, the Ministry of Transport made it known that the new by-pass was to commence in building at the end of the year. Its seven mile length was to contain a bridge over the Usk, twin tunnels under Brynglas and five access points - more than in any other similar conurbation in Britain, excluding the bigger cities. This fact alone is indicative of the influential position that had always been held by Newport as the conjunction of all the important main roads emerging from England, inner Monmouthshire and West Wales.

This was, in essence, the same scheme as drawn up by Hugh Jones the Divisional Road Engineer, in 1944 and it would probably have come about a lot sooner but for the negative nit-picking indulged in by earlier councils.

A House of Commons committee approved the Newport Corporation Bill for the second river crossing. The originally planned 220 feet span clearance was considered to be insufficient for shipping so it had been amended to 450 feet, and this was to be achieved by means of a cable suspension bridge. A start on the construction was scheduled for February 1962 but demands by the Corporation for a six-lane carriageway instead of four-lane, put the starting date back to July 1st after the Ministry insisted on four lanes.

So far, 160 houses and shops had been listed for demolition on the Morris Street, Corporation Road end. The date for the opening of the finished bridge was put tentatively at October 1963.

The other significant happening of the year, likely to have a telling effect on the town's future, was the Ministry of Transport's placing of a contract worth £2 million for the foundations and substructure of the Severn Bridge. The cable anchorages alone required 160,000 tons of concrete, and the towers when finished would be 480 feet high. The main span of 3,240 feet was to be supplemented by two side spans of 1,000 making this the fifth longest bridge in the world and only 60 feet shorter than the Forth Bridge.

The Mayor, Councillor J H Jones, looked forward to: 'more impressive buildings in Clarence Place, which does not look too hot for a town like Newport'. Nobody listened - two unprepossessing, multi-storey office blocks eventually rose here but the rest of this erstwhile prosperous little enclave gradually submitted to town planning indifference and lapsed into shabby semi-retirement.

This was a good year for new car models. Local showrooms advertised the Morris Minor at £598, Ford Anglia £667, Triumph Herald £699, Vauxhall Victor £745, Hillman Minx £854 and Ford Consul £862.

Following the delivery through the docks of the first 14,500 tons of Canadian iron ore, Spencer Works commenced manufacturing operations on Friday, September 22nd.

Public houses had been closed on Sundays in Monmouthshire since 20th April 1915. At that time, heavy drinking among munition workers seemed likely to effect the war effort so a Defence of the Realm Act closed the tavern door on the Sabbath. This wartime emergency measure was confirmed by the Sunday Closing Act of 1921 and ever since, no public house had opened in Newport on a Sunday. When restrictions were relaxed and the rest of Britain turned enlightened eyes towards its own licensing regulations, the strict religious principles and traditions of Welsh communities managed to exert a powerful influence over the licensing authorities to keep the Principality dry on a Sunday. The only exceptions made were to any small group which chose to charge a moderate annual subscription and form a drinking club. Needless to say, this type of establishment was as thick on the ground in the so-called devout areas as in the less reverent, heavily urbanised areas.

Come 1962 the people of Wales were allowed a national referendum on the subject, resulting in a victory for the drinking fraternity. All the South Wales boroughs and counties voted for Sunday opening and all the North Wales boroughs and counties (except Flint) voted against. November 11th was the first Sunday for 47 years on which the public houses of Newport opened their doors for the sale of alcoholic refreshment.

1962

The second oldest place of worship in Newport closed down at the end of April. Mill Street Chapel, erected in the 17th century as a dissenter's chapel was sold to the Ministry of Works as part of the site of the new Post Office building.

The years had shown that it was common practice for each generation of the town's guides and mentors to decide what advances were needed, to produce ideas and to shelve them for financial reasons, or simply fail to keep the pot boiling by inconsistency, irresolution and all sorts of other vacillations. How often has it been illustrated that something decided as the best for the town would, when finally given the go-ahead, emerge in an entirely different set of clothes often more like something originally discarded as impracticable? Mark the vituperation there was over the siting of or even the need for a second bridge or an inner ring road; recall those who had been vociferous in pointing out the bad effect a motorway would have, running through built-up areas - an attitude that led to the costly production of a plan for a southern by-pass and its subsequent rejection!

The new town centre plan was no exception, being very different from that which had been hailed as such a brilliant concept only twelve years earlier.

The 1962 scheme envisaged new skyscraper office blocks, several multi-storey car-parks giving 6,300 spaces and an inner ring road to take the traffic excluded from the pedestrianised High Street and Commercial Street. Dock Street was to become a major shopping centre and in a grand new precinct south of Llanarth Street another 16,000 square feet of shopping space was to be created in an atmosphere of ample squares, promenades, floral displays, coloured paving, murals and fountains. A superb, new bus station with a long frontage to Kingsway (and a longer walk to the railway station) was part of the package. It all sounded idyllic but the finished object turned out to be a travesty!

Some well established landmarks had to go - small but well-loved inns, the Capitol Cinema (the old Temperance Hall), the Capitol Car Park, the Town Fire Station, the Library, Museum and Art Gallery and the Little Theatre. To walk through the entrance arcade of the Kingsway Shopping Centre from John Frost Square is to tread the same ground as that which once fronted old Union Street with modern, plate-glass shop windows replacing Jaynes Buildings on the left hand side. To continue the full length of the precinct as far as the Emlyn Walk exit into Commercial Street is akin to promenading the remainder of old Dock Street as far as Emlyn Street.

Inevitably, a vast amount of demolition was required but, sentiment apart, it was regarded as a justifiable sacrifice insofar as 48% of the existing town centre and 80% of the houses had been built before 1875. This time the planners were destined to have their way and the project, when completed, was to bear close approximation to that which had been intended. However the grandeur and opulence which had been implicit in the advance publicity were not to be translated into hard fact. Nobody for instance ever questioned the absence of the fountains!

The latter days of 1962 were probably among the most frantically progressive since the canal and railway went through.

First of all, the Minister of Transport awarded a grant of £1 million towards the estimated £1,342,991 cost of the second river bridge which had already left the drawing boards of Mott, May & Anderson, constructional engineers, which was the first of its kind in Britain and which was subject to a plan that had been modified eight times to satisfy the Royal Fine Arts Commission.

In June, Henry F Spencer lit the first furnace at Spencer Steelworks.

A blast on a whistle was given by Alderman F V Cornford, Chairman of the Parliamentary and Improvements Committee, on July 2nd. This gave the signal to commence work on the building of the new bridge. Now the bulldozers moved in to create the approach carriageways between Coverack Road and Morris Street, and the realignment and widening of Wharf Road and George Street.

On September 10th, the first stage began for introducing the M4 Motorway into the suburbs of Newport. Because it was the most complicated and would therefore take the most time, the first section to be tackled included the 450 feet long, split river bridge and the 1,200 feet long Crindau Tunnels under Brynglas. This contract was let to Sir Robert McAlpine & Sons Ltd for £1,506,115. The term 'town by-pass' was finally laid to rest.

Queen Elizabeth and Prince Philip arrived to perform the official opening ceremony at Spencer Steelworks. Friday October 26th was a very busy day for them as it also embraced visits to the Civic Centre, St Woolos Cathedral and the Alexandra Docks. True to past traditions, the populace turned out in their thousands to line the various routes taken by the Royal cavalcade.

From a stately, double-staircased dais under a grand marquee, the Queen put her seal of approval on the giant engineering wonder and made it known that she wished the Liswerry approach road to the works to be named Queens Way. Of course this never happened although a nearby industrial estate was graced by the title. As a borough street name it had to wait some years before being assigned - without Royal approval - to the inner ring road from the Old Green to Bridge Street.

1963

A little before New Year's Day, snow began to fall steadily and more heavily than for many years. Within a few days, deep drifts lay everywhere - up to cottage eaves in rural areas - and were causing widespread chaos. Worse was to follow for when the snow finally stopped falling, there began a great frost that was to persist relentlessly for several weeks so that no thaw took place and snow clearance became doubly difficult. All forms of transport were dislocated, railway points and signals froze, postal, coal, milk and other vital deliveries could not be made, and work on the docks ceased almost altogether.

As temperatures continued to plummet, the frost sank more deeply into the ground to reach pipes carrying domestic water supplies. Whole streets found that their taps had run dry. Stand-pipes were raised from the mains and it became a normal sight to see men, women and children standing shivering in long queues awaiting their turn to fill buckets bowls and saucepans etc.

Home insulation was then a matter of low priority and this winter may have done much to promote it. Amongst the council house stock 400 burst pipes were reported in two days and 22 plumbers were employed full time to answer calls. In addition, hundreds of yards of guttering were brought down by the weight of snow and frozen water unable to escape. Walls were prone to sudden collapse. At the final reckoning, it was found that one estate of 200 houses alone had 149 bursts.

In the town centre another hazard materialised. Along the eaves of tall buildings, giant icicles formed and then began to plunge, spear-like and without warning, on to the pavements beneath. To avert a serious accident the fire brigade was called out regularly to break off as many as possible of these icy shafts.

Towards mid February, when the country had been layered in old snow for seven weeks, the thaw finally set in and proceeded to cause almost as many hazards as the freeze had done! Material damage became horrendous as thousands more burst pipes and water tanks were revealed, floodings were commonplace from backed-up drains and water courses with their usual trickles turned into instant torrents; the thick, dirty slush forming on the roads caused many accidents.

Inevitably, comparisons were made with the awful winter of 1947, and the conclusion drawn was that the former had longer spells of heavy snow but nowhere near the killing frosts.

As if to emphasise the eccentricity of the weather, the winter ended with the people of Newport little knowing that Tuesday 11th June would be the hottest day for 45 years!

Insurance companies issued figures to show that the expected damage claims for Newport would be in the region of £50,000. This might sound trivial to readers some thirty years later, but to put the figures into their true context it is only necessary to use the brewing trade as a yardstick. In March 1963, all the local brewers announced price rises in their mild ales; Mitchells & Butlers, Ansells, H & G Simonds, Webbs (Aberbeeg), Rhymney Breweries and William Hancock, all put 1d on a pint, bringing the price up to 1/4d (approximately 7 new pence).

Preparations were now being made to add a clocktower to the Civic Centre; the cost was to be £126,900, and the Welsh Office had advised that the decision to proceed could only be a local one.

The original plans, disturbed by the war, made provision for such a tower but the passage of time had blurred awareness of the initial concept; there was a powerful lobby of opposition to a venture involving a clock positioned where few could tell time by it and costing a sum regarded as a complete waste of money! Strength of feeling was such that it caused a private survey to be undertaken and this proved to be so popular that the original supply of forms catering for 5,000 signatures, was soon used up; a further rush order had to be placed.

The astonishing result of the poll, gleaned from 8,754 signatures, was 40 to 1 against the clocktower - not for total cancellation but only for postponement until the town was better able to afford it. At the time it was pointed out that £100,000 would provide two primary or junior schools, an old persons home, 50 old peoples bungalows or fifteen 78-seater omnibuses!

The Council's argument was that the reinforcing steel-work for the massive, 150 feet high tower was already built in, and that failure to complete would result in heavy compensation under previously signed contracts about which the Council seemed to have been overly reticent.

The protest was like baying at the moon!

On September 10th, the Council voted by 26 votes to 10 to commence building. The ratepayers were going to get their clock-tower whether they liked it or not!

For some years after this, ratepayers parties became very popular and their candidates began to win council seats, but gradually the fire seemed to go out of the debate on civic economies and a mood of reluctant acceptance set in. Ratepayers representatives quietly

The Salutation Hotel, 1963 - (Corner of Cardiff and Commericial Road)

departed the Council Chamber. Some, having tasted and liked the cut and thrust of town administration, chose to seek re-election under the guise of one of the main political parties and when successful seemed to forget their earlier aspirations as champions of the hard-pressed!

From March onwards, the area at the junction of Cardiff Road, Commercial Road and Commercial Street was never to be the same again after the demolition of the Salutation Hotel which had dominated this spot for 151 years. The famous tavern, older than Pillgwenlly itself, had long lent its name to label its immediate environment and it would take the passing of at least two generations before 'Salutation Corner' faded from the town vocabulary. Indeed, long before it did, the new layout of open, flower-bedded traffic islands at this busy junction became unaccountably endowed with the name 'Gilligan's Island' and no-one, not even the town council, seems able to explain why! From time to time, letters in the local press offer theories but always the origin remains vague. Certain it is that there has never been a Newport-born Gilligan celebrated enough to be honoured in this way!

The Boundary Commission rejected Newport's application for the transfer of Spencer Steelworks (and its million pounds of rateable value), into the borough. This pleased both the Magor & St Mellons Rural District Council and the Monmouthshire County Council.

A meeting of the Usk River Board on 29th July forecast that the only answer to the serious problem of erosion along the town reaches of the River Usk and as far up as Newbridge-on-Usk, would be a barrage.

The alterations and extensions to ancient St Woolos Cathedral -probably the most imaginative and substantial ever undertaken - were finally completed after a period of 3½ years, during which time the total cost of £85,000 was raised under the most difficult circumstances.

The work had consisted of a 33 feet long extension to form a sanctuary, choir chapel, organ chamber, sacristy, vestries and undercroft. The chancel arch and presbytery were rebuilt. The only existing parts of the building that were replaced were more recent 19th century works of no architectural merit.

Much thought and research went into the materials used and the most suitable stone was found in the old, derelict Church of All Saints, Kemeys Inferior, which when cleaned up blended beautifully with the ancient fabric of the Cathedral. The organ was replaced by the cannibalisation of the one already in situ and that of the Old Town Hall - worn out parts were replaced and modernisation followed. The dedication service on St Lukes Day, Thursday October 24th, took place in front of a congregation of 600.

On Sunday December 22nd, the last 30 feet section of road decking was fixed in the centre span of the George Street Bridge. A contractor's vehicle was the first to make the crossing.

Not to be left behind and conveniently synchronised as if in the same master plan, the period just before Christmas saw the connection of the steel mesh catwalks over the top of the 400 feet high towers of the Severn Bridge. The first man in history ever to walk across the River Severn from Beachley to Aust completed the 6,000 feet journey in 18½ minutes!

1964

A dream was realised on April 9th: a dream that had been in the melting pot for nearly half a century and which had been the subject of intense campaigning for the last 17 years. On this day, the Mayor, Councillor Trevor Vaughan, declared the George Street Bridge officially open and at long last Newport had its second road bridge.

The work had been completed in just 21 months, including delays caused by the terrible winter weather of 1963. The total cost was £2 million. The most recent census taken on the old town bridge showed 4,500 vehicles crossing in five hours.

On the £8 million, 3,000 unit, Bettws Neighbourhood Unit, 1,000 homes were completed by July. For the most part the early residents were delighted with their out-of-town estate but bewailed the absence of their own public house. Pentwyn House was soon earmarked for conversion.

In August, Newport closed down as a coal port, having been in its day the greatest of them all; compare the paltry 200,000 tons shipped in the first seven months of 1964 with the peak traffic figure of 7 million tons in 1923! From this time onwards all coal trade was to be concentrated on Barry Docks. In spite of this setback however, the Alexandra Dock managed to surpass its previous post-war traffic peak; two main items were responsible for this. The growing impact of Spencer Works caused iron ore imports to register 2,455,340 tons -over half a million tons up on the year before; on the export side, 539,106 tons of iron and steel goods were the best for 33 years!

The vacation of town centre properties was now well under way in the 7 acre Llanarth Street and Union Street Development Area. Until final clearance the empty, 19th century properties became more rat-infested and used by tramps to doss down in, but here and there still stood a solitary house inhabited by those unfortunates who were at the lower end of the rehousing list.

Demolition and clearance was due to begin on January 1st 1965 and it was hoped that the gleaming, new mall would rise in little more than 100 weeks.

These obvious signs of the sleeping monster stirring after so many false starts gave rise to much speculation about the shape of things to come. Rumour, often based on genuine enquiry from outside investment, ran rife, fuelled by press reports vividly illustrated by artists' impressions of what might be expected. Much proved to be ill-founded, and where not so, eventually materialised in heavily watered-down versions of the more fanciful predictions. Among other promises there was to be a vast entertainment centre spreading across Baneswell and containing grand concert and banqueting halls; a giant British Rail diesel servicing depot would revitalise Ebbw Junction Maesglas, and a jetty costing £18 million would project into the River Severn in order for ships up to 100,000 tons to discharge ore directly into Spencer Works. Much less ambitious but equally desirable, was the proposal that John Frost Square should be partly roofed over to create a sheltered, open-air piazza!

1965

Nearly one and a half decades after the days sometimes called 'golden', Newport Rugby Club added to them by producing the best finish yet - not quite invincible but, notwithstanding a small number of defeats, a performance to rank amongst the greatest. In winning their last home game against Ebbw Vale the club notched up an incredible 703 points - a mammoth total that left all the other senior Welsh clubs floundering in its wake!

Having set the pattern for scoring prolificity, the side continued in like manner over the next few seasons until in 1969/70 it eclipsed all previous efforts by recording the highest number of points in the club's history and this in one of its less satisfactory seasons. On Monday evening 27th April 1970, playing away at Bridgend, Newport were beaten by 21 points to 5. This, their 17th defeat, completed a disastrous programme in which they had lost more matches than in any season since the war, but the meagre 5 points that they earned gave them a record-shattering, history-making, seasonal total of 720 points - and this when a converted try was still only worth 5 points!

No more than eight miles from the outskirts of Newport , the Llandegveth Reservoir opened in early May. Just three years had seen the Sor Valley transformed into a large lake holding 5,530 million gallons of water. This new reservoir was intended to supply 9 million gallons a day to Cardiff, 5 million each to Newport and South Monmouthshire and 3 million each to Abertillery and Pontypool. Newport further benefited by the acquisition of an area of great natural beauty on its doorstep.

1966

The owners of the Union Development Area, Sovereign Securities Ltd, announced that a £2 million contract had been placed with Sir Robert McAlpine (South Wales) Ltd. Further details were now given of proposed attractions in the new shopping area.

The upper gallery of the covered mall was going to be accessible 'by stairs, ramps and escalators of a design that will enable them to be used by women with prams. The new museum, library and art gallery buildings will rise over the shops with a boldly sculptured elevation in stone and glass!'

The first of these proposals was fated to go the way of the fountains and the piazza. As for the library, museum and art gallery complex, the bold sculpturing in stone was to emerge as basic 'shoe-box' in uncompromising black engineering brick and roughcast, precast concrete panels. This, in the words of the planners, was a 'simplification of aspect' but everyone else recognised it as a lowering of standards and it was a typical feature of the whole development as it progressed. The end result was to prove a pale shadow of the marble, glass and chrome wonderland originally promised.

By February 1966, the whole of the town centre had become a mighty eye-sore as several large demolition sites were left rubble-strewn, waiting for the relaxation of Government restrictions on expenditure.

The Union site (Sovereign Securities Ltd) was the first and has already been described. The cleared Town Hall site (Chesterfield Properties Ltd) was silent until a start could be made on a 16 storey office block, a 4 storey multiple store, single storey shops and a basement car park. A similar development was intended for the Olympia Cinema site (Central and District Properties Ltd), while the Lyceum Theatre site stood vacant in anticipation of the ABC Cinemas' proposal to build a 1,300 seater super-cinema and six ground floor shops. Over on the river bank (Cinderhill Wharf) the great, stone bulk of the old Star Flour Mills no longer cast a shadow after having been reduced to space for the parking 100 cars.

Exploratory work on these sites in connection with the much deeper, stronger foundations required by much taller, more sophisticated, modern buildings, revealed a remarkable amount of water ('amazing' was the contractors' word for it), although this problem would not have been so unpredictable if a little more thought had been given to the history of the area!

It will be remembered that the Old Town Pill in its original form had cut deeply into this part of town - certainly as far as the Olympia site and most probably for some distance beyond. Instead of being just a tidal inlet it was also the mouth of a stream that had its source somewhere near the Civic Centre. Its route to the river must therefore have been along the line of Bridge Street. This may well have been the 'Histingiste' or 'Hurstons Ditch' mentioned as crossing the junction of High Street and 'Paynes Well' in the 1567 and 1630 post-mortem examinations of the estates of the 1st and 3rd Earls of Pembroke.

On its one side was the Baneswell Pump, reputedly served by a separate spring descending from St Woolos, and on the other the demolition of the Lyceum Theatre exposed two more forgotten, stone-lined wells under the basement. Not far away, in a house in Hill Street, a collapsing kitchen floor revealed a 50 feet deep well with 12 feet of water still at the bottom; this occurred in 1970 and there was fairly conclusive evidence that the well had been dug over 200 years before. A year later a floor cave-in in the George Street Furnishers' warehouse revealed yet another stone-lined well, 5 feet wide with 15 feet of crystal clear water at the bottom. Neither was it without significance that in Cambrian Road there was a brewery where, before the building of Newport's reservoirs, its main requisite was a copious supply of fresh water; was it not also from a stream in this same road that Mr Yorath the brewer, said that he once fished for salmon? (see chapter on Sewers)

Furthermore, a long-gone tavern which once stood on the corner of Baneswell Road, was pointedly called 'The Boat', and the remains of small rowing boats were known to have been found beneath the foundations of High Street shops.

Indeed, all the evidence points to the fact that there was water in abundance beneath the streets of central Newport but apparently only at levels where deep wells or probing drills could find it.

The first step was now taken in the redevelopment of Pillgwenlly. The Housing Committee recommended that a compulsory purchase order be made on 58 unfit houses between Frederick Street and Portland Street and in Broad Street. All these properties were over 100 years old and were severely effected by dampness, disrepair, instability and lack of sanitary conveniences.

The Newport Monmouthshire Order 1966 was laid before Parliament, and on 1st April the borough was enlarged by the addition of 3,501 acres from Caerleon and Bettws; Newport's population rose by 7,433.

The number registered as unemployed in the town fell from 911 in February to an incredible 780 in March (684 men and 96 women). This in spite of a recession which had recently caused the closing down of motor car exports from the docks and the operation of four day working at both Spencer and the Orb steelworks. It was however in the docks where hope lay of some remission in flagging fortunes and it came suddenly when the Minister of Transport, Mrs Barbara Castle, authorised a £2½ million improvement grant to create a basin with facilities for the unloading of 30,000 ton bulk carriers of Canadian timber. This would, in effect, make Newport one of three leading timber import points in Britain.

In April, great satisfaction was expressed in all quarters when it was finally decided that the toll for crossing the Severn Bridge should be fixed at half-a-crown (12½ pence). Within weeks of this announcement the last 60 feet long, road section was raised into position on the Wye Bridge, completing the total crossing of 9,120 feet including approaches.

On the Bettws Neighbourhood Unit in June, John Laing Construction Ltd put the finishing touch by completing the 3,000th house.

Shortly afterwards, the Queen Mother arrived to open the first phase of the £6 million, six storey extension to the Royal Gwent Hospital. The deed done, she was taken to Shaftesbury Park to be picked up by a helicopter and whisked away to Cardiff Rhoose Airport. It was on this occasion that Newport Police tightened security by using two-way, personal radios for the first time.

Royalty was again in the area on September 8th when Queen Elizabeth herself presided at the official opening of the Severn Bridge. In the three days following, 107,000 vehicles crossed over.

1967

Figures published for the docks suggested that an upward trend was beginning. The year 1966 was the best year since 1931. The throughput had been 4,321,000 tons as against 4,193,000 tons for the previous post-war best in 1964. Iron ore intake was 2,849,000 tons and imports increased to 3,461,667 tons - 428,000 tons up on the previous year. The main exports were still iron and steel goods and these suffered a modest reduction to 807,245 tons.

Coincidental with the release of these welcome figures another note of optimism inserted itself.

Plans for the once greatly popularised, giant ore terminal having fallen by the wayside, another diversification was showing promise. All the derelict coal hoists had been cleared from the north side of the South Alexandra Dock in the course of creating a 20 acre terminal with deep-water berths for three, 29,000 ton timber carriers then being purpose-built in Japanese shipyards. Japanese engineers had inspected the Alexandra Dock and were tailoring their ships accordingly - with 96 feet beams to clear the entrance lock by just 2 feet on each side. The first step had already been taken in this new enterprise with the recent arrival of a converted bulk carrier bringing 22,000 tons of packaged timber from British Columbia - the largest ever single cargo to arrive in Britain.

The western end of the M4 Motorway (Malpas to Tredegar Park) opened on February 23rd. Two weeks later, the twelve mile section from the Severn Bridge to the Coldra followed suit.

There was little left now of 19th century Newport and two of the remnants disappeared within 24 hours of each other.

The Town Abattoir was opened in 1864 and closed after 103 years of continuous operation on 31st March 1967. Never again, on hot summer days, would unsuspecting passers-by look in the open double doors in Wyndham Street and hurriedly move on, sometimes retching at the sight and foul smell of the piles of bones and a million feasting bluebottles!

On the following day another tradition ended when the 130 year old Borough Police Force merged with the County Force. On 1st April 1967, the Newport Borough Police Force became F Division of the Gwent Constabulary.

At least one of the town's legendary, underground tunnels proved to have substance but this one was completely unsuspected. In October, excavation of the Capitol Car Park site uncovered a small portion of an ancient tunnel just tall enough for a person to stand up in. Speculation as to its original purpose was inconclusive but from its geographical position it is almost certain to have been part of the Austin Friary with an entrance from the river bank or, some would say, from the castle itself!

1968

The new Library, Museum and Art Gallery in John Frost Square became ready for occupation and it was expected that the moving-in operation, using 35 staff, would take the first five weeks of the new year. Hardly had the 400 tea chests given up their thousands of books, documents and exhibits than disaster struck in the form of a flood caused by a fault in the ventilation and heating systems in the roof.

A torrent of water poured down walls, through all floors, deactivating all electrical installations including the lifts. Damage was sustained by many items which time had not yet been allowed to find their permanent storage places away from corridor floors and window sills.

The library staff faced a very difficult situation but dedicated application ensured that excellent order was restored in good time for the official opening by Princess Margaret on April 5th.

At this point it is timely to give final regard to Newport Docks. A dividing line has to be drawn between their traditional, historic performance on which the bulk of the town's economic growth had depended, and the new trade emerging as a result of the changing face of world commerce, advancing technology and the resultant revolution in the pattern of later 20th century life. 1968 is as good a year as any at which to start the comparison and, despite being outside the ambit of this history, 1981 an appropriate place to complete the illustration of the direction in which the wind was blowing.

	Imports (in tons)	
	1968	1981
Iron Ore	3,038,794	Nil
Iron & steel	154,000	5,400
Timber	139,274	214,700
General merchandise	149,513	48,500
Building materials	2,099	100
Oils & spirits	195,364	Nil
Fruit	Nil	104,000
	3,779,044	372,300

The import figure in 1968 was the highest in the docks' history and the resulting £248,000 profit more than the total made by Cardiff, Swansea, Barry and Port Talbot put together.

In contrast, exports rallied between these years. In 1968, the overall total was 801,337 tons whilst in 1981 the figure reached 1,087,200 tons, partially accounted for by the moderate recommencement of coal shipments.

A serious blow to the import tonnage came in 1975 when the new tidal harbour at Port Talbot took over the handling of all iron ore shipments into South Wales. Recovery could only come from diversification.

Newport had already become one of Britain's leading timber importers, and both sides of the River Usk possessed the first container terminals in South Wales. In 1980, the opening of the Jamaica Terminal in the South Dock put the port in the forefront of fruit importation from the West Indies and Israel. Meanwhile there was quick turn-around for ships carrying foreign motor vehicles as their shiny, colourful cargoes were off-loaded into the large, transitory parking area on the eastern side of the entrance lock.

There was of course still some activity in the traditional commodities which had for so long been the life-blood of the docks ie coal and iron, but now these only represented a form of lip service to fading markets.

It remained the great dockyard of old but shorn of all traces of the Victorian heritage that some would say had lingered over-long. Gone were the 'dark satanic' iron sheds and warehouses with generations of coal and iron ore dust coating every member of their framing. Here and there in much less profusion were bright, modern counterparts while the remaining acres, tidied and cleared of dereliction, beckoned invitingly to new investment, and the whole complex was made all the more attractive by virtue of a vastly improved connection with the national road transport system.

No longer was there need to haul huge loads through the congested streets of Pillgwenlly. The opening of Docks Way in 1976 introduced a road of almost motorway standard, stretching for a mile and a quarter from Junction 28 of the M4 (Tredegar Park interchange) right into the heart of the Alexandra Dock.

It was not far from the truth to describe Newport as a football town and, on occasions, a football-mad town! It possessed a moderate Football League team at Somerton Park that from time to time had its moments, and a world-famous rugby club at Rodney Parade. Between them they were guilty of the appropriation of a large percentage of the population on Saturday afternoons. There was however, another soccer club in the town which although not moving in such exalted circles, impressed just as markedly in the world of amateur and semi-professional players. This was a team with its own loyal following which in its day brought great prestige to the town.

Lovells Athletic was formed in 1917 as a works football team by Harold Lovell, managing director of the local confectionery factory known nationally for its celebrated 'Toffee Rex' - hence Rexville, a colloquialism for the Albany Street works and its near neighbourhood. The club ran two teams one in the Monmouthshire Senior League and the other in the Premier Division of the Welsh League. Their record made the club fully deserving of a place among Newport's meagre list of praiseworthy institutions.

It read:-

Western League Champions	1923-24 and 1938-39
Welsh League Champions	Three times between 1931 and 1939
Southern League Champions	1939
Welsh Amateur Cup Winners	Three consecutive years in the 1920s
South Wales & Monmouthshire Cup Winners	Three times
Monmouthshire Senior Cup Winners	Five times
Monmouthshire Amateur Cup Winners	Twice
Post-war Welsh Cup	1948
League Champions	Four times

In May 1969, the works management announced that at the completion of their current league programme, Lovell's Athletic was to be disbanded due to lack of support and the overriding need of their sports ground for urgent factory extensions. It was a sign of the times that such a rich tradition should end in such an unsatisfactory way.

It was at about this time that a Rogerstone-born, American businessman made the final of several offers to buy the Transporter Bridge for £1,000,000. His idea was demolition and re-erection on one of several possible sites in the United States. The scheme was genuine enough and found sufficient favour to receive serious civic consideration, especially in view of the enormous sum of £16,440 per annum that it was now costing to run the 64 year old bridge, but it came to nothing in the face of the division of opinion and bureaucratic wheels that turned far too slowly for the liking of impatient New World tycoonery!

The revived Newport Civic Society was now a mere three years old and a spokesman, more far-seeing than even he could probably imagine, gave his remedy for the rejuvenation of the old town. The River Usk, he said, was the biggest remaining blot on an otherwise promising landscape. Its ugly, pungent-smelling and litter-strewn banks needed to be tidied up and naturally beautified with attractive riverside walks! A quarter of a century later these self-same words were on everyone's lips but the most imaginative plan ever devised to correct the situation was to be sabotaged by a few purblind government officials!

Announcement now came of the crowning phase of redevelopment in the town centre, which would change it completely from anything that would have been recognisable to previous generations of townsfolk. The Old Green Improvement, costing £3,500,000, was intended to commence in 1971 and the works involved were to be gigantic in the extreme.

In order to eradicate the notorious traffic black spot, it was intended to bring the main road from the, north (Shaftesbury Street) straight through in the form of a dual carriageway, connecting the Harlequin (Rising Sun and soon to be born again as the New Rising Sun) roundabout with Kingsway, wholly unhampered by the convergence of any roads from other directions. In order to accomplish this the new highway would comprise an underpass beneath an open-centred roundabout where previously had been the Old Green cross-roads. For pedestrians, three subways would connect to a footbridge across the central void.

The canal together with its tunnel had been filled in southwards from the Old Green when Kingsway was built in the early 1930s. Ever since then it had terminated at the rear of the Castle Hotel, pouring its water down through a heavy iron grill to scour several of the river wharves. This section, stretching back to Barrack Hill, was soon to disappear.

Altogether, the scheme involved the purchase of parts of Moderator, Baltic and Bangor Wharves, properties in Dock Street, Kingsway, Shaftesbury Street, High Street, Mill Street, Dos Road and Queens Hill. Three of the more expensive premises were famous public houses: The Kings Head Tap, The Old Green and The Castle Hotel. The days of Screw Packet Lane were also numbered.

When completed in a few years, the project would result in the construction of five road bridges, two footbridges, one railway bridge, three pedestrian subways and a new wall for the Town Pill! Strangely however these colossal works of planning, demolition, engineering and reconstruction did little more than relieve the desperate traffic situation - once the crossing was made into High Street, one was once again confronted by the old fashioned town centre of yore!

1970

The town was stunned to learn that the Alexandra Docks would have to close down completely for up to four months - the first time for 77 years!

Routine inspections of the entrance had revealed that the outer sill was crumbling badly, allowing increasing amounts of water to leak out. The sill had to be rebuilt, and so the giant lock had to be sealed in from August 1st. The cost was anticipated to be £1,250,000 but the loss in trade would be worth many times more.

The immense task was carried out in a most efficient manner. A wall of concrete blocks weighing 16,000 tons was built up from the riverbed on the outer side of the damaged sill to hold back the tides; 18 million gallons of water were drained from the lock. Repairs to both the inner and outer sills, now high and dry, were carried out by a term of Cornish stonemasons who might well have been direct descendants of the experts who had installed the original sills. It was said that the precision required in the tight spacing of the joints was comparable to that required in setting the tiny gap of a spark plug in a motor car engine!

Four hundred and fifty dock workers were dispersed around Cardiff and Barry Docks and the only port traffic remaining was fuel oil through the Shell Mex & BP terminal via a temporary pontoon dock built out into the river from its eastern bank.

In just four months - three days ahead of schedule - the gates were rehung, the great concrete barrier demolished, and the docks declared open again on December 7th. The whole operation had cost less than anticipated - just £900,000 - but 2 million tons of cargo had been lost to the port.

On December 10th, crowds gathered at the lock to watch as the first ship for four months entered the docks; the Liberian registered 'Prometheus' brought in 9,000 tons of bauxite ore from Toulon.

1971

Final collapse of all Newport's aspirations in regard to revival of one of its older, traditional industries came with the announcement by the Newport Shipbuilding & Engineering Company, that at the end of its present contract no more orders were to be accepted. Thus, the last of a long line of River Usk yards was to close down, never to reopen.

The warning signs had been flashing for several years and for most of the 20th century Newport had lived in the shadow of the larger centres where shipbuilding had been inherent and the only source of virtually all the world's shipping requirements. Now, with even these well established yards failing in the face of dwindling merchant fleets and cheaper foreign competition, there was no place in the scheme of things for Newport's meagre contribution.

It seemed that only one requirement remained to confirm the town's earlier, questionable description as 'the gateway to South Wales', and this was the missing portion of a broad, new highway system giving faster, uncomplicated access from the Midlands and the North.

Construction work had been in progress for some years resulting in the connection by means of the M50 motorway at Ross-on-Wye to the M5 just to the north of Tewkesbury. By the end of 1971, the much improved A40 (thereafter to be known as the A40M) from Ross, through Monmouth, to Raglan was complete and from there a brand new A449 of motorway standard curled away southwards down the picturesque lower Valley of the Usk, to meet the M4 at the Coldra Junction 24 on Newport's eastern boundary. This final link, then commencing construction, was intended for completion by December 1972.

On September 6th, the first of 2,000 piles was driven in a £60 million extension at Spencer Steelworks. This was to involve the building of another blast furnace - the largest in Europe and one of the largest in the world. The result hopefully, would be to raise production from 2 million to 3½ millions tons.

The population of Newport was shown by the 1971 Census to have dropped by 1,190 to 111,810, with only 2% speaking Welsh.

With the story now approaching its conclusion, the Borough Council once again came under attack for its alleged, continuing apathy towards preservation of the past. This narrative has already had its say in this matter and the latest criticism was only the most recent in a long campaign of showing concern by prominent citizens whose views still seemed to be in a minority and whose point was reinforced by the fact that Newport was one of six Welsh local authorities that had so far failed to designate any areas or buildings under the 1967 Civic Amenities Act; accusers held that this was tantamount to an admittance that the town had nothing worth preserving!

But the public also had to take some share in the blame as demonstrated by the widespread disinterest that caused the early demise of the seven year old Civic Society.

The voices of censure were as one, both in the degree of their bitterness and the parallelism of their argument, saying: 'Newport is in the grip of a characterless clutter of concrete', or: 'too much has been replaced by impersonal concrete and glass!'

The Principal of Newport College of Art did not mince his words. His view was that the Civic Society had been formed 50 years too late and that anyone looking at the town would see the result of 'the most ugly, terrible town planning!'

No matter how the critics chose to phrase their comments, they all agreed that there was now no remedy to the problem of preserving any buildings which 'whilst not beautiful or historic in themselves, would have reflected the character and lifestyle of the past'.

The Kingsway Centre was still a ghost precinct of empty shops, despite refurbishment by the new owners Town & City Properties of London. There was strong talk of transferring Newport Market Traders to the closed-in basement of the Centre so that the Market Building itself could be redeveloped. This caused feelings to run so high that a 9,000 signature petition in opposition to the idea caused the defeat of the motion by 23 votes to 16.

In 1973, the Mayor said: 'The Kingsway Centre is no credit to Newport'. A representative of the Market Traders followed up with:

'It is a cold desolate place where those who have already moved have gone bankrupt!' Even the retiring Town Planning Officer who admitted to being satisfied with the appearance of the Centre, stated that if he had been responsible for it the design would have probably have required drastically different treatment before acceptance!

In this pessimistic atmosphere however, an altogether different note was struck by a lady speaker at the 30th annual dinner of the Newport Business and Professional Women's Club (the Mayor also present) who was quoted as saying: 'There is much of historical and aesthetic interest to preserve in the borough, including the Castle, St Woolos Church, the Westgate Hotel with its Chartist associations and the '*Civic Centre with its beautiful murals!*' Thus came further condemnation, albeit unintentionally, from the woefully short list of obvious, standard items, and at the same time confirmed what every one else was saying.

On December 8th 1972, the new road to the Midlands and the North was opened after having taken seven years to connect Newport to the M50 at Ross-on-Wye. The final eight mile section from Usk to the Coldra made it possible to drive on good quality, dual carriageway from South Wales to Scotland.

With only 12 months left before the introduction of a revolutionary reorganisation of the local government system, a huge sigh of relief was almost audible within the confines of the borough when the Secretary of State for Wales finalised the titles of the new local authorities and revealed that Newport would be allowed to retain its ancient name. At one time there had been a real danger of the borough losing its historic identity to become the much less appealing South Monmouthshire District Council.

'How are the mighty fallen?' is an expression frequently used to indicate an alarmingly retrograde step in the course of otherwise excellent performance, and this was never more apparent than in the case of Newport Rugby Club's 1972/73 season. Only three years after piling up the largest number of points that they had ever scored, the club suffered a 60 to 15 points defeat at the hands of the Barbarians, to reverse all records and create a devastating total of 786 points against - 215 more than the previous seasons aggregate! This was Newport's 28th defeat of the season and the heaviest in the club's 98 year history!

1974 was the year that closes this particular era, ending a word picture unsatisfactorily documented and so often disputable in fact. It is not inappropriate therefore that the curtain should fall on an act of momentous proportion. The Local Government Act of that year introduced sweeping restructuring of local government, accompanied by boundary divisions the like of which had hardly been seen since William the Conqueror drew his original manorial maps.

On April 1st, 440,000 people found that they now lived in the official Welsh County of Gwent instead of the arguably English County of Monmouth of King Henry VIII'S creation. Many who had gone to bed the night before in Monmouthshire, woke up to find that they now resided in Glamorgan, and the inhabitants of Brynmawr and Llanelly Hill in Breconshire became domiciled in Gwent!

Twenty-two old local authorities, urban and rural, were divided between five new 'districts', all of which were given the opportunity of applying for the style of borough council. Newport, Torfaen and Islwyn did so - Monmouth and Blaenau Gwent opted not to. The titular head of a borough was designated as mayor - that of a district as chairman.

The effect on Newport was emphatic and wide-ranging. Overnight the county borough of nearly 12,000 acres and 108,000 souls became a new super borough of 45,103 acres (70 square miles) with a population approaching 130,000. Absorbed into the borough were the areas of Caerleon Urban District and Magor & St Mellons Rural District, except for the parishes of Marshfield, Michaelstone-y-Vedw, Peterstone Wentlooge and St Mellons. Over 20 village communities were included.

Some major powers were lost by Newport to the new Gwent County Council: the responsibilities for education, fire and ambulance services, social services, food and drugs and libraries. The ancient office of alderman was abolished.

Sunday March 31st 1974, was marked, as the last day of the old regime by an old-fashioned procession of the Mayor and the retiring council to take part in a service at St Woolos Cathedral.

Epilogue

The point where reference to the past becomes 'just the other day' instead of 'once upon a time', would seem the most opportune at which to call a temporary halt in the story of a town which has been evolving from the moment that native Welshman and invading Saxon settled down together in an uneasy truce.

Having from the earliest days submitted to the might and oft-times anger of the great River Usk tides, through the eras when those same surging waters dictated Newport's role in the race for growth and prosperity, the town now stands at another brink. This time however, there has never been bigger incentive for the slave to become the master!

Contrary to ill-conceived supposition, it has been shown quite unequivocally that Newport *does have* a creditable history whose revelation has been obscured and sabotaged in a variety of ways by the mindless mayhem of ancient vandals resulting in a serious dearth of documentation, anecdotal evidence and other pertinent historiography, the insensibility of later generations in the keeping of important records and the 20th century compulsion to obliterate the past in layers of concrete!

Admittedly it is not a story that has generated a richness of famous personalities or one studded with gems of derring-do but nevertheless it is one that has progressed in steady, subservient support of a more illustrious if sometimes infamous national progress and which, for a while in the 19th century, made the port of Newport a leading standard-bearer for the nation.

Hopes of a rebirth as a major shipbuilding centre flourished momentarily and died. The largest steelworks in Europe never did live up to its original promise, although it leaves one to wonder what kind of a town there might have been without it. The evidence of a more than acceptable number of empty shops, the endless activity in the job centres and the sky high council taxes - all these things belie the prognostications of a hundred, jubilant, after-dinner speakers way back in 1959!

Many of the conditions required to keep the town in the front ranks of urban advancement were fulfilled however. Newport has so far attained many of the goals for which it has struggled over a century or more - plus the unexpected bonus of Spencer Steelworks for which its citizens had to withstand a battering as probably no other town in history has been required to endure in order to enhance its prospects.

The second river bridge duly arrived, and also a third if one counts the crossing of the M4 motorway. The long-awaited town by-pass finally snaked through the suburbs in the shape of that very same motorway, and the town centre received a massive face-lift when the Kingsway Shopping Centre rose from the demolitions.

Unfortunately, the first attempt misfired badly and a mixture of poor planning and ill-judged economising resulted in a cold, featureless warren of unfaced, concrete shop fronts and malls, aesthetically unattractive to prospective tenants and customers alike and put beyond the reach of many established traders by escalating rents and rates. In the light of mounting losses due to the snails-pace take-up of leases, the owners embarked upon a desperate refurbishment which, despite bringing a marked improvement, still fell far short of what one would have expected from a town trying to protect a reputation of once-renowned creativity. What was lacking here was the architectural daring, freshness and inspired presentation of similar centres elsewhere.

The shabby, poorly designed facade of the Borough Library, Museum and Art Gallery was a dominant feature of this development and in 1995, 27 years after its opening, a brave attempt was made to improve matters as part of a face-lift costing something in the region of

£800,000. However the result only showed that the passage of time had made little impact on the lack of imagination common to successive administrations.

The grimy, rough-cast concrete and a portion of the black brickwork is now obscured by aluminium panels in two-tone beige enamel. This is undoubtedly an improvement but not with the look of classical or traditional permanence looked for in such public buildings.

Three large, colourful mosaics fill one corner but the subjects are vague, beyond the comprehension of most citizens and by no stretch of the imagination can be associated with anything native to Newport. Moreover, the designs are supposed to be computer-generated (meaning 'blurred') and, situated as they are, high up on the building frontage, their message will probably remain as much of a mystery in years to come as several of the town's other artistic refinements!

Some semblance of the promised inner ring road, originally planned in 1950, managed to progress a few hundred yards through the old railway goods yard to the top of Bridge Street, and terminated at an insignificant little roundabout offering no more than the choice of a slightly more direct approach to the Civic Centre, escape into a maze of side streets or a circuitous return back into the town centre! The true ring road - almost a by-pass in itself - was to come in the form of the Docks Distributor Road from Kingsway, via the docks to Tredegar Park.

Serious traffic and flooding problems have been all but eliminated and the skyline kept respectable by a not-excessive proliferation of multi-storey office blocks and car parks. Slum clearance proceeds to good effect and much has been done in rebuilding the mouldering portions of Pillgwenlly, but as promising as recent events appear to be there is still a long way to go. One has only to study the 1992 publicity literature for the ill-fated River Usk barrage to obtain the Borough Council's own candid view:-

'Today, most of the traditional industries associated with the river and its docks are gone; remaining buildings have become derelict, and the waterfront, with its vista of mud and litter, has become a major eyesore. The area is so unattractive that past development has turned its back on the river. The prominence of the run-down areas bordering the river confirm the visitor's impression that Newport is a lacklustre town with environmental problems.'

These were almost the exact sentiments expressed by the Civic Society 23 years earlier!

As things have turned out, it appears that turning the dream of a clean river into reality has suffered a setback that may take a long time to overcome. Superficial stopgaps, thumbs in the dyke, can ultimately prove only to be an expensive waste of time. Attractive riverside walks and tree-lined avenues are a contradiction in terms alongside an extremely unattractive river, and tenants for architecturally pretty, riverside offices and flats will be hard to find if their picture windows only face a panorama of muddy dereliction. Nor will the current trend of _inventing_ town traditions by glamorising past calamities or resurrecting baseless legends be any more effective than raising abstract monuments whose meanings need to be explained in arduous detail to an incredulous public!

Does Cardiff, for instance, suffer because it possesses a goodly selection of lifelike stone or bronze images of celebrated Welshmen? Is anything more admired than the action-man pose of a remarkably accurate Gareth Edwards in the St David's Shopping Centre?

Even the euphoria accompanying the massive inward investment of the late 1990s must be regarded with some suspicion in view of the fact that as far as Newport is concerned there could be some element of déja-vous lurking in the background!

It has been stated elsewhere in this narrative that yesterday's happenings have already become history, albeit too recent to qualify for true historical representation. The process is infinite. This account ends therefore in the certain knowledge that the building of the town will never end.

When a further hundred years have passed, someone undoubtedly will be compiling a 21st century continuation of all that has appeared in these pages, and a daunting task it will prove to be for it is most unlikely that the concentrated advancement of the past two centuries will ever again take place. The special circumstances that gave rise to Newport's galvanic projection into the 19th century and its transformation from brutish village into Victorian super-town, will almost certainly never be repeated. Time alone will tell, but as these words are being written only one more option seems open to a town which appears to have run the gamut.

The priorities must be the taming of the highest tides in Europe, the detoxification of the appalling River Usk 'stew' by the banishment of several dozen raw sewage outfalls and the concealment forever of the reeking mudbanks. Then, and only then, might it be possible to predict that the next story will be that of the elegant *City* of Newport, a prosperous commercial centre with attractive marine aspect and carefully controlled urbanism from Castleton to Penhow.

No doubt it will happen one day and when it does Newport will have its second flowering. The big difference will be that this time the town's destiny will no longer rest in the hands of home-grown entrepreneurs but those of faceless civil servants and government accountants of indeterminate loyalties.

If, after the relocation of his statue from Park Square to Bridge Street (May 1992), Charles, 1st Baron Tredegar, still feels inclined to take his legendary, moonlight walks, it is not inconceivable that he returns to his pedestal shaking his head in bewilderment at the weird and ghoulish monuments that he finds are his only company. Is it too much to hope that one day a wealth of classical statuary might grace a redesigned town centre, devoid of basement bazaars and giving its lucky inheritors no further cause to continue asking: 'Whatever happened to the fountains?'

It will be a far cry indeed from the tiny cluster of hide and bracken covered hovels that stood, nameless, a thousand years before, on the bank of the River Usk at the edge of the 'beneweork' fields!

The End

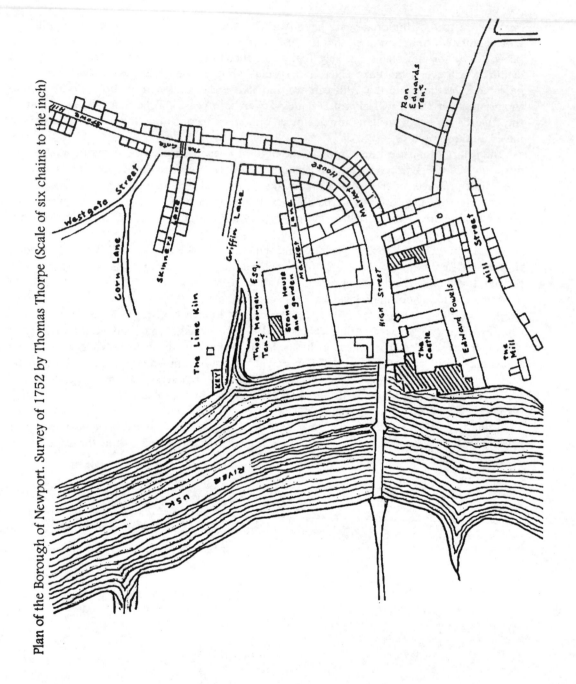

Plan of the Borough of Newport. Survey of 1752 by Thomas Thorpe (Scale of six chains to the inch)

344

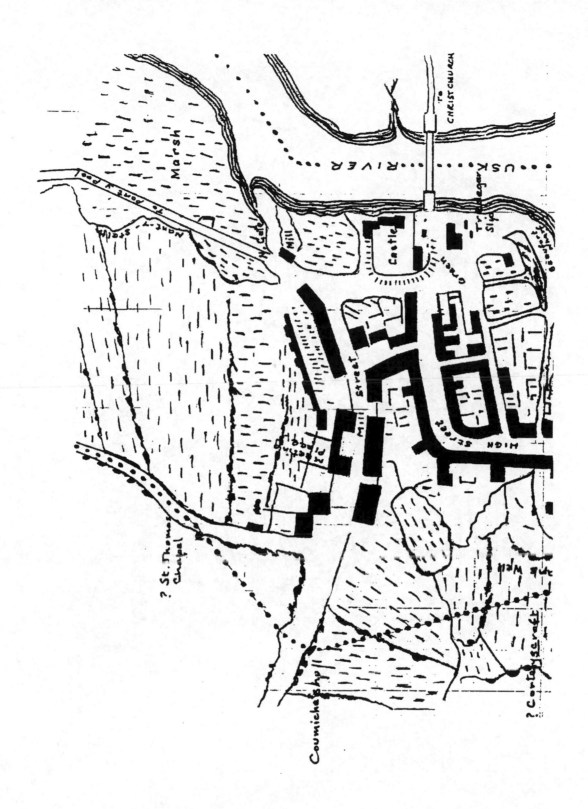

345

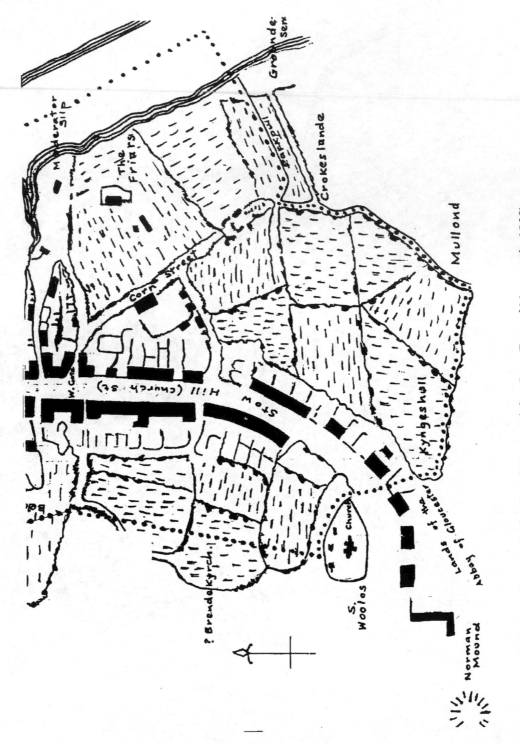

Plan of the Town and Liberties of Newport (after Coxe, Tour of Monmouth, 1802)

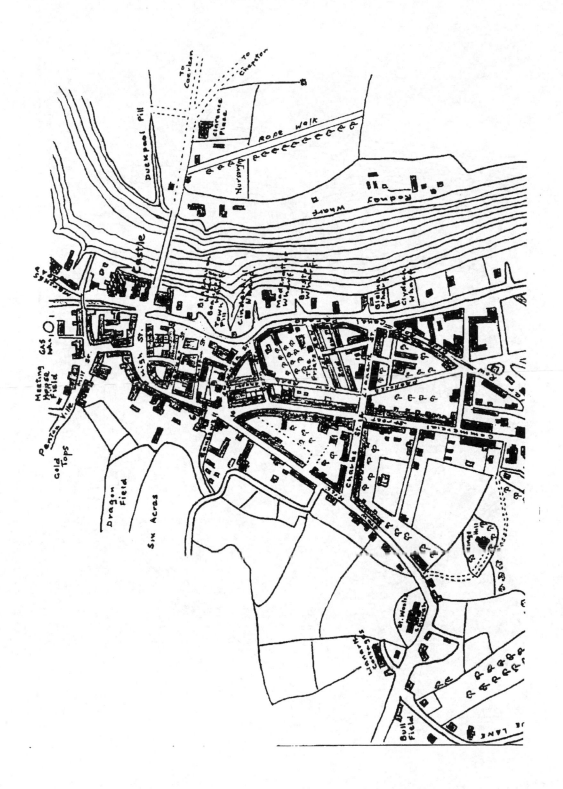

347

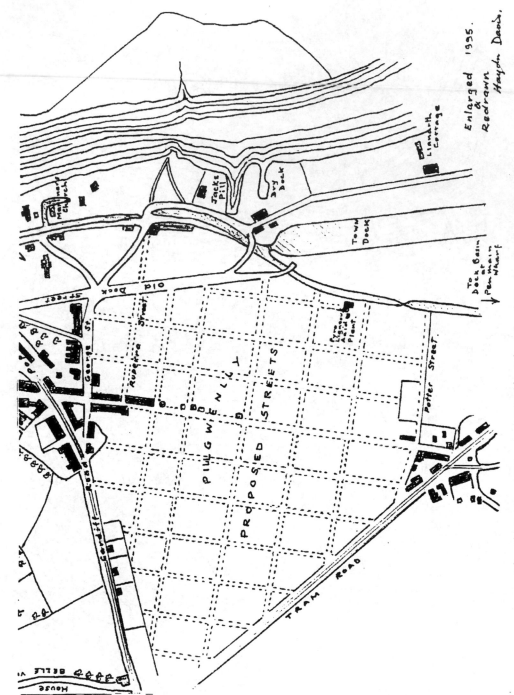

After the Survey of Newport 1836 by John Wood (Scale: six chains per inch)

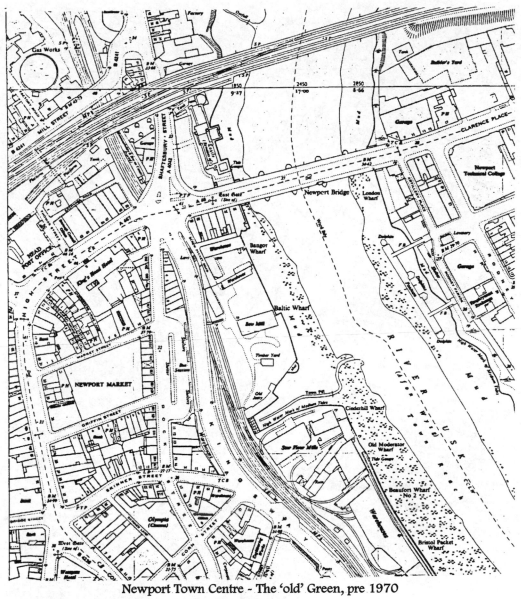

Newport Town Centre – The 'old' Green, pre 1970

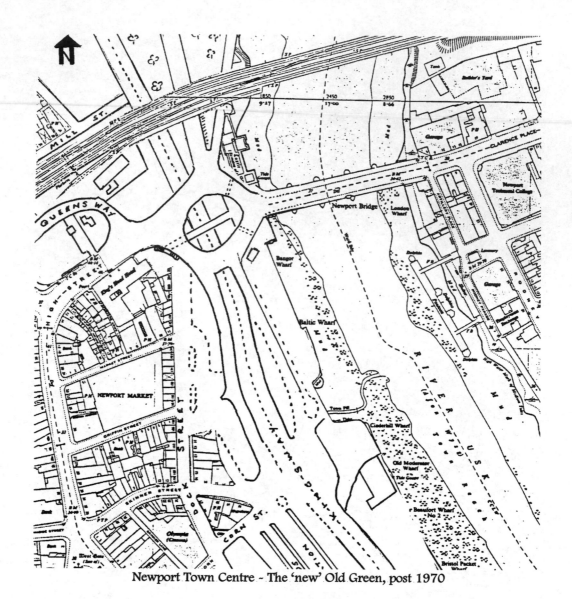

Newport Town Centre ~ The 'new' Old Green, post 1970

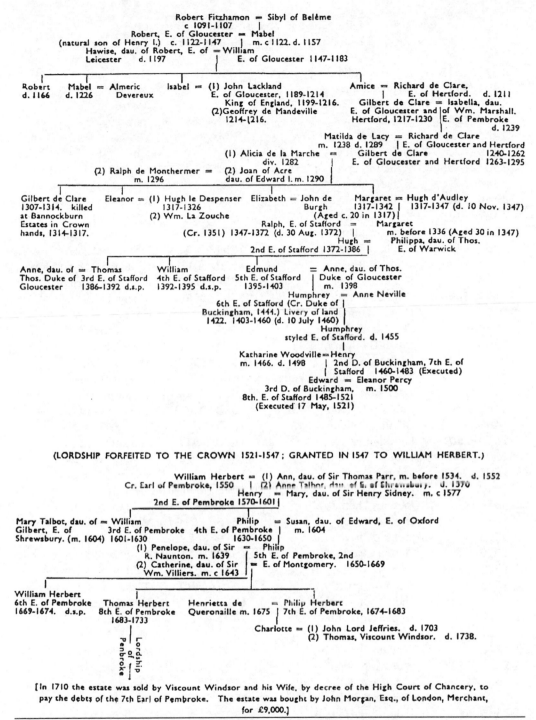

Robert Fitzhamon = Sibyl of Belême
c 1091-1107
Robert, E. of Gloucester = Mabel
(natural son of Henry I.) c. 1122-1147 | m. c 1122. d. 1157
Hawise, dau. of Robert, E. of = William
Leicester d. 1197 | E. of Gloucester 1147-1183

Robert   Mabel = Almeric   Isabel = (1) John Lackland   Amice = Richard de Clare,
d. 1166   d. 1226 Devereux   E. of Gloucester, 1189-1214 | E. of Hertford. d. 1211
                                      King of England, 1199-1216.   Gilbert de Clare = Isabella, dau.
                                      (2)Geoffrey de Mandeville   E. of Gloucester and | of Wm. Marshall.
                                      1214-1216.   Hertford, 1217-1230 | E. of Pembroke
                                                                                             | d. 1239
                                              Matilda de Lacy = Richard de Clare
                                              m. 1238 d. 1289 | E. of Gloucester and Hertford
                          (1) Alicia de la Marche =   Gilbert de Clare   1240-1262
                                    div. 1282   E. of Gloucester and Hertford 1263-1295
        (2) Ralph de Monthermer = (2) Joan of Acre
                m. 1296   dau. of Edward I. m. 1290

Gilbert de Clare   Eleanor = (1) Hugh le Despenser Elizabeth = John de   Margaret = Hugh d'Audley
1307-1314. killed   1317-1326   Burgh   1317-1342 | 1317-1347 (d. 10 Nov. 1347)
at Bannockburn   (2) Wm. La Zouche   (Aged c. 20 in 1317)|
Estates in Crown   Ralph, E. of Stafford =   Margaret
hands, 1314-1317.   (Cr. 1351) 1347-1372 (d. 30 Aug. 1372) | m. before 1336 (Aged 30 in 1347)
                                                                        Hugh =   Philippa, dau. of Thos.
                                                    2nd E. of Stafford 1372-1386 | E. of Warwick

Anne, dau. of = Thomas   William   Edmund   = Anne, dau. of Thos.
Thos. Duke of 3rd E. of Stafford 4th E. of Stafford 5th E. of Stafford | Duke of Gloucester
Gloucester   1386-1392 d.s.p. 1392-1395 d.s.p. 1395-1403 | m. 1398
                                                 Humphrey = Anne Neville
                                        6th E. of Stafford (Cr. Duke of |
                                        Buckingham, 1444.) Livery of land |
                                        1422. 1403-1460 (d. 10 July 1460) |
                                                          Humphrey
                                                styled E. of Stafford. d. 1455

                                        Katharine Woodville = Henry
                                        m. 1466. d. 1498 | 2nd D. of Buckingham, 7th E. of
                                                          | Stafford 1460-1483 (Executed)
                                                  Edward = Eleanor Percy
                                        3rd D. of Buckingham, m. 1500
                                        8th. E. of Stafford 1485-1521
                                        (Executed 17 May, 1521)

(LORDSHIP FORFEITED TO THE CROWN 1521-1547; GRANTED IN 1547 TO WILLIAM HERBERT.)

                    William Herbert = (1) Ann, dau. of Sir Thomas Parr, m. before 1534. d. 1552
        Cr. Earl of Pembroke, 1550 | (2) Anne Talbot, dau. of E. of Shrewsbury. d. 1370
                                    Henry = Mary, dau. of Sir Henry Sidney. m. c 1577
            2nd E. of Pembroke 1570-1601|

Mary Talbot, dau. of = William   Philip = Susan, dau. of Edward, E. of Oxford
Gilbert, E. of   3rd E. of Pembroke 4th E. of Pembroke | m. 1604
Shrewsbury. (m. 1604) 1601-1630   1630-1650 |
                            (1) Penelope, dau. of Sir = Philip
                            R. Naunton. m. 1639 | 5th E. of Pembroke, 2nd
                            (2) Catherine, dau. of Sir | = E. of Montgomery. 1650-1669
                            Wm. Villiers. m. c 1643 |

William Herbert
6th E. of Pembroke   Thomas Herbert   Henrietta de   = Philip Herbert
1669-1674. d.s.p.   8th E. of Pembroke Queronaille m. 1675 | 7th E. of Pembroke, 1674-1683
                      1683-1733 |
                                                  Charlotte = (1) John Lord Jeffries. d. 1703
                                                            (2) Thomas, Viscount Windsor. d. 1738.

[In 1710 the estate was sold by Viscount Windsor and his Wife, by decree of the High Court of Chancery, to
pay the debts of the 7th Earl of Pembroke. The estate was bought by John Morgan, Esq., of London, Merchant,
for £9,000.]

Table of the Lords of the Manor of Newport

Mayors of Newport 1314 to 1990

Researched and recorded (in manuscript)
by the staff of Newport Reference Library.

1314/1315	Ralph & Philip Dory	1536/1537	Henry Vaughan (alias
1401/1402	Roger Thomas		Baker) and/or Thomas
1406/1407	John Clerk		Boytre
1407/1408	John Watkins	1538/1539	John Taylor
1431/ 1432	Jenkin Vethyk	1539	Thomas Boytre
1433	Richard Batten	1540	John Taylor
1434/1435	William Berne	1541/1542	Richard ap Howell
1444	William Kemys	1545	Thomas Boytre
1446/1447	William Kemys	1546	Richard ap Hopkyn
1447/1448	Richard Adam	1548	John Lloyd
1448/1453	William Kemys	1550/1551	Richard ap Hopkyn
1453/1454	William Kemys and/or	1551/1552	John Lloyd
	William Berne	1552/ 1553	Win. Morgan ap Morris
1454/1455	Richard Adam	1556/1557	Rowland Morgan
1455/1456	William Berne	1561/1562	Morgan Griffith
1457	Hugh Mantell	1562/1563	Henry Parowe
1459	Thomas Vaughan	1563/1564	Morgan Edward
1463	David Gwilym Merick	1564/1565	Lewis Thomas
1464	John Merick	1565/1566	Morgan Griffith
1465	Thomas or Richard Vaughan	1566/1567	Morris Thomas
	ap Rosser	1567/ 1568	Giles Morgan
1491	Morgan David ap Gwillim	1568/ 1569	Morgan Griffith
1497	Griffith Tailleur	1569/1570	Thomas Morgan
1499/1501	Llywelyn ap Ieuan Vaughan	1570/1571	Morgan Griffith
1501/1503	Thomas Bulke	1571/1572	William Watkins
1503/ 1504	Roger Kemys	1572/1573	Edmund Morgan
1510	John Morgan	1573/1574	Lewis Thomas
1514	John ap Thomas	1574/1575	William Philip
1515	Ieuan Ralphe	1575/ 1576	Morgan Griffith
1516	John ap Thomas	1576/1577	Thomas John Lloyd
1519	Thomas ap Hopkin	1577/1578	Roger Williams
1521/1522	Thomas ap Hopkin	1578/1579	William Pritchard
1523	William Huws	1579/1580	Giles Kemys
1524/1525	Thomas ap Hopkin	1580/1581	Miles Herbert
1526	Thomas ap John	1581/1582	Miles Herbert
1527	William Watkins	1589	John Hollis
1528	William Huws	1590/1591	Miles Herbert
1528/1533	William Llewellin	1591/1592	Miles Herbert
1533/1534	Thomas ap Robert (alias	1594	John Jones
	Thomas Boytre)	1599	Thomas Morgan
1535	Richard ap Howell	1605	Morice Nicholas
1535	William Llewellin	1606	Morice Nicholas
1535/1536	Maurice Vaughan (alias	1607	Thomas James
	Baker)	1614	Rowland Morgan

1615	John Jones	1716/1722	Charles Ward
1619	Morice Nicholas	1722/1723	John Jones
1623/1624	John Priddy	1723/1726	Richard Pettingell
1625/1626	Morice Nicholas	1726/1727	Thomas Williams
1626/1627	John Jones	1727/1730	Thomas Edwards
1627	Roger Williams	1730/1732	Charles Morgan
1628/1629	John Plumley	1732/1733	Francis Jenkins
1629/1630	Morgan Meyrick	1733/1734	Thomas Morgan
1630/1631	Richard Williams	1734/1735	David Seys
1631/1632	Thomas Abrahall	1735/1736	William Seys
1632/1633	Henry Nicholas	1736/1740	Thomas Williams
1633/1634	Walter Jenkins	1741/1746	Thomas Morgan
1634/1635	William Rees	1746/1747	William Seys
1635/1636	Thomas Harris	1747/1750	John Cadogan
1636/1637	Thomas Young	1750/1754	Thomas Dumayne (Scott says 1748/1754)
1637/1638	James Williams		
1646	William Woolph	1755/1758	John Cobb
1655	Walter Nichols	1759	Adam Barber
1656	James Young	1762	John Cobb
1658	Thomas Young	1764/1766	John Blethin
1667	William Morgan (of the Friars)	1766/1767	William Keene
		1769/1772	Andrew Weaver
1669	Charles William	1773/1777	William Keene
1676	George Morgan	1778/1781	Thomas Richards
1682	Charles Williams	1782	John Thomas
1685	Francis Pettingell	1783	Thomas Morgan
1689	Nehemiah Williams	1784	Thomas Griffiths
1690	Thomas Bassett	1785	John Morgan
1695/1696	Nehemiah Williams	1786	Charles Morgan
1697	Charles Williams	1787	Robert Darch
1698	Charles Williams	1789	Edward Harries
1698/1699	Nehemiah Williams	1790	Richard Griffiths
1699/1700	John Morgan	1791	John Thomas
1700/1701	Roger Williams	1792	Edward Bliss
1701/1702	Henry Herbert	1793	Thomas Morgan
1702/1703	Francis Pettingall	1794	Robert Darch
1703/1704	Charles Ward	1794	Charles Price
1704/1705	Charles Ward	1795	Edward Harries
1705/1706	Charles Morgan	1796	Richard Griffiths
1706/1707	Thomas Morgan	1797	Charles Morgan
1707/1708	John Plumley	1798/1800	Sir Robert Salusbury
1708/1709	John Plumley	1800	Rev. Thomas Leyshon
1709/1710	Nehemiah Williams	1801	William Phillips
1710/1711	Lewis Morgan (of the Friars)	1802	Edmund Harris
1711/1712	Henry Herbert	1803	John Thomas
17 12/1713	Charles Herbert	1804	William Foster
1713/17 14	John Jones	1805/1808	Morgan Williams
1714/1715	Roger Williams	1808	Sir Robert Salusbury
1715/1716	Charles Morgan	1809/1812	Robert Jones

1812	William Foster	1862	George Wm Jones
1814	George Griffiths	1863	Wm Williams Morgan
1815	William Williams	1864	Edward J Phillips
1816	John Williams	1865	Thomas Floyd Lewis
1817	William Foster	1866	Willam Graham
1818	John Owen	1867	Thos M Llewellin
1819	William Brewer	1868	James Murphy
1820	Abraham Jones	1869	Thomas Beynon
1821	David Harrhy	1870	Lorenzo A Homfray
1822	Thomas J Phillips	1871	David Harrhy
1823	William Williams	1872	Wyndham Jones
1824	George Griffiths	1873	Nelson Hewertson
1825	William Brewer	1874	Benjamin Evans
1826	Abraham Jones	1875	Henry Pierce Bolt
1827	David Harrhy	1876	George Fothergill
1828	Benjamin Thomas	1877	John Moses
1829	Richard Rogers	1878	Joseph Gibbs
1830	Edward Jones	1879	Henry Russell Evans
1831	John Owen	1880	John Rosser Jacob
1832	John Williams	1881	Thomas Beynon
1833	John Jones	1882	Oliver Goss
1834	John Owen	1883	John Wm Jones
1835	Joseph Latch	1884	Charles Lyne
1836	John Frost	1885	Edwin James Grice
1837	Lewis Edwards	1886	George Hoskins
1838	Sir Thomas Phillips	1887	Thomas Pugsley
1839	Thomas Hawkins	1888	Henry Faulkner
1840	Thomas Hughes	1889	Mark Mordey
1841	Lewis Edwards	1890	Samuel Batchelor
1842	Richard Mullock	1891	Henry John Davis
1843	John S Allfrey	1892	Thomas Jones
1844	Edward Dowling	1893	Frederick Phillips
1845	Joseph Latch	1894	James C Sanders
1846	Thomas M Llewellin	1895	John R Richards
1847	William Jenkins	1896	Thomas Goldsworthy
1848	William Evans	1897	Alfred Robert Bear
1849	T B Batchelor	1898	Thomas Henry Howell
1850	Wm Childs Webb	1899	George Greenland
1851	Henry John Davis	1900	William H Brown
1852	Stephen Iggulden	1901	Henry John Davis (3rd term
1853	James Brown		in 50 years)
1854	Samuel Homfray	1902	John Holman Dunn
1855	James Nelson Knapp	1903	W Clifford Phillips
1856	Charles Lyne	1904	Robert Wilkinson
1857	William Williams	1905	John Liscombe
1858	Henry Shepherd	1906	Frederick Phillips
1859	Thomas Gratrex	1907	Thomas Parry
1860	James Brown	1908	Graham W White
1861	James Brown		

1909	Wm Miles Blackburn	1956	Frederick V Cornford
1910	John Henry Williams	1957	Frederick J Hopton
1911	John McGinn	1958	Herbert R Nock
1912	Charles P Simmonds	1959	Edwin Aston
1913	John Lloyd Davies	1960	George H Coulson
1914	Frederick P Robjent	1961	Herbert H Jones
1915	Charles Thomas	1962	Reginald Pook
1916	Alfred Swash	1963	William T Vaughan
1917	William Evans	1964	Percy C Jones
1918	Henry Charles Parfitt	1965	Alfred G Lovell
1919	Peter Wright	1966	Thomas L Pardoe
1920	Wm Augustus Linton	1967	Cecil A Stone
1921	Edwin Ambrose Charles	1968	William C Huckle
1922	Edward Davies	1969	Lilian Mabel Bowen
1923	Charles F Williams	1970	Sidney Teece Miller
1924	Wm Ellis Robertson	1971	Stewart McDougall Watson
1925	Cyrus T Clissitt	1972	Frederick Arthur Edwards
1926	A T W James	1973	Eric William Rowthorn
1927	Frank Quick	1974	John Marsh
1928	Walter T Griffiths	1975	Roger Williams
1929	W H B Williams	1976	Stanley Pritchard
1930	Thomas Crowther	1977	Aubrey Hames
1931	Griffith A Jones	1978	Edna Bosley
1932	Walter J Wall	1979	G Mathias
1933	Frank J Humphries	1980	Roy Morris
1934	William F E Smith	1981	Cliff Knight
1935	William Casey	1982	Ruby Kehmstedt
1936	Isaiah C Vincent	1983	Betty Clifford
1937	Mary Ann Hart	1984	Rev Cyril Summers
1938	John Robert Wardell	1985	Trevor Warren
1939	Richard Davies	1986	Reginald Lloyd
1940	John Henry Swallow	1987	Robert Allen
1941	William George Rudd	1988	Mrs V J Brydon
1942	George Scott	1989	Rosemary Butler
1943	Harry Godfrey Barter	1990	Harry Jones
1944	Alfred Henry Pursey		
1945	George William Armstead		
1946	Sarah Jane Hayward		
1947	Reginald Silas Tyack		
1948	Thomas Francis Mooney		
1949	Mary Josephine Dunn		
1950	Albert Henry Wills		
1951	Albert Edwin Pugh		
1952	Arthur F Dolman		
1953	William Pinnell		
1954	Maurice Selby		
1955	Letitia Bell		

Hotels and Inns in Newport in 1885
per Town Commercial Directory

Temperance

The Alexandra, Alexandra Road
Lockes, 11 Dock Street
Morleys, 30 Commercial Road
Morrishes, Pentonville
Raymonds, Baneswell Road
The Victoria, 5 Bridge Street
Watkins, Baneswell Road
Webbs, 9 Stow Hill

Inns and Hotels (Full Licence)

Albion, 57 Canal Parade
Alexandra Dock Hotel
Angel, West St.
Bluchers Arms, 11 Griffin St.
Borough Arms, Dock St.
Bridge Hotel, 1 High St.
Bunch of Grapes, High St.
Caledonian Hotel, Dock St.
Castle, 28 Commercial Road
Castle Hotel, Old Green
Commercial Hotel, Old Dock
Commercial, 37 High St.
Cross Hands, Chepstow Road
Cross Keys, 11 Market St.
Crown Hotel, Albert Avenue
Devonshire House, Dock Parade
Dock Hotel, The Docks
Dolphin, 6 Dolphin St.
Eagle, 54 Dock St.
Eastern Valleys, Marshes Road
Engineers Arms, Albert Tce
Exchange, 125 Commercial St.
George Hotel, Chepstow Road
George & Dragon, Mill St.
George St Tavern, George St.
Globe, 54 Canal Parade
Greyhound, 49 High St.
Handpost, Stow Hill
Hare & Greyhound, Commercial
Hope & Anchor, 103 Dock St.
Isca Hotel, Clarence Place

Isca Tavern, 59 Commercial St.
Kings Head Hotel, High St.
Kings Arms, 133 Commercial Rd.
King of Prussia, Somerton
Lamb, 5 Baneswell Rd.
Liswerry Hotel, Liswerry
London, 13 Baily St.
Lord Raglan, Commercial St.
Maindee Hotel, Chepstow Road
Masonic Hotel, 73 Dock St.
Moulders Arms, Marshes Road
Nelson, 2 Canal Parade
New Bridge, Bridge Street
Old Bush, Commercial St.
Old Green, High St.
Old Ship, 21 High St.
Old White Lion, Mill St.
Potters Arms, Dock St.
Princes Head, Lower George St.
Prince of Wales, Cardiff Road
Queens Hotel, Bridge St.
Railway Hotel, 42 Dock St.
Red Lion, 104 Stow Hill
Richmond Hotel, 53 Dock St.
Rising. Sun, 38 Marshes Road
Rodney Arms, Lower Cross St.
Rose & Crown, 26 Canal Parade
Royal Arms, Llanarth St.
Royal Exchange,161 Commercial Rd
Royal Oak, Courtybella Tce.
Ruperra Arms, Commercial Rd.

Salutation Hotel, Commercial Rd.
Ship Hotel, 15 Mill Parade Ship & Castle, Canal Parade
St. Ship & Pilot, Commercial St. Six Bells, Stow Hill
Star Hotel, Duckpool Rd.
Steam Packet, Old Green
Talbot Hotel, 148 Commercial St.
Tradesmans Arms, Commercial St.
Tredegar Arms, Church St.

Waterloo Hotel, Alexandra Dock
Wellington, 9 St Woolos Rd.
Tredegar Arms, High St.
Trout, 16 Market St.
Vulcan 78 Dock St.
Westgate Hotel, Commercial Rd.
White Hart, Cattle Market
William IV, Commercial St.
Windsor Castle, Dock St.
Windsor Castle, 56 Commercial Rd.
Wyndham Arms, 76 Commercial St.

Beer Houses

Alexandra, 89 Commercial Rd.
Alma, 7 Commercial Rd.
Black Horse, 1 Blewitt St.
Black Horse, Somerton
Black Swan, Market St.
Brewery, 12 Llanarth St.
Britannia, 55 Blewitt St.
Britannia, North St.
Cambrian, 112 Commercial Rd.
Cambrian Arms, Canal Parade
Cardigan Bay, 62 Canal Parade
Carpenters Arms, Church St.
Carpenters Arms, Chepstow Rd.
Castle, Castle Precincts
Cherry Tree, 5 Club Row
Church House, 14 Portland St.
Clifton Tavern, 48 Jones St.
Crown, Liswerry
Cumberland House, Courtybella Terrace
Custom House Inn, 33 Dock St.
Devon & Cornwall Hse,Dock Pde.
Dolphin, 30 Castle St.
Engineers Arms, Commercial Rd.
Exeter, 9 Clarence St.
Fair Oak, Chepstow Rd.
Falcon, 66 Commercial Rd.
Fishguard Arms, Lower Cross St.
Flag & Castle, 9 Castle St.
Foaming Tankard, Cross St.
Foresters Arms, New St.
Foresters Arms, Reform Blgs.
Fountain, 9 Canal Terrace
Gloucester Eating House, Thomas St.
Globe, Chepstow Rd.
Golden Hart, 33 Cardiff Rd.

Harp & Shamrock, 66 Commercial St.
Hastings, 93 Commercial Rd.
Herbert Arms, Church Rd.
Homfray Arms, 22 Jeddo St.
Horse & Jockey, Mill St.
Hope, 26 Church St.
Irishmans Arms, Mellon St.
Ivy Bush, 17 Clarence Place
Kings Head Tap, Old Green
King William, 44 Llanarth St.
Little Crown, Crown St.
Mariners Arms, Commercial Wharf
Masons Arms, 21 Dock Parade
Mechanics Arms, 70 Commercial St.
Neptune, 2 Dock St.
New Inn, Pentonville
New Inn, 1 Jones St.
Oddfellows Arms, 78 Commercial St
Oddfellows & Foresters Arms, 39 St Mary St.
Oddfellows Inn, Duckpool Rd.
Olive Branch, 134 Commercial Rd
Orange Tree, 21 High St.
(Now St Michael St)
Picton Arms, 14 Commercial Rd.
Plimsoll Arms, 120 Commercial St
Porters Arms, 30 Club Row
Prince of Wales, St Woolos Rd.
Prince of Wales, Kings Parade
Railway Inn, Thomas St.
Riflemans Arms, Granville St.
Rising Sun, High St. (now St Michael St)
Robin Hood, 3 Llanarth St.
Royal Albert, Albert Avenue
Royal George, 13 Church St.
Royal George, 1 Potters Parade

Royal Oak, Chepstow Rd.
Sailors Home, 30 Kings Parade
Shepherds Pride, Chepstow Rd.
Station Inn, Marshes Rd.
Ship & Pilot, 21 Church St.
S W Railway Inn, Albert Terrace
S W Luncheon Bar, 1 Griffin St.
Steam Packet Tavern, Dock Parade
Talbot Inn, 65 St Mary St.
Three Salmons, Lower Cross St.
Three Salmons, Griffin St.
Three Tuns, Thomas St.
Victoria, Liswerry
Welcome Home, 46 Commercial Rd; West of
England, Mill Parade; William III, Chepstow
Rd; Wiltshire House, 2 Cross St;Winning
Horse,17 Marshes Rd; Luncheon Rooms,53
High St.

Buildings in the Borough of Newport listed as
outstanding under the provisions of the Historic
Buildings and Ancient Monuments Act 1953, and the
Local Authorities (Historic Buildings) Act 1962.

Over 120 buildings are listed in the rural areas added to the old County Borough in 1974.
For the purpose of conciseness and relevance to this history only those properties within the
old borough are shown here.

Grade II

Newport Castle
Newport Transporter Bridge
Bridge St. Queens Hotel
Bridge St. Nos 20, 24
Bridge St. Lord Tredegar's Brynglas Rd.
Brynglas Gardens Cottage
Brynglas Rd. Brynglas House
Cardiff Rd. No 13
Chelston Place, Crindau Hse
Clifton Place, Nos 2-6, 7, 8
Commercial Rd. Nos 174,181-183
Commercial St. Nos 1-8, 13
Commercial St. St Pauls Church
Commercial St. Royal Albert PH.
Commercial St. Westgate Hotel
Friars Rd. Nos 9,11,13
Friars Rd. The Friars
Friars Rd. Bellevue Park
Drinking Fountain
Gold Tops, St Marks Church
Gold Tops, No 11
Gold Tops, Lamp Standard at No 11
Graham St. Elec. Transformer
High St. Old Post Office
Nat. Westminster Bank
High St. No 35
High St.Murenger Public House
Hill St. Nos 13,14
Lower Dock St. Masonic Institute
Lower Dock St. Nos 69,77,78
Park Square,   Nos 9,10,11
Park Square Electricity Transformer
Pentonville, Old Tredegar Estates Office
St Johns Rd. Cambrian House
St Johns Rd. St Johns Church
Stow Hill,   St Marys Church
Stow Hill, Nos 37,81,91,93,103,40, 108
Upper Dock Street, Newport Market

Victoria Place, Nos 1-14 (consec)
Victoria Road, United Reform Church
York Place, No 54

Locally Listed

Chepstow Rd. Nos 173, 175
Clifton Place Nos 9, 10
Commercial St. No 144
High St. Nos 14,15,27,27A,28, 29, 30, 31,
32, 33, 36 , 37, 38, 38A
39,40, 40A, 41,42,43,45,46,47
Kensington Grove, The Lawn Kensington Place, Nos 1-21
Lower Dock St. Nos 102,103,104,
105,106, 107, 108,110,111,58,74,
75,76,86, 87, 88,89,90,91, 112,
113, 114,115,116,117,121.
Park Square, Nos 1,1A,4,5,6,7,8
St Johns Rd. No 2
Stow Hill, Midland Bank
Stow Hill, Nos 25,27,29,31,33, 35,57,59,87,89,95
HighSt.97,99, 101, 105.
Victoria Lane Nos 3,4

The Coat of Arms of the Borough of Newport
(Based upon a publication by Newport Borough Public Relations Office.)

The badge adopted by the Newport Borough Council was formerly the Coat of Arms of the County Borough of Newport. As a Coat of Arms it was unusual for two reasons. Firstly in the placing of a cherub above the shield of arms, and secondly in that one of the supporters is a winged sea lion. The latter is something of a rarity in English heraldry and it appears that Newport was the first Civic Authority to be granted a supporter of this type.

A Royal Charter of Incorporation was granted by James I in 1623. The Town was governed under this charter until the Municipal Corporations Act of 1835 named Newport as a Municipal Borough.

For over four centuries, ever since the 3rd Duke of Buckingham was attainted and beheaded on 17th May 1521, Newport had used the arms, a gold shield charged with a red chevron reversed being ensigned by a cherub.

These arms, however had never been granted by the kings of arms, and consequently were being used without lawful authority. To put the matter right, a grant of arms was obtained and as no other body or person bore a red, reversed chevron on a gold shield, these arms were duly granted by letters patent dated April 17th 1927.

The shield is that of the Staffords, Earls and Dukes of Buckingham, Lords of the Manor of Newport in the 14th and 15th centuries - but with the chevron upside down in order to make the Borough Arms different from those of the family.

The face and wings of the cherub are in natural colours. The placing of a cherub above a shield of arms is unusual.

In 1957 it was decided to petition the Earl Marshal for the supporters which all boroughs are entitled to possess and the College of Arms granted on 7th May 1958, a winged sea lion and a sea dragon. These indicate that Monmouthshire, including Newport, had been for some centuries alternately officially designated either as part of England or part of Wales.

The animal and fish parts on the supporters, and the fact that they are winged, make them also representative of strength on land, sea and in the air. The lion is gold and the dragon red, except as regards their fish tails which are in natural colouring; the fins, however, are tinctured gold

The motto 'Terra Marique' which was adopted in 1958, means 'by land and sea'.
The official description is:-

(arms) or, a chevron reversed gules, the shield ensigned by a cherub proper. Supporters: on the dexter side a winged lion or, and on the sinister side a sea dragon gules, the nether parts of both proper, finned gold.

Citizen Soldiers of Newport

Reproduced from the Original Chart of B. Owen Displayed in Newport Museum

Occasioned by the 1797 French landing in Pembrokeshire and the following Napoleonic Wars, Colonel Sir Charles Morgan of Ruperra raised the Monmouthshire Voluntary Militia - 8 companies each of 75 men. Also known as the Wentlooge Infantry because of the moorland parishes from which they were drawn,they were absorbed, in 1805, into the Western Regiment of Monmouthshire Local Militia with their Headquarters in Newport. Thereafter:-

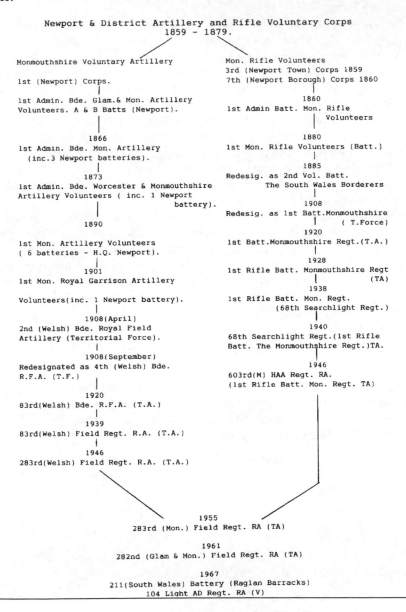

```
              Newport & District Artillery and Rifle Voluntary Corps
                                  1859 - 1879.


Monmouthshire Voluntary Artillery         Mon. Rifle Volunteers
                                          3rd (Newport Town) Corps 1859
1st (Newport) Corps.                      7th (Newport Borough) Corps 1860
         |                                         |
1st Admin. Bde. Glam.& Mon. Artillery             1860
Volunteers. A & B Batts (Newport).        1st Admin Batt. Mon. Rifle
         |                                           | Volunteers
        1866                                       1880
1st Admin. Bde. Mon. Artillery            1st Mon. Rifle Volunteers (Batt.)
(inc.3 Newport batteries).                         |
         |                                         1885
        1873                              Redesig. as 2nd Vol. Batt.
1st Admin. Bde. Worcester & Monmouthshire     The South Wales Borderers
Artillery Volunteers ( inc. 1 Newport                |
                          battery).                1908
         |                                Redesig. as 1st Batt.Monmouthshire
        1890                                       | ( T.Force)
                                                   1920
1st Mon. Artillery Volunteers             1st Batt.Monmouthshire Regt.(T.A.)
( 6 batteries - H.Q. Newport).                     |
         |                                         1928
        1901                              1st Rifle Batt. Monmouthshire Regt
1st Mon. Royal Garrison Artillery                  | (TA)
                                                   1938
Volunteers(inc. 1 Newport battery).       1st Rifle Batt. Mon. Regt.
         |                                    (68th Searchlight Regt.)
    1908(April)                                    |
2nd (Welsh) Bde. Royal Field                       1940
Artillery (Territorial Force).            68th Searchlight Regt.(1st Rifle
         |                                Batt. The Monmouthshire Regt.)TA.
    1908(September)                                |
Redesignated as 4th (Welsh) Bde.                   1946
R.F.A. (T.F.)    |                        603rd(M) HAA Regt. RA.
                1920                       (1st Rifle Batt. Mon. Regt. TA)
83rd(Welsh) Bde. R.F.A. (T.A.)
         |
        1939
83rd(Welsh) Field Regt. R.A. (T.A.)
         |
        1946
283rd(Welsh) Field Regt. R.A. (T.A.)


                              1955
                     283rd (Mon.) Field Regt. RA (TA)

                              1961
                  282nd (Glam & Mon.) Field Regt. RA (TA)

                              1967
                  211(South Wales) Battery (Raglan Barracks)
                        104 Light AD Regt. RA (V)
```

Bibliography

The groundwork of British History.	Warner & Martin.
A History of Great Britain.	Mowat.
The Oxford Popular History of Great Britain.	Edited by K O Morgan.
The Pleasant Land of Gwent.	Fred J Hando.
The King's England - Monmouthshire.	Arthur Mee
When was Wales?	Gwyn A Williams
Wales	Peter Sagar
Renewal & Reformation in Wales 1415 -1642.	Glanmor Williams
The Story of Gwent.	David Oates
A History of Gwent	R Howell
Monmouthshire. Its History & Topography	C J O Evans
A History of Monmouthshire	Sir Joseph Bradney
Historic Newport	James Matthews 1910
The History of Newport	Scott
Tour of Monmouthshire 1802	The Rev Coxe
History of Monmouthshire 1796	Williams
Boroughs of Medieval Wales	R A Griffiths
Lordship & Society in the March of Wales 1282 - 1400	R R Davies
The Charters in the Borough of Newport	Newport Library
Newport Lordships 1317 - 1536	A C Reeves
Life in Medieval Newport. The Rise and Progress of Newport 1789 - 1896 From Elizabeth to Victoria.	Henry John Davies
The Government Of Newport 1550 - 1850	Brynmor Pierce Jones
An Ecclesiastical History of Monmouthshire	E T Davies Canon of Monmouth 1953
Some Ancient Churches of Gwent	Mrs Mitchell of Llanfrechfa 1907
The Monmouthshire Antiquary 1985 - 1988	
The Monastery of Austin Friars at Newport	Thomas Wakeman 1839
Testaments of the Herbert Family in Monmouthshire 1469 - 1700	Newport Library
The Black Death in England and Wales as Exhibited in Manorial Documents	Dr W M Rees
Historical & Genealogical Memoirs of the Morgan Family	G Blacker Morgan
Survey of Newport for the Countess of Pembroke 1630	James Palmer
The History of Newport and Historical Landmarks	Abraham Morris
The Co-operative Congress Survey and History of Newport 1908	Co-operative Society
Commerce and Customs. A History of Newport & Caerleon	James W Dawson
Historical Traditions and Facts relating to Newport and Caerleon A History of Modern Wales 1536 - 1990 British Social and Economic History Documents & Debates	W H Johns Philip Jenkins Neil Tonge & Michael Quincy

The Normans in Britain. Documents & Debates   Donald Wilkinson & John Cantrell
Tudor Wales   Edited by Trevor Herbert &
   Gareth Elwyn Jones

19th Century Britain. Documents & Debates   Richard Brown & Christopher Daniel
Newport Castle & St Woolos   Octavius Morgan
Raglan Castle & the Civil War in Monmouthshire   Arthur Clarke
Summonses of the Footmen of the Caldicot Hundred
1638   Richard Herbert
The Royal Army in 1646   Sir Joseph Bradney
A Short Account of Newport Castle   John Kyrle Fletcher
The Newport Overseers 1776 - 1812   Newport Library
Local Government in Newport 1835 - 1935   John Warner
Newport Corporation Markets - a History   Newport Library
Newport's Coat of Arms   Newport Library
The Chartists of Blaenau Gwent   Norman Wybron
Chartists and Chartists   Joe Finn
South Wales and the Rising of 1839   Ivor Wilks
The Chart ist Movement   Mark Howell
The Chartist Collection   Newport Library
Chartism   Edward Royle
The Early Chartists   Dorothy Thompson
Labour & Reform 1815 - 1914   Clive Behogg
Radicals & Protest   Chris Steer
The Book of the Bastilles 1841   G R Wytham - Baxter
People & Protest, Wales, 1815 - 1818   Trevor Herbert &
   Gareth Elwyn Jones
Victorian Radicalism   Paul Adelman
Scotch Cattle and Chartism   David J V Jones
A History of Wales 1815 - 1906   D Gareth Evans
The Matter of Wales   Jan Morris
Newport Mon Gas Co. 1843 -1943   Newport Library
Through Seven Reigns. History of Newport Borough
Police   Islwyn Bale
The History of Newport Corporation Waterworks   Newport Library
Newport County Borough Electricity
50th Anniversary Committee 1895 - 1945   Newport Library
Trains & Buses of Newport 1845 - 1981   D B & E A Thomas
Illustrated Guide to Newport   Newport Chamber of Commerce
A Guide to Newport 1907   Edward J Burrow
100 Years in Newport 1834 - 1934)
House of E G Taylor & Sons   )   John Kyrle Fletcher
Newport after the First World War   W J Hamilton-Jones
Newport's Needs   W J Townsend Collins ('Dromio')
The Commercial Outlook for Newport 1926   W Mordey
A 1928 Guide to Newport   Stanley G Walters
Newport Docks Historical Notes   British Transport Docks Board
'Johnny'. The Story of a Happy Warrior   Alan Roderick 1990

Recollections of a Boxing Referee   Joe Palmer 1927
Bombers over Wales   Western Mail & Echo Cardiff
Revolutions and Revolutionaries   A J P Taylor
The Shrinking Shilling   James O'Donald Mays
Dictionary of Welsh Biography Down to 1940 Honourable Society
                                            of Cwmmrodorion

Directories: E Hunts, Percy & Butchers, Websters, Slaters,
                Morris's, Pigots, Kellys and Johns.
                Monmouthshire Reviews, Newport Christmas Annuals,
Periodicals: The Williams Monthly, Newport Year Books 1885-1931
                Household Almanac & Guide 1857 - 1898 W N Johns
Newspapers: Monmouthshire Merlin, Newport Gazette, South Wales
                Daily Telegram,Monmouthshire Record,Evening Star,
                Western Mail, South Wales Argus, The Pictorial World
                The London Illustrated News.

Index